CAMBRIDGE LATIN AMERICAN STUDIES

GENERAL EDITOR
MALCOLM DEAS

ADVISORY COMMITTEE
WERNER BAER, MARVIN BERNSTEIN,
AL STEPAN, BRYAN ROBERTS

40

OIL AND POLITICS IN LATIN AMERICA

OIL AND POLITICS
IN LATIN AMERICA

NATIONALIST MOVEMENTS AND
STATE COMPANIES

GEORGE PHILIP

*Lecturer in Latin American Politics,
the London School of Economics and Political Science, and
the Institute of Latin American Studies, London*

CAMBRIDGE UNIVERSITY PRESS

Cambridge

London   New York   New Rochelle

Melbourne   Sydney

Published by the Press Syndicate of the University of Cambridge
The Pitt Building, Trumpington Street, Cambridge CB2 IRP
32 East 57th Street, New York, NY 10022, USA
296 Beaconsfield Parade, Middle Park, Melbourne 3206, Australia

First published 1982

Printed in the United States of America

Library of Congress catalogue card number: 81-38531

British Library Cataloguing in Publication Data

Philip, George
Oil and Politics in Latin America.—(Cambridge
Latin American studies; 40)
1. Petroleum industry and trade—Latin America
—Political aspects
I. Title
338.2'7282'098   HD9574.L

ISBN 0 521 23865 X

The publisher wishes to thank the Publication Committee of The London School of
Economics and Political Science for its assistance in the publication of this book.

Contents

List of tables

vii

Preface

I began working on the oil industry when I started my doctoral thesis on the Peruvian oil industry in 1972. I am grateful to Alan Angell, Laurence Whitehead and Rosemary Thorp for their excellent supervision and to Malcolm Deas who, as one of my examiners in 1975, suggested that I should write a general book on the subject of Latin American oil.

Apart from my interview sources, acknowledgement is due to Rory Miller, Christopher Abel and Brian McBeth for their help on the 1920s; to Alan Peters and Fred Parkinson for help on the post-war environment; to Jorge Katz and Paul Cammack for help with the section on state companies; to Peter Alhadeff, Colin Lewis, Ed Early, Julio Fidel and Celia Szustermann for Argentina; to Laurence Whitehead and Manuel Contreras for Bolivia; to Charles Gedge, George Hawrylyshyn, Hari Bhat, Sue Cunningham and Getúlio de Carvalho for Brazil; to Malcolm Hoodless, Miguel Basañez, Manuel Tello, Andrés Viesca and Lief Adelson for Mexico; to Stan Rose for Peru; and to Dave Corkill and Norman Cox for Ecuador. I must also thank Seibke Hirst for her translations from Dutch (the other translations are mine) and Eileen Gregory for her secretarial help. Any errors which remain are entirely my own.

For reading and library facilities, I owe a debt to Shell, Lloyds Bank International, Chatham House, University College, London, the Public Record Office and the Institute of Petroleum (all in London); to the Instituto Argentino de Petróleo and Cepal in Buenos Aires; to the Banco Central, the Ford Foundation, Price Waterhouse and *El Comercio* in Lima; to the Banco Central, CEPE and the Ford Foundation in Quito, to YPFB and the Ministry of Mines and Hydrocarbons in La Paz; to the Banco Central in Caracas; to *O estado de São Paulo* in São Paulo; and to PEMEX in Mexico City. For access to, and permission to quote from, the Pearson archive, I would like to thank S. Pearson and Son.

I should also mention the London School of Economics, Senate House and British Libraries in London, and the Bodleian and Nuffield College Libraries in Oxford. Finally, I owe a debt in more direct fashion to the Social Science Research Council and the Institute of Latin American Studies, who together financed my four separate trips to Latin America.

Note

Although foreign sources have been translated, English language ones have been reproduced in their existing form; on occasion the English has suffered from telegram or telegraph requirements but has nevertheless been rendered here as in the original.

Glossary

adeco: supporter or member of Venezuelan AD party.

aprista: supporter of Peruvian APRA party.

asesor: personal advisor or member of personal staff.

Banco Central: Central Bank.

cateo: exploration permit from the government for oil or mineral development.

caudillo: independent political-military leader of a personalist kind.

Cepal: United Nations Economic Commission for Latin America.

Cono Sur: the three southernmost countries of Latin America; Argentina, Chile and Uruguay.

copeyano: supporter or member of Venezuelan COPEI party.

de confianza: literally 'confidential', in practice, a position reserved for a management appointee in Pemex.

desarrollismo (desarrollista): developmentalism (developmentalist); in Spanish this connotes political moderation and economic technocracy.

entreguismo (entregnista): Selling out to foreigners (one who favours this).

estaca: unit of territory leased by the (Argentine) government for mineral or oil prospecting.

Fedecámeras: Venezuelan business association.

Frente Cívico: Ecuadorian political coalition opposed to the military government of Rodríguez Lara.

gerente: manager; *gerencia:* management.

hacienda: literally 'business', but more usually a large land-holding or ranch.

Instituto Nacional de Planificación: National Planning Institute.

laudo: literally 'award', but in the case of Peru (1922) settlement or agreement.

majors (also Seven Sisters): seven large oil companies which dominated the post-War international oil industry (Jersey Standard, Royal Dutch/Shell, British Petroleum, Gulf Oil, Texas Petroleum Co.,

Mobil and Standard Oil of California).

Ministerio de Economía: Economics Ministry.

Ministerio de Fomento: Peruvian Ministry of Development (abolished in 1969).

Ministerio de Minas e Hidrocarburos: Mines and Petroleum Ministry.

Ministerio de Minas y Energía: Mines and Energy Ministry.

Ministerio de Planificación: Planning Ministry.

pertenencia: unit of land allocated by government for oil development.

'O petróleo é nosso': (Portuguese): 'The oil is ours' – slogan used by oil nationalists in Brazil.

reivindicación: legal recapture of a property held illegally plus damages to compensate for any depreciation during illegal tenure.

Secretaría de la Presidencia: Presidential Office.

sexenio: six-year Mexican presidential term.

Abbreviations

AD	Acción Democrática, Venezuelan political party; *adeco:* supporter of AD
AID	see US AID
ANCAP	Administración Nacional de Combustibles, Alcohol y Portland (Uruguay)
API	American Petroleum Institute
APRA	Alianza Popular Revolucionaria Americana (Peruvian political party)
Aramco	Arabian–American Oil Company
BNDE	Banco Nacional do Desenvolvimento Económico (Brazil)
CADE	Conferencia Anual de Ejectivos
CAEM	Centro de Altos Estudios Militares (Peruvian Centre for Higher Military Studies)
Cepal	see ECLA
CEPE	Corporación Estatal Petrolera Ecuatoriana
CFP	Compagnie Français de Pétrole
CGT	Confederación General de Trabajo (Argentina and Mexico)
CNP	Conselho Nacional do Petróleo (Brazil, 1938–53)
COB	Confederación de Obreros de Bolivia
Copec	Corporación Petrolera Chilena
COPEI	Comité de Organización Política Electoral Independiente (Venezuelan political party)
Corfo	Corporación Chileno de Fomento
CROM	Confederación Regional Obrera Mexicana
CTAL	Confederación de Trabajadores de América Latina
CTM	Confederación de Trabajadores Mexicanos
CVP	Compañía Venezolana de Petróleo
DASP	Departamento Administrativo do Serviço Público

ECLA	Economic Commission for Latin America
Ecopetrol	Empresa Colombiana de Petróleo
ENAP	Empresa Nacional de Administración de Petróleo (Chile)
ENI	Ente Nazionale de Idrocarburi (Italy)
EPF	Empresa Petrolera Fiscal (Peru, 1939–68)
ESG	Escola Superior de Guerra
FO	British government Foreign Office (index to general diplomatic correspondence)
FSB	Falange Socialista Boliviano
GOU	Grupo de Oficiales Unidos (sometimes known as Grupo de Obra Unida; Argentine army faction in 1940s)
HAR	*Hispanic American Report*
IBRD	International Bank for Reconstruction and Development (also known as World Bank)
ICA	International Co-operation Administration
IDB	(also known as IADB) Inter-American Development Bank
IMP	Instituto Mexicano de Petróleo
Ing.	Ingeniero (engineer)
IPC	International Petroleum Company (a Jersey Standard subsidiary)
ISI	Import Substituting Industrialisation
IVP	Instituto Venezolano de Petroquímica
LA	Latin America
LNG	Liquefied Natural Gas
MEP	Movimiento Electoral del Pueblo (Venezuelan political party)
MNR	Movimiento Nacionalista Revolucionario (Bolivia)
MSP	Movimiento Electoral del Pueblo (Venezuelan political party)
n.a.	not available
NACLA	North American Council on Latin America
neg.	negligible
OPEC	Organisation of Petroleum Exporting Countries
PDC (Bolivia)	Partido de la Democracia Cristiana
Pemex	Petróleos Mexicanos
Petrobrás	Petróleo Brasileiro
Petroperú	Petróleos del Perú
Petroquisa	Petrobrás Quimica, SA

Petrovén	(also PVDSA) Petróleos de Venezuela
PNR	Partido Nacional Revolucionario (*see* PRI)
POR	Partido Obrero Revolucionario (Bolivia)
PRI	(formerly PRM and PNR) Partido Revolucionario Institucional (Mexico)
PRM	Partido de la Revolución Mexicana (*see* PRI)
PSD	Partido Social Democrático (Brazil)
PTB	Partido Trabalhista Brasileiro
PDVSA	*see* Petrovén
STPRM	Sindicato de Trabajadores Petroleros de la República Mexicana
STOB	Standard Oil of Bolivia (a subsidiary of Jersey Standard)
UCR	Unión Cívica Radical (Argentine political party)
UCRI	Unión Cívica Radical Intransigente (faction of the UCR)
UCRP	Unión Cívica Radical del Pueblo (rival faction of the UCR)
UNAM	Universidad Nacional Autónoma de Mexico
UDN	União Democrática Nacional (Brazil)
UNE	União Nacional dos Estudantes (Brazil)
US AID	United States Agency for International Development
YPF	Yacimientos Petrolíferos Fiscales (Argentina)
YPFB	Yacimientos Petrolíferos Fiscales Bolivianos

A note on currencies and other units of measurement

I have tried to use current US dollars and cents as common currency throughout this book although there have been places where it was not practicable to do so, such as when a country operated a multiple exchange rate or when figures were expressed in constant units of a local currency. I have also converted many petroleum measurements into barrels (bbl) and daily barrels (b/d) in order to facilitate international comparison. When such figures have had no comparative significance, I have left them in their original form (normally either metric tons or cubic metres). For those interested in making their own calculations, one barrel of crude oil is roughly equivalent to 0.136 metric tons and 0.159 cubic metres. Conversion factors vary significantly for other oil products. Readers interested in pursuing the matter further should consult the last page of the *British Petroleum Statistical Review of the World Oil Industry* which is published annually. For all very large numbers, I have used the US system whereby a billion is 1,000,000,000.

I have used statistics for natural gas production in the form in which I have found them; for those wishing to standardise, one cubic metre is equivalent to 35 cubic feet.

Crude oil is not a homogenous substance. It rather varies according to the relative proportions of carbon and hydrogen in the compound; the higher the proportion of hydrogen, the 'lighter' (or less dense) the crude and the greater its commercial value. The conventional measure of the density of crude oil is the American Petroleum Institute schedule; around 28–32° API is the median. Crudes below 28° API are regarded as heavy and those above 32° API are light; some are as low as 11° API and some as high as 46° API.

I have also followed conventional usage in measuring exports 'free-on-board' (f.o.b.) and imports 'cost, insurance, freight' (c.i.f.). In other words, import costs include the cost of transportation whereas export prices do not.

1920

0   500 miles

0   1000 km

MEXICO

CENTRAL AMERICA
AND CARIBBEAN

VENEZUELA

COLOMBIA

ECUADOR

BRAZIL

PERU

BOLIVIA

PARAGUAY

CHILE

ARGENTINA

URUGUAY

Importing countries
(production less than half
domestic consumption)

Exporting countries
(production at least twice
domestic consumption)

Countries approaching
self-sufficiency

1940

0   500 miles
0   1000 km

MEXICO

CENTRAL AMERICA
AND CARIBBEAN

VENEZUELA

COLOMBIA

ECUADOR

PERU

BRAZIL

BOLIVIA

PARAGUAY

CHILE

ARGENTINA

URUGUAY

Importing countries
(production less than half
domestic production)

Exporting countries
(production more than twice
domestic production)

Countries approaching
self-sufficiency

1960

0   500 miles

0   1000 km

MEXICO

CENTRAL AMERICA
AND CARIBBEAN

VENEZUELA

COLOMBIA

ECUADOR

BRAZIL

PERU

BOLIVIA

PARAGUAY

CHILE

URUGUAY

ARGENTINA

Importing countries
(producing less than half
domestic consumption)

Exporting countries
(producing more than twice
domestic consumption)

Countries approaching
self-sufficiency

1981 (estimate)

0   500 miles

0   1000 km

MEXICO

GUATEMALA

CENTRAL AMERICA
AND CARIBBEAN

VENEZUELA

GUYANA

SURINAM

COLOMBIA

ECUADOR

BRAZIL

PERU

BOLIVIA

PARAGUAY

CHILE

ARGENTINA

URUGUAY

Importing countries
(production less than half
domestic consumption)

Exporting countries
(production at least twice
domestic consumption)

Countries approaching
self-sufficiency

Introduction: The politics of oil in twentieth-century Latin America

For many Latin Americans, oil is *el excremento del diablo*. [1] More recently similar perceptions have come to be shared in far wealthier oil-importing countries. In the popular imagination, and not only there, the progressive and beneficial side of the oil industry – provision of lighting, heating, travel opportunities and the astonishing innovations in petrochemicals – has been tied in inextricably with a darker side which has featured massive corruption, the fomentation of political upheavals within particular countries and the concentration of power on an international scale in a way which has led to large-scale but unpredictable shifts in the structure of the world oil system.

Market economists have tried to explain the oil industry in terms of the familiar logic of cost and price, supply and demand, but have always found it necessary to bring the concept of oligopoly into their explanations. Oligopolies are rarely popular and some writers appear to have believed that by denouncing Standard Oil or OPEC, they could persuade them to go away. Others have tried to demonstrate that the oil market is inherently unstable unless controlled – for a time – by some form of cartel, even though cartels themselves may collapse in the long term. The fact of oligopoly, however, denotes at least some distance between the imperatives of the market and the decisions of the major producers. In any case, it is clear that there is a political as well as an economic aspect of oil which limits, although it does not invalidate, the usefulness of narrow economic analysis. Certainly as far as oil is concerned market economists have proved poor prophets.

Another group of writers, generally to be found on the political left, has seen the oil industry as a classic example of twentieth-century imperialism. The development of the oil industry in the underdeveloped countries has clearly responded to the needs of the richer countries, which at times searched for market outlets but more usually were concerned with sources of supply. Those few companies which discov-

I

ered large oil reserves in Latin America, Africa and the Middle East generally looked to their parent governments for support and in many cases obstructed the efforts of local governments to exert more control over the industry. A threat to international oil supplies has often been seen by the main consuming countries as a strategic matter requiring diplomatic and possibly even military intervention. Again, however, the 'imperialist' picture needs to be modified. US or European consumers who have seen the world price of crude oil increase from under $2.00 a barrel in 1970 to around $35.00 a barrel in 1980 may have reason to reflect upon either the ineptitude of twentieth-century imperialists or the limitations of twentieth-century imperialism.

Any useful study of the international oil industry must take into account both the commercial logic of finding, developing, refining and selling oil and the political environment in which this has taken place. Here the aim will be to consider the way in which these factors interacted and combined to produce the world in which we have lived and continue to live. The oil market will thus be considered here as the outcome of actual behaviour and not as a set of logically interacting principles, although the latter will often prove valuable in interpreting the former. The book is therefore a history rather than an economic study but it is nevertheless focussed on a particular (even if wide-ranging) topic with general relevance. Essentially it aims to provide an account of the conflict that has been played out within the Latin American oil industry between the claims of international capitalism – in the shape of semi-oligopolistic transnational companies with variable support from their parent governments – and the at once older and more recent claims of national sovereignty and state control. Thus far at least, supporters of state control have had by far the better of the conflict, and the book will explore the reasons for this and the consequences.

Latin America provides a rich field for the study of oil politics. Mexico and Venezuela were among the earliest and largest-scale exporters of oil and, although later overtaken by the Middle East, continued to supply a significant proportion of the world's oil. The importance of Mexico is clearly growing and oil companies and their parent governments are increasingly turning their attention to sources of supply within Latin America as part of their efforts to diversify away from Middle Eastern oil. Moreover, having been among the first large-scale exporters of oil, both Venezuela and Mexico in their different ways pioneered oil politics which had major international repercussions. The

Mexican oil nationalisation of 1938 was the culmination of a series of measures on the part of successive Mexican governments which directly challenged the central assumptions about international law and contractual obligation underlying earlier foreign investment. The nationalisation led to a considerable change of attitude on the part of the companies which made itself felt in later dealings with Venezuela and the countries of the Middle East, while the resulting diplomatic activity did much to change Washington's own perspectives on the oil industry. Mexico meanwhile developed its own state oil company with reasonable success at a time when such a venture was widely believed to be beyond the capacity of any underdeveloped country. The Venezuelan government for its part pioneered forms of international collective action among producer governments which led to the formation of OPEC in 1960 and the oil market revolution of the period 1970–4.

By no means all of Latin American oil history has been of such international significance but many developments within Latin America, as well as being domestically significant, have highlighted more general features of the international industry. This is true, for example, of the major investment decisions taken in Latin America by the international oil companies, of cases of government – company conflict which have culminated in nationalisation and of the development of state oil companies within Latin America.

This book begins with the international dimension. The first part considers the choices or lack of choice faced by Latin American governments at different times in this century as a result of both the technical and political conditions prevailing in the international marketplace. To what extent have international conditions operated 'systematically' or in sinister fashion to close off avenues to Latin American governments and to what extent are present market conditions within the continent the result of freely made choices?

The discussion also considers the extent to which the behaviour of the major oil companies and the other significant international actors could be explained by immediate consideration of profitability under particular market conditions and how far it is necessary to bring in the international distribution of oil power as an explanatory factor. The second part considers the internal political implications of international oil investment by focussing on some of the major conflicts which have resulted – those which ended in nationalisation. It will consider the motivations of host governments which extended state control over their oil industries and will examine their bases of internal political support. Finally, the third part discusses the development of state oil companies in six key Latin American countries in order to see how these have coped with the complex pressures surrounding oil operation in these countries.

PART I

The world oil environment

1

The corporate ascendancy 1890–1927

The starting point of the modern oil industry has traditionally been placed in 1859 with the drilling of the Drake well in Pennsylvania. During the rest of the nineteenth century, the USA in general and Standard Oil in particular established a dominant, even if not entirely unchallenged, position in the world oil market. In the mid-1860s the USA, by far the world's largest producer, exported well over half of its total production, having first refined most of it. In 1879 Standard Oil carried out its first foreign investment, in a marketing outlet in Spain.

The last three decades of the nineteenth century were also a period of rapid technical change. The oil industry, partly in consequence, became increasingly concentrated as Standard Oil built up its dominant position within the USA while facing increasingly intense political attack from its Populist and Progressive opponents. In the international market, Standard Oil was also a major force but nevertheless faced competition from Russian oil (which began to be produced around 1880) marketed by, among other companies, Shell and Royal Dutch (which merged in 1907).

Until the First World War, crude oil was abundant. Standard Oil built up its position by controlling transportation and refining within the USA and, to a lesser extent, marketing outlets outside it. Thus, at the turn of the century, the US oil industry was in an almost classic vent-for-surplus situation. As a contemporary observer put it, 'the output of crude petroleum has mounted so rapidly, under a stimulus arising only in part from demand, that domestic markets for refined products were unable to keep pace; thus the vigorous construction of foreign markets became an economic necessity, as exemplified in the efforts that have gone into sending kerosene to the four corners of the globe'.[1] Thus, as Wilkins points out, Standard Oil's 'few [foreign] refineries were all built with marketing considerations in mind. It had no investments in foreign oil production . . . [only] by the turn of the century

7

[was] Standard Oil . . . beginning for the first time to consider purchasing oil producing properties as well as merely buying foreign oil'.[2]

The economic climate changed early in the twentieth century, partly
because of the merger of Royal Dutch and Shell. This new combine,
under the energetic leadership of Henri Deterding, put increasing
emphasis on developing new sources of oil supply in order to cut transport costs and win competitive advantage through complete vertical
integration. The very rapid increase in world oil demand from the
turn of the century – mainly in the form of fuel oil after around 1905
and gasoline after around 1910 – made this strategy increasingly effective.

In 1911, the structure of the international oil industry changed
again when Standard Oil was broken up into a number of its constituent parts, as a result of US anti-trust legislation. Jersey Standard was
the largest of these newly independent companies and was also the
most involved in Latin America. Jersey Standard had been left 'crude
short' by the break-up and felt the need to build up fresh crude oil
supplies in order to feed its stronger refining and marketing network.
Rather than risk further conflicts with US law, Jersey concentrated on
expanding abroad and particularly in Latin America.

The economic climate changed even further with the coming of the
First World War and a growing appreciation of the strategic potential
of oil supplies. This change coincided with a real, although temporary,
fear that US supplies would prove inadequate. As De Novo pointed
out,

geologists who appraised the domestic petroleum supply gloomily predicted
that it was inadequate for the future needs of the nation. According to the
most informed estimates, the known oil fields in the United States would last
less than thirty years at the prevailing rate of consumption . . . The Secretary
of the Interior cautioned in 1915 that the known available supply of petroleum
in the United States would be exhausted in about twenty-three years, or by
1937, at the current rate of consumption and export.[3]

As supply shortages seemed more likely, so the climate of opinion
within the USA changed. In the 20 years prior to 1911 Standard Oil
had faced very strong domestic criticisms and even political attack.
Later, however, the climate changed and various fiscal measures were
adopted within the USA to encourage US companies to invest abroad.
In 1916, a ruling from the Internal Revenue Service permitted companies to write off 'intangibles' against US income irrespective of

whether these costs had been incurred at home or abroad. In 1918 the Revenue Act introduced a tax allowance for oil depletion (the rate was increased to 27.5% in 1926) for both home and foreign fields. Thus, in addition to diplomatic action, which will be considered below, the US government became prepared to subsidise and in other ways to encourage direct foreign investment in oil exploration.

Immediately after the end of the First World War, therefore, there was something of an 'oil rush' into Latin America. Jersey Standard was looking for geologically interesting possibilities throughout the continent and Royal Dutch/Shell had been operating under similar principles for some time. As one of its *Reports* pointed out,

> business has been built up primarily on the principle that each market must be supplied with products emanating from the fields which are most favourably situated geographically . . . we are now reaping the benefits resulting from this advantageous position.
> We must not be outstripped in this struggle to obtain new territory. Our interests are therefore being considerably extended; our geologists are everywhere any chance of success exists.[4]

It would, however, be a mistake to see the Latin American oil industry, as some writers have done, as little more than a battleground between these two giant companies. Literally hundreds of other companies were active in the oil industry at one time or another and several of these – the Pearson interests and Doheny in Mexico, Lobitos in Peru, Gulf Oil and Standard Oil of Indiana elsewhere – were of quite considerable importance.

Developments in Latin America

These global changes clearly had their effects upon Latin America. At the turn of the century most Latin American countries were seen by the major companies as a backwater where high tariffs and poor communications inhibited sales. As late as 1898 Standard Oil exported fewer than one million barrels of products to all of South America together and 'all shipments of kerosene to that area continued to be in cases and cans. In most countries tariffs were high and the market for petroleum products comparatively underdeveloped.'[5] This situation induced scepticism on the part of the larger oil companies as to the value of investing directly in the continent. Regarding Peru, for example,

Standard Oil had since the 1870s been aware of the existence of commercial
oil resources in Peru, but had not been interested in drilling for oil; they were
more intent on marketing US-refined oil in Latin America . . . As late as 1910
Standard Oil visitors to Peru reported 'It will be more profitable to buy production than to hunt for it, and to buy oil than to run the risks in this territory
of producing it.'[6]

As late as 1913 Lord Cowdray (head of the Mexican Eagle Company)
instructed Murray, then negotiating for a concession in Colombia, that

We must avoid, whatever the temptation may be, of [sic] having to find big
capital sums. The only safe procedure is to limit your capital expenditure to
a moderate sum in the first instance and to develop out of profits.

We have also to remember that the best of markets for oil is the local
market . . . Probably a production of 10,000 barrels a day . . . would dis-
place the whole of the coal now being used between Panama and the Magellan
Straits. If the oil were of a high grade it would, of course, pay to ship through
the Canal to Europe, but if it were only a fuel proposition or primarily a fuel
oil proposition, then the only lucrative market for such grade of oil would be
the countries bordering on the Pacific south of Panama.[7]

By 1920, the position was dramatically different. During the 1920s,
the oil industry in Latin America, even more than elsewhere, underwent dramatic expansion. There had already been some foreign investment in Peru and Mexico and this became vastly more important,
while in countries such as Venezuela, Colombia and Argentina foreign
oil companies came to play a major part in the domestic economy. The
main changes can be seen in tables 1.1, 1.2 and 1.3, although it
should be noted that non-US foreign oil investment would further
intensify the (relative and absolute) importance of Mexico, Venezuela
and, to a much lesser extent, Argentina.

Naturally investments of this magnitude would not have been made
in Latin America unless profitable opportunities had appeared to present themselves. Before discussing these, however, a few preliminary
points should be made. First, the oil industry, particularly in its exploration sector, has always been one in which there is high risk and in
which capital cost has often been high. Secondly, the period between
1918 and 1927 was particularly favourable to successful oil producers;
they could sell all the oil they could produce at prices that were historically high, even though some decline took place after the spectre of
surplus reappeared around 1926. Low cost sources were being developed in Latin America at a time when oil products were competitive

Table 1.1 *Oil production in Latin America 1916–28*
(000 *b/d*)

	1916	1918	1920	1922	1924	1926	1928
Argentina	2.4	3.7	4.5	7.9	12.7	21.5	24.8
Colombia	0	0	0	0.9	1.2	17.7	54.5
Ecuador	neg.	neg.	neg.	neg.	0.02	0.6	3.0
Peru	7.1	7.0	7.7	14.6	22.9	29.5	32.8
Venezuela	0	0.9	1.2	6.0	24.7	101.1	289.7
Mexico	111.1	174.9	430.3	499.4	247.7	137.4	108.3

Source: US Department of Energy, *Petroleum Yearbook* (1978).

Table 1.2 *Market share by company in 1928*
(*Percentages*)

	Jersey Standard	Shell	YPF	Atlantic	Texaco	Other
Argentina						
Gasoline	45.79	27.65	14.63	n.a.	n.a.	11.93
Fuel oil	3.61	28.76	31.43	n.a.	n.a.	36.2
Gas and diesel	44.34	20.47	2.68	n.a.	n.a.	32.51
Brazil						
Gasoline	47.40	20.40	0	17.56	13.20	1.44
Fuel oil	4.54	50.88	0	0	0	44.58
Gas and diesel	5.87	36.71	0	2.31	0	55.10
Chile						
Gasoline	61.45	37.3	0	n.a.	n.a.	1.25
Fuel oil	31.59	8.23	0	n.a.	n.a.	57.31
Gas and diesel	44.86	2.82	0	n.a.	n.a.	52.32

Source: Wilkins, 'Multinational Oil Companies in South America in the 1920s', *Business History Review*, vol. 48 (1974), p. 418.

with almost anything else (as indeed they have continued to be) and demand was rising rapidly. World output more than doubled between 1900 and 1912 (from 149.1 million barrels to 352.4 million) and nearly tripled again by 1924, when it reached 1,014 million. Thirdly, oil investments in Latin America needed to compete with other ventures in a world which was still largely colonial and predominantly capitalist. If we consider only dividends paid on nominal capital (an imperfect but nonetheless readily available indicator), we find that

Table 1.3 US *investment in Latin America, and in Latin American oil, and Jersey Stan-*
dard's investments in Latin America
($m.)

	Total investment (1929)	Total oil (1914)[a]	Total oil (1929)	Jersey Standard (1927)
Cuba	919.0	0	9.0	n.a.
Mexico	682.5	85	295.9	8.66
Chile	422.6	0	n.a.	n.a.
Argentina	331.8	0	29.8	11.6
Venezuela	232.5	neg.	226.2	27.0
Brazil	193.6	0	23.0	n.a.
Colombia	124.0	neg.	55.8	23.5
Peru	123.7	15	68.5	71.8
Bolivia	n.a. (neg.)	0	n.a.	11.4

[a] Production of oil only; there was a very limited amount of investment in refining and marketing.
Note: These figures must inevitably be rough given the difficulty of breaking down investment by nationality.
Source: M. Wilkins, *The Maturing of Multinational Enterprise: American Business Abroad from 1914 to 1970* (Cambridge, Mass., 1974), p. 56, for the first and third columns; G. Gibb and H. Knowlton, *The Resurgent Years 1911–27: History of Standard Oil Company, New Jersey* (New York, 1956), for the fourth; and C. Lewis, *America's Stake in International Investments* (Washington, 1938), p. 221, for the second.

Anglo-Iranian paid an annual average of 17.1% between 1920 and 1950, Burmah Oil paid 24% between 1906 and 1950 (over 40% p.a. for most of the 1920s) and Royal Dutch/Shell paid 40% in 1920, 31% in 1921 and at least that amount until 1929 when only 23% was paid.[8] Even these rates were well below those paid on natural rubber, gold and diamond interests within the British Empire. Finally, it must be borne in mind that the 1920s was a period of technical dynamism in the oil industry in which oil finds were made and developed which in many cases provided long-term advantage to the host countries well after the bonanza years for the companies were over.

These considerations should be borne in mind not to explain away, but to put into perspective, company profitability in Latin America. Some of the most complete figures available come from Jersey Standard, where one striking point is the lucrative nature of oil marketing.

As we can see from table 1.4, Jersey Standard could generate up to 40% of its worldwide profits from Latin America in a good year and, in general, made more than it did in marketing within the USA. Although fluctuations were significant and there was the occasional year in which losses were made, the rate of return on capital which could be achieved was staggering. Thus in Argentina, 'one company with a cash outlay of $300,000 US dollars remitted to the United States from Argentina, between 1921 and 1929, $90 million US dollars translated at current rates of exchange. Another company, on a cash outlay from the parent company of $100,000 (US) remitted to the home office $2 million from Argentina in the 1920s'.[9]

Argentina is likely, in fact, to have provided the lion's share of the West India Oil Company's earnings if only because of the size of its domestic market. It has been estimated that in 1930 Argentina (together with Paraguay) consumed some 52,000 b/d as against a Latin American total of some 138,500 b/d. For gasoline, the figures are even more striking: 19,974 b/d out of a total of 33,800 b/d.[10] One should also note that the very high profits earned during the war years must be attributed in large part to the interruption of coal supplies from Britain. It is interesting that Royal Dutch/Shell believed, in 1915, that the price of fuel oil in Chile was 'too low to be attractive' and entered the market only after the end of the war.[11]

These huge marketing profits illustrate two important points. The first is that they were extremely vulnerable both to governmental control and to price competition between companies. The latter could, on occasion, be bitterly fought. The best documented example we have is the conflict in Mexico after 1908 between the Pearson interests and Henry Clay Pierce, whose company, Waters-Pierce, was 67% controlled by Standard Oil but in fact operated semi-independently. Lord Cowdray noted that in 1908 'the total refined oil trade of the Republic amounted to 700 bbls. per day'. Waters-Pierce had made an annual profit of £300,000 ($1.5m.) in the years 1903–7 on the basis of a local monopoly supplied by refining imports of crude oil. Cowdray attempted to negotiate a quota of the local market after his own oil discoveries in Mexico in 1904 but failed. The price war began in June 1908 and by October 1909 Cowdray noted that he had taken 40% of the market but 'the competition for the trade was of a cut-throat nature and prices were cut to a third.' Later a truce was agreed, but Cowdray was never in any doubt as to the strength of his position:

Table 1.4 *Jersey Standard's earnings from marketing*
1912–27
(000$)

	1912	1913	1914	1915	1916	1917	1918	1919
West India Oil Co.[a]	934	1,126	837	2,003	4,130	6,232	6,613	(435)
Standard Oil of Brazil	451	484	426	987	2,131	3,805	1,302	1,089
All Latin America	1,474	1,707	1,247	2,999	6,224	10,077	7,915	654
All USA	1,445	1,442	680	2,243	2,797	3,427	3,791	4,086
World total (marketing)	8,839	12,368	8,372	13,479	16,256	20,347	18,420	8,472

	1920	1921	1922	1923	1924	1925	1926	1927
West India Oil Co.	1,588	1,338	2,875	1,041	4,689	7,694	8,876	8,008
Standard Oil of Brazil	(955)	(2,009)	(680)	(732)	909	3,156	3,387	1,933
All Latin America	633	(761)	2,195	309	5,878	10,870	12,459[b]	9,959[b]
All USA	5,149	(1,878)	6,534	12,774	10,416	4,406	9,753	14,993
World total (marketing)	15,444	1,404	18,004	19,165	20,863	23,190	30,972	32,639

Note: Figures in parentheses indicate losses.
[a] Supplying Spanish America and the Caribbean.
[b] Includes a small 'other' figure.
Source: Gibb and Knowlton, *The Resurgent Years*, pp. 182 and 566.

C.P. [Pierce] fails to realize that his competition can only affect our profits to the extent of 5 to 10%. We produce our own oil, he has to buy his . . . If we have to make no profit from the domestic trade, he assuredly would make none. But our export trade is ours alone; he cannot touch it, and it will give us a profit of nearer £2,000,000 a year than £1,000,000, whereas we never estimated that the Domestic trade, the trade and only trade in which C.P. is or can be interested, would be worth more than £120,000 a year to us.[12]

The second point, which relates to the first, is that vertical integration was desirable, and sometimes absolutely necessary, if an oil company was to enjoy the bargaining power to make these quasi-monopoly profits or simply to respond to changes in the balance of the world market. Taken together, they presented a strong commercial argument both for absolute size on the ground that this made risk-avoiding policy easier and, where possible, for some form of cartel arrangement. During the 1920s, however, both of these represented tendencies rather than absolute facts and some companies, such as Lobitos, which did not integrate, continued to do well.

Jersey Standard's refining profits in Latin America were lower but still significant. They were particularly good between 1923 and 1926, probably as the result of the opening of the Barranca Bermeja refinery in Colombia in 1923; in 1927 an actual loss was recorded, possibly as a result of competition from the newly opened state refinery at La Plata in Argentina. Even so, Jersey Standard's best year in the entire decade – $2,670,000 profit recorded in 1925 – yielded less than the profits from marketing in Brazil alone during the course of that year.[13]

The biggest variation came in the production sector. Peru appeared to yield some of the highest returns from its accessible fields on the north coast. Here Jersey Standard seems to have timed its entry into the country with consummate skill, purchasing London and Pacific in 1913. Lobitos, on the other hand, began exploration in 1901 and drilled its first successful well in 1905 but did not pay its first dividend until 1912. After considering the case of Lobitos, Miller concluded that 'successful participation in Peruvian oil was, in fact, fraught with problems. The early history of Lobitos showed how much capital, tenacity, patience and luck it needed'.[14] As for London and Pacific itself, it was reported by Williamson of Lobitos that 'Keswick would be only too glad to get rid of his white elephant. It has been a sink of money and never paid. In short, a *disappointment* from first to last. Are we *sure* Lobitos will prove different? Not yet, I think.' (Original italic.)[15] The case of Peru does demonstrate beyond doubt, however, that once the difficult early stages had been surmounted, considerable profits could be made from oil production. According to estimates presented in table 1.7 below, IPC made $16.3m. in 1922 on an investment generously valued at $48.1m. (33.9% on capital) and $26.1m. in 1927 on an investment of $71.8m. (36.3% on capital).[16]

The Mexican case is perhaps even more interesting. Here it is necessary to distinguish three stages. The first ten years of the century, when oil exploration got seriously underway, were disappointing. The Mexican Eagle, apart from having to fight a price war with Waters-Pierce, suffered a serious blow-out at Dos Bocas at a total loss and in any case committed itself financially well beyond its original intention. The American Doheny, together with Cowdray, did make major finds in 1910 and these inaugurated a tremendous oil boom. The period of optimum profitability was between 1910 and 1921, largely because of the abundance with which the oil flowed but also because Mexico, undergoing a revolution, was in no position to raise taxes to what would even then have been regarded as a realistic rate. Thus, Mexican Eagle's dividends, which had remained as low as 8% in 1914 and 1915, rose to 16% in 1916, 45% in 1919 and a peak of 60% in 1920. The third period, between around 1922 and the eventual nationalisation of 1938, was relatively disappointing to the companies. Part of the reason for this was the decline in exploration success. Between 1919 and 1933 the Atlantic Refining subsidiary lost some $25m. in unsuccessful exploration. Between 1922 and 1925 the companies mounted what was described, in 1975, as 'the most intensive exploration campaign Mexico ever experienced'.[17] This included seismic work for the first time, but encountered little success.

It is also important, however, that Mexico acquired a more-or-less stable government in 1920 and progressively increased its tax rates to far higher levels (see table 1.5). Although the companies protested and tried to involve the State Department, they had to pay. Even though these rates do not appear onerous, the Mexican Eagle in 1934 told the British Embassy that

during the last ten years, 90% of our gross revenue has been returned to Mexico by way of wages, taxes and material. At least 5% of the 10% remaining abroad goes towards the cost of representation, insurance and losses on tank steamer operations; the average profit has not exceeded 5% . . . The government, in fact, have received from the company's operations fourteen times more revenue than that paid to the ordinary stockholders. In the same period of ten years, an amount of 196 million pesos [some $65.5m.] had been

Table 1.5 *Mexican oil output, taxes and taxes per barrel 1915–30*

	Output (000 barrels)	Total taxes ($ 000)	Taxes per barrel (US cents)
1915	32,911	966.7	2.9
1916	40,546	1,536.3	3.8
1917	55,293	3,757.7	6.8
1918	63,828	5,974.1	9.4
1919	87,073	8,622.9	9.9
1920	157,069	25,529.3	16.3
1921	193,398	31,206.3	16.1
1922	182,278	43,671.1	24.0
1923	149,585	31,041.7	20.8
1924	139,678	27,098.0	19.4
1925	115,515	23,282.6	20.2
1926	90,421	20,028.5	22.2
1927	64,121	12,069.0	18.9
1928	50,150	8,830.1	17.6
1929	44,688	9,344.6	20.9
1930	39,530	9,202.8	23.3

Note: These figures are probably the best available but should be treated with care. Company estimates of their tax payments are consistently higher. In 1922 Jersey Standard estimated that it would have to pay $0.36 a barrel under existing legislation, leaving the company $0.15 profit from a selling price, after transportation, of $1.43 (Gibb and Knowlton, *The Resurgent Years,* p. 363). In 1926 Mexican Eagle estimated that its total tax bill was 50.7 cents a barrel (Pearson Collection, box C 43, file 1).

Sources: Meyer, *México y los Estados Unidos en el conflicto petrolero,* pp. 21 and 35, provides figures for oil production and tax payments in pesos. I have converted to dollars using the exchange rates provided in Mexico's *Anuario estadístico de los Estados Unidos Mexicanos* (Mexico, 1939) and several copies of *Anuario de estadística* for the early 1920s.

spent by the company in new developmental work, modernizing refineries, etc.[18]

It is unfortunately true that, as Kane points out, 'data concerning rates of return on American investment are either too fragmentary or too unreliable to allow for meaningful generalisations'.[19] However, it is interesting to compare the attitude of Lord Cowdray with that of Jersey Standard during the Mexican boom. Cowdray always regarded the boom years of the 1910–20 period as extraordinary and unlikely to last. He made several efforts to sell his Mexican holdings, or at least to share ownership, with both British and US interests. When, in 1919, he finally arranged to sell a minority shareholding and offer a management contract to Royal Dutch/Shell, he explained to the British government that 'I was not prepared to carry, indefinitely and single-handed, the financial burden of this huge business'.[20] When the British government complained, Cowdray retorted:

We made the suggestion to HMG that it should take half the risk with us at a time when the El Aguila's property was considered by everyone conversant with the position to be gravely endangered, not only by the general unrest in Mexico (which was particularly acute in the region of the oilfields) but owing to the possibility of the Mexican government coming to active loggerheads with the United States. In the latter event it was the declared intention of members of the Mexican government to at once destroy all the oil properties.[21]

Thus, although Mexican Eagle did make large profits during the period, these were at least in part the reward for running extraordinary political risks. Moreover, even so large an operator as Cowdray did not wish to stay in the oil business unless he could spread his risks beyond Mexico; this was a further element in the logic of concentration in the oil industry.

Jersey Standard, on the other hand, for a time regarded Mexico with enthusiasm. As in the case of Peru, it began by purchasing oil for its marketing apparatus, later began buying up oil leases and, in 1917, bought out Transcontinental for $2.5m. Subsequently, it undertook a major expansion; its investment 'shot up from $4,429,000 at the end of 1918 to $32,247,000 in 1922, the highest point reached. In addition, very large sums were loaned by the parent company to finance operating expansion by the affiliate.'[22] Policy changed abruptly, however, after taxes were raised in 1921 and Jersey Standard calculated that it was making no more than $0.15 a barrel in profit from its exported Mexican production while paying $0.36 a barrel in taxation. Moreover, with the political situation still uncertain and as the company's labour force became increasingly militant, the company took the decision to disinvest as quickly as possible. As Gibb and Knowlton recounted,

by 1928 the liquidation of Jersey's Mexican venture had been carried far. Loans to Transcontinental, which in 1922 were outstanding in the amount of $12,000,000 . . . had all been repaid by 1924. From 1925 through 1927 every possible penny had been wrung out of the Mexican affiliate. Dividends paid over these three years totalled $35,131,000 . . . assets were depreciated, reserves and inventories liquidated and outstanding accounts settled. The investment in Mexico, which stood at $32,247,000 in 1922, had been pared to $8,660,000 by the end of 1927.[23]

The weakening of the world oil market after around 1925, and the prolonged dispute with the Mexican government between 1925 and 1927, were also important factors here; in 1927 an executive of Transcontinental wrote that 'unless low-cost production is found somewhat similar to Panuco and Southern field production the leases cannot be operated profitably at anywhere near today's market'.[24]

Data from Venezuela confirm that profits could be extremely high for those willing to invest heavily, take risks and wait for the returns – if, of course, they were lucky enough. Royal Dutch/Shell entered Venezuela in 1913, and began commercial production in 1919, but its *Annual Report for 1926* nevertheless complained that, although production was increasing, "the shareholders in the companies to whom this development is due receive as yet no or very little benefit'. By the time the bonanza arrived, the world price of oil had already begun to fall and the real financial rewards were not forthcoming until the middle 1930s. Nevertheless, as can be seen from table 1.6, the late 1920s did prove highly satisfactory for at least some of the companies involved, although one must again enter the caveat about dividends relating to nominal rather than actual capital; and it is also true that some smaller companies did make losses in Venezuela.[25] Indeed, as elsewhere in Latin America, Jersey Standard needed to acquire what it had difficulty in discovering for, prior to its first commercial find in Venezuela in 1928, it 'had to show for its investment of $27,000,000 over nearly a decade of time [*sic*] only unexplored concessions, inland watercraft, drilling rigs, much disappointing experience, miscellaneous camp facilities and forty-two dry holes'.[26]

To complete the picture, at least on the basis of such data as are available, it may be reported that in Colombia in 1927, which was Jersey Standard's first year of commercial operation, profits came to $6.9m. on an investment of $23.3m. On the other hand, the company made no money at all from Bolivia where it had up to that point invested $11.4m. Argentina was a paradise for marketing companies but profits from oil production were low and a number of companies, including Standard Oil of California, failed to find oil. In Ecuador, profits were also low; at no time before 1936 did Anglo-Ecuadorian Oilfields (the main operator, which had entered the country in 1921) pay more than 10% and in 1938 the company told the British govern-

Table 1.6 Net declared profits by selected companies in Venezuela 1920–33

	Venezuelan Oil Concessions Ltd K = £500,000		Venezuelan Oil Concessions Holding Co. Ltd K = £3,000,000		British Controlled Oilfields Ltd K = £2,604,167		Lago Petroleum Corporation K = $20,000,000	
	Profits (£ sterling)	Percentage of K	Profits (£ sterling)	Percentage of K	Profits (£ sterling)	Percentage of K	Profits ($)	Percentage of K
1920	100,000	20	n.a.	n.a.	n.a.	n.a.	n.a.	n.a.
1921	237,805	48	n.a.	n.a.	n.a.	n.a.	n.a.	n.a.
1925	n.a.	n.a.	n.a.	n.a.	410,100	16		
1926	715,325	143	426,820	14	186,389	7	1,458,197	7
1927	1,237,848	243	863,713	29	n.a.		7,558,886	38
1928	1,206,430	241	971,790	32	n.a.		n.a.	n.a.
1929	1,079,759	216	1,206,430	40	n.a.		n.a.	n.a.
1930	1,260,757	252	n.a.	n.a.	165,553	6	n.a.	n.a.
1931	697,124	139	n.a.	n.a.	(37,937)	(1)	n.a.	n.a.
1932	915,912	183	n.a.	n.a.	n.a.		n.a.	n.a.
1933	691,851	138	n.a.	n.a.	164,085	6	n.a.	n.a.

Note: K = share capital. Figures in parentheses indicate losses. £1 = $5 during the 1920s.
Source: McBeth, 'Oil in Venezuela', p. 11.

ment that 'the average rate of dividend paid to shareholders during 19 years amounts to only 2¾% per annum on the nominal capital and only about 1¼% per annum on the actual investment in Ecuador'.[27]

Given the extreme differences in the geological and political circumstances in which the companies operated, even in so apparently similar an environment as Latin America during the 1920s, it is not surprising that rates of return on capital varied widely. While it will be better to consider the political dimension in more detail before drawing any sweeping conclusions, it is perhaps clear that the average profitability of foreign oil investment in Latin America during this period is less than has sometimes been assumed. Even when average profits were high, successful companies took considerable risk and needed to wait for long periods before their initial investments came to full fruition. Often, actual losses were made. Even though it is certainly true that foreign companies enjoyed more favourable circumstances in Latin America than they were ever to do again, it was only occasionally that the balance between host governments and foreign companies could be described as wholly unreasonably in favour of the latter. This will be clearer when we have considered the question of returned value.

In comparison with these profits, tax rates were often modest. The overall average was considerably reduced by three particular cases which we considered above. These were the exceptionally favourable position of IPC in Peru (table 1.7) as a result of its exemption from almost all taxes in return for an immediate cash settlement in 1922, the very high profits made by the most successful operators in Mexico during the Revolution and the high distribution profits made in Latin America during the First World War. One might also add that Jersey Standard for a time enjoyed an exceptionally favourable position in the Argentine market after it was allowed to escape duty on refined oil imports by using a small topping plant at Campinas; this loophole was closed after 1925.

The remarkable example of IPC can be placed in better perspective when set beside Lobitos Oilfields (table 1.8), which was subject to the normal taxes and duties operating in Peru at that time.[28] As Thorp and Bertram point out, 'for IPC the profits on its sales of products *within* Peru were sufficient to meet the entire local currency cost of producing for export, with the result that the IPC, despite its role as the leading single export enterprise of the 1920s, played virtually no part in the actual supply of foreign exchange to the market'. (Original italic.)[29] It is fair to note that IPC did build up its investments in Peru

Table 1.7 *IPC and the Peruvian economy 1916–34*
(000 US $)

	Local payments to			Total local payments	Local sales income	Total sales income	Est. profit
	Labour	Government	Other				
1916	875	250	111	1,236	702	7,018	4,243
1917	803	364	115	1,282	1,118	5,993	3,014
1918	739	444	116	1,299	2,059	7,756	4,926
1919	1,230	590	182	2,002	2,007	11,631	7,710
1920	1,538	574	211	2,323	2,744	8,827	4,025
1921	1,393	484	188	2,065	2,191	15,353	5,960
1922	1,455	1,875	231	3,561	1,956	21,837	16,312
1923	1,648	937	255	2,840	2,885	18,618	12,408
1924	1,669	1,385	304	3,358	3,495	24,814	17,649
1925	2,240	988	324	3,552	4,948	23,132	15,100
1926	2,448	1,704	417	4,569	3,984	27,082	15,966
1927	2,678	1,690	436	4,804	4,916	37,352	26,132
1928	2,755	2,152	492	5,399	5,923	45,675	36,227
1929	2,452	2,676	452	5,580	5,884	50,520	41,140
1930	1,878	1,878	374	4,130	5,080	24,968	18,508
1931	1,057	1,589	265	2,911	3,867	15,760	11,260
1932	1,581	1,193	277	3,051	2,500	15,643	11,803
1933	1,327	2,122	345	3,794	2,312	17,926	13,171
1934	1,796	3,349	514	5,659	3,486	28,194	20,554
Total	31,562	26,244	5,609	63,415	62,057	408,099	286,108

Source: R. Thorp and G. Bertram, *Peru 1890–1977: Growth and Policy in an Export Economy* (London, 1978), pp. 105.

considerably during the period and expanded the Talara refinery in 1919–20. Nevertheless Lobitos, by this time also a profitable company, made local currency payments during this period (1916–34) which amounted to 43% of total sales income. Without going into details on the different position of the two companies,[30] it is worth noting that IPC owed its exceptionally favourable position, at least in part, to the fact that it had a monopoly of the domestic market. Thus, in 1918, in the midst of a taxation dispute with the Peruvian government, IPC cut its supplies of oil to Lima, following which the Peruvian government came to terms with the company. It is also worth pointing out that Jersey Standard used its good offices several times on behalf of Peru within the USA in order to secure loans for the Leguía government (1919–30), many of which were subsequently defaulted.

Table 1.8 *Lobitos Oilfields Ltd and the Peruvian economy 1916–34*
(000 US $)

| | Local payments to | | | Total local payments | Total sales income |
	Labour	Government	Other		
1916	245	58	29	332	495
1917	230	115	34	379	898
1918	206	153	37	396	1,214
1919	349	202	54	605	1,712
1920	450	161	60	671	909
1921	458	94	54	606	1,097
1922	481	212	69	762	2,067
1923	736	436	119	1,291	2,478
1924	1,041	587	162	1,790	3,009
1925	1,324	720	204	2,248	4,292
1926	1,432	826	227	2,485	4,479
1927	873	1,015	190	2,078	5,450
1928	699	985	167	1,851	5,264
1929	856	1,032	188	2,076	6,980
1930	646	858	152	1,656	4,900
1931	371	792	117	1,280	2,913
1932	606	580	119	1,305	3,322
1933	558	522	107	1,187	2,252
1934	792	765	156	1,713	3,229
Total	12,353	10,113	2,245	24,711	56,960

Source: Thorp and Bertram, *Peru 1890–1977*, p. 107.

Evaluation of Venezuela is complicated both by the unreliability of most statistics and also by the fact that companies entering the country at different times were able to make different financial arrangements. Thus Royal Dutch/Shell, which was the first major company to enter Venezuela, found itself in a particularly fortunate position. According to Brian McBeth, 'Shell between 1922 and 1935 accounted for 43% of total production, but only paid 34% of the total tax bill for the period'.[31] Moreover, large-scale profits were not generally made during the boom years of the early 1920s; only in 1928 did capital, on balance, flow out of the oil industry and only after 1930 was the net capital outflow pronounced. Taxes were, in fact, based mainly on concession area rather than production and therefore tax revenue per tonne fell from a high point in 1922 to a far lower level after 1925. Companies which entered the country under the 1922 law paid rather less than 10% of the international value of their crude oil up until 1935, whereas Shell, as we have seen, paid significantly less. To these tax revenues must be added the cost of acquiring concessions, which also varied considerably between companies but which (as we shall see in chapter 2) was in general significantly less than payment of taxes. Perhaps it is not surprising that in May 1930 *World Petroleum* declared that 'probably nowhere else do oil companies enjoy advantages equal to or greater than those which the government of Venezuela grants them for the purpose of stimulating operations'.

The most interesting case, however, is that of Argentina, for here there is available information on the terms Lord Cowdray and Deterding were willing to offer in return for the right to take over the government's oilfield in Comodoro Rivadavia. This oilfield was particularly tempting because of both its considerable size (later found to be over one billion barrels) and the availability of a ready market. As Masters wrote to Cowdray in 1913, 'If oil was found in quantity in the Argentine it would surely have one of the best home markets that could possibly be found, and therefore the Argentine will appeal to me before some of the other industries that we have been giving attention to.'[32] In 1915 Deterding wrote:

I would propose to make an arrangement with the governments for the development of petroleum areas in South America whereby we would furnish the capital. Of the net profit, after depreciation, we will take 5% cumulatively on capital, while we would be willing to give to the government 25%, even 50%, of the remainder. I think that the government of China only receives ⅜ from Standard . . .

[Regarding Argentina] In negotiating with the government about the money which she has already invested in the industry we could give her, in the case of our obtaining the territory, 5% preference shares on the amount she has already invested. Outside this 5% they would, of course, have no share in the profits. If the government was to ask why it could not share in the excess profit, we could give them the answer that this money has already been spent and with less money we could get better results than the government obtained.[33]

In 1919 Cowdray was willing to offer the government a 65% share in the profits of a joint venture, but only on condition that the government provided all its field assets (which were the result of 12 years' work) to the company and continued to invest on equal terms. Otherwise Cowdray would be willing to take over these assets, carry out all further investment and offer a 50–50 split, provided that no taxes or price controls applied and that, before any profit were shared, each party would receive a 7.5% return on its share of the capital. Neither offer was accepted.

Until the late 1940s there was no general acceptance of what equitable taxation or profit-sharing arrangements might be and practices, as we have seen, varied widely. Nevertheless, despite some important differences between companies and despite the fact that the data for the 1920s are very incomplete, it is clear that taxes were often nominal and even when they were more realistic they had nothing in common with those prevailing after 1945. Taxes, of course, were not the only or necessarily even the most significant element in returned value. Labour costs were still an important part of company spending; as we have seen (tables 1.7 and 1.8) both IPC and Lobitos in Peru spent more on labour costs than on taxes and this was also the pattern with the oil companies in Venezuela (see table 2.3). There are no reliable figures for Mexico in the 1920s, but in 1936 (when there was little active investment by the companies) labour costs were estimated at 49m. pesos ($13.6m.) against total tax payments by the industry of 50m. pesos ($13.8m.) – in other words, at $0.331 a barrel against $0.336.[34] Even more important, as we shall see in the next section, there were several Latin American countries in which the lion's share of all returned value went to local elites or regional governments.

Even with these qualifications, it is clear that the 1920s was a period in which tax rates were low, local elites relatively undemanding and profit opportunities seemingly unlimited. The gain to Latin America from the activities of the oil companies came less through any immediate return than through the opportunities provided for the longer term. Once major discoveries had been made and important fields developed, host countries would be in a much better position to take advantage than they had been at the start of operations. The companies themselves could argue that the oil industry was relatively competitive during the 1920s and that profits were the reward for extraordinary risk taking, for adapting to rapid technical changes and, above all, for opening up a genuinely new international industry.

Local and international capital

When considering the Latin American response to foreign oil investment in more detail, it must be borne in mind that the oil industry as a whole was undergoing a period of very rapid expansion. One striking

feature of the period, however, is the lack of any strong performance
by the Latin American bourgeoisie; by 1928 practically all significant
activity in the oil industry was in the hands of the transnationals or of
state companies. There are two essential reasons for this, which are
theoretically very distinct but in practice largely complementary; the
first involves the capital and technical requirements of the oil industry
and the second concerns the nature of the domestic capitalist class in
Latin America at the time.

It is evident that the technology required to extract oil will vary
according to the geological conditions, and that the technical possibilities will vary along with new developments and discoveries. Nevertheless, at the risk of generalising too sweepingly, it would appear that
technical and capital requirements for developing oil in Latin America
on a significant scale were always considerable and sometimes vast. It
is also undeniably true that the 1920s was a period of rapid innovation
in both drilling and refining techniques. Moreover, seismic exploratory
work began seriously in the 1920s in both Mexico and Venezuela.
Thus, in its *Annual Report for 1924* Shell stated that 'in many fields,
the old fashioned driller has had either to train himself into a drilling
engineer or make place for others'. In the case of the Lobitos Oilfields
in Peru, the field manager in 1927 'estimated that 65% of production
came from the deep-drilling programme commenced in 1923'.[35] Deep
drilling was naturally a very relative concept, for in 1927 Shell drilled
the deepest well in Latin America, a dry hole, of some 600 feet. Nevertheless the replacement of cable by rotary drilling was a major landmark; in 1928 Jersey Standard at last found oil in Venezuela by using
a rotary rig in a place where an earlier cable-drilled well had proved
unsuccessful.[36] Refining techniques were also transformed by the use
of the hydrocracker to convert heavier into lighter end-products for
which demand, mainly in the form of gasoline, was continually
increasing.

These technological innovations were not monopolised, but they
were expensive and thus increased the minimum size necessary for a
company to operate effectively. Moreover, the demands upon managerial competence increased. This was not just a barrier to Latin American companies but to foreign companies without particular expertise in
oil exploration; the British-owned Peruvian Corporation drilled for oil
in the early 1920s but withdrew shortly after being told by one of its
consultants that 'progress has been such as would not be tolerated by

a company prospecting for oil alone, without other means of income'.[37] It should also be pointed out that oil exploration was high risk. Even in Venezuela between 1912 and 1929 there were 152 wildcat wells drilled, of which only 22 proved successful. Thus, no company would rationally enter oil exploration unless it had either secure alternative sources of income or enough resources to be able to risk losing several million dollars on an abortive exploration venture.

Even on the Peruvian north coast, which was particularly favourable to oil development, Miller found that

> the amounts needed for the *development* of an oilfield were high; extensive investments were required in continued drilling, in the erection of storage capacity, tankers and possibly a refinery. There was no room for small operations. Small amounts of oil could not be exported; a tanker had to be completely filled from storage tanks as rapidly as possible . . . Lobitos was capitalised in 1908 at £360,000 [$1,800,000]. Even this did not suffice, for further investment had to be found from the operating surplus . . . In such a context, the expenditure on a few wildcat wells would have been a worthwhile risk, but the exploitation of a field even of the size of Lobitos would have demanded much more investment. No Peruvian capitalist could have found such funds, even if he had taken the risk of devoting all his resources to oil. A company the size of Lobitos, which was short of capital, would have been larger than any other in Peru and the venture would have involved high risks and a long time lag between investment and return.[38]

A local entrepreneur, Faustino Piaggio, did discover a small oilfield and was technically able to run it until the 1920s but his venture remained small-scale and even he offered to sell to Lobitos in 1908.[39]

In Venezuela, on the other hand, local operation was completely out of the question. As early as 1922 one major company reported that 'there is no doubt that the area is no paradise for the small producer with limited capital. The concessionaires on the whole are necessarily large and need a large capital for their effective exploitation.'[40] Later, in 1928, Jersey Standard took over an area which was 'geologically blind' and hired geophysical crews from its US subsidiary. This later proved to contain one of Latin America's most important oilfields. In Bolivia and Mexico the story was similar, the capital requirements were too great and risks were excessive to tempt local capital seriously.[41]

Rather than involve themselves seriously in oil development, many Latin American entrepreneurs and landowners preferred to seek speculative fortunes by taking out concession areas or using the privileges of land ownership to attract the interest of a foreign company. There are literally hundreds of such proposals in the files of the Mexican Eagle Company. One such, from Ecuador in 1914, read as follows:

> The petroleum business has during the last few years come to be of such very great importance that all the petroleum grounds which are known to exist on the coast have been petitioned for by private parties . . . the interested parties in this business have endeavoured to secure the greatest possible number of mining rights, which accounts for the greater number of these being in the hands of the few persons who are now the owners and of whom I am the representative.
>
> The exploitation of petroleum is at present carried on in Ecuador by the most primitive form of hand-sunk wells which are easily and cheaply made – the petroleum being usually found quite near the surface.[42]

The depth at which oil could be produced was between 7 and 12 metres; even so, this association of landowners was willing to sell out to Cowdray in return for the right to hold 40% of the capital of any company formed.

In Mexico, at least, payment to landowners played a fairly significant part in the overall financial calculations of the companies. Here it was necessary to pay a royalty which

> is fixed by law at a minimum of 5% of the value of the contents of the barrel. It can, however, be increased in the contract between the owner of the surface and the exploiter of the land. In fact, I believe that the average is about 10% rising in certain cases as high as 15%.
>
> Mr Assheton [of Shell] gave me some rough figures the other day which he promised to confirm; as far as I can remember, he told me that no less than thirty million pounds [$150m.] had already been paid out to Mexicans for royalties.[43]

Unfortunately these figures were never confirmed (or, at least, confirmation never appeared in the British records) but, if true or even slightly exaggerated, they are very high indeed. As we have seen (table 1.5), all companies together had paid slightly more than $200m. in total taxation to the Mexican government in the years up to 1926. Moreover, since El Aguila enjoyed concessions on a good deal of public land (awarded under Díaz), it probably paid fewer landlords than did its latecomer rivals. However, since Assheton's figures were not confirmed, it is best to treat them with reserve and merely to note that they are much higher than Meyer's estimates.[44] It is also notable (as we shall see in chapter 10) that in 1934 El Aguila contemplated offering Calles a bribe of 5m. pesos ($1.4m.) to settle a single minor, if troublesome, dispute; in that year total taxation paid by the oil industry was 45.6m. pesos ($12.67m.). It is quite clear, therefore, that payment to landowners, law-suits arising out of disputed claims and bribes to settle these were of significant economic as well as political importance in Mexico.

The same conclusion holds true of Argentina where the Mining Law of 1886 ensured that oil parcels could be allocated only in small blocks, thus increasing the potential for speculation. Argentina was hardly exceptional and Le Breton, the Minister responsible for oil in the mid-1920s, summed up the situation clearly:

> By maintaining an application for only ten pesos, the cost of the stamp, mining rights can be secured for as large an area as 2,000 hectares, with exclusive domination over that zone of land, without employing capital, without undertaking work, and without taking steps towards the production of petroleum. This has become a profession. This type of person solicits mining rights and then seeks a buyer; until he meets one he hinders progress and prolongs judicial proceedings, and thus it is that work which should have been commenced within thirty days has been held over for five and a half years without anything being done until the desired purchaser is encountered, and then that mining right which cost only ten pesos is sold for as much as 100,000 pesos.[45]

During the 1920s the central government in Argentina gained practically nothing from the existence of the private oil companies, although a number of well-placed private citizens made fortunes.

It is unfortunately quite impossible to quantify the returned value paid by the oil companies to local elites via rents, royalties or bribes. This amount is likely to have been significant but to have done little for the cause of economic development. It helps to explain why many local elites welcomed foreign oil investment. Even so, it is true that the larger foreign oil companies did have considerable competitive advantages over local entrepreneurs and that the barriers to entry into oil were, in general terms, large enough to have made it unreasonable to expect local capital to play more than a peripheral role. It should be remembered, after all, that the oil industry had already gone through some 50 years of development within the USA before the Latin American industry really took off and that only in a few Latin American countries were private fortunes of sufficient size to make large-scale private oil ventures realistic. It should also be noted, however, that selling out to foreigners was an option for most Latin American concession holders, and one that was in almost every case eagerly pursued.

Consequently, while foreign capital did not in any meaningful sense 'drive out' local capital, it may have inhibited the full development of the latter by its very existence.

There is a further point which was more obviously damaging to Latin American development and this concerned the politics of oil. Few foreign companies looked for technical expertise or large amounts of capital from their local Latin American allies. Almost invariably they were concerned directly either with landowners or with those who had access to political or regulatory power. Indeed, under a number of conditions, collaboration with well placed Latin Americans became a necessity for the foreign companies in view of the confusing and restrictive tangle of legislation within which they had to operate. As Mayo makes clear for the case of Argentina,

> in every case, the success of the [foreign] company did not depend only on its capital, organizational and technical resources, but also on the extent to which it was connected with the influential circles in the country . . . The securing of *cateos* and *pertenencias* in favoured areas, as well as requiring adequate technical and legal advice, created problems which only a close relationship with officials, professionals, politicians, and local businessmen could resolve in a relatively satisfactory manner.[46]

Thus there grew up a subclass of semi-politicians — often lawyers — who were in a position to sell their access to the state to the foreign companies (and sometimes vice-versa) rather than embark on the more dangerous course of serious entrepreneurship.

The other possible alternative to foreign investment was state enterprise. Argentina developed, with limited success, a state oil company, Yacimientos Petrolíferos Fiscales, which showed clearly that there might be some alternative to foreign investment if the public sector was well enough organised and determined enough to provide one. YPF's achievement is worth a brief examination here, although it will be considered in more detail below.

YPF had the inestimable advantage of taking over a large oilfield which had been accidentally discovered in 1907 by the state, which was drilling for water at the time. Thus, although limited government help was provided, there was no question of a large-scale and speculative venture being necessary. Even so, prior to 1914 it was a very open question whether the Argentine government would persevere with the venture or find some accommodation with a foreign company. After 1914, the increasing price of coal imports as a result of the outbreak of war enabled YPF to become essentially self-financing. After various managerial changes, culminating with the appointment of General Mosconi as head of YPF in 1922, YPF began to pose a serious challenge to the private oil companies operating in the country. Its success demonstrates clearly that the market for skilled personnel and technical services was relatively open during the 1920s. Much of the early work in the state oilfields was carried out by Europeans, and as late as 1925 an eyewitness reported that 'Drillers from the Carpathians and the distant Steppes of Russia mingle and hobnob with Germans and Polish drillers from the Baku and the Galician fields.'[47] Moreover, the crucial element in YPF's strategy, the construction of the La Plata refinery, was carried out under turnkey contract since, in Mosconi's words, 'in the first place, no firm was in a position to construct more than one part of the many and varied elements necessary for the distillery and secondly it would not be practicable to carry out a comparison of prices given the diversity of existing patents and systems'.[48] YPF could, therefore, easily find a US contractor able and willing to oversee and construct a large modern refinery which was beyond the immediate capacity of YPF even to supervise in detail. But it needed to be able to afford one.

The state apparatus in other Latin American countries was, of course, weaker and their economies far less developed. Nevertheless, YPF's success and Mosconi's deliberate attempt to persuade other countries of the advantages of state-owned oil were to become important in the future. It is indeed interesting that the Chilean government first took a minor but significant interest in its oil industry almost immediately after the major reform in public administration which took place in 1925. An effective, even an operational, state company had to be run on lines which were radically different from those of a traditional Latin American public sector bureaucracy.

The political response to foreign oil investment

We have already seen that the 'returned value' from foreign oil investment did not flow only, or even mainly, to governments. It will be useful, then, to draw a rough distinction between countries where landlords or state governments took the majority of the oil revenue and those in which the central government was the major beneficiary. As we shall see, oil nationalist movements in Argentina, Brazil and elsewhere can be understood only if we bear in mind the fact that these represented in large part an assertion of the rights of the central gov-

ernment over those of provincial authorities or landowners. Oil nationalists also tend to believe that foreign oil companies had a particular
interest in keeping the central government weak in order that they
might exploit local rivalries to their own best advantage. In fact this
was not always the case. In a remarkably frank letter, Ribon told Cowdray in 1913 that

I have no doubt that you realise that the sort of concession that we are trying
to get does not appeal to any government and that it is very difficult to obtain
it in a country enjoying a real parliamentary system; it is to my mind only
easy in countries of a one man government like Mexico under President Díaz,
Venezuela under Gómez or Colombia under Reyes.[49]

Most foreign companies prefer a 'strong man'; in such cases, they know
where they stand. In any case, they need to concern themselves with
what is politically possible.

In cases where governments could expect to share significantly in the
oil wealth, political strategy was often both corrupt and largely coherent. Generally speaking, the first priority of any regime is its own
survival and Latin American governments with dubious moral authority frequently found it useful to reinforce their positions with something more substantial. On other occasions the motive for corruption
appears simply to have been greed. Bertram summed up the situation
in the case of Peru:

governments operated with short time horizons and under constant pressure
to keep up their patronage payments. The great advantage of foreign firms
was that they could open the way to foreign loans which might otherwise have
been condemned as 'unsound', that they could often provide emergency support to a government when revenue was hit by local recessions; and that they
were prepared to pay bribes.[50]

Dr Bertram has in fact shown that the whole tortuous history of the
relationship between successive Peruvian governments and the International Petroleum Company can be explained in terms of the governments' desire for ready cash and IPC's pursuit of longer-run advantages.
We have already seen (pp. 22–3) the extent to which this strategy paid
off for IPC but not for Peru. Dr Miller reached almost identical conclusions with regard to Lobitos.[51]

Naturally in countries where Congress was powerful, it sought to
get in on the act as far as possible. In Peru, for example, Congress
almost invariably criticised agreements between incumbent governments and foreign companies in the frequently justified hope that

congressional wishes would have to be taken into account when any benefits from the agreements were distributed. Nevertheless, as the 1918 oil crisis showed clearly, Congress was never prepared to take such criticism to its logical conclusion. In the case of Bolivia the emergence of a similar pattern was prevented only by the absence of oil production. Even so, the British Minister reported in 1930 that Jersey Standard 'have experienced no serious difficulties beyond various attempts at blackmail which it is presumed they managed to buy off in order to avoid heavier legal expenses in the law courts. Blackmail is a thriving business and gives occupation and a means of livelihood to Senators, Deputies and others who have studied it and brought it to a fine art.'[52] Indeed, even at the beginning,

the gentlemen who conducted the negotiations on the part of the Standard Oil Company told me that at the outset the President had suggested that his company should advance the government as much as twenty million dollars. He said that if he had been so foolish as to inform his principals of the demand they would have 'gone up in the air' and at once recalled him. He had, however, adopted a policy of merely diverting attention from the subject and had eventually secured his concession without having to make any advance.[53]

It should be pointed out that it was no excess of scruple that bothered the negotiator, but merely the belief that Bolivian aspirations were far too ambitious.[54]

Gómez in Venezuela was able to use oil revenue for both personal enrichment and political consolidation. In some cases the rights of landowners to deal with foreign companies were respected but more often concessions were transferred from the government to foreign companies via various intermediaries. Here, political prudence did something to temper private avarice as when Gómez in 1923 tried unsuccessfully to bring in the German Stinnes group to counterbalance the Anglo-Dutch and American interests which were dominant in the industry.[55] Thus, although the central government never lost control over oil policy, there was created a group of concession holders and hangers-on of various kinds which had a strong financial interest in the rapid development of the oil industry.

It is interesting that several Latin American governments, including that of Gómez, were interested not simply in oil revenue but in persuading the companies to carry out various kinds of public works. The companies generally resisted such pressure, refusing in particular to site their export refineries in Venezuela when they could instead take advantage of the political position of Curaçao. Moreover, in 1923 the Mexican Eagle representative in New York reported that

Very large group leading Venezuelans desire form Development Company for national resource and industries of country and willing to subscribe one third capital to be used for office expenses and reports on project prior to directors deciding whether development feasible or warranted . . . For expansion there are at least eleven profitable industries . . . now controlled by Venezuelans who will enter . . . The entire project has the approval of the government of Venezuela.[56]

The main aim was to attract the participation of the oil companies, but these were not interested in business other than oil. Only Doheny, who was keen to find some means of getting into Venezuela, was at all positive.[57] Moreover, in (abortive) negotiations in Colombia in 1914 Ribon reported to Murray that 'we had to show that we were not after an oil contract alone but that we would take an interest in the development of the company in other directions if we became established in Colombia'.[58] He later reported that the construction of railways and ports were 'really the things in which they are interested'. Even in his contract negotiations in Ecuador, Murray was advised by the local representative to begin work on local construction projects and only then to declare an interest in oil.[59]

Apart from the obvious financial advantages that foreign companies appeared to offer, it was the general economic orthodoxy of the time that foreign investment was a desirable and 'modernising' force within Latin America. As Randall summarised the position in Colombia, there was 'a broad consensus among the Colombian élites and American officials, who perceived foreign capital and entrepreneurship as the most pragmatic route to modernization. There was no sustained, radical alternative to the pro-American position to which Colombian moderates adhered.'[60] One may make too much of this point since, as we shall see, there was often at least some degree of nationalist opposition to foreign oil investment, but oil nationalism was generally either a gut reaction or a tactical position. Until the success of Mosconi in Argentina, it did not seem to be more than, at best, a bargaining position rather than a genuine radical alternative.[61]

Oil diplomacy and its effects

It should already be clear that the economic and political advantages of the oil companies in Latin America during this period were such as greatly to limit their dependence upon diplomatic intervention from London or Washington. However, since a great deal has been written about great power involvement in Mexico during this period, it might be best to consider first Washington's behaviour in countries both geographically more distant and politically more stable than Mexico. As one might expect, there was considerable variation in this behaviour according to the situation and the ambassador of the day, but it is a reasonable generalisation that Washington's aid to its own companies in dispute with host governments was both modest and limited in its effects.

In the case of Argentina, for example, Mayo has concluded that

The State Department and the US Embassy acted as a base for support for the entry of Jersey Standard and were disposed, in principle, to support its demands. This fact . . . comes as no surprise considering the period under discussion. The interesting thing is that, while this attitude existed . . . the positions adopted by Ambassador Bliss and his superiors lacked the aggressiveness and the tough statements of policy which United States diplomacy adopted in other, similar, instances.[62]

In the case of Argentina, moreover, there was a real possibility that some form of oil nationalisation would be adopted at the end of the 1920s.

When pressures from Washington were more severe they were not always effective. For example, the cancellation of the Barco concession (belonging to Gulf Oil) by the Colombian government for legal reasons in 1926 first led to quiet US diplomacy. Later, however, the State Department appointed John Stabler to deal with the dispute and to adopt a much tougher line:

Stabler precipitated a crisis in Bogota. As a former State Department official, he assumed the responsibility to interfere with [US Ambassador] Piles and undermine his position both in Washington and Bogota. His outspoken criticism of Colombian policies aroused such intense public hostility that for the Colombian government to rescind the Barco forfeiture decree would have been political suicide . . . Stabler had become a political liability and was ostracised until his departure from the city in the summer of 1928.[63]

In general, serious political interventions by the USA over oil questions would have been costly, uncertain in their effect and generally unhelpful.

The case of Mexico is far more controversial. Whereas some scholars have seen 'dollar diplomacy' very definitely at work in Mexico, partic-

ularly during the 1910–17 Revolution, one recent study has nevertheless concluded that 'the oil companies failed to exert effective influence
on the foreign policy process'.[64] These very different interpretations
must be considered in terms of a number of distinct issues in Mexican–
US relations during the period.

The series of civil wars and local conflicts which made up the Mexican 'Revolution' several times placed the foreign companies' oil installations in actual physical danger. Since this was a time of world war,
there could be no doubt that such physical attack would have led to
armed intervention by the USA, at least on a local scale. Indeed this
was openly admitted. Whether, as US policymakers intended, such
intervention would have been limited in time and space (as were other
US interventions during the period), or whether it would have escalated
into something more drastic, remains an open question. There can,
however, be no doubt that US policymakers were reluctant to intervene
by force unless it was absolutely necessary to do so.[65]

For one thing, open warfare or serious escalation of conflict would
not be without its cost to the USA. It would be financially expensive
and politically embarrassing and, in the eyes of some key US policymakers, morally wrong. There were also special difficulties during the
First World War when Germany was looking to Mexico, or at least to
groups within it (and Carranza appeared particularly promising), to
divert US attention away from Europe. As Secretary of State Lansing
wrote after the outbreak of war,

Germany desires to keep up the turmoil in Mexico until the United States is
forced to intervene; therefore we must not intervene.

Germany does not wish to have any one faction dominant in Mexico; therefore we must recognise one faction as dominant in Mexico.

When we recognise a faction as the government, Germany will undoubtedly seek to cause a quarrel between that government and ours; therefore we
must avoid a quarrel regardless of criticism and complaint in Congress and the
press.[66]

Naturally these considerations limited the impact of oil upon policy.

After 1917 the position changed. The Carranza government had
more or less established itself in Mexico even though it was weak and
armed revolt appeared as a permanent threat. At the same time, this
government claimed the right to repudiate contracts with oil and other
companies made under the pre-revolutionary regime and to insist that
foreigners accommodate themselves to the new order. Under this new
order, as set out in Article 27 of the Mexican Constitution of 1917,

the Mexican state was the owner of the subsoil. If foreigners were to be allowed to exploit it, they had specifically to acknowledge the rights of the Mexican government and to rule out any recourse to any foreign government. The principles thus embodied had a long history in Latin American diplomacy and stemmed from a position formulated by Carlos Calvo, an Argentine diplomat of the nineteenth century. Until that time, however, they were of little practical importance since no foreign company would enter a country unless it considered its legal rights to be sufficiently guaranteed. Now that oil companies had already established themselves in Mexico, however, the Calvo Clause appeared to represent a clear threat since it challenged the principle of the universal validity of contractual obligation after the investment had already been sunk.

Company reaction took two forms. On the one hand, the companies formed a united front which successive Mexican governments tried in vain to breach. Secondly they looked for support, including armed intervention if necessary, from the US State Department. Without covering the period in detail, it may be worth considering one specific phase of this at times latent, at times overt, conflict: the period 1925–7. It begins with the passage of the Mexican oil law of 1925 which required all foreign companies to apply for 'confirmatory concessions' on their holdings; it offered 50-year terms (from the date of issue) for claims which had already been worked and 30-year terms for those which had not. This involved a symbolic invasion of what the companies regarded as their property rights and might, if legal titles were investigated too closely by an unsympathetic government, have had real economic consequences.

This legislation was a matter of concern to both Washington and the companies. However, even from the start key US policymakers were clear that they would not push opposition to its limits. In June 1926 US Secretary of State Kellogg told the British Ambassador that

He had told Mexican Ambassador some days back that he did not see what advantage American citizens derived from money spent in patrolling frontier so as to prevent importation of arms into Mexico and he thought this had given Mexican government considerable food for thought. He did not seem to think, however, that either withdrawal of recognition or raising arms embargo, either of which might result in renewed civil war, would be practical politics. It would probably be better to leave Mexican government and people to feel full pressure of financial boycott which would ultimately bring them to their senses.[67]

One of the reasons why more drastic action was not 'practical politics' lay in the weakness of the Executive in the USA at that time and the hostility of Congress to any form of foreign intervention.[68] Indeed, in 1927, the US Senate, by a vote of 79 to 0, called for international arbitration to settle the dispute and made clear that it disapproved of an excessively hawkish stand by the US government.

The US Ambassador in Mexico, Sheffield, took a line which was much closer to the intransigence of the oil companies than to the greater flexibility preferred by his superiors.[69] On the other hand the Mexican government, which had no wish to confront the USA, could not afford an open retreat. As a result there followed a long period of impasse; the oil companies refused to make any concession to Mexico, but had few ideas about how a settlement might be reached. Some of this intransigence appears to have been tactical; the General Manager of El Aguila told the British Ambassador in 1927 that 'the companies had nothing to gain by an early settlement. There was at present an extremely bad market for oil owing to over-production. The companies accordingly stood to gain more by menacing the Mexican government with closing down, than by making concessions at the moment with a view to the immediate unshackled resumption of productivity.'[70]

Neither side was particularly interested in pursuing this conflict to its end. Too many US interests were involved in Mexico for the latter to prefer any genuine destabilisation of the regime, while President Calles of Mexico needed US support too badly to risk overt conflict with the oil companies. The problem was not so much fundamental irrecon- cilability of position as diplomacy without imagination; in 1927 the British Ambassador pointed out that 'with goodwill a solution could easily be reached but this goodwill is entirely lacking on either side'.[71] Thus, once Dwight Morrow was sent to Mexico by President Coolidge to arrange a compromise settlement in 1927, he encountered little difficulty in doing so.

The Mexican case is extremely interesting but does not lend itself to sweeping conclusions. Mexico was not the first country in the world to restrict the rights of foreign oil companies while continuing to seek to attract them; this was already the situation in Romania and French Algeria. The question of retroactivity was crucial, and it is also worth noting that Mexico, heavily in debt as a result of the Revolution, was in no position to buy out oil company interests. Actual confiscation would have been followed by active intervention from Washington although this would probably have stopped well short of war. It is most unlikely, however, that any of the weak Mexican governments of the 1920s could have forced the oil issue and remained securely in office even without strong countermeasures from Washington. Against this, Mexico's right to tax the companies was left unchallenged; the US State Department did involve itself in negotiations on the tax question, but was mainly concerned to avoid a complete breakdown in relations between Mexico and the companies.[72] Beyond this, there lies ambiguity; we do not know at what point, if any, Mexican nationalism would finally have triggered aggressive foreign intervention. Certainly it is significant that the Calvo Clause in the Mexican Constitution was never openly repudiated by Mexico. Indeed, in 1925 the State Department in Washington resisted pressure from the oil companies to launch a 'preventive' protest against the oil bill which later became law, although Kellogg did take the matter up informally with the Mexican authorities and Sheffield also went as far as he could to comply with the oil companies' requests.[73] In 1928 Ruben Clark, for the State Department, went so far as to say that the 'adoption by other countries of theories of nationalisation is not our business; our only concern is with specific cases of injury and violation of legitimate rights'. Diplomacy was played out between the principles of unqualified national sovereignty and of the inviolability of contract. With nationalisation unlikely on economic grounds, compromise was still possible on the legal formulae.

If the picture drawn here is one in which US policymakers often acted with restraint and foreign companies were more often politically naive and obstinate than defiantly imperialist, this was not always how it appeared to contemporaries. The spectre of the 'trusts', the widely held assumption that the Mexican Revolution was little more than a conflict between British and American oil interests, and the Anglo-American rivalry which genuinely existed up to a certain point,[74] all seemed to threaten the sovereignty of the Latin American republics. Thus in Colombia in 1914 Ribon told Murray that

Mexico did us a great deal of harm also, for although people agree that the firm have had nothing to do with the revolutions which have been going on in that country they all feel convinced that what brought the first one about was the success of the British oil venture and that it was financed by some American oil interests with the object of having the Pearson concessions cancelled.[75]

The 'demonology' of oil is as old as the industry itself, and it is possible to find literally hundreds of examples of this kind of attitude among Latin Americans both at the time and later.

On the other hand, even if we make allowances for exaggeration, the reputation of the big companies and their home governments was often daunting. Thus, as we have seen, until the release of government records modified the picture, it was almost universally believed that the oil companies, Washington and London all played a far more direct role in the Mexican Revolution than was in fact the case. Like the actual behaviour of these actors, these beliefs reflect an essential ambiguity in which the shadow of imperialism haunted much of Latin America even where its substance was altogether smaller and less formidable. Company strength stemmed mainly from economic rather than political power.

Oil companies and governments in Latin America 1890–1927

This chapter has presented an outline of the economic structure of the oil industry between 1890 and 1927 and the major political developments. A more detailed political analysis of Argentina and Mexico during the period will be provided in chapters 8 and 10. Some readers will no doubt consider that the evidence presented largely vindicates the oil companies from at least some of their most severe critics while others will feel that corporate imperialism during the period was genuine enough. Certainly the 1920s was the peak of international corporate capitalism and there can be little doubt that the balance of international power favoured the companies in a way that would never again be fully the case. Latin American governments were also weaker than they would be later. Whether the power enjoyed by at any rate the larger oil companies was in any way matched by their contribution to Latin American development is a more difficult question.

It would certainly not be difficult to show that few governments in Latin America prior to 1928 had enjoyed more than very modest returns from foreign oil investment and that the companies benefited disproportionately. In some cases, notably in Mexico during the Revolution and in Peru under Leguía, it would appear that a stronger host government or more considered policy might have changed this position significantly. In other cases, much of the returned value that was provided by foreign oil investment was taken by land-owning or other elites. Nevertheless, even this amount probably took no more than a minor proportion of oil company profit from Latin America.

Before the balance of advantage could change decisively in favour of the host countries three developments needed to take place. Central government needed to be strengthened in various Latin American countries; this was partly a matter of administrative machinery and knowledge of the oil industry (in the 1920s, for example, Venezuela did not even have a Central Bank). The main factor, however, was political; governments which were later to challenge successfully international oil companies and their domestic allies were in most cases more secure and more strongly based than those of Leguía, Carranza or Gómez. Secondly, the climate of international opinion had to undergo some changes. As we shall see, the adoption of a 50–50 profit-sharing formula owed a great deal to the Second World War and its consequences; and in the oil industry as elsewhere, changes beyond Latin America have often influenced developments within it. Finally, a Latin American oil industry needed to be brought into existence. Once this had been done, the way was open for some governments to demand higher taxes from private capital which had already been committed and from discoveries which had already been made; governments which were less well placed could at least learn from the private companies and set up their own industries by taking advantage of foreign expertise and technology. Argentina's YPF had already committed itself to the second path by the end of the 1920s. Only the third of these changes can be attributed directly to foreign oil investment although there may also have been a limited impact on the first. In any case, foreign oil investment contributed to oil development in Latin America mainly through the long-term changes which it facilitated.

Other questions can be answered with less hesitation. For one thing, elements of open or threatened force were by no means decisive in preserving the status quo. It is not clear how far Washington would have responded to a widespread and determined challenge to the position of its companies; the situation simply did not arise. The companies could in most cases rely upon the support of Latin American elites whose nationalism, where it existed at all, was either a vague aspiration, a bargaining position or a tactical stance on the part of opponents of the government. Only in the cases of revolutionary Mexico and radical Argentina, which will be discussed in more detail below, were there any real threats to the position of the companies. In other countries, oil companies were welcomed by governments only too anxious for the access to international finance that could be expected to result.

Moreover, company profitability within Latin America was generally governed by contemporary expectations of what was reasonable rather than by the shameless use of monopoly power. Although the oil com-

panies often did stand together in their dealings with local governments, this was nevertheless a competitive phase of the oil industry in
which independent companies ventured much and sometimes gained
proportionately. Moreover, it is only fair to point out that the oil companies did invest heavily, they did run real risks, they did introduce
technical innovation into a rapidly developing industry and that, even
when oil was found, they often needed to show remarkable patience
before seeing the full fruits of their labours. The rewards were there,
but they hardly consisted of a 'free lunch'.

This point leads to a further conclusion, perhaps the most important
of all. Although research into some industries in Latin America during
this period appears to show that the Latin American bourgeoisie tended
to sell out from positions of strength – to yield its birthright for a mess
of pottage – this does not seem to have been the case with oil. While
it is quite certain that Latin American landowners proved eager sellers,
it does not seem reasonable to have expected the local bourgeoisie to
have undertaken serious oil development on its own, except possibly in
a very small minority of cases.[76] Even the Argentine state required an
almost remarkable combination of favourable circumstances before
committing itself determinedly to a policy of state oil development
under Mosconi, although it cannot be doubted that the success of Mosconi later did much to change Latin American perceptions of what was
possible, with consequences which we shall consider further below.
Nevertheless, it would be hard to argue that the 'YPF solution' made
any real sense to governments further north in which large-scale oil
exploration was being undertaken by the companies.

It is true, however, that foreign oil investment may have damaged
Latin American development in a more subtle way, by strengthening
certain local elites or central authorities which were in other respects
profoundly reactionary. It might seem unfair to single out oil companies for this particular charge since most Latin American elites have,
throughout history, sought collaboration with metropolitan sources of
economic power when this has seemed to be available. It is difficult to
know whether such an attitude has, on balance, made Latin America
more underdeveloped or less so. In any case, allowing for the fact that
the oil companies played a role in this process, it must be concluded
that this was more subtle than has been allowed for by the cruder
conceptions of 'imperialism' as well as being more important than has
been generally accepted by those with an excessively narrow view of
'economic development'.

2

Retrenchment and concentration 1928–41

For Latin America, the 1920s was a decade of open, expanding, competitive capitalism of which foreign companies took full advantage. Nowhere was this more true than in the oil industry. While the expansion of the foreign oil companies was underpinned by the support of the US State Department and the British Foreign Office, it was certainly not based entirely, or even mainly, on coercion. Latin American elites generally welcomed the inflow of foreign oil investment in the hope of quick fortunes. The 1930s, however, were years of retrenchment and concentration; oil had become abundant and the industry became concerned to avoid the consequences of oversupply. Management rather than discovery became the key to oil company behaviour.

The 1930s was made up of two distinct periods. Until 1934, the slump led to a fall in demand and the companies cut back production wherever they could. After 1934, however, there was a partial recovery and production and profits picked up, but the market was still vulnerable and vertical integration remained essential to the position of the major companies. In the late 1930s, war appeared increasingly probable and strategic aspects of the international oil industry became more and more important, although these were by no means uniform in their effect.

Achnacarry and the slump 1928–34

For the oil industry, the pattern of the 1930s was largely shaped by the Achnacarry agreement of 1928, which was made by the major oil companies just before the depression but after it had become clear that the world market was in fundamental oversupply. One of the major factors making for this oversupply was the rapid development of Venezuela[1]. When agreement was finally reached, it centred around the principle of 'as is'. In other words, the participating companies' market share would remain roughly constant in each country. Subsequently these companies agreed on the need to cut or hold down production in the major producing companies and to institute various forms of co-operation among themselves.

The series of agreements which followed set apart a group of companies – subsequently called (among other things) the 'majors' – whose size, international experience and interconnections gave them an almost permanent advantage over the others in the international marketplace. In 1929 only Standard Oil of New Jersey, Royal Dutch/Shell and Anglo-Persian (later Anglo-Iranian and finally BP) were in this sense major companies but after the Second World War they were joined by four others, Texas Petroleum, Gulf Oil, Standard Oil of California and Mobil (formerly Socony Vacuum), to make up the 'Seven Sisters'. After Achnacarry, the atmosphere prevailing in the 1920s had been totally reversed and the new pattern of oligopolistic co-operation among the major companies was to last a very long time.

The Achnacarry agreement was not a simple blueprint for inter-company co-operation but rather provided a common pricing system and a framework within which specific cartel arrangements could be made. Marketing quotas were widely put into force and were specifically agreed throughout Latin America. The evidence regarding oil production is more ambiguous. In Peru, for example, Shell appears deliberately to have refrained from making any attempt to exploit IPC's unpopularity with the Sánchez Cerro regime which took power in 1930 and the British Embassy reported that 'British petroleum interests appeared to look upon Peru as the private preserve of the Standard Oil Company'.[2] On the other hand, the widespread belief in Colombia that the Anglo-Persian had withdrawn its interest in favour of Standard Oil was firmly denied by the former. Perhaps the main difference was that although Shell would not challenge Standard for an existing concession, Anglo-Persian had no objection to exploring new territory.[3] Indeed, it should be pointed out that although economic concentration did increase considerably during the 1930s, the major companies by no means controlled the entire industry and smaller operators continued to exist in Latin America as elsewhere in the world. Where the major companies did control production, however, cartel arrangements were generally explicit.[4]

Nevertheless, the move toward concentration is undeniable. Within Latin America, one of the major features of concentration was the expansion of Jersey Standard which, having previously been at its strongest in marketing, now made a determined effort to balance its position by increasing its holdings in oil production. This could be seen in Venezuela where Gulf Oil faced severe problems because of its lack of overseas marketing outlets and in 1937 sold half of Mene Grande to Jersey Standard for $100m.; Jersey, in turn, sold half of its share to Shell. Already in 1928 Jersey Standard had bought a majority stake in Creole of Venezuela for around $18m. Its most important purchase, however, was that of Pan American's Latin American holdings in 1932 for $140m. From then on, Jersey Standard was clearly the largest foreign oil company in Latin America, with major holdings in Venezuela and Mexico to add to its earlier position in Colombia and Peru. As to the reasons for the sale,

since 1929, Pan American had been spending millions to build up its foreign marketing organisations. To firmly establish a place for itself in overseas markets would require an additional outlay of money. It could be done but it would not be easy. If a tariff or embargo were levied on oil imports to the United States, which was being discussed in Congress, the expenditure would be even greater. Moreover, Pan American's huge investment in Venezuela and Aruba would be seriously jeopardised by reason of its inability to market most of its products in the United States. The prospect of losing Pan American's entire investment in Mexico, due to the nationalisation of the oil industry, also weighed heavily.[5]

The effect of these changes on Standard Oil's production in Latin America can be seen in table 2.1.

Shell essentially maintained its position in Latin America and expanded its crude oil production more slowly while it devoted most of its attention to securing marketing outlets elsewhere. In 1928 Shell produced an average of 142,710 b/d from Venezuela – almost a third of its total global supply – while its production from Mexico (including Mexican Eagle) was only 28,000 b/d. In 1937, these figures were 206,628 b/d and 84,219 b/d respectively.[6] In 1937 Shell and Standard Oil accounted for 92% of total Venezuelan production while Venezuela provided around a third of Shell's global production, which remained at around 10% of the world total. Apart from very small-scale output from Argentina, Shell had no other producing interests in Latin America although it did take exploration concessions in Ecuador, Guatemala and Colombia.

Similar moves towards concentration took place in the USA, where the aggressive expansion of the 1920s gave way to the depression. Oil production in the USA, which had risen from 443 million barrels in

Table 2.1 *Jersey Standard's production in Latin America 1927–39*
(ooo *b/d*)

	Venezuela	Colombia	Peru	Mexico	Bolivia	Argentina
1927	0.4	36.7	21.3	9.8	0.1	0.8
1928	14.2	48.2	26.0	6.4	neg.	1.2
1929	18.6	49.3	29.6	5.0	0.2	1.9
1930	17.1	49.1	26.8	4.5	0.1	2.1
1931	20.4	43.8	21.0	4.1	0.1	3.3
1932	82.4	39.3	20.9	13.5	0.1	4.7
1933	123.9	31.6	30.7	21.3	0.3	6.4
1934	160.4	41.6	38.7	27.3	0.4	6.6
1935	181.1	42.3	40.4	18.6	0.4	5.8
1936	198.6	45.3	41.3	11.9	0.3	5.2
1937	236.6	49.5	40.3	16.1	neg.	5.2
1938	233.3	52.5	36.0	2.0	0	4.9
1939	273.0	54.5	29.6	0.0	0	4.6

Source: Larson, Knowlton and Pople, *New Horizons,* p. 114.

1920 to 1,007m. in 1929, fell back to 898m. barrels in 1930. Prices declined even more drastically, most of all in East Texas where falls to the catastrophic levels of $0.12 a barrel were common; but even within the USA as a whole per barrel prices fell from an average of $1.68 in 1925 to $1.19 in 1930 and a low of $0.65 in 1931. As a consequence of this, and of the New Deal, there developed in the 1930s a series of state-wide pro-rationing arrangements which deliberately restricted US output. More significantly for Latin America, there was now created a powerful protectionist lobby made up of small producers in conflict with the larger companies whose interest continued to lie in importation from lower-cost foreign sources. In 1932 crude oil imports into the USA were restricted through a prohibitive tariff; the effect of this was to block off the US market to Latin American oil exporters although, as we shall see, there was some relaxation at the end of the decade in the case of oil coming from Venezuela.

The immediate effect of the slump was also felt keenly in Latin America. World-wide company profitability fell sharply. Dividends paid by Shell fell from 24% in 1928 to 17% in 1930 and 6% in 1931–3, although there followed a gradual recovery, with 17% being paid in 1937 and 1938.[7] Moreover, in Peru the profits of the IPC fell from

Table 2.2 *World oil output and output of main Latin American countries 1932–7*
(b/d)

	1932	1933	1934	1935	1936	1937
World	2,963,371	3,883,894	4,102,854	3,894,268	4,913,765	5,566,426
USA	1,784,560	2,462,922	2,490,978	2,690,534	3,009,773	3,496,050
USSR	340,801	410,428	462,100	460,290	525,826	525,627
Venezuela	318,418	331,215	389,273	408,247	427,185	512,247
Mexico	90,517	92,902	104,582	109,601	112,405	128,511
Colombia	35,956	36,051	39,773	49,320	50,647	55,542
Argentina	37,404	37,516	38,447	39,170	42,341	44,926
Peru	36,328	38,154	38,412	44,926	48,200	52,077
Ecuador	4,438	4,446	4,532	4,653	5,342	5,928

Source: Compiled from *Revista de economía argentina* and the US Department of Energy, *Petroleum Yearbook.*

some $41m. in 1929 to around $11m. in 1931 and 1932 before again recovering sharply (table 1.7).

The worst year of the depression was 1932; the oil industry recovered fairly quickly. As early as November 1934, the British Minister reported from Colombia that

During the past six months, interest in Colombian Petroleum Deposits has been renewed by both political and commercial trends. Monsieur Beauvois told us that the petroleum expert of the National City Company had drawn his attention to the fact that oil supplies were again becoming a chief preoccupation of the United States government and oil industry . . . it is a fact that United States companies have been paying much more active attention to Colombia of late.[8]

Indeed, as can be seen from table 2.2, world production did increase quite rapidly in the mid-1930s, with Venezuela playing a significant part in this expansion. Profits picked up with this increase in production, although the maintenance of vertically integrated channels was crucial to the companies; Romanian crude, which did not have a long-term buyer, was sold at rock-bottom prices throughout the 1930s; and the profitability of Mexican Eagle was calculated very differently according to whether it was treated as a full subsidiary of Shell and a vertically integrated operation or whether its assertions that it was operationally independent were accepted as valid. Thus, in the years

1934–6, the Mexican government calculated that companies operating in Mexico earned an average of 16.81% on their non-amortised assets on the assumption that all exports were made at the internationally operating Texas–Gulf price. The companies' figure, based on what it claimed were actual prices, was 7½%.[9]

Companies that were genuinely vertically integrated possessed considerable advantages during this period. Since sources of supply could be controlled more easily than market shares (given the vast capital resources that had gone into opening up Venezuela, Persia, etc.), profitability was generally allocated to the 'upstream' stage. Consequently, the base of the major companies' market power came to be located in their control over the main oil reserves of Latin America and – somewhat later – the Middle East. This control, in turn, enabled them to extract near-monopolistic profits from oil once the international market recovered.

Moreover, as a result of the potential or prevailing world surplus of oil, the companies had considerable opportunities for allocating profitable production by country according to political or any other convenient criteria. This gave them great bargaining power particularly since, until the emergence of war economies in Germany and Japan, there were few other purchasers of oil. Open-market crude, deprived of entry into the USA as a result of protective tariffs, had to be sold at rock-bottom prices on the open international market.[10]

As we saw in the previous chapter, taxation from the activities of oil companies during the 1920s was not high and there was therefore little scope for major reductions following the depression. Nevertheless, the case of Venezuela shows that the effects of cutbacks in company spending could be significant to other areas of returned value. The best estimates available appear in table 2.3. These show clearly that major reductions in wage payments and concession purchases (essentially investment items) sharply reduced oil company costs in Venezuela. Moreover, the depression came at an extremely unfortunate time for Venezuela. After a decade in which the growth of the oil industry had exceeded all expectations, the Venezuelan government was beginning to consider at least the tightening up of existing legislation (which the companies had not always obeyed) and the development of a centre of expertise in the Development Ministry and possibly an actual renegotiation of the terms; the appointment of Torres as Development Minister in 1930 was regarded as a step in that direction. Unfortunately the time was inopportune and the government had to retreat. It was

Table 2.3 *Oil and returned value in Venezuela 1925–35*

	Returned value ($m.)					Tax per barrel (US cents)	Returned value per barrel (US cents)
	Government	Concessionaire	Labour	Local purchases	Total		
1925	4.05	3.28	6.95	3.86	18.14	19.15	85.79
1926	3.40	3.60	9.09	3.79	19.88	8.90	52.08
1927	3.98	3.60	11.74	3.79	23.11	6.22	36.10
1928	8.85	5.58	11.92	3.85	30.20	7.89	26.89
1929	9.00	2.68	15.32	3.83	30.83	6.19	21.20
1930	8.55	3.27	12.18	3.64	27.64	5.79	18.71
1931	7.83	0.83	6.33	3.33	18.32	6.21	14.54
1932	6.62	0.15	4.12	2.94	13.83	5.29	11.04
1933	8.49	0.19	6.42	3.77	18.87	6.70	14.89
1934	13.33	0.77	11.95	5.12	31.17	9.04	21.14
1935	15.05	5.35	12.76	5.10	38.26	9.79	24.86

Note: The main reason for the sharp falling off in per barrel taxation after 1925 was that most revenue came from surface taxes levied at a flat rate; there was also a small amount of royalty income and some other minor taxes. Much of the increase in returned value after 1932 stemmed from an appreciation of the bolivar against the dollar from 7.00 in 1931 to 3.00 in 1934.

Some other points relating to Venezuela may be noted. Shell paid substantially less in taxes than the US companies as a result of entering the country earlier when terms were more favourable. Shell was therefore more profitable but it is fairly clear, even with the difficulty of calculating an 'open-market' price for Venezuelan crude, that all three big companies did very well out of the country. In 1942, Jersey Standard's Lago Company told Shell that its pre-war production cost ex-Aruba (where the oil was refined) was $0.09 a barrel whereas Mene Grande (owned by Gulf Oil) estimated its costs at $0.08 a barrel. These costs even included some minor taxes. Even allowing that the provisions made for depreciation were somewhat conservative and that much returned value did not come directly from the production cost but from overheads or exploration/development expenses, nevertheless it is likely that the companies after 1928 took out in profits at least double Venezuela's returned value and around five times its tax level.

The bolivar–dollar rate fluctuated greatly during this period, particularly since there was no Central Bank in Venezuela which might have stabilised the rate. The rate was around 6.5 per dollar in 1925, it fell to 7 per dollar in 1931 and rose to 6.40 in March 1932. By 1934, when a two-tier arrangement was introduced, the rate had improved to nearly 3.00. The recovery in the bolivar's value in 1933 explains much of the increase in retained value during that year.

Sources: McBeth, 'Juan Vicente Gómez', pp. 236 and 239 provides returned value figures in bolivars; he also makes separate calculations for Shell and the other companies. McBeth's figures are slightly higher than those provided by David Knudson in 'Petroleum: Venezuela and the United States 1920–41' (PhD thesis, Univ. of Michigan, 1975). I have converted the figures into dollars and used oil production figures from data provided in Venezuela's *Anuario estadístico* (1938), pp. 132 and 419. Company cost figures were reported by Shell in FO 371, A 11945/503/47, Van Hassalt to Godber, 23 December 1942.

not until Gómez's death in 1935 and his replacement by López Contreras that significant further efforts were made to increase tax revenue
from the companies. Although there was no major breakthrough, some
improvement occurred through the creation in 1936 of an artificially
high oil currency in which taxes had to be paid by the companies.[11]
Nevertheless there were clear limits to the government's bargaining
power during the 1930s, as could be seen when the tougher 1938 oil
law governing new concessions remained a dead letter because the companies refused to apply for any new concession area.

Although the oil companies were somewhat apprehensive immediately after the death of Gómez, there was no serious nationalist threat
to them. A major oil-workers' strike which began in December 1936
was settled after presidential intervention, while the companies sought
to win over the political elite by increasing their production of oil
rather than the tax yield. A small export quota in the USA was negotiated for this purpose and, as can be seen in table 2.2, oil production
did increase quite sharply after 1933. In 1938, following the Mexican
expropriation, the British Minister in Caracas reported that

there are occasionally references in the press to eventual nationalization of the
oil industry as a desirable aim but I can find no indication that these references
are in any way connected with events in Mexico and oil companies are not
uneasy for the present. Position of companies is normal and there are no indications of endeavours from outside the industry to gain a foot-hold. From
discreet enquiries I have been able to make, I learn that Venezuelan officials
are inclined to regard Mexican expropriation as an unwise measure.[12]

In Peru the IPC at least found that decapitalisation could be profitable. Apprehensive about the political climate in the years following the
depression and believing (correctly) that its extraordinarily favourable
tax position could not be maintained indefinitely, the company max-
imised output while cutting investment. As Thorp and Bertram point
out,

production was pushed to the technically feasible limit while new exploration
was neglected. By the mid-1930s output at Brea–Parinas – 83 percent of total
Peruvian output – was some 50% higher than in the late 1920s. Without an
enormous increase in exploration effort, this level of output simply could not
be sustained, and by 1938 production at Brea–Parinas was falling steeply.[13]

It was during the years 1935–8 that IPC's return on investment 'was no
less than 100% annually for four consecutive years'[14] in spite of a limited increase in taxation in 1934. Despite this level of profitability, the

government of Benavides (1933–9) was more interested in persuading IPC to expand its output than increasing the tax rate and was on the point of offering IPC a major new exploration contract when the plan was frustrated by a change of government.[15] The fact that IPC continued to be willing to make small loans or gifts to Peruvian government figures, and also to the government itself, was undoubtedly an important reason for its continuing popularity.

Colombian oil policy during the 1930s was little different from that of the 1920s. It was aimed at increasing production rather than tax revenue per barrel and in 1936, encouraged by the hardening of world markets, the Colombian Congress passed a new law which aimed to facilitate oil exploration. Successive governments found oil concessions to be an avenue to credit-worthiness and local landowners, lawyers and so forth continued to trade in concessions. Indeed, successive oil laws continued to be drawn up with an eye to strengthening the position of such local intermediaries.

Oil nationalism appeared to have taken a somewhat stronger hold in Ecuador. Here Anglo-Ecuadorian, following a number of difficult years, suddenly began making reasonable profits in the late 1930s; in 1937 it was able to pay a dividend of 15%. Such an increase in affluence did not pass unnoticed and in January 1939 the Enríquez government gave the company fifteen days' notice of its intention to renegotiate its contract. The company responded by offering to increase its royalty payment from 7% to 10% and the government used the extra income to negotiate a foreign loan. Following this, and some brief excitement following the Mexican expropriation,[16] the companies were again left in peace. A bill submitted to Congress which called for the nationalisation of domestic oil marketing was allowed to lapse after the government extracted loans from Anglo and Shell. A Petroleum Congress, which the government had called in Quito in February 1939, was left with nothing to cheer.

In these four countries, therefore, there was some slight increase in tax revenue from oil towards the end of the decade together with a significant increase in output. Governments did not bring very significant pressure to bear on the companies, perhaps because of a sense of relative well-being but also because the position of the companies themselves remained strong. International conditions worked strongly against oil exporters in the early 1930s, and when conditions picked up towards the end of the decade governments showed themselves to be rather easily satisfied. It should also be noted that the short-term effects of the Mexican nationalisation did little to foster confidence in state oil companies. Even though the rise of the Axis powers did something to break up the vertical integration of the international oil industry, the major companies' cartel was for a long time effective enough to protect company positions in the main exporting countries. This was not true of Mexico or Bolivia, for reasons which will be explored in detail below, and neither was it generally true in the main oil-importing countries of Latin America. To these we now turn.

The oil-importing countries

There were no dramatic nationalisations in the oil-producing countries (if we exclude the Bolivian expropriation of 1937 which does not fit easily into any category and which will be discussed in further detail in chapter 9) but instead a gradual extension of state control. In Chile, Argentina and Uruguay oil nationalists did secure most of their objectives (as we shall see in chapter 9), although a degree of company unity and the active support of Washington and Whitehall in the initial 1929–33 period allowed the foreign investors to fight a reasonably effective rearguard action. In the early 1930s, London and Washington worked together in Latin America. Although the attitude of each did occasionally appear to the other to be tiresome, it was felt that the advantages of co-operation outweighed the importance of disagreement on particular policies. In Chile and Uruguay, for example, London was far better placed than Washington partly because oil nationalism in these countries included a certain amount of specific anti-Americanism and partly because Britain traded more heavily with them than did the USA. Nevertheless, Britain continued to co-operate with the USA largely because it relied almost absolutely upon Washington in the far more important case of Mexico (although to what advantage is not entirely clear).

These trading links made expropriation without compensation unthinkable to the Southern Cone countries, Argentina, Uruguay and Chile. Expropriation with compensation, however, was made difficult for countries with weak trade balances by the lack of international credit facilities and by Anglo-American refusal to accept deferred payment. The position was summed up with great clarity by a minute in the British archives which pointed out that 'we realise that effective (i.e. transferred) compensation is impossible for the present and probably for many years to come; and that therefore in warning the Chileans that in the event of expropriation we should press for such compensation is warning the Chileans off expropriation altogether as a luxury they cannot afford.'[17]

On the other hand, this prevention of nationalisation did not seriously interfere with the objectives of the various governments, which were not to attack the companies *per se,* but rather to check the outflow of scarce foreign exchange and, later, to move directly into those parts of the industry (notably refining) from which the companies themselves had held back. In the period of crisis following the slump – notably in 1930 and 1931 – the companies were quite unable to repatriate their funds from several countries and they found that their profits were in any case small because of the heavy depreciation of the local currency. Companies were unable to raise prices in order to compensate fully for currency depreciation without risking confrontation with hard-pressed governments. At this time, a member of Shell's subsidiary in Chile told the British Embassy

that his company were not at all keen on continuing to carry on their business in Chile, that they were unable to get their money out of the banks, and that they are always afraid that at a time of crisis the Chilean authorities may on some pretext or other seize these funds. They realised fully that the country is quite bankrupt. Speaking quite confidentially this member of Shell-Mex said that they would not in the least mind being bought out entirely provided the figure were not absurdly low.[18]

Later, however, 'international considerations' changed the minds of the companies about this question.

In Chile the question of nationalisation came up apropos of an offer by the Soviet Union to supply crude oil to Chile as a part of a barter arrangement in exchange for nitrates; the companies were asked unofficially if they would handle Soviet crude and unequivocally refused. Shell was backed in its refusal by the British government despite the fact that a British shipping company hoped to win the contract to transport the Soviet crude and the Chilean nitrates. In Argentina, a similar offer from the Soviet Union led to serious negotiations with Mosconi who was head of the state-owned YPF at the time but these were broken off after the military coup of October 1930. In Uruguay, however, a limited trade agreement was signed with the Soviet Union and ANCAP was set up as a state distribution company to handle the imported oil.

As the decade wore on, ANCAP, YPF and Copec (a nominally private but in fact partially state-backed company formed in 1935 to market oil in Chile) came to take over an increasing part of the domestic markets of the Cono Sur; in all of these countries, marketing quotas which included these countries had been agreed by the late 1930s. At the same time it proved impossible for the companies in conditions of oversupply (no matter how well concealed by cartel) to maintain the high domestic prices prevailing in the 1920s. In some cases, notably Argentina, prices were forced down by aggressive competition from the state company, whereas in others taxation played its part in soaking up company income. There were several such tax changes in Brazil and when, in 1939, the Chilean Popular Front government increased taxes on oil distribution, Shell reported that

the profits of the companies have not been large and they will be considerably smaller in future because of a new tax of 10½ cents per litre on gasoline, which represents 12 million pesos and which cannot be passed on to the consumer. Allowing for the new tax, the Shell company's profits at present would only be equivalent to about 4% on their capital.[19]

In Argentina company profitability was also low – much lower than it had been in the 1920s – and Jersey Standard in 1936 offered to sell its holdings to the Argentine government for around $40m. but the offer was refused. Even in Mexico the companies reported to their parent governments that 'the prosperity of Mexican companies depends almost entirely on exports, domestic prices being lower than in other countries'.[20] Taking Latin America as a whole, it was calculated that although Jersey Standard in 1938 had 40% of the Latin American market and that its sales of oil products had doubled since 1928, 'operating earnings had fallen in 1938 to approximately a quarter of the earnings in 1927' and the company after 1933 'as a matter of policy priced its products lower, relative to prices elsewhere, than it had formerly done'.[21]

Even more important than marketing was refining, because a state company in control of a domestic refinery was in a position to determine access to its market. The German commission entrusted by the Chilean government with preparing a refinery project in 1939 was scarcely exaggerating when it concluded that 'Oil refining is an obvious and secure investment for the state; apart from other advantages, it allows the Government direct and effective control over the marketing of oil and oil products . . . installation is simple, management relatively straightforward and construction can be carried out in less than twelve months.'[22] Not only did a refinery add a further stage of added value to the domestic oil industry, it also broke up the vertical integration of the industry. State companies could now buy cheap or barter for Soviet oil; Uruguay, when its La Teja refinery was completed in 1937, did both of these things. Even if the logic of scale and global rationality argued against these advantages, they weighed heavily with Latin American governments. As we shall see in more detail below, Brazil, Uruguay and Chile took effective control of their refining sectors during the 1930s, although war broke out at a time when only Uruguay had finally succeeded in building a refinery of its own.

Diplomatic pressures in the 1930s

The 1930s were very different from the 1920s in so far as they involved the willingness of the USA to support its oil companies overseas. There were several reasons for this. There had been a reaction against the 'war scare' with Mexico in 1927 and this had intensified after the depression and the election of a reforming Democratic administration in 1932. Up until the inauguration of Franklin Roosevelt in 1933, Washington had continued to offer diplomatic support to its oil companies. It supported and even encouraged the hard line taken by Jersey Standard in Chile when the government fell behind in its payments (see chapter 9), and it 'embargoed' a loan from IPC to Peru which was to have enabled that country to go to war with Colombia (in which IPC also had interests), probably in response to the wishes of the company itself. After 1933, however, US policy became far less favourable to the oil companies, as could be seen first in the case of Mexico.

The behaviour of Josephus Daniels, appointed Ambassador to Mexico in 1933, dismayed the British, who were extremely anxious to be able to rely upon the strong support of Washington in the event of any conflict over oil. Daniels, who had been a hawkish Secretary of the Navy in the First World War, was now anxious to atone for his previous sins by adopting an extremely friendly attitude toward the Mexican government. As a former US embassy official noted, 'Mr Daniels would never willingly make representations to the Mexican government; his past lay over him like the sword of Damocles, it had fallen once and he would never if he could help it give ground for it to fall again.'[23] Thus, when the companies became involved in their dispute with the Mexican oil-workers and, later, the Mexican government, Daniels took the view that it was scandalous that the companies should not have raised their wages to the level demanded without any necessity of a strike. He did not say this to the Mexicans, he said, but it was nevertheless his view. Personally [said the British Minister] I am by no means sure that he would not say so to the Mexicans or that he would not at any rate assert tacitly to this view if it were put to him, as undoubtedly it has been, by the Ministry of Foreign Affairs.[24]

Moreover, a British Embassy minute from London recorded that 'Mr Daniels' views may not correspond exactly with the official opinion of the State Department but, I suspect, they are shared privately by a number of officials of the present administration.'[25]

US Under-Secretary Welles was similarly out of sympathy with the companies. In 1937 he had come to believe that oil nationalisation was likely,[26] but he felt that as long as Mexico continued to act legally there was little he could do and that premature intervention on the part of the USA would only increase Mexican nationalism.[27] It is probable that his attitude also owed something to his opinion of the companies, which he revealed to the British Minister:

Conditions in Mexico to which present developments were mainly due were not present in other countries in the same degree, and [Welles] then launched into a diatribe against oil companies in Mexico who, with certain honourable exceptions, had obtained valuable concession and had always extracted maximum profit with minimum consideration for labour or any other interest. With such, he said, he could feel no sympathy.[28]

It certainly cannot be said that the entire New Deal administration was as sympathetic to Mexico as this, but the balance within it was far different from the Harding or Coolidge administrations of the 1920s (though even these, as we have seen, were more pragmatic than is sometimes believed). This became clear following the Mexican oil nationalisation which was carried out on 18 March 1938. Subsequently, although Secretary of State Hull sent a very strongly worded note to the Mexican government, Daniels completely blunted the initiative by agreeing with the Mexicans that the note should not be officially delivered. While this was certainly bold personal diplomacy, Daniels's concern to avoid a crisis over the issue was shared by Franklin Roosevelt as well as by influential members of his Cabinet. As a consequence, very little was done. In Gellman's words,

Throughout the period of oil confrontation, the United States government was unable to formulate any consistent policy. Events, rather than leadership, tended to dictate solutions. Roosevelt offered little direction . . . When settlements were reached, they resulted from the Roosevelt administration's commitment to hemispheric solidarity taking priority over the interests of the oil companies in a period of international tension. Even then, the United States tried to satisfy all parties.[29]

In retrospect, this seems to have been a very wise policy. The British, in contrast, were far too energetic in hurling protests and insults upon the Mexican authorities until the latter broke diplomatic relations.[30]

Company pressures proved more effective than those of either London or Washington, but before considering these in more detail it will be useful to compare events in Mexico with official US reaction to an earlier nationalisation, that of Standard Oil of Bolivia in 1937. Here the expropriation was of symbolic importance only, since the properties taken over were worth very little indeed to Jersey Standard. In this case, as with Mexico, a policy of simple defence of US property could not easily be reconciled with a further objective of Washington's foreign policy which became increasingly important towards the end of the 1930s: the elimination as far as possible of Fascist influence within Latin America. A hard line against Bolivia, it was feared, risked driving it into the arms of Nazi Germany. Consequently,

the US intial response to the Bolivian seizure was mild, limited mainly to an expression of regret and hope that friendly discussion would resolve the issue. The Department of State did not question the legality of the seizure decree and the subsequent decisions of the courts, nor did it pass on the company's claims or insist on any specific means of settlement. The department did, however, take the position that the company was entitled to some form of compensation.[31]

Washington also felt that an over-reaction might further undermine the already shaky political stability in Bolivia.[32] Thus it continued quiet negotiations with La Paz in the hope that it could secure an agreement to go to arbitration. However, without the support of Argentina, which was more than willing to purchase Bolivian oil, the leverage Washington possessed was very limited.

Indeed even the (by the standard of the time) very muted degree of economic pressure actually applied did not meet with universal approval in Washington. According to Wood, in 1940

the question was raised within the Department of State whether it was wise to continue to refuse aid to Bolivia. Officials of the Bureau of Mines suggested to the Assistant Secretary Breckenridge Long that the Standard Oil dispute prevented any exploitation of Bolivia's oil reserves with United States capital, and that there was a danger that 'German agents . . . will get the concession for German account and will open up credits in blocked marks as the payment for furnishing the mining materials necessary to deal with drilling and production.'[33]

Consequently, Washington resolved to offer economic aid to Bolivia if a settlement could be reached. This allowed an agreement in 1941, which followed a change of government in La Paz, according to which Jersey Standard received token compensation from the government in return for the latter's maps of Bolivia and other technical information. The USA then authorised a far larger loan for Bolivian development.

Over all, therefore, despite some differences within the US government apparatus, the direction of policy was decidedly more unfavourable to the oil companies than had been the case in the 1920s. Under these circumstances, the companies needed to maintain the unity they had developed in the late 1920s and to act alone where necessary. Following the Mexican nationalisation, for example, they instituted a remarkably effective boycott not only of Mexican crude exports but also of inputs destined for use in the Mexican oil industry. The effectiveness of this boycott increased after the outbreak of war in Europe, which closed off Mexico's major export markets. Even before this, however, the boycott had had its effect. Mexican exports could now only take place at cut prices (since Pemex owned no tankers) and, with regard to inputs,

by the end of 1938, 24 United States companies had refused to sell equipment sought by Pemex despite the fact that Pemex had offered to pay cash for its acquisitions. In 1939 at least sixteen companies continued to refuse to meet requests from Mexico . . . In the face of this tactic Mexico had to obtain part of its equipment from Germany in exchange for petroleum and to use intermediaries who would send the machinery to Cuba where it would be redirected to Mexico.[34]

During this time, relations between the State Department and the major companies continued to be somewhat strained. The State Department, while lacking any sympathy with Cárdenas and the expropriation, essentially wanted an amicable settlement on terms which both parties would accept, whereas the companies wanted to secure the return of their properties in Mexico and were not keen to make arrangements about compensation, feeling that these would make it more difficult for them to keep up their pressures. Thus, when the US-lawyer Richberg went to Mexico in 1939 to negotiate on behalf of the companies, he had clear orders not to discuss with the Mexican government under any circumstances the value of the expropriated properties.

While the companies were able to put considerable pressure on Mexico, however, they were not able to achieve the political breakthrough they had sought. The Mexican oil industry proved able to keep going despite all difficulties, and in 1940 Mexico was able to break the united front of the companies by making compensation agreements with Sinclair and Cities Service. Meanwhile the State Department, having made several abortive efforts to find a compromise between Mexico and the companies, found settlement increasingly urgent in 1941 since this was essential if the navy was to negotiate the right to establish naval bases in Mexico. Consequently, after some further negotiation, the State Department, without company support, agreed to a Mexican plan that compensation should be decided by a US–Mexican commission on which each government had one member. The total agreed was not large; the US companies were offered $31.75m., to which a further sum was added in respect of interest due for the period between 1938 and actual payment. Shortly after the war, El Aguila arrived at a similar agreement and received $81m. plus interest. The companies were still reluctant to accept the US–Mexican agreement of April 1942 and Secretary of State 'Hull told the companies that they were under no obligation to accept the terms of this award, which was the best which Washington could obtain; but they had to be aware that from then on they could count on no official support for any other question of this kind. Standard waited more than a year before accepting this solution.'[35] As we shall see in the next chapter, however, this did not settle the Mexican question but merely proved to be preliminary to a further set of negotiations.

Corporate stability and economic nationalism 1928–41

Between 1926 and 1930 the world oil market changed from a condition where there were fears of a shortfall of supply to one in which there was an actual or potential surplus of crude oil which was effectively suppressed by cartel. This new situation gave the companies considerable flexibility *vis-à-vis* producer governments and this increased further after the mid-1930s when modest supply increases became possible over and above simple recovery from the depression and when there was a limited recovery in exploration activity. With the major exception of Mexico, and the minor one of Bolivia (which we shall consider in chapters 9 and 10), the companies were able to use this position to ensure that there was little change in relationships with producer governments, which rarely showed real discontent with the course of events. Low taxation remained the rule, with payment to landlords, *ad hoc* loans to governments and simple bribery adding to this modest host country income.

If the companies essentially maintained their position in those producing countries which they regarded as most important, they did, however, lose considerable ground in Latin American importing countries. Consuming countries in a world of surplus acquired a bargaining power which was often used to set up domestic refineries and to establish state control over marketing. Thus, the governments of Brazil, Argentina, Chile and Uruguay expanded national control in varying degrees over the downstream sections of the oil industry.

The other major change which took place during the period was more temporary. Between 1933 and 1938 the US government effectively withdrew support except of the most routine kind from its foreign oil companies. After the Mexican nationalisation, State Department concern increased somewhat, but a punitive attitude toward Mexico (and Bolivia) was effectively ruled out by the priority attached to preventing or minimising contacts between these countries and Fascist Europe. The Mexican nationalisation and the Second World War did have very important effects upon the outlook of the State Department but these were not seen until later. Only the British continued to press for an undiscriminating hard line, believing that Mexico really was a semi-colony where resistance would crumble before a combined Anglo-American offensive. Fortunately Washington realised that things were not quite this simple, but neither the USA nor the companies had evolved a credible answer to the Mexican challenge by 1941.

Within Latin America, the depression led first to economic crisis in a number of countries, and the companies faced problems of controlled prices, blocked foreign exchange, non-convertibility of currencies, etc., although these did not in themselves have lasting effects. More important in the long term was the gradual development of ideas of import-substituting industrialisation which encouraged governments to seek an increase in the domestic added value of the oil industry. Although Chile and Uruguay had both made serious moves in this direction by 1941, the full effect of this transformation was to be seen after the Second World War.

3

The making of the post-war oil world 1942–55

If the position of the oil companies and their parent governments appeared highly insecure in 1941, apparent stability had returned by 1955. A part of this stability depended upon the 'Pax Americana', for the USA had emerged from its pre-war isolation to take over the leadership of what came to be known as the 'Free World'. As a result, although the countries of Latin America enjoyed considerable attention from the USA during the war years, they came to be regarded increasingly as peripheral after 1945 when Washington's relations with Europe and the Middle East came to take priority. Moreover, the full importance of the oil discoveries in the Middle East became increasingly clear in the decade after 1945, and the attention of the major companies was also directed eastwards.

For the major oil-exporting countries, the 1942–55 period fell into two distinct phases. Until around 1948 the oil market was tight; the war had increased demand for oil and destroyed capacity, and the immediate post-war reconstruction also sharply increased world demand. Demand continued to rise after 1950 but could now easily be met from the prolific oilfields of Iran, Kuwait and Saudi Arabia; even the boycott of Iranian oil between 1950 and 1953 (which followed the nationalisation of Anglo-Iranian) barely affected the international market. As a consequence, the power of producer governments – considerable in the 1940s, when the Venezuelan government was able to pioneer a major shift in profit-sharing arrangements between government and company – was far less in the 1950s. The famous 50–50 profit-sharing agreement, pioneered by Venezuela in 1948 and accepted in the Middle East in 1950, marked the limit of the progress made by host governments. The Iranian conflict of 1950–3 ended in defeat for Iran.

Moreover, by the late 1940s US policy had largely killed the hopes of certain Latin American countries that, in a world chronically short of dollars, they could secure indirect finance from the USA as an alternative to direct investment in oil. Some finance of this kind was made available during the war years, but US policy hardened after the ending of hostilities, and the overt rejection of Pemex's request for an Export–Import Bank loan in 1950 proved to be Washington's last word on the subject until very much later. Consequently, a number of countries (although, significantly, not Brazil or Mexico) began to open their doors to foreign investment in the mid- and later 1950s. These developments now need to be considered in more detail.

The oil companies, Washington and Venezuela 1941–8

In 1941 Venezuela openly committed itself to seeking a renegotiation of the terms under which previous Venezuelan governments had granted concessions to the oil companies. This provided a good testing ground for Washington and the companies, which had to consider whether to maintain their earlier position that such concessions, once granted, were inviolable and risk precipitating a confrontation, or whether to acknowledge the right of the Venezuelan government to seek renegotiation and risk the gradual erosion of their position. The position was somewhat complicated by the Venezuelan government's threat that if renegotiation were refused, it would examine closely the legal status of all of the contracts; not all of these would stand up to detailed investigation.

Over all, the position of the companies was not easy. For one thing, some of them were doubtful about the extent to which a hard company line could be maintained in the face of the competition that still existed for access to Venezuelan oil resources (a competition which was intensified by the war).[1] On the other hand, it was also felt that 'a continued policy of appeasement is unlikely to result in permanent solution of difficulties'.[2] But where could the balance be struck?

Tactically the position of the companies was complicated by a division within Jersey Standard between younger executives who were concerned to respond to changes in the international climate and the old hard-liners; Shell, meanwhile, tended to follow the advice of its local manager, Van Hassalt, who was himself a veteran of the Mexican fiasco. This division within Jersey Standard was aggravated by the very bad relations which existed between the hard-line local managers of Jersey Standard and the US Ambassador to Caracas. As the British Embassy was well aware, Ambassador Corrigan was a Democratic political appointee, whereas company executives, 'Linam, Crebbs and Greer, but especially Linam, are violent anti-New Dealers and opponents of the Roosevelt regime'.[3] Consequently, 'The American oil companies are very distrustul of the United States Ambassador whom they consider an out-and-out New Dealer and one who is personally opposed to their interests.'[4]

It was not surprising, therefore, that the initial approach of Caracas to the companies did not yield the hoped for response, and after conflicts within the government and some embarrassing leaks to the press, the government of Medina Angarita (1941–5) decided not to continue bilateral negotiations. Instead, it turned to Washington and asked for assistance. The State Department proved helpful. For the Department, 'the issue was the avoidance of any conflict between Venezuela and the oil companies that would limit or diminish the production of petroleum in wartime . . . the Department of State felt that it could not simply be a bystander when Venezuela and the oil companies appeared to be on the way to a repetition of the Mexican experience'.[5] Moreover, 'the controversy was of nearly vital importance because Great Britain was at this time obtaining the major part of its oil requirements from Venezuela'.[6]

It should be pointed out that Washington's perceptions were not self-evidently correct since they heavily discounted information from Jersey Standard as a result of the differences between Linam and Corrigan. The Petroleum Department in London, which remained close to Shell during the period, believed that if left to themselves the companies were capable of coming to an agreement with Caracas. Shell also doubted whether Caracas's determination and intransigence were really as great as Washington suggested. Thus, when Manrique Pacanins, the Venezuelan attorney general, told Washington that the government of Venezuela was under pressure from public opinion, the Shell manager (Van Hassalt) suggested that this was 'a typical example of a war of nerves' since 'there is no such thing in Venezuela as yet, as a public opinion which the government, in the last instance, cannot control or direct'.[7]

However, at the insistence of President Medina, who refused to negotiate with Jersey Standard, Washington began to put pressure on the company, precipitating an internal crisis and a subsequent transformation of policy.[8] It is not clear how far differences of opinion within Jersey Standard were aggravated by the actions of Caracas and Washington in seeking to isolate the local management, but the latter – and particularly Linam – now seemed to be badly out of touch with events. According to the official history of Standard Oil, Linam's 'standing with the [Venezuelan] government had been predicated on close personal relations with the group in power, with whom he had considerable influence, but that group had changed since the death of Gómez'.[9] Linam opposed the making of concessions to Caracas, fearing 'action elsewhere' if sanctity of contract were broken and any advantages were given to Venezuela. Against this, there was a younger group which had been involved in the Mexican case and understood the dangers of complete intransigence. This group felt that, by giving greater revenues to the government of Venezuela, the oil companies would tie Caracas into an acceptance of a modified status quo. This argument was to be heard even more forcefully later in the decade.

Washington's pressure was effective, then, because it corresponded to a strong current of opinion within the company where perceptions had been modified by the Mexican experience.[10] Under these conditions, Jersey Standard was willing to give the State Department a major role in helping to negotiate a settlement, and the other companies followed suit.[11] Moreover, the final agreement, voted into law in Venezuela in 1943, according to US Under Secretary Welles, 'went a good deal further than the oil companies had earlier believed to be necessary'.[12] As if to prove this point, it resulted in the resignation of Linam and other members of the Standard 'old guard'.

The companies needed to go still further after Acción Democrática came to power in Venezuela in 1945. AD had voted against the 1943 oil law on the grounds that the regime of Medina Angarita had failed to exert its full bargaining strength.[13] Thus, in 1945, the AD government imposed an extraordinary levy on company profits, designed in such a way as to fall most directly upon the oil companies, while in 1946 the oil law was modified and profits tax raised again. Finally, in 1948, the principle was laid down, and accepted by the companies, that 50% of total company profits should be paid to the government in one form or another.

The ease with which the companies accepted these later changes may appear surprising after the internal conflicts surrounding the far milder provisions of the 1943 law; having strained at the gnat, the companies appear to have swallowed the camel. A part of the reason for this lay in the fact that profits taxes levied by Venezuela could be deducted by the companies from taxes paid to the US government, so that they were in fact little worse off. Moreover, there was the state of the world market.

Post-war reconstruction stimulated European demand which the Middle East was not yet in a position to supply. Venezuelan production nearly doubled between 1944 and 1948 and continued to increase sharply thereafter. To emphasise the importance of Venezuela the *Petroleum Press Service* reported in 1948 that Shell had raised $250m. in New York to develop production in the Caribbean. This

serves as a reminder that the oil resources of South America, notably of the Caribbean area, are just as much in the forefront of new development as are the fields of the Middle East . . . While oil development in Colombia is rather slow owing mainly to difficult geological and geographical conditions, restrictive mining legislation and social unrest among the oil workers, progress in Venezuela is lively and incessant.[14]

A third major factor lay in the greater control which the 'reforming' group within Jersey Standard appear to have gained in Venezuela after the resignation of Linam. Arthur Proudfitt took over in Venezuela as head of Creole (the Jersey subsidiary) in 1945 and immediately set himself the aim of reaching a long-term accommodation with AD. Proudfitt 'had started in the oil business as a drillers' helper with Huasteca Petroleum in Mexico and he had profited much by his experience in those old, unhappy Mexican days'.[15] Proudfitt almost immediately set up a 'professionally staffed public relations department' and worked hard to increase the employment of Venezuelan nationals in skilled and managerial jobs; at the end of 1948 out of a total workforce of 20,500, 19,000 were Venezuelans and the company wages bill was proportionately lower.[16]

Proudfitt's most important moves, however, came in his relations with the workforce. Following the Mexican nationalisation, labour relations had become a particularly sensitive matter for the companies. The Communist Party after 1945 worked hard to try to stir up labour militancy in the oil industry throughout Latin America as part of a coherent anti-American programme and was fairly well placed in the Venezuelan workforce. However, AD were major trade union rivals of the Communists and had the advantage of controlling the government as well as a rival union of oil-workers. Consequently, after some initial hesitation, Creole worked with Shell and the AD government to eliminate Communist influence by building up their opponents. According to *Fortune,*

the new (AD) government encouraged the formation of a federation of some forty oilworkers unions, which included a flock of Communist-inspired demands that were frighteningly reminiscent of the [Lombardo] Toledano expropriation programme in Mexico. Creole, as the chief bargainer on the industry's side of the table, responded by offering unexpectedly liberal wage and benefit gains while firmly rejecting all demands involving an invasion of management prerogatives. In the showdown the government backed Creole's position, and the workers came out with 1946 and 1948 contracts granting total wage and benefit gains of 86 percent, but no seat in the board room.[17]

Some of the smaller and less profitable employers, notably Gulf, were unhappy with Creole's generosity and even complained to the US Embassy, but for Creole itself the advantages of winning the loyalty of the workforce, the technical and managerial staff and the government itself, in return for a share in the benefits, far outweighed the immediate loss of revenue.

Similar logic persuaded the companies to accept Venezuela's request in 1948 for formal agreement on a 50–50 share of the profits on crude oil. Shell agreed to this proposal because it felt that 'although it would cost some money in good years, it would be well worthwhile since it would tend to stabilise and improve all our relations with the government'.[18] Certainly during this time booming demand and higher world prices combined to maintain the attractiveness of Venezuela to the companies. Indeed, although taxes paid by the companies increased from $0.31 in 1943 to $0.86 a barrel in 1948, net profit per barrel increased even more rapidly, from $0.18 to $0.79 a barrel. There seemed to be more than enough for everybody; indeed in 1948, around one-half of Jersey Standard's total profits came from Venezuela. There is no reason, therefore, to doubt the *Fortune* report that the 1948 coup 'was disheartening and disappointing to Creole and the responsible leaders of the oil industry. The industry, while carefully non-political, had spent much time and effort on the establishment of a co-operative and stable relationship with the AD government.'[19]

It is also worth remembering that the US companies operating in Venezuela were able to deduct the direct taxes paid to the Venezuelan government (which took a progressively greater share of all taxes) from taxes due in the USA. The same arrangement – a formal 50–50 profit share with the companies able to deduct their tax payments from their US tax obligations – was extended to Saudi Arabia in 1950 and thence spread throughout the Middle East. Indeed, US companies which generally saw the need to make these arrangements early on avoided the difficulties facing the more intransigent Anglo-Iranian company in Iran. The 50–50 arrangement appeared to provide the answer to the

Table 3.1 *Venezuelan oil production and income 1943–8*

	Output (m. barrels)	Direct taxes ($m.)	Taxes per barrel (total)	Profit per barrel ($)
1943	179	55	0.31	0.18
1944	257	94	0.37	0.37
1945	323	146	0.45	0.28
1946	388	163	0.42	0.37
1947	434	262	0.60	0.57
1948	477	411	0.86	0.79

Source: Petroleum Press Service, July 1949.

most severe problems of government–company relations and to the question raised by the Mexican expropriation. It is now clear how the companies would try to prevent nationalisation in the future.

Other Latin American countries

Venezuela was one of the most conspicuous winners in the world oil market during the 1940s. As we can see from table 3.2, the increase in the government's per barrel take did not prevent a very sharp increase in Venezuelan production, which continued until the late 1950s. The country owed its success to its market position but also to its awareness of both its strengths and their limitations. Although it secured a great deal, it did not press for more than the companies were willing to offer. Other Latin American countries, however, either were less well placed or for political reasons were unwilling to pursue a similar bargaining strategy. As a result, Venezuela became even further removed from conditions prevailing in the rest of Latin America.

Conditions began to move against the other Latin American oil producers as early as 1949. In July of that year, the *Petroleum Press Service* remarked that 'barely six months have passed since the world's post-war shortage of petroleum was overcome, and there is already talk of over-supply'.[20] In the same year, it pointed to the withdrawal of some companies from exploration in Colombia:

It is particularly striking that one of the companies to suspend search work – Stanolind Oil and Gas Co., affiliate of Standard Oil of Indiana – only entered the field as recently as 1948, at the height of the world petroleum shortage

Table 3.2 *World and Latin American oil output 1940–55*
(000 *b/d*)

	1940	1945	1950	1955
World Total	5,874	7,109	10,419	15,413
USA	3,697	4,675	5,407	6,807
Venezuela	502	885	1,498	2,157
Mexico	120	119	199	245
Argentina	56	63	64	84
Other Latin American countries	177	167	202	254

Source: Banco Central de Venezuela, *La economía venezolana, 1940–73* (Caracas, 1975), p. 125.

. . . As oil has now become generally more plentiful, it is understandable that there should be so much the less willingness to face the unfavourable conditions to which operators have hitherto submitted.[21]

Thus, the 'boom period' was brief and not all countries were able to take advantage of it. In Peru, as we have seen, the need for new exploration had become obvious after the beginning of a decline in production from La Brea in 1938, and in 1939 initial discussions were held over a proposed Sechura venture. When negotiations broke down,

IPC from 1940 to 1946 devoted its attention and $22 million to an unsuccessful attempt to locate a new oilfield on the coast of Ecuador. The departure of President Prado in 1945 coincided with the abandonment of the Ecuadorian venture, and IPC proposed to the incoming Bustamante government that the Sechura negotiations be revived.[22]

When the Sechura contract was finally agreed (involving an advance payment, a 12.5% royalty and various other taxes), the agreement was destroyed by congressional opposition, which appeared to be motivated essentially by considerations of political tactics.[23] When a new government finally brought into force a new petroleum law in 1952, IPC, along with other companies, did explore the Sechura desert, only to find that it was almost completely dry.

IPC continued to be active during the entire period, although, as we shall see in chapter 12, its aim seemed to be limited to compensating for the decline in the La Brea field.[24] Shell, however, which had earlier shown some interest in Peru, abandoned interest in the country after the Sechura contract was blocked. In 1947 a Shell spokesman told the

British Minister that 'Peru, which is far less worth developing from the financial point of view than the Middle East or even, say, Venezuela, has rapidly become not worth developing at all.'[25] The reopening of Peru to private investment in the early 1950s resulted in the partial filling of this gap by local interests; Gildemeister, Wiese and Beltrán spent considerable sums in exploration but found relatively little to show for their efforts.[26]

Colombian governments also tried hard to stimulate the development of their industry, which had been held back to some extent by legislation which was cumbersome rather than nationalist. After the election of Gómez in 1950, however, exchange restrictions were eased and a number of other changes were made which facilitated further foreign investment. In 1951, however, the government moved directly into oil production after the De Mares concession reverted from Jersey Standard to the state at the end of 40 years of operation. According to the official historians of Jersey Standard, the Colombian government in 1948 originally offered the company a minority stake in a joint venture which would continue to operate the field. After some debate within the company, this offer was rejected 'for reasons of policy'. Instead the company agreed to provide technical help for the new state venture – Ecopetrol.[27]

As a result of these various changes, Colombia enjoyed a boomlet during the 1950s, with oil output increasing from 65,000 b/d in 1948 to 151.585 b/d in 1960. Colombia also made efforts to expand its refining capacity. Almost immediately after its creation in 1951, Ecopetrol undertook a modernisation of the Barranca Bermeja refinery with the help of various loans, including $10m. from Jersey Standard, while Standard was also given permission to construct a refinery of its own. Colombian refining capacity therefore increased from 23,800 b/d in 1950 to 78,200 b/d in 1960.

Colombia's negotiating position was relatively weak since it was a high-cost country where exploration involved an unusually high degree of uncertainty. *World Oil* pointed out on 15 August 1954 that 'the heavy expenses required for exploration . . . plus high taxes and import duties which total up to 60 percent in the higher income brackets, have retarded development'. The companies also had to contend, at any rate in the 1940s, with a militant workforce apparently largely under the control of the Communist Party. After a major strike in 1946, the US Ambassador reported that the head of the oil-workers' union, Pineda, called for 'energetic movement on part of all labour for

nationalization of petroleum industry'.[28] There were further strikes in
1948 and the US Embassy was in no doubt that 'the labour unions in
the petroleum industry are Communist-controlled and strikes brought
about by Communist leadership are aimed less at obtaining economic
benefits for labour than at obtaining for the Communist labour leaders
control of management of the oil companies'.[29] Despite the Embassy's
fears, the companies were able to change the situation by following the
Venezuelan strategy of offering high wages while refusing to surrender
any power. In May 1951 a State Department memo recorded that
'labor conditions in the oil industry have been relatively stable due in
large measure to increased salaries and other financial benefits obtained
by labor under negotiated contracts'.[30]

In the other countries there was less to report. Shell and Esso undertook a major but unsuccessful exploration venture in the Amazon
region of Ecuador, but the Bolivian government was unable to attract
foreign investment into oil exploration. Shell commented of Bolivia
that 'the geological information is rather scanty but such evidences as
exist are not lacking in possibilities for eventual oil production . . .
[but] it seems most unlikely that the central areas of South America
will be developed for some time to come in view of the tremendous
distances to be covered between these regions and the coast'.[31] In 1946
Shell dismissed as 'not very attractive' a Bolivian offer of a concession
in the north of the country.[32]

Although the companies were willing to share profits on an increasing scale with host countries, they insisted upon maintaining full
operational control. Countries which were unwilling to offer this had
no chance of attracting foreign investment. Both Chile and Brazil were
willing to offer forms of joint venture to the majors but neither
received a positive response. As we shall see in more detail in chapters
9 and 11, this was a major factor in persuading both countries to create
full-scale exploration monopolies.

Indeed there was no reason why the major companies should have
accepted terms which were not of the most obviously favourable kind.
They were now in control of what had turned out to be the massive
discoveries of the Middle East, some idea of which can perhaps be seen
from table 3.3, although estimates of proven reserves are always highly
conservative. The main reason why Venezuelan oil remained attractive
and Colombian and Peruvian oil marginally attractive to the companies
was that oil transport costs remained high. In 1949 the *Petroleum Press
Service* calculated that Venezuela had an advantage of $1 a barrel over

Table 3.3 *Proven oil reserves by country 1945–55*
(*m. barrels*)

	1945	1955	Reserve: production ratio[a]
USA	19,942	30,060	13.0
Saudi Arabia	3,000	36,000	103.5
Kuwait	4,000	27,500	79.1
Iraq	4,750	14,500	63.5
Iran	6,000	13,000	609.9
Venezuela	7,000	10,919	15.8
Mexico	870	2,000	23.9
Colombia	500	525	13.3
Argentina	300	300	10.3
Peru	160	225	13.1
Bolivia	50	36	17.7
Brazil	1	35	35.3
Chile	0	40	23.0
Ecuador	25	23.5	7.6
WORLD TOTAL	58,027	154,539	30.8

[a] Production of 1954, reserves of 1955.
Source: World Oil, 15 August 1956.

the Persian Gulf in New York ($0.23 against $1.23) and, surprisingly, a $0.54 a barrel advantage at Southampton ($0.50 against $1.04). These advantages, however, were gradually eroded.

The activities of the companies in the Middle East have been well documented elsewhere and need not be recounted again here.[33] However, we need to keep in mind the fact that all seven major companies were making very large profits in the Middle East, where their control over the main sources of supply was guaranteed by the massive size of the concessions, the closely worked out set of interlocking joint ventures between the majors, the sales of crude at discounted prices to even out supplies between the major companies, and the various arrangements enabling the companies to keep substantial control over levels of production. Thus, although the potential world surplus of oil was considerable (as could be seen from the effectiveness of the boycott against Iran between 1950 and 1953), prices were nevertheless kept up at the high post-war levels. All of this was underpinned by support from Washington and London which sometimes went far beyond the purely diplomatic. Under these circumstances, it is not surprising that Latin America (with the exception of Venezuela) came increasingly to be seen as a backwater.

State oil companies and US policy

By no means all of the countries of Latin America, however, were interested in coming to terms with the multinationals. Nationalist campaigns of the 1930s and 1940s had led to the establishment of state oil monopolies of various types in Chile, Mexico, Brazil and Uruguay while Argentina and Bolivia, which still welcomed foreign investment under certain conditions, also had important state companies. All of these faced financial problems of one kind or another and in some cases looked for help from Washington in overcoming them.

During the Second World War Washington did make two loans to Latin American state oil companies. The first of these was made to Bolivia, where Washington had already agreed to provide a loan for development as part of the compensation agreement with Jersey Standard which followed the nationalisation of 1937. Although held up by various political factors, agreement was reached in 1945, after La Paz agreed to re-admit foreign investment into its oil industry.[34] Subsequently, although little serious interest was actually forthcoming from the foreign companies, the Bolivian state oil company YPFB was able to borrow $8.5m. from the Export–Import Bank.

Efforts by Chile and Argentina to secure similar finance, however, were less successful. In Argentina, the State Department had for several years been concerned with what it viewed as the unsatisfactory nature of Jersey Standard's position there, where the company was restricted to its existing exploration territory and a market share which was fixed by a quota. Thus, according to Fanning, himself a State Department official,

unless the private companies obtain the right to explore for and to produce oil in Argentina or to import it to the extent of their requirements, their continuation in business is precarious indeed. The Argentine situation has been discussed almost continuously with the US State Department, which has made repeated efforts to straighten it out.[35]

In 1942, the State Department offered preferential treatment in the supply of oil equipment to YPF (a significant offer under wartime conditions) if Buenos Aires would permit 'mixed companies' including foreign capital to explore areas reserved for the state by the law of 1935.[36] However, any prospect of agreement was ended by the pro-Fascist GOU coup of 1943 towards which Washington reacted extremely aggressively.[37] After this, no agreement was possible for several more years.

The Chilean government also made a serious effort, this time in 1946, to secure a loan for its fledgling state oil industry, but its applications for loans from the Export–Import Bank, the World Bank and the British government all failed. The State Department considered the question after a request from Chile in February 1946 and a letter from a Standard Oil executive to Under-Secretary Braden asking the Department not to agree to it. There was a discussion within the State Department on 26 March 1946 in which some differences of opinion were voiced, but in conclusion Braden 'stated that this Government stood for private enterprise and that it was therefore fundamental – in order to follow a consistent policy – that we not encourage state trading abroad through public financing. In other words he wouldn't give the Chileans 'a plugged nickel' on their oil.'[38] This position was taken despite the fact that the Chilean government was willing to offer exploration terms to private companies which might have allowed profitable operations although these stopped well short of the concession terms that foreign companies and their parent governments wanted.[39]

Ultimately the most significant case, however, concerned Mexico. Here the issues raised were not marginal to the USA's main concerns (as they had been in the other countries) but quite central in view of Mexico's promise as an oil-producing country. Moreover, the question of how to react to Mexican requests for indirect finance led to an important debate within the USA, and the relatively conservative position supported by the State Department and the major oil companies was not finally adopted until 1950.

The Mexican oil expropriation of 18 March 1938 was not necessarily intended to provide the definitive solution to the question of foreign oil operations within the country. Until around 1950, by which time Pemex had effectively demonstrated its technical and organisational capacity, the question was still under discussion. Nevertheless, there were major differences between the Mexican government (itself divided into more and less nationalistic factions) and the major foreign companies for whom the US Embassy in Mexico (after the retirement of Josephus Daniels in 1942) and the State Department emerged as spokesmen. The Mexican government passed a petroleum law in 1941 which provided for joint ventures between the Mexican state and foreign capital in oil exploration ventures, provided that the state took 51% of any partnership and provided that all the oil produced was exported. The objective of this legislation appears to have been to win over some smaller US oil producers in order to break the boycott which the major oil companies still maintained over the provision of supplies to Mexico. It should also be pointed out that during this time Pemex's performance gave little confidence to those who believed that Mexico could 'go it alone'.

At the same time, if Pemex was to avoid the return of direct foreign investment of the traditional kind, it needed to finance its acquisitions of foreign equipment and technology. There was little possibility, at least at first, that Pemex could generate the necessary funds internally. Thus, the Mexican government began to search for indirect financing from the USA. Its efforts in this direction did not meet with the unqualified rejection that might have been supposed, despite the fact that the compensation agreement with the companies made in 1942 appeared extremely generous to Mexico. This was because the Interior Department under Harold Ickes, which had been given the responsibility for ensuring that oil supplies were adequate to meet wartime requirements, was far less interested in the question of ownership than was the State Department. Moreover, on a number of crucial questions, the Interior Department could count on the support of the President.

The interventionist position of the Interior Department was not confined to Mexico. Indeed, in 1943 the Department, together with the US navy, persuaded President Roosevelt to set up a new parastatal corporation to give the US government a controlling interest in the Aramco concession in Saudi Arabia.[40] When this plan met with opposition, Ickes made an alternative proposal which was that Washington should build a thousand-mile-long pipeline in Saudi Arabia to enable the US companies to export their oil in return for company provision of cut-price supplies to the US navy. This plan also proved abortive.

It is clear that the Interior Department, often with the support of the US military, for national security and other reasons, was interested in involving the US government directly in the world oil industry, in contrast to the State Department, which preferred to protect, and perhaps influence occasionally, the position of the US oil companies. Certainly the Interior Department and the US military for several years pursued the idea that Mexican oil could be treated as a strategic reserve by the USA and developed by means that were more acceptable to Mex-

ico than simple concession arrangements made with the major companies. This view was close to Mexico's idea of a series of limited technical and drilling contracts with the smaller private companies,
financed from Washington, but under the direct supervision of the
Mexican government. This conception was also welcome to a number
of smaller US oil companies which were only too willing to enter Mexico under such guaranteed terms.

The State Department and the major companies decidedly did not
share this view. The outbreak of war brought the State Department
closer to the major oil companies, with whom it operated a system of
international rationing and distribution. In 1943 the State Department
implicitly accepted the companies' position that

> private enterprise is the best medium for oil development, and that oil con-
> trolled by American corporate interests is equally available for the needs of
> national security with that owned wholly or in part by the United States
> government. Secondly, the American petroleum industry should be encour-
> aged to expand its plans for developing the world's resources.[41]

The difficulty with the harder-line position taken by the State Department was that it was clearly unacceptable to the Mexican government.
One of the chief principles under which the major companies operated
was an absolute unwillingness to take part in oil exploration activity in
joint ventures with host governments. Thus, although the major companies were willing to abandon their claims over the Mexican subsoil
and accept contracts for limited periods of time rather than in perpe-
tuity, they insisted upon maintaining full operational control, a
requirement which would have necessitated amendment to the Mexican oil law of 1941 and thus an open retreat by Mexico. However,
quite apart from the need to avoid 'action elsewhere', neither the State
Department nor the companies saw any need for compromise in the
Mexican case. Both believed that, partly as a result of the boycott
(which remained in effect for some time after the compensation agreement) and partly for organisational and technical reasons, Pemex could
not provide a viable long-term alternative to some form of foreign
investment. By the time this belief had been clearly shown to be false,
the companies had established production in the Middle East on such
a scale that Mexico ceased to appear important.

Between 1942 and 1950, the Mexican government tried to deal with
the USA on terms that were acceptable to the Interior–Defence faction
but found that the State Department – major company axis blocked

anything which would strengthen Pemex. Mexico did, however, achieve one important success when in 1943 it secured an Export–Import Bank loan of $10m. (with the express approval of President Roosevelt) for a refinery at Atzcapotzalco. This was completed too late to influence the war effort but proved helpful to Pemex in supplying the Mexican market.

Between 1943 and 1946, however, no further decisions were made. Since the period has been covered elsewhere in quite considerable detail,[42] there would be no point in discussing it again here. It should be pointed out, however, that even the State Department's oil policy was of secondary importance to its overall concern for political stability within Mexico. In March 1945, for example, the US Ambassador (Messersmith) told Washington that 'the political situation is of so serious a nature that it would be futile at this time' to pursue the oil question.[43]

Despite certain hopes within the USA, moreover, the accession of Miguel Alemán to the presidency in 1946 did not lead to the change in oil policy that would have been necessary to attract foreign investment on a significant scale (see chapter 17). The Mexican government, however, and particularly Antonio Bermúdez, who became director of Pemex in 1947, made a very determined effort to secure indirect finance and technical help from the USA on his own terms. Bermúdez proved himself adept at playing upon differences within the USA, much to the annoyance of the State Department, and in 1948 invited the Wolverton Committee of the US House of Representatives to see the oil industry for themselves. Their report was favourable to Bermúdez's proposed project.

This project involved a massive loan to Pemex from the Export–Import Bank, amounting to some $475m. which was to be used to discover and develop around one million barrels of oil, roughly doubling Mexican oil reserves and production which at that time amounted to some 160,000 b/d. Following the visit of the Wolverton Committee, Bermúdez in 1949 signed a number of drilling contracts with independent US companies and, later in the year, returned to Washington to seek a loan from the Export–Import Bank, this time scaling down the request to $150m. and emphasising that this would be used to develop downstream activities. Even though Bermúdez received support from President Truman, the State Department did not change its attitude, which was frankly spelled out in a memo of May 1950. Although, it said, it had earlier agreed 'to make loans for the construction of transportation, storage and refining facilities', it now felt that the question was more symbolic than substantive since the Mexican Ambassador 'clearly implied that Mexico does not attach great importance to the utilisation of all the credit'. Moreover, to offer the credit to Pemex would be to favour the political position of Bermúdez who had, after all, largely frustrated the State Department's efforts to secure the return of concession contracts. Bermúdez 'is the official most interested in the loan. He aspires to be elected President in 1952 and he believes that the granting of a petroleum loan will improve his chances'. The main objections, however, were strategic:

an unconditioned [*sic*] petroleum loan would be interpreted in Mexico and throughout the world as United States government approval of a nationalistic approach to the problem of oil development. This interpretation would be in direct contrast to established United States foreign economic policy. This interpretation would weaken the position of the strategic Venezuelan industry.[44]

Remarkably, the State Department's position was not supported by President Truman. Earlier in 1950, Truman had said:

I want a loan granted to Mexico for refinery and pipeline development. I want private arrangements made with our wildcat drillers for the proper extension of drilling. Something is slowing the programme. Get me all the facts. Watch the successors of Teapot Dome and see if we can't help Mexico and the Mexican people.[45]

When faced with the State Department memo, he '*rejected* this and told Webb he definitely wanted an *oil loan*' (original italic).[46] Dean Acheson, however, took a very different position and claimed that 'Mexican officials in Washington have asserted that such a loan would 'consecrate' the principle of expropriation, and the Mexican Ambassador in Caracas recently urged Venezuelan officials to nationalize the one billion dollar oil industry.'[47] Eventually a compromise was worked out; the Export–Import Bank made a loan of $150m. to Mexico for non-oil projects following which the Mexican government passed on a similar sum in pesos to Pemex.[48]

The Mexican case helped US policymakers to iron out internal conflicts and arrive at a coherent policy. Although, as we have already seen, it is important to note that US–Mexican relations were by no means typical of US relations with Latin America as a whole, it was now decided that no concessionary finance was to be made available to state oil companies in Latin America or to countries in dispute with

foreign companies. The 'strategic' considerations which had underpinned the more interventionist strategy of the Interior Department
appeared less pressing with the ending of the Second World War and
with the massive Middle Eastern discoveries which transformed a
potential world shortage of oil into a threatened world glut. Moreover,
after the Mexican nationalisation and the internal divisions over Venezuela, the companies had come round to a position which offered good
possibilities of protecting their own long-term interests in ways which
did not require constant resort to Washington; indeed, it is likely that
the companies responded to the wartime activities of the Interior
Department by drawing the conclusion that help should be sought
from Washington as rarely as possible.

The new US strategy on the oil question was strengthened by the fact
that the World Bank adopted similar policies. Under the presidency of
Eugene Black, the World Bank adopted a strong position in favour of
private enterprise and was unwilling to finance public sector projects
in areas where private investors might be interested. Indeed, the whole
question of 'development aid' was still open at this stage; the World
Bank had begun by concentrating on post-war reconstruction and only
gradually came to specialise in development lending to the Third
World. However, as early as 1949 the Bank referred to events in Mexico

which began, in April 1947, with the application by Mexico for a large loan
for a series of hydroelectric, irrigation, oil pipeline, railway, port and highway
projects . . . Extensive further development of the country's oil resources still
awaits adequate prosecution [sic]. Although the difficulties are appreciated, it
would appear that one course which might bring about a quick transformation
of Mexico's economic situation would be the conclusion of appropriate
arrangements for oil exploration and production of a type which has proved
successful in other countries.[49]

In fact, the Bank did lend quite heavily for electric power projects but
no loan was made to the oil industry.

Under the Democrats, the US refusal to grant loans to state oil
monopolies was intended primarily as a defensive measure, aimed at
eliminating a possible alternative to concession arrangements for countries interested in large-scale development of their oil industry: sometimes loan finance was supplied quietly as part of a package. Under the
Eisenhower Administration (1953–61) the USA became more ambitious
and began to use the promise of aid to induce Latin American govern-

ments to open their territories to foreign companies for oil exploration. This change can be seen in the cases of Bolivia and Argentina where it had the most impact.

The Bolivian Revolution of 1952 brought to power a political party, the Movimiento Nacionalista Revolucionario, whose relations with the USA had previously been bad because of Washington's suspicions that the MNR had Fascist sympathies. The MNR promptly added to these suspicions when it nationalised Bolivia's tin mines. For various reasons, however, including Bolivian fear of bankruptcy and US concern with the dangers of chaos or undue Argentine influence if the MNR fell, Washington and the MNR began to move closer together and the State Department began to consider supplying aid to Bolivia. One of the conditions for aid, however, was that Bolivia show itself independently friendly towards foreign investment and 'agreements with McCarthy [oil company], Gulf Oil and other US and foreign interests became the touchstone of the MNR government's willingness to collaborate with foreign capital in the development of the country'.[50] Although, as we shall see in chapter 13, the Bolivian authorities were independently favourable towards a return of foreign investment, the USA made a great deal of the running on this question. The Bolivian oil code was drawn up by the US law firm Schuster and Davenport and, once drafted, was passed 'without debate or modification by the Bolivian authorities'.[51] US aid then followed.

The importance lent by the Republican Administration to the granting of oil concessions can also be seen in the case of Argentina. During the 1950s there was a constant stream of diplomatic efforts aiming at persuading Argentina to open its doors to foreign capital. It did achieve some success, but Argentine nationalists, as we shall see in more detail below, were able to reverse both Perón's and Frondizi's efforts to attract foreign companies into oil exploration.

In many other countries, however, Washington's pressures proved ineffectual, largely because they were outweighed by factors which had more to do with the economics of the oil industry.[52] The state oil companies of Chile, Brazil and Mexico expanded during the period with a major stimulus coming from the growth of consumption (see table 3.4). This expansion encouraged domestic refining which, in turn, became the backbone of state oil companies.

Even without finance from Washington few governments had difficulties with refinery projects. The Brazilian government in 1949 used frozen credits to buy French equipment for the first government-owned

Table 3.4 *Oil consumption in selected Latin American countries 1930–53*
(000 *b/d*)

	1930	1935	1940	1945	1950	1953[a]
Argentina[b]	52,059	52,260	79,395	100,299	152,760	174,870
Brazil	14,070	17,085	25,125	25,125	86,631	130,650
Mexico	30,954	37,386	73,968	101,505	154,770	198,990
Venezuela	2,412	2,211	9,246	10,653	30,150	48,240

[a] 1952. The figure for 1953 (40,200 b/d) was based on a different series which excluded oil used by the companies themselves.
[b] The figures for Argentina include products re-exported to Paraguay.
Source: Petroleum Press Service, 1950 and 1954.

refinery of any real economic importance, at Cubatão, while a smaller refinery was expanded by Kellogg. Subsequent refineries were financed partly by trade credits and partly by companies looking for an outlet for their crude. ENAP's first refinery, constructed by Kellogg at Concón, came onstream in September 1954, while Pemex invested heavily throughout the late 1940s in a number of refineries capable of servicing Mexico's new or expanding industrial centres.

Moreover, while state companies sometimes faced financial problems, they were certainly not held back by technical difficulties. Capital goods suppliers from both Europe and the USA (and later Japan) were only too eager to find Latin American buyers, whether for refineries, drilling equipment, tanker terminals or pipelines. Indeed, a number of state companies came to rely heavily on small, specialised suppliers of particular services who also worked under contract from the multinationals. In the USA in 1955, for example, 'small companies or specialists drilled three-quarters of all new oil wells . . . a large proportion of the drilling was done by specialists under various risk-sharing agreements with the largest companies'.[53] Similarly, refining gradually became the province of specialised builders; according to Adelman, 'no refiner builds his own plant; there is a separate and well-known group of construction firms whose name is legion around the world. Many important processes are patented, but these are all duplicated by competing processes and royalties are low'.[54] This list of activities could be extended further; Williams Bros. built most of the pipelines which integrated YPFB's distribution network in Bolivia during the 1950s, and specialist geophysical companies were widely used in exploration by the state oil companies of Latin America.[55] In these circumstances, state companies had little difficulty in securing access to the technology needed for them to operate on a single-country basis, even though the major oil companies continued to play an important role in the international markets. Thus, for example, in Chile 'ENAP has contracted whatever specialised or technical work it required; it has explored the vast continental extent of Chile with geological and geophysical surveys and has followed up with drilling, realising that the hydrocarbon reserves discovered and tapped in the Magallanes zone would not last forever.'[56]

The USA and the companies in post-war Latin America

The war years and their immediate aftermath would provide a good deal of material for a student of internal US policymaking processes as they affected oil policy. Certainly internal conflicts were more in evidence at this time than they had ever been before. However, too much should not be made of this apparent internal disunity since the US government was nevertheless able to act on a number of measures; insiders may see conflict at times when those affected by particular policies may be only too well aware of their underlying continuities. What were the underlying continuities of US and corporate policy during this period?

Here we must make a distinction between those countries (notably Venezuela and much of the Middle East) which were central to the world oil industry and those (including the rest of Latin America) which were increasingly peripheral. With respect to the first category, the top priority of government and company policymakers was to protect major company investments in these countries. During the negotiations with Venezuela leading to the 1943 law, those who believed that this could best be done by making limited concessions prevailed over those who preferred an unambiguous hard line. Subsequently the companies, supported by Washington, made a concerted effort to win the support of their labour force, their technical staffs and their host governments by increasing the payments made to each. At the same time, there could be no question of sharing power; the companies were determined to maintain control of the market, partly to protect their immediate profitability but also in order to guarantee security of supply and to maintain intact the highly sophisticated system of transactions which had grown up between them. Thus, although the companies were willing to concede more than had been the case before the war, there were limits. As Iran found to its cost, the velvet glove still concealed an iron fist.

In countries which were less important to the overall world pattern, the US government was still concerned to encourage the opening of oil to foreign capital. Here there was some dispute between the Interior Department, which was eager to see a greater US government interest, and the State Department, which backed the interests of the major companies and thus tried to insist that terms were offered which were acceptable to them. By 1950 the latter position had prevailed, although its impact upon Latin American policymakers was surprisingly limited, with neither Brazil nor Mexico making concessions to the US position.

It would be a mistake to see this support for foreign investment in purely economic terms. In the 1940s and 1950s the USA did have a very ideological view of the world, and state enterprise, like neutrality, was seen as immoral. Economic development was to be brought about in the underdeveloped countries by means of private investment, with foreign aid playing only a very secondary role in those infrastructural projects which private capital would not touch. Foreign oil investment was often seen as a 'good thing' irrespective of its immediate effects upon the USA. Thus, for example, the US Ambassador to Bolivia, which was not the most central of US concerns, reported in 1950 that

since my arrival here I have worked diligently on the project of throwing Bolivia's petroleum industry wide open to American private enterprise, and to help our national defense program on a vast scale . . . I know that you would be interested to hear that Bolivia's petroleum industry and the whole land is now wide open for free American enterprise. Bolivia is, therefore, the world's first country to denationalize or have nationalization in reverse and I am proud to have been able to accomplish this for my country and the administration.[57]

Subsequently, after the 1952 Revolution, the entry of Gulf Oil into Bolivia proved to be a prerequisite for serious help from the USA, although it would be nonsense to claim that the aid was intended to protect Gulf's investment; given the magnitude of US aid between 1955 and 1964 it would be as true to suggest the reverse. In fact, it seems to have reflected the US assumption that, in pursuit of development, 'all good things go together'.[58]

4

The major companies in retreat 1955–70

The middle 1950s was a high-water mark for the major companies. The Iranian challenge had been defeated and producer governments were quiescent. Rapidly increasing demand in Europe allowed the progressive development of the highly profitable Middle Eastern finds without creating major tensions elsewhere. The major oil-exporting countries were still being developed almost exclusively by consortia in which the major companies had controlling interests, and elaborate schemes had been arranged to regulate the supply of oil from these countries.[1] In the following 15 years, however, this position was steadily eroded; the actions of producer governments, although essentially defensive, became increasingly important after the formation of OPEC in 1960, but the immediate challenge to the majors came from the independent companies – the newcomers – who were becoming increasingly prominent in the search for foreign oil supplies. Under these circumstances, world prices began to erode and this erosion brought further tensions and conflicts into the international oil market.

The first significant erosion of the major companies' control over the most important non-US oil reserves came in Venezuela, where in 1956 Pérez Jiménez offered a massive new round of concessions to the highest bidders. Good oil prospects, proximity to the USA and a government eager to supplement its major source of income all attracted independent US companies which were willing to undercut established suppliers in order to find marketing outlets. In the early 1960s the rapid development of Libya by predominantly independent companies reinforced this effect. Prices began to weaken almost immediately after the Suez crisis and the majors, after trying to take on board these changes by various forms of discounting, finally cut posted prices (which had come to act as tax reference prices after the agreement with Saudi Arabia in 1950) in 1959 and 1960.

The weakening world price also had its effect elsewhere in the world.

Since the effect of this weakness was not felt mainly in across-the-board cuts made by the companies (despite the reductions of 1959 and 1960), but rather by a piecemeal process of discounting, importing countries struggled to take maximum advantage of these reductions. The position of the importing countries was strengthened by offers from the USSR, made in the late 1950s and early 1960s, to supply crude oil at rates cheaper than those which the majors were willing to match. At the same time, eroding prices led to protectionist pressures within some of the importing countries; although some efforts were made in Europe to protect coal against fuel oil, the main effect of protective measures was felt in the USA, where import controls, applied on a 'voluntary' basis from the mid-1950s, became law in April 1959. At the same time, weakening world prices increased tensions between producer countries and the operating companies. Although the formation of OPEC in 1960 was essentially a defensive move, the producer countries did markedly improve their position in the 1960s as their per barrel income remained broadly steady while that of the oil companies fell heavily. Finally, the effect of weakening world prices, together with a rapid rate of world-wide economic growth, led to a massive growth of investment downstream and of oil-using activities.[2] By 1970 these had fundamentally altered the supply and demand position of the world oil industry.

One of the major effects of these developments concerned company profitability. As might have been expected, the decline of oligopoly led to a decline in company profits. In 1955 and 1956 the US companies earned 30.2% and 28.8% respectively on their direct foreign oil investments.[3] Upstream, rates of return were even higher and, according to one calculation, annual rates of return were 56.6% in Iraq between 1953 and 1962, 69.3% in Iran between 1954 and 1964, 57.6% in Saudi Arabia between 1952 and 1961, and Gulf (with its heavy investment in Kuwait) averaged 40.7% on its Middle Eastern assets between 1952 and 1963.[4] Although not quite this high, profitability was more than adequate in Venezuela, and Shell and Jersey Standard probably earned more than the average (see table 4.1). By the late 1960s, US oil companies were earning no more on average than manufacturing or service sector companies (about 12.5% a year).[5] Much of this transformation was due to the reduction in per barrel company income from producing countries where there took place a considerable shift in revenue from companies to governments during this period. This can be seen from table 4.2.

Table 4.1 *Profitability in Venezuela 1947–57*
(percentage return on average net fixed assets)

Year	Percentage	Year	Percentage
1947	22.54	1953	23.10
1948	27.44	1954	25.69
1949	14.89	1955	30.38
1950	19.30	1956	33.38
1951	23.63	1957	34.62
1952	23.81		

Source: Tugwell, *The Politics of Oil in Venezuela* (Stanford, 1975).

Table 4.2 *Producer government and oil company per barrel income 1957–70*
(Selected years; US cents a barrel)

	Iran	Iraq	Venezuela	Libya	Company take
1957	86.8	93.1	103.0[a]	0	78.0
1960	80.1	78.6	89.2	0	56.5
1965	82.9	81.7	95.6	83.8	41.8
1969	80.9	91.4	103.6	100.0	35.4
1970	80.8	94.2	109.2	109.0	32.7

[a] Artificially high, because it includes bonus income from concessions awarded in that year. The bonus was subsequently tax-deductible.
Source: Z. Mikdashi, *The Community of Oil Exporting Countries: a Study of Governmental Co-operation* (London, 1971), and *Petroleum Press Service,* July 1967 and September 1972.

As overall prices fell, so demand for oil rose strongly. Much of the impetus for world-wide demand increases, which consistently averaged 7–8% a year, was the transformation of Western Europe from a predominantly coal-burning area to a predominantly oil-burning one (see table 4.3). Of perhaps even greater long-term significance, however, was the change in the attitude of the USA. The USA had been the earliest and largest supplier of oil; indeed, it remained the world's largest single producer until the mid-1970s. Its legal system encouraged overdrilling,[6] and the abundance of oil encouraged massive consumption. The USA resisted the import of cheap oil from the Middle East and Venezuela by the imposition of an import-quota system in 1959, but US imports nevertheless continued to increase and in 1970 rose above 3 million barrels daily.

Table 4.3 *Use of energy: percentage use of different fuels*

	1950				1970			
	Coal	Oil	Natural gas	Hydro/ nuclear	Coal	Oil	Natural gas	Hydro/ nuclear
USA	37.8	39.5	18.0	4.7	19.1	43.9	32.7	4.3
Western Europe	77.4	14.3	0.3	8.0	27.4	55.6	6.1	10.8
Latin America	9.8	72.9	8.3	9.0	4.9	67.8	18.4	8.8
Japan	61.9	5.0	0.2	32.9	22.4	68.8	1.3	7.5

Source: J. Darmstadter and H. H. Landsberg, 'The European Background', in 'The Oil Crisis in Perspective', *Daedalus,* vol. 104 (Fall 1975).

Table 4.4 *World oil production 1955–70*
(b/d average)

	1955	1960	1970
USA	6,807	7,035	9,635
Venezuela	2,157	2,846	3,760
Kuwait	1,091	1,624	2,735
Iran	330	1,068	3,845
Saudi Arabia	965	1,247	3,550
USSR	1,397	2,952	7,090
Mexico	245	271	485
WORLD			
TOTAL	15,413	20,994	47,800

Source: Banco Central de Venezuela, *La economía venezolana,* p. 125.

During all this time, Middle Eastern output continued to rise strongly, as can be seen from table 4.4. Thus, between 1945 and 1970 there was a transformation of the industry from a situation in which effective control was operated by a small group of major companies to one in which potential control had fallen into the hands of an even smaller group of producer governments.[7] The period also saw the emergence of other, smaller, companies, many of which played important roles in the oil politics of the period. Some, like Occidental Petroleum, emerged from the more controlled but less oligopolistic environment of the USA to seek concession areas outside and, in doing so, were willing to compete for business with the major companies. Others,

Table 4.5 *The role of the majors in world oil*
(percentage control)

	1953		1972	
	Majors	Other	Majors	Other
Refining				
Latin America	67	33	51	49
Western Europe	65	35	55	45
Middle East	98	2	63	37
Far East	77	23	34	66
Africa	32	68	30	70
Production				
Latin America	81	19	73	27
Middle East	92	8	83	17
Far East	94	6	71	29
Africa	92	8	47	53

Source: Jacoby, *Multinational Oil,* p. 211.

such as the Italian state company ENI, grew up in consumer areas and subsequently tried to link backwards by establishing control over centres of production; they aimed to do this by distinguishing their strategies sharply from those of the 'Seven Sisters'. Still others, notably in Latin America, were state companies which took advantage of national monopoly legislation to set up important local concerns. Consequently, during the course of the period, the grip of the majors was eroded and, as far as the companies were concerned, the world oil industry in 1970 had become far more competitive than it had been at any time since 1928.

Consequences within Latin America

During this time Latin America became increasingly marginal to the central developments of the world oil industry, although Venezuela played a major role in the formation and early history of OPEC. Although particular countries (notably Argentina, Bolivia, Brazil and Chile) achieved major increases in production, these were not of global significance. Apart from the case of Venezuela, therefore, the importance of the period lay in the effect of world conditions upon Latin America and not the other way around.

Venezuela, however, continued to be in the forefront of the major develoments in the world oil market during the period. Moreover, after the fall of the dictator Pérez Jiménez in 1958, the Venezuelan government resumed its political orientation of the 1940s and once more began to press hard for the interests of producer countries. This pressure began shortly after the 1958 elections. These were won by Acción Democrática, but before it could take office the Provisional Government, which had run short of funds, unexpectedly increased oil taxes. The effective increase was some 13%, increasing the rate from 52% to 65%; this increase led to an angry riposte from the head of Creole, the Jersey Standard subsidiary.[8] Although AD was not responsible for this tax increase, it allowed the new rate to remain in force, and relations between Venezuela and the companies remained uneasy during 1959 and 1960.

A further complicating factor for the Venezuelan oil industry was the US imposition of mandatory import restrictions on crude oil and oil products in April 1959. The decision to impose these was taken on behalf of the US producer interests; the strategic argument was also deployed to some effect. In fact, the reversal in US policy on imports in general was more apparent than real. In the 1930s the USA had imposed protectionist measures, although these were gradually relaxed as the economy picked up. After the war the extent of imports came to be controlled informally by the major US oil companies. These were able to use their oligopolistic position to limit imports to a level which did not trigger off politically significant domestic resistance. By the mid-1950s, however, imports into the USA by independent producers had become a serious threat to domestic oil interests and various forms of import restriction were imposed after 1956, culminating in the adoption of a mandatory quota in April 1959.

From the Venezuelan perspective, the most interesting point about these oil quotas was their distribution. In particular, Venezuela, which had been exempted from earlier import restrictions and had historically been given favoured treatment in the US market,[9] was suddenly subjected to the quota with no preference whatever, while Canada was given full exemption and Mexico was given a useful 30,000 b/d 'loophole' through which it could export crude oil at premium prices.[10]

The imposition of import quotas by the USA added considerable impetus to the efforts of the Venezuelan Oil Minister Pérez Alfonzo to create a similar pattern of regulation of the oil industry on a world-wide basis. Within Venezuela, Pérez Alfonzo announced his intention of granting no new oil concessions and set up a Co-ordinating Commission within the Ministry of Mines which was given 'broad powers over the production and marketing of the country's petroleum',[11] with the immediate aim of halting price discounting by the operating companies. Pérez Alfonzo was even more active at an international level and played a major role in the setting up of OPEC.

Although OPEC did not play as active a role in the international oil market as Pérez Alfonzo would have liked and was unable to evolve a workable system of production sharing, it did play a significant role from the beginning as a defensive organisation. No further cuts were made in tax-reference prices, and the burden of falling prices during the 1960s was borne exclusively by the companies. OPEC was a contributory factor to this development. Moreover, OPEC did have a significant educational impact upon its members, and

if Venezuela failed in its central goal during the years before the oil price and producer control revolution in the 1970s, the country's influence in the organization remained strong as it continued to make important political and technical contributions to OPEC. It was this sharing of experience that aided the Middle Eastern producers in gaining the greater tax benefits that Venezuela already enjoyed in their negotiations with the companies.[12]

Venezuela's relationship with the USA became far closer after the election of President Kennedy in November 1960. For Kennedy the Venezuelan government was a vital counter to Castro, geographically, economically and ideologically. Ideological factors were especially important since Venezuelan democracy (established only in 1958) would have been threatened seriously by any major conflict with the companies. Washington, therefore, used its influence to persuade the oil companies to moderate their opposition to the government in Caracas and also worked to reduce the impact of US oil quotas on the Venezuelan industry. Exports of fuel oil, which were crucial to Venezuela,[13] were gradually released from the restraints of the programme after 1961 until, by 1966, the US administration retained only 'the skeleton of a control programme' on residual fuel oil.[14] By this time the Venezuelan industry was expanding slowly on the basis of previous investments and discoveries: by raising taxation to 65% the government had brought about a sharp reduction in company activity (see chapter 15).

In other parts of Latin America, the 1955–70 period saw a deliberate attempt to move away from the logic of the world market. If Pérez Alfonzo had tried to control this logic, other oil ministers in less well-placed countries tried to ignore it. Thus, Petrobrás in Brazil carried out intensive exploration efforts, despite the fact that its domestic finding and development costs were high, whereas some naturally low-cost producers such as Mexico deliberately avoided emphasising the comparative advantage they appeared to have in crude oil production. Other countries, such as Bolivia and Argentina, relied upon foreign investment in oil production but did so only reluctantly, and in both countries policy was subsequently reversed; in Argentina contracts were cancelled in 1963, while Gulf Oil was nationalised in Bolivia in 1969. One of the most interesting cases of a retreat from the export market, however, can be seen in Peru.

The transformation of the Peruvian economy from being a substantial net exporter of oil to a substantial net importer was not the result of policy. As Thorp and Bertram point out, 'the overriding feature of the oil industry's history from 1948 to 1970 was the fact that thirty years of exploration had failed to locate new oil fields'.[15] Consequently, the profitability of IPC – a Jersey subsidiary and the largest oil company in Peru until its nationalisation in 1968 – fell sharply as the domestic price level, which was now crucial to its operations, was kept low. Thus, although IPC made a far more positive contribution to the Peruvian economy in the years 1955–68 than it had in the past, its economic weakness invited political attack. Moreover, its isolation in Peruvian politics increased as the Peruvian capitalists who eagerly began exploring under the 1952 oil law pulled back after several disappointments.[16] This situation, as we shall see in chapter 12, encouraged Peru to expropriate the company in 1968–9. Peru thus joined the ranks of those countries in which the oil industry was substantially under state control. When the Bolivian government nationalised Gulf Oil in 1969, Ecuador, Argentina, Colombia and Venezuela remained as the only Latin American oil producers that continued to rely significantly upon foreign investment in oil exploration.

Those countries which relied more extensively on state enterprise frequently defended their activities in terms of the extent to which, in their view, the oligopolistic structure of the world industry inhibited the workings of a free market. Thus, Salas, the President of the Chilean state company ENAP, justified government investment in oil exploration on the grounds that geologically, Chile is a country poor in oil opportunities with only very small areas of sedimentary basins compared with Venezuela and Middle Eastern countries. The prospects, therefore, of Chile becoming an oil exporting country are remote and any production can only be for local consumption. If this were to be developed by the international companies, their Chilean operations would be only a very small percentage of their total operations and in times of price weakness their marginal costs in the main producing areas would almost certainly be much below their marginal costs in Chile such that there would be a natural inclination on their part to import rather than to produce locally.[17]

In other countries, moreover, it was argued that if concessions were given to the major companies (the 'trusts'), they would use them as reserve areas only for as long as they could rely on lower-cost Middle Eastern production.

While there is some truth in these arguments, they perhaps underestimated the uncertainties and flexibilities still remaining in the oil market as well as the extent to which independent companies were moving into exploration ventures, even if it remains true that some companies did face difficulty in marketing their newly developed supplies.[18] Certainly, despite the world surplus of crude, Gulf Oil undertook considerable exploration activity in Bolivia (admittedly under a highly favourable tax regime) and, in conjunction with Texaco, in Colombia and Ecuador. President Arturo Frondizi of Argentina also attracted considerable quantities of foreign investment into Argentina, mainly from independent US companies (under various forms of contract system). A large part of the explanation for this lay in the desire of the companies to hedge against uncertainty in a world which was itself highly uncertain. As Vernon pointed out,

a feature of the corporate environment encountered in these studies was the pervasive presence of ignorance and uncertainty in the decision-making process. The justification for many major actions could only be explained as a hedge against the murky future, or a commitment to a learning process. . . .

This is not to say that rational textbook decision-making based on the certainties of discounted cash flows, linear programmes, and all the rest, is not employed by large corporations that were the object of this study. But it is a good generalisation that formal decision-making criteria of that sort were much more influential in the small decisions than in the large.[19]

Uncertainty, involving the geology, the appropriate development technology, the political risk and possible developments elsewhere in the world, is inevitably extensive in any exploration venture.[20] Even during the 'Golden Age' of Middle Eastern production there had been serious upsets; these included the Iranian nationalisation, the Suez closure of 1956, the formation of OPEC in 1960 and the closure of the Suez Canal again in 1967. Consequently there operated, in the minds of the major companies, a kind of insurance principle according to which it was better to invest and be certain than stay behind and risk missing out on a major project. As Hartshorn noted, 'there remains, even after so many years of search throughout the world, a strong element of pre-emptive bidding. If one company does not look for oil in even an unlikely place, the next may find it there. Geology is not an exact science.'[21]

The point should also be made that the US Treasury absorbed many of the costs of oil exploration throughout the world. According to US legislation (until this was amended in 1975), US companies exploring abroad could write off against income earned anywhere in the world (including the USA itself) the costs of drilling dry holes and of certain specified exploration and development costs. To this should be added the considerable tax allowances (including the world-wide operation of the depletion allowance) that could be claimed when any oil discoveries were actually in production.

Moreover, for countries in which any oil production would be intended mainly for the home market, the prevailing international surplus did not take on the same importance. Here, governments could act to give preference to local production over imports over and above the natural barriers which were provided by transport costs. In Argentina under Frondizi (1958–63), for example, a deliberate attempt was made to attract medium-sized US oil companies in the belief that Shell and Exxon, which had a long history of involvement in Argentina, were more interested in maintaining their import and marketing businesses than in further exploration. After a number of these contracts had been signed, Shell and Exxon approached the government and offered to explore, provided that their own market share was protected. This offer was then accepted.[22]

Thus, although it remains true that oil exploration activity continued to be based overwhelmingly within the USA (which took 92.7% of the wells drilled in the 'free world' in 1950 and 76.6% in 1972), development was nevertheless possible elsewhere. Indeed, according to Sampson, some major companies were still enthusiastic explorers: 'After long arguments within the board, in the early sixties, Monroe

Table 4.6 *Latin American refining capacity 1950–8*
(ooo *b/d*)

	1950	1955	1960	1965	1967	1969
Argentina	151.7	189.1	237.5	423.5	434.1	457.2
Bolivia	7.2	12.3	11.2	12.2	14.0	11.6
Brazil	6.5	105.8	208.1	364.9	379.9	501.6
Colombia	23.8	39.5	78.2	99.9	129.1	140.7
Cuba	7.3	7.7	86.9	86.6	93.0	93.0
Chile	0.4	20.0	48.0	83.6	91.0	91.0
Ecuador	4.4	6.0	13.2	19.2	20.4	33.0
Peru	35.1	47.5	48.6	63.2	90.0	91.5
Uruguay	25.2	28.0	28.0	35.0	50.0	40.0
Venezuela	258.5	520.8	680.0	1,199.9	1,337.7	1,324.4
Mexico	160.4	408.5	393.0	421.0	517.5	494.5
Others	0	0	0	104.0	135.5	189.3
TOTAL LATIN AMERICA	680.5	1,385.2	1,832.7	2,913.1	3,292.2	3,467.8

Source: United Nations, ECLA, *La industria del petróleo en América Latina: notas sobre su evolución reciente y perspectiva* (New York, 1973), p. 20.

Rathbone the [Exxon] chief executive, pushed forward a massive programme for exploration. It was to cost $700m. in the three years from 1964 and it concentrated on territories outside OPEC.'[23] Indeed, as we shall see, many Latin American governments during this period attacked the oil companies as undesirable rather than as impossible to attract.

In many Latin American countries the 1955–70 period saw a sharp expansion of state ownership of the oil industry. One of the main growth sectors for state enterprise was domestic refining. As can be seen from table 4.6, the refining industry underwent massive expansion in several Latin American countries during the period. Apart from Venezuela the most dramatic example was undoubtedly Brazil, where Petrobrás built up a large refining industry from almost nothing. A similar degree of expansion took place in Chile and Mexico.

The development of a state-controlled refining sector effectively broke up the vertical integration of the oil industry. It is true that the major companies were less hostile to state refining ventures than they had been to state participation in oil production. Thus, in the 1960s Shell and Esso offered to buy a share in ENAP's Concepción refinery, offering in return a guaranteed supply of oil, but this offer proved unsuccessful.[24] The advantage of state refineries lay in the fact that these were not tied to any particular source and, in a world market where oil was in surplus, the larger buying companies were able to wield considerable bargaining power. Thus, whereas the offer from the Soviet government to sell crude oil directly to the government of India provoked a major crisis in the latter's relationship with the companies, Brazil was able to accept a similar offer without serious complications[25] and during this period Petrobrás developed into a large-scale and efficient purchaser of crude oil.

Some countries, however, notably those in the Caribbean area, had hopes of becoming exporters of refined crude. Such countries needed to rely on private companies to build refineries in order to take advantage of their international marketing and distribution network. The most striking example was that of pre-revolutionary Cuba, where the 1950s saw a refinery building boom. Thus, according to *World Oil* in 1956, 'a decisive factor in these refinery expansion plans has been a recent law decree granting substantial tariff and duty exemptions both to new refinery projects and to expansion of existing units. It further provides that no additional taxes will be levied during the 20 year period [!] and offers new refineries many of the advantages accorded entirely new industries.'[26]

Had these refineries not been capable of processing Soviet crude oil in 1960, the history of the Cuban Revolution might have been very different.

The marketing of natural gas, whose consumption increased rapidly in several Latin American countries during the post-war period, was also largely carried out by state companies; the most active were Pemex in Mexico, the CVP in Venezuela and Gas del Estado in Argentina. Interestingly enough, the Inter-American Development Bank was willing to finance natural gas production even when this was in the hands of state companies. Between 1969 and 1971, for example, the IDB made a series of loans to Gas del Estado (with the US Export–Import Bank also financing a part of Gas del Estado's investments). Until 1970, most natural gas was sold in the same country as it was produced; the growth of consumption can be seen in table 4.7.

The marketing of oil products was also left substantially in the hands of the state. The importance of oil in Latin American economies increased with the very sharp rise in consumption during the post-war period. This increase was less dramatic than that which took place in Europe because there was less scope for substitution from coal, but it

Table 4.7 *Natural gas consumption in Latin America (excluding re-injection)*
(m. tons of oil equivalent)

	1945	1950	1955	1960	1965	1969
Argentina	408	464	626	1,203	3,673	4,634
Bolivia	o	o	o	15	74	n.a.
Brazil	o	o	o	58	98	95
Colombia	179	190	209	252	760	1,061
Chile	o	o	70	244	450	435 (est.)
Mexico	641	1,144	1,465	2,808	7,769	10,275
Peru	neg.	neg.	46	46	90	131
Trinidad and Tobago	n.a.	n.a.	n.a.	666	1,021	1,396
Venezuela	750	972	2,371	4,007	5,688	6,943
TOTAL	1,978	2,770	4,787	9,299	19,623	24,970

Note: Not available totals (n.a.) are not included in the final total.
Source: United Nations, ECLA, *La industria del petróleo*, p. 15.

Table 4.8 *Total consumption of commercial energy in Latin America 1937–69*
(m. tons of oil equivalent)

	1937	1948	1958	1963	1966	1969
Solid fuels	6.2	5.7	6.0	6.0	7.1	7.8
Oil derivatives	12.0	25.7	53.0	70.0	78.0	98.3
Natural gas	0.0	2.2	7.0	15.0	21.3	25.0
Hydroelectricity	2.2	4.6	11.0	12.4	17.1	21.6
TOTAL	20.4	38.2	77.0	103.4	123.5	152.7

Source: United Nations, ECLA, *La industria del petróleo,* p. 9.

was impressive nonetheless. Part of the increase can be attributed to the relatively low level of Latin American prices although there are important exceptions to this, and it should also be remembered that the cost of hydroelectricity was also kept down by subsidy and heavy lending to this sector by the international aid organisations.

It is difficult to generalise extensively about prices in Latin America owing to problems of exchange rate comparison (particularly when there is a multiple exchange rate or a black-market rate) and also to the fact that, in some countries at least, prices have changed rarely but then sharply, so that there are problems in selecting a typical year.

However, two general statements can be made. First, in almost all countries prices, and frequently market quotas, have been set by governments so that there has been little real competition (except of certain non-price kinds). Secondly, prices tend to be lower in exporting countries than in importing ones. For exporting ones, low domestic prices, as well as being justified on grounds of cost, were frequently seen as a way of spreading the wealth received by the country from its oil income. As Betancourt explained of the 1945–8 government of Venezuela, which deliberately pursued a policy of low domestic prices, 'the government was convinced that the industrial development of the country and the opportunities for the well-being of all of its inhabitants were closely linked to a policy of cheap fuel'.[27] As a consequence, internal oil consumption in Venezuela grew spectacularly, rising from 7,076 b/d in 1940 to 12,460 b/d in 1945, 28,957 b/d in 1948, 106,333 b/d in 1955 and 192,813 b/d in 1969.[28] For much of this time, internal distribution was run at a loss, a fact which continued to be true after the nationalisation of oil at the end of 1975.[29]

Cheap oil, however, did not necessarily rule out private profitability. Up until 1968 in Peru, the largest part of the domestic market was in the hands of a Jersey subsidiary (IPC) which also controlled the largest domestic refinery. Between 1948 and 1968 domestic oil consumption grew from 18,579 b/d to 86,612 b/d and Peru moved from being a net exporter to a net importer of oil.[30] IPC nevertheless continued to be able to fulfil its marketing role with only one major conflict with the government, in 1959, taking place over the domestic price level. As we shall see in chapter 12, this was a complicated and rather unsatisfactory relationship with an acrimonious conclusion but it remains true that IPC could supply the domestic market at low cost for as long as the government was willing to allow it to do so. In Ecuador, moreover, foreign companies actually received government subsidies to operate their refineries and supply low-priced oil products to the public; Ecuador, like Peru, was a former exporter of oil turned importer, again becoming an exporter during the 1970s.

Importing countries, on the other hand, tended to keep prices high. It may seem surprising, therefore, that with profitability reasonably high and with no need of sophisticated technology or bold entrepreneurship private distributors have tended to maintain a share of the markets of otherwise nationalised industries such as those of Chile and Brazil. In the case of Chile, one observer noted that 'Shell and Esso are apparently content to jog along in a protected market which ensures their profitability but which gives them practically no independence whatsoever.'[31] In the case of Brazil, Petrobrás at first declared its unwillingness to move into marketing,[32] although it later did so and gradually moved its share up to around 33% of the market. The operation of foreign companies in this area ruffled few political sensitivities, since under these circumstances distributors had little actual power, while national capital could be devoted to those areas which were more widely regarded as strategic.

The state also generally took a significant role in petrochemical ventures which became increasingly important to at any rate the larger Latin American countries during the 1960s. Although there has been scepticism over the value of petrochemical investments in developing countries,[33] it appears that at least the larger and more developed Latin American countries had good reasons for seeking the establishment of a national petrochemical industry. Certainly the reasons were not always wholly economic; in many cases the lure of what was described in the 1960s as 'one of the most glamorous, advanced and potentially profitable branches of modern industry'[34] was decisive, while the argument that petrochemical production increased domestic returned value from oil production was also important. As a Venezuelan petrochemical expert argued, 'Conceived as an industry of high added value, it had the elements and conditions necessary to transfer primary material into intermediary and final products and inputs of high value, and was therefore a genuine creator of wealth.'[35] The companies themselves (sometimes oil but more usually chemical) were often willing to invest in Latin America in order to help spread their research costs as widely as possible.

Undoubtedly some very dubious ventures were set up, of which none was worse than Venezuela's IVP. This was created by Pérez Jiménez and its main complex was built at an inconvenient site on land belonging to a principal figure of the Pérez Jiménez government. It was located some distance from a port, with the arrangement that another insider of the regime could transport the raw material by tank truck from Puerto Caballo.[36] A later government estimated that supplying companies overcharged for their materials by around 30–40%. Moreover, since the complex was also intended to provide employment for an underdeveloped area, workers were taken on with few restrictions; by 1959 there were 3,223 workers in the complex and wages made up 27.5% of operating costs. Productivity was correspondingly low and rationalisation was, for political reasons, very difficult. As Acosta Hermoso pointed out, 'petrochemicals became transformed into the centre of social services of the town of Mora and even of its neighbours'.[37]

The larger Latin American countries, however, were better placed to develop the petrochemical industry and in each of these countries there developed a 'tripartite structure' within the industry, featuring multinational corporations, host governments and domestic capitalists. In a number of cases, the domestic private sector, which was the weakest of the trio, was encouraged by the prospect of finance from the IDB. Some of the projects financed help to give a flavour of the kind of ventures undertaken. Thus, in 1963, the IDB lent $25m. for a petrochemical plant in Argentina and $0.7m. to Mexico for a carbon black plant. In the latter case, the IDB claimed that the Salamanca plant 'will produce about 15,000 metric tons of carbon black per year at a cost competitive with that of the imported product'.[38] The company involved, Negromex, was majority owned by local capital, but Phillips Petroleum had a 10% stake and an agreement to provide the technology. In 1965, the IDB lent $10m. to Petrosur of Argentina[39] for an ammonia complex, 'the first such major installation in Argentina'.

In 1967 the IDB turned its attention to Chile and Colombia. In that year it reported that 'as part of its 1964–74 National Economic and Social Plan, the government of Chile is seeking to develop the nation's petrochemical industry'.[40] In fact, Petroquímica Chilena (a joint venture between ENAP and Corfo) was formed in 1966 and its first venture was to be an ethylene plant. This was to be set up on the site of ENAP's Concepción refinery and the IDB loan was to go towards the $15.9m. plant for which ENAP was to provide 41% of the capital, the IDB 41% and Esso, which had the technology contract, a further 18%. Petroquisa also took 30% of a joint venture with Dow Chemicals to build up a polyethylene complex in the same place.[41] In the same year the IDB lent $5m. to Colombia for a polyethylene plant with the familiar tripartite ownership structure. The Colombian industry is interesting in that it was set up to provide consumer goods and subsequently integrated backward; the polyethylene plant would now replace an imported input. The IDB was to provide 48.6% of the finance for the $10.3m. project, with the state company Ecopetrol a further 19.4%, Dow Chemicals 19.4% and domestic capital 12.6%.

Host governments were generally favourable to these kinds of joint venture arrangement. The state company could guarantee access to the market, while foreign capital would provide the technology and a significant proportion of the finance. Domestic private capital was encouraged chiefly for its political convenience. In Mexico, for example, it was decided in 1957 that Pemex should have control of 'basic' petrochemicals (although these were developed with the help of trade credits and foreign suppliers) with private capital, up to 40% of which could be foreign controlled, allowed into secondary ventures. Nearly 20 years after serious development of the industry began, it was reported that

because it is a priority development sector for the Mexican government, the petrochemical industry enjoys many advantages. Companies in the sector report no difficulties in negotiating tax incentives for decentralised industries, getting technology contracts approved and obtaining import permits. The industry is also favoured as a priority area for the channelling of scarce domestic credit resources. Further, companies that have associated with Pemex report a good working relationship with the super agency.[42]

Although the really spectacular phase of Brazilian petrochemicals expansion took place in the 1970s, the essential groundwork was laid in the 1960s. The development of Brazilian petrochemicals was very much the result of official policy. Thus, according to Peter Evans, 'no simple geographical or technological explanation provides any leverage. Brazil had, throughout the fifties and sixties, very poor luck in its search for petroleum. It has no obvious comparative advantage in petrochemicals at all. The development of the industry cannot be attributed to the unseen and unconscious accretative results of a general process of economic development.'[43] Indeed, it appears that private Brazilian capital played a crucial role in persuading the state to set up Petroquisa (see chapter 18), which in turn made the important arrangements with foreign companies which permitted the large-scale developments of the 1970s. The foreign companies themselves were not only attracted by the size of the Brazilian market, but also proved willing to share ownership with the other partners because, as one executive explained, 'It is better to share with local capital and let the state harmonize the operation than to have it all taken away from us later on.'[44]

Thus, there continued to be a major role for the oil companies in Latin America between 1955 and 1970, although state enterprise was far more prominent than had been the case earlier. With the exception of a few oil exporters, the state was concerned to break up the vertical integration which had previously characterised the industry and to take control of the sectors which it regarded as strategic – generally, refining and exploration. Foreign companies continued to play a significant role in domestic marketing as well as being invited to explore in countries which had hopes of exporting oil. Despite the general conditions of world oil surplus, some companies did so.

Another significant development during this period was the increasingly active role played by domestic capital in the oil industry. It is true that domestic capital had never withdrawn entirely from oil, but its relative importance increased perceptibly in and after the late 1950s. It is notable that some of the most successful domestic companies were located in Argentina. Here, large capital-goods producers such as Bridas and Pérez Companc were able to take advantage of the Frondizi government's liberal policies and of the problems besetting the state oil company YPF (of which more in chapter 19) in order to hire local geologists and engineers and win orders from the Argentine government. In Brazil, as we have seen, local companies were most active in the petrochemicals sector after 1964, as also were local companies in Mexico. These trends became still more important after 1970 and will be considered in rather more detail in part III of this book.

The position of Washington

Once the major oil companies had established themselves satisfactorily in the Middle East, Washington and London tended to withdraw their diplomatic interest in company activities. This process was accelerated by the victory of President Eisenhower in the elections of 1952 in the USA and by the Suez crisis and the subsequent retreat of Britain from the Middle East. Engler summarised the change as it affected the USA:

over the years, the State Department came to accept that the industry had grown up and was now the best instrument for protecting the energy base of the nation. It abandoned its network of petroleum attachés and retained a minimum of independent experts at its command. The oil industry dealt directly with the two central sources – Saudi Arabia and Iran – keeping the State Department generally informed, but the need for direct involvement was no longer assumed.[45]

A very similar statement was made by an Exxon executive: 'although in earlier years, the US government had participated actively, during the sixties there was little need for it to do so. The fact is that, up until 1970–1, there was no need for the government's active involvement or intervention.'[46]

In Latin America also, the State Department tended to provide broad rather than specific support for the companies. However, there were two major differences from the Middle East. First, in Latin America state companies had already taken over much of the oil industry, and the Eisenhower government was concerned to try to 'roll back' state enterprise in the oil sector. This attitude was abandoned after the election of President Kennedy but the State Department then needed to concern itself with securing compensation for various US oil companies which were nationalised during the 1960s. Secondly, anti-Communism played a significant part in Washington's attitude towards Latin America. At least for a few years after the Cuban Revolution, the US government modified its concern for the short-run interests of its oil companies in order to protect the position of various anti-Communist Latin America governments. The major watershed in US policy towards the area, therefore, was in 1960–1.

Indeed, in some ways 1959 marked the high point of Washington's identification with the oil companies in Latin America. According to one influential US critic, in 1959,

intoxicated with the success of the assistance it had rendered US oil companies in breaking down resistance to the granting of concessions in Argentina and Bolivia on terms wholly inconsistent with current industry practice and as such prejudicial to the Latin Americans, by a skilful use of promises of financial assistance by the US government, the Department had made an all-out effort to break down Brazil's resistance. Despite the fact that the marketing situation for its chief export commodity was such that normally special assistance would have been thought in order, the word went out now that Brazil must be broken. It was now or never. There could be no further accepting of Brazil's resistance to introduction of the petroleum companies, particularly those where there was a special association with the administration on a personal basis, into exploration and exploitation of Brazil's petroleum potential.[47]

Although one may argue with some of the judgements made in this passage, the essential point that the State Department did seek to break down Brazilian resistance to foreign companies (as it had earlier done in Argentina) has never seriously been disputed. Indeed, as early as 1958 Roy Rubottom (a senior State Department official) was quoted as saying that 'Brazil refuses to yield to US pressure to give foreign companies a significant role in oil development'.[48]

At least until 1960, US financial pressures were real enough. Until then, no other Western country had the financial means to lend abroad on a significant scale, let alone to challenge the USA in Latin America.

Most of Western Europe had received 'Marshall aid' from the USA and suffered from a chronic shortage of foreign exchange, alleviated only by various controls. Moreover, until the death of Stalin in 1953, the USSR took a very patronising attitude to Latin America, regarding it as at worst Fascist and, at best, an ally of the USA.[49] Consequently, until the 1950s, US hegemony in the area was not seriously challenged.

Under Khrushchev, however, Soviet policy became far more open towards Latin America and in the late 1950s the USSR became willing to offer an attractive inducement to the oil-short Latin American countries: relatively cheap Soviet crude. Thus, the USSR offered a trade pact to Brazil in 1957 which included the possibility of supplies of crude oil and equipment. The Hispanic American Report commented that

Khrushchev's bait appealed to the national oil monopoly Petrobrás, which has been buying US equipment on a businesslike basis out of its limited budget. Public pride in Petrobrás and the nationalistic desire to reduce dependence on the United States were powerful factors astutely capitalised on by the Kremlin.

Publicly, Petrobrás was cool to the . . . offers, but privately it awaited a top governmental decision. Congressional and army opinion was building up for a resumption of both trade and diplomatic relations with Russia.[50]

A trade agreement was signed in 1959 and this 'envisaged vaguely but significantly "the possibility of refining in Brazilian plants the import of Soviet crude oil" '.[51]

The Soviet Union also offered aid to Bolivia. The offer was made in January 1958 when Dr Ruiz González, a Bolivian technocrat returning from Moscow, met President Siles Zuazo (1956–60) and conveyed an offer of technical aid which had come from the USSR. Siles then asked two YPFB technicians to go to the Soviet Embassy in Buenos Aires since Bolivia had no diplomatic relations with the USSR at that time. The USSR promised that, if diplomatic relations were restored, it would offer a package of financial aid and technical co-operation which, at rough foreign exchange equivalents, might have been worth some $60m. – 80m. Siles, however, did not intend to accept the offer, but was nevertheless willing to publicise it in the hope of receiving more from the USA.[52]

Once this offer was made public, it became a political issue within Bolivia, with the YPFB management and the left wing of the ruling MNR supporting the Soviet offer, and comparing it with persistent US refusals to lend to state oil companies. The matter was taken up in

Congress where, 'after conducting an investigation of YPFB to find out if its financial problems were the result of mismanagement or of the failure to adequately investigate avenues of credit, the Senate recommended that the purported offer of a $60m. loan and technical assistance to YPFB be more fully explored through official channels'.[53] As the Soviet Union no doubt anticipated, however, the debate over the offer quickly became more extensive. Thus, according to a *New York Times* report,

an important though now minority sector of the governing National Revolutionary Movement is pushing for closer ties, including the establishment of diplomatic relations, with the Soviet Union. Rubén Julio announced this week that he and a group of senators, including Juan Lechín . . . had accepted an invitation to visit Moscow after the May 22 national election. For this group, the state oil company is a symbol, and its continuing decline is used as justification for seeking aid in the Communist sphere if it cannot be obtained elsewhere.[54]

Although the conservative wing of the MNR was eventually able to surmount this challenge, Siles was able to succeed in his objective of securing further aid from the USA. Indeed, Washington was so concerned about this Soviet offer that 'the Eisenhower administration reversed its previous policy of not aiding state-owned enterprise in Latin America, and in April 1960 YPFB . . . was allowed to apply for US credits for the purposes of re-equipment'.[55] YPFB was eventually offered $10.5m., and the justification offered in Washington was that private companies had been allowed to explore for oil in Bolivia. However, as the *Hispanic American Review* pointed out 'the United States had firmly and unequivocally broken its formerly inflexible policy of giving no governmental support to state-owned entities. Most observers felt that this was perhaps the most important change in US policy in many years'.[56] A main factor in this transformation was the Cuban Revolution.

Relations between Fidel Castro and the USA had never been easy after Castro came to power in January 1959. However, the final breach did not take place until June 1960 when the Cuban government expropriated oil refineries belonging to Shell, Jersey Standard and Texaco after these had refused Havana's demand that they refine Soviet crude oil. The incident which led to the takeover of the oil refineries sheds an interesting light on the relationship between the oil companies and Washington which is worth considering here, especially since it has sometimes been alleged that Cuba provides an example of 'private diplomacy' by the oil companies acting on their own.[57] One crucial witness provides a very different picture. Thus, according to US Ambassador Bonsal, there was a meeting between himself and a senior oil executive on 4 June 1960. The executive recounted that

until very recently the companies' position had been that of going ahead with the operation [of refining Soviet oil] under protest and attempting to secure recognition of their rights through the Cuban courts, he added that this position had been predicated on the assumption that the United States government would not wish to take a stand on the matter. This assumption had now proved contrary to fact.[58]

The US Treasury, without the advance knowledge of the State Department and against the wishes of Ambassador Bonsal, had advised the companies not to refine the oil; this advice was accepted. The companies were then confiscated and the break with Washington completed. Thus, the major companies did not initiate policy but rather followed a lead from Washington (as they had earlier done in Iran). Even if the substance of policy was interventionist, the style was cautiously bureaucratic.[59] The companies had, moreover, invested considerably in Cuba during the 1950s and, at least at first, tried hard to avoid conflict with the incoming regime.[60]

The Cuban Revolution sharply changed the tone of relations between Washington and Latin America. In the years 1945–60, Latin America had been largely ignored by Washington which, with no other overriding policy objectives, devoted its main interest to the protection of US property and the discouragement of state companies which might provide an alternative to foreign investment. It was not that these policies were particularly high priority (although Eisenhower was the most pro-business US President since the 1920s) but rather that there were few other US concerns involving Latin America. The attempts to 'open up' Brazil in 1959 were the high-water mark of this policy. Even without the Cuban Revolution it is likely that these policies would have come under strain as, from the late 1950s, European (notably French and Italian) suppliers of capital goods proved willing to provide trade credits for state oil companies; Pemex and YPF both benefited in and after 1959. After the Cuban Revolution, the policy of discouraging state oil companies became even less valuable and was quietly dropped. After 1960, US lending policy became less restrictive.

This can be seen from the setting up of the Inter-American Development Bank in 1960 and the launching of the Alliance for Progress in 1961. The IDB's attitude to economic nationalism and state enterprise was altogether less restrictive than that of the World Bank (which at this time reviewed but left essentially unchanged its previous policy of not lending to state oil companies).[61] This can be seen particularly in the IDB's lending to Chile where the danger of Marxism appeared to be greatest. Thus, in 1962, the IDB made an $11m. loan to ENAP towards the cost of an oil refinery and followed this up with various petrochemical loans both to Chile and to other Latin American countries. Thus, although it was still reluctant to lend towards the cost of oil exploration (understandably, in view of the world surplus of oil at that time), the IDB did significantly broaden US lending policy. By this time, it was quite clear that access to international finance was no longer, if it had ever been, a serious obstacle to the expansion of the state oil sector.

The Alliance for Progress, however, by no means ended Washington's concern to protect the property of US companies. Indeed, this concern was to some extent intensified after around 1962 by the Democratic Administration's fear of a right-wing backlash from within the USA. The nature of this could be seen most clearly in the Hickenlooper Amendment to the 1962 Foreign Aid Act, which called upon Washington to withhold all aid from a country in which US property had been nationalised unless 'prompt, adequate and effective compensation' were paid. This Amendment was tested in Latin America for the first time when Argentina cancelled its oil contracts with foreign companies in 1963. This was a crucial event since it gave Washington the opportunity of developing its response to nationalisation in the post-Cuban environment.

The US Ambassador's first concern was to keep the companies united and thus avoid any breaking of ranks. Moreover, as Ambassador McLintock pointed out, 'all agreed that publicity would sound the death knell of a successful renegotiation'.[62] This line corresponded to that of the smaller US companies, which wanted positive results from Argentina, rather than that of the larger ones, which were more worried by 'worldwide implications'. Thus, the 'main concern of Union–Cabeen is that one or another of the big companies in New York or Chicago will take a hard-nosed line and jeopardize the chances of quiet negotiation in Buenos Aires', especially since Standard Oil of New Jersey 'is more concerned about the principle involved than money'.[63] McLintock's immediate aim, therefore, was to set up a *modus vivendi* with the Argentine government which prevented the actual takeover of the companies while other forms of pressure could be applied; as he put it, the situation resembled 'a common-law marriage. Later perhaps it might be possible to negotiate a more permanent relationship and make the marriage legal.'[64]

As time passed, Washington's attitude hardened.[65] Negotiations were going on between Buenos Aires and the companies, but

the US runs the risk of becoming prisoner of developments which could seriously affect our relations with Argentina and in which we did not play a role. We worry, in a word, about leaving relations entirely to discussions between private oil companies and the Argentine government . . .

On the question of the application of the Hickenlooper Amendment, if worst comes to worst we are giving thought here to quietly cutting back on aid, including military aid, without a formal invocation of the Amendment. We could leave a token program or programs going as proof that we have not applied sanctions and if pushed by press justify in an off-the-record way the cutback on the grounds of failure of Argentina to take self-help measures or some other line . . . The companies [US Under-Secretary] Mann has talked to here seem to be fully aware of the disadvantages to them of formally applying the Amendment and the importance of keeping doors open and playing for time.[66]

What appeared to worry Ambassador McLintock (who was one of the more activist US Ambassadors) was the possibility of some of the companies settling for a separate peace and thus embarrassing the others and perhaps creating an undesirable international precedent.[67] If, however, those companies which had found no oil were successfully to reclaim their capital plus interest, as the Argentine government originally offered, this might make it difficult for the other companies to receive more; the Argentine government would be 'politically frozen' on the matter.[68]

By early 1965, it had become clear that Buenos Aires was prepared to negotiate seriously with the companies over the compensation which was due. 'Pan Am and Tennessee initiative. Loeb Rhodes had engaged Robert Anderson to go to Europe and contact banks in the UK, France . . . [etc.] with view to establishing consortium to finance oil settlement. Anderson has completed his mission and obtained, in general, agreement of seven banks to go ahead. Loeb Rhodes will also participate financially.'[69] The banks would pay the companies directly and be repaid over ten years by the government of Argentina.

In some ways, the Argentine case was a clear success for US policy. Washington had learned the lessons of Cuba and thus the importance of seeking to prevent any escalation of the conflict. Although successful on the matter of principle, however, the US government and the foreign companies needed to make a number of concessions on matters of substance whose full significance was to become clear only later. First, the companies had actually taken the initiative in finding a source of loan finance to enable the Argentine government to pay compensation; the US government was to play a similar role in Peru at the end of 1973. Consequently, it was no longer possible to rely, as the companies and their home governments had in the 1930s, upon the inability of the host governments to pay compensation as a protection against expropriation. Not only had a government borrowed money from abroad for its petroleum industry, but it had actually done so to finance expropriation. International financial obstacles to policies of oil nationalism had practically disappeared. Secondly, the compensation actually paid by governments was generally based on the book value of assets; this, however, was normally lower than replacement cost or market value and lower by definition than the value of profit expected to be achieved by any successful venture. While the US government did not welcome this, it was unable to make alternative arrangements effective in view of its concern to ensure that some kind of compensation was paid and its unwillingness to put excessive pressure on expropriating governments lest these radicalise further in consequence.[70]

The Peruvian experience showed that a policy of quiet pressure was not always effective. While it will not be possible to provide a full account of the IPC dispute here (for which see chapter 12), it should be pointed out that the company remained intransigent as political pressure against it mounted. Moreover, rather than pressing IPC after 1963 to accept the minimum demands of what was a very moderate Peruvian government, the US Embassy preferred to try to pressurise President Belaúnde (1963–8) to settle on the company's terms. Levingstone and De Onis reported that 'throughout the IPC dispute, the US Embassy in Lima constantly equated US interests with the interests of IPC. In 1965 when Robert Kennedy visited Lima on his trip throughout Latin America, he had a fierce argument with the deputy Secretary [on the matter].'[71] Thus, after IPC's legal status was formally declared null by Congress in 1963, US aid was quietly cut. Goodwin quoted one official as saying, 'the idea was to put on a freeze, talk about red tape and bureaucracy, and they'd soon get the message. Unfortunately, they believed we were as inefficient as we said, and it took about a year for them to get the message.'[72]

Once it had been taken, this decision was not easy to reverse. After the Cuban missile crisis and the general triumph of conservative politics throughout Latin America, Washington saw less need for generosity and the State Department correspondingly lost influence within the US government. Subsequently the business community, expressing its feelings through the US Treasury and, even more so, through Congress, forced the State Department on to the defensive.[73]

Aid to Peru was resumed in 1966, following a change in the personnel of the State Department, but a year later was cut again over a separate dispute. It is not clear how far the cancellation of aid contributed to the fall of the Belaúnde government, but IPC's failure to reach a settlement with Belaúnde prior to 1968 was to prove costly. When, finally, in 1968 IPC did find it possible to make the concessions for which Belaúnde had been asking in 1963, it was too late. Seizing on certain irregularities in the 1968 agreement, a relatively small number of military officers took the opportunity to launch a coup, confront the IPC and use the consequent tension to consolidate itself in power. In February 1969 IPC's whole property was taken over by the state and compensation was refused.

The vigour and determination of the Peruvian government's attack caught Washington by surprise. The Peruvian military was not Communist and nor could it be so described but it had openly and deliberately challenged Washington over a property issue. The takeover of IPC immediately raised the possibility that the Hickenlooper Amendment would be applied to Peru. This would have involved not only cancellation of aid, but, far more seriously, of the Peruvian sugar quota. While difficult to quantify exactly, such measures would have amounted to a serious, though not a decisive, blow to the Peruvian economy – a loss of perhaps $45m. to a country whose exports in 1968 were just under $840m. If international semi-commercial bank loans from such sources as the Export–Import Bank, the World Bank and the IDB were included, the figure might perhaps have reached $100m. a year. In early 1969, however, the Peruvian balance of payments was relatively strong.[74]

Moreover, Washington's position was not free of difficulty. For one thing, IPC was a relatively small investment; its own valuation was

$200m., but this was a vast exaggeration of its true worth; Peru's valuation was $71m. and this was more realistic. Other American properties in Peru were much more important. Indeed, one of these, W. R. Grace, which was the only large American-owned sugar company in Peru, was particularly vulnerable if Washington imposed its most damaging sanction – suspension of the Peruvian sugar quota. In that case, the Peruvian regime threatened that it would restrict its protected home market to domestic producers and force Grace to sell its full output at cheap international prices. Moreover, the Peruvian regime had declared that IPC was 'a special case' and that, as things stood, other American interests were not threatened. However, it did hint broadly that it might radicalise in response to US pressure and thus put at risk not only US property but all US interests in Peru. As the Peruvian foreign minister, General Mercado Jarrín put it, 'We all remember what happened in Cuba.'[75]

Thus, for Washington there was a wider dimension. Moreover, application of the Hickenlooper Amendment to Peru, especially by an incoming Republican Administration, would certainly have strained relations with other Latin American countries, many of which would have felt bound to provide at least diplomatic support for Lima. Finally, there were domestic political considerations. President Nixon cannot have been eager to bury openly the principles of the Alliance for Progress in one of his first acts in office. With the Vietnam War at its height, 'another Cuba' might have had explosive effects.

Nor could Jersey Standard effectively pressurise the Peruvian regime. Peru was not an exporter of oil and so could not be boycotted by the companies; moreover, given the world surplus of oil at that time, there could be no question of mounting an embargo. Indeed, Jersey Standard was not even capable of dissuading other US companies from investing in Peru. In October 1968, only days after the initial seizure of IPC's properties, Belco Petroleum announced such an investment programme continuing its exploration of the offshore area. Indeed, Occidental Petroleum went so far as to offer to help Peru to develop the expropriated properties and this at a time when the Hickenlooper Amendment was still being considered officially.[76] The major companies no longer dominated oil exploration and IPC's long history of intransigence had lost it many friends.

After a period of intense diplomatic activity, the USA finally decided not to apply the Hickenlooper Amendment, a decision which was

widely seen as a victory for Peru.[77] However, Washington did quietly
apply a set of modified economic sanctions. These were described by
Einhorn:

the policy, when implemented, came down to US Government denial of
Export–Import Bank credit to businesses seeking investments in Peru, no new
AID authorisations and a policy of preventing loans, in so far as possible, from
going to Peru from the international financial organisations. The policy was
part of a negotiating scenario which suggested doing everything you possibly
could without having to admit it. If something came up that would force an
admission, then give in.[78]

Such sanctions were never intended to provide a knock-out blow to the
Peruvian regime. Rather they operated quietly in the hope that, once
passions had cooled, the disadvantages of continued intransigence
would make themselves felt.

After further manoeuvring and counter-manoeuvring, agreement
was reached at the end of 1973. The negotiations ended with a settlement according to which Peru would make a lump-sum payment to
Washington to cover the cost of compensating a number of expropriated properties; Peru stated that the sum was not to be used to compensate IPC, but the USA was not bound by this statement and $24m. was
in fact paid to the company late in 1974. Once the principle was
agreed, Peru was once more able to rely on help from the Export–
Import Bank and other aid agencies.

The nationalisation of Gulf Oil in Bolivia reflects in a different way
the difficulties Washington encountered in combining a vigorous anti-
Communist strategy with the defence of its own transnationals. Indeed
(as we shall see in chapter 13), the nationalisation itself could be seen
in large part as a reaction against US intervention in Bolivia – an intervention which had earlier been largely responsible for the drafting of
the liberal 1955 oil legislation. The nationalisation itself was not a
particularly devastating blow either to Washington or to the company.
In this case, since Bolivia was an exporter of oil and potential exporter
of natural gas, the position of Gulf Oil was a good deal stronger. Moreover, at the instigation of Gulf Oil the World Bank had become
involved in financing the pipeline to Argentina through which Bolivia
hoped to begin exporting natural gas; this loan, and the project itself,
were therefore automatically frozen until a compensation settlement
could be announced.

Gulf nevertheless felt that it needed to move quickly in search of a settlement, fearing that Bolivia might find a market for its crude oil in Cuba or Brazil.[79] At the same time, Gulf wanted to be sure that any compensation agreement that was made would in fact be honoured. Thus, at the beginning, it sought the aid of Hispanoil (in which Gulf had a small share). Fairly soon after the expropriation it was provisionally agreed with La Paz that Hispanoil would give technical help to Bolivia in return for a fee and would market the expropriated crude for Bolivia by selling it back to Gulf Oil. However, according to the *Peruvian Times,* which broke the story of the proposed agreement early in 1970, 'the reason this "secret" deal was linked to our associate is that some members of the government don't, it seems, like it and the relevant documents were therefore made available'.[80]

Bolivian objections were not so much to the fact of compensation, which was based on book value, as to the manner of payment. Some government ministers in La Paz feared that if oil was pumped at the maximum rate in order to finance compensation, Bolivian oilfields would be depleted too quickly, to the detriment of Bolivia's own plans for industrialisation.[81] Moreover, as 1970 wore on, Gulf became increasingly disenchanted with Hispanoil, which was eventually 'cut out of the picture when she became too greedy'.[82] Nevertheless, what appeared to be the final agreement with Gulf was signed in September 1970.

There is evidence, however, that this agreement was renegotiated under Torres, who replaced Ovando as President of Bolivia in September 1970 and was replaced in his turn in August 1971. Thus, the agreement that finally went into effect in September 1971 made no mention of Hispanoil; instead, it was now the World Bank which guaranteed compensation for Gulf Oil. This was to be paid out of an earmarked portion of the revenue which Bolivia received for exporting natural gas to Argentina. The World Bank guaranteed the agreement and helped finance the pipeline. This appeared to meet one of the Bolivian objections to the agreement of September 1970 and also enabled Gulf to dispense with the services of Hispanoil. Moreover, it resolved a problem which became obvious after world prices began to rise in 1970–1, namely that the balance of advantage was shifting from consumers to producers of oil and that there was no longer any 'single market price' upon which compensation could be based. Thus, in early 1971 Bolivia found that it could secure a higher price by selling its oil to Peru rather than to Gulf Oil.[83] Bolivia's gas sales, however, did not have this flexibility.

It is also noteworthy that the final agreement with the IBRD came only in August 1971, just after a right-wing coup had succeeded. Indeed, there were suspicions in Bolivia that the World Bank had held up its loan approval for political reasons. Thus, on 3 May 1971, the *Guardian* reported that Torres's move to the left 'can also be linked with Bolivian displeasure over what is seen as American hostility to the building of the gas pipeline'. In Washington, however, the postponement of aid to the Torres regime was explained in terms of the

Bolivian nationalisation of a $2.3m. property of the International Metals Processing Corporation, which was run by a fellow Texan, Frank Tye. Bolivia's nationalisation of the IMPC on 12 January 1971 was unacceptable to the new Secretary [of the Treasury, John Connally] though a settlement for the expropriation of Gulf properties in October 1969 had been agreed upon. It was unacceptable to Connally because it was an expropriation without *immediate* compensation.[84]

In a country as weak as Bolivia this kind of pressure could still be made to tell, but there were few other Latin American countries of which this was true in 1970.

The expansion of state enterprise in Latin America 1955–70

By 1970 Venezuela was one of the few Latin American countries in which foreign oil companies still controlled almost all of the domestic industry. Moreover, Venezuela was far from being a passive hunting-ground for the major companies; it had played a major part in the creation of OPEC and was to play a further aggressive role in the transformation of the world oil market in 1970–1. In most of the other important countries – Mexico, Chile, Brazil, Peru, Uruguay and Bolivia – the industry was in 1970 wholly or substantially nationalised. Thus, there was a clear retreat of foreign investment in the Latin American oil industry not, as has sometimes been alleged, mainly because of the attractiveness of other economic sectors, but because of the expulsion of foreign companies from a number of significant investments. US policy could ensure that some form of compensation was paid in cases of nationalisation but could achieve very little else.

Within Latin America the creation of state enterprise was intended to give policymakers a new freedom from the dictates of the world market and an opportunity to move their industries in the direction which they chose. As a consequence there developed considerable emphasis on self-sufficiency, which involved an increase in exploration in Brazil, Chile and (later) Peru, and a reduction in Mexico. Self-sufficiency in refining and petrochemicals, however, invariably indicated a policy of rapid growth. As in the 1930s, low crude oil prices led governments to place more emphasis on ventures downstream. For this expansion, access to technology or finance posed few problems; technology had never been under oligopolistic control, while finance was becoming easier to obtain once the immediate post-war scarcities were over. As a consequence of these changes, Latin America, with the exception of Venezuela, became increasingly marginal to the major developments in the world oil market. The centre of the industry was focussed on the main OPEC countries, on the USA and on the main importing countries of Europe and the Far East. For Latin America the Cuban Revolution was very much more important than broader international oil factors, regarding both US policy and the attitude of Latin American elites themselves. This position was to change considerably during the 1970s.

5

The oil market revolution and its consequences for Latin America 1971–9

The 1970s saw a fundamental shift of power over oil markets from the oil companies and their home governments to the most important producer governments. Oil prices increased sharply, ownership of oil passed from the oil companies to the host governments and key members of OPEC began to take effective responsibility for the level of world oil production.[1] On the other side of the same coin, there was clear loss of influence on the part of the USA and a massive transfer of income from the importers of oil to the exporters. This transformation was also largely (although not solely) responsible for a general slowdown in the rate of economic growth in the OECD countries after 1973, which was reflected in slackening demand for oil and oil products. Nevertheless, with little effective substitution for oil, the balance of market power was not greatly altered by world recession, although at the end of the decade Mexico was emerging as a new world supplier on a significant scale. Over all, the fundamental market strength of the main OPEC countries appeared more and more evident as the decade went on, and the effect of this transformation upon Latin America was very marked indeed.

Latin America's oil exporters

Venezuela was one of the main beneficiaries of this oil market revolution. As can be seen in table 5.1, export prices and income increased sharply in the 1970–4 period, despite the fact that the volume of crude oil production actually fell. Although a much smaller producer, Ecuador's gains were proportionately even greater since that country only began exporting on a large scale in June 1972. There was also a major transformation in the Mexican oil industry. Pemex, which had encountered some difficulty in maintaining self-sufficiency in the late 1960s (as we shall see in more detail in chapter 17), made a string of major

Table 5.1 *Venezuela's export prices, income and volume of production 1970–4*

		Export price declared ($ per barrel)	Government oil income ($m.)	Output (b/d)
1970		2.011	1,406	3,760
1971	15 Feb.	2.016	1,702	3,620
1971	1 June	2.647		
1972		2.647	1,948	3,305
1973	1 Jan.	3.094		
	1 May	3.524	2,670	3,460
	1 Aug.	4.16		
	1 Oct.	4.92		
	1 Nov.	7.26		
1974	1 Jan.	14.26	8,700	3,065

Sources: British Petroleum, *Statistical Reviews of the World Oil Industry, Petroleum Economist,* September 1976, and *Petroleum Intelligence Weekly,* 22 April 1974.

Table 5.2 *Oil and the Ecuadorian trade balance 1972–9*
($m.)

	1972	1973	1974	1975	1976	1977	1978	1979
Exports f.o.b.	323.2	583.3	962.4	897.2	1,127.3	1,191.6	1,493.8	2,030.5
Oil exports	59.2	226.0	527.5	516.9	565.2	502.1	614.6	1,035.2
Imports c.i.f.	294.2	396.8	617.6	829.2	911.5	1,226.4	1,320.7	1,319.6

Note: Export figures relate to permits.
Source: Banco Central de Ecuador, *Información estadística,* various issues.

discoveries in the Chiapas and Tabasco area after 1972. The effect of oil on the Mexican balance of payments can be seen in table 5.3 (see also chapter 17).

The policies of Venezuela, Ecuador and Mexico, Latin America's most important exporters, varied with the pattern of ownership within the industry. Venezuela, following many of the major Middle Eastern and North African exporters, nationalised its industry at the end of 1975. However, this move was far less radical than might have appeared on the surface. The majority of the oil concessions which were nationalised had been due to revert to the state in 1983 and the transfer was simply brought forward by a few years. Moreover, the nationalisation followed a decade or more in which Venezuela took the bulk of

Table 5.3 *Mexico's oil balance of payments 1973–80*
(US $m.)

	1973	1974	1975	1976	1977	1978	1979	1980
Exports								
Crude Oil	0	61.9	393.7	420.0	987.3	1,760.3	3,811.3	9,449.3
Natural Gas	0.3	0.1	0	0	5.4	0.1	0	447.8
Refined Oil	28.8	62.0	25.4	25.8	22.8	9.3	67.6	384.2
Petro-chemicals	4.7	9.5	4.3	0.3	3.3	67.5	107.7	120.5
TOTAL	33.8	133.5	423.4	436.1	1,018.8	1,837.2	3,986.6	10,401.9
Imports								
Crude Oil	88.7	79.5	0	0	0	0	0	0
Refined Oil	193.4	271.9	225.6	126.1	51.7	144.0	208.6	243.1
Petro-chemicals	21.5	70.4	57.0	103.8	156.5	163.6	331.6	522.8
TOTAL	303.6	421.8	282.6	229.9	208.2	307.6	540.2	765.9
Oil balance	(269.8)	(288.3)	140.8	206.2	810.6	1,529.6	3,446.4	9,636.0

Source: Pemex, *Annual Reports.*

the company's oil income in taxation and effectively controlled both the level of oil production (subject to world conditions) and the price at which it was sold. Indeed, the effective rate of taxation was so high in Venezuela that, as we saw in the previous chapter, the companies cut back sharply on their investment programmes and allowed Venezuela's oil reserves to level off, so limiting the level of production that could be sustained over the long run. One of the objectives of the nationalisation was precisely to permit the oil industry to increase its investment, reverse Venezuela's production decline and maintain a stable rate of output in the long term. The early years of Petrovén will be discussed in chapter 22.

In order to build up its investments, Petrovén needed to maintain close relationships with the large multinationals (notably Shell and Jersey Standard) whose properties had been nationalised. This requirement was foreseen at the time of the nationalisation and a series of sales and technology agreements were negotiated with the former owners. These proved to be highly acceptable to the companies, which found that they could take a lump sum in compensation (based on the low book value rather than on the much higher replacement or market values) while continuing to earn revenues in some cases similar to those which they had previously. As an official in the US Commerce Department pointed out, 'Returns per barrel of output may be slightly less than before, but output is rising, so the difference won't be noticed. Besides, the settlement frees up capital that can be used in exploring for new oil. All told, net profits could conceivably be higher than before the nationalisation.'[2]

The sales agreements reached were fairly straightforward in character, although they involved hard bargaining and were renewable every three months (see also chapter 22). Essentially, Venezuela chose to deal, for the bulk of its output, with relatively secure and stable purchasers who had a well-organised marketing network rather than taking the far more dangerous path of seeking the best short-term arrangements available. The consequence was greater stability all round: Venezuela lost some opportunities to make windfall profits in return for a degree of international credibility and the knowledge that Petrovén would not be squeezed too severely when market conditions were adverse. Although Venezuela did sell an increasing amount of oil outside these integrated channels, generally in government to government deals, the continuing relationship with the major purchasers was undoubtedly important to both sides.[3] It was clear evidence, however, that the impact of nationalisation upon the international market was limited. In 1977 an Exxon (Jersey Standard) spokesman could claim that,

like the high-technology manufacturing companies, the vertically integrated oil multinationals possess a unique advantage that host countries cannot afford to dispense with. These companies have developed a world-wide system of marketing contracts that cannot easily be duplicated. So, although the OPEC powers thought they had the upper hand when they nationalised oil-company property within their borders, they soon discovered that it wasn't easy to sell the oil they had wrested from the multinationals.[4]

However, this arrangement, by which OPEC governments marketed oil almost exclusively through the major oil companies, seems to have been only transitional. During 1979 the position changed again as more and more oil was withdrawn from these channels by OPEC governments so that it could be sold on the more lucrative 'spot' market, where prices (as in 1973–4) jumped sharply as a reflection of temporary scarcity caused by the Iranian Revolution. As the *Petroleum Economist* pointed out in September 1979,

The Iranian revolution . . . sharply accelerated the movement whereby control of crude oil supplies was gradually being shifted from international oil companies to governments of exporting countries. That process, which began in the early 1970s, is still far from complete, but it will certainly not be reversed. It will have long-term implications that are well worth pondering.

This is perhaps an issue for the 1980s, but it suggests that the impact of oil nationalisations in the main exporting countries may be even greater in the long term than it has been so far.

Following the nationalisation in Venezuela (see chapter 22), the government also agreed technology contracts with the main foreign companies (mainly Exxon, Shell and Gulf), which received a fee based on each barrel produced in return for an agreement to provide a given number of technical advisers purely at the cost of their salaries. The size of the fee – $0.15 and $0.20 a barrel, depending on the case – and the very limited amount of real technological transfer both led to criticism of these arrangements within Venezuela. In fact, the generosity of the initial contracts (which came up for renegotiation after four years) appears to have been a *quid pro quo* for company acceptance of compensation paid only at net book value, which totalled just under $1,000m.[5] As we shall see (chapter 22), these contracts were renegotiated at the end of 1979.

There was also a nationalisation in Ecuador, where Gulf Oil was taken over by the government at the end of 1976 (see chapter 14). This was interesting partly because the proposal for the nationalisation came from Gulf Oil itself early in 1976. This proposal showed the extent to which the international oil industry had changed in the preceding few years. In the late 1960s the International Petroleum Company hung on desperately to an essentially unrewarding operation in Peru and refused to make any significant compromises with the government because of its fear of 'actions elsewhere'. By the beginning of 1976, however, these 'actions elsewhere' had largely taken place, with the large-scale liquidation of oil company property in the main OPEC countries. There had been full-scale nationalisations in Venezuela, Algeria, Iraq and Iran and partial nationalisations in Libya, Kuwait, Saudi Arabia and Nigeria; the companies were now concerned to maintain profitability rather than property *per se* and much of the inflexibility which had earlier stemmed from company insistence on the same basic mode of contract in all countries had now gone.

Gulf Oil's offer to the Ecuadorian government was inspired by the fact that the company had far more potential control over that country's exports than it had over its taxation legislation. Ecuador had set its taxes high and, since Gulf Oil needed to sell its own crude oil on the open market, it found that its rate of return was as little as 5% as against the 15–20% for which it had been looking.[6] The situation was somewhat complicated by the fact that Gulf Oil was part of a joint venture with the operating company, Texaco, whose policy (as we shall see in chapter 14) was to maintain its position in Ecuador and wait for a more favourable climate.

During the course of 1976 Gulf Oil was able to pressurise the Ecuadorian government into carrying out the desired nationalisation (see chapter 14), with the consequence that at the end of that year Texaco was the minority partner in a joint venture with the Ecuadorian state company CEPE; CEPE had already taken 25% of the consortium in 1974 and now increased its share to 62.5%, leaving Texaco with the remaining 37.5%. Nevertheless, Texaco remained the operator and provided the experience and expertise in the subsequent investments made by the consortium.

In both Venezuela and Ecuador, however, policy was complicated by this transfer of ownership which for a time superseded decisions about production. In Mexico this was never a problem because the state oil monopoly, established in 1938, remained inviolate although Pemex did come to rely on limited amounts of technical help in certain areas.[7] On the other hand, the changed international climate ensured that it was no disadvantage for a state company to export oil through privately owned channels; a certain amount of government to government selling did take place, but many customers were private US concerns only too happy to buy at arm's length from a reliable and politically stable producer.

Another major question which needed to be faced by the oil exporters was that of conservation. Should oil be pumped at the maximum technical rate, or should it be left in the ground until later? There were four main arguments for producing oil at less than the technical maximum, which were logically distinct but often effectively the same. The first was simply a matter of price expectation. This played a part, for example, in Ecuador's unhurried renegotiation of concession terms in 1972–3; the Oil Minister, Captain Jarrín Ampudia, believed that the price of oil would rise and that the country could best be developed by exporting oil at a slower rate but at a higher real price. On the whole, however, given the extreme uncertainty prevailing about the long-term price of oil, governments have preferred to be certain of a steady flow of oil over time commensurate with their real spending plans (a distinct point) than to take the risk of speculating with the future.[8]

The second argument was simple fear of depletion. While such a fear is rarely economically respectable, since oil is costly to find and develop and the cost must usually be met by producing and selling existing oil, it has often proved politically powerful. At times oil companies have played upon these fears by selecting oil reserve figures which best fitted their own arguments. In Ecuador, for example, the oil companies in early 1974 told the Oil Minister 'with interesting optimism that the final recoverable output from their reserves was of the order of 3,400 million barrels, and that they could plan a rate of production of 320,000 barrels a day if permission was given to them to increase output from the authorised rate of 250,000 barrels daily'.[9] Admittedly only 1,726 million barrels had been proved but, the consortium implied, the rest could easily be discovered if the go-ahead were given. After it was refused, however, and the Oil Minister made his own conservationist strategy apparent, the company position changed. In May 1975, the new Oil Minister, Admiral Salazar, reported on the basis of company statistics that Ecuador's proven reserves amounted only to 1,500 million barrels and that, if oil exploration activity was not made profitable once more, Ecuadorian oil output would start to fall in 1981.

It was not only the private companies that used figures in this way. Pemex, which made a series of major oil finds in and after 1972, stubbornly refused to increase significantly its estimates of proven oil reserves. As we shall see (chapter 17), a part of the reason for this was technical but the main reason was political; a high reserve figure would increase the pressure for sharp increases in Mexican output and exports and would, therefore, turn Mexico into a focus of international attention. In this case, however, a part of the decision was taken out of the hands of Pemex and the Mexican government. In October 1974, the *New York Times* reported that 'high-ranking United States government officials said tonight that they had received reports from sources in the oil industry of a major petroleum discovery in Mexico . . . A large discovery could give Mexico the capacity to break the high prices that have been fixed by the 12 members of the Organisation of Petroleum Exporting Countries.'[10] While this report if anything underestimated the true size of the Mexican discoveries, its leaking at that time was clearly strategic. The first sign of the availability of such information came on 12 September 1974 with a report in *Platt's Oilgram* that 'estimates in Mexico's . . . oilfields now range as high as 18 billion to 19 billion barrels'. This information, like that published by the *New York Times*, was made available by a US company which later explained that 'the OPEC stranglehold is threatening the world economy. Psychologically it is not a bad idea to remind OPEC countries that there might be oil elsewhere. We just want to give them a gentle reminder that new oil fields still can be found.'[11]

This raises an interesting point. The USA's reason for making these oil finds public was similar to that of the Mexican government for keeping them secret; however, in order to justify its position, Mexico had to make it appear that oil reserves really were low and that the pure depletion argument was still relevant. In any case, the Mexican government remained highly secretive about the extent of its real oil deposits. In March 1975, for example, the *Financial Times* remarked that 'it is apparent that the Government is intentionally holding back all possible information about its new deposits. Even within the administration, there is little known about the Chiapas–Tabasco reserve, while Ministers admit privately that the secrecy has helped Mexico escape pressure from both producers and consumers.'[12]

When the new López Portillo regime took office in December 1976, policy changed; the proven reserve figure was immediately upgraded from 6.3m. barrels to 11.8m. and this has been further increased to reach 50 billion barrels (of all hydrocarbons) in March 1980. Even so, however, there has continued to be *sotto voce* criticism within Mexico warning against an excessively rapid growth of oil production. As the position was summarised in one article:

the fact that oil and gas are non-renewable natural resources and thus constitute a source of wealth that inevitably tends to deplete . . . leads to the argument that Mexico should keep this source of wealth for its own needs.
. . . the fact that Mexico depends on hydrocarbons for 90% of its oil consumption makes this argument more dramatic, for, as is known, Mexico is poorly endowed with other conventional raw materials such as coal and hydraulic river power.[13]

The third major argument for conservation was essentially that of international solidarity. Since 1973 there have been years of price weakness (notably 1975 and 1977) as well as of price strength and, at times when the price has seemed about to fall, the international solidarity of OPEC has been called upon to dissuade governments from cutting prices in order to expand output. In Ecuador, for example, where 1975 proved to be a particularly difficult year domestically as well as internationally, there was a debate between domestic conservatives who favoured a policy based strictly upon local conditions and radicals who wanted a broader dimension to be added to policy. One of the latter, Admiral Vásquez, argued in May 1975 that Ecuador should,

act in close harmony with the marketing policy decided by OPEC . . . It is crucial to maintain price levels and increase state participation in the profits of the companies by means of a vigorous OPEC policy which should bring supply and demand for oil into balance on the world market and guarantee the conquests which the country has already made in this matter.[14]

The conflict was closely fought within Ecuador and, although the conservatives eventually achieved many of their objectives, the radicals left their mark upon Ecuador's long-term oil policy, not least by keeping company profitability sufficiently low for Gulf Oil to offer to sell to the Ecuadorian government in 1976.

Venezuela faced a similar choice at the beginning of 1976, just after the nationalisation itself. As Tugwell recounts it:

In preparation for takeover, a group of Venezuelan experts worked out a price list they felt was in line with OPEC standards, and offered to sell 2 million barrels a day to the companies. The companies then responded with offers to buy, but at prices that ranged from 20c to $1.00 per barrel below those asked by the government.
   There followed a period of tense negotiations . . . the government decided to stand firm by its proposals. The risk was substantial, since the budget for the following year was dependent upon a full 2.2 million barrels per day in export sales. Just sixty hours before the nationalization ceremony on New Year's Day, the government announced that agreement had been signed for just under 1.5 million barrels per day at the prices fixed by the government – too little, but as much as the companies would buy at the prices demanded.[15]

Early in 1976 demand picked up and Venezuela was able to increase its output without difficulty. Indeed, Venezuela has always been a key member of OPEC and, despite its long-term contracts with the oil companies, its pricing and production policies have always shown a keen sensitivity to international conditions.
   The final argument for conservation concerned the impact of massive

and uncontrolled oil income upon a country unused to affluence on such a scale; events in Iran after 1974 reinforced suspicions within several governments that such a bonanza was not always an unmixed blessing. Such a position had already been taken by Jarrín when he was Oil Minister of Ecuador. Jarrín was concerned that an oil boom might develop only those sectors with a high short-run elasticity of supply (such as construction) at the expense of more valuable projects which required longer gestation periods and a degree of careful planning.[16] It is likely that he also wanted the oil revenue to be used to finance major structural reform within Ecuador and believed that if the wealth was not held back until the government was ready with plans for such reforms, its effect would be to strengthen the status quo, since the local dominant classes would benefit disproportionately. However, as we shall see in chapter 14, Jarrín's position was not widely enough shared within the Ecuadorian government. When production fell back from the high point reached in early 1974 the government began to look for ways of lightening the burden on the oil companies, and Jarrín was removed from his position in October 1974.

The possibility that oil wealth might prove socially corrosive also proved to be of considerable concern to the Mexican government as oil-export income began to accumulate on a large scale during 1978. In Mexico the fear was that oil wealth might bring about changes of a kind with which the government – which traditionally ruled Mexico by manipulation and co-optation rather than large-scale repression – would not be equipped to cope. If oil exports led to a massive increase in non-essential imports, the internal distribution system might prove unable to cope without widespread disruption to important programmes. If oil-fed economic indigestion led to a rising rate of inflation, then organised labour which had already been squeezed severely in the aftermath of the 1976 devaluation might become genuinely militant.[17] Moreover, if the oil revenue were to be wasted conspicuously then the way might be open for a radical change in policy under a new president after 1982. Clearly some of these problems could in theory be alleviated by banking excess income abroad and enjoying the interest payments, but this course of action was ruled out by President López Portillo for political reasons at the end of 1978.

In the case of Venezuela, the question of conservation raised a series of issues concerning the relationship between Petrovén and the rest of the Venezuelan government. In 1976 Petrovén argued strongly for, and eventually secured, the right to base its sales on short-term judgements about the state of the market rather than longer-term but more rigidly imposed criteria laid down by the Mines Ministry based on considerations of long-term capacity. Subsequently the question of production levels became something of a 'boundary dispute' in Petrovén's relations with the government. Petrovén took the view that, once politicians took responsibility for the level of oil production, long-term calculations would be sacrificed to the need to cope with short-term financial crises and that, in general, the level of production would tend to rise above that determined by technical prudence. For the rest of the government, however, the level of oil exports played an essential part in budgeting and financial planning and there was considerable pressure to produce according to the political and economic strategy of the government of the day.

Questions of oil conservation have not been resolved and, indeed, are likely to become more rather than less pressing as it becomes clear that governments and not companies now control the major production decisions and that error can prove very costly indeed. Although the international context and various international pressures will continue to be important, the ability of an oil-rich country to control its rate of production must be a great advantage in any strategy of economic development.

Other Latin American producing countries

The sharp rise in the world oil price combined with more specifically political developments in many Latin American countries to bring about a large-scale return to the logic of the free market. Although state companies continued to play an important role, foreign investment was invited back into Latin America (excluding the major oil exporters) on a scale unknown since the 1920s. Uruguay, Chile and Brazil reversed long-standing state monopoly arrangements to bring foreign companies into oil exploration. In Bolivia and (after 1976) Argentina previous nationalist policies were reversed and policy swung back in a direction favourable to foreign investment while in Colombia oil policy became far more pro-producer. Even in Peru and Ecuador, where promising earlier oil finds had pushed policy in a markedly nationalist direction, new governments which believed that their predecessors had exaggerated their bargaining power swung the direction of policy in a markedly neo-liberal direction. Moreover, in most of these countries state oil companies took an increasingly active role in

Table 5.4 *Proven oil reserves in Latin America 1973–8*
(m. barrels, end of year)

	1973	1974	1977	1978
Argentina	2,312	2,459	2,317	2,424
Bolivia	223	216	130	135
Brazil	774	779	1,094	1,126
Chile	220	210	515	578
Colombia	688	627	779	850
Ecuador	1,500	1,424	1,500	1,450
Peru	544	830	750	774
Mexico	2,846	3,086	10,428	28,407
Venezuela	13,812	14,568	18,043	18,228

Source: World Oil, 15 August, annually.

oil exploration and development. However, given the time-lags in exploration and development, these changes have not yet been reflected fully in increased oil production. It is likely that the early 1980s will see a fairly substantial transformation in the hydrocarbons sector of several Latin American countries since there are already signs of an increase in oil reserves, although only in Mexico and to a more limited extent in Peru, Brazil and Argentina has production increased significantly above earlier high points.

There was still one important obstacle facing countries which sought to boost their oil reserves via foreign investment: the oil companies were not always willing to come. A part of the reason was the sheer pressure of opportunity as a large number of geologically promising areas were offered in different parts of the world at the same time; there was the North Sea, large parts of Africa and South-East Asia and, as we have seen, a large part of Latin America. As the *Petroleum Economist* reported of Argentina in April 1977,

the contract system is now widely used elsewhere . . . Given the present strong competition among developing countries for foreign expertise and capital in this high-cost sector, Argentina's offshore terms are likely to be more favourable than otherwise and to provide for the retention by the contractor of a substantial percentage of production as well as appropriate price incentives.[18]

There was another reason, however, which had to do with more fundamental changes in the world market system. The rise of OPEC and the withdrawal of the major companies from their large blocks of cap-

Table 5.5 *Production in main Latin American countries 1973–9*
(000 *b/d*)

	1973	1974	1975	1976	1977	1978	1979
Venezuela	3,384	2,987	2,353	2,294	2,239	2,165	2,356
Mexico	525	652	806	896	1,040	1,330	1,616
Argentina	421	413	395	397	431	452	471
Brazil	175	187	177	172	166	166	171
Colombia	191	175	163	152	143	136	131
Ecuador	209	177	161	187	182	202	218
Peru	72	79	72	77	92	151	192
Chile	43	39	35	33	33	17	21
Bolivia	47	46	40	41	35	32	25

Source: Briefing Service, Shell Transport and Trading, and *Petroleum Economist.*

ital in the main exporting countries effectively ended the period in which the companies or their parent governments had any real control over the governments of producer countries. Even in the 1960s Washington found it increasingly difficult to secure compensation for expropriated oil properties in Latin America; only when the companies were able to take matters into their own hands was compensation likely to be secured and even then compensation at book value was not particularly attractive. On the other hand, host governments were now effectively able to set the tax rates upon the companies according to their own preferences, with the OPEC countries serving as models. Under these circumstances and with no stigma attached to expropriation, there could be no real difficulty about renegotiating contracts. Thus, successful oil companies might expect a modest profit but would be most unlikely to achieve the really large returns which would have tempted them into exploration in the first place.[19]

Certainly it is difficult to generalise about company behaviour. By the early 1970s a fairly large number of companies were actively involved in overseas exploration; to the majors were added various independent US enterprises which were eager to make up for their dwindling crude oil supplies within the USA and also a number of European concerns linking backward from marketing into exploration and production.[20] These companies often had different assessments of political risk and even of what was attractive geologically. Moreover, some companies had specialised knowledge and experience (such as British Petroleum in difficult offshore territory) which may have made certain kinds of venture (offshore Brazil?) particularly appropriate. However, it remains a good generalisation that the effect of the oil market revolution of the early 1970s was to reduce the attractiveness to the oil companies of oil exploration in 'politically difficult areas', although not all Latin American countries were considered as such. It should also be pointed out that amendments to the petroleum taxation system of the USA worked in the same direction. Following legislation passed in 1975, US oil companies could no longer write off the costs of foreign exploration and development against their US income. This had the greatest impact upon companies entering a country for the first time. Once income was already being earned from a venture, profits could more easily be reinvested. This might reduce the overall tax liability of a company (although this would depend upon the manner of host country taxation) and would certainly provide a kind of political insurance for existing ventures. There were also economies of information and organisation to be gained from operating in a single country.

Further problems were created for foreign exploration by an Internal Revenue Service ruling of 1977 (since challenged by the companies) that crude-oil-sharing contracts with host governments did not involve payment of taxation and that these payments could not therefore be offset against taxation within the USA. Despite these obstacles, however, certain companies proved far more willing to continue to explore abroad than others and those companies which were willing to brave Latin American conditions were then able to enjoy a relatively privileged position by virtue of the barriers to entry created for their rivals.

Many of these trends can be seen clearly in the case of Peru. Between 1971 and 1973 the Peruvian military government was able to attract a considerable number of firms into oil exploration in Amazonia on the basis of crude-oil-sharing agreements varying from 50–50 to 54–46 to the host government.[21] Sixteen contracts were signed for exploration of the Amazon area and a further two for exploration offshore. However, although the geological indications appeared extremely promising and the early drilling results highly successful, disappointment quickly set in. Partly because a number of dry holes were drilled, but largely because of changing political conditions within Peru and the US tax legislation of 1975, all but two of the companies pulled out without finding oil in commercial quantities. The Peruvians, intoxicated by the scent of oil, had begun to put pressure on the companies before new discoveries really improved the bargaining position of the host country; the Mines Minister even announced that Peru was preparing to join OPEC. Once most companies had pulled out, those which remained – Belco, which had long operated the Peruvian offshore, and Occidental, which had been extremely keen to explore the Peruvian Amazon[22] – found their bargaining power to be considerable, especially when (as we shall see in more detail in chapter 20) the state oil company encountered severe problems.

The Bolivian government also attracted considerable initial interest with its offer of contract blocks in the years after 1972. Between 1973 and 1976 17 contracts were signed with foreign companies but at the end of 1979 all but two of these companies had withdrawn, often without drilling, and only Occidental Petroleum was producing crude oil in small but commercial quantities. The Ecuadorian government, despite its better bargaining position than that of Peru or Bolivia, also met some difficulties in attracting oil investment and, following the Gulf nationalisation of 1976, found it easier to persuade Texaco (already in joint venture with the state company) to expand its investment than to bring in other companies.

The position of Brazil was rather easier in that there already existed private companies in the marketing sector. As we shall see, however (chapter 18), there was some domestic opposition to any attempt to open oil exploration to foreign investment and it was not clear that Brazil could devise terms that would satisfy foreign investors; certainly the task did not prove easy. According to the initial arrangements, Petrobrás made a geophysical survey of the areas which it was willing to offer for bids and required all would-be contractors to purchase the data. Contracts were to be offered initially for three years; if oil was found in commercial quantities, this would then be bought by Petrobrás according to terms which were not immediately specified. At the beginning, moreover, no mention was made of any offer to purchase natural gas.

Although foreign companies' interest was slow to develop, BP did reach an agreement with Petrobrás in September 1976 and a contract was formally signed in December. According to this, BP guaranteed to drill at least two wells and would subsequently transfer ownership of its oil installation to Petrobrás. Any oil found by BP would be paid for in cash, whereas if natural gas were found, terms would be negotiated. Other companies quickly followed, and by the end of February 1978 a total of nine risk contracts had been signed (four with Exxon, three with BP and one each with Penzoil and Hispanoil). Contracts continued to be signed during the course of 1978 and towards the end of that year contract terms were offered to cover onshore areas as well. Since then, more and more territory has been opened up to private investment and, as we shall see in chapter 18, contract terms have become more generous. However, despite the evident success of Brazilian policy, none of the contracting companies has yet (March 1981) discovered oil. The Uruguayan government similarly changed its laws to allow the return of foreign investment in oil exploration but Standard Oil of California, after drilling two dry wells, pulled out of the country.

Chile also had some success in attracting foreign oil investment on the basis of rather similar provisions. The enabling legislation was passed in July 1975 (DL 1089) and according to the contracts offered the companies had to agree to a minimum spending requirement with detailed terms to be negotiated if any oil was found. So far, two contracts of this kind have been signed, one with an Arco–Amoco consortium (in November 1975) and the other with Phillips Petroleum (in early 1979). Arco also played a part in the development of Chilean natural gas by taking a 20% share in a consortium (31% ENAP, 20% Copec, 20% Air Products Company) which was to export liquefied natural gas from Chile to the USA. In 1979 negotiations were still in progress for a loan from the IDB for this project.

A similar change of policy took place in Argentina, tentatively during the last months of the presidency of Isabel Perón (President 1974–6) and more determinedly under the regime of General Videla. After the military coup of April 1976, the Argentine government moved quickly to liberalise its industry and on 6 July offshore blocks were opened to contract, although foreign companies needed to associate themselves either with domestic capitalists or with YPF. Some private oil companies, which had survived the rather difficult political conditions preceding the coup, were given more territory to explore. Indeed, the Argentine offshore was generally regarded as highly attractive to foreign investors[23] and by the end of 1975 a number of companies were clearly interested.[24] However, Total was the first company to sign an exploration contract with the Videla government, which it did in April 1978, and Shell signed two further contracts in April 1979.[25] In November 1979 a further 16 blocs (six offshore) were put on offer.

While most of these countries were eager to attract foreign investment, state enterprise also played a significant role in oil and gas exploration. Prior to the oil market revolution, for example, Petrobrás, as we shall see in chapter 18, had partially de-emphasised domestic oil exploration, which it regarded as uneconomic in Brazilian circumstances, and concentrated instead on foreign ventures and developments downstream. After 1972, however, it devoted an increasing proportion of its budget to oil exploration and these resources were supplemented after 1976 by foreign investments.[26] In Argentina, YPF began offshore drilling for the first time in 1976 and in 1978 Gas del Estado revealed some ambitious plans to construct a $450m. pipeline complex to transfer gas from the Neuquén, San Juan and Mendoza areas to Buenos Aires. These appear to be developing according to schedule and even more ambitious developments are likely in the 1980s.

In Colombia, Ecopetrol led a recovery in oil exploration investment which had fallen away somewhat in the early 1970s essentially as a result of price controls within Colombia. These became more important as Colombia's exportable surplus of oil fell until in 1975 Colombia became a net importer of oil. From the middle of 1976, however, price controls were progressively eased and one source reported in July 1978 that

Foreign oil companies operating in Colombia are surprisingly optimistic about the future, and some even believe that the country could become an oil exporter again during the 1980s. But most think that the chances of finding sufficiently large oilfields to allow this are extremely small. Only about one fifth of the area covered by sedimentary basins has been explored so far.[27]

Exploration wells drilled rose from 15 in 1976 to 30 in 1977 and 35 in 1978, of which Ecopetrol drilled 26. This exploration initiative did not enjoy quick success although Elf–Acquitaine does appear to have made significant discoveries in 1979–80. It remains to be seen whether the optimism of the companies proves justified.

Despite this increase in investment, however, it was widely believed that the real potential of Latin America's geology had barely been touched. As OPEC raised the world price of oil and as doubts grew about world supplies in the long term, so interest continued to focus on Latin America and the wide gap that continued to exist between the continent's energy potential and its actual levels of production became increasingly noted. One influential survey by Bernardo Grossling, for example, concluded that 'from a long-range point of view, the energy position of Latin America has to be judged in terms of its energy

Table 5.9 *Latin America: evolution of consumption of petrochemical products 1970–7 (indices (1970))*

	Oil industry views	Grossling	USSR Ministry of Geology
Latin America	150–230	490–1,225	620
Africa	120–70	470–1,220	730
South/S.E. Asia	55–80	130–325	660

Source: P. Odell, 'A personal view of "missing oil" ', *Petroleum Economist* (January 1980).

resource base. Yet, the published energy resource data seems to be utterly insufficient and to grossly underestimate the energy resource potential of Latin America.'[28] Grossling concluded that ultimate recoverable reserves for Latin America could range from 490 to 1,225 billion barrels of oil (compared with 74 billion barrels of reserves thus far identified). Even these figures 'do not allow for giant size accumulations as in the Middle East, which cannot be excluded in Latin America'.[29] A comparison between Grossling and some other estimates appears in table 5.6. If Grossling's figures are even close to the truth, and some recent oil discoveries (notably those in Mexico) suggest that they may be, then vast amounts of oil have still to be recovered from Latin America and the international oil balance may well be altered as a result.

Thus, despite the return of foreign investment into some areas of Latin America and the increased activity undertaken by state oil companies, it was by no means clear that Latin America would benefit from sufficient exploration to permit full realisation of its hydrocarbon potential. Under these circumstances and in view of the changing world position, the World Bank began to reconsider its lending policies. Until 1973 the World Bank had refused to lend money to state concerns for petroleum development (except, as we have seen, in a few very special cases) on the ground that private investment was available for the purpose. After 1974, however, this policy was reversed and the Bank continued to try to smooth various kinds of joint venture arrangements in oil exploration between host governments and various foreign companies and it sometimes went even further. In 1974 the Bank lent $200m. to the Indian Oil and Gas Commission for the development of its Bombay High offshore oilfield. In 1978, in a still more ambitious development, the Bank agreed to help finance oil development in Pakistan in a joint venture between the World Bank, the state oil company and Gulf Oil (which would take upon itself the initial exploration risk, with the other partners entering only if commercial quantities of oil were discovered). In the same year the Bank began serious negotiations with Bolivia over a $32m. loan to YPFB. After agreement was reached in 1980 the company was able to continue its exploration activities which were being threatened by a relative lack of success and by the general financial problems of the country as a whole, as we shall see in chapter 21.[30] In 1980 the Bank made a $32m. loan to Petroperú for onshore oil development.

Over all, there can be little doubt that the events of the early and mid-1970s brought about a massive improvement in the position of existing oil exporters. When added to the gains which these had already achieved during the 1940s (with the 50–50 arrangement) and in the 1960s (when the world oil surplus mainly affected company profitability rather than payments to host governments), they brought about a fundamental transformation in the economies of a relatively small number of oil exporters. Almost overnight Venezuela was changed into a country whose economy had a significant financial surplus and into a sub-regional power with a significant aid programme and a domestic standard of living comparable with that of a Mediterranean country. Although it continued to deal with the oil companies at arm's length and to rely on the sales outlets and technical help which the majors could provide, it was well capable of financing the continuing development of its own oil industry. Mexico, with a well-established state oil company and an abundance of relatively low-cost domestic crude oil, was in a similar enviable position. Both were major winners in the oil market revolution. Some smaller exporters (Ecuador, Bolivia and, after 1977, Peru) earned some welcome foreign exchange from the price increases which went some way, but only part of the way, towards financing a substantial programme of domestic oil exploration. For several other countries, however, the oil price increases worsened rather than improved economic prospects and increased the urgency of stepping up domestic production of crude oil.

Most of these countries, as well as Ecuador, Peru and Bolivia, came to rely on foreign investment for a substantial part of their requirements, especially since the most promising areas for the location of oil tended to be either offshore or in remote and high-cost onshore locations. However, the very success of the OPEC countries in breaking the power of the major oil companies and their parent governments increased the difficulties of attracting such foreign investment. Because it seemed clear that renegotiation would afford the companies only a modest profit, there was a marked reluctance by the companies to enter particular countries or at least to explore thoroughly if the initial indications were unfavourable. Those companies which did undertake such activities were therefore very strongly placed. In general, while most Latin American countries could attract at least a certain amount of foreign investment, this was often of a lesser quantity and on more onerous terms than had earlier seemed likely. While these countries had acquired greater policy flexibility and greater power *vis-à-vis* the oil companies as a result of the oil market revolution, it was not at all clear that they had gained significantly in terms of achieving their economic objectives. It remains to be seen whether the greater flexibility that undoubtedly followed the effective abandonment of the long-term concession contract and the greater willingness of international agencies to finance oil development permit new institutional arrangements to be found which can tackle these problems and allow full development of the oil resources of these countries.

Oil consumption and the downstream sector

The rise in world oil prices did little to check the upward trend of oil consumption, which increased rapidly in the 1970s in almost every country but Chile, where political upheaval outweighed the general trend. A principal reason for this was that, at least until 1979, domestic prices rarely varied to take full account of these changes. The main substitute for crude oil was natural gas, and here there were signs of increasing consumption during the course of the decade (except by Chile, for reasons already noted) as we can see from tables 5.7 and 5.8, although these do not show the effect of the ambitious gas marketing projects in several countries, notably Colombia and Argentina, which were planned or still underway in 1976. Gas consumption was still highly unequally distributed between Latin American countries, although the 1970s did see the beginnings of an international trade in natural gas. Bolivia began exporting substantial quantities of gas to Argentina and a possible gas pipeline from Bolivia to Brazil was under discussion for most of the decade. Chile began to consider seriously the possibility of LNG exports from around 1974;[31] it was expected that a

Table 5.7 *Oil consumption in Latin America 1960–77*
(000 *b/d*)

	1960	1965	1970	1975	1977
Argentina	243,189	380,860	422,573	454,556	475,145
Bolivia	6,063	9,099	11,444	20,479	21,830
Brazil	263,844	327,490	506,775	868,276	961,786
Chile	47,923	59,907	88,471	91,381	89,910
Colombia	54,981	68,477	101,986	139,726	157,260
Ecuador	12,273	14,712	23,901	27,441	50,778
Mexico	297,066	340,529	503,173	735,312	1,016,000
Peru	48,549	76,441	90,935	116,408	119,000
Venezuela	154,626	175,808	200,386	243,392	256,732

Source: Compiled from *Latin America and Caribbean Oil Report,* published by *Petroleum Economist* (London, 1980).

Table 5.8 *Marketed natural gas production in Latin America 1972–6*
(*billion cubic feet*)

	1972	1973	1974	1975	1976
Argentina	218	238	256	273	259
Bolivia	38	58	61	60	62
Brazil	9	9	18	25	19
Chile	144	145	127	120	122
Colombia	65	65	66	66	67
Ecuador	1	1	1	1	1
Mexico	496	542	561	584	578
Peru	31	34	32	35	36
Venezuela	388	460	476	450	480

Source: Latin America and Caribbean Oil Report, p. 67.

project would be onstream by 1982. Most important of all, there were serious negotiations between Mexico and the USA about the possible export of natural gas. These negotiations, however, proved unexpectedly difficult, as we shall see in more detail below (pp. 141–3).

While most of the major Latin American countries were either oil exporters or at least close to self-sufficiency, Brazil fell into neither of these categories and suffered particularly heavily as a result of the oil price increases. We shall consider its responses in detail in chapter 18. At the same time, the size of the Brazilian market made it possible for

Table 5.9 *Latin America: evolution of consumption of petrochemical products 1970–7 (indices (1970))*

	Argentina	Brazil	Mexico	Andean area	Total
1970	100.0	100.0	100.0	100.0	100.0
1971	116.5	134.8	111.8	125.6	122.2
1972	137.0	171.6	132.7	156.9	149.8
1973	139.5	245.6	151.9	182.1	185.4
1974	164.5	345.0	175.1	210.6	217.2
1975	159.4	354.5	186.1	215.8	220.2
1976	147.3	421.0	211.1	239.1	256.0
1977	157.0	481.7	244.4	271.0	310.0

Source: Industria y quimica, 1979, p. 29.

the state to initiate a number of major petrochemical developments in which foreign investors played an important part and local capitalists also participated. Because of the rapid expansion of industrial demand, petrochemicals in Brazil was 'a sellers' market' in which Petroquisa (a subsidiary of Petrobrás, set up for the purpose of initiating and controlling petrochemical developments) was eager to take its share of the profits.[32] As the result of a relentless pace of expansion, Brazil had by 1979 acquired capacity similar to that of a number of European countries (see also chapter 18).

A number of other countries undertook more or less ambitious developments in petrochemicals. Peru got its industry underway with a carbon black plant and an ammonia plant, and even Bolivia was pursuing plans for a pesticides plant with the more or less reliable promise that the other Andean Pact countries would provide a market for the production. Indeed, the Andean Pact, founded at the beginning of 1971 with the aim of providing the economies of scale and common policies that would aid industrialisation in the countries of the west coast of Latin America,[33] did have ambitious plans for petrochemicals although the hoped-for integration in this sector has not really taken place. Consequently, development of petrochemicals and oil refining has tended to take place in line with the capacity of local markets.

The most interesting exception to this rule was in the case of Mexico where the government, after the major oil discoveries in the south and the 1973–4 energy crisis, took a conscious decision to export refined oil and petrochemicals as well as crude. A number of very large-scale

Table 5.10 *Latin America: evolution of the market for petrochemical products* 1970–7
(*m. metric tonnes*)

		1970	1976	1977
Argentina	production	0.65	1.00	1.12
	imports	0.19	0.25	0.26
	exports	0.06	0.10	0.15
	consumption	0.78	1.15	1.23
Brazil	production	1.04	4.84	5.43
	imports	0.62	2.15	2.57
	exports	0.01	0.02	0.03
	consumption	1.65	6.97	7.97
Mexico	production	1.54	4.36	4.57
	imports	0.39	0.58	0.62
	exports	0.10	0.07	0.06
	consumption	1.83	4.87	5.13
Andean area	production	0.37	1.21	1.39
	imports	0.36	0.66	0.75
	exports	0.02	0.16	0.20
	consumption	0.71	1.71	1.94
TOTAL	production	3.60	11.41	12.51
	imports	1.56	3.64	4.20
	exports	0.19	0.35	0.44
	consumption	4.97	14.70	16.27

Source: Industria y química, 1979, p. 29.

ventures were planned and investment was channelled into these sectors. In current dollars, investment in refining and petrochemicals increased tenfold between 1972 and 1978, from $44.9 and $44.8m. respectively to $464m. and $493m. (see also chapter 17). Under these circumstances, it is likely that Mexico will become a major exporter of oil products and petrochemicals during the 1980s.[34]

Taken as a whole, the growth of the petrochemicals sector in Latin America during the 1970s was impressive. It owed more, however, to growth of demand within the continent and to import substitution, both stimulated by the pressure of industrialisation, than to exports. The nature of these developments can be seen in tables 5.9 and 5.10.

International diplomacy and Latin American oil and gas

As we have seen, the US government's direct interest in the overseas oil industry declined after the early 1950s and it came to rely to an increasing extent upon the judgement of the oil companies. It was extremely badly placed, therefore, as it became clear in the early 1970s that the companies themselves could not effectively resist the increasingly ambitious demands of the main producer governments. Moreover, Washington's concern with Israel, and thus with Arab 'moderation', and its anti-Communism, which remained something of a reflex even though the Cold War was now quieter, ensured that the needs of the oil industry were not immediately at the centre of attention. Since the part played by Washington in the oil price revolution of 1970–4 has been discussed elsewhere,[35] it will merely be noted here that the US State Department had great difficulty in arriving at a policy which was even consistent, let alone at one which was effective. This is not to say that Washington's position provided the main reason for the transformation of the oil market but only to emphasise that it would be difficult to speak of 'a US oil policy' during this period.

A part of the reason for this lay in the increasingly apparent, and increasingly complex, interconnection between Middle Eastern oil and strategic questions involving Israel. Moreover, the effects of the Vietnam War and the Watergate scandal within the USA considerably weakened the power of the Federal Executive in the conduct of foreign policy. It was also true that the effect of the oil crisis in the USA (as in parts of Europe) was to increase the unpopularity of the oil companies, and particularly the major companies, and thus to reduce their capacity to influence US policy.[36] Finally, within the USA and also in parts of Europe, there was at first a considerable reluctance to accept that the transformation in the oil market was real and not something created by the major companies for some ulterior purpose. The demonology of oil, whose effects in the USA had long been nullified by the close post-war relationship established between the major companies and the State Department, once more emerged (as it had to a lesser extent in the 1930s) as a constraint upon policy. In the 1930s, however, the USA was still an exporter of oil and the changed political climate was of only peripheral importance to international arrangements; in the 1970s, with the USA a major oil importer and profligate consumer of energy, the consequences were far more striking.

The effect of all of these changes on US policy was twofold. On some occasions (notably under the Ford Administration) State Department policy was motivated by a desire to attack OPEC, or at least to exert pressure sufficient to break the organisation. Since this policy was not supported by the major oil companies (which were concerned to keep the oil flowing and so wanted to avoid any kind of confrontation) or by important European countries, notably France, it did not enjoy a great deal of success. On other occasions the aim was to build up close understandings, and even special relationships, with the main oil-producing countries in the hope that goodwill would provide an effective antidote to market forces and the increasingly uncertain political balance within the Middle East. It is evident that the latter policy had only a limited effect.

When discussing policy, however, it should be remembered that on a number of occasions the logic of what was, after all, a very rapidly changing situation was simply not understood and US policymakers, particularly when in 'tougher' mood, tended to overplay what was in reality a very weak hand. In the case of Venezuela, for example, the Nixon Administration began by trying to use admission into the US market as a pressure tactic in order to persuade Caracas to favour the oil companies. Throughout the period, and even as late as 1972, the USA tried to bargain on the assumption that access to its own market was some kind of gift which could be bestowed upon a grateful Venezuela in return for the latter's pursuit of pro-company policies. The fact that US import requirements were instead a major liability appears to have occurred to nobody.[37]

Much the same lack of realism or tendency to bluff lay behind Washington's anti-OPEC offensive of 1974, which followed a series of 'hawkish' statements made, to singularly little effect, on the question of Middle Eastern oil.[38] Immediately after the sharp price increases of 1973–4, Washington tried to split Saudi Arabia from Iran and the more militant OPEC members; at the time the CIA believed that there was a real chance that Saudi Arabia might defect from OPEC.[39] Thus, on 23 February 1974, the *Guardian* reported that 'the American view, currently being urged on King Faisal, is that OPEC is in many ways irrelevant and that Saudi Arabia could go it alone.' It is not difficult to see what the effect of any such unilateral decision would have had upon Saudi Arabia, but the Saudis did agree to lobby quietly from OPEC for a modest price reduction, and at the beginning of June 1974 Sheik Yamani called for a cut in the price of oil to $9 a barrel.

As the expected price cut failed to materialise, however, Washington put increasing public pressure on the other OPEC governments. In July 1974, 'in a highly unusual move', the State Department publicly criticised Gulf Oil for paying what it said were excessive prices for Kuwaiti oil.[40] In the same month, US Treasury Secretary Simon publicly described the Shah of Iran as 'a nut'.[41] Similarly, Ecuador's decision in May 1974 to order a production cutback from 250,000 b/d to 210,000 b/d resulted in scarcely veiled criticism from Washington; US Treasury Under-Secretary Bennet remarked that 'any new reduction in oil production, by any government, at the present moment, will clearly be regarded by the USA and other consuming nations as a counter-productive measure'.[42]

By the end of August, Washington's diplomatic offensive against OPEC had clearly failed. The signal of this failure was the publication of the decision of Saudi Arabia not to cut its oil price but to cut its production instead. Consequently after OPEC's meeting of September 1974, Ford and Kissinger made aggressive speeches to the United Nations which appeared to be aimed at persuading the non-oil-exporting developing countries to turn against OPEC, and seemed also to threaten some form of trade boycott against OPEC members. Kissinger asserted that 'the World cannot sustain even the present level of prices, much less continuing increases . . . what has gone up by political action can be reduced by political action'.[43]

Washington did not limit itself to making rhetorical attacks upon OPEC countries but also adopted commercial pressures as well. At the beginning of 1975 it issued its Trade Act, which denied tariff concessions to those Third World countries which were members of OPEC. Although this law was aimed essentially at the Middle East, it had a considerable effect in Caracas and, even more so, in Quito, where membership of OPEC had always been controversial, and in Mexico, which was considering whether to apply for membership of OPEC. Moreover, the USA did at least consider trying to prevent the main international aid agencies from lending to members of OPEC,[44] but was apparently dissuaded through the argument that OPEC aid-giving had an important part to play in limiting the effect of the world price increases upon the developing countries.

It is not clear how seriously all of this should be taken. Certainly talk is cheap and Washington's hard line did help to persuade the other main consuming countries that they had interests in common, while Kissinger negotiated the formation of the International Energy Agency and tried to discourage Japan and the main European countries from establishing separate arrangements with OPEC.[45] Moreover, the US Trade Act did persuade Mexico not to apply for membership of OPEC and, as we shall see, was able to bring considerable pressure to bear on the government of Ecuador. Since most of the day-to-day contact with OPEC governments was made by companies, Kissinger could afford some extravagance in his rhetoric.

Nevertheless, when 'hawkish' statements are repeatedly made without effect they tend to lose credibility, and Washington's intervention in 1974, as well as providing ammunition for its more radical opponents, showed only too clearly that the crucial decisions concerning the international oil market were now beyond its control. The weakness of the US position had become clear for all to see. Moreover, Washington's outspoken attacks upon OPEC tended to reinforce the sympathy felt for that organisation by many Third World governments who were already inclined to see OPEC as a model to be emulated rather than as a threat to their own trade balances and who were now convinced that it was possible to challenge the existing world economic order. Kissinger had lost the loyalties of the Third World far more effectively than OPEC ever could.

Within Latin America, the most important diplomatic consequence of this situation was that Venezuela had shown that it could 'stand up' to US pressures that were often personal as well as political.[46] Within Ecuador, however, the open split between OPEC and the USA did cause considerable concern to practically all conservative forces, including both traditional politicians and established social classes. When this effect was reinforced by a sharp reduction in the oil companies' production from the country after June 1974 (when the oil market changed from shortage to surplus), it led to the removal of the radical Oil Minister, Captain (later Admiral) Jarrín, who had earlier been elected President of OPEC when that organisation met in Quito in June 1974. The fact that such a meeting was held in Quito at all, as well as the election of Jarrín as President, suggests the importance of the latter in the behind-the-scenes deliberations of OPEC.[47] Although Ecuador did not in fact withdraw from OPEC, as some conservatives had suggested it should, it subsequently played a far more minor role in the organisation.

While Washington was concerned about the behaviour of OPEC, questions of property ownership were generally left to the companies. Thus, when Venezuela was negotiating for control of its oil industry in 1975, the former US Ambassador Robert McLintock (who had been involved in similar negotiations in Argentina in 1963), 'recommended . . . that the United States government take a leading role in direct negotiations with Venezuela concerning oil rather than leaving them to several private American companies'.[48] But these proposals were rejected by the State Department.

In Ecuador, however, Washington did continue to press on more narrowly focussed property issues. Thus, in October 1974, just after the removal of Jarrín, the US Embassy believed that the time had come to discuss an earlier dispute with Quito over the cancellation (in late 1972) of a concession earlier granted to a US consortium (Ada) under circumstances which were questionable under Ecuadorian law. However, its call for a return of the concession to Ada was rebuffed. The Carter Administration was very much less aggressive on oil matters than its immediate predecessors. This is partly the result of its own preference for a softer line, partly because of the domestic political difficulties which have reduced US presidential power, but perhaps mainly because there has seemed little that could usefully be done. By the end of 1976 the world had become accustomed to high oil prices, the main oil-exporting countries had completed their partial or total nationalisations of foreign companies, and the attempt to turn 'Third World' loyalties against OPEC had clearly failed. Moreover, the swift collapse of the Shah of Iran at the beginning of 1979 further emphasised, if emphasis was necessary, the extent to which the USA (and Britain) had lost influence over the Middle East and the inability of material goods to fill a political vacuum. All that seems to remain is the threat of open military involvement, and its dangers are such as to ensure that this is regarded only as a last resort.

Following these changes in the Middle East, the USA became increasingly concerned with nearby sources of supply, particularly with the huge oil and gas discoveries made in Mexico during the 1970s; although here, as we shall see, US policy was no more coherent than it was anywhere else, it did turn out to be more successful.[49]

After the inauguration of López Portillo as President of Mexico in December 1976 it became increasingly clear that Mexican oil reserves were massive even by international standards. In late 1978 the CIA calculated that Mexico could at some future date produce as much as 10m. barrels daily — more than enough to alter decisively the world-wide balance of supply and demand. As we shall see, Mexican policy, although less cautious than it had been earlier, was by no means committed to total expansion. However, it was in the interest of the USA that Mexico produce as much oil as possible. Publicly the US government remained scrupulously aloof and declared that Mexican production levels were a matter for Mexico, but it is clear that the Mexican government was aware of US preferences. Indeed, there was something of a debate within the USA as to the best way of dealing with Mexico, and a number of US Senators suggested that inducements might be found to persuade Mexico to increase its level of oil production.

The question of Mexico's natural gas exports appeared, if anything, even more difficult. The idea that Mexico should export large quantities of natural gas to the USA was born in 1977 after a cold winter which made it clear that there were shortages of gas within the USA but a surplus within Mexico. The remedy appeared obvious and once negotiations began between Pemex and several US oil companies there appeared to be little difficulty in securing an agreement. A letter of intent was signed in August 1977. Although, as we shall see in chapter 17, there was some nationalist criticism of the agreement within Mexico, López Portillo made clear his intention of proceeding with the project.

The economics of the arrangement appeared excellent. The export income earned would pay back the cost of the pipeline within a year and there would then be left some $2,000m. a year of extra revenue for Pemex. Moreover, since the gas discovered was associated with the oil finds of the south, it would be difficult to leave the gas in the ground; much of it had either to be sold or flared. When agreement was reached, therefore, with a price of $2.60 per thousand cubic feet (which was linked with the c.i.f. price of diesel oil into the USA), everything appeared to be settled. At this point, the US administration put an end to the deal on the grounds that it was too expensive, especially if the same price had then to be offered to Canadian gas imports.

This change in US policy caused intense anger within Mexico. The López Portillo government felt that it had gone some way to meet US needs despite pressure from its own nationalists, and now had the door slammed in its face. Against this, the Mexican negotiating position was relatively weak. Much of the natural gas which was to have been exported was associated with oil and would therefore have to be flared if no market could be found for it. The cost of constructing an LNG export terminal (which some nationalists would have preferred) was vastly above that of transporting gas by pipeline, and there were very strict limits to what could be absorbed by the domestic market even at heavily subsidised prices. Publicly, therefore, the Mexican government called off all negotiations but privately the door was kept open. López Portillo relieved his feelings by giving President Carter a stern public lecture about US imperialism when the latter visited Mexico in February 1979. Nevertheless, a gas pipeline capable of transporting 2,000 million cubic feet of gas daily continued to be built as far north as Monterrey so that it would be an easy matter to extend it the few miles further necessary to reach the US border. The gas pipeline to Monterrey was officially opened on 18 March 1979. The gas contract was also renegotiated during the period between Carter's visit in February and September 1979 when final agreement was reached, just before a further meeting between Carter and López Portillo. Renegotiations were made easier by the sharp increase in world oil prices during 1979, so that although Mexico conceded the principle that the gas price should be tied to that of fuel rather than diesel oil, it nevertheless received a far higher price than it had originally demanded. The final agreement was for the export of only 300 million cubic feet daily, although it was understood that the volume could be increased gradually, and the price agreed was $3.625 per thousand cubic feet, adjustable every three months.

The extent of Mexican hydrocarbon reserves and the difficulties of transporting gas over long distances made a pipeline solution logical, but agreement was possible only after hard bargaining. Moreover, the rather clumsy US bargaining posture led to a serious loss of goodwill toward the Carter Administration within Mexico. The US government certainly felt that there was a good deal at stake in these negotiations, partly because it would have needed to concede 'parity' to Canadian gas exports if it had treated Mexico more generously and partly because natural gas exports have been the subject of a good deal of international negotiations in 1979 and 1980 as exporting countries have tried to capitalise on OPEC's success in raising international oil prices. Against this, there was a cost to Washington in that its earlier hard line helped strengthen nationalist opposition to Mexico's oil and gas export policies. Perhaps the most important conclusion, however, is that agreement was finally reached and marks a significant step in Washington's efforts to switch its source of oil and gas supplies away from the Middle East.

6

Latin America in the twentieth-century oil system

There are, broadly speaking, two ways in which the international oil system can be analysed. One of these is essentially derived from liberal economic theories and stresses the importance of factor endowments and comparative costs in explaining international trade. The other is basically Marxist (although shared by some conservatives) and argues that trade, even where it does not follow the flag, is nevertheless mainly determined by international power relationships. Now that evidence has been presented, it may be interesting to consider how these different approaches can be applied to the oil system in the twentieth century.

To begin with the first approach, it is certainly true that the history of international oil has been made up in large part by such environmental factors as the international distribution of population and potentially oil-bearing territory. Moreover, policy can very often be understood in terms of these factors. Let us therefore consider the geological conditions that have existed in Latin America during the course of the century and their effect upon policy.

Two Latin American countries, Venezuela and Mexico, have been actually or potentially oil rich during most of the century in the sense that there was not only enough oil to be found and exported on a large scale but also adequate technology for the purpose as well as geological conditions which made these sources relatively low cost. In other words, not only were these countries endowed with 'easy oil' which could be discovered by the techniques available during and even prior to the 1920s, but also with 'difficult oil' which can still be extracted on a large scale, albeit at higher cost and with more sophisticated techniques. In Venezuela nearly every major exploration venture achieved a significant measure of success and reserves only appeared to be dwindling in the early 1970s because little exploration had taken place since 1958. More recently, not only has Petrovén found important reserves offshore, but it has begun to consider seriously the development of the Orinoco oil belt from which, it is now believed, 500 billion barrels may eventually be recovered. Mexico has not been quite so prolific, but Mexican oil history has nevertheless revolved around three major oil developments; the Golden Lane in and after 1910, the Poza Rica find of 1932 and the Chiapas–Tabasco discoveries beginning in 1972. The first and third of these converted Mexico into a large-scale exporter, while the second, as we shall see in chapter 17, helped Pemex survive the difficult early years following the nationalisation of 1938. Given this impressive resource base, it is not surprising that both Mexico and Venezuela have played important parts in determining the evolution of the international oil system. Mexico pioneered the path of nationalist self-assertion following the Revolution, and the 1938 oil nationalisation was a significant event in world politics. Subsequently it preferred to withdraw from the international oil system to the greatest possible degree and to concentrate instead upon fostering domestic industrialisation on the basis of cheap oil. Very recently it has returned to its previous position as an oil exporter, with results that are not yet fully clear but which will undoubtedly be important. Venezuela, in contrast, remained inside the international oil system and sought to play a constructive role within it. Venezuelan policy did a great deal to improve the position of all producer governments both in the 1940s and during the formation and early years of OPEC (essentially 1959–63). Later, when overtaken in economic importance by Iran and Saudi Arabia, Venezuela continued to play an important although essentially second-level role in the counsels of OPEC and took decisive action in 1970–1 and again in 1974–5 to further the interests of all oil producers.

It is interesting that Venezuela and Mexico, although they have been explored more intensively than some other Latin American countries, have not had anything like the amount of exploration that has been carried out in the USA or Canada. This has been even more true of a second group of countries (Peru, Argentina, Bolivia, Ecuador and Colombia) in which exploration success has been significant but erratic. The most promising areas in these countries – offshore Argentina, Peruvian Amazonia, the Ecuadorian and Colombian trans-Andean area and the Bolivian Chaco – have been high cost, technically difficult and more than usually uncertain. Clearly the position has changed in all of these countries as a result of oil depletion in some areas (Comodoro Rivadavia in Argentina, the north-west onshore fields in Peru and the coastal fields in Ecuador) and the increasing possibility of developing others as technology has developed. Nevertheless one may generalise roughly by saying that most of these countries (though perhaps not Argentina) have for most of the century aspired to become large-scale oil producers, but that for the most part they are still living in hope. The Ecuadorian Amazon has almost but not quite (at least yet) yielded enough to change this position. While the volume of reserves required to bring about such a transformation is obviously influenced by domestic population and oil demand, it is worth pointing out that proven oil reserves in these countries at the end of 1978 varied from 776 million barrels in Peru to 1,450 million in Ecuador and 2,424 million in Argentina (which has the largest market of the group). Bolivia had much less oil but extensive reserves of natural gas. This compares with proven reserves of over 18,000 million barrels in Venezuela and (as announced in March 1980) some 50,000 million barrels of all hydrocarbons in Mexico.

These countries, therefore, have had to balance their desire to achieve national control over oil with their concern to increase exploration and production. On the whole they have relied to a considerable extent upon foreign investment in oil exploration. Nationalisations have taken place, but sooner or later foreign investment was invited back to supplement the resources of the state company. There has also been a certain amount of exploration by state companies, but the difficulties and high costs have often made this disappointing or, at best, of only limited value. Consequently, and because of their continuing aspirations, they have been rather more dependent on prevailing international arrangements and rather less able to change them than Mexico or Venezuela, even though they have often been able to bargain quite effectively with foreign companies.

If we exclude those countries in which no oil was developed, and Guatemala where it has been developed only very recently, we are left with a group of countries (notably Chile and Brazil) which have discovered oil reserves in some quantity but have never achieved full self-sufficiency and may never do so. Even so, oil development has assumed considerable economic importance and has provided considerable relief to the balance of payments. Since these countries believed, almost certainly correctly, that they had little chance of persuading the multinationals to explore heavily at a time of world surplus, state companies were set up in order to carry out the exploration. A key factor in this decision was that both governments were, in the 1940s, forced to make a choice between a policy of complete state control and one of total reliance upon the discretion of foreign companies; had a policy of joint ventures or limited contractual arrangement been available, this outcome might have been different. It may, of course, be argued that large-scale oil exploration in these countries was economically irrational during a period when oil was cheap and capital relatively scarce, but governments in Chile and Brazil were more concerned with the logic of domestic industrialisation than with that of the international oil system. Moreover, even the relatively small amounts of oil produced in these countries have done something to offset the impact of the oil price increases of the 1970s. It is interesting that Brazil and Chile were both willing to allow foreign oil investment in the 1970s on terms which they might have accepted earlier had they been available. Subsequently, foreign investors have been investing quite heavily in Brazil and to a significant degree in Chile, even if so far without very much success.

Market size has also been important to oil development. This was particularly true in the oil industry where, at least until very recently, international distribution was in the hands of the major companies, but where host governments have generally been successful in controlling their internal markets when they have wished to do so. Where domestic industrialisation has been a major objective of policy, governments have often played a major role in developing such sectors as oil refining and petrochemicals. Under these circumstances, the importance of market size is apparent. It was easier for Brazil and Mexico to develop modern oil-refining sectors and large petrochemicals industries than it was for Peru, and easier for Peru than it was for Bolivia. One should also point out that the very rapid growth in oil consumption in most Latin American countries after around 1930 transformed the economics of state enterprise by increasing the commercial viability of refining and (later, although to a lesser extent) of petrochemicals production for the domestic market. It is extremely interesting that Mexico is now moving aggressively into the export of petrochemicals (as we shall see in more detail in chapter 17), but the industry was developed on the basis of an expanding home market and, up to now, almost all downstream investments in Latin America (except in Venezuela and a few strategically placed Caribbean countries) have been aimed at the domestic market. The size of the Brazilian market, or more accurately of the Brazilian oil import bill, has also led the state oil company, and the country itself, to take an increasingly active international role, with consequences which will be considered in more detail below.

When these factors are taken together, it becomes clear that a treatment of the Latin American oil industry based essentially on geological and market variables may prove far more adequate than is apparent at first sight. Certainly some writers have seen power relationships or even sinister conspiracies at work in cases where an elementary knowledge of economics could be applied to far better purpose. However, it would be equally misleading to assume that the international oil industry operated 'purely' as a response to essentially environmental conditions. One can see power relationships in a number of ways, from the perspective of long-term patterns of oil exploration, the price at which oil has been sold and the ownership of the means of production.

The question then arises as to how far power has been inherent and 'systematic' in the oil market and how far it has been transient and unexpected. This raises many issues, but it will be useful to begin by discussing one topic which has excited controversy both at specific and more abstract levels, namely whether it makes sense to assume that the most potentially powerful forces in the international oil industry have generally acted with sufficient energy and harmony to make their superiority effective. Those close to the centres of power often talk of drift, muddle and indecision, whereas those further away tend to see patterns which are clearer and designs which are more ambitious. Who has the clearer vision?

If we take the case of the US government, it has been clear from these chapters that domestic political conditions have been important to international oil policymaking. The effect upon US policy of the depression and the New Deal in the 1930s or of Vietnam, Watergate and the oil crisis in the 1970s could perhaps be exaggerated but this would certainly be difficult. Critics from the left have generally regarded it as 'normal' for the US government to back up its oil companies whether or not these had a valid legal or moral claim. Certainly there have been periods of US history (1920–8, 1953–60 and 1963–72) when US policy has been substantially pro-company, although even then only within limits. By no stretch of the imagination, however, could the 1933–40 period be seen in these terms; wartime conditions also led to some important departures from conditions prevailing during the years of peace. Similarly the Alliance for Progress, in its early years, marked a significant even if short-lived change in US policy.

Since 1973 the position has been rather different; quite apart from any underlying changes in direction, the ability of governments in Washington to pursue a particular strategy has been sharply curtailed and, as a result, so has the political influence of the international oil companies.

Moreover, within any US administration, key appointments have often greatly influenced the conduct of policy; there is a proconsular tradition within the US foreign service which does something to vindicate students of bureaucratic politics.[1] Some ambassadors and other key officials have carried out what almost amounted to a personal foreign policy; consider, for example, the different roles played by Sheffield, Morrow, Clark and Daniels in Mexico between 1925 and 1940, or the relationship between Ambassador Corrigan and Linam of Jersey Standard in Venezuela in the early 1940s. Obviously one can make too much of this point, since there certainly are continuities and similarities in US policy, but no history of the international oil system can safely concentrate on these alone.

Ultimately, however, one does need to consider the systematic nature of power in the international oil system and the way in which it has been and can be exercised. To a considerable extent this can also be understood in terms of the economics of the industry. Without going so far as to say that the oil industry is inherently oligopolistic,[2] one can certainly identify a number of factors – geological, technical and institutional – which facilitate oligopoly. For one thing, it has always been true, and is now more than ever apparent, that the short-run price elasticity of oil is very low. Refiners will bid up the price of oil in order to maintain full capacity, since there are large financial penalties for failing to do so. Motorists, railways and airlines will, at least in the short run, consume oil at almost any price because of the relatively high capital costs of cars, trains and aeroplanes. Householders will continue to warm their dwellings if they can possibly afford to do so, and government agencies are notoriously slow to cut back on anything scarce. Even in the medium term the elasticity of demand for oil is not high, particularly since oil, even when sold at historically high prices, is still cheaper than almost all other forms of energy.

This low demand elasticity does not make oligopoly inevitable but it greatly increases the rewards available to those who are able to control the main sources of supply, for even a limited cutback in world oil production will permit a very large increase in oil prices. Moreover, given the essential cheapness of the lowest-cost supplies of oil, at any rate at the margin, uncontrolled oil production has threatened to destroy the profitability of a number of oil-competing industries while also proving disappointing and sometimes disastrous to oil producers themselves. One consequence of this has been that there has always been protectionist pressure when the challenge of oil became too great; some European coal producers were hostile to imports of low-cost oil after 1955, but the most important protectionist measures took place in the USA with the imposition of import restrictions in 1933 and again in 1958. Another consequence has been that oil producers have had great incentives to form common organisations rather than see profits destroyed by uncontrolled competition. This was true of small producers who helped form the Texas Railroad Commission and put into force the Texan pro-rationing system after 1933. It was also true of the larger companies, as could be seen from the Achnacarry agreement of 1928 and the subsequent development of the Seven Sisters. Finally, it was true of the main oil-exporting countries. It was the Venezuelan government's initiative of 1959 that led to the formation of OPEC and this was followed by a series of deliberate and ultimately fairly successful efforts to form an effective producers' cartel.

While the price elasticity of oil is low, its income elasticity is extremely high; world oil production increased by more than 100 times between 1900 and 1974, from 194.1 million barrels to 20,334 million. The financial requirements posed by this pace of expansion, together with the uncertainty of oil exploration, have tended towards a situation in which only a few companies were able and willing to invest aggressively in the relatively small number of hitherto poor countries under whose territory the bulk of the world's oil has been found. As it turned out, these countries came to play an increasingly decisive part in the world oil market.

None of this is to say that oligopoly was inevitable, but only that there was a tendency for it to develop. The years between 1911 and 1928 were relatively competitive but, following the Achnacarry agreement of 1928, a system of co-operation among the major companies kept the industry solvent during the depression. The period following the depression also saw the development of a regulatory system within the USA and a greater degree of concentration within the overall oil system. Until around 1955 the system of oligopoly was sustained even though the control exercised by the major companies was strategic rather than comprehensive. Between 1955 and 1970 company oligopoly eroded and subsequently the producer governments rather than the oil companies came to determine the fate of the international oil market.

Naturally these arrangements had their effect upon Latin America. Until around 1970, one of the most important consequences was that most foreign companies would explore for oil in a country only on the basis of a concession contract which gave them essential control of development. Established producer governments could in practice exercise some influence over company strategy, but even this was very limited. Otherwise, countries unwilling to offer such terms had essentially to go it alone. Moreover, the major companies largely controlled and were in many ways able to manipulate the international movement of oil. They were also able to persuade the US government and the international aid agencies, with some limited exceptions, not to offer financial aid to state oil companies, and particularly not to do so for the purposes of oil exploration. Moreover, in cases of expropriation on terms unacceptable to the companies involved, the major companies were able to exert considerable economic leverage against the host government – leverage which was complemented in most cases by similar action from Washington, even though Washington was frequently anxious to settle disputes on terms which were sometimes less than satisfactory to the oil companies. Taken together, these powers were limited but nevertheless they were real enough.

Even so, surprisingly little that has taken place in the international oil system during the century can be explained in terms of the exercise of metropolitan power directly upon oil-producing countries (rather than through classes or groups within these countries, which is an altogether more complicated matter). On the contrary, one of the most striking features of the international oil system has been the way in which it has been changed in the interests of the main oil producers. These countries have been able to influence tax rates and (later) price levels on a world scale. They were able to carry out expropriations on what were often highly advantageous terms. They have also been able to call upon metropolitan sources of finance and technology at the very time when they were changing the international system to the disadvantage of the major oil companies and the metropolis as a whole. Such changes suggest two conclusions. The first is that the international oil system (and, by extension, the international capitalist system) is far more flexible and capable of far more change than is often supposed. The second is that it is worth exploring why the balance of international power during the 1970s swung so drastically in favour of the large oil producers. Here we shall need to look not just at Latin America but at the world as a whole.

As was suggested above, factor endowments have much to do with the explanation. As is well known, the oilfields of the Persian Gulf and North Africa are much larger and much lower cost than the world average. Moreover, partly as the result of deliberate policy, production potential from the extensive even if higher-cost oilfields of the USA had fallen off and output began an absolute decline after 1970. During the mid-1920s, the USA produced around 70% of the total world output; in 1974 the proportion was 17.3%. By 1970, therefore, the main oil-exporting countries had developed an effective stranglehold over the world's oil supplies and they could maintain a high level of production even at far higher prices than those prevailing in 1970.

Nevertheless, factor endowments are far from providing the whole story. A number of political and commercial factors had also contributed to this situation. The major companies, which still carried out the bulk of international oil exploration, were obviously reluctant to do anything to compromise their apparently strong positions in the oil-exporting countries. This reluctance inhibited them from too much exploration elsewhere, lest new discoveries and pressures to produce from new areas upset their finely balanced calculations. Even more important, the major companies were unwilling to accept exploration terms in other countries which offered more to host governments than was being offered in the main producing areas; had they done so, they would have been faced with pressure to generalise such terms internationally, to their own disadvantage. Moreover, terms then acceptable to governments in oil-abundant countries could not always be acceptable in countries where oil production was higher cost. Specifically, many host governments feared that the absolute control of exploration and development demanded by the companies would remove any guarantee that serious exploration would take place. Finally, in countries where private oil companies were not free to explore, it was decided by the USA and the international aid agencies that exploration by state companies should also be discouraged. As a consequence of all these factors, one observer writing in 1979 pointed out that Third World countries 'contain almost 50% of the world's total potentially petroliferous regions but, to date, the petroleum efforts in these regions have been minimal. Even including the considerable amount of work undertaken in OPEC countries such as Venezuela and Nigeria, it is less than 5% of the world total.'[3]

Perhaps most important of all, however, has been the fact that the main oil-exporting countries have been able to use their market power in a spectacular manner without either meeting vigorous international resistance or allowing their differences on other matters to undermine their unity. The reasons for this are clearly political and relate to the logic of 'imperialism' more than to oil as such. One may begin by pointing out that there is a lack of symmetry between the interests of metropolitan governments and those of oil-producing countries. For example, for the US government, the fate of its oil companies abroad and the international price of oil have been important but by no means the main factors in foreign policy. Great power conflicts have always been far more important. Thus, the USA was far more concerned about German and, subsequently, Soviet influence in Latin America than with Mexican or Venezuelan oil policies, as was made clear by its relatively muted response to the Mexican expropriation of 1938 and its very muted reaction to Venezuela's pro-producer policies of 1958–63. Similarly, the USA's Middle Eastern policies have been greatly complicated by its support for Israel. Conversely, the most important element in the policy of a major oil-exporting country is a concern to make the most of its resource. Governments such as the Mexican and Venezuelan have been extremely determined in their oil nationalism even when their other policies have been negotiable or even in natural accordance with US interests. As a result of this, successive US governments have tended to leave oil to the oilmen and, if anything, sought to mediate between the interests of the oil companies and those of friendly host governments. When the oil companies were no longer able to hold the line, partly because of growing disunity (after various 'newcomer' companies were attracted into foreign oil exploration by the promise of high profits) but also because of changes in the location of the world's oil reserves, there was very little that the US government could do.

It is in any case difficult for a metropolitan government to decide upon an appropriate response to economic conflict. Unless the position is desperate, military intervention is likely to be seen as far too drastic. On the other hand, commercial and financial pressures are notoriously unreliable and may even, as in the case of Cuba (and Rhodesia), play into the hands of hard-line adversaries. Moreover, even allowing that economic sanctions had some value against oil expropriations, they were quite useless in cases such as tax increases or supply restrictions, which brought direct financial benefit to the government involved.

In fact, the US government and the major oil companies appeared to believe after 1945 that a 'reasonable' tax arrangement with the main producer governments would prove mutually satisfactory and that growing oil-based affluence would discourage these governments from any rash nationalistic moves. For a time, this logic worked well; companies could shift their investment and production to reward 'moderate' governments and punish excessively nationalistic ones by a boycott, possibly accompanied by internal destabilisation. However, when the main consuming countries had become sufficiently dependent upon cheap OPEC oil this relationship broke down. Producer governments found that militancy visibly paid dividends – indeed in 1971–4 and again in 1978–80 it appeared that the main oil producers could hardly lose – and the rewards for co-operation were far exceeded by the rewards for taking control of the oil industry and forcing up the price internationally. The advantages of such action were so apparent that the 1970s saw a remarkable degree of unity amongst countries that in many other ways had very little in common and within countries where political cleavages were otherwise very deep. Nothing less than military invasion would now break up the unity of the producer countries and military force on the required scale would have highly dangerous international implications as well as threatening to make an already scarce commodity even scarcer.

The US government, as well as a number of independent observers, have also been surprised by the ability of the main OPEC countries to remain essentially united over oil prices even when differing sharply over other matters. Clearly a part of the reason lies in the awareness of the main OPEC countries of how much they have gained from co-ordinated actions and how much they could still lose from disunity. There is also the fact that the option of 'leaving oil in the ground' has appeared increasingly attractive to the main oil exporters as it has become clear how vulnerable OPEC dollar surpluses have been to international inflation and acts of political revenge. Even so, some weight must still be given to what might be called the ideology of oil production. This is essentially based on the argument that deteriorating terms of trade are internationally unjust and that producer power needs to be exercised in order to protect exporters of raw materials against the greater bargaining power of exporters of manufactured goods. It was this ideology which lay behind the creation and strengthening of OPEC in the 1960s and was thus a necessary precondition of any attempt to exert real market power. Until then, exporting countries had been concerned to increase their production rather than to control it.

This raises an important general point. It has often been asserted by Marxists that 'imperialism' operates in such a way that elites in underdeveloped capitalist countries are psychologically and structurally so tied in to the international capitalist system that they are unlikely to take decisive action against metropolitan interests even when their own countries would clearly benefit thereby. It is doubtful that this hypothesis can be applied very satisfactorily to Latin America and it certainly falls down very badly when applied to the Middle East and North Africa.

It can be accepted at once that transactions between nation states form only a part of the international oil system; at least as important are conflicts within them in which foreign actors are involved. We shall consider oil politics within Latin America in part II of this book, but meanwhile it will be sufficient to mention the modern history of Iran as an example of how national and international factors can interact. However, the Iranian case also highlights two very different points. For one thing, even when there is internal political conflict there is no guarantee that pro-US forces will triumph. Secondly, even relatively conservative regimes have sometimes taken the lead in pressing for high oil prices, in much the same way as the otherwise very pro-US regime of Betancourt took the lead in setting up OPEC and limiting the freedom of foreign oil companies. As we shall see in the next section, it is far too simple to regard conservative governments in developing countries as being pro-US in every issue, or even in the most important ones.

PART II

The major expropriations

7

Politics and the concession contract

We have already considered the international dimension of oil conflicts in Latin America. It remains to look at conflicts which have taken place within particular Latin American countries. Ten case studies will be presented, all of them culminating either in some form of expropriation or exclusion of foreign companies, but, as will be apparent, they differ in a number of significant ways. They include a number of genuine confrontations (Mexico 1938, Peru 1968 and Bolivia 1969) but also a number of more ambiguous cases in which conflict coincided with a considerable degree of mutual accommodation. Naturally, selecting as case studies relations which culminated in expropriation does focus the presentation clearly on conflict; cases can be found of long-term and relatively harmonious relations between foreign company and host government and these have been excluded here, or at best considered only when they came to an end. However, while it should certainly be recognised that fairly harmonious government–company relationships have occurred at various times, with differing consequences for the domestic economy and political society, cases of overt conflict have been more frequent. All of the oil-producing countries of Latin America (with the very recent exception of Guatemala) have set up state oil companies and most have promoted the expansion of these companies by some combination of expropriation or exclusion. The more spectacular nationalisations or nationalist campaigns, moreover, have entered the Latin American folk memory, even if not always quite in the manner in which they actually took place.

Although the theoretical approaches to these questions will be considered in more detail when the empirical material has been presented, it is worth outlining the key assumptions of the more influential writings in order to introduce the topic. One influential approach corresponds closely to the assumptions made by theoretical economics which have been applied to the question of foreign investment by means of a bargaining model. This abstracts from internal political concerns and assumes that host governments and foreign companies are both max-imisers. According to this view, host government – foreign company relations are best understood in terms of a two-person non-zero-sum game.[1] In other words there are interests in conflict but also interests in common; it is in the interests of both parties to arrive at some form of agreement or negotiated settlement as complete breakdown is likely to be mutually damaging.[2]

While the difficulties that lie behind any assumption of 'maximisa-tion' on the part of host governments may be readily apparent after the empirical material has been presented, it should be pointed out that, because of its rigorous assumptions, the bargaining model has been able to identify a number of analytic relationships. The most interest-ing of these have concerned changes in the way interests are shared or held in conflict during the course of an investment, and particularly in investment in oil exploration. The essential arguments are that, in the case of a successful venture, unless there is renegotiation during the course of a concession contract, conflict of interest between government and company is likely to increase over time. However, if a strategy of renegotiation is realistically employed, then the potential advantages of the investment to the host government increase over time as the discovery of oil dispels the original uncertainties, as the ratio of sunk capital to potential new investment increases and as the host country learns more about the nature of the industry. It is generally agreed, however, that there is some point at which the balance of advantage can be struck.

A second influential position is essentially Marxist. The essential tenets of Marxism will be known to most readers; what is most inter-esting here is the denial that there can be a 'maximising' state in any value-free sense. States do not 'maximise'; they pursue political and economic strategies which are as likely to be in conflict with national interests as with the interests of the multinationals or the USA. In this context, imperialism may be an internal reality as much as an external reality. It would be difficult to argue (although such argument has been attempted) that a host government would knowingly refuse to take advantage of a situation in which it could easily extract more money from a foreign oil company, but it is easy to present the case in a more sophisticated manner. It can often be asserted, and has on occa-sion been documented convincingly,[3] that particular host governments have been more interested in a quick pay-off than in providing long-term advantages to the country (however its interests have been defined), that they have been unreasonably risk-averse when a little determination would have yielded real dividends, and that they have neglected to learn about the oil industry (and, indeed, about other industries), even when it would clearly have paid them to do so. Above all it can certainly be argued that 'technocratic' bargaining has generally been subordinate to the overall ideological orientation of the government in question.

While these arguments have generally been used to explain *entreguismo* and the absence of conflict with foreign companies, similar logic can easily be used in pursuit of a different conclusion merely by pointing out that, even in Latin America, broader and more popular pressures have frequently impinged upon the processes of economic policymaking. Marxists would argue that, when they have done so, oil policy has been conflictful and even confrontational and, as such, in keeping with the real interests of the country concerned.[4]

Essentially, therefore, the literature can be divided into one branch which has seen host government – company conflict as essentially technocratic and situational and the other which has focussed on broader and more sociological factors; given the extent to which ideological considerations have predominated in this type of literature, the 'is' has often been quietly transposed into an 'ought'. However, while it is excessively limiting to take one of these approaches on its own (and to dismiss factors external to the model as 'irrational nationalism' or *entreguismo*), a combination of both may prove to be helpful.

8

Argentina: YPF, Yrigoyen and the 1935 oil law

Argentina was the first Latin American country to set up an effective state oil company and one of the first to take strong legislative measures limiting the activities of the private companies. The underlying motive for these measures lay as much in Buenos Aires's distrust of the provinces as in the behaviour, or even the presence, of the oil companies themselves. Moreover, to a considerable extent the story of Argentine oil nationalism is that of the growth and development of the state oil company, Yacimientos Petrolíferos Fiscales (YPF). If these were the underlying factors, however, it is also true that Argentina saw the first major oil nationalist campaign, led by Yrigoyen in 1928, which raises questions about the nature of the political support that a movement of this kind could attract. All the same, it is best to begin with a discussion of the way in which the industry itself developed.

The Argentine oil commission 1907–22

In December 1907 a team belonging to the Argentine Ministry of Agriculture was apparently drilling for water at Comodoro Rivadavia when it struck oil in a shallow depth of what proved to be a huge field from which one billion barrels were ultimately recovered.[1] Some observers have expressed doubts as to whether this find really was accidental and there was certainly an air of mystery surrounding its immediate circumstances.[2] Whatever the truth of the matter, the discovery of oil in such potential quantity antedated serious interest in the area by either British or American companies.

Although of little immediate economic importance, the find did have major political implications. Even though oil policy had not been formulated in any way at that time, there was certain to be political resistance, even in a country where liberal economic orthodoxy was official policy, to any attempt to give up what had already been found.

Moreover, those Argentines working the field soon became convinced (correctly) that it had considerable economic potential. As early as 1913, an agent of the Anglo-Mexican petroleum company met Hermitte, one of the senior engineers working on the field, who told him that 'the wells they had bored covered an area of 15 [square] kilometres, so that they were quite certain in their minds that they had a big field but owing to the lack of funds they had not been able to go ahead in the way they would like.'[3] Later in the year he reported that both Hermitte and the Agriculture Minister, who had overall responsibility for oil development, were 'very optimistic . . . they go so far as to say that in a very short time they will have sufficient oil to supply the whole of the needs of the Republic.'[4] Even if expectations did outrun performance, they clearly had important effects upon policy.

Moreover, those engineers and technicians responsible for the development of the field provided an influential pressure group interested in its further development in the hands of the state. They were an obvious source of opposition to any measures to bring private investment into the field, and were able to use the 'demonology' of Standard Oil to good effect. It seems that they did use it in this way deliberately; in 1913, the Anglo-Mexican representative declared that 'everybody seems to have the same opinion of the Standard Oil Co. which is, to put it mildly, loathed'.[5]

None of this is to say that the transition to a nationalist policy was easy. On the contrary, the nationalists themselves were, at the beginning, concerned only to keep the Comodoro Rivadavia field in state hands. Under the constitution at that time, mineral claims were the property of landowners or, in the case where the land was public property, of the provincial governments. In 1907, almost immediately after the oil find, the government reserved an area around the Rivadavia field – a reservation confirmed, although diminished in size, by the law of 1910. Provincial governments, particularly in the north and west of the country, where oil appeared to exist, and private landowners or claimants to mineral rights under the 1886 mining code, made up a powerful interest opposed to any attempt to exert central control over the oil industry.

Quite apart from those directly affected, there was also a considerable feeling that an inexperienced government department could not, on its own, effectively develop the Rivadavia field. Those who felt in this way argued, with *La razón* (19 January 1914), that 'the Minister of Agriculture has locked himself up with his treasure', and called for more ambitious measures to get the industry effectively under way. One possible solution was large-scale funding of the state oil commission but, although some small sums were approved for this purpose, Congress had insufficient faith in this organisation to grant it any really important capital. Another possibility, put forward in 1915 by Alfredo Demarchi, President of the Unión Industrial Argentina and a Federal Deputy, was for a 'mixed' company in which a foreign company (but not Standard Oil) would directly associate itself with the state oil commission in order to bring about rapid development of the field. This proposal, however, had the critical disadvantage that it involved the handing over of existing state property to a foreign company. As *La razón* objected in 1916, 'There is no Minister, President or Congress who would venture to dispose of one iota of that National Wealth, who would compromise it in private speculations, who would allow it to be shared by syndicates or foreign companies, whatever the nature of compromise they may contract or the safeguarded conditions under which the agreements are made.'[6] Early in 1917 the Anglo-Mexican representative, who had been keen on a contract of this nature, reported that 'There is no doubt that it will be difficult for the government to hand over or sell the fields to a foreign company, in view of the strong feeling against it – although mostly political [*sic*] – and the only reason could be their inability to raise money during the war for development.'[7]

It is certainly true that this oil production was of negligible importance to the Argentine economy as a whole until the First World War, as can be seen from table 8.1. Apart from lack of experience on the part of the management, the main problems were financial. As the government later reported, 'despite admitting the necessity of the work, the Commission was not able to manage its funds effectively, but despite this the materials were bought under the responsibility of engineer Luis A. Huergo who promised that, if the government did not meet the cost, he would pay out of his own pocket'.[8]

The outbreak of war, however, brought about some major changes. One of the most important was that coal supplies, already interrupted several times as a result of strikes within the UK, became increasingly unreliable and expensive. As a result, domestically produced oil became increasingly competitive and, despite some administrative and accounting problems and continuing difficulties with acquiring supplies from abroad as a result of the war, production increased considerably, as can be seen from table 8.2.

These changes made it inevitable that the Argentine state would

Table 8.1 *Argentine oil production, imports and consumption 1907–14*
(cubic metres)

	Production	Imports	Consumption
1907	16	106,913	106,929
1908	1,821	124,000	125,828
1909	2,989	145,000	147,989
1910	3,293	162,000	165,293
1911	2,082	170,000	172,082
1912	7,462	204,000	211,462
1913	20,733	280,000	300,733
1914	43,795	235,000	278,795

Note: There is a very slight discrepancy between the 1914 figures here and those in table 8.2.
Source: Solberg, *Oil and Nationalism in Argentina,* p. 10.

Table 8.2. *The Argentine oil commission: drilling, output and sales 1914–20*

	Wells drilled	Output (cubic metres)	Sales (m. pesos)
1914	2	43,740	n.a.
1915	9	81,580	1.9
1916	16	129,780	5.4
1917	14	181,621	10.0
1918	26	197,578	14.9
1919	20	188,092	11.7
1920	21	222,545	13.1

Note: The (paper) peso before 1933 was valued at US $0.425 but was not always freely convertible.
Source: Compiled from YPF, *Desarrollo de la industria petrolífera fiscal 1907–32.*

keep direct control over its Rivadavia field, even though there continued to be dissatisfaction over the way this was being run. In October 1917 the Anglo-Mexican representative wrote that

the more difficult preliminary period is now passed, the presence of paying quantities of oil and gas has been demonstrated, large amounts of public funds have been invested in the operations and in the acquisition of three tank steamers, and the exploitation is meeting with success. Under these conditions, I doubt if any government could stand against the cry that would go up if control of the field were placed in private, and especially foreign, hands.[9]

Anglo-Mexican had been trying to secure a management contract of some kind ever since 1913, at the same time as a number of other foreign companies, including Royal Dutch/Shell. In 1920, after yet another proposal was rejected, this time by Yrigoyen, the company finally abandoned its efforts.

The private oil companies 1907–28

The state oil commission was concerned only with a fairly minor part of Argentina's potential oil-producing territory, although it was always by far the largest single producer of crude oil. The main private companies tended to link backwards from their market interests into production. Thus Jersey Standard in 1911 had only a marketing presence in Argentina. As we have seen in chapter 1, the profits to be made in marketing were immense, but they could not be secure while the company remained vulnerable to the imposition of a tariff. While there is some evidence that Jersey Standard discussed entry into oil exploration as early as 1914, the company history states that it was in 1917 that Standard's geologists first made such a recommendation.[10] The company had little difficulty in finding suitable local allies with which to associate (see chapter 1), but nevertheless proved much less successful in finding oil than it had been in marketing it. The company drilled a number of dry wells in Rivadavia and worked hard in Salta and Huincul to establish very modest amounts of oil prodution.

Royal Dutch/Shell also moved into Argentina in a similar way, after its earlier effort to negotiate a management contract for the state oil commission was rejected. Shell encountered some exploration success and also developed a marketing network, but its output was held back at first by a lack of refining capacity and it produced only 15,900 cubic metres in 1927. Anglo-Persian produced some oil from the Rivadavia area, just outside the borders of the state reserve, but the only other politically significant company at that time was the Ferrocarriles, composed of three British railway companies. These also had a concession area near the state reserve and in 1912: 'the government approached the railway companies with a view of [*sic*] forming a company in which the railway companies would take shares, but the railways refused to join hands, and I am informed that this was solely due to the fact that the government had been squeezing them on other matters and their relations were not very friendly'.[11] By 1920, relations were evidently more friendly, for in that year the railway company took over certain of the oil commission's territories in return for a royalty and a percent-

Table 8.3 *Oil production by the main private companies 1920–9*
(*cubic metres*)

	1920	1922	1924	1926	1928	1929
Ferrocarriles	9,722	26,615	60,274	185,760	212,588	246,373
Astra	22,014	74,701	90,537	155,880	182,318	96,855
Anglo-Persian	0	4,233	29,849	142,720	98,042	83,953
Diadema (Shell)	0	0	0	2,054	57,817	n.d.
Jersey Standard[a]	0	0	4,622	9,861	68,658	118,534
Imports	795,000	n.a.	n.a.	929,688	1,517,405	1,916,678

[a] Not including Astra production, but including Challacó.
Source: Compiled from *Revista de economia argentina,* 1927, 1930.

age of the output.[12] It used the oil to power its own railways which were increasingly converting away from British coal supplies, although by 1930 its concession territory was beginning to become depleted.[13] It is worth pointing out this activity on the part of the railway companies in order to dispel the notion, sometimes put forward by writers on the subject, that the railway companies – or even the British in Argentina as a whole – were generally hostile to the development of the local oil industry. The level of output achieved by these companies can be seen in table 8.3. It will readily be apparent that the amounts involved were not large. Until the 1930s YPF continued to produce very much more than the private companies and Argentina's imports of oil continued to increase during the 1920s. The main reason for this appears to have been that Argentina's geology was not particularly attractive at the given level of technology, with the important exception of the Comodoro Rivadavia field which had been found accidentally in 1907. In the 1920–6 period the private companies drilled a total of 103 oil wells and found oil on only 21 occasions; statistics for pure wildcatting (which are not available) would have been very much less favourable and it is also important to note that even successful drilling did not lead to any really major discoveries. A number of companies, including Standard Oil of California, failed to find any oil from their explorations and pulled out of the country.

YPF 1922–30

By far the most important development of the 1920s was the expansion of the government's oil company. As we have seen, the state oil com-

mission had by 1920 reached an economic scale and had developed a
political constituency sufficient to discourage Hipolito Yrigoyen (President 1916–22) from handing over the agency to a British company.
During this time, however, there continued to be serious problems
with the operation of the agency. Given that YPF's production had
continued to increase, Solberg may be overstating the case slightly but
nevertheless has grounds for his conclusion that by 1922,

the [state] industry had virtually lost credibility as a serious business enterprise . . . The Ministry of Agriculture . . . had for years failed to formulate
coherent budgets for the oilfields, supervising finances simply through arbi-
trary decrees. Because the oilfields had no budget for the year 1922, for example, the state had hired hundreds of unnecessary workers and administrators.
Accounting was in miserable shape and often there were no records of costs or
sales. The almost total lack of control over expenditures was paralleled by the
rankest lack of concern for the actual needs of the oilfields.[14]

In response to considerable press and congressional criticism of these
various, mainly financial, abuses, the state oil company was reorganised, renamed Yacimientos Petrolíferos Fiscales (YPF) and put under
the charge of General Enrique Mosconi. Already in 1922, despite the
difficulties referred to above, the government's oil output was almost
eight times what it had been in 1914 and the company appeared to
operate profitably even if its own figures are questionable. Given the
advantage provided by its Comodoro Rivadavia field, such profitability
is perhaps not surprising. In 1922 YPF made a new find at Huincul
although this was not of comparable importance. In the following year,
YPF's drilling performance was improved by the purchase from abroad
of new 'rotary' drilling rigs; the company's drilling increased sharply,
as we can see from table 8.4. Although General Mosconi was later
accused of paying too much attention to development and production
and insufficient to exploration,[15] it is clear that the Comodoro Rivadavia reserves were sufficiently important to permit continuing
increases in production.

YPF's success after 1922 was, as we have seen in chapter 1, mainly
due to its organisational rather than its technical capacity. One former
employee described Mosconi as being 'a military man . . . [who] ruled
the Yacimientos Petrolíferos Fiscales as a czar, and established an excellent discipline, although his rather positive opinions prevented the best
co-operation of his department chiefs'.[16] Economically, YPF's advantageous crude oil position stemmed from its ability to continue to
develop the Comodoro Rivadavia find of 1907. Apart from doing this

Table 8.4 *The progress of* YPF *in the 1920s*

	Wells drilled	Production at Rivadavia (cubic metres)	Total YPF production (cubic metres)	Sales (YPF) (m. pesos)
1923	46	365,700	372,600	16.6
1924	55	465,700	474,600	18.3
1925	129	596,400	610,300	22.5
1926	141	707,960	730,100	32.0
1927	127	772,670	802,000	50.1
1928	140	742,200	789,700	56.7
1929	165	807,200	871,960	58.5
1930	165	721,600	827,900	65.9

Source: Compiled from YPF, *Desarrollo de la industria petrolifera fiscal.*

rather more effectively than hitherto, YPF in the 1920s developed its position decisively by constructing a large oil refinery at La Plata. This enabled it to break into oil distribution which had up until then been the main (and highly profitable) stronghold of the companies. Mosconi and the Alvear government (1922–8) made refining a priority. In a speech of 24 September 1923, Le Breton, who was Alvear's Agriculture Minister, claimed that 'the advantages of a large refinery are indisput-able. It is calculated that with the production of next year alone, a million pesos monthly will be lost in the boilers and that in only a year a refinery would repay its cost.'[17] As we saw in chapter 1, YPF decided to offer a turnkey contract for the project to Bethlehem Steel and, after a partial opening in December 1925, the refinery went into full pro-duction at the beginning of 1927. A fuel hydrocracker was subse-quently installed in 1928.

This refinery abruptly changed the structure of the Argentine mar-ket, as can be seen from table 8.5. In 1925 YPF had one service station, although in that year it did contract on a small scale with a local dis-tribution company. In 1926 it had 680; in 1930 it had 2,320 and in 1932, 3,860. We have already seen that marketing was the key to company interest in Argentina since it was the greatest single source of profitability. YPF's position now posed a real threat to the companies, while the companies' entrenched market position similarly provided a major handicap to YPF.[18] Under these circumstances, company reac-tion was one of alarm, but there was little to be done in the face of YPF's offensive.[19]

Table 8.5 *Production and consumption of gasoline in Argentina 1922–30.*
(cubic metres)

	Consumption	YPF production	Other production	Imports
1922	181,962	1,118	22,323	158,451
1923	213,998	2,357	34,452	177,189
1924	286,949	4,689	45,093	237,167
1925	400,808	5,849	47,440	347,519
1926	524,250	48,525	56,991	418,734
1927	562,386	75,784	118,129	368,473
1928	693,812	99,212	195,811	398,789
1929	947,558	140,168	382,001	425,389
1930	961,795	178,650	442,998	340,147

Source: Solberg, *Oil and Nationalism,* p. 93.

The politics of oil

The developing situation 1926–30

It was against this background that the nationalist campaign unfolded.
There were two main economic issues: YPF's battle for a share of the
domestic market and its concern to wrest control of as much potentially
oil-bearing Argentine soil as possible from the state governments and
their potential allies, the transnational corporations. However, the
most important developments during the late 1920s were political. Up
until the mid-1920s, the heterogeneity of Argentine political groups
– particularly the Radical Party – had made it impossible for the government to secure any effective oil legislation. In 1920 a Pearson executive asked a Sr Oxyhanante, a lawyer who was close to Yrigoyen, what
the Radical Party's principles were; the lawyer 'replied that they had
no particular principles as any statement of principles would be sure to
cause them the loss of many supporters'.[20] Moreover, any chance of
effective policymaking was further reduced by the power of Congress,
which served as a focal point for various interest groups because party
unity was slack.

There had for a long time been some discussion of the possible federalisation of the oil industry. This would give the central government
the power to decide whether, and on what terms, oil concessions
should be granted. The proposal was first made in 1916 by Melo and
Moreno, both Federal Deputies representing Buenos Aires although in
different parties. This proposal met strong opposition from the prov-

inces of the interior, as did Yrigoyen's rather similar proposals made in 1919. This position was then taken over by Alvear after 1922.

Federalisation proposals, therefore, were common ground between Alvear and Yrigoyen, although these were opposed by the provincial authorities in Salta and other interior provinces. In 1927, however, Yrigoyen went beyond these and called for the 'nationalisation' of the oil industry, in a move which represented almost a complete change of position during the course of a year.[21] It is likely that Yrigoyen's motives were essentially tactical. Alvear, who was a personal and political friend of Mosconi, had been a moderate nationalist, protecting and promoting YPF's interests where possible; if Yrigoyen was to capture this issue for the 1928 elections, he needed to go further. Moreover, when in opposition to the Alvear government, Yrigoyen had lost some of his more conservative and provincial supporters, leaving him with fairly solid support among the Buenos Aires middle class. Indeed, two influential oil nationalist pressure groups were set up in Buenos Aires during the years 1927–8, the Junta Nacional pro-Defensa del Petróleo in August 1927 and the Alianza Continental in 1928.

Thus, Yrigoyen staked out his position for the 1928 elections. He had touched upon an issue whose remoteness ensured that it would not split his own faction of the party, which would therefore be able to use its majority to full advantage. In 1927 Yrigoyen's section of the Radical Party and the Independent Socialists, who were also nationalist on oil, together had a majority in the Chamber of Deputies which was sufficient to secure passage both of the federalisation proposal (by 88 votes to 17) and of the more controversial state monopoly proposals (by 65 to 55). The Senate, however, would be a different matter.

This essentially electoral perspective is reinforced if we look in more detail at Yrigoyen's 1927 proposals. These involved a refusal to grant any concessions to the private companies, which would nevertheless continue to operate existing territories, and also a guarantee that YPF would not be forced to take part in any joint ventures with private capital. It would also involve a transport monopoly (essentially involving tanker transport), a prohibition of exports and a 10% royalty on the production of oil by private companies. The main aim appeared to be to allow YPF various forms of advantage over the private companies while also restricting their activities but without eliminating them entirely. They would still be allowed to import and market oil as well as to produce it from their existing concession areas.

It was the companies themselves who first argued that this arrangement would not be workable and that full-scale nationalisation would be necessary.[22] Since it is unlikely that the companies would genuinely have welcomed their own nationalisation, it is probable that they considered that Yrigoyen was engaged in brinkmanship and were resolved to call his bluff.

Certainly there is no reason for believing that the companies were seriously alarmed. The State Department took a very low key position in the issue[23] and the British Minister contented himself with remarking that

the cry has been raised that the petroleum resources of the state are in danger of being captured by foreign companies which would constitute a menace to the state in time of war. The popular distrust of the United States has caused many tales to be spread of the sinister activities of the Standard Oil Company . . . [but] the majority of Senators resent the proposals to remove from the jurisdiction of the provincial governments matters over which they now have authority and to place them under the control of the Federal Government.[24]

Moreover, the British Minister believed that, in the event of the bill's passing the Senate, which was unlikely in view of the latter's all-but built-in conservative majority, it would be rejected as unconstitutional by the Supreme Court, which explicitly provided that expropriation could only be carried out with full compensation. After this comment, the British Embassy had little more to say about the oil nationalisation question even when it became a major domestic issue.

The economics of the industry also worked against the more radical of Yrigoyen's proposals. Argentine oil consumption had been growing rapidly in the 1920s as a result of the substitution of oil for coal; as we can see from table 8.6, however, this increase in demand was not fully met by domestic production. As a result, imports continued to increase and consequently so did the bargaining power of the oil companies. If the government did nationalise existing holdings, they would certainly need to compensate generously in order to avoid trade sanctions either from the companies or from their parent governments. This, in turn, would seriously strain YPF's budget (to say nothing of its organisational capacities) and reduce its ability to undertake new investment, which would in turn increase Argentina's dependence on imports. It would have been a political impossibility for such compensation to have been financed out of general taxation, which was the only way this dilemma might have been avoided.

For these reasons, therefore, the threat to nationalise seems inher-

Table 8.6 *Production and consumption of oil in Argentina 1925–9*
(Metric tons)

	National production	Imports	Total apparent consumption
1925	873,335	718,601	1,591,936
1926	1,146,135	929,688	2,075,823
1927	1,231,291[a]	1,237,518	2,468,809
1928	1,318,362	1,517,405	2,835,767
1929	1,361,882	1,916,678	3,278,560

[a] Includes a small amount exported to Uruguay.
Source: Revista de economía argentina, 1931, p. 4.

ently implausible, as indeed it was to contemporary observers. The position taken by Yrigoyen seems clearly to have been electoral. This conclusion ties in with Peter Smith's broader finding that 'by the mid-1920s, at least, cleavage within the Radical Party did not correspond to any particular problem of social policy. It apparently began as a political dispute, then spread across a wide variety of issues.'[25] Under these circumstances, it is not difficult to see why the oil question was so useful to Yrigoyen. He could take a clear stand on an apparently defined issue but on terms which made it most unlikely that he would be called upon to put his programme into practice; conservative groups would block the legislation in the Senate and he would then be able to blame them for doing so and for acting as 'agents of Standard Oil'. The stronger the rhetoric used against the company, the more uncomfortable would be the position of his opponents.

It was also true that the oil companies were politically weak and with few important domestic allies, at least with regard to their production interests. These were of little real economic importance and were in any case located in areas with little political leverage. Thus it was possible to attack Standard Oil and the north without antagonising powerful domestic groups and British capitalists with their apparently powerful base in Buenos Aires and on the pampas:

in this fashion the *yrigoyenistas* had discovered by 1927 an ideal popular slogan. They found a way of advocating change, and with it their old goal of class harmony, without implying any sacrifices by the established primary export interests . . . Oil was largely set apart from the primary exporting economy and from the various configurations of power and political influence it had produced.[26]

It is likely that the oil issue contributed somewhat to Yrigoyen's electoral victory of 1928 although it should also be noted that his electoral opposition in that year was feeble; the conservatives had very little taste for electoral battle and Alvear did not use his position to support a challenge to Yrigoyen from the divided Radical Party. However, it appears that the oil issue did win the support of much of the Buenos Aires middle class. If, for example, one takes the students,

the *Federación Universitaria,* the principal student organisation at the University of Buenos Aires, became a strong and vocal supporter of Yrigoyen's petroleum policy. Throughout the capital, the Federación organised public meetings, distributed leaflets, and lobbied vigorously to alert the public 'to protect our rich subsoil resources from the avarice of capital'. Students at technical and industrial schools, which had begun to train petroleum technicians in 1926, joined the university students in directing a steady stream of petitions to Congress in support of a state oil monopoly.[27]

On the other hand, as Solberg points out, 'the anarcho-syndicalist and socialist trade unions, including YPF's own FOP, remained openly hostile to a state monopoly over the oil industry'.[28] Rock therefore concluded that

the introduction of a state monopoly meant that the bureaucracy and the groups directly or indirectly involved in it could be funnelled into a new range of activities. They could remain dependent on the State, but the State would have an additional range of activities at its disposal to respond to them.
    The clarity with which this programme was developed and enunciated forms a striking contrast with the amorphousness and lack of definition of Radical doctrines before 1922. For the first time, the *yrigoyenistas* had something practical and concrete to campaign on beyond their previous abstract appeal to 'democracy' and the 'defence of the constitution'.[29]

Nevertheless, the oil issue could be, at best, only a short-term substitute for a capacity to govern. When in the local elections of March 1930 the Radicals again campaigned in Buenos Aires on the oil question they were convincingly defeated.

The domestic market and the Salta question
Triumphantly re-elected President earlier in 1928, Yrigoyen on 26 July presented a bill to the Chamber of Deputies calling for the complete nationalisation of oil production. It was only around the middle of 1929 that Mosconi, who had previously been wary of Yrigoyen, joined the rhetorical battle on a large scale. Mosconi's position, how-

ever, remained distinctive. Although quite capable of violently attack-
ing the oil companies, he preferred the policy of setting up a joint
venture between the state and Argentine capital (an 'Anglo-Persian'
solution) to a pure state company, since he was concerned above all to
maintain the political autonomy of the enterprise management. Moreover, he made it clear that his main concern was with oil and not with
broader issues; as he later wrote, 'We are not and cannot be enemies of
foreign capital, but we prefer unhesitatingly that such activities with
characteristics which are as special as oil development which we can
carry out ourselves should be reserved absolutely to Argentine
capital'.[30] Finally, Mosconi was opposed to a policy of actual expropriation and preferred simply to close off any possibility of future expansion on the part of the private companies.

It was surely not coincidental that Mosconi's rhetorical offensive
against the companies took place at the same time as YPF's commercial
offensive. In 1929 YPF began cutting gasoline prices and forced the
private companies to do the same. It is clear, moreover, that Mosconi
was finding it difficult to break into the domestic market; in 1929 YPF
asked the Ministry of Agriculture (which retained formal jurisdiction
over the oil industry) for

its intervention against the provincial authorities of Santa Fé, Entre Ríos,
Córdoba and San Juan, in order that they should secure from the municipal
authorities of their respective provinces the repeal of ordinances which were
drafted in terms which favoured exclusively the private companies and hindered the work of gasoline stations allied with the state company.[31]

In 1929 YPF also approached Jersey Standard with a view to achieving
an agreed quota of the domestic market but was refused.[32] After this,
YPF began negotiating with the USSR in order to try to secure a source
of low-cost crude oil imports which could be processed at La Plata and
sold cheaply on the domestic market. In 1930 YPF continued its marketing offensive by asking the government that pending new legislation private companies should be forbidden to open any new gasoline
service stations.

YPF's commercial offensive took place at much the same time as
another conflict, this time specifically with Jersey Standard, over exploration rights in the northern province of Salta. Jersey Standard had
always been well connected in Salta and closely tied in with the local
elite. A number of mining permits had been handed out here between
1905 and 1910 and 'among the claimants figured the prominent names

of the Salta oligarchy. Most were young men in their 20s and 30s who through their families and personal dynamism emerged as the dominant patriarchies of the Salta oligarchy in the 1920s and 1930s and as staunch allies of Standard Oil.'[33] There can be no doubt that Standard thought highly of the geological possibilities of the area[34] and, as we have already seen, Argentina was not so rich geologically that prospects of this kind could be ignored.

As early as 1923 Jersey Standard formally proposed a contract with the provincial government of Salta for 90,000 hectares of state territory with a 10% royalty. The government of the province accepted instructions from President Alvear and rejected this proposal, but it was renewed after a conservative victory in the provincial elections of 1925. Subsequently more concessions were offered by the local government and taken up by local allies of Jersey Standard. However, YPF also coveted this area and as the 1920s wore on, competition between the two intensified. In 1926 YPF offered a 15% royalty against the 10% offered by Standard for the same territory but its offer was rejected. In late 1926, at the same time as the oil question was taken up in Buenos Aires, *La nación* published an article claiming that Standard Oil had illegally been granted concessions by the Governor of Salta and almost immediately afterwards YPF began to challenge Standard at its own game. In 1927 YPF contracted with one Francisco Tobar for the transfer of 29 *estacas* in Salta but found that these did not contain the most promising territory. YPF continued, therefore, to put pressure on Standard. In 1928 the Radical Party again achieved power in Salta and the new governor cancelled the series of concessions which had been granted by his predecessor. Standard then appealed to the Argentine Supreme Court.

To many contemporary observers it seemed inevitable that Standard would win its case. Indeed, after the coup of 1930 the federal interventor of Salta (a Radical) tried to forestall the court hearing in order to protect the province against possible damages and came to a provisional agreement with the company in which he offered to return its concession in exchange for payment of a 10% royalty to the province. This agreement was cancelled in Buenos Aires, however, on the ground that the interventor had exceeded his authority.[35]

The connection between oil nationalism and the Salta question helps to explain two points which were prominent in the oil debate. First, the question of federalisation was likely to lead to conflict between

Buenos Aires and Salta. Buenos Aires had good reasons for its position. Apart from Alvear's (and later Yrigoyen's) desire to strengthen YPF, there was also the point that Jersey Standard had acquired concession territory over the border in Bolivia and there were suspicions, by no means completely ill-founded,[36] that the company might try to win greater leverage by combining the nature of the two operations in some way. Secondly, the conflict over Salta was very evidently with Jersey Standard rather than the British companies; it is therefore understandable that nationalist rhetoric should have been directed at the USA more than at Great Britain, despite the importance of the latter in the oil industry as a whole.[37]

The aftermath 1930–5

The coup of September 1930 abruptly cut short the oil nationalisation debate. Later Radicals have often asserted that the coup was financed or instigated by Standard Oil. This accusation is highly implausible. Indeed, there is evidence that internal conflict over oil policy was far less important than has often been assumed. For one thing, it was clear the Yrigoyen had no real interest in pushing through his proposals for oil expropriation, which he seems to have considered more as a bargaining position with apparent tactical advantages than as a policy to be determinedly pursued. Thus, at the end of 1929 Yrigoyen called on the Senate to pass an oil bill, whether the one passed by the Chamber (in which Yrigoyen had a majority), or 'whatever other measure which in its judgment will be the best for our interests'.[38] However, by the middle of 1930 the Senate had not acted on the oil nationalisation bill and there was little expectation that it would ever do so. Moreover, not only was Yrigoyen more flexible on the oil issue than some later historians have believed but the same was perhaps also true of his conservative opponents. Smith certainly found that

there are solid indications that his [Yrigoyen's] economic policy would have been acceptable to the landed rural interests, as suggested by the affinity between Radical and Conservative deputies on socially definable roll-call voting factors. This was not the issue; what mattered was the distribution of political power. In 1930 the Congress bickered from May until August about the legality of elections in several provinces; the UCR was flaunting its superiority and the opposition, hopelessly outnumbered, could only boycott sessions in an effort to prevent quorums. As a result the legislature passed no laws at all in 1930.[39]

The third piece of evidence that oil was not a key factor in the coup stems from an analysis of the oil policies of the incoming government which, as we shall see, certainly did not represent any sharp reversal of earlier ones.

To recapitulate, there were essentially three proposals which had been considered by the legislature in the 1920s. The first was federalisation, which had been supported by most of the Deputies from Buenos Aires and nearby provinces, but opposed by the northern provinces and other far-flung regions. The second, put forward by Yrigoyen in 1927, amounted effectively to the nationalisation of future development in the oil industry although the companies would be allowed to operate their existing properties. The third, put forward by Yrigoyen in 1929, implied the total nationalisation of the oil industry; this would have been economically costly since Argentina was in no position to refuse compensation and in any case it stood almost no chance of success in the institutional climate of 1928–30. The first two projects were supported by Mosconi, who had serious reservations about the third. The first two projects but not the third were enacted by the governments of the 1930s.

Although the key figures in the 1930 coup and in the incoming government of General Uriburu 'looked like the local directorate of a multinational enterprise',[40] it remains true that the army as a whole did not have an overriding view on the oil issue; 'some officers, for whom General Mosconi was the symbol and spokesman, not only hailed the industrialising trend but identified themselves with an incipient economic nationalism that sought to develop Argentina's petroleum resources under state control'.[41] Others, like Justo, had been essentially laissez-faire.

Nevertheless, the limits of the oil question had already been set by the political conflicts of the 1920s. The incoming military governments – Uriburu to 1931 and Justo 1931–8 – were concerned above all to depoliticise the oil issue rather than run the political risks of reversing earlier lines of policy. These governments tried as far as possible to avoid publicity over the oil issue and took care to remove Mosconi as well as the ageing Yrigoyen from any position of influence, although Alvear continued to play a role behind the scenes. Moreover, in 1932 the government passed a law to cover YPF's activities which had the effect of sharply reducing the latter's autonomy; in future, YPF was forbidden to deal directly with state authorities without the prior approval of the federal government. Indeed, the bureaucratic structure of centralised control, which was to prove so damaging to YPF in later years (as we shall see in chapter 19), dates back essentially to the 1932 law.

In 1932 the Supreme Court also handed down its judgement on the Salta dispute and ruled in favour of Standard Oil. In the same year the Justo government made a further effort to secure passage of a comprehensive oil law. Justo's proposals were similar to those put forward by Alvear in 1927; the bill would federalise the oil industry and give control of oil territories to YPF. This could then develop new national oilfields either on its own or in joint ventures with private companies. Although a section of the Radical Party held out for total state control (and some Radicals had boycotted Congress), most of the civilian parties took positions which were broadly in line with these proposals. However, before these proposals could become law, Salta, in almost direct defiance of Buenos Aires, approved a new contract with Standard.

The political influence of the northern senators was such, however, that Buenos Aires preferred to agree to this contract rather than to risk a confrontation over the issue.[42] Once this contract had been signed (and it proved to be economically disappointing) the government resorted to executive decree to avoid any possibility of a repetition. Its action was precipitated by YPF's discovery of oil in the province of Mendoza, which created the danger of a new conflict between YPF, the provincial authorities and the private companies. As the editorial of *La nación* stated, 'this decree ensures that the benefits from possible oil developments by the state company remain within the country where the oil is produced and, although it does not guarantee that such development will take place, it ends any possibility that the private sector will develop it outside the control of the state'.[43]

Following the executive decree, Congress at last passed the required legislation. According to the 1935 law, there were to be no further concessions although joint ventures were to be permitted between private investors and YPF on a 50–50 basis; otherwise the companies were to be confined to their existing holdings.

The depression further limited Standard Oil's willingness to develop its Salta oilfields, as did changes in the distribution system which followed the 1935 law; in 1939 foreign-owned Argentine oil production was only 8.4% above its 1932 level. A similar pattern could also be seen in the distribution sector, where YPF continued its offensive in a now declining market. In 1932 a 'uniform price' was established nationally and subsequently YPF tried, by political action, to extend its network in Buenos Aires, where the private companies were most entrenched and where, after the 'uniform price', the market was most lucrative.[44] In 1934 YPF applied to the municipality of Buenos Aires for a 60% sales quota in the city (its actual market share in 1933 was 36%). Although this initiative was blocked, it was clear that there would be others. Thus, in 1936, the private companies, responding to official pressures, opened negotiation with YPF and in 1937 gave a 50% quota share of the market to YPF. In that year, Jersey Standard's offer to sell to the government was refused. The private sector was now firmly under control and seemed condemned to a lingering death instead of immediate execution.

The continuity of Argentine policy

As we have seen, therefore, the oil nationalisation controversy in Argentina was less dramatic than is often believed. The Chamber of Deputies voted almost unanimous support for the federalisation of oil reserves in 1927 and this became policy in the oil law of 1935. The 'no more concessions' policy which Yrigoyen had supported became a *de facto* part of the 1935 law, although theoretically provision was made for some form of foreign investment in joint venture. YPF's battle at the end of the 1920s for access to the Argentine market was also won by 1937, when the companies agreed to a quota system. Most of the policy initiatives which had stemmed from the Radical period came to fruition under the conservative governments of the 'infamous decade'.

The 1930 coup was important, however, for its effect on the politics of oil. The nationalist campaign was aborted before there could be anything, no matter how dubious, to show for its efforts. The Radical Party always felt cheated of the issue and were to return to this theme time after time in subsequent decades, by which time circumstances had changed considerably. The incoming conservative governments, in their concern to take the oil issue out of politics, downgraded YPF and thus set back the possibility of efficient development of the industry through public ownership. In that respect, the nationalists' victory was to prove an empty one, but most of the Radical Party were more concerned with questions of politics and ownership than with efficiency.

When one considers the main factors behind the nationalist campaign, it may be interesting to take into account a report made by the

Pearson representative in 1920 who, after talking with 'several leading men of both parties', concluded that

Their ignorance of the whole subject of Petroleum is complete. There is a remarkable unanimity of conviction of the immense (?) quantities of oil existing in this country and of the necessity of preserving it from the rapacity of some colossal foreign Trust. They are all agreed that the government cannot work the fields successfully and must have foreign assistance, but they are also agreed that this assistance must not jeopardize the national control of their own property which is so immensely (!) valuable.[45]

It is only natural that, once Mosconi showed that YPF could be managed effectively without foreign assistance, this same set of values could be enlisted in support of oil nationalism. The key elements, therefore, may be considered as the accidental discovery of large-scale oil reserves at Comodoro Rivadavia, the increasingly effective operation of such reserves by YPF under Mosconi and the strong feelings of nationalism felt throughout Argentine political society.

Such an interpretation may appear to play down the importance of Yrigoyen's role as against that of Mosconi. Nevertheless, the middle-class nationalist oil campaign mounted by Yrigoyen in 1928 did have importance not so much in determining the final outcome of the oil issue as in demonstrating that a nationalist platform could, under the right circumstances, generate significant political support. Had it come to full fruition it is highly likely that YPF would in later years have received more support than in fact proved to be the case.

Finally, reference should be made to the generally weak position of the foreign companies themselves. They were divided into a number of competing units, divided by interest and nationality and quite incapable of forming any kind of united front. Economically, they faced a challenge from YPF for the domestic market and were in no position to export from Argentina; to put it briefly, they were dispensable. They could not easily be expropriated without expensive compensation or trade sanctions, but they could certainly be prevented from expanding, as eventually they were.

9

Some nationalisations of the 1930s: Chile, Uruguay, Bolivia

Following the example of Argentina and facing the general withdrawal of American capitalism during the 1930s, many Latin American countries took steps to increase state control of their oil industries. Generally speaking these steps were not as dramatic as the Mexican nationalisation and not as fully and popularly debated as the Argentine oil campaign had been (or as the Brazilian campaign was later to be), but they nevertheless played their part in the politics of oil in Latin America. Three less well-known cases will be discussed in this chapter.

Chile

Until the mid-1920s Chile had not found it necessary to define its oil policy. Chilean territory had, immediately after the First World War, attracted a certain amount of company interest.[1] However, survey results were not promising and as a further disadvantage there was no specific oil legislation in operation at the time, with the consequence that the oil companies would have found it necessary to buy up small land titles piecemeal from local landowners. Company interest therefore subsided.

The first company to take a major initiative in Chile was Pan American which, at the end of 1926, persuaded the Chilean Congress to pass a draft law permitting oil companies to take concessions up to a maximum of half a million hectares. This also made it clear that an area of this size would shortly be offered to Pan American (a subsidiary of Standard Oil of Indiana). This would easily have covered all of the potential oil-bearing land in Chile. The proposal united the other major companies (British and American) in opposition and the British Embassy in particular was able to call upon allies in the Chilean Senate to block the contract. Instead it was agreed that the government would not issue concessions for the time being and would instead undertake survey work before deciding finally upon oil legislation. A part of the reason for this relatively restrictive attitude stemmed from the fact that virtually all of the promising oil territory lay in the far south of the country where Argentine currency circulated freely and where Santiago was far from securely in control.

Shell and Jersey Standard, which between them supplied the Chilean market, were by no means dissatisfied with this outcome; they had no real interest in exploring in Chile when they could import from other parts of Latin America where production costs were very much lower. In retrospect, however, the 1928 law came to play an important part in shaping Chilean oil policy since it enabled the state to take an effective monopoly of oil exploration at a later date without the need for further legislation.

The next major stage in the development of Chilean oil policy came with the depression, which hit the Chilean economy particularly hard. In 1931, moreover, the USSR offered to supply crude oil to Chile in exchange for nitrates and also offered assistance in setting up a domestic oil refinery; this was a tempting proposition since Chile was now finding it extremely difficult to sell nitrates on the open market for any price at all. Following these developments, Congress began debating a law which would have created a national oil company and authorised the state to build a refinery. This proposal was regarded with scepticism by the companies, which felt that 'there is small possibility of sufficient funds being forthcoming to enable the national refinery proposition to be implemented.'[2] In early 1932, however, the Chilean Senate dropped the refinery project and instead introduced the idea of a national monopoly of oil imports, distribution and sales. The bill authorising the setting up of this agency was passed unanimously, while a proposal to exclude all non-Chilean capital in the agency was passed more narrowly (15 votes to 11). The law (law 5124, 16 May 1932) was permissive in character rather than mandatory and does not appear to have been supported by the Chilean administration. The US Ambassador reported that

my conversations with the President and the Foreign Minister indicate that the government does not favor the strongly nationalistic features introduced into the measure by the Senate . . . I regret that the President did not see fit to insist on amendments to this law prior to its promulgation but, confronted by other and more pressing differences with Congress, the Cabinet apparently decided in this case to follow the path of least resistance.[3]

During this period, oil marketing was causing considerable difficulty and friction. The slump had drastically reduced Chile's export earnings and its economic position was little short of desperate. In 1931 the Chilean government imposed exchange controls while allowing the currency to depreciate drastically. Naturally this squeezed the oil companies, which found that 'while all petroleum products bought for sale in Chile have to be paid for in sound currencies, any profits made are received in the most worthless Chilean currency and even this money cannot be got out of the country.'[4] Moreover, as the Chilean government began to show an increasing interest in the Soviet Union's barter offer, the companies indicated clearly that they would refuse to handle Soviet oil.

The slump also led to a crumbling of political order in Chile. The fall of Ibáñez in July 1931 was the first of several changes of government. Moreover, during this time no government could feel securely in control of the military, which was restive in view of the austerity measures imposed. These led to an unsuccessful navy mutiny in August 1931. Under these circumstances, the control of oil prices was particularly significant because of the potential for revolt that would be created by any price increases. These conditions of political instability also made it increasingly difficult for the oil companies to establish their habitual relationships with governments in Santiago. Indeed, frequent changes of regime made the establishment of close relationships extremely risky. Thus, for example, 'During the late Ibáñez regime Mr Laing the Standard Representative knowing that the administration were in urgent need of cash had offered to let them have in advance a substantial sum in cash to which the government would become entitled in the ordinary way in due course as a result of taxation.'[5] However, after the change of government in 1931, this offer was found in the archives by political opponents of the Ibáñez government, who created a scandal over the issue.

Low petrol prices created a major problem for the companies. In March 1932 they decided to raise the prices to compensate for currency depreciation but agreed to a temporary postponement at the request of the Chilean government. A few weeks later, however, seemingly at the initiative of the US Ambassador, the companies again announced their intention to raise prices and thus precipitated a crisis. The Chilean Interior Minister

described the companies' decision as an unfriendly act to Chile in the present circumstances, and in declaring that he would resign this morning, added that serious disorder would be inevitable. With this view the Governor of Santiago and the Prefect of Police who were also present fully agreed, going so far as to suggest that the expected riots by omnibus drivers, taximen and other interests affected might well lead to armed revolt. The situation was then fully discussed with the United States Ambassador, the managers of oil companies and members of our [British] staffs and I found that we were alone in deprecating any action which would precipitate a crisis. My United States colleague was almost violent in calling for 'a show-down' . . . As matters stand, the companies are in danger of being manoeuvered into an impossible position vis-à-vis public opinion.[6]

Again, a last minute postponement was secured and this might well have been decisive in preventing a full-scale nationalisation. It was the classic position of a weak government with strong and angry pressure groups which was unable to take any firm decision but might well have been able to deflect popular antagonism away from itself and on to the oil companies if the price increase had gone ahead. Indeed, the British Ambassador later reported that 'either by deliberate manoeuvres or purely accidentally as the result of a lack of co-ordination among themselves, the President and the Cabinet were in the position of portraying the oil companies to the public as bandits suddenly holding up the state and people without mercy'.[7]

Matters became worse for the companies with the fall of the conservative but ineffective Montero regime in June 1932 and its replacement by various radical military juntas. Financial stringency and the sheer impermanence of all regimes at this time, however, prevented any of the short-lived radical governments between June and October 1932 from carrying out their undoubted intention of expropriating Shell and Standard. Thus, following a far-left coup on 4 June, the British Minister reported that 'Standard Oil company manager has been informed by authority concerned that Junta intend as soon as they are financially able to expropriate supplies, oil storage tanks etc. belonging to both companies. Had funds been available, they would already have acted.'[8] Indeed, the junta were 'contemplating immediate seizure of oil companies' installations and getting their tanks ready'.[9]

Before any such action could take place, however, a new government took over on 16 July and initially informed the companies that there would be no expropriation. The incoming regime also made it clear that the government intended to make its own arrangements to secure oil supplies as cheaply as possible. It made another effort to persuade Shell and Standard to distribute Soviet oil but met another refusal.

Meanwhile, faced with continuing late payment, the companies reduced their oil supplies until the situation became serious.

On 30 August the Chilean government set up a commissariat with power to ration and control a wide range of products including oil, and on 5 September 'there appeared in official Gazette dated the previous day decree law number 519 establishing state control over import, distribution and sale of all petroleum products . . . it may be said to confer upon the state the right to interfere almost to any extent with commercial activities of oil companies'.[10] The British Minister commented that this law 'may be regarded as further evidence of anxiety of administration to give effect to their "socialist" principles and incidentally to provide posts for office seekers',[11] although the serious supply situation prevailing within Chile at that time might also have been mentioned.

The government also began to consider various rationing schemes. Some respite had been afforded by its ability to cut purchase taxes on gasoline sales, as had been done by the Montero regime in May, but this could be no more than playing for time as the Chilean currency continued to lose international value. The British Minister continued to be pessimistic.[12] Nevertheless he urged caution on Shell and on Washington, arguing that a rise in the price of petrol might be the spark to start a conflagration going and 'it would be most disconcerting if we had yet another change of government which could in any way be laid at the door of foreign companies and highly embarrassing to us'.[13]

With the conservative coup of September 1932 and Alessandri's election victory in the following month, the position of the companies improved. In December of that year a major increase in the price of gasoline was permitted, though the price to buses was not raised. A certain amount of strike action followed, but the new regime was able to prevail. The new Alessandri regime also dropped plans to import oil from the USSR and as the economic situation improved so the government became increasingly willing to allow the oil companies to repatriate profits.

The years 1931–3 were ones of panic and disorganisation; all longer-term trends and features of Chilean oil policy were lost behind the immediate prospect of disaster. The effort to alleviate immediate balance of payment problems by bartering oil supplies from the USSR, the attempt to avoid political unpopularity by pinning the blame for any oil price rise upon the companies and the concern to control the outflow of dollars at all costs were the key factors in Chilean policymaking at this time. Given these extreme circumstances, oil nationalism was a response to unforeseen emergencies and to the political disorganisation to which they gave rise. Indeed, the absence of a planned nationalist strategy or longer-term nationalist campaign were essentially responsible for the lack of any real policy during this time and for the eventual return of the initiative to the oil companies.

The conservative restoration of 1933 ended the immediate threat of total nationalisation. This was followed by some economic recovery and a partial return to laissez-faire policies. In 1934 the government tried to persuade Congress to reopen the country to foreign oil exploration, but this met opposition from a wide coalition of forces including the Socialist Party and the Chilean Mining Society and, in the absence of any real sign of foreign interest, the government's proposals died quietly in Congress. In the same year, a group of private Chilean businessmen set up an oil distribution company, Copec.

It is likely that Copec was set up independently of the government but it could nevertheless count on some state support. It enjoyed certain minor government favours over the location of petrol pumps and was also allowed credit on its customs duties. These did not amount to a great deal, but when the foreign companies cut their prices in 1935 in order to compete with Copec the government did intervene. Finance Minister Gustavo Ross told the Shell representative 'that he would regard himself as free to afford CPC [Copec] such assistance as it might require';[14] Ross made it clear that he was influenced by memories of the supply squeeze mounted by the companies under the Montero government and wanted Copec to take at least 20% of the market in order to ensure that this would not happen again.[15] At the same time, he did not want to pay compensation for any actual takeover of assets.

In 1936 the question of a full state monopoly was seriously considered. The necessary decree (under the legislation of 1932) was approved and signed by Alessandri, but was not enforced; it is clear that Gustavo Ross was a major obstacle to such a step. Indeed, years later the British Minister recalled that 'in 1936, Señor Wachholz was President of the Copec company and had obtained President Alessandri's approval for introducing law no. 5124 of 17 May 1932 creating a petroleum monopoly in favour of Copec. When, however, he brought the decree to Don Gustavo Ross, at that time Minister of Finance, Don Gustavo simply tore it up in Señor Wachholz's presence.'[16] After further negotiation it was agreed at the end of 1936 that the nationalisation proposal would be dropped in return for company agreement to freeze gasoline prices until after the congressional elections of 1937. (Copec was meanwhile allowed to borrow from the Bank of Chile in order to survive the necessary period.)

Copec was run by established Chilean businessmen, all but two of whom, if the British Embassy is to be believed, voted for Gustavo Ross against the Popular Front candidate Pedro Aguirre Cerda in the 1938 elections; the exceptions were Wachholz (who had resigned from the board in 1936 when the plan to expropriate was dropped) and Cerda himself. The rest of the board was satisfied by an agreement made in 1937 that Copec would take a third of the domestic market and operate a cartel along with Shell and Jersey Standard.

With the election of a Popular Front government in 1939, Sr Wachholz was made Finance Minister and given a new chance to implement a more radical strategy. By this time, the need to save foreign exchange was no longer a short-run imperative but was rather a part of a longer-term strategy, that of domestic industrialisation. Wachholz wanted to give Copec, or the Chilean state, a marketing monopoly in order to use the revenue to finance exploration within Chile. Already the Chilean government had undertaken a certain amount of survey work in the south of the country[17] and the British Minister felt that 'a scheme for petroleum drilling at Punta Arenas or elsewhere in order that Chile should not have to import oil from abroad, is dear to the heart of the Minister of Finance'.[18] It appeared at first, in fact, as though an amicable settlement might be reached along these lines. Shell and Esso offered to carry out some oil exploration in the south of Chile in return for permission to continue their existing marketing operations; this was intended as a possible gesture of goodwill to the government rather than representing any real desire to explore on the part of the companies themselves.[19] Although Wachholz appeared at first to be interested in this offer, he later declared that it was unacceptable because it would involve a change in the (1927) law which would be politically impossible. Although the government did have the power to expropriate, it hoped that Shell and Esso could be persuaded to sell voluntarily but the companies were not interested in doing so. As they explained,

Shell-Mex (Chile) Ltd and the Standard Oil Company have replied . . . that they are strongly opposed to the suggestion that they should sell voluntarily to Copec on the grounds that their oil interests in other countries would be more seriously affected if they withdrew from Chile. The companies feel that the Finance Minister is anxious to avoid forcing the issue of expropriation as such a step may make certain difficulties for Copec and this may also prejudice the floatation of a foreign loan which he is anxious to obtain.[20]

Accordingly, the companies agreed to sell voluntarily if this was still government policy after the expiry of the first cartel agreement with Copec in 1942, but refused to come to any agreement in the meantime. By mid-1939 the government felt the need to stage a tactical retreat on the question. Wachholz had been keen to set up a national oil refinery and began to look for a foreign loan for this purpose. Washington, however, made it clear that it would not lend to an expropriating government (even if compensation were paid) and the Santiago regime preferred to make peace with the companies rather than lose momentum upstream. The government also looked to Germany for help with its refining plans.[21] In August 1939 a new agreement was made which guaranteed Shell and Standard their existing position (and even allowed a limited extension at the expense of the few remaining independent distributors) in return for a loan from the companies for road-building projects. When the cartel agreement did expire in 1942, Copec extended its quota to 50% of the domestic market.

Subsequently, despite being forced to postpone its refining project by the outbreak of war, Chile began to make real progress in its oil-exploration ventures. In 1940 Corfo (the state investment bank set up by the Popular Front government in 1939 with the aim of promoting Chilean industrialisation) hired an American geologist, Glen Ruby, to carry out preliminary exploration for oil in the south of the country. In 1943 it followed this up by contracting United Geophysical and United Engineering Co. to carry out surveys. Although operations were held up by the war, Corfo was able to drill for oil and made its first discovery in 1945. Meanwhile the government began preparing a law to regulate the Chilean oil industry and to set up a state company to take on the responsibilities then being discharged by Corfo. The draft law was released in 1942; this would have allowed foreign investment to return under short-term contract but not to obtain concessions, while the state kept control of refining. This draft law was passed by the Chamber of Deputies in 1944 and then sent for consideration in the Senate.

Further modification of Chilean legislation proved to be the result of circumstances rather than of fresh political developments. For one thing, foreign capital proved uninterested in the terms offered by Chile; indeed, London and Washington actively discouraged their nationals from entry on these terms.[22] Given that oil production equipment was scarce and that London and Washington could control its distribution, this position explains a great deal. Chile was faced with the choice of liberalising its legislation or doing without foreign capital altogether. Once Corfo had struck oil itself, as it did in 1945, Chile's response was predictable. Although denied credits from London and Washington for the purchase of refining capacity, Corfo nevertheless proved capable of developing its discoveries and oil production began in 1950. In the same year, the Chilean Senate passed the government's original legislation, with the modification that the government should now have a complete monopoly of oil exploration and development as well as of refining. ENAP was set up as a separate agency in order to discharge these responsibilities.

Uruguay

Like Chile, Uruguay was geologically unpromising and had attracted little exploration interest in the 1920s. Partly for this reason, and partly because of the strong interventionist nature of the Uruguayan state at that time, the transition to a nationalist policy in the 1930s was relatively easy and thorough. The depression had two main effects. First, it increased the willingness of what was already a very interventionist Uruguayan state to provide middle-class employment now that this was less easily available elsewhere. Public employment in Uruguay rose from 30,000 in 1930 to 52,000 in 1932, and in 1931 a law was passed which

called for the establishment of a seven-man board of directors for each of the state *entes* [agencies] and the appointment of all employees and labourers by party affiliation in proportion to the strength of the two parties in the previous election. A separate act passed at the same time called for the appointment of day labourers to all public works projects in the same proportional manner.[23]

ANCAP fitted easily into the same employment-creating mould when it was set up in 1931 and given responsibility for domestic marketing of cement, fuels and alcohol. Of these, oil proved to be the most important.

Balance of payments motives also became increasingly important with the collapse of Uruguayan exports during the depression. Inability on the part of the Uruguayan government to pay for oil imports was, as we shall see in more detail below, an inconvenience to the companies but the company reaction – raising domestic prices sharply and in mid-1932 holding back supplies – was certain to strengthen Uruguayan determination to set up an effective state company. In the short term, the balance of payments would be aided by a barter deal with the USSR by which Uruguay could import Soviet oil products on the understanding that these would be substituted by crude oil following the construction of an oil refinery. The refinery, however, was the crucial step, and one which was first considered seriously in 1931.[24] In 1933, when firm plans had been made for the refinery construction, the aim was clearly to set up a complete state monopoly. As Pérez Prins recounted, 'If indeed ANCAP at that time controlled no more than approximately 50% of the market, it was expected that this project would allow the creation of the complete monopoly which was in accordance with the law of 1931.'[25]

Naturally these developments were regarded with apprehension by the oil companies, for whom outlets for crude oil were now tremendously important as a result of world-wide oversupply.[26] The companies, as we have seen, also needed to respond to the balance of payments crisis within Uruguay which led to the imposition of exchange controls on 29 May 1931, after which the oil companies had great difficulty in securing the withdrawal of money from the country. However, the parent governments, feeling that Uruguayan public opinion was adverse, did not want to polarise the situation and preferred instead to adopt quieter means of pressure. Thus, in 1934 London decided 'that the position of British oil companies in any countries in which trade negotiations are pending should be reviewed and the opportunity afforded by the negotiations should be taken to safeguard, as far as possible, our interests in the oil industry'.[27] As an important buyer of Uruguay's agricultural produce, Britain was in a strong bargaining position.

The Uruguayan government acted with considerable skill to achieve most of its objectives in the face of this pressure. At first it pressed ahead rapidly. In April 1932 Uruguay contracted with the USSR to receive oil for marketing and by November of that year Shell remarked that 'ANCAP pumps are very numerous and are installed all over the city'.[28] While the companies claimed that this competition was unfair, ANCAP blandly denied the accusation.[29] ANCAP's actual market share can be seen from table 9.1. In 1933 Shell and the US companies agreed to offer a quota arrangement to ANCAP. The offer was seriously considered but declined. Meanwhile the marketing companies continued to have financial difficulties. As the British Embassy reported in its *Annual Report for 1932,*

The oil companies have been busily employed throughout the year addressing protests to the National Administrative Council, which receive little attention, and when they placed their complaint before the President of the Repub-

Table 9.1 *Gasoline sales:* ANCAP *and the private companies*
1932–7
(*percentages*)

	ANCAP	Others
1932	39	61
1933	37.5	62.5
1934	42.2	57.8
1935	52.8[a]	47.2
1936	48.6	51.4
1937	49.8	50.2

[a] The figures for 1935 were distorted by a partial and temporary withdrawal from the market by the companies by reason of low prices.
Source: ANCAP, *Annual Reports, 1934–8.*

lic that they were unable to secure any foreign exchange, his Excellency recommended them to invest their frozen credits either in land and property in Uruguay or in the government's gold bonds.[30]

Company hopes were briefly raised by the 1933 coup but 'when the matter came before the Junta these hopes were entirely falsified, the Junta not only confirming the existing privileges of the ANCAP but also determining to proceed with arrangements for the construction of a petrol refinery'.[31]

ANCAP relied very heavily upon help from YPF in its refinery construction. Tenders had first been called for the refinery at the end of 1932, but the operation had been badly organised and the bidding was therefore unsatisfactory. Technicians were then contracted from YPF and a new tender was called in 1933.[32] This time the contract went to the British subsidiary of Foster Wheeler, possibly for diplomatic as well as for strictly commercial reasons since British opposition to the refinery project was necessarily muted in consequence. The refinery came onstream in early 1937 and, according to Pérez Prins, 'When the refinery began to operate, YPF deprived itself for several months of its best operators in order to respond to the request of ANCAP for technical assistance.'[33]

Possibly in order to avoid the need to expropriate with compensation, but more probably because of the hardening of the world oil market in the years after 1933, ANCAP found it advisable to reach a quota agreement with the private companies. According to the arrangement actually made in 1937, ANCAP would take 50% of the domestic market, leaving the private companies to share out the rest, while ANCAP would refine the companies' oil for a fee as well as refining oil destined for its own share of the domestic market. This guaranteed that ANCAP's refinery would be working at full capacity while at the same time protecting the country from the threat of oil shortages or trade reprisals. Moreover, ANCAP could use its market position to keep domestic prices low – just high enough to enable it to remain profitable[34] – and force the private companies to do the same. As a partial nationalisation, it proved extremely successful.

Bolivia

Unlike Chile and Uruguay, Bolivia had once hoped strongly for a successful export trade. The first Bolivian oil concessions had been granted as early as 1867 and the first oil find anywhere in Latin America took place in Santa Cruz in 1875. As a result of this, several Bolivian companies were formed to develop oil in the Bolivian Oriente but serious action began only when US companies showed an interest after 1918.[35]

After a series of complicated manoeuvres, Standard Oil of New Jersey came into the country. Its entry, however, did not pass without criticism:

Such men as Daniel Salamanca had argued as far back as the early 1910s that Bolivia's petroleum potential should be developed by native capitalists rather than foreign interests. This position was supported by a host of conservative leaders and it was the pro-clerical and anti-labour deputy, Abel Iturralde, who led the fight throughout the 1920s against the Standard Oil. While these same men never questioned the introduction of foreign capital in every other economic activity of the nation, to them petroleum represented a kind of mystique of national sovereignty and for the next fifteen years Standard Oil remained one of the most bitter issues in national politics.[36]

The arguments presented by the opposition were political and relied heavily on the anti-Standard arguments which had been developed throughout the world. Iturralde, for example, quoted a book by a John Burns which had been published in the USA:

this book contains very many details about the policy pursued by Taft and by Wilson and about the situation in Mexico and the government of Carranza which resulted from the manoeuvres of the Standard Oil Company. Frankly, in view of this, I have formed a bad opinion of this company and I considered the following question: If Mexico, which is a rich country with 14 million inhabitants, has not been able to free itself from the pernicious influences of this company, what will happen in Bolivia, which is a country of few economic resources and with a population of two million inhabitants?[37]

There were, it must be said, other reasons for this nationalist opposition. President Saavedra, who seized power in a coup in 1920, wished to take advantage of international capital in order to win himself a power base in the urban areas through lavish spending policies. He used the Standard contract to attract foreign loans, and the oil contracts in turn 'became major political issues with which the Liberal and *Genuino* [rival party faction] opposition could attack the government'.[38]

The Standard contract, however, did not have the expected economic significance. The main bottleneck to rapid oil development was transportation, and here Argentina proved to be the obstacle. As Rout explains,

The creation of the Argentine national oil company in 1922 was followed by the rapid transfer of many Standard Oil agents and engineers to Bolivia. Having rejected a trans-Chaco oleoduct the company sought permission from the Argentine government in 1925 to construct a pipeline from Bolivia to a deepwater port on the Parana River. It was perhaps coincidence but in 1927 not only was Standard Oil's construction petition refused but also Argentina raised the tax rates on Bolivian oil so high that export became prohibitive. Stymied in its efforts to market Bolivian petroleum, Standard Oil capped its Bermejo wells in 1931, adjusted production to meet local needs, and began to ship equipment out of the country.[39]

This ended the good relations between Bolivian political leaders and Jersey Standard. Difficulties began with a Bolivian claim for backtaxes for the 1920s period and gradually increased as further issues were raised. The Bolivian government continued to hope that Standard could be persuaded to expand production – as late as 1932 Bolivia raised the question with Chile of a possible export pipeline through Arica[40] – and became increasingly disappointed when Standard would not co-operate.

Bolivian hopes had earlier been high[41] and now attacks on the company increased. As we have seen, there had already been some criticism of Jersey Standard and this now intensified.[42] To make matters worse Jersey Standard resorted to deception in order to try to hide the truth that the company was no longer interested in Bolivia, both playing down the potential of some of its reserves[43] and 'clandestinely moving parts of a dismantled refinery into Argentina' in 1935.[44] It did not help that this last move was discovered.

The really decisive event, however, was the Chaco War. This war was initiated by Bolivia with the objective, among other things, of securing access to the navigable Parana River in order to develop its oil reserves. According to Rout,

La Paz concluded that effective exploitation of the petroleum wealth would necessitate a port on the Paraguay River for oil shipment and enough territory across the Chaco for the construction of a pipeline. But under existing circumstances, Bolivia held no frontage on the lower Paraguay River. To negotiate with Asunción to obtain such space would be tacit admission that Paraguay held *de jure* rights to the Chaco.[45]

The war proved to be a disastrous miscalculation as Paraguay, with help from Argentina and from Bolivian ineptitude, destroyed the Bolivian army and with it the Bolivian political system.

Meanwhile Standard Oil's lack of co-operation with the Bolivian authorities continued. Thus, in 1933 the Bolivian government requested that Standard increase its output of refined aviation gasoline for the Bolivian Air Force but Standard agreed to do so only on condition that the government bought, at higher prices than before, the complementary products that would be produced by the refining process.[46] The government at first refused and expropriated the refinery for the duration of the war, but later had to back down. As the British Minister reported, 'The government were never, in fact, in a position to take over the refining at Camiri and have therefore been obliged to accept the company's terms . . . the Government are in arrears with their payments and the company are now drawing up a contract to assure prompt payment for additional supplies provided for in the new resolution.'[47] It is not difficult to see why the Bolivian government and the Bolivian military in particular did not regard Standard with affection.

Standard's attitude, however, was only one factor in an increasingly complex situation. The main other features in this stemmed from Bolivia's defeat in the Chaco. Bolivian politics were radicalised in consequence; the Trotskyist POR was set up in 1934 and various other left-wing organisations followed. The existing military leadership was discredited and yielded power to a generation of younger, radical officers.

One of these, Toro, seized power in May 1936 and declared that the new government's 'firm intention is to implant state socialism with the aid of the parties of the left'.[48] Under pressure from other officers, Toro moved against Standard. Thus the regime quickly set up the Petroleum Ministry for the first time and confiscated a number of unworked oil concessions belonging to Standard. In December 1936 the regime set up a state oil company, YPFB, and the powers of this agency were expanded several times during 1937. In January YPFB took over all of the oil concessions not worked by Jersey Standard, in March it was given an import monopoly and in May a five-man directorate was set up and given a ten-year tenure. Standard was expropriated in March 1937.

Up to a point, therefore, the nationalisation of Standard Oil could be seen as the consequence of its own past actions or inactions. Much later, in September 1942, a British Embassy official who had formerly worked with Standard recalled that 'The Bolivian army often asked for small concessions and favours which were always turned down on the plea of their (painful) neutrality. The result was that feeling against them grew quietly but firmly, even with some level-headed Bolivians like the late President of the Republic, José Luis Tejado Sorzano with whom I personally often discussed the matter.'[49] It is also noteworthy that the Bolivian left had, after the defeat, taken up the story apparently begun in Paraguay that Standard Oil had somehow forced Bolivia to go to war with Paraguay in order to secure oil concession areas in the Chaco.[50] Nevertheless there were other behind-the-scenes factors which may have been decisive. At least part of the reason for the oil nationalisation stemmed from Bolivian foreign policy.

With the defeat of the Bolivian army, the country's only internationally valuable resource was its oil supply, something it knew it could use as a bargaining counter. Thus, in 1936 the Bolivian government offered the President of Uruguay 'all the petroleum that its refineries would need' in return for Uruguay's help at the Chaco peace conference, although this gambit was unsuccessful.[51] Argentina, however, was more interested. Indeed, in Buenos Aires a special committee had been set up to examine the Chaco question and reported in November 1935; the Argentine navy had pointed out that 'Today we have to import, as has been stated many times, an enormous amount of oil for the people of the Republic. Today we import from Mexico and Peru, countries distant and uncontrollable; tomorrow we ought to replace that importation with the Bolivian product.'[52]

In September 1936 Finot became Bolivia's Minister of Foreign Affairs. His main concern was apparently to save the Bolivian oilfields from the victorious Paraguayan army. The US Embassy at any rate believed that this was why Finot went to Buenos Aires in December 1936. Very shortly after this visit the Embassy reported that 'the Argentine government . . . is alleged to have gone so far as to promise that if the Argentine obtains advantages in this matter and the Bolivian government expropriates the fields held by the Standard Oil Company and allows their purchase by the "YPF" the Argentine will guarantee that Paraguay will not again go to war with Bolivia'.[53] To this end, Argentina agreed to extend its railway from Yacuiba to Santa Cruz in return for joint exploration arrangements in the Santa Cruz area and in December 1936 YPFB was set up explicitly to discover and develop these new fields.

It is difficult to know exactly how much weight to give the 'Argentine' factor in explaining the expropriation of Standard Oil. It is a key question, for it suggests a very much more 'rational' motivation for the action than the explanations which focus on the state of Bolivian politics or disappointment on the part of Bolivia with Standard's failure to produce more oil. It is possible that the foreign policy aspects of the takeover were heavily emphasised in Washington because the US Embassy was itself out of touch with rapidly changing political developments within Bolivia, but it is striking that the Embassy referred to the Argentine connection two months before the actual nationalisation took place.

Moreover, some of the other evidence for this perspective does seem quite strong. For example, the Yacuiba – Santa Cruz railway project which linked the Bolivian oilfields to Argentina was announced in April 1937, only a month after the announcement of the nationalisation itself. Standard Oil itself, like the US government, evidently believed that the decision stemmed from Argentina since it first took the matter up with the authorities in Buenos Aires rather than in La Paz.[54] Moreover, it is also true that if Toro had imagined that the takeover of Standard Oil would strengthen his domestic political position then he miscalculated badly, for he was removed by another left-wing nationalist coup only a few months later, in July 1937.

To these specific points may be added the general consideration that fear of Argentina appears to have been a strong motive in the minds of Bolivian policymakers during this period, and it was this which apparently prompted even the left-wing Villarroel government (1943–6) to

seek aid from the USA. Certainly the British Minister believed that
'There are grounds for believing that the present government would
welcome American co-operation in the development of its oil fields
. . . [partly] in order to be guaranteed against feared aggression on the
part of Brazil and the Argentine.'[55]

Nevertheless, the nationalisation could only have taken place in the
form in which it did as a result of the extreme weakness of Standard
Oil in Bolivia. The company did have a national presence in the country but it patently had no serious interest in this investment nor any of
the political influence that is normally associated with major economic
presence. Moreover, the state of domestic politics in Bolivia at that
time made it far easier for the nationalisation to take place even if it
was indeed intended as a concession to Argentina, for it could at least
be made to appear as an issue of domestic politics and as a triumph
rather than as a further surrender. In some manner, therefore, the
nature of which is not entirely clear, all three factors combined to produce this particular effect.

Concluding reflections

Although there were clear differences between Chile, Uruguay and
Bolivia, some of the same forces were at work in each case. Indeed, the
trend towards greater state control of oil in the 1930s was so general
throughout Latin America that it can only be explained by continent-
wide factors. The most important of these was the change in the world
economy itself; in the 1920s, US and to a lesser but still significant
extent British capital was moving into Latin America looking for
opportunities. Powerful interests in most Latin American countries
believed that their advantages lay in co-operation with foreign enterprise. By 1930, however, the momentum had halted; those countries
which were not already established exporters could see little opportunity in continuing to be linked with international companies which by
then had formed a cartel to stabilise and hold back the growth of production, and had little interest in making large investments in new
countries.

The depression also had a more subtle effect. As the USA withdrew
into itself, it lost power and prestige in Latin America, in many cases
at the expense of more nationalist, or even Fascist, influences. Moreover, in the south of Latin America, the star of Argentina rose as that
of the USA fell. Argentina's influence was considerable both in the Uru-

guayan decision to form and develop ANCAP and in the Bolivian decision to expropriate Standard Oil (YPFB itself was named after the Argentine state company YPF).

The depression had other effects. For the oil-importing, raw-material-exporting countries, it made obvious the balance of payments costs of continuing to rely upon the major private companies for imports, for private investments related to global profitability and not to the balance of payments positions of particular countries. In the very short term, the depression brought about balance of payments crises in a number of Latin American countries, which took desperate measures to try to save foreign exchange and thus to mitigate the already very harsh austerity measures which they felt it necessary to apply. Under these circumstances Uruguay and Chile were particularly tempted by the offer of barter arrangements with the USSR which would save hard currency, while Uruguay's acceptance of a Soviet offer led it to develop its own marketing system in order to distribute the imported oil (which private marketing concerns would not touch). Of the three countries, however, only Uruguay had a political tradition which made possible this immediate response. In Chile, although many were similarly tempted by the Soviet offer, the laissez-faire tradition was too strong and the governments in power too weak to permit a short-term break with previous patterns of supply. The conservative restoration in October 1932 appeared to bring this option to a close.

In the slightly longer term, however, the depression led to a major change in the intellectual climate within Latin America. Advocates of domestic industrialisation who had already played a significant role in Argentina and Uruguay quickly became part of the intellectual mainstream. The ideology of import-substituting industrialisation had taken hold. Domestic industrialisation almost inevitably came to involve construction of a domestic oil refinery and often involved a search for domestic oil reserves in order to free scarce foreign exchange for imports of capital goods and other requirements for industrialisation. Argentina's YPF, which showed that it was technically possible for a Latin American state enterprise to develop oil deposits and to operate a refinery, naturally became an important influence.

Popularity, as such, played a relatively minor part in oil policy. None of these nationalisations, not even the Bolivian, was designed simply as a crowd-pleaser. Such domestic political base for oil nationalism as existed was generally middle class and involved those who hoped to benefit from the expansion of state employment; this was a major factor in Uruguay (as it had been in Argentina) and a significant one in Chile. In Bolivia survival rather than patronage was the issue. Thus, in Chile and Uruguay it was the idea of domestic industrialisation rather than the promise of flamboyant attacks on foreign oil companies that won popular support for the nationalists; indeed, in both Uruguay and Chile governments were concerned to avoid a confrontation over oil and instead preferred to secure their limited objectives by a mixture of bluff and negotiation. In neither case were the property rights of the companies directly affected; governments had no wish to provoke confrontations which would only have interfered with their other objectives. Cárdenas might be spectacular, but governments further south preferred to tread carefully.

10

Cárdenas and the Mexican oil nationalisation

The Mexican oil expropriation was one of the most dramatic in Latin American history and it had major implications both for the international oil industry and for the Mexican Revolution. The Cárdenas presidency (1934–40) did much to institutionalise the Mexican Revolution as Lázaro Cárdenas looked for support beyond the small secular elite which had triumphed under Carranza. He organised the Mexican working class and peasantry and incorporated his supporters into the Revolutionary Party. The oil nationalisation of 18 March 1938 was one of the high points of his programme and Mexican politics subsequently evolved in a far more conservative direction. The nationalisation marked a dramatic assertion of economic independence from the major oil companies and their parent governments and it was certainly widely supported within Mexico. Beyond this, however, lie some very difficult problems of interpretation and many of Cárdenas's own motivations remain shrouded in mystery, as do his relationships with key political insiders. The British diplomat who complained at the beginning of 1938 that 'a kind of oriental fog of secrecy and intrigue and misrepresentation covers the struggle going on all the time between the President, his advisers, the syndicates, the Generals and so on'[1] was probably no less well informed than many later historians.

The Constitution and its consequences

It is certainly clear, however, that the initial impetus towards oil nationalisation came not from diffuse popular pressure but from the political elite. This can be seen as far back as the framing of the 1917 Constitution whose Article 27 claimed national ownership of the Mexican subsoil and first embodied the Mexican perspective which lay behind the eventual expropriation (see also chapter 1). As Meyer summed up the Constitutional debate, for such pro-peasant tendencies as Zapatismo, the important thing was to resolve the problem of the land and the oil industry only entered into their demands in a very marginal way; the Villistas took the same attitude. Only at the convention of Aguas Calientes did the representatives of these currents consider the problem. In reality, after Carranza himself, it was the conservative writers who were most concerned with the question. If on the oil question there was a certain unanimity among the power contenders, this could be explained because the main interest affected was foreign and the main gainer would be the group which won power.[2]

Smith goes even further and attributes a tactical element to oil nationalism in 1917 which, in his view, acted as a substitute for redistributionist policies.[3]

Certainly, oil nationalism was not particularly popular during the revolutionary period. After a study of the revolutionary years, Knight concluded of nationalist propaganda: 'it is striking how ineffective it was; the politico-cultural standards which went with it were confined to a relatively small group, and their roots in the mass of the population were tenuous. Mexico was too stratified, too fragmented, too disunited to produce a powerful grass-roots nationalism'.[4] Moreover, such nationalism as there was frequently took on a highly conservative tone, 'this theme of Latin, Catholic civilisation resisting Anglo-Saxon Protestant barbarism cropped up frequently and denotes a set of attitudes – Catholic, conservative, hierarchical, anti-materialist – with a long pedigree in Mexican culture'.[5]

If one is to see oil nationalism in class terms at all, then the only possible source to select is the urban middle class. Lorenzo Meyer does so:

the nationalist oil policy originated in the militant nationalism of the urban middle-class sectors represented by *carrancismo*. This nationalism was an indispensable part of the attacks made by this faction against the Porfirian political system which had entrusted the development and management of the modern sectors of the economy to foreign capital. One of the reasons for its rebellion was the attempt to gain for itself the greatest possible degree of control over the economic system, for which reason it needed to dominate and subordinate foreign capital.[6]

Without altogether denying this interpretation, it is important to point out that the majority of those actively involved in the drafting of the Mexican Constitution were military officers serving with Carranza in the course of fighting that was still continuing. It is likely that these officers were considerably irritated by US intervention in the Mexican Revolution and that they, like Carranza, held the oil companies largely responsible.

There can be no doubt that the oil companies did find it necessary to finance in some manner or other various rebel factions in physical control of oil-producing areas. There was inevitably some ambiguity in such arrangements which would be seen, by the enemies of the companies or of the rebel groups, as indicating some form of political commitment by the companies. This was not necessarily true, although not always quite inaccurate (see chapter 1). However, as a Huasteca representative told the Fall Committee, 'This form of contribution to the need or caprice of controlling forces in Mexico cannot be prevented except by the abandonment of properties which, in the case of oil producing properties, cannot be considered.'[7]

To this form of political involvement had to be added the fact that the companies claimed a legal position which, if respected, would have given them entrenched rights independent of the policies or desires of any post-revolutionary government. For Carranza himself, the continued existence of foreign oil companies who claimed a privileged status in Mexican law was a permanent threat to the government of Mexico. He believed that 'in Mexico, North American private interests were in operation which, on losing the support provided by the regimes now overthrown, have for some time actively opposed the Revolution and are now demanding that their home government should intervene against it'.[8] Consequently, he was determined to assert 'the principle that Mexico is free to repeal or modify its laws which – without being retroactive or, if it is necessary to do so, even retroactively – must be obeyed by foreign interests, who ought to accommodate their activities to our laws instead of using their influence with their governments in order to force Mexico to accept legislation which is convenient to them'.[9]

Carranza's position was similar to that of the Calvo Doctrine, formulated by an Argentine lawyer in conscious opposition to the US insistence on the principles of international law which allowed foreign intervention where this was necessary to protect contracts. According to Calvo, foreign interests ought to obey the laws of the countries in which they operated, even if these should change over time, and should not be allowed to call upon the help of foreign governments in any dispute. Carranza was exaggerating only slightly, therefore, when he wrote that 'this is not only our cause, but that of the whole of Latin

America'.[10] Company opponents of Carranza's proposals agreed on this point at least and consequently remained intransigent.

Although the radical provisions of Article 27 became part of the Mexican Constitution of 1917, no Mexican president before Cárdenas proved willing to confront the oil companies, although Carranza himself went close to the brink. While the strength of the companies themselves and the backing which they received from Washington were important factors in this, it should also be noted that successive Mexican governments were in very weak positions and by no means all of them wished to confront the USA. The 1910–20 period had been one of constant internal warfare and there were three major armed revolts against Mexican governments during the 1920s. Consequently, most Mexican governments during this period found support from Washington to be essential if domestic political stability was to be maintained.

In 1919 Carranza did make an effort to translate Article 27 into law, but he faced determined opposition from the companies and the USA and appeared to draw back from confrontation. Before the situation could develop further, Carranza was overthrown by Obregón, who showed far less interest in pursuing the oil question. However, when General Elías Calles came to power at the end of 1924, he appeared ready to radicalise the Mexican Revolution partly in order to build up a power base with which to challenge Obregón and partly to reduce any possibility of independent political mobilisation. Although his main initiatives lay elsewhere, Calles persuaded Congress to pass a law specifically implementing Article 27 of the Constitution. This had been awaiting action since 1919 and the law finally received presidential approval in December 1925. According to the terms of the law, the companies were ordered to seek confirmation of their holdings in Mexico and these were also to revert to the state after a specific time limit (this was originally to have been 50 years from the beginning of operations). The law also forbade the companies from seeking foreign intervention in the event of a dispute with the Mexican government. For these and other reasons, these terms were unacceptable to Washington or the companies.

As we have seen (pp. 37–9), the USA took a far more narrowly ideological view of this issue than could have been justified by the nature of its interests in Mexico. This inflexibility has tended to obscure the fact that Calles's own motivations were essentially tactical; it is very probable that he was telling the truth when he explained to Dwight Morrow that

the Government of Mexico had never wanted to confiscate any property, least of all did they want to confiscate the oil properties; that they needed the revenues, and obviously 'they did not want to commit suicide', that the act of 1925 was a most necessary piece of legislation at the time because the country was in considerable disorder and there was an extreme radical wing whose interests had to be met in that legislation, that he had thought the grant of the 50-year old right as good as a perpetual right to take out the oil, and that such a grant would satisfy every practical purpose, but that the oil companies had not co-operated with him at all, but in fact their representatives had boasted all over Mexico that they did not need to obey the laws of Mexico.[11]

Certainly, Calles had to balance his administration between a pro-US and national development wing led by Pani and a more nationalist wing led by Morones. As Calles became more established and as other dangers threatened (notably the Cristero rebellion which broke out in 1927) so Calles showed decreasing interest in the oil question. It was the companies themselves which held up an early face-saving settlement.

The position of the companies

By far the most important company in Mexico in terms of oil production and reserves was the British-owned El Aguila. Although nominally independent, this company was managed by Royal Dutch/Shell which had, from the mid-1920s at least, moved into informal alliance with Jersey Standard. This in turn relied for its position upon the support of the US State Department. In view of the justified reputation of the companies for blind intransigence and lack of sympathy for Mexico, it is worth looking a little more closely into the reasons for company behaviour.

It will be useful to begin by considering the peculiar management system in operation at El Aguila. As we have seen, Pearson in 1919 sold a minority shareholding and management contract to Royal Dutch/Shell in return for an undertaking that the company continue to be managed in the interests of the El Aguila shareholders. This arrangement would probably have provoked conflict in any case, but it was complicated by the death of Wheetman Pearson in 1926 and the personal behaviour of Henri Deterding who, after around 1925, became increasingly eccentric and pro-Fascist. There were, therefore, considerable disagreements between the local management of El Aguila, the board of Royal Dutch/Shell proper and the Mexican Eagle Company, which still retained an advisory role.

The main evidence for this conflict comes from the papers of the Mexican Eagle itself.[12] On 9 April 1934 Clive Pearson noted that 'Our fear sometimes is that the RD [Royal Dutch] may be too ready to limit the programme of the company because of some trouble or other.' The following year, on 2 August 1935, R. J. Body complained that 'Mexican psychology is not understood by the management and it is likely that many of the troubles can be attributed to the lack of being in touch with the situation.' Moreover:

the present policy not only restricts expenditure in Mexico, but actually causes the company to lose money. It is rather significant to remember that the Aguila company succeeded in making fair profits during 1934, which may be considered as probably one of the worst years in Mexican history from a legislative and industrial aspect.

There would seem little doubt that the Aguila company's and the Group's interests have now arrived at a pass where policies must diverge, unless the former's shareholders are prepared to sacrifice themselves for the good of the combine.

It is to be noted that the Management have instructed Assheton [the local manager] not to open any negotiations with the authorities regarding an attempt to smooth out the company's present troubles, and to come to some arrangement whereby the company can carry on their present activities less molested. These instructions have virtually tied Assheton's hands.

The Group methods in Mexico are unacceptable to any Mexican government and the only effective approach is the friendly personal one.

The effect of this position upon El Aguila's behaviour can be seen from a report presented by a former US Embassy official, Ruben Clark, who had been commissioned in 1935 by the Royal Dutch/Shell group to investigate the Mexican company. In his view, El Aguila

had to learn that her [Mexico's] sovereignty and independence had got to be respected. The Mexican government had got to be persuaded and satisfied to do in their own interests, and not compelled to do, what the companies wanted. . .

Another thing was that, without mentioning names or criticising individuals, Mr Clark thought it essential that the board of the Aguila would be careful never to send to Mexico anyone, whatever his position, who in Mr

Clark's words suffered from a race complex. . . . [regarding negotiations with the Mexican government] there would have to be someone with a quite different mentality from anyone at present in charge of the company's business. Again, Mr Clark would urge that the Company should try and get more Mexican capital interested in the Aguila. He had heard too, that lower paid staff were discontented. He would urge also that the question of employing more Mexicans in higher posts should be sympathetically studied.[13]

Assheton himself had complained to Clark that Deterding 'was incapable of conceiving Mexico as anything but a Colonial Government to which you simply dictated orders. He, Mr Assheton, had tried to disillusion him without success – indeed Sir H. Deterding had accused Mr Assheton of being half a Bolshevik.'[14] In his report, Clark 'makes a point of the advisability, if not the necessity, of placing reliance on the knowledge and judgement of the local management in Mexico and giving them freedom of decision'.[15] Royal Dutch responded by agreeing to this recommendation, but only on the understanding that Assheton was himself replaced, a stipulation unacceptable to Mexican Eagle; interestingly enough, Deterding had been a keen supporter of Assheton when the latter had been given his appointment in 1925.[16]

Apart from this management structure, El Aguila faced a real problem in that its main source of active political support, the US government, could only be reached through an alliance with US companies which were far less economically committed to Mexico. Thus, although El Aguila was by far the largest company in Mexico, it was by no means the most important power diplomatically. At the same time, the company seems never to have considered breaking the united front and dealing directly with the Mexican government. The Achnacarry agreement of 1928 would probably have ruled out such a strategy but even in 1926 the British Minister reported that 'The Mexican Eagle, instructed by Sir Henri Deterding, are collaborating very closely with the Americans. They say with right that they must not show a gap in their united front.'[17]

The US companies also formed a united front, under some prodding from the State Department, effectively under the influence of Jersey Standard. We have already seen (chapter 1) that after 1928 Jersey's financial interest in Mexico was quite small. Moreover, as the official company historian points out, as a result of this fact, Standard

transferred its ablest executives in Mexico to more active operations . . . Thus, poor prospects brought an attrition of Jersey management as well as of investments and operations in Mexico. This same policy of curtailment was followed by other companies. This, in turn, weakened the operations of the Mexican oil industry and contributed to the increasing criticism of foreign investment in that country.[18]

At no time was the company seriously interested in the goodwill of the Mexican government; instead, it sought to protect its position by requesting US intervention whenever it felt threatened to any extent. Well before 1938 many officials in Washington (as well as Ambassador Daniels in Mexico) had lost patience with this attitude and come to expect that the companies would cry 'Wolf' at the slightest provocation.

Company attitudes to Mexico also reflected the fact that most of the companies had entered the country either during the dictatorship of Profirio Díaz or during the revolutionary years when they survived by dealing with the immediately powerful *caudillos* according to the needs of the moment. As we have seen, 'high' politics for the companies consisted in complaining to the State Department whenever they felt their rights to be threatened. At an intermediate level the companies were willing to deal with, and where necessary bribe, local power-holders and even senior politicians in Mexico City. These activities largely replaced, in the minds of the companies, any need for bargaining with or conciliation of the Mexican government.

It is a striking fact that the US oil companies seriously considered financing Calles in his conflict with Cárdenas in 1935. Cárdenas's genuine belief that money had in fact changed hands was almost certainly a factor in his decision to expropriate the oil companies.[19] El Aguila had been approached by Ruben Clark on this matter but had refused to act on it.[20]

At a lower political level, the oil companies found themselves in what must have seemed an interminable series of disputes with local landlords and workers. Huasteca had to deal, in Tampico alone, with no fewer than 4,500 landlords any of which could have had their titles challenged or themselves made some kind of claim against the oil company.[21] Landlords only too happy to sell out for cash before the discovery of oil quickly became discontented when they found out how much wealth could be produced from a successful find and tried to coax or blackmail the companies into increasing their original prices.[22] At times, oil companies would try to resolve the more serious of these disputes by taking them up at a high political level. This course of action, however, was not without its dangers for, as Assheton told the British Ambassador in 1934 (apropos of a property dispute),

sum required as a bribe by Calles was about 5 million pesos [$1,338,889] and that they were now seriously considering whether it would not be cheaper to bribe a majority of the judges of Supreme Court. He told me that on last occasion each side thought they could count on two judges but that the fifth judge was supposed to be such an honest man that it was thought inadvisable to tempt him. The court divided against the company by a majority of three to two and they discovered that the honest man had been given an extra large bribe by the other side; he hoped that would not happen again.[23]

Calles was regarded as 'extremely expensive' but El Aguila was told a little later that Cárdenas 'was extremely innocent in these matters and did not properly understand business conventions as understood in Mexico'.[24]

It should be pointed out, however, that even where bribery took place it did not result in any easy solution to the company's problems. Regarding the Amatlán case, for example, in 1934 the British Foreign Office noted that Assheton

states with illustrations that the present administration, with a view no doubt to their early departure, are engaging in blackmail and graft against foreign companies on a scale unprecedented even for Mexico, and he asks for discretion to spend two to three million pesos [$500,000–800,000] in settling this case. On this point Mr Hutchinson informed me that their opponents have actually offered to settle for four million pesos [$1.1m.] and this offer and Mr Assheton's request have been considered by the highest authorities here [London] and a decision taken to refuse all accommodation and go through with the case. The decision is based upon the belief that to yield to blackmail in this case would lead to endless further demands and would therefore in the long run be useless.[25]

There was also the point that, to be effective, bribery must not only work but be invisible; if corruption were 'common knowledge', repercussions would quickly come to outweigh any initial advantages which the company might gain.

It is not difficult to see why, as a result of these various attitudes and activities, the companies were not popular with the emerging Mexican political elite. Since almost all authors on the period say the same, it will be useful to quote a single source, that of López Portillo y Weber, a Mexican technical expert who later played a part in the 1937 oil commission, to the effect that, 'unfortunately with [a few exceptions] company executives were hard, egotistical, racist, and discriminatory, and many of them contributed effectively to the creation of resentments and hatreds felt for the United States and Anglo-Saxons in general'.[26] Under these circumstances, it was not surprising that key figures in the Mexican elite naturally believed all company statements to be false unless they had positive proof to the contrary.

The emergence of Cárdenas

A number of factors came together in making for Mexican oil nationalism in the 1930s – a nationalism which was far more sophisticated than that of Carranza. For one thing there was the state of the oil industry itself. Although, as we have seen (chapter 1), the tax increases of 1917 and 1921 had done something to improve the Mexican share of returned value from oil, this by no means satisfied Mexico. Even though Mexican governments of the 1920s generally shared an economic strategy of export-led growth, it was becoming increasingly unlikely that oil had much of a part to play in this. Moreover, even earlier,

figures like Joaquín Santaella, Vásquez Schaffino, Aquiles Elourduy, Gonzáles Roa and Manuel de la Peña, active in the Technical Commission set up by Carranza in 1915 to examine the problems of the oil industry, were responsible for demands for stricter control over the exploitation of oil. Voicing their opinions through the *Boletín del Petróleo,* this group was convinced that it was essential for Mexican development to determine policy concerning oil utilisation according to the country's own development needs rather than in the interests of the oil companies, whose basic concern was to maximise profits. Since by purchase, lease or concession, the companies controlled vast portions of oil bearing land, the only way to assert effective control over resource utilisation was by replacing the Anglo-Saxon concept of absolute ownership, imported by Díaz, with the older Spanish concept of ownership vested in the nation.[27]

The strength of this view increased as it became more and more clear that the oil companies were switching their interest to lower-cost Venezuela. In fact, Mexican oil production, which had increased sharply between 1916 and 1921, fell back subsequently despite continuing foreign investment activity and declined sharply after 1926. By 1931 Mexican oil exports had effectively lost all international importance.

By this time, the damage done to Mexican oilfields by the drilling practices of the companies had become obvious and Mexican officials

Table 10.1 *Mexican oil production 1916–37*
(*b/d*)

1916	111,082	1928	137,399
1918	174,872	1930	108,301
1920	430,325	1932	90,517
1922	499,393	1934	104,582
1924	382,680	1936	112,405
1926	247,729	1937	128,511

Source: Pemex, *Annual Reports.*

had few expectations concerning the economic advantages provided by the foreign oil companies. Writing in July 1929, one of the Mexican intellectual elite, Silva Herzog, noted that 'mining and oil production in Mexico, advanced from the technical point of view, is in the hands of foreign companies which remit their profits and thus increase the capital resources of other countries, leaving us only starvation wages and tiny tax revenues.[28] In fact, it would not be entirely true to say that the companies treated Mexico purely as a reserve area, to be held back in the interests of international market stability, although it would not be surprising if some Mexicans believed this to be the case. On the contrary, much of El Aguila's frustration stemmed from the fact that it had in 1932 discovered a major field at Poza Rica. Assheton told Ruben Clark 'in strict confidence that the Company had secured a great new field but that this was at present known only to themselves; this discovery was of such importance that to secure the right to exploit it, it would pay them to accept any terms the government might impose.[29] The problem was, however, that this field lay in part under federal land and that fresh arrangements would have to be made with the government before it could be developed.

There was also the question of labour relations. The Mexican oil-workers appear to have been typical of workforces in mining or oil enclave areas where political authority was unpredictable and distant and labour relations primitive and violent. At the beginning labour was recruited by subcontractors (*enganchadores*) who were held responsible for the workers. The workers' first struggle, therefore, was for the right to form trade unions and to strike. In 1917, for example, a manager of Huasteca Petroleum in Tampico responded to a strike threat by saying that 'the management of the company do not object to the workers taking part in strikes, petitions and the like, but it advises everybody that the employee who is absent from work without a valid excuse, such as the sickness of himself or his family, will be dismissed from employment'.[30] After repeated strikes, El Aguila granted union recognition for the first time in 1921 and other companies then followed.

After 1921 there were two major features of the labour scene. The oil companies, which were now running down their investments in Mexico, made periodic attempts to discharge labour, thus meeting union resistance. At the same time the central government and some state governors made efforts to win control of oil-workers by setting up their own trade unions or by seeking to manipulate existing organisations. This led to inter-union conflict with dismissal being the usual penalty for the losers.[31] Indeed, officially sponsored unions, notably the CROM, were mainly concerned to protect their own members and almost eager to see the others fall victim to company retrenchment. As a result of these conflicts, the officially sponsored CROM had, by 1928, effectively won for itself the leading position in the oilfields with the anti-government and Communist-led CGT largely destroyed. After 1928, however, Calles became increasingly conservative and the CROM declined in effectiveness, leaving the workforce largely unprotected against the avalanche of redundancies and wage reductions put through by the companies during the depression.

It is perhaps not surprising, therefore, that the oil-workers behaved in extremely militant fashion after their industrial and political strength began to increase in 1934. In that year, with Calles losing his grip on the government machine, El Aguila complained that

Labour affairs are reaching the stage where it is practically impossible to control workmen . . . the Federal Inspectors act as agitators instead of mediators. The government Department of Labour deliberately foments agitation and insists upon the recognition of the particular union which at this moment the head of the Department desires to aid.[32]

In June of that year there was a strike at El Aguila and the British Embassy reported that

the PNR were unable to resist the temptation to make political capital out of this strike, and have published a manifesto in the press to the effect that, as friends of the working classes, they were sending down a prominent member of the Party to distribute food and other necessities of life amongst the starving men. The fact, however, that the gentleman who was sent down by the party is their official candidate for election as Deputy in the particular district where the strike is taking place would seem to prove that their action is not so disinterested as it would appear on the surface.[33]

There followed federal arbitration which ruled in favour of the workers.

In January 1935, moreover, El Aguila described a strike which had taken place when,

a few months ago, the two rival unions had fused with the result that the more extreme elements, consisting chiefly of young boys and clerks in the sales department of their office in Mexico City, had managed to get control of the union and, in order to show their power, had deliberately fomented a strike by the submission of totally unacceptable demands.[34]

This was followed by a sympathetic strike at Jersey Standard. A few months later, the El Aguila management complained of new disturbances and claimed that 'the moral responsibility for the recent unrest and agitation amongst the men which culminated in the murder of Mr Chabaud [a Swiss employee of El Aguila] . . . lay with certain Federal Labour Inspectors who, to the companies' certain knowledge, had countenanced and even tacitly supported threats of violence against its foreign employees.[35] And in November 1936 'past successes seem to have gone to the heads of men's syndicates so that general strike affecting all oil companies is quite on the cards within the next three weeks. Attitude of government on the other hand is reasonable and indeed friendly over this issue but politically their hands are to a large extent tied.'[36] It is clear, therefore, that the 'labour issue' was not simply created by Cárdenas. On the contrary, the oil-workers had a militant tradition of their own and although they proved easy to mobilise in opposition to the companies they were later to prove far more difficult to pacify.

Another set of pressures on the oil companies came from domestic consumers. The period following 1924 saw in Mexico a deliberate attempt to foster domestic industrialisation. As a consequence, there grew up something of an industrial bourgeoisie, which in many cases stemmed directly from the revolutionary political elite. One key indication of this process can be seen from the development of a consumers' pressure group for the Mexican electricity industry. According to Wionczek's study of this industry, the lobby grew up in order to influence the regulations relating to a new electricity law:

Sooner or later the new group was bound to find a common issue on which to test its strength. Cheap power was a perfect issue on many counts. First, electricity rates still were widely considered to be exorbitant. Second, despite all the secrecy surrounding company records, the disparity between prices paid by large and small consumers had become widely known . . . Third, no known substitute for electricity was then available in the country. Fourth, the owners of the industry were foreigners.[37]

The parallel with the oil industry hardly needs to be laboured.

In fact it was the Calles regime which first set up a state oil company in Mexico. Calles gave the national railways the right to explore some areas in which oil was believed to exist (indeed, in which it was later found) close to certain railway routes. Later the government created a specific agency for the industry.[38] At the beginning of 1934, Petromex was set up in order to develop those potentially oil-rich territories still in the hands of the state with the objective of supplying the domestic market. These changes represented a statement of intention rather than an immediate fact of economic importance, but they clearly related to the increasing significance of the Mexican domestic market. Thus, although the companies claimed that 'the price of gasoline, less tax, is less than in any other country in the world', price increases were resisted by domestic consumers. In 1934, following an arbitration settlement which raised wages in the industry, the companies put up prices and, in the words of the British Minister, 'as was to be expected, a violent agitation was worked up in the daily press against the oil companies, who were accused of exploiting the public for the benefit of foreign share-holders, with the result that the various unions of motor-bus drivers and taxi-drivers came out on strike'.[39]

It is clear, therefore, that Cárdenas harnessed, rather than created, political forces hostile to the oil companies, although it is also true that he had a strong personal commitment to establishing state control over the oil industry. His first report to Congress at the beginning of 1935 included the promise that:

The state will intervene to bring about equilibrium in the economic forces of the oil industry stimulating the development of national undertakings and creating a semi-official organism for their support and control . . . [he believed] that the exploitation of oil in Mexico has, for many years, taken place in a way characteristic of foreign companies; that is to say, our country, though independent and enjoying advanced social ideas, permits the extraction of its wealth and natural resources by the foreigner without preserving for itself any permanent benefit.[40]

Moreover, he promised a draft law to give the state sufficient power to regulate development of the oil industry since 'the application of the petroleum law of 1925 in regard to ordinary concessions was found not to comply properly with the fundamental principle of Article 27 of the Constitution'.[41]

There is clear evidence that Cárdenas was interested in exerting state control over the oil industry, but it is equally apparent that he would have preferred to do so gradually and quietly; it is likely that he would have been satisfied with establishing effective government control while stopping short of outright expulsion of the foreign companies. What is less clear is the extent to which his actual policies were governed by his own independent preferences and how far they were influenced by factions and tendencies within his administration or by circumstances which he did not foresee and could not control. It is certain, however, that some of Cárdenas's advisers, notably General Múgica and almost certainly Lombardo Toledano, were more radical in oil (and indeed other) matters than Cárdenas himself; in the eyes of the British, Múgica 'was in violent opposition to all of the companies'.[42] There appears also to have been a more moderate wing within the government which urged more gradualist policies but which was ultimately unable to avert the confrontation which led to the expropriation. The picture that emerges is not one which easily affords a simple explanation but rather one which emphasises the importance of various unforeseen and conjunctural factors in determining the way in which the actual expropriation took place. The most immediate of these was the mobilisation of the oil-workers.

By 1934 there were some 10,000 oil-workers grouped together in 19 different unions. Under Cárdenas, however, determined efforts were made to federate oil-workers into the STPRM and thence into the CTM which had been set up in 1936 under the leadership of the pro-Communist Lombardo Toledano. The original aim of the organisation was to strengthen the position of Cárdenas in his conflict with Calles. Following the defeat of Calles, however, the CTM continued to be important and, although it is not necessary to accept the British Minister's evaluation that it was a 'Frankenstein's monster',[43] there is no doubt that the CTM and Lombardo himself came to play key roles during the Cárdenas presidency. It is interesting that when the Dutch Ambassador questioned the Under-Secretary of Foreign Relations, Beteta, about the relationship between Cárdenas and Lombardo, 'while admitting that no distinction could be drawn between labour issues and politics, Sr Beteta said that this factor constituted a permanent unknown and commented no further on it'.[44]

In July 1936 an assembly of the STPRM was held in Mexico City with the aim of drawing up a demand for a collective labour contract. The companies rather welcomed the possibility of a comprehensive settlement but felt that the demands made were clearly excessive. There can be little doubt that the Mexican government encouraged the high wage claim; Cárdenas himself had earlier stated in public that wage levels should be set, not in order to balance supply and demand, but to reflect the companies' ability to pay. At the same time, the government's underlying radicalism became increasingly apparent during 1936. In one of the high points of the year, the regime responded to a series of class conflicts in Monterrey by passing a law of expropriation which permitted industries to be nationalised if compensation were paid. At the same time, Cárdenas made a speech in which he said that if entrepreneurs did not want to take the trouble of maintaining their businesses in the face of labour militancy, the government would be only too pleased to do this for them.

Moves towards confrontation

During 1937 these radical pressures came to centre increasingly on the oil industry. At the beginning of the year, a draft bill was leaked to the press in which, in the words of the British Minister,

Mexican government propose in place of Petromex to create a government petroleum corporation to take over and operate all national reserves.

The new corporation being 100 per cent government-owned will presumably be free of all taxation and however inefficient should nonetheless be able to undersell existing companies in local market. American companies whose entire output is sold locally appear likely to be worse sufferers and if government carry out their intention some at least of them may withdraw from the country. It is doubtful if this project is constitutional but this consideration is unlikely to deter government whose main aim would appear to be the gradual nationalisation of the industry.[45]

When this plan was leaked, the Mexican denial was extremely half-hearted.

At the same time, the government was considering further taxation of the oil companies. In March the British Minister reported that 'the government contemplate the issue of a more onerous oil law which would undoubtedly prove to be very unfair to the existing companies, and apparently the President takes the line that he is not doing any harm to foreign capital so long as his decisions do not result in confiscation of their properties'.[46] By July these had become firm plans, and in August the British Minister reported that 'Finance Department is now working at claims for backtaxes against all the oil companies'.[47] It is possible that such plans would have led to crisis had the labour question not already done so. Certainly they contributed to the companies' own feelings of isolation in Mexico.

Meanwhile, in May 1937 the companies replied to the oil-workers' pay demand. Against the workers' demands for wage increases totalling 65m. pesos the companies offered 14m. It is not clear whether this offer was made in the expectation that it would be accepted. In March 1937 the British Minister reported that 'men are proving intransigent over negotiation for collective contract, are evidently looking forward to general strike for which warnings have been sent to local unions to be prepared'.[48] On the following day the Embassy was even more explicit:

Van Hassalt [El Aguila manager] feels that it will be impossible to avoid a strike in May which will very likely be general. The government are most anxious to avoid trouble with the unions and they will therefore probably demand impossible concessions from the companies and Van Hassalt anticipates that we may then have to dig in our toes and take the consequences . . .

The President seems convinced that the government could handle any quantity of oil which they might have on their hands and that therefore there would be no difficulty whatever of the government developing the Poza Rica field themselves and disposing of the production.[49]

The companies' forebodings proved to be justified, for the oil-workers struck at the end of May and almost immediately appealed to the government for arbitration. The government then called upon a commission of experts to look into the situation. Since this commission (of three) included Silva Herzog, who was known as an oil nationalist, it might appear that the government was looking for a report which would prove unacceptable to the companies. In August 1937 Under-Secretary Beteta told the British Minister that

although attitude of oil companies was justifiable from their point of view, they and Mexico were engaged in a struggle of a politico-economical more than labour character and conflicting interests were irreconcilable. Presence of big foreign companies was symptomatic of semi-Colonial system of Mexico incompatible with economic sovereignty of Mexican nation. 'We have conquered Mexico politically, we have still to do so economically'. Under-Secretary of State for Foreign Affairs does not speak for the government but represents current of opinion influential in government circles.[50]

Certainly, when the commission reported, it provided a massive indictment of the operations of the oil companies in Mexico as these appeared to the more radical supporters of the government and went clearly beyond the terms of reference that would have been appropriate for a purely labour dispute. Some of the major points made were the following (numbers as in original):

1. The main oil companies which are operating in Mexico are part of massive economic units owned by British or Americans.
2. The principal oil companies operating in Mexico have never been connected to the country and their interests have always been foreign and on occasion in effective opposition to those of the nation . . .
6. The great oil interests have influenced the political events which took place both within the country and internationally on more than one occasion . . .
24. The prices at which the companies sell their oil products in Mexico are considerably higher than those at which the same products are sold in the exterior . . .
29. The prices at which the oil companies sell their oil products in Mexico are so high as to constitute an obstacle to national economic development . . .
40. The oil companies have obtained in the three years [1934–6] very considerable profits and, consequently, it may be stated that, without prejudicing their situation in the future, for at least the next few years they are perfectly capable of accepting the demands of the STPRM up to a value of approximately *26 million pesos* [$7.2m.].[51]

While many of these recommendations were challenged by the companies, it is probable that they were honestly arrived at, although it is clear that Silva Herzog, the key member of the experts' commission, made little secret of his hostility to the companies; he later referred to company spokesmen as 'men without respect who were unaccustomed to speaking the truth'.[52] Beteta was certainly close to the mark when he told the British government that

most of the key men in the present government were drawn from a group of Revolutionaries who had a natural bias against big capitalistic enterprises which could scarcely fail to influence their attitude . . . [and it was intolerable for Mexico] to have the development of her natural resources subordinated to the decision of persons in another country or another continent who might for instance debate whether to increase production in Poza Rica or retard it in favour of some Venezuelan oilfield . . .

If there are signs of prejudice in the report, and he [Beteta] was quite prepared to admit that there might be, this was due to the difficulty which the experts had experienced in trying to penetrate to the truth through the complexities of the companies' accountancy which might have been designed specially for the purpose of concealing the real state of affairs . . . The conviction that he [Beteta] was faced with a misleading or incomplete picture of the position had been borne in upon him when he himself had investigated the question of the income tax paid by the oil industry and he knew for a fact that it weighed strongly with the experts.[53]

Although it will not be possible here to consider the accountancy in detail,[54] it is clear that the commission planned to go to the limit of the companies' ability to pay and probably overstepped it, although the actual cash involved may not have been the main issue. The companies were also worried by reports that this demand would only be the first of many. Thus, in September the British Minister reported that 'the communist Professor [*sic*] Jesus Silva Herzog, who was by far the most active of the three experts, expatiated on the vast profits made by the industry and abjured them [the workers] to regard the verdict as merely a stepping stone to further demands'.[55]

Up to this point, the story appears straightforward. Whatever the merits of the case, the report of the commission appeared to provide the government with the means to expropriate since the companies made it clear that they would not pay the 26m. pesos demanded. Moreover, the nationalisation of the railways in June 1937 was widely regarded (and apparently regarded by Cárdenas himself)[56] as a trial run for the nationalisation of oil. At this point, however, Cárdenas appeared to draw back. In October 1937 the British Minister reported that oil had become

the subject of a subterranean struggle in which external as well as internal influences are probably playing their part. There are many indications that the government would like to be generous and to condemn the companies to paying no more than their highest offer at the time of the strike. On the other hand, I cannot but see that it will be difficult, and perhaps impossible, for internal reasons, for them to award the men less than the Committee of Experts have recommended.[57]

These internal reasons were clear enough: any obvious concession from Cárdenas to the oil companies would strengthen domestic industrialists in their opposition to the pro-labour policies of the government and there were clear signs that Mexican politics was becoming increasingly polarised and that an incipient right-wing backlash could be detected, especially after the outbreak of the Civil War in Spain, which had a considerable psychological influence in Mexico.

On the other hand, this same consideration would have argued strongly against a policy of confronting the companies, which would have involved the risk of diplomatic intervention and the creation of a focal point around which opposition could rally. In September 1937 the US government made its first diplomatic representation on behalf of its oil companies. Moreover, it became increasingly apparent during the course of 1937 that the oil-workers were no longer (if they ever had been) under effective political control. After July 1937 there was a series of wildcat strikes in the oil industry and Cárdenas was increasingly losing patience. In October 1937 he stated that one of these strikes (at Poza Rica) 'is due on the part of the workers substantially to the lack of cohesion of the organisations which form the [STPRM]' and that the government felt 'anxiety [over] the deception which the workers may suffer at the hands of those who are within the ranks of the workers and who are serving antagonistic interests'.[58] At the end of October there was a further strike at Poza Rica and the men were simply ordered back to work. By this time the consequences of the men's action had been to cut off oil supplies to Mexico City and to cause considerable domestic disruption. Labour militancy of this kind clearly raised questions as to whether an expropriation could be made to work since, as Cárdenas himself pointed out to the oil-workers, no part of the commission's award would be paid in the event of an expropriation and the workers might, indeed, have to take a wage cut rather than a wage increase.

There was also the fact that the Mexican economy itself was experiencing increasing difficulties during 1937 and would certainly be seriously damaged by any confrontation with the oil companies. Cárdenas's original economic policies had been aimed at strengthening Mexican capitalism through a series of reforms which would fit in well with the populist orientation of the regime.[59] Public investment, which doubled in real terms under Cárdenas, was crucial to this strategy. As Hoodless pointed out, the *Plan sexenal* for 1934–40, which had been drawn up in 1934 but which was expressly endorsed by Cárdenas,

reinforced the role of the state as regulator of economic activity. Through a vast public works programme, the national economic infrastructure was strengthened, providing opportunities for young Mexican capitalists to earn easy profits with little risk . . . Cárdenas himself expressed the essential difference between Calles and himself as being a preoccupation with production as against consumption and distribution.[60]

It is unlikely that the conflict between the *desarrollista* and labourist elements in the Mexican Revolution, which was to be so important in the 1940s, was perceived with any real clarity in the mid-1930s, when it seemed that the middle-class and popular interests could be united against 'imperialism', Fascism and a few recalcitrant employers. By 1937, however, the cracks were beginning to appear. The militant labour activity of 1936 had led to a withdrawal of investment and the Mexican balance of payments position had become discouraging. In 1936 the government began efforts to get a loan from New York and future financing of this kind naturally required an accommodation with the oil companies. This was a further argument against confrontation.

In late 1937, therefore, several attempts at compromise appeared to come from Cárdenas himself. In November El Aguila was finally given permission, which had been held up for a long time, to develop the Poza Rica find. This was an important decision. For one thing, it appeared to go a long way towards solving the Mexican government's increasingly pressing economic problems. Since the oilfield was partially located under government property, Mexico was to receive a royalty which varied from 15% to 35% according to the area. As Suárez later recounted, 'this contract, clearly favourable to the national interest and signed by highly honest officials assured the federal government of an important and secure income which had not been anticipated in the tax laws'.[61] Suárez himself had personally blocked several attempts by General Tapia (the Secretary of Economy) to give control of the government's part of this area to a third party – the Sabalo Transportation Company had earlier come close to receiving a contract of this kind – on the ground that this would lead to wasteful overdrilling.[62] Moreover, this decision provides clear evidence that Cárdenas had not then made any decision to expropriate El Aguila; it is possible that he was hoping to divide the companies or perhaps it was a signal that the companies could expect better treatment from the Mexican government if they would only go along in public with the 26m. peso demand.[63]

Moreover, at the beginning of November, the British Minister reported that the government's

present intention is that the verdict shall embody the substance of the Experts' recommendations, requiring the companies to make additional disbursements

stated by the Experts to amount to 26 million pesos . . . Against this, however, an increase in the internal price of oil and petrol would it is believed be
authorised (which would in practice benefit the American companies more
than the Mexican Eagle), and the companies be given guarantees against
further strike action and facilities in regard to drilling permits, confirmatory
concessions and so forth.[64]

Although the British Minister advised the companies to seek some
compromise on these lines, they were in fact rejected out of hand. By
now, the conflict had become a matter of principle and the companies
felt that they could not back down. They also refused to consider a
Mexican proposal that they should bring in the government as a full
partner in the oil industry, with the implication that the Mexican government would in return make concessions on more narrowly focussed
financial issues.[65] There appears therefore to have been some justice in
Silva Herzog's assertion that

the companies were not concerned at all about the payment of the sum specified, but rather about the possibility that a precedent would be established in
Latin America of intervention in their finances by legal methods or otherwise;
they were not willing to admit that the government of a weak country would
fix financial norms lest this example be followed in other countries.[66]

It is also clear, however, that Cárdenas had not fully established the
credibility of his threat to nationalise; there was a marked difference of
opinion within El Aguila between the local management and the London directors who remained convinced until the end that Cárdenas was
bluffing. The US companies appeared to share the latter view.[67] The
companies in fact appeared to pin their hopes on the assumption that,
with its economic situation deteriorating, the Mexican government
could not afford drastic action.

   Indeed, it is difficult to escape the conclusion that, whereas in 1936
and 1937 it was the government which had been pressurising the companies, in late 1937 and early 1938 it was the companies which took
the more aggressive line. Their publicity within Mexico suggested a
desire to polarise the issue and face down the Mexican government
which, it was widely believed, could not afford the economic consequences of an expropriation and would in any case be unable to work
the expropriated properties. This polarisation, however, appears to
have crystallised Cárdenas's determination; if in late 1937 he had
sought an agreement with the companies (as well as becoming more
moderate in other areas), he was still far stronger than the companies

believed. The steps which he had already taken to assert control over the PNR (which was reorganised on 18 December 1937) were designed to increase government control whether or not there was an expropriation, and the slowness with which the government acted reinforced the conclusion of many Mexicans that the companies rather than the President were seeking confrontation.

The expropriation

Once the companies had openly attacked the award, Cárdenas was left with little choice. As he himself explained in a speech on 24 February 1938:

the companies [had] abruptly repatriated their funds and deliberately carried out a campaign of publicity in order to cause concern to businessmen and to bring about the restriction or refusal of credit to industry as if they were trying to use illegitimate coercion in order to provoke a definite solution for the benefit of their own commercial interests and to prevent the normal and correct development of the matter through the appropriate institutions.[68]

Indeed, it is clear that the activities of the companies had succeeded in raising once again the question of national sovereignty in the mind of the President.[69]

Moreover, the low-key position of the USA was important; just after the expropriation, the British Minister reported that 'Sr Rodríguez, a former Mexican President who interviewed the President on Wednesday last is of the opinion, which I fully share, that the inaction of US government has been largely responsible for the present situation.'[70] Nevertheless, while international conditions were important (as we have seen in chapter 2), the key factor was surely that Cárdenas had been forced into a corner, partly by his own earlier policies, but also by the rejection of several efforts at compromise after the 26m. peso award had been announced. Had compromise been reached, some form of nationalisation would probably still have followed but more gradually and probably less completely than in the event proved to be the case.

Indeed, and not for the last time, the companies vastly overestimated the importance of economic, as opposed to political, factors. Although the Mexican economy was in serious difficulty, the popular support which Cárdenas had built up, and the length of time which it had taken for the confrontation to develop, made the step of oil nationalisation politically safe. Nothing less than military invasion would have protected the companies and such a step would have been inconceivable in the international context of the time. No opponent of nationalisation within the country dared open his mouth, for

the support which the President received as a result of his decision had few precedents in the modern history of Mexico. It is true that the mass demonstrations which began immediately after 18 March, and which were repeated in the following years, were in part organised by the regime. However, they went well above the limits of the 'staged' mobilisations and became a massive demonstration of unity achieved by practically every group in the country – including some entrepreneurial groups and the ecclesiastical hierarchy – in support of the government's action . . . If the public collections and issue of bonds to pay for the companies taken over did little to solve the economic problems created by the nationalisation, they were impressive demonstrations of public opinion in support of the change of ownership in the oil industry.[71]

Certainly things had changed since 1934 when, following the establishment of Petromex to supply part of the domestic market, the government reluctantly took over full control 'due to the reluctance of the public to take up their half-portion of the shares in such a high risk industry'.[72]

Cárdenas and the companies

The Mexican oil nationalisation provided a paradigm in the sense that it contained nearly all of the elements to be found in later nationalist movements, many of which modelled themselves more or less consciously on the Mexican experience. At the same time, it was particularly dramatic precisely because it was the first major act of its kind – the expulsion of foreign oil companies from an underdeveloped country in the name of national sovereignty. Later expropriations would be easier because of the Mexican example.

Certainly it would be difficult to find anything good to say about the behaviour in Mexico of the oil companies, whose arrogance was legendary and whose attitudes made their eventual loss of position almost inevitable once Washington had become less willing to spring to their defence whenever they felt threatened. While it appears that the companies' ultimate intransigence did no more than hasten the effective oil nationalisation that was already being planned, it would be difficult to exaggerate the longer-term effect of their general unwillingness to respect Mexican claims of national sovereignty. No government would indefinitely tolerate a situation in which any attempt to change the regulations governing its oil industry became a matter of international concern and diplomatic intervention. The Cárdenas government chose to expropriate not because it preferred confrontation to bargaining, but because a bargaining relationship did not seem available. The companies consistently acted on the belief that they did not need to justify their presence to the Mexican government and that the threat of reprisal was more effective than conciliatory behaviour or any sensitivity to Mexican aspirations. In 1926 a British Foreign Office official complained that the oil companies' 'main idea of negotiation appears to be bluff, with graft if bluff fails';[73] since then they had learned nothing and forgotten nothing. Under these circumstances, expropriation was the only way in which national sovereignty could be defended.

The Mexican nationalisation resulted above all from the claim to effective national sovereignty. Discontent on the part of the Mexican government with particular aspects of company behaviour, while important, was subordinate to a greater discontent with the status claimed by the companies themselves. Nevertheless, changing circumstances in Mexico during the 1930s did much to determine how the processes of conflict led up to final expropriation. Thus it was important that the balance of supply and demand within Mexico was switching perceptions of the oil industry from a possible engine of export-led growth to a potential obstacle to domestic industrialisation. Some fears were expressed that the economic practices of the companies might lead to the premature depletion of existing Mexican fields just as they had led to the destruction of the Golden Lane fields in the early 1920s. Indeed, the Arbitration Commission had reported to Cárdenas that 'the exploration of new fields and the drilling of new wells is a problem of national importance which it is essential to resolve. If this is not done, there is a danger that Mexico will run short of oil in a relatively short period and will be obliged to import.'[74] By the late 1930s, some 60% of Mexican oil output was destined for the domestic market.

Even more important was the labour question. It is, of course, true that Lombardo Toledano, like Morones and Portes Gil before him, hoped to further his own political objectives while ostensibly supporting the Mexican proletariat. However, the militancy of the oil-workers themselves was a major factor. The crucial decision, in retrospect, may well have been STPRM's resolution to reject the companies' wage award of 1936, to threaten to strike and thus to involve the government.

Given Cárdenas's general pro-labour orientation and the extent of his alliance with Lombardo, it was evident that he would regard such involvement sympathetically. Once he decided to set up a commission of inquiry, he needed to appoint influential Mexicans who were well informed about the industry; in 1937, almost all Mexicans in this position were hostile to the companies and it was therefore almost certain that the arbitration award would be hostile. Once this commission had reported, however, compromise became far more difficult and the only chance revolved around the possibility of the companies publicly accepting the terms of the award while a way was found to reimburse them in secret. Such an agreement would have required a high degree of mutual confidence between government and company, and this was evidently lacking. Moreover, it is likely that at least some of the companies would have refused to accept an award of this kind for reasons of principle, and, even if the money involved was fairly small, principles are indivisible.

While the oil nationalisation certainly appears to have been a popular act, public opinion played a role which was essentially subordinate. There is no sign that there existed any general public opinion which played a real part in pressing Cárdenas to move against the oil companies; there were a number of sectional interest group demands (mainly from workers and consumers) which were channelled in a nationalist direction by the political leadership, but there was no inevitability that they should be so channelled. Indeed, some oil-workers' leaders were concerned to keep secret the terms of the companies' final offer to the workers (which was 19m. pesos) for fear that it might prove acceptable. For the Cárdenas regime as a whole, land reform and broader economic policies won far more support than oil, where the popular support for nationalisation appeared to be essentially defensive and protective of Cárdenas himself.[75] Indeed, the mass mobilisation triggered off by the oil nationalisation died away soon after 1938 and the political elite subsequently came to prefer far more conservative policies than those initiated between 1935 and 1937.[76] After the nationalisation, the oil-workers never in fact received the award of the arbitration commission. Moreover, between 1940 and 1952 Presidents Avila Camacho and Alemán pushed Mexico firmly back into the world capitalist orbit and there was even serious discussion of the possibility that the oil companies might return. The expropriation laid the foundations for a nationalist oil policy, but certainly did not guarantee that such would be pursued.

11

The formation of Petrobrás

The great depression set in motion a train of events which completely transformed the Brazilian economy. The past 50 years have been a period of rapid industrial growth while other sectors of the economy have also maintained a considerable momentum. This industrial growth and the consequent rise in oil consumption have brought the question of oil on to the political agenda in a way quite unknown in Brazil before 1930. Moreover, in the years after 1930 there developed two tendencies whose interaction was largely to determine the course of Brazilian politics and which were to take on new and important forms during the course of the post-1945 oil debate. On the one hand, there was the gradual development of a centrally directed technocratic state, as successive governments came to concern themselves increasingly with the pursuit of industrial development. On the other, the process of urbanisation and industrialisation generated possibilities of popular mobilisation and opportunities for radical politicians. Nowhere was the uneasy compromise between these two more clearly revealed than during the debate over Petrobrás.

In the years before 1930, and for some time afterwards, there was no oil issue. In 1930 Brazil's oil industry was almost classically underdeveloped. Oil consumption was less than a third of that of Argentina, less than one half of that of Mexico and oil made up less than 10% of Brazilian imports. Distribution was in the hands of foreign companies which scarcely troubled to provide a service beyond the coastline. There was no domestic refinery and a congressional attempt to persuade the government to alter its excise taxes so as to encourage local refinery construction was opposed in 1926 by the Domestic Finance Committee.[1] Exploration for oil was hindered by the legal framework of the time, which emphasised the rights of the provinces and of local landlords, and by lack of interest on the part of foreign companies.[2]

Oil and national security 1930–41

During the 1930s, however, this position changed. This was due partly to the impetus afforded to Brazilian industrialisation by the depression and the consequent increase in local oil consumption and partly to the increasing centralisation of Brazilian politics under the presidency of Getúlio Vargas (1930–45). In the early 1930s there was some movement towards an active oil policy, mainly taking the form of a number of bureaucratic reorganisations which led up to the formation of the CNP in 1938.

Although there was general agreement within the government that a more activist oil policy should be pursued, there was no clear idea about exactly what should be done. As Martins put it, 'the official position was undecided. On the one hand, "nationalist spirit" was recognised; this suggested the country should "protect the wealth of its subsoil as a national asset". On the other hand, there were warnings against "extreme nationalism" which, it was said, brought about the decline in oil production in Mexico.'[3]

The main difference of opinion within Brazil during the 1930s was between 'technocrats' and 'entrepreneurs'.[4] The most vocal of the 'entrepreneurs' were private speculators interested in discovering oil but with a greater flair for publicity than for oil exploration.[5] The most notorious of these 'entrepreneurs', Monteiro Lobato, wrote a book called *O escândalo do petróleo,* published in 1936, which was a no-holds-barred attack on the government agency concerned with oil; this, according to Lobato, was engaged in trying to destroy entrepreneurial initiative and to leave the oil in the ground for the benefit of the 'trusts'. The book sold well and created considerable public interest and the government reacted by setting up an inquiry which found against Lobato.

Although it is true that entrepreneurial groups were fairly weak in Brazil during this period and the state bureaucrats relatively strong,[6] the problems raised by this conflict appear to relate more to the structure of the oil industry than to anything more sociological. The fact was that Brazil was a high-cost environment for oil exploration and very little success could be expected at so early a stage. The government agency was certainly inefficient, if only because of its lack of experience, but the domestic private sector had no real solution to this. As Soares Pereira pointed out, 'In fact, Lobato did not see that the dimension of the problem made private enterprise solutions unviable for Brazil. It was possible in other areas, under other circumstances such as the existence of abundant capital allied with favourable geology. In Brazil the oil geology was very difficult and private capital very scarce.'[7] The 'technocrats' in the state sector, on the other hand, had made a number of embarrassing mistakes during the early 1930s and the publicity that followed these, culminating in Lobato's book, made it more important for them to reassert control. The small state sector was in any case strongly nationalist.[8] However, while oil exploration remained important, the increasing interest shown by the private sector in oil refining soon became more pressing. As we have seen in chapter 3, oil consumption grew steadily in Brazil throughout the 1930s, and fiscal policy slowly changed in the direction of encouraging oil refining in Brazil. As a result, a number of small refineries were set up by Brazilians; these could import oil from low-cost non-integrated producers (such as Lobitos of Peru) and sell domestically. One Brazilian company, Brania, had even set up a local distribution network. These moves, together with pressure from some sections of the Brazilian government, led the major supplying companies to offer to set up refineries in Brazil.

Oil refining, however, was seen by the Brazilian military as a question of national security. By the mid-1930s the military influence on economic policymaking was already considerable and the army moved to the centre of the stage with the declaration of the Estado Novo and suspension of Congress by Vargas in 1937. Already in the 1920s

in coordination with the efforts of Ildefonso Simões Lopes in Congress, the jurist Solidónio Leite published a series of articles, on 'Petroleum and Duty in Brazil' in which was asserted the need for state intervention in the sector and for the nationalisation of reserves. These articles were inspired directly by General Olímpio do Silveira who represented in this case the thinking of the Estado Maior of the army.[9]

This orientation became stronger in the 1930s. In 1936 the Estado Maior created a Departamento Nacional de Combusiveis and in the same year General Horta Barbosa wrote to the Minister of War indicating that Brazil needed access to oil in time of war and pointed to YPF of Argentina as an example to be followed.[10] Horta himself was an officer well within the mainstream of army thinking; according to

Wirth he was 'a professional officer of the old school, an apolitical general who now staked his career and reputation on creating a petroleum industry'.[11]

Following the establishment of the Estado Novo, Vargas set up a secret commission to look at oil policy. The head of the committee, Fleury de Rocha, was influenced by oil nationalists who wanted to impose total state control but felt it prudent to put forward a more limited recommendation. Thus he proposed that the government set up a new agency, the CNP, with extensive powers over all sections of the oil industry although these did not include a monopoly of exploration for oil or the expropriation of existing holdings. Although there were some misgivings about this recommendation within the government, Vargas set up the CNP in 1938 and gave control to Horta Barbosa. As Wirth put it, 'the government . . . sprang its national oil legislation deliberately before foreign and domestic pressure groups could mobilise'.[12]

It is clear that the security question was paramount in the thinking of the key officers. As a later government document put it, 'the military conception of the oil problem, which was expressed in terms of national security, was decisive and served as a touchstone for the formulation of the most nationalistic path'.[13] Cohn added that 'In 1938, in the prevailing international conditions, this conception imposed itself upon the military. As a result, the military came to be entrusted with tackling the problem.'[14] In 1938, with war in Europe highly probable and a conflict with Argentina also likely, the CNP was seen as the answer to a security problem rather than as an approach to a longer-term strategy. This question of security could also be seen in the operation of the agency; CNP was given a degree of administrative autonomy which was quite exceptional by contemporary standards[15] and which incurred the bureaucratic jealousy of other agencies.

The CNP's first step was to try to take the steam out of an earlier conflict. In 1939 it drilled for oil in Bahia in the place where its existence had long been suspected (and had previously been denied by the state) and, upon making a discovery, reserved future exploration in the area to the CNP. In Pedro de Moura's words, 'under the circumstances, it was necessary to get rid of accusations of sabotage, unpatriotism and complaints, stifling any rebirth or resurgence of agitation on the basis of mystical obsessions'.[16]

Even more important, Horta blocked the attempts of the private oil companies to build further refineries in Brazil. By this time a number of refinery projects had reached the preliminary stage and there had been some support within the government for construction of privately owned refineries. However, Horta Barbosa himself was greatly influenced by his findings during a visit to Argentina and Uruguay in 1939; after discussing the question with Mosconi, Horta became concerned that the existence of privately owned refineries might limit the power of the federal government to regulate the oil industry and felt that they might act as Trojan horses for undesirable foreign capital. Although Vargas was unwilling to go so far as to make refining an official state monopoly at a time when he needed the support of the USA for his steel plans, he did agree to regulations which ended all activity on the part of private refinery companies.

As for the CNP itself and the army as a whole, there is no doubt that the objective was broadly a state-controlled oil industry even if not necessarily a state monopoly. As Martins summed up the army's attitude,

> private interests were seen as being in conflict with economic integration and the assertion of national power; as Juarez [Távora] put it, in conflict with the interest of the collective. It appeared that, at this time, the officers wanted a 'clean capitalism' without the calculating manoeuvres of Monteiro Lobato, the automatic profits that were earned by the refiners, or the rip-offs (*vols*) of the powerful 'trusts', without the 'egotism of the owner' as Juarez put it. This was also the attitude of the technocrats who took upon themselves the role of guardian of the public welfare, which was in danger of being pillaged (*engloutie*) by the 'enterprises' of Monteiro Lobato.[17]

This was to become an attitude characteristic of much of the post-war Brazilian state elite.

Nevertheless, despite its discovery of oil in 1939, the CNP proved to be better at keeping its opponents out of the oil industry than at developing it on its own. Partly because of the difficulty of obtaining supplies during the war, but also because of errors made by the CNP itself, Brazil in 1945 was still without a significant refinery and oil production remained negligible. These factors, together with Brazil's wartime alliance with the USA, decided Vargas against a policy of uncompromising nationalism. From mid-1941 onward Horta found himself on the defensive, blocking initiatives from Jersey Standard which was now keen to set up a refinery in Brazil; when his position became impossible, he eventually resigned in 1943. Subsequently a more liberal orientation was given to oil policy.

Oil and economic development 1941–8

Colonel João Barreto took over from Horta as head of the CNP in 1943 and began to press for a more liberal oil policy. Several factors appeared to be working in his favour. For one thing, as the war was drawing to a close, emphasis within the Brazilian political elite shifted from a concern with security to an interest in economic development. Brazilian industry had boomed under the stimulus of the war and oil consumption rose sharply, from just over 25,000 b/d in 1940 to nearly 89,000 b/d in 1950. Just as important, the wartime alliance with the USA, and US support for a steel complex at Volta Redonda, led to Brazilian hopes that after the war the USA might be persuaded to co-operate in developing the oil industry in Brazil. Thus in January 1945 Barreto asked the government to liberalise its oil laws and also to permit foreign companies to invest in oil refining, which could be done without any changes in the oil law. Despite some opposition from within the CNP, Barreto appeared to be able to count on support from Vargas. Thus, at the end of March 1945 the US Ambassador reported that 'the President indicated an interest in . . . the possibility that a joint Brazilian–American exploration company might be formed'.[18] The US reply, however, was in the negative; the State Department and the major companies were interested only in concession contracts and not in joint ventures.

In September 1945 the US Ambassador reported a further conversation, this time with Barreto, who wanted to change the Brazilian Constitution in order to permit foreign companies to explore for oil. Barreto

indicated that while this subject has been the subject of discussion in the Petroleum Council as well as between Barreto and President Vargas, he, Barreto, wanted to be on very safe ground and for that reason had referred it also to the Army and Navy and the Airforce . . . He seemed quite confident that all of these services fully appreciate the importance of developing a petroleum industry in Brazil, but he was not clear as to whether there would be any unity of thought or opinion as to how the present petroleum law could be changed to permit the entry of foreign capital.[19]

Later in 1945 the government prepared to open the refining industry to domestic capital and, although Vargas was overthrown by a military coup soon afterwards, this direction of policy did not immediately change.

Between the election of President Dutra (1946–50) and the opening of the full-scale oil nationalist campaign in July 1947, efforts were made within the political elite to find a formula that would permit foreign investment to re-enter at the lowest possible political cost. It was clear that an acceptable formula would be difficult to find. The major companies were not particularly interested in exploring in Brazil, and certainly not to the point of finding it advisable to offer terms that might have repercussions upon their arrangements elsewhere in the world. In 1947 the *Petroleum Press Service* reported that 'any development of Brazil's own oil reserves will be a useful contribution to the national fuel bill, although the estimates of prospective reserves make it unlikely that the country's importance as a market for foreign oil will be affected thereby to any major extent'.[20] Under these circumstances, foreign capital would enter only under conditions which gave them effective operating control.[21] Such conditions could not be acceptable to Brazilian nationalists.

It was clear, therefore, that the commission set up by Dutra in February 1947 to prepare a new oil law would have to make a choice. Anything less than a return to concession contract terms would fail to attract the major oil companies into oil exploration, while independent US companies were not greatly interested in Brazil. The supporters of liberal oil legislation believed that such legislation could be passed only in a climate of public acceptance; for this reason, General Juarez Távora, a former nationalist turned liberal, in April 1947 began a campaign of speeches in favour of allowing foreign investment to return to the oil industry. His main aim was to persuade the army.

Essentially Juarez Távora based his arguments upon the need to maintain the Brazilian–US alliance. The entry of foreign capital into the Brazilian oil industry was not an end in itself but rather a way of guaranteeing national security and the defence of the American continent. Since oil production was a matter of strategic importance, and since it could only be developed effectively through direct foreign investment, it was necessary to allow this. Although these views encountered some support they were attacked by Horta Barbosa, who in July 1947 embarked upon a series of lectures of his own. Horta argued that if the USA really needed Brazil to develop its own oil industry then it should lend Brazil the money to do so.

In Horta's view, the best way of developing the oil industry was through a state enterprise; this could construct the refineries necessary to provide oil products for the domestic market and could use the profits on refining to mount an extensive exploration campaign within Brazil. Horta was also concerned with national security and asserted that

In principle, I am not sympathetic to the ideas of an industrialising state. However, I am a firm defender of it in matters of energy and, particularly, of petroleum . . . although the crude oil market is competitive, refining is essentially monopolistic and is controlled either by the trusts or by the state.

Exploration, development and refining are parts of a whole, which is capable of ensuring political and economic power . . . It is not permissible to give outsiders the responsibility for an activity which is tied in with national security.[22]

Oil and political advantage 1948–53

Although Juarez Távora's views were welcomed by some members of the government, there could be no doubt that Horta's position was the more attractive to the army as a whole and his supporters were quick to capitalise on this fact. In April 1948 the Centro de Estudios de Defensa do Petróleo was set up and it began a full-scale campaign on the oil issue. As Wirth described it,

a small group of pro-Horta army officers . . . in mid-1948, in consultation with an advertising expert, made a massive direct effort to influence policy and opinion makers. Using a Military Club letterhead, they sent out 3,000 copies of Horta's lectures to a specially prepared list of recipients that included . . . all those judged capable of influencing public opinion.[23]

This appeal struck a deep chord within the Brazilian military which by the end of 1948 was 'overwhelmingly pro-Horta',[24] with the middle and higher ranking officers increasingly being won over against their formal superiors in the high command. This situation appeared to the British Minister as one in which 'the Army' supported liberal legislation but 'some 70 Generals' were nationalist.[25] General Sodré later wrote that

hundreds of army officers, faithful to the democratic traditions of our armed forces [*sic*], publicly pledged their support to the [nationalist] campaign. On 21 June 1948, in a telegram to General Estillac Leal, the entire command of the 3rd Military Region, 54 officers of the garrison of Santa Maria, declared themselves in favour of the state monopoly. These were followed by another 122 officers – students and 15 professors of the Army Technical School. Another 245 officers of the 1st Military Region also declared themselves in a collective telegram.[26]

Moreover, as far as the nationalist officers were concerned,

no other issue encountered such strong feelings among the military. Certainly
the issue aroused strong feelings throughout the whole of Brazilian society,
since the position taken by the military campaign was so uncompromising
and was adopted and defended so strongly and with such publicity. In order
to bring about victory for the position taken, it was necessary for the military
campaign to create a climate of war, an attitude in every respect similar to
that which was created when preparations were being made for a military
campaign.[27]

A persuasive explanation for the attitude taken by the military has
been put forward by Martins. According to this, the overthrow of Vargas and the return of Brazil to civilian rule in 1946 partially removed
the officer corps from the centres of power which they had enjoyed
under the Estado Novo and they were now looking for a way of returning. The quiet forms of pressure which had proved so successful under
the closed politics of the Estado Novo were now ineffective and army
officers therefore believed that the military needed to use forms of pressure that were more appropriate to a democratic form of politics. If the
campaign were successful, moreover, a state oil monopoly would give
the military something to control and would provide 'an extra political
resource to strengthen its position in the centre of the system'.[28]

The nationalist campaign went some way beyond the ranks of the
military itself. It involved a large section of the Brazilian middle class
which, often for similar reasons to the military, supported the idea of
a strong state vigorously promoting the goal of economic development.
The students union, the UNE, for example, played an important role
in the nationalist campaign in terms of organisation as well as numbers.[29] The campaign was also vigorously backed by a section of the
press; for example, there was the *Jornal de debates,* which was 'a struggling Rio weekly that needed a new issue as its middle- and lower-
middle-class readers lost interest in the usual fare of crime and corruption in the old Estado Novo. Circulation soared when it "discovered"
oil.'[30] There were also a number of other nationalist newspapers.

Finally, and perhaps most important of all (apart from the military)
there was the Brazilian Communist Party. This had made a promising
start to the new period of democratic politics. While unable to campaign openly, it nevertheless won 10% of the vote in the 1946 elections. At first the party was keen to maintain its legal status and consequently tried to avoid taking too many controversial positions. When

it was in any case banned in 1947, it came to focus on the oil issue partly out of opposition to the Brazilian–US alliance and partly in order to seek allies within 'progressive' sections of the army. Once it did join the Petrobrás campaign it came to play a major role. Its full significance is difficult to evaluate but according to the US Embassy,

the Communists created and led the attack against American capital in the development of Brazil. Through an extremely clever and able use of the press and by influencing the young people in schools and colleges they have made opposition to foreign capital appear to be of spontaneous origin rather than of Communistic origin. They developed the slogan 'Brazil for the Brazilians' which appears all over Brazil in the press and on posters.[31]

This judgement may have been exaggerated, but there could be no doubt of the Communists' energy in this respect.

While it is not possible to rely upon more than somewhat impressionistic evidence, it seems overwhelmingly likely that oil nationalism was essentially a middle-class issue. Soares Pereira described the campaign as mobilising 'all of the immense range of men who were representative of the Brazilian middle class'.[32] Few of the members of the working class were involved[33] and, according to Martins, 'Brazilian industrialists seemed more interested in a rapid solution to the problem than in the nature of the solution'.[34] At the same time, classically middle-class groups – the military, the students and the press – tended to support a nationalist line and were in all cases extremely interested in the issue. What was remarkable and distinctive about the issue was the informal alliance that grew up between much of the army and the Communist Party, although real power was always in the hands of the army. The nature of this alliance was perhaps summed up by the British Ambassador in 1948 when he reported that 'a nationalist meeting, led by seven generals but, according to eye witnesses, composed chiefly of Communist rabble' was broken up violently by the special police, thus winning further public sympathy for oil nationalism.[35] This unlikely political alliance would not last for long.

When considering this period it is important to distinguish between the operations of the oil industry and the politics of oil. When Dutra sent an oil bill to Congress at the beginning of 1948, without his own recommendation, it was already effectively dead; it was not acceptable either to the oil companies or to the nationalists and had clearly been overtaken by events. Nevertheless, as Brazilian oil consumption continued to increase rapidly, something needed to be done. Consequently, in May 1948 Dutra proposed a plan to Congress, known as the SALTE plan, which was based upon the need to resolve immediate problems, while the more fundamental questions remained pending. This plan was based on a proposal from a bureaucratic rival of the CNP, the DASP, which, although originally a budgetary agency, had expanded its functions and wanted to enter the oil industry.[36] The head of DASP was also close to Horta Barbosa and was therefore more nationalist than Barreto of the CNP. Essentially, DASP proposed to press ahead with a number of oil projects, including the construction of a new refinery, the expansion of an existing refinery (at Mataripe, still under construction in 1948) and the acquisition of a number of oil tankers.

These projects were to be financed by credits held by Brazil in Europe. The most important, a 45,000 b/d oil refinery, was financed from credits blocked in France. Dutra did modify the DASP's proposals so as to allow the two private refineries which had responded to the government's call for bids in 1945 to go ahead with their own small projects. The SALTE plan was then quickly approved by Congress and serious development of the Brazilian oil industry began.

From mid-1948 to the 1950 elections the oil issue was effectively dead in as far as it related to actual policymaking. Plans were now underway to make the country self-sufficient in refining and the state was preparing to take effective control of this sector; once this had been done there was little possibility of such control ever being relinquished. At the same time, it was certain that the oil companies would not be offered the long-term concession contracts which they required if they were to search for oil in Brazil. While the political drama continued in full swing, this reveals more about the politics of oil than about the policy opportunities open to Brazil.

Getúlio Vargas won the 1950 elections on a campaign that had very little to do with the oil question. He had stressed nationalism in a low-key way similar to that of his opponents but was clearly content to follow opinion on this question rather than to lead it. By 1950, however, the oil question had become complicated by a number of even more directly political matters within Brazil. Perhaps the most important change was that the focus of conflict within the army was shifting away from oil to questions of military participation in politics and the alliance with the USA. These issues greatly strengthened the military right wing. The Escola Superior de Guerra had been set up in 1949 by a group of officers who had taken an active part in the Second World

War and in the anti-Vargas coup of 1945. This group was particularly close to the USA: it opposed military participation in populist forms of politics and preferred instead to maintain the primacy of discipline within the military institution. It also stressed the importance of good relations with the USA. As late as May 1950 (when Estillac Leal and Horta Barbosa won the military club elections on a nationalist programme) this group was still in a minority, but the position changed abruptly with the outbreak of the Korean War in July. When an article in the *Revista do Clube Militar* accused the USA of starting the war in Korea, it triggered off a pro-US reaction which was to sweep the 'Democratic Crusade' to power in the elections of 1952.

The implications of this change were ominous for Vargas. For one thing, he had never been close to the ESG officers, who tended to associate themselves with the opposition UDN, for reasons which were personal and historical as much as ideological; for Vargas an alliance with this group was out of the question. Secondly, although most of the army was still nationalist on the oil question (a poll conducted in 1952 by General Lima de Figueiredo, President of the Commission of National Security, found that 80% of the officer corps was nationalist on oil),[37] this was no longer a particularly salient issue except for the minority of officers who opposed alliance with the USA. These officers could be dangerous allies of the President but they were necessary if he were to avoid even more dangerously complete dependence upon the pro-UDN officers. In fact, Vargas made Estillac Leal his Minister of War, which was a risky but probably unavoidable move. Finally, Vargas was himself basically pro-US, as indeed he needed to be in order to survive, but while remaining primarily a political tactician and conciliator he had nominal supporters on the left whose objectives were essentially contrary to his own. Vargas therefore had to manoeuvre between the ESG and his own left wing.

Neither were civilian politicians likely to be helpful to Vargas. The Communist Party, which had gained most from the oil campaign, was not about to allow its advantage to slip by meekly supporting Vargas's proposals. Moreover, the political campaign had now reached such a pitch as to make quiet settlement of the issue impossible. Yet Vargas could not put himself at the head of the extreme nationalists without playing into the hands of his more conservative opponents who still controlled a congressional majority. He resolved instead to search for a technocratic solution to the oil question.

Vargas set up a commission composed of technocrats and headed by

Rómulo de Almeida, which was to come up with a proposal on the oil question. Almeida recalled that

I consulted very few people, either civilian or military, and only when authorised by the President and on specific points. Various people sought me out, among them Oswaldo Aranha and Amaral Peixoto, to express their anxieties and to furnish political information. But it is important to emphasise that nobody within the close circle of the President put pressure on me or demonstrated any desire to be told about the nature of the project which was put together in conditions of exceptional secrecy.[38]

The model upon which the proposed project was based was that of the Volta Redonda steelworks.[39] This had been the first major state-led industrial project in Brazil and it had essentially been an act of Brazilian–US co-operation.[40] The technocrats were not seriously thinking in terms of a state oil monopoly, but of a government holding company with broad powers of discretion to seek foreign finance and technology where it best could.

Thus, when Vargas submitted his Petrobrás bill to Congress in 1951 he met opposition. He had proposed to set up a new state agency, Petrobrás, which was to be 51% government owned and would act as a holding company for further oil development and refining. Petrobrás would be financed by the transfer of existing state property, by selling 49% of the shares to the private sector and by a set of earmarked taxes on certain luxury goods. One of the main reasons why the private sector was invited to take such a significant share was to build up the capital of the state company. Oil consumption within Brazil was continuing to increase and the capital needed to find large oil reserves and to construct oil refineries capable of handling perhaps 300,000–400,000 b/d by 1961 was certain to be large and, the government believed, the full amount could not easily be secured from taxation (which was to have been increased considerably in any case). There were also various disadvantages with a total state monopoly in terms of its potential for operation in other countries[41] and in terms – it was thought – of getting congressional approval.

The provision of 51% state ownership and the large amount of discretion given to Petrobrás under the proposed legislation were not acceptable to the oil nationalists, who wanted tighter legislation to prevent 'backdoor' dealing with foreign companies. Martins argues that these objections 'were essentially political and revealed, in the last analysis, the nationalists' perception of the fragility of the political controls which they retained'.[42]

Technocratic solutions, no matter how elegant, were not acceptable to those who were fighting and appeared to be winning a political battle over the oil issue. Even so, it was not immediately obvious that nationalist objections would carry much weight when in January 1952 Euzébio Rocha of the PTB left wing introduced an alternative bill which provided for a total state monopoly of oil to cover all phases of the industry. Vargas's calculations were finally upset when in May 1952 the opposition UDN, which was traditionally liberal on economic issues, surprisingly declared its support for a complete state monopoly. This was essentially an opportunistic anti-Vargas move; since it was believed that some form of state monopoly would eventually be set up, it was important for Vargas's opponents to deprive him of as much political capital as possible for bringing it into existence. It was also important for the UDN to keep faith with the military which, as we have seen, was still nationalist on oil but now wanted the issue to be settled quietly. The military was largely satisfied by a decree of June 1952 which declared oil to lie within the area of national security.

The political implications of the UDN's manoeuvring were ominous for Vargas. If it had remained an ideologically pro-free-enterprise party, Vargas's brand of ambiguous, or moderate, nationalism might well have appealed to army officers who wanted a state oil company but who were increasingly unhappy at allying themselves with the Communists. As things stood, however, the UDN was able to maintain the support of the increasingly anti-Communist (but not anti-nationalist) army, while Vargas's own Minister of War (Estillac Leal) became increasingly isolated over the Korean War question and in 1952 was forced to resign by the senior right-wing commanders. By changing ideas on nationalism (and even outflanking Vargas), the UDN was able to concentrate its attack on areas where Vargas was weakest.

It was now even more evident than it had been in 1948–9 that this was a debate which had more to do with politics within Brazil than with the possibilities of actual policymaking. The issue was now about who was to control Petrobrás and who was to take the political credit for having created it. Thus, once it had made its gesture, the UDN prepared to compromise with Vargas. While the left continued to try to mobilise around the Petrobrás question, Vargas later in 1952 made a deal with the UDN according to which the Petrobrás bill would be amended so that the state would take a definite monopoly of the whole refining industry except for the two private plants already in operation. Following this agreement, a modified bill was sent to the Senate where a number of outspoken liberal Senators were able to amend the law again, this time in a less nationalist direction. These amendments were then cancelled when the bill returned to the Chamber and the bill creating Petrobrás passed into law in October 1953.

Petrobrás formally began operations at the beginning of 1954. In April Petrobrás received the government oil holdings and assets, which up until then had been managed by the CNP which had (after the modification of the SALTE plan in 1951) finally won its bureaucratic battle with the DASP. These were valued at $165m.[43] and included a certain amount of drilling equipment, a small refinery in operation and a larger one still under construction, and a tanker fleet. The immediate aftermath of the Petrobrás campaign was disappointing for the nationalists; the real beneficiaries of the politics of the period were the UDN and those army officers most closely associated with them who carried out the anti-Vargas coup of 1954. The Petrobrás campaign reasserted the importance of the military in Brazilian politics and showed the political limitations upon the kind of moderate nationalism pursued by Vargas. Brazil was already beginning to polarise and Vargas was one of the first casualties of this polarisation.

Oil policy and oil nationalism in Brazil

From a technocratic point of view, the creation of Petrobrás was quite unexceptionable. The national bank and holding company, the BNDE, which was of similar economic importance, was created by Vargas in 1952 and its creation was a technocratic affair, barely noticed in Brazilian politics. Earlier, during the war years, the Volta Redonda steel project had laid the basis of the Brazilian steel industry on terms in which the state, while retaining essential control, worked closely with a number of private companies. During the same period the Brazilian government canvassed similar arrangements for oil with the US government only to be told that a middle way was unacceptable in the oil industry. If Brazil was to maintain a significant state presence in the industry, then this would have to involve establishing an effective monopoly of the production and refining stages. Brazil was too unimportant a market for the major companies to be willing to make exceptions. Given the nature of Brazilian economic development – its lateness, the central role of the state, the ideology of import substitution – the creation of Petrobrás under such circumstances could cause little surprise.

The real significance of the Petrobrás debate, therefore, was political. In earlier and perhaps romantic accounts of the period, the Petrobrás campaign was presented as consisting of a mass mobilisation of public opinion against foreign imperialism in the shape of 'the trusts'. Later, revisionist historians – notably Martins – have stressed how important the army was in the campaign, how the pro-US orientation of the army remained essentially unchanged and how important the Communists were in organising popular support for oil nationalism. While the popularity of the campaign was evident enough, in organisational terms the Petrobrás campaign consisted of an 'impossible alliance' between the Communist Party and the army. Yet whereas the Communist Party regarded the Petrobrás campaign as a victory and as a springboard to further success, many officers regarded their new bedfellows with profound distaste. When the army was forced to choose, order, discipline and alliance with the USA won out over populist nationalism both in 1954 and in 1964. In that sense, the Petrobrás campaign was inherently deceptive; a community of interest which was only minor and relative came to be seen later as something far more important than it really was. The Communists had fought for a military and elitist objective; they could not expect such support to be reciprocated when more genuinely popular objectives were in question.

The ultimate victor, therefore, was the Brazilian army. In 1938 the army had taken control of the oil industry on the ground of national security. When in the mid-1940s security arguments appeared to point in a different direction, they were able to put forward a different claim for control – this time in the name of economic development. Such development was to be brought about by a state elite willing to manipulate popular support if necessary but in no sense interested in following the views of the majority when these conflicted with their own. Moreover, the army benefited directly from the setting up of Petrobrás: thus in July 1960 *O estado de São Paulo* complained that 'one has the impression that instead of belonging to the country, Petrobrás is a monopoly of the army. From the information that has been furnished to us, more than 200 officers of our army are working in Petrobrás.' Perhaps the army had taken the slogan 'O petróleo e nosso' rather too literally.

12

The nationalisation of the IPC in Peru

The history of the International Petroleum Company in Peru was so varied and dramatic that it provided at one time or another a case study of nearly every conceivable permutation of host government – oil company relations. Essentially, the IPC took over a dubious legal title in 1913, used force and bribery to establish itself in the country and earned fabulous profits in the 1920s and 1930s. Subsequently its fortunes changed and IPC spent nearly a decade under economic pressure and political attack before its final expropriation in 1968. The expropriation was dramatic and the refusal of compensation led to serious conflict between Peru and the USA which, as we have seen, ended in 1973 with a compromise agreement which gave IPC only a fraction of the market value of its holdings.

The IPC in Peru: from exporter to supplier of the domestic market

The periods before and after about 1952 were very distinct. In the first period IPC, as an exporting company, was able to buy political support and retain extremely high profits for itself. Between 1913 and 1922 it was able to establish for itself an exceptionally favourable long-term position in Peru by its willingness to offer ready cash to governments with immediate financial problems. The pattern of offering short-term loans in return for favours was established early and continued until late. In 1938 the British Minister remarked that 'the demand for a loan from this company is nothing new. Indeed, the International and the Cerro de Pasco Copper Corporation have for years been the cows supplying milk for the government's necessitous children.'[1] This pattern continued for at least some time after the war. Thus, in 1946 IPC lent a further $5m. to the Bustamante government and in 1953 it made a

$10m. loan to Odría's government at the same time as a minor increase took place in the domestic price of gasoline.[2]

While IPC remained a central part of Peru's export economy, its position was secure. By the late 1930s, however, the centre of IPC's output, the La Brea field, had reached the limits of its production and further exploration by IPC – notably in the Sechura Desert – did not yield significant results. IPC did not explore offshore but in 1957 it did take a 50% share of the Lima field operated by the Lobitos Oil Company and worked hard to expand output from there. Although this did pick up to some extent, it did not keep pace with growing consumption. Consequently, IPC needed to devote an increasing proportion of its production to the Peruvian home market; after 1962, when Peru became a net importer of oil, almost the whole of IPC's output was consumed domestically. By this time IPC was both politically exposed (as by far the largest supplier of the Peruvian market) and able to produce only a more-or-less fixed level of output. IPC's financial position and economic power consequently declined.

Within the home market, prices had been frozen by President Prado in 1939 and remained controlled by the government. Whereas earlier Peruvian presidents felt able to avoid serious conflict with the company by allowing taxes to remain low and seeking loans from the company when in difficulty, post-war governments could less easily protect IPC's position when this involved raising prices and antagonising the all-important urban electorate while also provoking public disturbances which might trigger off a military coup. After the Second World War, the price issue became increasingly central to the unfolding of the IPC conflict. As Goodsell has pointed out, IPC lobbied incessantly for price increases after 1949 with very little result; there were small price increases in 1953 and 1954 but these did not amount to a great deal and by the late 1950s the issue had become a serious one for the company.[3]

Another source of difficulties for the company was its inability or unwillingness to maintain good relations with key members of the Peruvian elite. A part of the reason for this lay in the fact that the company's high-handed behaviour during the First World War still rankled. This was particularly true of the Miró Quesada family which owned *El comercio,* the most important newspaper in Peru and the most consistent and outspoken critic of IPC. Other important Peruvian families, such as Beltrán and Gildemeister, were supporters of laissez-faire policies but naturally felt more strongly on the issue when they were

Table 12.1 *Oil production and exports in Peru*
(m. *barrels, annual average*)

	Production	Exports	Internal consumption (including imports)
1935–9	16.3	14.0	3.0
1940–4	13.3	10.1	4.2
1945–9	13.6	6.4	6.5
1950–4	16.1	7.2	9.9
1955–9	18.3	6.8	14.5
1960–4	20.9	4.8	21.9
1965–9	25.1	3.3	31.3

Source: Thorp and Bertram, *Peru 1890–1977,* pp. 164 and 222.

themselves in a position to benefit from such policies (see chapter 4). As the interest of the elite in the domestic oil industry declined, so did its enthusiasm for IPC, particularly as the company increasingly became a political liability. Beyond these factors it is likely that more personal questions were also important but it is difficult to provide conclusive evidence about these. One interesting episode occurred, however, when in 1960 the Prado family (one of whose members was at that time President of Peru) formed a joint venture with Standard Oil of California to construct a small domestic refinery which would compete with IPC. The company opposed this project and persuaded the 1962–3 military government to cancel some of the tax concessions given to the refinery. For this reason the project did not prove profitable and the Prado family never in fact put up their share of the money. IPC's relations with Belco Petroleum (itself well connected with the Peruvian elite) were also bad. It is in fact likely that IPC's concern to keep a near monopoly of the Peruvian industry and its generally uncompromising attitude helped to deprive the company of valuable political allies.

If these factors were at the root of the question, it was IPC's legal position that quickly came to dominate the forefront of the debate. In fact, IPC itself first raised this question in 1957 by seeking to transfer its legal status from that prevailing under the *laudo* of 1922 to that of the petroleum law of 1952. The 1952 law was more advantageous both because the *laudo* was due to expire in 1972 and because the 1952 law offered specific guarantees over the domestic price level which the *laudo* did not. As a consequence of IPC's request, the pricing and legal questions interconnected. The Prado government (1956–62) was at first unwilling either to allow legal transfer or price increase. As IPC continued to press for a domestic price increase, Prado tried to disguise such an increase and smuggle it through Congress, but this move was discovered and aborted. IPC then, in 1958–9, cut back on its activities and began to lay off its workers.⁴ At this time Peru was already in the middle of an economic crisis and Prado in 1959 called upon Pedro Beltrán, an orthodox economist and hitherto a critic of the government, to become Prime Minister and impose his remedy. Among other moves, Beltrán allowed IPC to raise its domestic price substantially and recommended to Congress that it should be allowed to convert its status to concessionaire under the 1952 law.

Political developments 1959–63

This move almost proved fatal to the company. Congress could not effectively oppose the price increase (or any of Beltrán's other measures, many of which proved unpopular) because this was carried out by decree, but it could certainly use the legal question to attack the company. Consequently a relatively small group of vocal nationalists within Congress sought to cash in on the unpopularity resulting from a large rise in the price of gasoline by bringing up the whole legal history of IPC which the *laudo* of 1922 appeared to have settled. Opponents of the company were given free rein to develop their own version of legal and commercial history according to which IPC's position in Peru had always been illegal and could not be regularised by the transfer which the government proposed.

This was not the first time Congress had taken a nationalist stand on an oil question. Given the extreme weakness of political institutions within Peru and the consequent tendency toward political fragmentation, it was rarely difficult for congressional opponents of any government to deny it a majority on a controversial piece of legislation. Moreover, opposition to an unpopular foreign company could provide an excellent focal point for any congressional opposition. Opposition was a role which Congress was always able to play. It opposed a number of contracts between the Peruvian government and foreign companies (including the IPC contract) in the early part of the century⁵ and wrecked President Bustamante's proposals of 1946 to allow IPC to explore the Sechura Desert. Even during the Odría period of semi-dictatorship, Congress still modified the proposed petroleum law quite substantially. In institutional terms, therefore, this attack upon IPC in 1959–60 was nothing new.

It is difficult to evaluate this nationalist opposition in broader and more political terms although it is clear that one of its main features was a dislike of the Prado government and its alliance with APRA, the former radical party which had now made its peace with the Peruvian establishment. It does not appear that the leaders of the nationalist campaign (Benavides Correa, Montesinos and the Miró Quesada family) had a great deal of independent strength, although the support of *El comercio* was very important. The nationalistic attack, however, did have the huge tactical advantages of uniting the government's political opponents. These included the main opposition party, Acción Popular, and, even more important, sections of the army which had their own reasons for wishing to embarrass Prime Minister Beltrán. Consequently, in February 1960 the high command of the army declared its opposition to the proposed terms of the conversion of IPC's legal status and their dissatisfaction with its existing status, effectively killing the proposed settlement. IPC maintained its existing status on a provisional basis, and nobody was satisfied.

The years 1959–63 cover a fascinating period of Peruvian politics. They were years of very rapid economic growth, particularly concentrated in manufacturing, construction and urban services. For politicians of the moderate and extreme left they seemed to be years of great political opportunity. The traditional radical party, APRA, was now in alliance with an openly conservative government and there seemed to be great opportunities for appealing to newly emerging groups for which the existing parties would have little appeal. Thus, a whole series of left-wing groups were formed at about the same time – the Christian Democrats in 1959, the APRA *rebelde* in 1959 and the Movimiento Social Progresista (MSP) in 1960 – while the Cuban Revolution added a new dimension to politics on the left. Under these circumstances, it is likely that the anti-IPC nationalists were staking a claim to some of this potential new popular support.

If one considers the election results of 1962, however, it is striking how little headway the oil nationalists made. In the election, the broadly conservative vote came to 60%. This included 32% for the *aprista* party and 28% for the party of ex-dictator Manuel Odría (UNO). For APRA, this represented something of a decline on previous expectations, but for Odría it represented a considerable increase. Belaúnde's moderately reformist Acción Popular, which had polled well in 1956, achieved a slightly lower percentage (31.12%) in 1962. Belaúnde had opposed the IPC conversion in 1959, but it was clear that he had done so for tactical reasons and that he was basically interested in a settlement with the company. The parties of the left fared badly, although the Christian Democrats, with 3% of the vote, did better than the other splinter parties. Ruiz Eldredge of the MSP, who had campaigned almost exclusively on the IPC question, came bottom of a nine-man poll with 9,000 votes from the entire Peruvian electorate – just 0.53% of the vote. As a result of this election, the major leaders of the anti-IPC campaign in Congress (Benavides Correa and Montesinos) retired from or were forced out of politics.

Electoral statistics, therefore, do not support the view that Peruvian voters held strong nationalist views on IPC in 1962–3. Indeed, they are as dismissive of this hypothesis as it would be possible to be. Moreover, there is no sign that (mainly rural) illiterates, who were not able to vote, cared any more strongly about the issue than did the electorate itself. The 1963 elections (which took place after the 1962 elections had been annulled by the military) resulted in victory for Belaúnde after most of the parties of the left had withdrawn in his favour. During the election campaign Belaúnde did promise to settle the IPC dispute 'within ninety days', but he said nothing about the method by which he would do so. Moreover, during Belaúnde's presidency the electorate continued to be unwilling to support anti-IPC nationalists. When support for the governing coalition began to erode, it was the conservative opposition (APRA and UNO) which benefited most.

None of this is to argue that IPC was popular with Peru. Questionnaire data suggest that IPC in particular and foreign companies in general became far less popular as the 1960s wore on and as the Peruvian economy became increasingly dominated by foreign investments,[6] although it is not clear how far the IPC issue contributed to this change in sentiment and how far it reflected it. Thus, there can be little doubt that the military regime of General Juan Velasco did increase its popularity by confronting IPC in 1968–9. Against this, however, it must be said that this popular sentiment appears to have been extremely diffuse and that it was easily 'containable' by Peru's civilian political leadership (of all major parties), which had no desire to bring upon itself the economic setbacks that confrontation with the company would involve.

The story of the 1960–8 period, therefore, is not primarily one of rising popular nationalism directed against IPC, although it is probable that there was some adverse change in public opinion during this time; rather it shows the inability of successive governments to reach a generally acceptable settlement with the company. The failure of several attempts at solution eventually helped swing the initiative to a group of military nationalists who were willing to act decisively against IPC. The military veto of Beltrán's proposals effectively shelved the IPC issue until the 1962 elections. These elections were followed by a military coup and the 1962–3 military government did not take any kind of stand on IPC, despite the hostility which the army commanders had earlier shown to Beltrán's proposals. It is likely that this inactivity was partly due to the regime's desire to use the American business community in Lima to win the favour of the Kennedy Administration in Washington whose initial reaction to the coup was hostile. In any case it seems quite clear that there was an internal dispute within the military at this time in which the IPC case figured. Some officers apparently wished to confront IPC and to use this and other policies to generate sufficient popular support to 'manage' the 1963 elections in favour of a military man.[7] The dominant faction of the army, however, intended to keep its promise to hand over power to an elected civilian in 1963 and thus avoided taking any controversial measures in the meantime.

Belaúnde and IPC 1963–8

With the election of Belaúnde in 1963, settlement again seemed likely. Belaúnde was something of a political outsider, coming from the southern city of Arequipa, but he was no radical. He was, instead, extremely keen on regional development within Peru and enthusiastic about the Alliance for Progress which, he believed, would provide the necessary funds for large-scale public works without creating too many political difficulties. Thus, there can be no doubt that Belaúnde wanted an agreement with IPC, but he was now caught between his own earlier rhetoric and the intransigence of the company. It is also true that both Washington and IPC would have preferred to deal with APRA than with Belaúnde, who came to be regarded with considerable (and quite unjustified) suspicion in these quarters. Moreover, the conservative opposition (including APRA) now controlled Congress and were very willing indeed to use the IPC issue as an attack upon Belaúnde as part of their overall strategy of obstruction of the government. Thus, as the US Embassy remarked late in 1963: 'It was clear that Executive

Branch is not prepared to take sole responsibility for reaching agreement with company because of its suspicion, perhaps well founded, that opposition would use "petroleum flag" to rally popular support against [the government].'[8]

Even so, settlement might still have been reached had IPC been willing to make any real concessions to the Peruvian position. Belaúnde would have been willing, in 1963–4, to allow IPC to remain as operating manager of La Brea for 25 years in return for the formal return of the oilfields to Peru. IPC, however, still insisted on 'full control' and limited its offer to a slightly higher tax rate.[9] This was not acceptable to Belaúnde.

Meanwhile, it had become the established view of almost everybody within the Peruvian political system that the *laudo* award of 1922 was illegal. This view had been argued within the Peruvian legal community for a long time and was greatly strengthened by the army's declaration in 1960 that it regarded the *laudo* as null. No political group dared contradict the army and Beltrán responded by setting up a commission to look into the legal status of IPC. This reported that the *laudo* was indeed illegal but could not be repudiated unilaterally; instead, the Peruvian government should open negotiations with the company to try to establish a mutually acceptable legal regime for its continued operations. By 1963 this position had become common ground among Peruvian conservatives.

In 1963, therefore, Congress annulled the *laudo* formally and also repealed the law of 1918 which had enabled the then President of Peru to take the case to arbitration; it was more or less understood that a negotiated settlement would replace this old legal status. Against this perspective, however, there was a radical view, that IPC was liable for damages because it had made profits from the illegal exploitation of La Brea ever since 1922. No matter how these damages were calculated (and the amount varied from $50m. to the eventual claim of $690m.), they posed a growing problem for another potential solution of the La Brea question, namely expropriation with compensation while IPC continued to operate its other investments in Peru. In the nationalist view, the Peruvian authorities should enforce the law and confront the illegal company.

IPC meanwhile continued to resist any compromise. La Brea had now lost all economic importance and IPC began to cut down its drilling in the field after 1963. By now IPC's position in Peru had become wholly dependent upon the domestic market and the company was barely profitable; in 1961 IPC declared its post-tax profits to be no more than $8m. and they probably fell slightly afterwards. Barring a major new discovery (which seemed unlikely at the time) IPC could never again expect to make significant profits from Peru. Instead, it used its vertically integrated operation as a training centre for its younger executives.

Since they had little to hope for, IPC executives came to see the La Brea question as one of principle. If they voluntarily surrendered or were seen to be dispossessed of property rights which they claimed, the unfavourable publicity might well outweigh the advantages of a quieter life in Peru.[10] Under such circumstances, no agreement was possible with the government.

The impasse which resulted provided an excellent opportunity for opponents of the company to step up their pressures. None took better advantage of this than Ruiz Eldredge, the MSP leader, who responded to his setback in the 1962 elections by cultivating the military increasingly carefully. Thus, according to Pinelo,

the opportunity to mingle with the military came when MSP's leader, Alberto Ruiz Eldredge, was invited to speak to the students and staff of the Center for Higher Military Studies (CAEM). Ruiz Eldredge used this opportunity to the fullest. He developed close relationships with several CAEM officers – much to the annoyance of the IPC management, which had for years sponsored an annual four-hour review of the Peruvian petroleum industry at the Center . . . Eventually, an officer friendly to IPC attempted to alert the armed forces command to the close relationship between Social Progressist activists and CAEM officers, only to be told that the CAEM curriculum called for the officers to be exposed to all types of philosophical orientations, including Marxism. By the middle 1960s, even though IPC continued to send lecturers to the Center, the officers began to react more and more belligerently towards the company's general manager and his staff, thus indicating that to a very large extent the Social Progressists were able to persuade CAEM officers that their position was valid.[11]

It should also be pointed out that *El comercio* had extremely good contacts with the military and used them to promote a nationalist perspective on the IPC issue.

Thus, although opinion within the army did not crystallise until 1968, there was undoubtedly a growing current of military opinion against the company during the 1960s. The activities of the company itself, however, were only part of the reason for this change. Another important factor was the increasing dissatisfaction within the Peruvian military with what they regarded as unwarranted US interference in Peruvian affairs. First, there was Washington's initial refusal to recognise the 1962 coup,; secondly, there was the CIA's interference with the Peruvian military command structure during the counter-guerilla of 1965; and thirdly, there was Washington's refusal to supply supersonic aircraft to the Peruvian air force in 1967 and its cutting of aid to Belaúnde after the purchase of Mirages instead.[12] While hard evidence is difficult to find, it is likely that these interventions were more important than anything else in converting key army officers in Peru to a nationalist perspective. Washington had clearly exaggerated the degree to which it could continue to influence Peruvian politics by the granting of relatively small amounts of aid without generating serious side-effects. As a consequence of US policies, Belaúnde's followers had become bitterly disillusioned and a number of army officers became prepared increasingly to take strong measures to reduce the degree of US influence.

These changes were particularly important because they tied in with a change in the way these officers viewed Peruvian politics. Between 1930 and 1955 the Peruvian army was engaged in defending the social order against the challenge of the militant and apparently threatening APRA party. Subsequently the Cuban Revolution opened the possibility of insurrection from the left and Peru's own Castroists rose against the regime in 1965. With the defeat of this rebellion, increasing numbers of army officers came to concern themselves less with the need for short-term repression and more with the need to take advantage of the quieter political conditions to press for policies of social reform and economic development. Anti-IPC nationalism fitted in much better with this perspective than it had with the previous conservative orientation of the military.

The Act of Talara and after

Despite all of this, however, it was not until 1968 that the fate of the company was settled. Indeed, at the beginning of that year IPC's general manager held discussions with two prominent generals, including the army chief of staff, and 'found them well-disposed towards the company'.[13] However, IPC did become increasingly concerned about its position during 1968 and on 25 July made a new offer to Belaúnde in which it proposed to hand over the La Brea field in return for guarantees on its other operations. These were actually better than the terms which Belaúnde had wanted in 1963–4 and which the company had refused. There were probably several reasons behind this change of mind. For one thing, IPC was becoming increasingly aware that there was oil potential in the Peruvian Amazon on a large enough scale to turn Peru into a net exporter of oil. A major find in Ecuador in 1967 had increased foreign interest in Peruvian Amazonia, but IPC could not take any advantage of this until the La Brea question was settled. Moreover, there had been political changes in Peru as the 1969 elections came closer. Belaúnde's party was beginning to split and its more conservative section (led by the President) seemed to be moving into some form of alliance with APRA. In June 1968 APRA agreed to give Belaúnde 60 days of emergency powers to settle all outstanding issues. Since APRA had close links with IPC through the workforce, through some of its senior (Peruvian) management and also through the good offices of the US Embassy, it is likely that APRA prevailed upon IPC to make its offer at a time when too much congressional scrutiny could be avoided. It is also possible that APRA feared a military coup if the IPC issue was not satisfactorily resolved.[14]

Despite these favourable circumstances, the settlement was nevertheless abortive. The Act of Talara of 13 August provided for the handing over of La Brea to Peru, but in return the company was given a number of other concessions such as the right to expand its Talara refinery, to manufacture and sell lubricants and, it appears, to take a concession in the Amazon under a different name. At the same time, the US government began putting together a large package of aid for the Belaúnde government.[15] The almost complete discrediting of this agreement in the subsequent six weeks and the preparation and planning of the military coup of 3 October have been well discussed in the literature and will not be considered in detail here, but it will be useful to sketch out the main factors involved.[16]

The key factor was undoubtedly the fact that preparations for a military coup had been underway since the spring of 1968. A number of conspirators were in very good positions to seize upon any weaknesses in the Act of Talara in order to discredit the government. Zimmermann, the editor of *El comercio* and a close friend of Loret de Mola (who was head of the small Peruvian state oil company), General Maldonado Yáñez, the military representative on the board of EPF, and Pedro Beltrán, the editor of *La prensa* and opponent of the government's tax reforms, were all in good positions to influence perceptions of the

agreement. At the same time the government handled the tactical situation rather ineptly both by leaving a number of confusions and
ambiguities in the original agreement and by failing to respond effectively to the criticisms which followed. Finally, and most important of
all, opinion, particularly within the army, had now hardened decisively against IPC after its years of intransigence. It was therefore fairly
easy for opponents of the company (and the coup leaders) to whip up
opposition to the Act of Talara, the effect of which would have actually
increased IPC's presence in Peru. Thus, in late September, 36 senior
army officers held a meeting to discuss the Act of Talara; Velasco later
described the outcome as being 'Twenty-nine against the agreement
and seven traitors'.[17] The coup took place on 3 October.

The incoming military government immediately made it clear that
it would take some form of action against IPC, but it was still not
evident how far the new regime would go. It was clear that it would
repudiate the Act of Talara and seize the La Brea oilfield; on 9 October
it did so, and also took over the Talara refinery, but it was unclear
what would follow. Certainly, US business was not seriously worried at
this early stage, and regarded the military move as an act of showman-
ship which would be followed by a fresh set of negotiations. Diplomatic discussion with the USA and informal contacts with IPC continued for the rest of the year.

Clearly the issue of total confiscation seriously divided the government. The hard-line opponents of IPC (who included both President
Velasco and a group of radical colonels mainly recruited from the intelligence services) achieved an initial success in late October when Ruiz
Eldredge, the leader of the MSP, who also happened to be the senior
lawyer on the Lima bar, was entrusted with preparing the government's case against the company. This ensured that a recommendation
would be made for the *reivindicación* of IPC – in other words, there
would be full confiscation as part of Lima's claim for backtaxes against
IPC in respect of the latter's 'illegal' operation of La Brea since 1922.
The amount eventually claimed came to $690m.

A hard line against IPC also had considerable tactical advantages for
Velasco and the military radicals. This was partly because a nationalist
challenge to the USA would be likely to rally popularity for an incoming government which had no obvious source of civilian support, and
partly because decisive action of this kind would help to legitimise the
military coup (at least in the eyes of the army) by maximising the
contrast between the allegedly hopelessly compromised and ineffectual

Belaúnde and the bold new military leadership. Given that there was no obvious crisis in Peru in 1968, bold action of some kind was necessary in order to create a political consituency for the new regime. Thus, General Velasco was able to use the IPC issue to establish his own personal ascendancy. He immediately adopted a hard line against the company and successfully identified himself with the hard-liners (although there were a number of other senior officers who were also willing to take drastic measures against IPC). According to one report, 'the petroleum crisis and its symptoms (silence) have not afflicted all members of the Junta in the same way. In fact, General Juan Velasco Alverado has hardly spoken about anything else in the last few days than petroleum and the threats flying about in consequence.'[18] Consequently, Velasco was able to win the personal endorsement of *El comercio* which, under the influence of Zimmermann, believed that Velasco was the most determined nationalist on IPC. This nationalist reputation helped Velasco to combine support from the 'radical colonels' and the more conservative nationalists and therefore to prevail in the struggle for the leadership which followed the coup.

Once he had secured his position, Velasco moved decisively against IPC. In February 1969 the remainder of IPC's property was taken over and the government announced its final refusal to pay compensation (see also chapter 4). This final takeover coincided with a diplomatic initiative which aimed to co-ordinate this move with the establishment of closer relations with the Socialist bloc and with a concerted effort to unite Latin America behind the Peruvians. It is clear that these moves had been well prepared.

The IPC and Peruvian nationalism

By 1968 IPC had become an obvious target for a radical military regime which was no longer interested in the friendship of the USA. The company was economically weak; as it did not export oil, it had no easy way of putting pressure on the regime and its distinctive legal status severely limited the extent to which it could attract the support of other property owners. Indeed, as we have seen (chapter 4), other American-owned oil companies were willing to do business with Peru even after the confiscation.

It appears, moreover, that the company had made a series of political miscalculations. In 1963 IPC's unwillingness to offer La Brea to Belaúnde, at a time when such an arrangement could have been presented as a triumph for a moderate reformist government, was an act of extraordinary insensitivity. Jersey Standard could claim that it feared 'action elsewhere', but it hardly seems likely that its highly profitable fields in the Middle East or Venezuela would come under attack as a result of a minor property adjustment in distant Peru (and in Venezuela company property rights had been explicitly confirmed by the agreement of 1943).

Nevertheless, it is clear that IPC's position had become extremely difficult well before 1968. Certainly, in the 20 years prior to the nationalisation IPC's profits in Peru cannot have been high and were certainly very much lower than Jersey Standard's earnings from its major producing areas. No matter how the La Brea issue might have been settled, there was no good reason to believe that these profits would have been much higher in subsequent years. Accordingly, there was evidently at least a surface plausibility in IPC's strategy of amortising its investments as quickly as possible (most of its assets in Peru were written off well before 1968), avoiding any concessions to the government which might have been internationally embarrassing and hoping that Washington would be able to press Lima into a favourable settlement. The company could not expect to be popular, it was in no position to bargain from strength, it had relatively little to lose from even the worst possible outcome in Peru (the true value of IPC's holdings in Peru cannot have been more than $80m. on the most generous estimate) and, until 1968, it had in any case seen little sign of a genuinely dangerous political threat. Had it been more generous earlier, it might well have succeeded in reducing its political visibility but would also have threatened the limited profits that were being made. Under any circumstances, IPC's continued operations in Peru were of little value to either company or government and, had it not been for nationalist claims for recovery of the 'debt' from IPC, a plan of nationalisation with compensation might have appeared the obvious outcome. The legal problem, however, made this impossible.

The IPC expropriation also provides a fascinating example of the politics of oil nationalism. While the takeover was certainly popular, it would be inadequate to explain the measure in terms of 'public opinion'.[19] Instead, one must consider the complicated tactical situation which had existed during the previous ten years. Until 1968 Peru's dominant economic attitude stressed the importance of US aid and foreign investment to develop Peru. While this view was widely held within the political elite (military as well as civilian), it seemed clear that no Peruvian president would attempt to confront IPC. Moreover, when opposition groups took nationalist stands on the issue (as they did in 1959–60 and again in 1963–7) they did so more in order to embarrass the government than from any ultimate conviction. During this time public opinion may have been opposed to the company but it was too diffuse to have any major impact, and the issue played little part in electoral politics.

It is likely that 'public opinion' (i.e. the opinion of the Lima middle and lower middle class) did swing against the company during the 1960s and hardened significantly during 1968. However, it is extremely doubtful whether this alone would have been enough to bring about confrontation. Rather, the crucial event in the fate of the company was the military coup of October 1968. The nationalist army officers who were chiefly responsible for the coup found that the IPC in general and the Act of Talara in particular provided an excellent focal point for their political attack. The existence of a large and unpopular but relatively weak foreign oil company clearly provided an excellent target which could unite a coalition of nationalist forces which might otherwise have had great difficulty in coming together. In the longer term, the long controversy over IPC provided something of a catalyst in changing the perspectives of a number of key army officers away from a willingness to act as the 'watchdog of the oligarchy' and towards a more ambitious and more radical interpretation of the role of the military. These officers now wished to carry out reform and to cease defending unpopular targets in order (they hoped) ultimately to make armed repression unnecessary in Peru. Without the IPC case, this transformation might still have occurred, but its immediate political consequences would almost certainly have been less.

13

The nationalisation of Gulf Oil in Bolivia 1969

For some observers, the nationalisation of Gulf Oil appeared sudden and dramatic and a reflection of little more than the political instability within Bolivia.[1] It will be argued here, however, that while there is a 'spur of the moment' element in any decision there were also a number of longer-term aspects of this nationalisation and that there was a broad 'logic' to this outcome. There were three elements in this. First, there was the nature of the initial Gulf contract itself and its effect upon the state company, YPFB. Second, and more important, there was the existence and growing strength of the nationalist faction within the army. Finally, there was Bolivia's own revolutionary tradition and history. In order to bring these out it will be necessary to begin this account in the mid-1950s.

The MNR period

The MNR leadership, which came to power with the 1952 Revolution, had never been opposed to all foreign investment in principle, although it had taken strong nationalist stands at various points in its history. Moreover, President Paz (who had earlier been Finance Minister in the 1943–6 government) believed that there were plentiful oil resources in Bolivia and that these needed to be developed if the country was to escape from its unrewarding and dangerous dependence on tin. However, given the lack of success with which pre-1952 governments had sought to attract foreign oil investment, it was evident to the MNR leadership that active co-operation from Washington was necessary. Certainly Washington was eager to open Bolivia to foreign investment in oil, partly as a matter of general policy and partly as a symbol of Bolivian faith in Washington's economic remedies.

Thus, although the actual formulation of the 1955 oil code was carried out largely by North Americans, there was no reason to suppose that this was simply forced on an unwilling or 'bought' Bolivian government, or that it was unpopular at the time (see chapter 3). Alexander, indeed, asserted that 'virtually no political opposition was raised within the MNR to the granting of these oil concessions'.[2] Certainly the code was generous, but it needed to be, given the prevailing world surplus of oil, the high cost of exploration in Bolivia and the country's previous political history.[3]

Interest in Bolivia increased considerably after the Suez invasion, in 1956, which emphasised the political uncertainties of the Middle East, and a number of companies took concessions. All but one of these subsequently pulled out, having invested a total sum of $50m., while Gulf Oil spent some $80m. before discovering commercial quantities of oil.[4] After making its first find in 1960, however, Gulf followed this up with a run of success which took its reserves well above those of YPFB. Once this had happened, the difficulties and uncertainties of earlier exploration were quickly forgotten.

Until the later 1950s the state company itself played a significant role in oil development. For several years YPFB had benefited from the government's eagerness to strengthen the oil industry. While the hyperinflation of the period makes detailed accounting impossible, YPFB's rate of drilling, production and employment generation all increased after 1952 and by 1956 Bolivia had reached self-sufficiency in oil even after earmarking specified quantities of oil which had to be exported to Brazil and Argentina as part of a treaty arrangement. This position changed, however, with the stabilisation policy which was implemented in 1956. This cut heavily into YPFB's investment programme and forced it to reduce its activities. (YPFB's position will be discussed in detail in chapter 21.)

These developments inevitably had political consequences. These became more important as the unity of the MNR came under increasing strain. After the stabilisation measures of 1956, President Siles tried to impose austerity measures against the opposition of, or at best with only the reluctant acquiescence of, the Lechín wing of the MNR. Indeed, after 1956 Juan Lechín came to be seen increasingly as the leader of the left wing inside the MNR and was naturally willing to defend national pride (in the shape of YPFB) against the *entreguista* government and foreign imperialism (in the shape of George Jackson Eder of the Stabilisation Council as well as of Gulf Oil). Moreover, as frustration built up within YPFB, there developed a powerful nationalist lobby. This had allies on the left – the Communist Party attacked the

oil code in 1957, and in 1958 Sergio Almaraz published his criticisms
of it in his *Petróleo en Bolivia*. Almaraz's book influenced the intellectual
community in the Universities of San Andrés and San Simón; subsequently Almaraz left the Communist Party and went to work for the
left-wing of the MNR. The YPFB workforce, worried about their jobs,
also supported such nationalism; in December 1958 the fifth national
congress of oil-workers met in Sucre and called for changes to the 1955
code. They then followed this by going on strike in November 1959.

By 1959 the FSB (the right-wing opposition to the MNR), recognis-
ing a promising issue when it saw one, also came out against the oil
code. In the same year the national federation of oil-workers asked the
government to recapitalise YPFB. Moreover, within YPFB events 'intensified a feeling of frustration among the engineers of YPFB, who understood perfectly well that the first battle, that directed towards maintaining oil reserves, might be lost and the future of the state enterprise
would then become uncertain'.[5] The event that really polarised the
situation, however, was the USSR's offer of a loan to the mining and oil
industries in Bolivia.

As was discussed in more detail above (chapter 4), the offer was
made in 1958 and finally rejected in 1961 in favour of a higher level of
aid from the USA. As a result of these developments, relations between
certain members of YPFB (notably Mariaca himself, who subsequently
wrote a history of this period and, as we shall see, was an important
political figure) and the Lechín wing of the MNR became increasingly
close. Thus, in 1962 the Confederación de Obreros de Bolivia (the
Lechín-led MNR trade union) called for a change in the oil code, which
was also criticised by the MNR student assembly. During the same year,
Deputy Benjamín Miguel (of the right-wing Social Christian party)
presented a bill calling for YPFB to be given more acreage, but this
attracted little support.[6] By 1964 even President Paz himself found it
necessary to pay some attention to these demands, despite his statement that 'half his cabinet and half the country were Gulfmen', and he
appointed a nationalist oil minister who ordered Gulf to turn over
much of its unexploited concession area to YPFB. However, the US
presence in Bolivia was still so strong that the government found it
difficult to find a newspaper which would publish this decision and the
resulting decree, and both had to be presented to the Cabinet as *faits
accomplis*.[7]

During this period oil nationalism did indeed appear to be a lost
cause. US aid had long been crucial to Bolivia, but its importance

intensified after 1960. Thus, aid had risen from $12m. in 1954 to $24m. in 1955, falling to $14.6m. in 1960 but then rising to $32m. in 1961, $52m. in 1963 and $64m. in 1964. In every year except 1957 and 1960, US aid exceeded Bolivian taxation as a source of revenue for La Paz. Consequently, much of Bolivian politics came to surround access to American aid and aid administrators came to play a major part in the Bolivian economy.[8] No Bolivian president would jeopardise his connections with Washington in order to placate YPFB.

Nevertheless, the opposition to Gulf Oil which had manifested itself prior to 1964 played a decisive role in the eventual nationalisation. Mariaca's book, which recounted the history of the period, was widely read within Bolivia and greatly impressed General Ovando, who subsequently carried out the nationalisation.[9] For some time, however, Barrientos, who seized power in a military coup in November 1964, was able to bury the issue.

The Barrientos regime 1964–9

Indeed, as far as oil was concerned, Barrientos's position seemed particularly strong. The oil code of 1955 could be attacked and blamed on the MNR, while a moderate nationalist line might be acceptable both to the nationalists (who would at least get something) and to Gulf Oil (which could only expect worse if Barrientos fell). Thus Barrientos, while accepting helicopters from the company, was able to make public statements such as: 'Our oil code is an act of folly (*una ingenua*) for which my government was not responsible, but which was carried out by the *movimientistas* who were, in power, the worst *entreguistas* and servants of imperialism that the history of Bolivia has ever known.'[10]

This line was not without its danger for Gulf Oil. Barrientos might be able to run with the hare and hunt with the hounds, but there was no guarantee that his successors would be able to do so. Military nationalism lay deep in Bolivian politics; the army had already nationalised one oil company and many senior officers could still remember 1937. Take, for example, a speech by General Hugo Suárez, the Minister of Mines, in May 1968 (which was extensively circulated by the regime): 'The defence of our natural resources has always occupied a prominent place among the military . . . Toro . . . Busch . . . Villarroel . . . represented the genuine spirit of patriotic fervour.' Suárez went on to defend Barrientos and the need for a negotiated settlement with Gulf. Others might interpret these sentiments in a different way.

Indeed, the army's active concern in oil matters can be seen in several minor ways. For example, on 30 March 1967, General de la Fuente Soto sent a sharp enquiry to the Minister of Mines and Petroleum: did Parker Drilling have the right to move *combustibles* from Santa Cruz over the border to Paraguay? No such authorisation had in fact been given.[11]

The first major issue with which the Barrientos government had to deal concerned natural gas, which Gulf was already hoping to market in the Santa Cruz area. Gulf first suggested that it sell limited quantities of natural gas in Santa Cruz in 1962 and, although the offer led to Mariaca's resignation, nothing came of it. In September 1964, Gulf apparently wrote to the government offering to build a gas pipeline to Santa Cruz and to involve itself in any gas-based industry that might be set up, while at the same time selling gas to YPFB for domestic marketing. There were legal questions over whether the 1955 code actually mentioned gas, which added to the political dispute that centred on Gulf's apparent attempt to break into the domestic market and compete directly with YPFB.

The gas issue was raised publicly for the first time on 5 January 1965 by *La jornada* (a La Paz evening newspaper), which led the Minister of Mines and Petroleum to reply that, although gas was not mentioned in the Gulf contract, there was a need for 'a conciliatory interpretation . . . which will preserve the rights of YPFB'.[12] This reply led the leader of the pro-government Christian Democratic Party to say that his party opposed the 1955 code and that 'even though the code was not sufficiently clear when referring to "accessory or subsidiary concessions", there remains in force the principle that natural gas is the inalienable possession of the nation'.[13] Barrientos tried to defuse this issue by setting up the 'Gas Commission' (on 22 September 1965) which included Manuel Tejada, the General Manager of YPFB. Its terms of reference made it clear that some kind of joint venture with Gulf was under consideration. The commission reported on 28 March 1966. Its recommendation was technical in nature but did include the statement that 'the development of an industrial policy which is so complex and so basic and which involves both national interests and those of foreign markets or countries, will require constructive and mutual cooperation from private enterprise and state-owned or semi-state-owned business, irrespective of political and ideological positions'.[14]

From 1966 Gulf began exporting crude oil to Arica and thence to California. In the same year discussion of an export gas pipeline to

Yacuiba in Argentina got under way. In June 1966 Argentina agreed to pay for future deliveries of Bolivian oil and gas in convertible currency and later in that year YPFB made serious studies of the pipeline project and of the possibility of developing the Mutún ironworks. On 11 September 1966 YPFB told the Ministry that it intended to go ahead with the Yacuiba gasline and that it wanted control over the transportation.

The problem for YPFB was finance; the gasline would be expensive (its eventual cost was $57m.) and Gulf's participation was needed in order to attract foreign credit on that scale. For Gulf, this appeared to present a further opportunity of controlling what was clearly becoming an increasingly alarming political situation by bringing the World Bank into the agreement. As Ingram put it, Gulf 'had been disturbed by the various developments in Bolivia during the 1960s and hoped that the presence of the Bank would deter' possible nationalisation.[15] The World Bank was willing to lend $23m. and Gulf then arranged a commercial loan for a similar amount. A contract was then awarded to Williams Bros. for pipeline construction and work began.

Barrientos's aim of developing the petroleum industry as rapidly as possible can also be seen in the government's proposal in 1966 to set up a new state company to develop Bolivian petrochemicals. However, this proposal was criticised by YPFB as well as by Gulf, and was subsequently withdrawn. The regime continued planning the development of a petrochemicals industry; a paper circulated by the Ministry of Mines and Petroleum in 1967 stressed that 'the development of the petrochemicals industry has been regarded by the government as a regional project to be given the maximum priority since four years have now passed without anything being done'.[16] A commission was set up in November 1966 to study the development of the industry. It began by applying to US AID for a loan to carry out its studies, but nothing seems to have resulted.

Despite these efforts, Barrientos was unable to prevent Gulf Oil from becoming a major political issue during his presidency. In order to explain this, it will be necessary to discuss Bolivian politics in more detail. Barrientos's coup had drastically reduced the political influence of the MNR (which had split with many members supporting the military government) and the regime had shown itself willing to crush radical civilian opposition by force. There remained, however, several small right-wing parties which were vocal rather than powerful but which did gain some credibility with the reopening of Congress in

1966. After elections were held in that year, the CDC, which had incorporated various right-wing fragments, held the statutory 20% quota of congressional seats which were allocated to the running-up party.

Real opposition to Barrientos, however, came from within the army and particularly from General Ovando. Ovando was the senior military officer in Bolivia and had done much to build up the army after its near destruction by the 1952 Revolution. His political ambitions had earlier been disappointed, largely because of his shy manner and inability to speak in public (Barrientos, by contrast, was a born demagogue who was fluent in Quechua as well as Spanish). Ovando, therefore, had been forced to accept Barrientos as President, while Barrientos felt it necessary to keep Ovando as army commander, but neither really trusted the other and Ovando, in particular, was soon looking for ways of embarrassing Barrientos.

Ovando was also something of a nationalist, which perhaps resulted from his involvement with the ideology of national security. From around 1965 he began gathering in secret a group of *anti-barrientista* nationalists, some of whom he was able to place into Congress in the 1966 elections as ostensible supporters of the regime.[17] One of this group was Quiroga Santa Cruz, who quickly made his name by delivering a number of eloquent speeches in opposition to Gulf Oil. Another ally of Ovando was Alberto Bailey, the Editor of *Presencia,* which achieved prominence as a major national newspaper under Barrientos and which was one of the most forceful critics of Gulf Oil. The group also included Chacón, who had been adviser to Busch as a young man and had played a significant part in the nationalisation of Standard Oil in 1937, and Sergio Almaraz until his death in 1968. Perhaps surprisingly, Mariaca Bilbao was not a member, although his book was influential with Ovando and clearly influenced public opinion after its publication in 1966.

By 1969 it had begun to appear that Ovando was more in tune with the thinking of an increasingly nationalist army than Barrientos. There were several reasons for this. First, and most important, the CIA's growing penetration of the Bolivian security forces (which culminated in the successful campaign against Guevara in 1967) clearly upset certain institutional arrangements and precipitated a backlash. The most apparent sign of this was the Arguedas affair. Arguedas, Bolivia's Interior Minister, became increasingly frustrated with the penetration of CIA *gusanos* (Cuban exiles) in Bolivia and their interference in Bolivian politics[18] and reacted by sending Ché Guevara's diary to Cuba. Subsequently, in early 1969, *Presencia* ran a whole series of articles documenting the extent of CIA involvement in Bolivia, forcing Barrientos to admit its presence in the country. At the same time the Vietnam War and the consequent increase in the price of tin reduced Bolivia's financial dependence upon the USA. Although American aid continued, its key element – budgetary support – tailed off. Bolivia could now more easily afford gestures of independence. Thus, when early in 1968 Barrientos sought a $12m. loan from Washington to balance his budget, he rejected US 'technical' advice that tax measures should be tightened and administrative economies made. Instead he applied to the USSR for a $100m. loan.[19]

Gulf itself, however, was becoming increasingly important to the Bolivian economy, especially after it began exporting through Arica in October 1966, and the petroleum code, which had been generous in 1955, was by now absurd.[20] Thus, according to a report in *Latin America* in 1968, 'nationalist irritation with the US has spilled over into other fields and is particularly directed towards the operation of the Bolivian Gulf Oil Company . . . The nationalists maintain the Bolivian Gulf, the country's largest producer, pays only an 11 per cent royalty on its exports which, they claim, is far below the average for oil producing countries.'[21] However, it seems that the objections to Gulf were not so much technocratic (since Barrientos was in any case renegotiating the terms) as political, and Gulf was now vulnerable to a change in the political climate.

Already at the beginning of 1968 Ovando had sent an open letter to other senior officers which said that

in order that the country be ours, basic industries must belong to the state . . . National resources, and the terms of their exploitation, also constitute an inseparable part of national sovereignty. The country must move towards control of their full exploitation through its own resources and entities. . . . with reference to petroleum, the Davenport Code [1955] must be annulled as soon as possible, and a tax established that reaches 50% of gross production, special regulations for gas must be established and control for the state obtained over its refining, transport, marketing and industrialisation through YPFB.[22]

During 1968 there were signs of divisions within the army. Ovando broke openly with Barrientos and General Torres (who had been Barrientos's Labour Minister) was dismissed for publicly opposing the refining of Bolivian oil by Chile. In August 1968 General Vásquez tried a military revolt with support from the MNR and FSB, but was unsuccessful. In the same month Barrientos's Interior Minister, Argue-das, broke with the regime and gave a press conference which revealed deep CIA penetration, massive corruption and the basic insecurity of the regime.

The military coup in Peru in October 1968 and the Velasco government's nationalisation of IPC furnished an alternative model for military officers who were dissatisfied with what they saw as Barrientos's demagoguery and *entreguismo*. This apparent proof that military officers who were hitherto regarded as right-wing could nationalise an oil company with great fanfare and use the issue to rally support and win over much of the left was of great interest to Ovando and his allies. Could military nationalism perhaps succeed in creating a genuine popular base in Bolivia?

Siles, Ovando and the nationalisation

There are some indications that this question crossed Barrientos's mind as well as Ovando's, but before anything could develop Barrientos was killed in April 1969 in a helicopter crash. Consequently his formerly almost unknown Vice-President Luis Siles Salinas took over. Once in power, Siles worked hard to develop a political identity and one of his weapons was a moderate oil nationalism. Siles did not want to nationalise Gulf but did want publicly to renegotiate the terms with the company.[23] His objective was to commit Gulf publicly to acceptance of the principle of a 50% rate of tax (the 1955 law specified only a 30% tax rate and an 11% royalty but also left various loopholes, including a 27½% depletion allowance).[24] Gulf at first refused, either overestimating its bargaining power or believing that Siles was in no position to deliver an agreement. Gulf's position was probably reflected in a *New York Times* article which, as late as 2 September 1969, reported that 'Experts feel that if nationalisation pressure becomes too intense, Gulf might withdraw altogether, thus depriving Bolivia of her main outlet for petroleum . . . Despite the great leverage exerted by Gulf, political pressure against foreign business interest is mounting rapidly.' Gulf finally agreed to Siles's terms but by then it was too late.

Certainly Siles's political position was not particularly strong.[25] There is some doubt over whether Mariaca, whom he appointed as head of YPFB, was seriously interested in coming to an agreement with Gulf, or merely wanted to use the negotiations to show Gulf's intransigence and thus to justify further measures against Gulf. In any case, from the middle of 1969 the campaign against Gulf Oil appeared to gain considerable momentum.

The first issue which arose was that of the marketing of natural gas in Santa Cruz. The fact that nearly all of Boliva's oil and gas had been found in Santa Cruz had created a major policy complication, for the province had created serious problems for the government in La Paz. Ever since the 1940s successive La Paz regimes had fostered projects which would develop the promising but backward area of Santa Cruz, but after the mid-1950s the local economy 'took off' in a way that brought little comfort to the capital.[26] As it became wealthier, it became more vocal and rebellious. The natural gas issue can only be understood in terms of this change.

The first manifestations of conflict on petroleum matters began with the formation of the right-wing Pro-Santa-Cruz Committee in 1957. This almost immediately launched a campaign against the radical pro-MNR political leadership of the province,

> insisting that a higher proportion of the tax revenue generated from the new oil finds in the area should be earmarked for local expenditure. [The MNR leader] had accepted a central government formula which the Pro-Santa-Cruz Committee was determined to outbid. In practice the difference was not very great, but it was possible to inflate the issue into a matter of life and death for the local community.[27]

Although the government in La Paz and its local allies finally gave way, this issue allowed the Pro-Santa-Cruz Committee to achieve prominence and a position of power, which it later regained after being temporarily removed by armed invasion from La Paz in 1959.

While it is difficult to evaluate the motives of those concerned, it was certainly believed in La Paz that the Pro-Santa-Cruz Committee and Gulf Oil were moving into political alliance in a way that would seriously compromise the central government. It is notable that Gulf Oil's first attempt to supply hydrocarbons directly to Bolivan consumers took place in 1962, when it offered to supply natural gas to consumers in Santa Cruz – an offer which had precipitated Mariaca's resignation. In 1966, the Pro-Santa-Cruz Committee made an offer to set up a private company to manage the gas which was due to it as part of its royalty; but this offer was quietly turned aside by Barrientos. Instead, Barrientos set up a commission (the CNP) to fix the price of natural gas which was to be provided by Gulf Oil to YPFB and sold by YPFB in Santa Cruz. There was an obvious clash of interest between

YPFB (which wanted the gas kept expensive) and Santa Cruz (which wanted it cheap). On 18 April 1969 the CNP reported secretly (but the news leaked out) and called for a (high) price of $0.10 per thousand cubic feet. After the death of Barrientos, however, the Pro-Santa-Cruz Committee rejected the government's recommendations and tried to reopen the issue with a demand that gas should be supplied at $0.04 per thousand cubic feet.

Meanwhile further problems arose with respect to the gas pipeline to Argentina which had apparently been agreed in 1968. Criticism was levelled against the contractors, Williams Bros., for allegedly demanding an excessively high price for the construction and conniving with Gulf in order to get the contract. There seemed to be little evidence for these charges and the World Bank let it be known that it continued to have confidence in Williams Bros., after which the government decided not to seek a renegotiation of the contract.[28]

Faced with these developments, Siles in August 1969 introduced a bill into Congress nationalising natural gas completely and thus taking over the reserves which lay within Gulf's concession areas. The regime defended its position by pointing out that natural gas was not mentioned in the original contract. Gulf was clearly worried by these developments. Already it had sought World Bank help for the gas pipeline as a form of political protection. Moreover, its concern with public relations had led it to identify closely (probably much too closely for its own good) with Barrientos. According to Ingram,

the company had loaned YPFB money and had given it information. It had assisted Barrientos in financing and organising a Bolivian display for a trade fair in San Antonio, Texas. In the same year [1968] with no delaying tactics, Gulf had agreed to Barrientos' request for a suspension of the depletion allowance in order to raise badly needed government revenue, supposedly increasing the government's take from $6 million to $8 million.[29]

Ingram did not know that Gulf Oil also financed Barrientos more personally to a total of $460,000 between 1966 and 1968.[30] While it is possible that other companies were involved in rather similar activities, Gulf Oil stood out because of its size. Moreover, even though the secret was kept from the outside world, many Bolivians must have known or suspected the nature of this relationship, which is likely in any event to have gone further than Barrientos himself. Thus, in 1975 Gulf Oil stated that 'there are indications that various representatives of General Barrientos' political party may also have been involved, but we will not be certain of this fact until we finish the investigations',[31] but the Bolivian reaction was so strong that no other names were mentioned.

In any case, Gulf responded to Siles's attacks by looking for a new source of support and in August 1969 offered to supply gas free to Santa Cruz for a period of 20 years. This offer gave YPFB its chance. Mariaca had already been clearing the decks for action against Gulf after Silas had appointed him as head. In August there was a purge within YPFB of those who were directly associated with the Barrientos government's plans for the gas pipeline to Argentina. According to *Presencia,* 'the charge was brought about, it seems, as a result of pressure that was being exercised by the oil-workers' union movement which had given notice of a prolonged strike to demand the dismissal of employees of the company who participated in the negotiations relating to the Santa Cruz–Yacuiba gas pipeline'.[32] It would not be surprising if political loyalties were also considered.

At the beginning of September, therefore, Mariaca denounced Gulf's offer to Santa Cruz as 'an intervention in the affairs of the country and, moreover, it involves a blow against Yacimientos, which will probably face demands from other areas for similar treatment to that which Gulf is offering to Santa Cruz'.[33] In September YPFB's territory was again expanded at Gulf's expense and in the same month Geopetrole was commissioned to survey Gulf's assets.

Siles's policies led Ovando to seize power while he still could. Ovando had been attacked in Congress by supporters of Siles, and it appeared that the President was grooming the Mayor of La Paz as a rival to Ovando in the presidential elections which were due in 1970. Thus, on 26 September Siles was overthrown and Ovando came to power. Gulf Oil was nationalised on 17 October.

The composition of Ovando's Cabinet certainly suggested that the regime would take a nationalist line. Quiroga Santa Cruz became Oil Minister and Alberto Bailey, the ex-Editor of *Presencia,* became Minister of Information. Other confidants, such as Chacón and Canelas, played an important part from behind the scenes. There were, it is true, some negotiations with Gulf Oil which were carried out before the nationalisation. Accounts of these conflict. According to Alberto Bailey, 'the decision to nationalise . . . was made a week after Gulf offered a tax concession that would only give Bolivia an additional tax of $1m. annually'.[34] According to Gulf, however, the company had offered to double its royalty to 23%.[35] In any case, there seems little doubt that the regime was not seriously interested in further negotiations except as a means of buying time. It is interesting, however, that in 1969 Gulf had provided only about 6% of the budget of the central government, although it had made higher payments to the provincial authorities of Santa Cruz and contributed greatly to the Bolivian balance of payments.[36]

There were a number of reasons why Ovando should have moved against Gulf. Apart from his own nationalist convictions, the most important reason was perhaps his concern to carve out a political base which up until then had been lacking. His efforts in this respect, however, were clearly unsuccessful. For one thing, his background was unpromising for a would-be populist politician; Ovando had been directly involved in military repression, both of the tin miners in 1965 and of Guevara in 1967. Moreover, like many other army officers, Ovando believed fundamentally that civilians were meant to obey and rarely made a serious effort to pretend otherwise. Indeed, although some members of his Cabinet wanted to bring the political parties of the left into his regime, Ovando brushed aside these suggestions and continued to rely upon support from within the army.

The army itself, however, was too fragmented to provide a credible political base. Moreover, while officers were willing to see a reassertion of national sovereignty, their support wavered when they counted the cost. When faced with an embargo on oil exports, virulent opposition from Santa Cruz, loss of US aid and a generally deteriorating economy, the response was close to panic.[37] While remaining ostensibly loyal to Ovando for nearly a year, senior army officers lost little time in pressing him to dismiss those civilian radicals who had appeared chiefly responsible for the nationalisation, which had in fact been unanimously approved by the Cabinet despite some misgivings on the part of the civilian Finance Minister.[38] Thus, early in 1970 both Alberto Bailey and Quiroga Santa Cruz were forced to resign and compensation for Gulf was quickly agreed (as we have seen in chapter 4). Ovando's 'opening to the left', which was always half-hearted, ended only a few months later. Indeed, just before his downfall Ovando was reported in the press as saying that 'the government will set up a new oil policy' and 'will decide whether it is convenient to permit operations for foreign companies under oil concessions or under any standard industrial operations'.[39]

The remaining source of support for Ovando was a small *cepalista* technocracy. Indeed, an interesting indication of the regime's economic thinking appeared in *Estratégia socio-económica,* which appeared

in July 1970 and which, in a more durable regime, might have provided the basis for a plan. This accused Gulf of overproducing from its
wells from a national point of view and of operating in the manner of
a typical export enclave. It stressed the need to change the Bolivian
pattern of growth in a statist, industrialising and planned direction
based on internal finance and the domestic market. As far as oil was
concerned, more emphasis was to be given to increasing domestic value
added through local refining, a state-owned petrochemicals industry
and the development of a local market for natural gas.

The nationalisation of Gulf Oil, therefore, was the result of an
attempt by Ovando to create a variant of the military populism which
he believed to exist in Peru and in the Bolivia of the 1930s. It failed
partly for the reasons that so frequently undermine such regimes and
stem from the basic incompatibility of the military and any independent civilian left, and partly because Bolivia, a country with a revolutionary tradition, could not be won over by half-measures. There was
enough common anti-US feeling (in the aftermath of CIA operations
against Guevara and earlier operations against the MNR left) to make
such a strategy worth attempting, but not to ensure its success.

Gulf Oil and the Bolivian state

While an abrupt nationalisation may appear to signify failure, or, at
best, an admission that serious mistakes were made in the past, such a
conclusion would need to be qualified in the Bolivian case. Under the
1955 oil code, Bolivia attracted very considerable oil investment that
would not otherwise have been possible. Many companies pulled out
after unsuccessful exploration which saved YPFB the trouble of exploring those particular areas. Gulf Oil, however, did find and develop
commercial quantities of oil after investing an estimated $169m. It is
most unlikely that any code less generous than Davenport (the 1955
code) would have brought foreign investment to Bolivia in such quantities. The oil thus discovered, together with the world oil price
increases of 1971–4, played a major part in fuelling the Bolivian economic boom of the 1970s.

Any damage caused to the Bolivian economy by the oil nationalisation was short-lived. By 1971, with the gas pipeline to Argentina
under construction and with oil once again flowing freely from Arica,
the post-nationalisation disruption was over. Moreover, the fact that
YPFB was able to secure the return of considerable foreign investment

after 1973 (see below, p. 465–6) suggests that a nationalisation does not always cut off future policy options. For Gulf, meanwhile, compensation was adequate, if not generous, in that it covered not only asset or 'book' value but all costs which the company had incurred in Bolivia less income received. Given that at least some of these could be set against US taxation, it appears that Gulf did leave Bolivia with some kind of profit.[40]

Nevertheless, it is obvious that Gulf's presence in Bolivia posed serious problems for both company and government. The intensity of these problems can be seen from the shortness of Gulf's stay in Bolivia and the abruptness of the final takeover. Essentially, they hinged upon the weakness of the Bolivian state and its responsiveness to powerful interest groups.[41] For the 15 years after 1952, by far the most powerful of these was the US government. US aid frequently exceeded domestic tax revenue as a source of government income and, although the policies which it preferred frequently met opposition in Bolivia (the stabilisation plan, the entry of Gulf Oil under the 1955 code, etc.), US influence was clearly strong enough to make sure that its wishes prevailed. After 1964, however, the position changed. Washington continued to provide aid to Bolivia, but the amount of this and its relative importance tended to decline. At the same time Washington's demands upon La Paz increased drastically with the anti-Guevara campaign, which was a US priority of altogether a higher order than the influencing of any particular government in La Paz. In pursuing this campaign, however, Washington made enemies in the army through its interference with promotion prospects and its use of specialised counter-insurgency units. These enemies were more powerful politically than those who had opposed the stabilisation plan and the earlier opponents of the 1955 code.

After the defeat and death of Guevara, it was clear that there would be some kind of backlash against Washington. Dissatisfied army officers began to look for alliances on the left on the basis of some common nationalist programme. Under these circumstances, Gulf Oil became an obvious target since it was a large multinational which had succeeded where YPFB had apparently failed and which had clearly been manoeuvring in Bolivian politics. Gulf Oil's vulnerability increased further after the apparently successful nationalisation of IPC in Peru.

The activities of Gulf Oil under pressure provide a fascinating subplot to the whole period. There can be little doubt that Gulf realised the vulnerability of its position and the extent to which it had come to depend upon a strong US presence in the area. Once Washington's influence in Bolivia diminished, Gulf began to cultivate local political allies in order to improve its survival chances but it is likely that these actions only aggravated suspicions and hostility towards the company and made its longer-term position more difficult. Gulf's financing of Barrientos and its courtship of the *barrientista* appointments in YPFB are now public knowledge and illustrate the dangers to a company of excessively close involvement with the government of the day. Indeed, had the story of Gulf's relationship with Barrientos leaked out before compensation agreements had been made, Gulf's position would almost certainly have become far more difficult. Gulf Oil did achieve some real success by bringing the World Bank into the gas pipeline project; the Bank helped secure compensation for the company and might have been even more influential had it taken a more active role. Perhaps even more interesting is the way in which Gulf sought to cultivate the Pro-Santa-Cruz-Committee with its offer to supply cheap natural gas. Although the company may even have added to its own difficulties by further antagonising the government in La Paz and the executives of YPFB, its longer-run relations with Santa Cruz catalysed a major change in Bolivian politics as the right-wing Santa Cruz area came to exert an increasing national influence. In that respect, one might say that Gulf Oil was posthumously successful.

14

Oil politics in Ecuador 1972–6

When the Ecuadorian military took power in February 1972, it found
an oil industry which was economically quite well developed but which
remained a mystery to almost all Ecuadorians. Ecuador had produced
some oil ever since 1918 but the amounts had been small and successive regimes had hardly concerned themselves with oil policy. For
many years, Ecuador levied few taxes, had no state company and knew
extremely little about the industry. In some ways, therefore, the events
of the years 1972–6 may be regarded as providing something of a learning process for Ecuador, after which policy became less dramatic and
rather more settled. The 1972–6 period was extremely eventful, both
nationally and internationally, and a great deal was telescoped into a
very short period of time. Ecuador began large-scale exports of oil in
June 1972 and by 1974 the Ecuadorian Oil Minister had become President of OPEC. Only in 1977 did some kind of conservative 'normality'
return, and this was followed in 1979 by the election of a reformist
civilian government.

Expansion and renegotiation 1969–73

The Ecuadorian oil boom got seriously underway in 1967 when a major
discovery was made in the Oriente. Until that time Ecuador's small-
scale oil production had come entirely from the coastal area; it was
widely believed that there was oil to be found in the Oriente but until
then no commercially attractive discovery had been made. By 1972 an
independent survey by Rudolf Martin and Associates put the reserves
discovered by the main exploring companies – the Texas–Gulf consortium – at 3,200 million barrels (proved and probable) and added that
'Texas–Gulf have some twenty promising structures which have not
yet been drilled.'[1] A trans-Andean pipeline was under construction and

due for completion in June 1972 with an initial capacity of 250,000 b/d; expansion to 400,000 b/d or perhaps even more was very much in prospect.[2]

The prospect of production on this scale had already brought about some changes. There had been a major renegotiation of the original concession terms in 1969 and a new but non-retroactive oil law (the first since 1937) was introduced in September 1971. The 1969 negotiations had pushed expected government revenue up to reasonable levels in the short run but still left a great deal unclear or unsatisfactory. The question of government control had not really been tackled at all. Ecuador had no state oil refinery or even a firm contract to build one, although the question had been under discussion at least since 1966. Moreover, although the 1971 law had set up a state company, CEPE, the legal terms of its creation were so unsatisfactory that it had to be legally re-established in 1972. The question of acreage was also important; in 1972 Texas–Gulf's concession area amounted to 400,000 hectares, although this was still far less than it had enjoyed in the period before 1969. Other companies, however, had taken concessions which covered much of the rest of the potential oil-bearing area. Apart from the question of size, there was also the fact that at least one (offshore) concession had been granted under very doubtful circumstances, a matter which would later become important. Finally there was the question of administration itself; there was still much validity in the government's own complaint made in 1966 that 'the state does not dispose of sufficient personnel to be able to carry out satisfactorily the administration, control and regulation of all aspects of the oil industry'.[3] This lack of oil policy reflected the weakness and backwardness of the Ecuadorian state itself and was no different from the lack of policy on a number of other important questions.

This situation, however, did not relate simply to economic backwardness. The economy had grown rapidly in the years since 1948; the main growth point had been the banana-exporting *haciendas,* where a conservative but modernising 'oligarchy' had grown up. During this period there had also been a certain amount of industrialisation and urbanisation. The voting population expanded from under 300,000 in 1948 to 827,000 in 1968, out of a total adult population of around 2½ million. The impact of this change was limited, however, by the chronic weakness of Ecuador's political institutions; fragmented and disorganised populist parties merely replaced the older fragmented and disorganised conservative groups. If anything, post-war economic

growth made politics even less important than they had been formerly.
As Fitch pointed out,

the new economic prosperity promoted a substantial lessening of tensions
between the coastal oligarchy, the traditional landowning aristocracy of the
sierra, and the increasingly numerous members of the urban middle class.
With the increased opportunities for elite mobility outside of the political
system and the rapid increase in the number of middle class bureaucratic
positions resulting from the doubling of public expenditures, control of the
government ceased to be a highly salient issue.[4]

Bouts of serious instability coincided with periodic difficulties in the
export markets but these did not lead to any major change in successive
civilian governments' basically conservative approach. In good times,
change was not necessary; in bad times it did not seem possible.

The military itself had shown some signs of wanting to take an
active and possibly reformist role in politics but lacked sufficient unity
to press for reform in any coherent or effective way. Military intervention had been frequent prior to 1972 but was essentially inconsequen-
tial in as far as it related to any long-term change in the structure of
Ecuadorian politics or society. However, changes were taking place
within the military institution in Ecuador which were at any rate sup-
portive of a military attempt to take over the government in a more
long-term and decisive way than had been the case in the past.

These changes within the military were catalysed by the prospect of
oil. Few doubted that, when the oil began to flow from the Oriente in
June 1972, there would be important changes in Ecuador and this
general sense of anticipation no doubt encouraged the military to take
power directly. The coup of February 1972 was actually precipitated
by the efforts of civilian President Velasco Ibarra to use the military to
block the probable electoral victory in June 1972 of his populist rival
Assad Bucaram. Velasco's tactics misfired, however, and the military
took power in its own name. Indeed, for a number of officers the
motives for the coup were not purely negative; rather, they themselves
hoped to take the initiative in using the oil wealth to transform the
Ecuadorian economy and modernise its society. One of the most radical
of these officers was Captain Jarrín.

Although appointed to the Ministry of Natural Resources, Jarrín
had no background in the area. He had expected to become Minister
of Education but was given this more influential position after two
more senior and conservative naval officers had been vetoed by the

army. He was a military intellectual, and had previously been head of the naval academy, where he had propounded a radical form of the 'national security' ideology. Moreover, Jarrín was a determined nationalist who had been influenced by the creation of Petrobrás in Brazil and who immediately conceived a strategy of gradual oil nationalisation in Ecuador. In a sense, Jarrín followed an earlier tradition of Latin American military oil nationalism which can be traced back to Horta Barbosa of Brazil and even Mosconi of Argentina. In a different way, he shared the 'Third World' consciousness of the elites of many underdeveloped countries which has been able to assert itself only under the right material conditions.

Almost immediately, Jarrín collected together a team of oil nationalists which included both Ecuadorians and foreigners who had experience of the industry and were sympathetic to a nationalist line.[5] Organisationally, this group worked very well indeed. The World Bank later referred to a 'group of highly motivated and dedicated professionals, both at the Ministry of Natural Resources and at the national oil company. Indeed, the improvement in the public management of the petroleum resources has been remarkable.'[6] Within the team there was no doubt of Jarrín's personal ascendancy; one of his associates later recalled that 'for the first few weeks he took our advice, but after that he took charge'.[7]

Jarrín's position within the incoming government, however, was more difficult. There were some factors which worked in his favour. For one thing, the general orientation of the regime was nationalist; President Rodríguez Lara had no wish to repeat the experience of his military predecessor who had been severely criticised as an *entreguista* for coming to an understanding in 1963 with the USA over fishing limits. Many officers had also been influenced by the radical military regime in Peru. Moreover, once the military had taken power away from a relatively conservative civilian president, there needed to be a rationale for it to stay in office. More specifically, a fishing dispute with the USA which had flared briefly in 1970–1, had strongly implanted nationalist values within the navy, where Jarrín's policies were enthusiastically supported by the senior Navy Minister, Admiral Sergio Vásquez Pacheco.

In any case, the oil industry itself seemed ripe for a policy of oil nationalism; the oil had, after all, already been found and the foreign investment had already been committed so that the bargaining advantage now lay with the host government. Moreover, the international climate of the period was extremely favourable to host governments, as was being fully demonstrated by the governments of Venezuela and a number of countries in the Middle East. Finally, in a country with so little technical expertise in oil as Ecuador, the calibre and expertise of Jarrín's team went a long way towards neutralising any neoliberal criticisms that his opponents might make.

Against these advantages, however, there were serious potential weaknesses in Jarrín's position. The greatest of these was Jarrín's own lack of a political base. To some extent this was a result of choice. Jarrín was a military elitist who showed very little interest in coalition-building or even in cultivating a strong personalist image. He also sought protection against political attack by maintaining a fairly low profile and ensuring that all of his proposals were fully discussed within the government and within the military before they were implemented. These choices were, however, conditioned among other things by the fact that Jarrín was a naval officer who could not rely on strong personal loyalties within the army which was after all the most powerful of the services. Indeed, given the army's political power but its essential lack of cohesiveness – a lack which could be seen throughout Ecuadorian political society – Jarrín was forced to build his house upon sand. It could survive the clear weather of 1972–3 but was swept away in the storms of 1974.

The weakness of Ecuador's political institutions throughout the period 1972–4 and the consequent tendency toward drift and indecision must be emphasised. It is also necessary to point out the fact that major changes were taking place within a country which had no experience of exporting oil or of playing a significant role at an international level. Jarrín's team was the only source of independent knowledge about the domestic oil industry; the only alternative source was the Texas–Gulf consortium. At the same time, few Ecuadorians doubted that major changes were likely as a result of the oil discoveries, but hopes and fears were probably exaggerated. Nevertheless, for a short period everything seemed possible and the expectations of the main protagonists took on an importance of their own.

While Jarrín's oil policies had a number of different targets,[8] the most important issue concerned relations with the Texas–Gulf consortium. The first major step taken by the government was the issuing of Decree 430 (12 June 1972) which stipulated that those who had obtained concessions prior to 1971 would have to renegotiate them to take account of the 1971 law. The most important provisions of this concerned territory. Jarrín wanted to secure the return of enough of the consortium's territory to ensure that a significant part of the industry could be developed on terms other than the old-style concession contract system. This government decision was not taken easily; according to one source, Jarrín was close to resignation before his proposals were finally accepted.

Once the law was passed, however, Jarrín was given control over the process of renegotiation. Texas–Gulf tried to offer increased production as a bargaining counter to the government's demands and the company even hinted that reserves might justify a second trans-Andean pipeline if the terms were right.[9] Moreover, the consortium claimed that it had worked its entire concession area and initially asked for $70m. as compensation for its returned acreage. However, despite what may have seemed a strong position, the companies had little to offer Jarrín. He had no fear of prolonged negotiations and the consortium's offer of higher output was of no interest. Jarrín had always aimed at long-term nationalisation and his immediate aim was therefore to rescue as much as possible from the hands of the companies in order to entrust it to the state oil company for long-term development. Moreover, Jarrín was a conservationist; perhaps influenced by Venezuela, he believed, in 1972, that oil prices would continue to increase and that the value of oil left in the ground would therefore appreciate. Jarrín wanted Ecuador to export less oil than the companies wanted but over a longer period and at a much higher price. Even apart from these price expectations, Jarrín was willing to hold back output for fear of the domestic consequences of an uncontrollable flood of oil wealth; as we have seen in chapter 5, he wanted to spin out developments more gradually.

Others, however, were less patient. It is not clear whether consortium spokesmen quietly tried to put over their views to the more conservative Ecuadorians (although it would be surprising if they had not), but certainly there were those who wanted a rapid build-up of production and who were worried by disputes which concerned not only Texas–Gulf but also a number of other oil companies operating in Ecuador. It should again be remembered that the problems of oil policymaking were very new to Ecuadorians, many of whom seemed prepared to take the claims of the companies more or less at face value, or at least to prefer them to the views of the left-wing technocrats grouped around Jarrín. Thus, the conservative press kept up a line of criticism against Jarrín for taking too hard a line with Texas–Gulf, particularly when a number of smaller companies, disappointed with exploration results and uncertain about the political climate, gradually pulled out. Even *El universo,* by no means an organ of the unthinking right-wing, wrote on 15 February 1973 that 'there are growing doubts about whether the Ecuadorian government has miscalculated'.

It was certainly true that investment in exploration and even development had virtually dried up by the end of 1972, but the resulting criticism was muted since the government could point to rising revenue as the oil continued to flow and the price increased. Nevertheless, the rest of the government did become increasingly uneasy and began to pressurise Jarrín to settle. Finally, they presented him with an ultimatum: get an agreement or resign. When the agreement was finally signed in August 1973, Jarrín had a signed letter of resignation in his pocket.

According to the contract which was eventually signed, Texas–Gulf handed back much of their territory but were allowed to keep the rest until 1992. They would invest $60m. over the next three years in order to bring the level of production up to 400,000 b/d. The state oil company, CEPE, was allowed to buy its way into the consortium, taking 25% over four years at a price not revealed officially but believed to be $65m. Financially, the Ecuadorian government had already achieved its objectives through a complicated set of fiscal arrangements which could be regulated according to the changes in the tax reference price.[10] In a market where prices were moving rapidly and where there was in any case no single world price, it is almost impossible to evaluate a particular tax structure without inside information but the Ecuadorian government was certainly not generous. Already in mid-1972 the World Bank had calculated that 'comparing the Ecuadorian tax system with the prevailing Venezuela or Middle East tax structures – using similar sets of assumptions as to costs and tax reference prices – the level of most taxes resulting from the Ecuadorian system is higher than the other two'.[11] As world prices mounted, so did those set by Ecuador; they rose gradually from $2.50 in July 1972 for 28° API crude to $7.30 on 10 November 1973 and the ceiling rate of $13.70 set on 1 January 1974. While not exactly comparable, this rate has marked similarities to that set by Venezuela.

1974: the crisis

The dramatic world price developments of 1973–4 did more, however, than simply increase the tax take of the Ecuadorian government. They also raised the international dimension of oil politics more forcefully than ever before. The impact of international conditions was all the greater since Jarrín had deliberately tried to link Ecuador as closely as possible to the other oil-producing countries and had led the country into OPEC in November 1973. In the eyes of the more radical government ministers, OPEC membership seemed to have its advantages. Apart from the prestige of membership and the apparent international significance which it bestowed upon the country, it was hoped that membership might also strengthen Quito's bargaining position against the consortium. Certainly the regime entered OPEC with its eyes open and the matter was fully discussed within the government itself. However, membership was of particular importance to Jarrín himself; he was anxious to use the oil weapon internationally to bring about changes in the international balance of power while also transforming domestic political attitudes.[12] Membership of OPEC would help Ecuadorian nationalists ideologically and would therefore provide the backing to permit the gradual takeover of the consortium by CEPE and also for foreign economic policies which would have been unthinkable only two years before.

Nevertheless, Ecuador's membership of OPEC was always controversial domestically and it proved to be the more so as the costs of membership became more apparent. Essentially, domestic conservatives believed that it was an error to look a gift horse in the mouth. If the increased income from oil was in any case available, why put Ecuador's position at risk? It was not interested in the Middle East and not powerful enough to play a real part in international politics, so why not take the free ride? If it did so, it could enjoy both the oil revenue and its traditional alliance with the USA.

It was certainly true that the companies tailored their own strategies to the international environment, which included a temporary world surplus of oil after the middle of 1974 and a public anti-OPEC campaign mounted by the US government. At the same time, events within Ecuador also need to be considered. One important development which has to be explained is the sharp cutback in the output of the oil companies after June 1974. This did coincide with the world surplus and it is possible, although by no means certain, that Ecuadorian crude oil was overpriced (in terms of government revenue) internationally, but is impossible to dismiss the hypothesis that the companies determined to put pressure on Ecuador in order to try to bring about policy changes within the country.

It is likely that the key issue again involved conservation (see also chapter 5). After the contract with Texas–Gulf had been signed in August 1973, the consortium had intended to increase its output to 400,000 b/d.[13] Jarrín, however, was less co-operative than the consortium hoped and instead tried to use the issue as a lever to induce the companies to carry out further oil exploration on terms which cannot be regarded as attractive. Moreover, by delaying permission for the expansion, Jarrín clearly damaged the interests of the companies which, in early 1974, lay in expanding oil production to the maximum possible in order to offset the production cutbacks then being enforced in the Middle East. It is quite likely that it was this refusal which persuaded the companies that Jarrín was irreconcilably hostile. Nor would their attitude have changed after 22 May, when Jarrín ordered the consortium to cut back its production from 250,000 b/d to 210,000 b/d as a conservation measure. At the end of June, by which time Jarrín had again raised taxes (after the OPEC meeting of that month, he put up the royalty from 16% to 16.67%), the companies launched their counter-offensive.

There is an important point to be made here. In theory at least, most countries that produce oil for a long period develop some kind of relationship with their foreign companies (which may be called a bargaining relationship) which at any rate imparts a certain predictability to their mutual behaviour. The balance may shift over time but, for as long as the companies retain any power at all, host governments will find it desirable to press for gradual change rather than abrupt transformation. In the eyes of the companies, therefore, Jarrín's strategy must have seemed almost suicidally aggressive. Ecuador was after all a new and small producer, with little technical knowledge of or experience in running the industry, and yet Jarrín was turning down the prospect of increased revenue in the short-run and practically inviting retaliation once the balance of power shifted.

Jarrín's strategy was not so much misconceived, however, as oriented in another direction. He did not expect to last long enough in office to be able to enjoy a long-term bargaining relationship leading to eventual nationalisation. His aim, rather, was to use the short time which he expected to remain in office to bring about economic and political transformations of a kind that would be irreversible when (as he fully expected) the conservatives regained control. The objective, therefore, was to impart a few shocks to the system rather than to try and maximise the return from the market as it existed. While the matter is debatable, it appears to me that this was the only position Jarrín could reasonably have adopted given the extreme weakness of the Ecuadorian institutional system and thus the impossibility of any office-holder putting down firm roots. This raises the question, which will be taken up again, of whether it is reasonable to expect any kind of 'market rationality' from a country where political institutions are extremely weak.

In any case, rather than go on the defensive when the oil companies began reducing their production, Jarrín pressed on in the hope of achieving the maximum in the limited time remaining. In June 1974 he was able to complete CEPE's purchase of 25% of Texas–Gulf and in the same month he pushed through a decree which authorised CEPE to take gradual control of the domestic market; 100% control was to be achieved in two years. In October, when on the point of dismissal, Jarrín sent 'a signed bill to the Presidency for the purchase of up to 51% stock' in the consortium.[14] If implemented, this would have given CEPE formal control of investment decisions and would have made it more difficult for the companies to avoid raising their level of production. It is likely, however, that the proposed measure would have led the consortium to demand its own total nationalisation which would have given the responsibility for the industry to Ecuador at a time when market conditions were highly unfavourable and when the host country was probably still too inexperienced to manage effectively. In any case, Jarrín was dismissed at the beginning of October and this proposal was quietly dropped.

Eventually, therefore, Jarrín's opponents proved too strong for him. By this time, he was opposed by a number of old politicians whose positions had been threatened by the government's energetic moves against corruption (at least on the part of former regimes). These had connections with much of the press which, traditionally close to the private sector, in any case resented Jarrín's attacks upon itself, was mistrustful of his radicalism and afraid of a confrontation with the oil companies and with Washington. Similar sentiments motivated the Ecuadorian business community; quite apart from its misgivings about the development of a more powerful and efficient state, it feared the short-term economic consequences of a serious conflict with the companies. To this open opposition, which had to be somewhat muted for fear of encouraging pro-Jarrín sympathies within the military, must be added the more potent but quieter pressures working within the regime and the army. There was an Israeli military mission in Ecuador which had already proved influential; during 1974 Jarrín had several times requested but been refused permission to visit Arab members of OPEC, while several army officers paid semi-official visits to Israel. These efforts did not lead to the withdrawal of Ecuador from OPEC but they did bear fruit when Ecuador voted against the famous UN 'Zionism' resolution in 1975. Washington's influence was difficult to discern but was surely present; in 1974 the CIA's involvement in Chile and elsewhere had not yet come to light. Certainly during 1974 a number of rumours circulated within the Ecuadorian army to the effect that Washington would cut military aid unless Jarrín was removed from his post. Washington also had natural allies within the Ecuadorian Foreign Ministry whose traditionally pro-American outlook had been threatened by a man from outside the department. Moreover, when pressure mounted, Rodríguez Lara began to weaken; he was said to be increasingly concerned about the prestige accruing to his 'Superminister' and he certainly proved willing to dispense with him once he appeared a liability.

Over all, therefore, both domestic and foreign influences seemed to be at work in removing Jarrín. His internal position was never so secure that he could survive a major crisis although it had earlier proved sufficient to withstand the opposition of purely domestic conservatives at a time when the price of oil was still rising. It is notable that Jarrín's dismissal was precipitated by the rhetorical attacks he made upon the US administration. *El tiempo* explained that

Jarrín Ampudia, referring to the speech given by President Ford at the General Assembly of the United Nations, said that United States pressures were unacceptable and that statements of a 'neocolonialist' nature had been overtaken by events. These declarations were received with concern in conservative circles which branded them as demagogic. On the other hand, these same circles have said that the Minister had put leftists into his ministry.[15]

Jarrín still maintained support from those officers who were traditionally sympathetic to a nationalist line and who believed that Ecuador had been put 'on the map' by its participation in OPEC. His most valuable support lay within the navy and particularly with its head, Admiral Vásquez. These supporters did not have enough strength to protect Jarrín's position in October 1974 but they did make it difficult for the regime to repudiate his policies later. Retreat was also difficult for other reasons; Jarrín's own boldness was an important factor and it must also be remembered that Rodríguez Lara had earlier taken care to present himself as nationalist, as in June 1974 when he opened the OPEC conference in Quito. Consequently, although Jarrín's successors were willing to make a few quiet concessions to the companies, so much had now happened that these were no longer enough. The full restoration of 'investor confidence' would have required an open reversal of policy from Quito and this proved to be beyond the strength of the companies or their domestic allies.

Ecuador under siege 1974–5

Once Jarrín had resigned the companies tried to press their advantage. They were favoured by world market conditions and in particular by the growing surplus of crude oil which had become a glut by the middle of 1975. Moreover, the weakening world price, combined with the fixed tax reference price, increasingly forced the hand of the companies; there is no reason to doubt company claims that their profits in Ecuador between June 1974 and October 1975 were negligible or even negative.

Quito was willing to make some concessions to the companies in order to try to secure a resumption of exploration and a recovery in production which had fallen heavily from early-1974 levels. The first of these was its decision not to increase the price level in line with OPEC recommendations at the beginning of 1975. However, as world demand continued to fall, this did not prove to be enough and further price reductions appeared to be in prospect. Thus, according to the *New York Times* of 25 February, 'Ecuador . . . is likely to cut the price of crude within the next few weeks, following several months of strong pressure by United States petroleum companies.' In the same month, the Ecuadorian Finance Minister predicted serious economic consequences if the oil price was not cut. As the Quito government continued to hold out, company pressure intensified. On 19 March representatives of the consortium met Rodríguez Lara and threatened to pull out unless three demands were met: the tax reference price was to be cut from $13.70 to $10.25, the domestic selling price was to be raised and companies were to be paid $59.2m. which they said was owing as the result of local purchases by CEPE, CEPE's purchase of 25% of the consortium and the Central Bank's delayed repayment of money which the companies had banked in Ecuador.[16]

The Ecuadorian government, however, was unable or unwilling to act. The regime had now clearly lost what little radical momentum it once possessed, partly because the oil market had turned sour and partly because the military government had shown, in its removal of Jarrín and in other ways, that it had no stomach for a fight. At the same time it was unable to move convincingly in a more conservative direction; instead it tended to disintegrate as rival factions blocked each other's initiatives. For as long as the oil money was flowing on a large scale Rodríguez Lara, who was an adept political tactician although little else, was able to play off the rival factions. When conditions worsened, the result was simply impasse.

During the course of 1975 the civilian right began to recover confidence and returned to the political initiative. In May 1975 two civilian ex-Presidents, Camilio Ponce and Carlos Julio Arosemena, formed a *Frente Cívico* (civic front) to oppose the Junta in what was a deliberate carbon copy of the successful anti-military campaign of 1966 when a vaguely reformist Junta was toppled by concerted right-wing civilian opposition. However, the fight had not yet gone from all of the military; there were still military nationalists, strongest in the navy, who opposed any move in a conservative direction.

Nevertheless, the nationalists could do no more than mount a blocking and delaying action as the government gradually responded to the pressures put upon it. Already in March the government had decided not to press ahead with the takeover of 51% of the consortium after the latter had threatened to pull out if any such attempt were made. Even so, the government continued for a time to oscillate between promising concessions to the companies and threatening them with sanctions if they did not increase their liftings. On 14 April the government ordered the companies to maintain a level of production of 210,000 b/d and gave CEPE the right to take its 25% of production from this level irrespective of whether it was achieved.

However, the majority of the government remained convinced that some further concessions would have to be made to the companies. The real reason for this concerned the immediate revenue position which later in the year made it necessary for the government to impose some import controls, a move that was extremely unpopular in right-wing circles. However, it is also noteworthy that the companies and the government itself had dropped the assumption that Ecuadorian oil reserves were abundant and instead emphasised the need for further exploration if fresh discoveries were to be made.

At the end of June 1975 the government made its long-awaited

concession to the oil companies, cutting the tax revenue per barrel of
28° API crude oil by $0.43 a barrel (from $10.84 to $10.41). This
price cut, however, was very much a compromise. The government
claimed that its new price was still within OPEC guidelines and the
Venezuelan government, disappointed though it was, soft-pedalled its
reaction. The price reduction did lead to some increase in oil production but was not enough to persuade the consortium to resume its
investment. In August René Bucaram of Texaco was publicly pressing
for a new tax cut. The government certainly appeared willing to make
further concessions to the companies later in the year, but had now lost
all coherence and capacity to act.

At the end of September the regime was able to put down a bitterly
fought coup attempt, involving a right-wing general and the political
parties of the right. Nevertheless, the government was now too weak
to turn this situation to its advantage and a successful military coup
took place in January 1976. In many ways, the coup was a move to the
right. The head of the Junta and the senior army officer were both seen
as political conservatives. The continuing strength of the nationalists
could be seen, however, in the appointment of Colonel René Vargas,
ex-head of CEPE and a close friend of Jarrín, to the Natural Resources
Ministry. It would quickly become apparent, however, that Colonel
Vargas had views on oil which were somewhat different from those of
his superiors.

1976: the consortium splits

The major feature of 1976 was the conflict between Gulf Oil and the
Ecuadorian government. This conflict was accompanied by a growing
difference in outlook between the two companies of the consortium.
Texaco was more accommodating than Gulf, partly because it sold
Ecuadorian oil directly to its own subsidiary and so could charge itself
whatever prices were most convenient whereas Gulf had to sell on the
open market. There may also have been more subjective reasons. The
key figure in Texaco's operation, René Bucaram, had earlier worked in
the government bureaucracy and continued to enjoy good relations
with many of its members, some of whom seemed to derive their full
knowledge of the industry from what they were told by the companies.[17] Accordingly it is possible that Texaco picked up the importance
of the 1976 coup and the military's gradual move to the right more

quickly than did Gulf. Moreover, Gulf Oil's position in Latin America appeared less secure after 1975 when the company had admitted to bribing senior Bolivian officials during the 1960s.

In any case, even after the tax reductions of 1975 Gulf remained unhappy with its operations in Ecuador. Consequently, although the world oil market had improved somewhat after mid-1975, Gulf was nevertheless prepared to take a hard line in Ecuador with the option of pulling out if its demands were not met.

The incoming regime was apparently prepared to consider satisfying the companies provided this could be done reasonably cheaply. It began by trying to find out what Texas–Gulf's terms were for resuming their investments. It was not left in doubt for long. It was reliably reported that in March the companies demanded a further fall in the tax reference price together with a further reduction in taxation.[18] They wanted an extra $0.50 a barrel profit if they were to resume investment in their existing fields and a further $0.50 a barrel if they were to develop new sources.

Although these terms were not acceptable to the government, further negotiations continued behind the scenes. Ostensibly, complete breakdown had taken place in March and reports by the *Petroleum Intelligence Weekly* (8 March) and *Platt's Oilgram* (17 March) stated that the companies preferred nationalisation to their existing position. However, this did not prevent the consortium from asking in May for an increase of $0.10 a barrel in the cost allowed against tax and promising that, if this was granted, they would embark upon a programme of 'reconditioning' the wells in the concession area as set out by a study drawn up in March.[19] Although this request was granted at the end of May, negotiations continued and on 27 July the *Financial Times* reported that, 'although Texaco and Gulf have consistently denied that they would like to get out of Ecuador, it is an open secret that they have been discussing nationalisation terms with the military'.

Meanwhile, the government itself was divided over the oil issue. Colonel Vargas had presented a report to the government in March 1976 which responded to the consortium's call for a $1.05 tax reduction by calling for nationalisation. In a detailed presentation he explored the possibilities of nationalisation with compensation coupled with a short-term management contract with Texaco. Vargas claimed that nationalisation could be made profitable if the oil were to be sold to other Latin American countries. The revenue thus generated could be used to finance the required re-investment in exploration. While this programme was not regarded with much enthusiasm by a cautious and conservative Junta, it was impossible for the regime to reject this position out of hand. Nationalisation, therefore, remained on the political agenda; as the *Financial Times* put it,

though internal divergences among the military have so far prevented any direct move to oust the Junta, many people feel that its prestige has fallen so low that such a step [nationalisation] seems almost inevitable. In particular, a group of progressive army colonels is making its influence felt in the political arena. Even if the Junta would like to remove Colonel Vargas and the head of CEPE, Colonel Luis Piñeros, for their radical attitudes, the repercussions might cause its own demise.[20]

Moreover, in 1976 Jarrín had returned from his diplomatic post in London and in June he launched a strong defence of his own and Colonel Vargas's position at the University of Guayaquil. However, despite (or because of) these pressures, the regime still found itself unable to take a decision.

The storm finally broke at the end of July 1976 when Gulf, now determined to get itself nationalised, sued Arco for receiving crude from CEPE when, according to Gulf, in reality it belonged to the consortium. The dispute went back to the decree of April 1975 which gave CEPE the right to take 25% of Ecuador's potential crude oil production of 210,000 b/d rather than actual production: Gulf disputed CEPE's right to do this. Texaco, meanwhile, emphasised that it had nothing to do with the conflict.

On 31 August Gulf went further and demanded its own nationalisation. Piñeros, the head of CEPE, immediately demanded that Gulf deposit in the Central Bank a figure corresponding to oil exports between February and August which had not been paid (leave of 120 days was generally given for this). Gulf's move did, finally, lead the government to act and on 7 September Colonel Vargas announced that CEPE was negotiating for Gulf's share of the consortium. Vargas also claimed that Gulf owed $32m. in back payments and demanded that payment should be made within 30 days if Gulf was not to be confiscated.

Even at this point, conservatives continued to mistrust the direction of government policy although the regime had obviously been forced into nationalisation by Gulf and had no particular enthusiasm for the step. Consequently the regime felt it necessary to prevent the nationalist issue from spinning out of control and was therefore determined to avoid making political capital out of nationalisation or even turning it into a political issue. It discouraged the formation of a pro-nationalisation pressure group and in August banned a proposed 'march for the nationalisation of oil'. Colonel Vargas himself, who had earlier tried to attract civilian support for a nationalist oil policy,[21] was kept out of the decision-making process as far as possible. In September, when the government responded to Gulf's payment of its debts by setting up a special commission to discuss compensation arrangements, Vargas was excluded altogether, all the more remarkably since the commission included several representatives from CEPE and participation from the Central Bank and the Procuraduría (the Attorney General's Office). Negotiations in fact continued on a low-key note until a working agreement was reached in December. Although there were a few loose ends which still needed to be tidied up, Gulf's assets passed under the control of CEPE, which now had 62.5% of the consortium.

The outcome

By the end of 1976 the military radicals had been defeated politically; a conservative regime, largely in control, was paving the way for the elections of 1979. Oil policy similarly changed; CEPE, now the 62.5% owner of the consortium, reached a new series of agreements with Texaco that were expected to lead to a considerable increase in production over the next few years. New legislation was enacted to end CEPE's marketing monopoly and to restrict its activities to production and refining. When one considers broader questions, it is tempting to quote from Fitch's conclusions regarding an earlier phase of Ecuadorian history: 'after more than three decades of modernisation, the basic social structure remains intact, the economy remains wedded to externally controlled markets for primary products, and the political system still lacks legitimacy and institutions capable of mobilising support on a sustained basis'.[22]

On the other hand, one must remember how new the oil industry was and how much had indeed changed in four years. CEPE was now the majority partner in the main consortium and had a major role in the refining and marketing sectors. While CEPE's own management had not inspired a great deal of confidence, the state company had at least established itself as a possible alternative to the multinationals in the longer term. Ecuador was a member of OPEC, even if not a particularly important one, and was certainly far more aware of the international dimension of the oil industry than it had been earlier.

When one considers the broader issues it is clear that the immediate effect of the oil wealth was to increase greatly the financial power of the Ecuadorian state. Since the end of 1973 oil has accounted for around one half of Ecuador's exports, and government taxing and spending policies have become proportionately important. In the very short term the effect of this transformation was to give a tactical advantage to a brilliant authoritarian–nationalist who aimed to shake up Ecuadorian government, oil policy, foreign policy and social structure as a whole. He gained some impressive early successes with the help of favourable international conditions, taking Ecuador into OPEC, establishing a strict tax regime and taking a government share in the oil industry. These moves, and the military government's early interest in major social reforms, then triggered off a counter-mobilisation from those groups who felt threatened by this new political direction. The oil companies and the US government were predictable opponents, particularly in the oil crisis years of 1973–4, but Jarrín also antagonised the traditional political groups in Ecuador by his outspoken attack on errors made in the past. By 1976, moreover, there were clear signs that the rapidly expanding Ecuadorian business community was also pressing hard to limit the power of the Ecuadorian state. The bourgeoisie as a whole had benefited greatly from the oil boom, but with its new-found wealth came a feeling of dependence on government policy and a deeply-rooted fear that the tap might be turned off. When stripped of rhetorical exaggeration, it essentially feared two things: that the state might use its financial power to force through major social changes, and that it might 'kill the goose that laid the golden eggs' by taxing the oil companies to excess or by pricing its oil out of world markets.

The removal of Jarrín in 1974 effectively ended the chance that the military government might adopt any genuinely aggressive reformist policies, although the Ecuadorian establishment clearly preferred to see a military return to barracks such as occurred in 1979. Tax and pricing policy, however, continued to create problems, for here Jarrín's policies were not so easily reversed. His successors could halt his aggressive initiatives but they could not backtrack too openly – the 1975 price cut was very limited but yet turned out to be the maximum that the economic liberals could secure. It was in fact Gulf Oil that broke the deadlock; weary of waiting for a decisive change in the political climate, it demanded its own nationalisation. This gave CEPE a majority of national oil production and meant that concessions on price to Texaco and other private companies were both financially and politically cheaper to make. Moreover, in their efforts to bring about this nationalisation both Jarrín and Vargas allowed themselves to be politically isolated during the course of 1976 so that the military conservatives triumphed politically even while Gulf Oil was being nationalised.

The successful emergence of a civilian regime in Ecuador has further solidified the status quo in the oil industry. Democratic governments in oil-exporting countries expect to buy, or at least to maintain, political support by judicious public spending policies. Once these come to benefit the majority or even a large minority of the electorate it becomes crucial for any government to keep up the inflow of revenue. Under such circumstances confrontational or overly ambitious oil policies are generally avoided. The Roldós government, elected in 1979, has so far concentrated on gradually increasing oil exploration and production through a mixture of public and private investment.

15

The nationalisation of oil in Venezuela

The Venezuelan nationalisation took place 53 years after oil production first began. Although the roots of the nationalisation in some ways go back as far as the companies themselves, the takeover followed many years of relative tranquillity. Moreover, the nationalisation was (as far as any step of this magnitude can be) a quiet, consensual affair which showed, as clearly as anything could, the lack of serious political conflict within the country. Nevertheless, despite the lack of acrimony or drama at the time of the final takeover, the nationalisation was the logical, perhaps the only, response to a gradually woven web of political and economic constraints which fit into place during the 53 years of oil production.

During this time, massive income had found its way to the Venezuelan Treasury and Venezuelan society. The high profits which the companies earned for many years, the massive corruption of certain of Venezuela's rulers and even the relative weakening of the country's market position after about 1957 were not sufficient to check the impact of oil wealth. With its oil income, the country's political order had been consolidated by successive Venezuelan presidents. Gómez had contented himself with buying the allegiance of Venezuela's military and political elite; López Contreras and Medina Angarita expanded the public service to provide employment for the growing Caracas middle class and the civil service grew in size from 7,000 in 1935 to 47,000 in 1941 and 95,535 in 1954 (by which time it had reached 10% of the non-agricultural labour force). Acción Democrática governments subsequently spread the wealth among unionised workers (especially the oil-workers) and among a provincial, even rural, electorate in order to oil the party's efficient electoral machine. By the 1970s, practically the whole of Venezuela had benefited to some degree from the oil industry and none showed any eagerness to damage this source of fabulous wealth.

Indeed, well before the establishment of democracy in 1958, Venezuela's largest political party, Acción Democrática, had been able to mobilise a powerful electoral machine on issues of internal distribution while proposing or making only limited changes in national oil policies. The 1945–8 AD government, while pressing hard for tax changes, was able to achieve a *modus vivendi* with the oil companies based on a 50–50 tax split and very high wages for the oil workforce. AD had committed itself to eventual nationalisation of oil, but this was not expected before 1983, when the 40-year concessions which had been granted in 1943 finally expired. Indeed, both under the 1945–8 government and under the subsequent dictatorship, oil played a surprisingly small direct role in Venezuelan politics. This pattern was to continue with the democratic restoration in 1958 and with AD's electoral victory in December of that year.

In certain respects, however, nationalism still flourished. Venezuela had no wish to turn off the tap of oil wealth, but influential Venezuelans wished to control its flow and harness as much of it as possible for their own purposes. Thus, after 1958 the AD party enforced a policy of oil conservation. Companies continued to operate, but they were given no new territory to explore and insufficient financial incentive to make further heavy investment attractive. Changes in Venezuela combined with the increasing attractiveness of producing in the Middle East to impose a sharp deceleration on the hitherto rapid expansion of the Venezuelan oil industry. The fall-off in investment was not immediately reflected in a reduction in output (although growth slowed down considerably after 1958), but did lead to serious problems in the early and mid-1970s.

The Betancourt government 1958–63

After 1958, Venezuela's freedom was in any case severely limited by the world oil situation. World oil prices had begun to weaken, a trend which was strengthened by Washington's imposition of an import-quota system in 1959 (see chapter 4). Moreover, changes in technology were sharply reducing the cost of transporting crude oil from the Middle East and so exposed areas traditionally supplied by Venezuela to competition from lower-cost sources. Venezuela, therefore, was faced with the choice of making substantial tax reductions on the oil companies in the hope that this would encourage them to continue expanding production or maintaining high tax rates (which had been increased

Table 15.1 *Investment in Venezuela's oil industry 1957–64*
($*m*.)

	1957	1958	1959	1960	1961	1962	1963	1964
Total	1,140	775	515	315	220	205	210	210
Exploration and production	965	550	415	255	185	175	180	165

Source: Chase Manhattan Bank, *Report on the World Oil Industry*, 1958–65.

Table 15.2 *Venezuela's oil output 1956–72*
(000 *b/d, annual average*)

1956	2,463.5	1966	3,369.9
1960	2,846.6	1968	3,605.5
1962	3,200.0	1970	3,706.8
1964	3,391.8	1972	3,227.4

Source: US Department of Energy, *Energy Statistics*, 1972.

Table 15.3 *Oil prices and government take since 1958*
($ *per barrel*)

	Price	Fiscal take		Price	Fiscal take
1958	2.50	0.93	1966	1.87	0.83
1959	2.23	0.82	1967	1.90	0.89
1960	2.12	0.77	1968	1.92	0.91
1961	2.13	0.80	1969	1.92	0.89
1962	2.08	0.83	1970	1.93	0.98
1963	2.04	0.83	1971	2.52	1.30
1964	1.96	0.87	1972	2.99	1.63
1965	1.89	0.85	1973	3.17	2.52
			1974	10.45	8.48

Source: Fuad, 'Venezuela's role in OPEC', in Bond (ed.), *Contemporary Venezuela*, p. 150.

by the interim 1958 government) and accepting the inevitable slow-down of growth.

This choice, between emphasising per barrel income or total pro-duction, has always been central to the strategy of any producing coun-try. However, the situation in 1959 both sharpened this choice and made it clear which Venezuela would choose. Given the extent to which international circumstances had become adverse, only very sharp tax cuts could hope to stimulate output significantly over what it would otherwise have been. Any such tax cut would have been extremely unpopular, not only because of revenue forgone but also because the companies had themselves damaged their image significantly by their tacit (and sometimes not-so-tacit) support of the fallen dictator, Pérez Jiménez. Given that the new AD government was highly insecure, any move such as a tax cut that would unite the considerable opposition to the regime would have been impossible on political grounds alone. On the other hand, a policy of higher taxes and slower growth became easier to pursue after 1960 as a result of Washington's general support for the overall orientation of the regime (which was strongly anti-Castroist at a time when this was Washington's main concern). Washington could therefore press the companies to be relatively conciliatory in their approach to the government.

Under these circumstances, the distinctive mark of AD's Oil Minister Pérez Alfonzo was less his basic economic strategy than his energy and breadth of vision in pursuing it. Pérez Alfonzo was in many ways deeply conservative. He believed that the world price of oil would increase in later years and that there was therefore little point in pressing for short-term increases in production. Moreover, he believed that oil income should not increase more rapidly than overall GNP because 'excessive expenditure leads to waste and inefficiency, with the result that the community does not receive the full benefit; bonanzas inhibit hard-headed calculation'.[1]

Internationally, Pérez Alfonzo attempted nothing less than the creation of a world-wide pro-rationing system according to which world oil production would be decided upon by agreement between producing countries and governments would take the major responsibility for international marketing. Washington, however, was not receptive to Pérez Alfonzo's proposals that its oil quotas be allocated by country (on the lines of the sugar quota) rather than by company, if only because its own companies controlled the bulk of the trade. Nevertheless Pérez Alfonzo did play a major part in the creation of OPEC in 1960 although, as we have seen in chapter 4, his objectives for the organisation were excessively ambitious. Even within Venezuela, Pérez Alfonzo's attempts to regulate prices and production were not wholly successful, partly because the government lacked information and partly because the companies showed little desire to increase production even to the level desired by the government.[2] The oil companies, however, not only had to face Pérez Alfonzo's foreign economic policy but also his interruption of their domestic activities. Only part of this question was directly fiscal; there had been a large tax increase imposed at the end of 1958 by the Provisional Government which, as we have seen (chapter 4), provoked company anger. Betancourt, although 'privately shocked by the price increase',[3] did not change it during his term in office. However, he and Pérez Alfonzo successfully resisted pressure from within the AD party to increase taxes still further in 1961.[4]

Not less important for the companies was the decision of the AD government to end the granting of concessions and to set up a state oil company, the CVP, in 1960. The CVP provided a convenient focal point for conservative opponents of the government's oil policy and Pérez Alfonzo had to go somewhat against his personal inclinations by promising that the CVP would prepare and subsequently sign long-term contracts with the companies. These would permit a 'backdoor' return of direct foreign investment. This decision followed an attack on the CVP from a member of COPEI (a rival party which was nevertheless part of the government coalition between 1959 and 1963) and signs of unhappiness from within the government over what was seen as excessive nationalism.[5]

Given the extent to which oil policy changed in the years between 1958 and 1963, it is not surprising that there was considerable opposition to Pérez Alfonzo. Nevertheless, he received steadfast backing from within the government, particularly from President Betancourt. As a senior energy official of the time pointed out, 'if indeed Pérez Alfonzo owed a good part of his position as initiator of a new Venezuelan oil policy to his characteristics of combativeness, honesty and studiousness, one should not forget that this was possible as a result of the tremendous respect and operating freedom afforded to him by President Betancourt'.[6] Politically, therefore, Pérez Alfonzo was as secure as the government itself, for which other questions quickly became more pressing than that of oil. Moreover, as a nationalist, but not a nationaliser, Pérez Alfonzo was broadly in tune with popular thinking,[7] even though there was important opposition from both left and right.

The impact of left-wing opposition was greatly weakened by the fact that AD maintained secure control over the oil-workers' union. Indeed, it is significant that the first left-wing breakaway from AD occurred at the time of the drawing up of the oil-workers' new contract in February 1960. One of the leaders of the left wing, Rangel, who had himself played a part in the negotiations, publicly criticised the settlement. Consequently, 'the AD leaders among the petroleum workers were infuriated by Rangel's action and threatened to bring charges against him within Acción Democrática'.[8] This precipitated a split within the party but the oil-workers remained loyal. The main left-wing opposition came from students who had taken to the streets in 1958 in order to bring down Pérez Jiménez and now found themselves excluded from power by the middle-aged professional politicians of AD. There can in fact be little doubt that the aims of the far left, which involved forcing Caracas into alliance with Castro's Cuba and into confrontation with Washington, attracted very little sympathy within Venezuela, and once it resorted to violence (as it did in 1961) it lost any opportunity of influencing oil policy.

Criticism from the right was more formidable. Even this, however, was of only limited significance. Washington acted as a moderating influence to some extent under Eisenhower and to a very great extent under Kennedy. The military, which might have played a different role under other circumstances, was internally divided and in any case concerned far more with internal security than with domestic oil policy. Consequently, when criticism was made of AD's oil policies, it came from outside the mainstream of politics. The first major public attack on Pérez Alfonzo came during the 1963 election campaign and was voiced by Uslar Pietri, a right-wing former adviser to Medina Angarita (President 1941–5). As Martz described him,

more strongly opposed than most to any possibility of nationalising the industry, he looked askance at the state-owned oil enterprise in which the government took great pride. Viewing it as wasteful and inefficient, he preferred a clear encouragement of foreign interests. While his stand was somewhat softened as a bow towards public sympathies, informed quarters held little doubt that his approach reflected the Venezuelan elite that mistrusted the whole thrust of politics first instituted by Acción Democrática.[9]

Uslar Pietri had a plurality of votes in Caracas and came third nationally; although he was far from being victorious, it is significant that no left-wing candidate has ever put up such a good showing.

The oil companies themselves put a certain amount of pressure on the AD government, but it seems clear that this was mostly the result of orders from above, stemming more from the nature of the world oil situation than from any particular quarrel with the government of Venezuela. Thus, in August 1960, when Jersey Standard decided to cut its 'posted prices' of crude oil in all major producing countries, 'when the board instructed their man in Caracas, Arthur Proudfitt, to enforce the cut, he threatened to resign, believing that it would wreck Exxon's position in Venezuela, so the board climbed down'.[10] It was probably coincidence that at the end of August a senior Venezuelan executive resigned from Creole because of his disagreements with the company which

have become more serious as a result of the latest price cut dictated by Esso export and the defensive measures taken by the Venezuelan government . . .

I particularly object to a motion passed by a majority of the executive committee of the Cámera de la Industria del Petróleo (of Fedecámeras [the Venezuelan business association]) which sets in motion a publicity campaign demanding among other things the withdrawal of this government resolution (994) just in time to weaken the position of the Venezuelan representative at the forthcoming Oil Congress in Beirut.[11]

International pressures, therefore, appear to have been qualified by the nature of local conditions.

The Leoni Administration 1963–8

AD's victory in the 1963 elections, although not particularly impressive, nevertheless ensured an essential continuity in oil policy and was followed by the creation of another broad government coalition. One of the new President Leoni's first steps was to strengthen CVP operationally, particularly in the field of domestic marketing which, it was felt, was an area in which it could expand without upsetting the delicate balance of the international oil industry. Decree 187 of 1964 set a target for CVP to take 33% of the domestic market by 1970. However, company resistance, although passive, was strong and this target was not even nearly achieved. Subsequently, in 1964, Congress passed a law giving CVP 100% of the domestic market by 1971.

The companies put up more open resistance to the government's efforts, in 1966, to raise the tax rate. This move led to the most serious crisis of the Leoni government and to the resignation of Uslar Pietri from the government coalition. Conditions had changed in two respects since the early 1960s. The world market, which had softened consistently during the early 1960s, had shown some signs of changing. In 1965 Libya, until then an important source of low-cost oil, sharply raised its tax rate and also adopted a 'posted price' system; this ended the most aggressive price cutting on the world market and also marked the first clear-cut defeat of the international companies by a producer government. Venezuela, like pre-1965 Libya, did not have a system of tax reference prices and taxation therefore depended on the actual price at which crude oil was sold. This system proved very costly for Venezuela and in 1965 total government revenue from oil actually declined in the face of company price cutting. The second important change lay in Venezuela itself. As we have seen, capital spending by the oil companies dropped off sharply after 1959 with the result that the book value of the oil installations also fell. In 1958 the oil companies had produced 2.6 million barrels of oil daily from installations valued at $2,302m.; in 1966 they produced 3.4 million barrels daily from $1,922m. of invested capital.[12] Consequently company profitability increased; average rates of return on capital increased from 16.8% in 1958 and a low point of 12.1% in 1960 to 31.11% in 1966.

Under these circumstances, it came as no surprise that the Venezuelan government once again sought to increase its tax take. The government in fact sought to establish a tax reference price for future use and also to reclaim an amount of backtaxes in respect of earlier price cutting. At the end of June 1966, however, the government went further than this and informed the oil companies that it was about to introduce a new tax: a selective tax on all profits of more than 15% on net assets. According to Tugwell, who has provided an outstanding account of this episode, the selective tax was 'the brainchild of Pérez Alfonzo' who, although no longer a formal office holder, retained a great deal of influence over government policy'.[13] The tax package introduced in July also included a general increase in income tax and other domestic taxes.

This tax package faced united opposition from the right-wing political parties, from Fedecámeras (the businessmen's lobby) and from the oil companies. The oil companies had joined Fedecámeras in August 1959 after they had become conscious for the first time of the depth of hostility to their formerly close relationship with the dictator Pérez Jiménez. The Venezuelan bourgeoisie was happy enough with this arrangement, and particularly with the financial benefits to their organisation which the companies provided, and were willing to reinforce the company line on oil policy. In May 1966, while negotiations continued with the government over reference prices, Fedecámeras put out a report on the oil industry which essentially reflected the company position. It appears that the companies (and certainly the US Ambassador) wished to avoid open conflict with the government and pressed the government not to introduce the bill into Congress until a negotiated settlement was reached.[14] When this advice was disregarded, the proposals met intense assault from the press and Congress (which was boycotted for a time by the opposition parties so that there was no quorum). It is possible that the government regarded the selective tax as a lightning conductor, which would attract attention away from the rest of the package but which could be withdrawn after a compromise could be worked out. If so, it miscalculated and President Leoni quickly offered to retreat from his initial position while calling on the companies to ease the political pressure on his administration.[15] Finally, in September, an agreement was reached on all outstanding points. The companies agreed to pay a total of $155m. in backtaxes over five years. The government would in the future set tax reference prices but would not otherwise interfere with the operating freedom of the companies. The companies would, in turn, seek to increase their output from Venezuela, as they did later, especially after the Suez Canal closure of 1967. The selective tax was withdrawn but the ordinary profits tax was increased so as to add 3% to the government's own profit share − roughly one half of the amount that would have been raised by the initial proposals.[16] Finally, the Leoni government agreed in principle to introduce a form of service contract which would replace the old concessions when they expired in 1983 and which would in the meantime give the companies new opportunities to invest.

Such plans, however, met serious opposition from nationalists within AD (once again including Pérez Alfonzo) and were thus delayed.[17] Although Congress did approve the contract law in outline, it nevertheless insisted that any contracts actually signed should be returned to Congress for scrutiny. Nothing had been settled by the end of 1968, when COPEI won the presidential elections.

Caldera, the crisis and OPEC 1969–73

The Caldera Administration was perhaps the most crucial of the whole democratic period with regard to the oil industry. In 1968 there was a powerful conservative wing in Venezuelan politics which supported

the idea of a long-term accommodation with the companies to reverse
the disinvestment which had been taking place in the oil industry and
to ensure Venezuela's continued connection with international markets. By 1973, however, all of the major political groups had come to
favour total and almost immediate nationalisation. While not everything is yet clear about the dramatic events of 1970, it was then that
the turning point was reached.

Caldera's initial instincts were to favour the oil companies, upon
whom he came to depend increasingly for information after the dis-
bandment of the former AD government's oil policymaking group.
Thus, Caldera in his first years in office 'became increasingly preoccupied with production levels and showed little sympathy for Pérez
Alfonzo's policy . . . Until late in 1971 at least, he operated on the
assumption that low prices would continue for the foreseeable future,
as Creole and other companies repeatedly assured him they would.'[18]
Indeed, it was later reported that the Caldera regime 'seriously contemplated increasing production to five million barrels a day',[19] which
would have required very heavy private investment if reserves were not
to be depleted rapidly. Caldera's sympathy with the companies was
mirrored by his government's lack of sympathy with OPEC.[20]

Consequently Caldera at first made a serious effort to bring into
being those service contracts which Congress had earlier approved in
principle. In late 1969, the government submitted its detailed proposals to Congress (in which AD had retained its majority). Although a
number of smaller parties, notably the MEP (which was composed of a
group which had broken away from AD in 1968), supported Pérez
Alfonzo's opposition to all service contracts, AD as a whole agreed to
support the idea of service contracts in principle, but made little effort
to make them attractive to foreign companies. By February 1970 contract terms were approved, but these were such as to deter many of the
companies involved and only Shell, Occidental and Mobil were willing
to enter.[21]

In 1970, however, the balance of power in the world oil industry
finally tilted decisively in favour of the oil producers. In that year, the
Libyan government was able to secure a major increase in taxes and the
reference on which taxes were based: the companies objected strenuously, but in vain. By then the companies were disunited, their spare
capacity had largely disappeared, and the political guidance from
Washington and London was ambiguous and indecisive. Nevertheless
one of the few cards which Jersey Standard believed that it still pos-

sessed lay in Venezuela. Although Venezuela's oil reserves were not high (and fell from 16 billion barrels in 1968 to just over 14 billion in 1970), it was still just possible to squeeze an increase in production from the country. Output in fact rose only slightly in 1970, but Jersey Standard was at one point planning to increase production from Venezuela in order to put pressure on the Middle Eastern governments:

When we went into this negotiation in Tehran and Tripoli, we thought at one time that we could get Venezuela input. There are quite a few cables here of talking about the Venezuelan situation. That did not come to pass. The Venezuelans kept on acting unilaterally and we think it would be extremely damaging if the knowledge of the formation, attempted formation, of this was publicised in any way.[22]

The source of this 'unilateral action', however, was not the Venezuelan government but the congressional opposition.

In fact, the Caldera government in 1970 faced a severe budgetary problem as revenue had failed to keep up with expenditure. In October, Finance Minister Tinoco requested an increase in domestic taxes but not oil taxes. His timing was not opportune. Pérez Alfonzo, who had maintained his interest in oil and his international connections, was watching the oil market closely. By October he had 'decided that the government, preoccupied with production, was missing an opportunity to increase its income and enlarge its control of the oil industry'.[23] After the Libyan victory over the companies in September 1970 and with an OPEC meeting due in Caracas in December, Pérez Alfonzo looked for a way to force Venezuela on to the offensive.

When Tinoco presented his proposals, therefore, Pérez Alfonzo and his ally, Deputy Hernández Grisanti, called instead for an increase in oil taxation. The rest of AD wavered at first, but then found that such a strategy was politically too good to resist. The congressional majority met Tinoco's proposals, therefore, with a counter-proposal involving an increase in oil profits tax from 52% to 60% (not including royalties) and pressed for a law which would give the government the right to set oil prices unilaterally. After some vacillation, Caldera accepted this position.

Between 1970 and 1975 events moved quickly. By the end of 1970 the weakness of the companies' position was clear. They had expected their future to be secured by agreement on some form of service contract. The contracts finally agreed, however, after nearly a decade of discussion and in the teeth of strong nationalistic opposition, were extremely unattractive. Even if such terms were offered in 1983 (when the concessions ratified by the 1943 law were due to expire) it is not clear that the largest companies would accept them, but there was certainly very little chance that more generous terms would be available. Secondly, by 1970 the oil companies found themselves almost without domestic allies. The major part of their problem was that executives in Venezuela had been largely constrained by the global perspectives of their head offices and, as we have seen, this required them to put pressures on Caracas in ways that were certain to be politically costly to themselves in the long term. Caldera, in particular, turned strongly against the companies in the years after 1970, no doubt feeling (with some justification) that they had misled him. For others, CVP's frustrating experience in trying to secure distribution outlets in the face of passive resistance from the companies was important in changing attitudes.[24] *Business Venezuela* could quote an influential although anonymous Congressman as saying 'We have been told so many lies by the oil industry that if an oil executive told me it was raining, I'd have to go outside and check before I'd believe him.'[25] Under these circumstances, the end was closer than anybody realised.

In 1971 the congressional opposition raised a further question: what was to be done with the oil industry after the companies' concessions reverted to the state in 1983? The companies had been disinvesting ever since 1958 as a result of falling world prices and local tax increases. Moreover, their hope of an eventual transfer to a regime of service contracts had done something to check the decline in oil activity but, with the service contracts on offer being so unattractive, this option appeared to be closed. In March 1971 the MEP leader, Silva Calderón, introduced a bill to 'resolve' the issue by guaranteeing state control of the industry after 1983. Companies were to deposit a sum which would be returned provided that the fields were turned over in good condition. This bill was then supported by the 'nationalist' wing of AD and the rest of the party followed reluctantly; subsequently the other parties agreed to go along with the proposals.

During these years there also came about a major change in COPEI's attitude. Formerly an ally of the companies, it now became nationalist and determined to outbid AD on the issue. Thus, in 1970 Caldera nationalised the natural gas industry and subsequently COPEI adopted a political strategy of 'more nationalist than thou'. One reason for this change was that COPEI felt that AD had 'broken the political rules' by enforcing changes in oil policy on the government in 1970; until that time, Congress had never reversed government policy on a major issue. Perhaps more fundamentally, it had become obvious that the oil companies had lost their power; their credibility had gone, their days in Venezuela were clearly numbered and the rising world price of oil more than offset the immediate impact of a fall in production. Indeed, between 1971 and 1974 the rate of disinvestment grew and Venezuelan output fell back sharply. In 1974 this averaged 3,065 million b/d, which was below the level of 1964 and only just above that of 1960. Caldera introduced tax penalties for underproduction but with little result.[26] It appeared that the companies had effectively written off their investments in Venezuela and were hoping for some compensation from nationalisation. Thus, in the 1973 elections 'privately, company representatives did little to hide their strong preference for an AD victory'.[27]

Although pressures for nationalisation were building up during the Caldera period, the matter was rarely mentioned explicitly; all politicians clearly realised that premature or irresponsible discussion of the question might do serious harm at a time when relations with Washington were still difficult (see chapter 5) and when public opinion was not totally predictable. Indeed, it seems that during this period the political elite were determined to decide upon this issue themselves and to prevent it being discussed more widely than was necessary. Certainly, as Gall points out, 'many politicians privately say that the movement to nationalise comes not from any public clamour, but from pressures from within the smaller community of politicians and from recent dramatic changes in the oil industry outside Venezuela'.[28] But when did these pressures arise?

As late as 1972, nationalisation was seen as 'an alternative voiced by only two minority groups'; these included the MEP which, significantly, defended its position on the grounds that 'in OPEC, the international conditions are now such that for Venezuela this step is necessary'. Pérez Alfonzo still opposed nationalisation but criticised the government for not taking an equity stake in the companies on the OPEC 'participation' model.[29] At this time, however, most of the political elite preferred to wait until 1983 when reversion of most of the oil properties to the state was to be automatic; for this reason, the Venezuelan government in 1972 was 'not particularly concerned with the outcome of the participation talks at OPEC'.[30]

In the 1973 elections, only the parties of the far left openly advocated nationalisation, although the AD candidate Pérez was careful to keep his options open, arguing that,

because the oil companies in Venezuela were investing minimum amounts, the state was running the risk of inheriting an out of date and run-down industry when it took it over in 1983 . . . [consequently] 'We may proceed immediately to a nationalisation which would ensure our sovereignty in the industry and which would set out new formulas for the participation of foreign companies in those spheres in which we need their technical resources.'[31]

Indeed, the *Guardian* remarked that 'there is a widespread feeling that either Fernández [the COPEI candidate] or Pérez will move quickly to begin the process of taking over property, especially of the major foreign producers such as Shell and Gulf'.[32]

Thus, it appears that key Venezuelan politicians made up their minds to nationalise the oil industry in 1973 but were determined not to publicise the fact too openly lest it become an election issue. This is not to say that they deliberately did not seek to pick up votes on the issue; it is by no means clear that votes were to be won by a nationalist stance and more likely that fears of 'instability' would have rebounded against a stridently nationalistic candidate. Certainly, the left fared miserably in the 1973 elections, winning only around 12% in total and with even this proportion divided among four candidates. Uslar Pietri had done far better in 1963 on an openly pro-company platform. Rarely in Latin America can radical oil nationalism have been less popular than it was at this time in Venezuela.

The nationalisation 1974–5

Once the election was over, however, the move toward nationalisation began. In January 1974 COPEI spokesmen, including Caldera, began calling for nationalisation and in February President-Elect Pérez promised to carry out such a measure 'within two years'. The only question to be answered was what form this nationalisation would take. The incoming AD government could tackle this problem with remarkably few difficulties; the party maintained its congressional majority and could therefore if necessary force through a nationalisation law on its own. The companies were willing to be nationalised and simply sought satisfactory terms. Problems, therefore, were technocratic rather than political; as an AD leader, Pérez Guerrero, pointed out, 'Our greatest political problem is management capacity.'[33]

In early 1974 Pérez set up a commission, ostensibly to study ways of nationalising the industry but in fact in order to take away any political pressure that he might have faced. In fact the most influential figures behind the commission were a small group of AD leaders, Betancourt, Pérez Guerrero and Valentín Hernández as well as Pérez himself. Meanwhile, in 1974 the government nationalised the iron-ore industry as a kind of trial run for the larger and more complex oil question. This nationalisation was probably intended to reassure the companies and Washington rather than the more militant domestic nationalists. In March 1975 the government finally issued its draft nationalisation law. The most controversial part of this was Article 5, which enabled the state to contract particular private companies, with prior congressional approval, to carry out particular activities within the oil industry. This permitted

the signing of agreements or contracts with private companies for the execution of particular tasks or the provision of particular services which may be paid for in cash or kind, although payment should not be made through a fixed proportion of production from a particular field or the provision of a substantial quantity of oil which would change the character of the contract into a simple one of service or operation.[34]

More extensive contracts could be signed, for a fixed period, under conditions of emergency.

These provisions were enough to unite an opposition which was clearly looking for a place to attack. According to the *New York Times* this article was 'inserted at the last minute by the government'.[35] The aim was merely to give the regime the maximum freedom to negotiate; there could be no question of company pressure at this stage. The same *New York Times* article quoted an oil executive as saying, 'We're frankly very much in the dark because, so far at least, there have been few contacts between government and the industry. The sporadic talks between representatives of Shell, Exxon and Gulf and the government haven't got very far.' It added that 'Government officials nevertheless insist privately that the administration does not wish to be seen negotiating with the oil companies until nationalisation.' Moreover, there was no question of the government allowing itself to be pressed by its political opposition into an unreasonably hard line *vis-à-vis* the companies. As Valentín Hernández, Venezuela's Oil Minister, pointed out, 'I consider that it is much better for the country not to have [nationalised] "heroically" because that would not have allowed the oil industry, when nationalised, to continue to bring in the income which the country requires for its development plans.'[36]

It is likely that the leading opposition party, COPEI, would have opposed anything that the government might have proposed. As Martz summarised its attitude:

Fighting to retain its position at the head of the opposition while determined to regain power in 1978, COPEI was therefore anxious to seize all available opportunities of criticising the government for 'anti-nationalist' actions.

Several currents of thought emerged in party discussions. The first saw the importance of national consensus on such a vital matter, contending that COPEI should contribute to the preparation of legislation. Other *copeyanos*, however, projected greater political advantage from relentless opposition to official proposals. They believed that the party's 1978 campaign could best be enhanced if COPEI presented itself as an unqualified critic of the *adeco* government and its policies. And yet another group, including Caldera's former Minister of Mines, Hugo Pérez la Salvia, had been disappointed by the party's failure to have nationalised the industry itself in 1973. Resentment of an AD government doing so was profound.[37]

The left was in any case certain to oppose anything which appeared to be a concession to the companies and its opposition to AD's proposals was therefore inevitable. Thus, although several attempts were made to reach a compromise on the question, the nationalisation was ultimately carried out with only the support of the AD party and the very small political right wing.

The nationalisation itself was defended by the government on psychological rather than economic grounds. In a sense, therefore, 'dependency' was the central motive for nationalisation, but it was 'dependency' as it influenced the political elite rather than broader social forces. Consequently, although nationalisation had long been aspired to by influential Venezuelans, it took place when domestic and international conditions were favourable and not before. Until 1973 the Venezuelan oil nationalists had worked to regulate domestic and international supply levels, to co-ordinate international producer agencies, to maintain a high rate of tax and to conserve resources. These policies avoided confrontation with the companies but were not without some cost. Between 1958 and 1973 the Venezuelan oil industry had been transformed from a dynamic and low-cost industry into one which had become largely decapitalised and unable to maintain production even at 3 million b/d. This transformation, together with a change in international conditions, lay behind the Venezuelan nationalisation.

From Creole to Lagovén

The Venezuelan nationalisation is one of the few in Latin America in which continuing co-operation with foreign companies was clearly bound up with the takeover itself. As we shall see in more detail below (pp. 469–80), the Venezuelan industry was to continue to be an essential part of the international economic system; only the terms and conditions of Venezuela's membership of the international economic system had changed. Consequently, one might see the Venezuelan nationalisation as a natural culmination of many years of operation by the private oil companies.

In many ways, company–government relations during this period must be accounted a success. The oil companies made good profits but at the same time contributed heavily to the Venezuelan Treasury. One might almost say that Venezuela floated to affluence on a sea of oil; certainly during the whole post-war period, and especially after 1973, Venezuela's oil income was sufficient to keep the country in the ranks of the wealthiest in Latin America. It is clear, moreover, that a secure source of oil income permitted Venezuelan political parties far greater latitude to pursue patronage politics than would have been the case in a more austere economic climate; consequently, it may be argued, oil resources and the companies themselves played a major part in safeguarding Venezuelan democracy. Admittedly it was far from inevitable that the oil industry should play such a role; the fact that Venezuela has a small and fairly coherent political elite, itself convinced of the virtues of democracy, was almost certainly more important for domestic politics. Nevertheless, criticisms of the arrangements prevailing in Venezuela, at least since 1958, need to be qualified heavily.

The relationship between Venezuelan democracy and the oil companies, however, did have its problems. For one thing, the relatively harmonious 1958–73 period was certain to be finite. The oil companies could continue to operate for a certain time from investments which they had already carried out, but production would be certain to fall eventually unless oil development continued. However, while the Venezuelan political elite could survive easily enough on the basis of high tax rates upon the oil companies, there were severe political difficulties in any strategy which would have allowed the oil companies to earn sufficient profits to make it worthwhile for them to reinvest. By 1970 severe problems appeared imminent but were postponed by changes in the international markets.

At a more political level, the difficulties stemmed from the fact that the companies could never be wholly outside the local political system, or wholly within it; instead, they occupied a kind of no-man's-land. This, in turn, stemmed from the fact that national sovereignty was both a universal aspiration and, in important respects, a physical impossibility. The nature of this conflict can be seen in several ways.

First, the companies were able neither to enter Venezuelan politics openly nor to withdraw from them fully. Under Pérez Jiménez, they responded to favourable treatment by strongly and vocally supporting a regime which was extremely unpopular within Venezuela, and thus they became discredited along with the fallen dictator. Relations with the subsequent AD governments were cool; the companies sought to use Fedecámeras and friendly journalists to present essentially critical positions while generally avoiding open attack. However, the way in which they used rather than joined the Venezuelan private sector can be seen from how they made a 'separate peace' with the Leoni government in 1966. Subsequently, under Caldera, the companies sought to move closer to the government but found that their own, and the government's, initiatives were blocked by the congressional opposition. When AD's predictions proved to be more accurate than those of the companies, the latter lost credibility still further and, with it, their last influential domestic allies. It is interesting that the companies lost more when they became closely associated with governments (such as those of Pérez Jiménez and Caldera) than when they remained at arm's length. However, for as long as the companies and their parent governments retained significant power, it was natural that Venezuelan political groups would seek credibility or direct financial rewards by associating themselves closely with them; gradually, however, their position eroded.

Secondly, the companies needed to balance their position in Venezuela with their 'worldwide commitments'. In 1960, Creole (the Venezuelan subsidiary of Jersey Standard) nearly launched itself on a collision course with the government in Caracas because it feared that action in Caracas would damage Jersey Standard's interests in the Middle East (as indeed it eventually did). But for the strong opposition to Standard's policies which came from within Creole, there would almost certainly have been a government–company confrontation in 1960. With the Cuban Revolution barely a year old, the consequences of this would have been incalculable for the whole of Latin America as well as for the world oil industry. In 1970 Jersey Standard again tried to play off Venezuela against the countries of the Middle East and, in doing so, brought about the company's definitive isolation in Venezuela (without significantly improving its position in the Middle East).

Thirdly, and perhaps most fundamentally, foreign oil companies remain foreign irrespective of the amount they pay in taxes or of their impact upon the domestic economy. The dominant opinion within Venezuela, at least since the Second World War, was that the legitimate owner of the oil wealth was not the company but the country. Thus, no matter how high taxation became, the government was getting no more than its due; no matter what the skills or the market power of the companies might be, they were entitled to no more than 'a reasonable return', and even that for only as long as Venezuela was technically incapable of managing the industry. In a world where profits were often very much higher than what Venezuelans would regard as a reasonable return, it was inevitable that there would be accusations of exploitation which would be widely believed. Consequently, the companies' defence was merely that of technical efficiency; that this was effective for so long in Venezuela had a great deal to do with the abundance of the returned value from oil and the responsible outlook of Venezuela's own democratic rulers. While unpopular oil companies have sometimes been able to survive for long periods under the protection of secure, if even more unpopular, domestic dictators, the coming of democracy to Venezuela practically ensured that oil would be nationalised once it had become clear that the step was expedient.

For these reasons, therefore, the symbolism of the change in ownership of the oil industry may well be far greater than one might expect purely from the operational changes involved. The responsibility for managing the world oil market has now been assumed by the producing countries, who can co-ordinate (or otherwise) their policies more openly than the companies ever dared and the political dimensions of the choices involved can now be made explicit. The existing situation should also prove far more satisfactory for Venezuela, now that the political and strategic decisions concerning the oil industry are openly in government hands (as in many ways they were previously, but less clearly). The companies can continue to provide technical services. We shall consider these arrangements in more detail in chapter 22.

16

Oil companies and governments in twentieth-century Latin America

In the introduction to this section (chapter 7) we considered the assumptions lying behind two influential approaches to government–company relations; the bargaining model and what, for want of a better term, may be described as a 'class' model. Now that the main cases of oil expropriation or exclusion of foreign companies have been discussed, it will be useful to return again to the question of how these conflicts are best conceptualised and understood. It should be said at once that all models are abstractions from reality and it would therefore not be difficult to uncover cases in which particular assumptions do not apply. While such an exercise might provide a useful antidote to an excessively dogmatic or arrogant presentation of a particular case, it would not by itself take us very far. It is much better to begin by considering the advantages of each framework before considering how they might usefully be combined, supplemented or modified.

If we take the bargaining model first, it is necessary to proceed by making an assumption of what host government objectives really are. Let us then assume that all Latin American governments wish to take control over their domestic oil industries to the greatest extent possible, and that they will therefore expropriate or exclude foreign capital unless the cost to themselves is high or unless the oil companies or their parent governments have a great deal to offer. In other words, nationalisation is assumed to be mainly the result of opportunity. Let us further assume that this is partly determined by the state of the industry in the country in question, but mainly by the international system.

Before testing this hypothesis in detail, it is important to explain why it has been preferred to other possible formulations relating to bargaining behaviour. The key factor is that it highlights governments' desire for control over oil rather than for maximum income from it. If we consider the various nationalisations that have taken place, we find that only those carried out in Brazil, Chile, Uruguay and possibly Venezuela were motivated by a desire to increase returned value from oil. Conversely those of Bolivia (twice), Mexico, Ecuador, Peru, Argentina (in the 1930s and also, as we shall see, in 1963) and Cuba were deliberately designed to foster political objectives even at the price of some short-term loss of national income. The 'maximisation of income' hypothesis, therefore, does not work well here. It may of course be objected that maximising governments do exist but generally do not nationalise. Certainly there are conditions under which maximisation of income is more likely than maximisation of control. These include occasions when the state apparatus is very weak, when foreign investment is expected to bring about proportionately very large increases in oil income (both of these conditions were generally applicable throughout Latin America during the 1920s) and when existing returned value is both large and precarious (Venezuela 1958–72). Moreover, in cases where foreign investment is available on terms more restrictive than the traditional concession contract, governments may find it easier to strike a balance between their desire for income and their need to maintain control. Even so, it is argued here, Latin American governments have historically been more likely to seek to maximise their control over oil rather than their income from it. Let us therefore consider the original hypothesis.

In the 1920s the only important oil nationalist programme was developed in Argentina where, as we have seen, oil nationalism tied in closely with the needs of the state company. In the 1930s Chile and Uruguay both extended state control over their oil industries for balance of payments reasons; these reasons also help to explain why no oil industry property was actually taken over. The existence of a world oil surplus and the possibility of securing supplies from the USSR were inducements to such policies but the main factor was probably the realisation that the international oil companies had no intention of carrying out further significant investment in Chile or Uruguay. This was also the case with Standard Oil of Bolivia prior to the expropriation of 1937. Moreover, there was little that either the company or Washington could do in response to the nationalisation which was therefore effectively cost free. The Mexican nationalisation of 1938 does not fit this pattern so well because the Mexican government suffered very real costs. However, even here the rather ambiguous attitude of the US government was a major factor in the decision to nationalise.

In the immediate post-war period, decisions made in Chile and Brazil to establish state exploration monopolies had much to do with the belief that foreign oil companies were unwilling to mount a serious exploration campaign within these countries. A refining monopoly was a natural extension of a monopoly of exploration largely because it provided a secure source of finance to set against the uncertainties of exploring for oil. The Cuban confiscation of oil company assets in 1960 does not fit the pattern, but this is not surprising since it took place in the context of a total break with the USA. The subsequent nationalisations in Peru in 1968–9 and Bolivia in 1969 appear to have related to US government policies more than to the oil industry as such. In the Peruvian case, IPC had been decisively weakened by around 1960 when it had lost its place in the export economy and come to depend upon the domestic market (and thus domestic price levels) for its continuing profitability. Had the Alliance for Progress not convinced influential Peruvian politicians of the value of good relations with the USA, it is likely that some form of nationalisation would have taken place sooner than it did. When Peruvian expectations gave way to disappointment with the USA and with the domestic pattern of laissez-faire capitalism, the Peruvian army moved abruptly and dramatically against IPC. The nationalisation of Gulf Oil in Bolivia was also tied up very closely with the decline of US influence in the country from the extremely high levels prevailing in the 1950s and earlier in the 1960s although this decline did not prevent the US government from exerting considerable pressure on Bolivia.

Finally, in the cases of Ecuador and Venezuela, nationalisation (partial in the case of Ecuador, total in the case of Venezuela) appears to have been a response to the 'oil market revolution' of 1970–4. In the case of Venezuela, desperate company efforts to break up the united front of oil producers lost the oil companies such friends as they still possessed within the country. Even more important, the dramatic rise in world prices, and the wholesale nationalisations taking place throughout the Middle East and North Africa enabled Venezuela to expropriate without serious consequences. Ecuador, on the other hand, was practically forced into a partial nationalisation by the attitude of Gulf Oil. Nevertheless Gulf's position stemmed essentially from the fact that between 1972 and 1974 Ecuador had pursued pro-OPEC policies from which it was subsequently unwilling to retreat.

It is perhaps stating the obvious to say that nationalisation of oil could only be carried out when international opposition was not overwhelming. Nevertheless, it is striking how far Latin American govern-

ments have moved into the oil industry, often by exclusion but sometimes by expulsion, as a consequence of perceived opportunity. Even
so, this explanation is clearly incomplete. In four cases – Peru in 1968,
Bolivia in 1969, Mexico in 1938 and Cuba in 1960 – oil expropriations
(in the form which they actually took) did trigger off strong opposition
from oil companies or Washington or both. Even allowing for some
possible miscalculation by host governments in the first two of these
cases, there remains something to be explained. In order to do this, it
will now be necessary to bring in a different kind of logic which relates
oil nationalism to the pattern of class conflict and class alliance within
Latin America. Here, the hypothesis which appears to work best is one
which connects oil nationalist policies to an urban class alliance with a
strong middle-class component (sometimes called a 'populist' alliance)
and to government policies making for domestic industrialisation.

The best 'fit' for such a hypothesis comes from Mexico in 1938.
Here, the oil expropriation took place as a result of combined action
from oil-workers, the wider Mexican trade union movement, radical
intellectuals and government officials. It would become clear later,
however, that while this action was directed against a common enemy,
it did not imply a genuine harmony of objective and it is not even
certain that the oil-workers welcomed the nationalisation in 1938.
Nevertheless, the combination was decisive. From the mid-1920s successive Mexican governments had sought ways of extending state control over the oil industry but the expropriation took the form it did as
a result of pressure from the oil-workers who were at least partly independent of central government at that time. The Argentine nationalist
campaign under the Radicals in the 1920s and the Petrobrás campaign
in Brazil also tie in well with this hypothesis. In both cases, the oil
nationalist movement was overwhelmingly middle class in character
and in both cases it essentially offered popular support to technocratic
aims. These were originally set out by men who had long been familiar
with the oil industry: Mosconi in Argentina and Horta Barbosa in
Brazil. In both cases the technocrats' recommendations were eventually
accepted by relatively conservative governments who nevertheless tried
hard to limit the political impact of the nationalist campaign. In both
cases, there was a gap between oil policymaking and the politics of oil.
Two other cases, Uruguay and Chile, further bring out the middle-
class character of many oil nationalist campaigns although oil did not
become a major political issue in those countries because even quite
conservative governments (those of Tierra in Uruguay and Alessandri

and later Videla in Chile) were basically in sympathy with oil nationalist objectives.

Other cases may be found even where it is, at first sight, more difficult to relate oil expropriation to any kind of urban alliance. In three
of these, however, an oil expropriation formed part of an unsuccessful
or only partially successful attempt to create such an alliance. Thus
Velasco was no Cárdenas but there is no doubt that he actively sought
support among the middle and lower middle classes, particularly in
Lima, and that his confrontation with IPC was intended, at least in
part, as a popular move. This was even more obviously the rationale
behind Ovando's expropriation of Gulf Oil in Bolivia, while Toro's
earlier expropriation of Jersey Standard, which was motivated by international considerations, was perhaps undertaken with half an eye to
popularity too. Over all therefore, only in the cases of Venezuela and
Ecuador does it appear that there is no relationship between urban class
alliances and policies of oil nationalism.

These class categories are undoubtedly rather crude, but they are as
useful as the data permit and the conclusion that emerges is a strong
one. State oil companies are a powerful means by which middle-class
professionals can exert control over a Latin American economy and
their creation is likely to command support from those who are professionals and those who aspire to professional status. That does not mean
that middle-class support for policies of oil nationalism is inevitable or
that it will always be decisive. Even so, it is an important element in
oil politics.

Both the bargaining and class alliance hypotheses put forward,
therefore, seem to fit the data quite well. When charting out the various cases considered, it is important to point out that we are concerned
with proposals which were actually made and with the actual form
which they took; a different kind of nationalisation or a different kind
of nationalist campaign might have met with very different responses.
Even with this qualification in mind, one striking conclusion emerges
from figure 16.1: in most cases oil nationalism as a class issue and as a
response to an international opportunity appear to be substitutes for
each other. It is in fact probable that a government seeking to confront
a foreign oil company when conditions are adverse will seek to maximise domestic support for the measures taken. Similarly, when there
is no real external obstacle to oil nationalist policies, no political head
of steam is likely to build up which would turn oil policy into a major

Figure 16.1 *Class alliance and bargaining hypotheses compared*

| | | International conjuncture | |
		Not unfavourable	Moderately unfavourable
Oil as class issue (actual or anticipated)	important	Argentina Brazil	Mexico Peru Bolivia (1969) Cuba
	unimportant	Venezuela Bolivia (1937) Chile Uruguay Ecuador	

political question. It now remains to consider some of the implications of these hypotheses.

When considering the bargaining hypothesis, it is important to remember that the emphasis was placed very much on international factors rather than on the outcome of a process of 'bargaining in one country'. Indeed, international factors sometimes need to be emphasised *at the expense of* internal ones. Thus, foreign oil companies have sometimes tried to 'maximise' on a global scale by refusing to bargain at all on a national one. The IPC in Peru in the 1960s, the US companies in Mexico and Shell and Jersey Standard in Chile in the 1930s were more interested in the 'international implications' of their activities than with their future in these particular countries. International logic has also played an important part in the calculations of rational host governments. Market leaders, such as Venezuela in the 1940s and again in the 1958–63 period, made changes in their taxation arrangements in the hope that other countries would follow suit. To the extent that they did so Venezuela benefited, but the Venezuelan government faced considerable right-wing criticism in the early 1960s from those who argued that it should compete with the Middle Eastern producers rather than co-operate with them. Once an important country has taken a market lead others are faced with the choice of whether to co-operate in the hope of creating a pattern of long-run solidarity or breaking ranks in order to take a quick profit.[1] The importance of such choices for the world oil system hardly needs to be emphasised. Finally, a small producer might benefit most of all from a position of neutrality. It need only wait until the more adventurous countries have fought the necessary battles and then move in quietly to share the benefits or to exploit the situation. A small producer is often a 'free rider'[2] and, as we have seen, one of the main differences of opinion in Ecuador between 1972 and 1974 lay between those who wanted the country to enjoy a free ride and those who wanted it to take an active and energetic role in OPEC.

If one focusses mainly on international factors, it is evident that these are likely to be similar for different countries at a particular time. Moreover, if the international oil system itself responds to other major changes taking place in the world environment, then one would expect there to be a strong combined effect. This is exactly what did happen during the depression. The Achnacarry agreement helped offset the worst consequences of the depression for oil-exporting countries, but did so at the price of creating a suppressed world oil surplus and a sharp reduction of company exploration interest in countries where prospects were not first class. The main oil exporters in Latin America did not therefore face any prolonged economic crisis as a result of the depression and their subsequent economic history reflected its absence; this appears to have been true of Venezuela, Colombia and Peru.[3] On the other hand, oil-importing countries were faced by an immediate balance of payments crisis, during which they could not always pay for oil imports. This helped implant a longer-term belief that it was crucial to save foreign exchange wherever possible. This belief later became systematised in the doctrine of import-substituting industrialisation. Together these factors induced Chile, Uruguay and Brazil to extend state control over oil while also making it possible for them to do so. As a final contributory factor, the depression also brought about political changes in the USA which led to a considerable reduction in US government willingness to defend the position of its oil companies; this was important in the Mexican expropriation.

A second, much smaller, extension of state control over oil took place in 1968–9 with nationalisations in Peru and Bolivia. The major factor in the Bolivian situation, and a significant one in the case of Peru, was reaction from within the military against excessive US influence. While there were various general reasons for this, important specific factors included open CIA interference in the command structure of both armies during the war against Castroist insurgents in 1965

(Peru) and 1967 (Bolivia) and open US support for particular parties or factions within domestic politics (APRA in Peru, Paz and later Barrientos in Bolivia). Those who suffered from these measures concluded that the price of foreign help could be too high.

The third major transformation took place in the years after 1973. The oil market revolution was followed by a vast extension of government control over oil throughout OPEC. In this context Venezuela's nationalisation was neither surprising nor fiercely resisted. Moreover, the oil market revolution decisively changed the basis on which international oil companies were willing to explore for oil in developing countries. The period of concession contracts was effectively terminated and a number of countries were able to bring in foreign investment under strictly defined terms reducing the conflict between their governments' need to control the domestic oil industry and their desire to expand it. World Bank finance also became available for oilfield development. Finally, international oil companies became less committed to maintaining an unsatisfactory status quo in particular countries because they feared that any change might have unwelcome international implications. Thus, whereas IPC hung on obstinately in Peru during the 1960s, Gulf Oil was very willing to sell up in Ecuador rather than undertake the slower path of negotiating a gradual improvement in conditions. By the mid-1970s nationalisation, as such, had ceased to be controversial.

In four earlier cases, however, Latin American governments carried out controversial nationalisations in the face of significant international pressure. The Cuban confiscation of 1960 was part of a revolutionary process which was possible only because of strong Soviet support and it therefore does not require detailed attention. There remain Cárdenas's nationalisation of oil in Mexico, Velasco's attempted confiscation of IPC in Peru and Ovando's expropriation of Gulf Oil in Bolivia; all of these had clear political motives but all were known to be economically damaging in the form which they actually took. These three cases warrant further investigation.

A key factor appears to be that civilian political institutions were weak in all of these cases. Cárdenas is perhaps the father of modern Mexican politics but he was largely unable (and not just unwilling, although there was an element of this as well) to exert real central control over sections of organised labour; we have seen how little control he had over the oil-workers. Moreover, he was genuinely concerned about the possibility that the oil companies might provide a focal point for some kind of right-wing revolt (and such fear was by no means completely unfounded). The companies themselves tended to behave as though they were in a semi-colonial country and always believed that US intervention would protect them from the worst consequences of their own unsympathetic actions. The oil nationalisation is rightly taken as a landmark in Mexican revolutionary history, but it is sometimes forgotten how difficult Cárdenas's position was immediately before it.

When considering Velasco and Ovando, it is also worth pointing out that there has always been a close connection between the military and oil nationalism. This was the case with Toro and Busch in Bolivia, with General Mosconi in Argentina and with General Cárdenas in Mexico. Horta Barbosa and the Brazilian army played a major part in the Petrobrás campaign and Admiral Jarrín of Ecuador was very much influenced by the Brazilian precedent. One may ascribe this to the social origin of military officers, with the argument that oil nationalism stems from aspirations for upward social mobility on the part of middle-class professionals, not excluding military officers who have often themselves found positions in state oil companies. Others may prefer an explanation in terms of the institutional perceptions of the military; some kind of state control over oil, particularly in importing countries, may be seen as essential for national security and the military may also have an institutional bias toward state control in general terms. For whatever reason, however, there is often likely to be a purely military constituency for policies of oil nationalism, quite apart from any suggestion of wider political appeal; this was clearly the case during the nationalist campaign in Brazil, Ecuador, Peru and Bolivia.

A pervasive military preference for oil nationalism, together with the disproportionate influence of military officers in Latin American politics, may be one reason why when civilian institutions are weak the political process tends to amplify rather than subdue demands for oil nationalist policies. A second reason is that nationalism may be formulated as an issue by the political elite as a more or less deliberate substitute for class politics. This ties in with one widely accepted explanation for Latin American 'populism', which is often defined as a political alliance in which a political elite, committed to policies of industrialisation, manipulates popular support by stressing urban class harmony and the importance of nationalism while suppressing or co-opting class-based left-wing opposition. Even if the manipulative aspects of *cardenismo* have sometimes been exaggerated, it is both true and important that the oil nationalisation in Mexico was intended to reduce rather than increase class conflict. In this respect, as in many others, it proved successful. Similarly there is an obvious connection between the banning of the Communist Party in Brazil in 1947 and that party's active and effective support for the Petrobrás campaign after 1948. Here again it may not be quite accurate to speak of manipulation, for oil nationalisation was dear to the heart of the Communist Party in Latin America during the Cold War. Nevertheless, there can be no doubt that oil nationalism proved during those years to be a substitute for political class-based activity within the law by the Communist Party.

The corollary of this argument is also interesting, for it suggests that there is little genuine working-class or peasant support for policies of oil nationalism. Evidence would seem to bear out this claim, at least in part. In Venezuela accommodationist politicians dominated the electoral process after 1958 and the Marxist left did very much worse electorally than the unreconstructed right wing. No Marxist candidate in any election prior to the nationalisation received as many votes as Uslar Pietri in 1963. In pre-1968 Peru, pro-US politicians dominated the elections and looked likely to continue to do so; admittedly, illiterates were not eligible to vote, but it is not likely that these would have been more willing to vote for nationalist candidates than, for example, were the Lima middle class. In Argentina, one of the very few indisputably popular Latin American presidents of the century, Juan Perón, did not nationalise the oil industry and, on the contrary, was removed from office in 1955 at least partly because of his agreement with Standard Oil of California.

Undoubtedly there has been popular support for particular oil expropriations. Very often, this amounts to little more than support for a popular government which has carried out extensive policies of redistribution in sectors other than oil. When a popular president, for example Castro or Cárdenas, nationalises the oil industry and announces that he is threatened by 'the imperialists', there is a genuine popular response, particularly when the threat from outside appears real. However, when similar steps are taken by a government which is less popular, such as that of Velasco or Ovando, the response is likely to be disappointing. Even where the takeover is generally welcomed, which was certainly the case with IPC, the response will not be enough to provide the regime with a lasting base of support. Presidents cannot live by oil nationalism alone.

A final reason why institutional weakness is likely to amplify the politics of oil nationalism comes from the nature of the issue itself. It is very difficult in Latin America to be publicly opposed to oil nationalisation or to speak up in favour of the interests of foreign oil companies or the US government. Consequently governments which have not wished to carry out nationalist policies have generally concerned themselves with keeping the issue off the agenda. If this fails, they may adopt a kind of 'me-tooism' and seek some kind of renegotiation with the oil companies as a substitute for more drastic measures. Under such circumstances, the political opposition is likely to demand, and may even force through, even tougher measures, secure in the knowledge that it has little to lose by doing so.[4] At the very least this is likely to move policy in a more nationalist direction than it would otherwise take, and the effect of cumulative failure to reach any compromise settlement may leave the way open for very drastic action indeed, particularly if the opposition reaches power and is trapped by its own rhetoric. Something of this pattern can be seen in Peru prior to the attempted confiscation of IPC.

The same two factors — international considerations and domestic political ones — will also be crucial in determining the success of an oil expropriation or nationalist campaign. Let us begin by drawing the distinction between campaigns which trigger off important domestic opposition and those which do not. This focus on opposition rather than support appears most useful when one evaluates the political success of oil nationalist campaigns. Apart from Cuba which was mentioned above, there are, in fact, only three cases in which domestic opposition to oil nationalist policies was considerable — Argentina prior to 1935, Bolivia in 1969 and Ecuador in 1972–6.

In the first two cases there was a major conflict between the capital city and an influential region of the country; although more muted, this tension was not completely absent in Ecuador. Thus the oil nationalist campaign in Argentina tied in very closely with an effort to assert central government control over the oil industry and to prevent foreign companies striking separate agreements with the provincial authorities of the north. In Bolivia the 1969 expropriation was partly aimed at preventing Gulf Oil from consolidating an alliance with the provincial leadership of Santa Cruz. Something of the same pattern can be distinguished in Ecuador where the Guayaquil bourgeoisie was uneasy at the use which a radical government in Quito might make of its new oil wealth.

Conservative opposition to oil nationalism in these countries therefore stemmed from fear of the centralisation and other possibly radicalising political changes that would follow an expropriation. Something must also be attributed to a lack of confidence in the ability of nationalist governments, particularly in Bolivia and Ecuador, to avoid inflicting damage upon the economy as a whole. The opposition did not actually try to reverse these nationalist policies – in the case of Argentina nationalist policies were actually implemented by a conservative government. Instead, it reacted with hostility to mobilisation politics, whether on oil or anything else, and also made determined efforts to seize control of the state from the oil nationalists. While never the only factor, oil played a significant part in the 1971 coup in Bolivia and in the ejection from office of the military nationalists in Ecuador in 1974 and 1976; the exact role of oil in the 1930 coup in Argentina is more doubtful but it was probably a factor of some kind. In these cases, therefore, oil nationalists were denied political victory even if some of their policy objectives were allowed to stand.

In other cases, there was little real domestic opposition to oil nationalism. Where foreign investment was excluded rather than expelled this is not difficult to understand. In Chile, Uruguay and Brazil foreign oil investment was excluded largely because it showed very little interest in projects which might have attracted support. The same could also be said of Jersey Standard in Bolivia. In the remaining three cases, where foreign companies were actually expelled, they had succeeded in isolating themselves from domestic allies. The companies in Venezuela had lost influence both by co-operating too well with Pérez Jiménez and by co-operating insufficiently with Rafael Caldera. Generally speaking, foreign oil companies tend to lose support when they invest little, build up alternative supplies abroad and make it clear that they are willing to be expropriated with compensation; in the case of Venezuela, these responses were themselves the result of earlier government policies but they underline the inevitability of the whole process. IPC in Peru had also isolated itself from local capitalists and even from other oil companies in the 15 years prior to 1968, partly because of its aggressive political tactics and partly because of its exposed economic position. In Mexico the oil companies had made little effort to come to terms with the post-revolutionary political order and instead preferred to depend almost entirely on the good offices of the US Embassy.

The mere fact that international oil companies have had to consider the international implications of their actions has made it difficult for them to maintain good relations with host governments over long periods. Companies have found themselves blamed for producing too much oil or too little; for exporting at too low a price or for importing too expensively. When governments have changed sharply, oil companies have been regarded with suspicion by incoming governments for being identified too closely with the *ancien régime*. In yet other cases they have suffered from a hostility really directed against the parent government of an international company which spilled over onto the company itself; consider Peru in 1968 and Bolivia in 1969.[5] For all of these reasons, it is unlikely that a simple alliance between domestic conservatives and foreign oil multinationals will last over time; such an alliance generally requires a regional dimension and this is not always available.

As we have already seen, international opposition to oil nationalist policies has not always prevailed, if only because the US government has generally preferred a compromise settlement to prolonged conflict over oil. The major exception to this rule in Latin America – Cuba after the Revolution – clarifies the position further; US hostility to Cuba reflected far more than Cuban oil policies, which might have been acceptable if taken in isolation. Only in Iran in 1953, where the British played an important aggravating role, did a conflict which was purely about oil lead to total confrontation. Conversely, Washington played an important role in pushing for compromise after the Mexican expropriation; as we shall see in chapter 17, it was willing to accept the nationalisation subject to acceptable compensation and tried also to secure the return of fresh foreign investment on different terms. In the case of Peru, Washington was not concerned with the expropriation of IPC as such, but with the refusal of the Peruvian government to pay compensation.

A classification of opposition to oil nationalisations is set out in figure 16.2. The relationship between opposition and outcome is clear. Where international opposition was high but domestic opposition low, Washington took the initiative in finding a compromise settlement involving payment of compensation and the re-entry of fresh foreign investment. This re-entry was not opposed by Peru but was blocked by Mexico. Where both domestic and international opposition was extensive, the expropriating government faced major problems. Cuba resolved its difficulties successfully by shifting to a new set of international alliances and new internal social structure; the break with the USA played a major part in this transformation. The military govern-

Figure 16.2 *Opposition to oil expropriations in Latin America*

		International opposition	
		Low	High
Domestic opposition	Low	Venezuela Brazil Chile Uruguay Bolivia (1937)	Mexico Peru
	High	Argentina (pre-1935) Argentina (1963) Ecuador	Bolivia (1969) Cuba

ment in Bolivia, which did not have this option, instead agreed to compensate Gulf Oil, agreed also to give a number of assurances that compensation would really be paid and began to talk once more of allowing direct foreign investment to return. After the ten-month Torres interlude, direct foreign investment was welcomed once more. Over all, the Bolivian position was far weaker than that of Peru or Mexico.

In cases where opposition was predominantly domestic, government changed more readily than policy. In the case of Argentina, the 1930 coup did not change oil policy itself but only the manner in which it was carried out. Much of Yrigoyen's programme was in fact carried through by Justo's conservative government during the 1930s. In Ecuador, however, there was a significant change of emphasis in oil policymaking, to some extent after 1974 and even more so after 1976. Even so, Ecuador remained in OPEC, and CEPE (the state oil company) continued to produce and sell the majority of Ecuador's oil. In Argentina after 1963 the partial oil nationalisation did not have dramatic political consequences but policy was reversed after the 1966 coup (itself quite unrelated to oil). This section, therefore, is something of a mixed bag but it is safe to say that, in the absence of strong international pressure, oil policy was generally secondary to the question of who was to run the government.

The variables explored in this chapter were important not only to the decision to nationalise and to the effect of nationalisation but also to the success or otherwise of the newly created state oil companies in developing the industry. The behaviour and performance of six state oil companies will be considered in the next section but it can be stated here that the international market and the domestic politics of oil were important factors in all cases. To the extent that the expropriation or exclusion of foreign oil companies determined these factors, they proved to be of key long-term significance. As we shall see in the next section, a historical perspective of this kind is crucial to the understanding of the present day operation of state oil companies.

PART III

The state oil companies

17

Pemex in Mexican politics 1938–79

In a political system as centralised and finely balanced as that of Mexico, the position of a major public sector company is particularly interesting. For Pemex itself, the question is how far the technical and financial needs of the state agency could be fulfilled within the fairly tight constraints of Mexican politics. For other sections of the Mexican government the emphasis has appeared differently; how could effective political control be maintained over this agency without the danger of seriously damaging its performance? For outside observers, the nature of this relationship casts an interesting light on the whole question of state ownership of the oil industry: if Pemex can be accounted a success, then what conditions have made this possible? If a failure, then what have been the most important obstacles?

Pemex in formation 1938–50

The birth of Pemex was not easy and the prospects of the infant were not generally regarded highly. Indeed, the US government took so dim a view of its future that it sought only to contain the agency in the expectation that it would eventually die an almost natural death. The early Pemex was itself deformed; it was well endowed with crude oil reserves, but there were difficulties with transportation equipment and a serious lack of refineries in a suitable condition to supply the increasingly important domestic market.[1] Moreover, most of the senior technical and administrative staff of the companies were foreign and left Mexico at the time of the expropriation. To add to this, there was the effect of the boycott which had been successfully mounted by the oil companies on Mexican oil exports and on supplies of capital goods to Pemex.

For these reasons, and also for political ones which will be discussed below, the decision to make Pemex a state monopoly was not made finally until 1950. During the subsequent 12 years its economic position was worked out against a background of political change. The 1938 oil nationalisation marked the high tide of radical government in Mexico. After that the Cárdenas regime was clearly on the retreat, its position compromised by economic crisis and civil discontent. The choice of Avila Camacho as President in 1940 was something of a move right. Avila Camacho, however, was more concerned to balance rival pressures than to take a pronounced position of his own and so the change in political direction was muted. The rightward direction of the Mexican government became far clearer with the election of Alemán in 1946. Alemán made a determined and largely successful effort to establish a personal ascendancy over the PRI elite and his very autocratic regime marked a decisive break with the radical politics of the 1930s. A major purge of party ranks in 1947–9, including the removal of Lombardo Toledano from the leadership of the CTM, only emphasised this point.

The debate over the future of Pemex was naturally influenced by this change of direction. The petroleum law of 1941 gave the first indication that Mexico might be more willing to allow the return of foreign investment into the oil industry than had earlier appeared likely. Subsequently, as we have seen in chapter 3, there was discussion within the Mexican government and also between the government and the USA over the terms and conditions, if any, under which foreign investment might return. The left, including Cárdenas (Minister of Defence for a time under Avila Camacho), were able to block any real reversal of policy.[2]

What is undoubtedly more interesting is that Alemán did not change this policy significantly despite his evident sympathy for the USA and his staunchly pro-Washington stand on Cold War issues. It is likely that a key figure in persuading Alemán not to make major changes was Antonio Bermúdez, who had been appointed Director of Pemex in 1946 and became perhaps the most influential Director in the history of the agency. There is no absolutely convincing evidence on this point, but among the voluminous correspondence dealing with the oil issue in US State Department files is an entry in January 1947. It stated that US Ambassador Thurston met Alemán and Bermúdez in order to discuss the oil question. Alemán stated

that the Mexican petroleum law (which could not be changed because of the political consequences that would follow any tampering with it) made it impossible for any other than strictly Mexican companies to operate in Mexico excepting under such contractual terms as were contemplated . . .

Antonio Bermúdez . . . had stated categorically that it is not the intention of the Mexican government to permit foreign capital to participate in the Mexican petroleum industry. I asked Sr Garfias (a local oil company representative) if he could suggest any explanation that would account for such a complete reversal of the views of Sr Bermúdez – who as recently as January 9 had submitted to Señor Garfias a draft of a press release in which it was stated that foreign capital was essential to the development of the Mexican petroleum industry. Señor Garfias stated that he was unable to account for the abrupt change but he suggested that it might be related to the presence in this city during the past few days of Mr de Golyer. Sr Garfias is of the opinion that Mr de Golyer, who has frequently served as adviser to Pemex, may have convinced the Mexican government that the re-organisation of Pemex now under way will enable it to operate and expand the Mexican petroleum industry through contractual arrangements with independent oil companies.[3]

Thus, although it is almost certainly true that Alemán did not wish to add to his political problems by bringing foreign investment back into Mexican oil, he was persuaded by Bermúdez that another option was available. This, however, required certain changes to the internal structure of Pemex, and in particular the reduction of trade union power and the emergence of managerial control.

The oil-workers, as we have seen in chapter 10, played a major part in creating the conditions necessary for the oil nationalisation and subsequently in keeping up production in the face of extreme difficulty. Moreover, in terms of size, solidarity and economic importance, the oil-workers were the most significant sector of organised labour in Mexico. At the beginning, however, the oil-workers' leaders sought not only material benefits but also effective control over the actual running of the enterprise. This led to a number of serious conflicts with the management, which were then referred to the President for decision. The atmosphere was further soured when the government had to announce the postponement of the wage award which they had originally demanded of the private companies and whose refusal had actually precipitated the expropriation. Although a series of compromises was eventually worked out, the situation remained tense and there was frustration on all sides.[4] Thus, for example, on 22 April 1946 Cárdenas himself wrote to his old protégé and friend Buenrostro, then Director of Pemex,

Esteemed and valued friend,
    I have followed with interest the situation that has arisen between the oil-workers' union and the management and I consider it my duty to tell you, as

your friend, of my opinion based on the fact of your belief that there are those in the Labour Ministry who are interested in creating a crisis in relations between the union and the management.

If you reaffirm this belief and the situation remains unresolved, I would advise you to resign immediately from your position.[5]

This position was particularly dangerous for Alemán. The Avila Camacho government had always been willing to seek agreement through compromise. Alemán's reaction, however, was very different. In December 1946 he sent troops to break a strike of oil-workers and relations with the oil-workers continued to be antagonistic. Between 1947 and 1949, moreover, there was a struggle for power within the oil-workers' union. The radical sector allied itself with Lombardo, who in 1947 left the official party and set up an organisation of his own. In January 1948 oil, mining and railway union leaders met and appeared ready to set up a counter-government union. By May the British Ambassador went so far as to report that

internal situation which has been slowly deteriorating for some time, seems to be approaching a crucial trial of strength between President and labour unions in the week following May 1st . . . If left-wing opposition takes definite shape, it will probably centre round ex-President Cárdenas as the only public figure who could turn President Alemán out.[6]

This was perhaps overstated and by the end of 1948 it was clear that Alemán had neutralised his opponents. Nevertheless, for a brief period the attitude of the oil-workers became a part of 'high politics' and not simply a matter relating to the running of the industry.

Under these circumstances, it was clear that Alemán would prefer to avoid the additional controversy that would be created by bringing foreign investment back into oil. As things stood, Bermúdez could go some way towards deflecting left-wing opposition by playing the nationalist card, which he did energetically when speaking, for example, to the Latin American Oil-Workers' Conference organised by Lombardo Toledano in 1948. At the same time, Bermúdez manoeuvred quietly to encourage a more syndicalist and less political leadership to win power in the oil-workers' union. Such a leadership did win real economic benefits for its members but, as we shall see in more detail below, it also had other means of winning support.

Of fundamental importance in Bermúdez's early years as Director was the re-establishment of managerial power. Although this responded in part to the rightward movement within the PRI, there is no doubt that the consequence of workers' participation in terms of wage demands, manning practices and strikes came as a severe shock to the Mexican elite as a whole. This was made clear, many years later, by the government's response to a similar demand by the electricity workers' union:

The Federal government has not forgotten past experiences, particularly in regard to two activities which were the headaches of their time, the railroads and the petroleum industry. The government did not purchase the electric companies at a cost of 600 million pesos in order to turn them over to the workers. From the experience gathered over the years, the government had recognised fundamental errors in this system of practice which was followed in the Ferrocarriles Nacionales and presently in Petróleos Mexicanos.[7]

The consequences of these arrangements could be seen in Pemex's accounts for, as Powell points out,

Prices set by the government were based largely on social and political considerations. The government tried to encourage domestic use of petroleum fuels and the political strength of labour added to the pressure for low prices . . . the accounting methods of the organisation were such as to make rational price setting on a cost basis an impossibility. . . . Cost accounting had been considered unnecessary until that time probably for two reasons; first, it was widely felt, especially by labour, that Pemex was not a business association required to make ends meet; and second, the management had little incentive to determine specific costs simply because prices were set by the government. Management, squeezed between pressures for low prices and high wages, seems to have developed an attitude of indifference since both prices and wages were set partially or wholly by government policy which was subject to political influence.[8]

Between 1940 and 1947 *per capita* consumption increased eightfold, while the price of oil products actually fell. Furthermore, non-payment of bills by other nationalised industries, particularly the railways, reached such a pitch that in 1947 Bermúdez threatened to cut off supplies to the latter unless they paid what they owed.

Under these conditions, Pemex management did not so much determine a strategy as resort to a series of expedients in order to keep the industry running at all. As we have seen (chapter 3), Pemex tried repeatedly and with some success to secure loan capital from the USA. Under Bermúdez, Pemex also signed a number of drilling contracts with small US companies. Bermúdez himself recounted that studies within the organisation were made between 1947 and 1949 on the best way of attracting a limited amount of foreign capital with a minimum of visibility and loss of freedom of manoeuvre to Pemex itself.[9] The contracts signed were for drilling only but did make the significant concession that payment was to be made to the contractor in crude oil. There was some opposition to these contracts (which became a political issue in the late 1960s) but this was muted; the nationalists were generally relieved that the government had not gone further in this direction.

The need for drilling contracts stemmed directly from Pemex's own position. Pemex gave highest priority to supplying Mexico's expanding urban centres. Distribution and marketing, very uneven in the years immediately following the nationalisation, clearly improved after the mid-1940s. A $10m. loan from the US government in 1943 helped Pemex to build a sophisticated refinery of 36,000 b/d in Mexico City and by 1948 Pemex had begun work on a new refinery at Salamanca. The Salamanca refinery, 'the most modern in Latin America at that time, was designed to produce 1,500 barrels of lubricants and 65 tons of paraffin daily, thus eliminating the large imports of these costly products. The estimated cost of the refinery construction was 75 million dollars.'[10] These projects were of particular importance given the state of Mexican refining capacity in 1938 described by Powell as being 'old, badly worn, inefficient and obsolescent'.[11] To get so far, under such adverse circumstances, was something of an achievement.

Refineries, together with pipelines and tankers, absorbed what resources Pemex had. Oil production rose by only 4.9% a year between 1939 and 1950 while consumption increased at an annual rate of 9.1%. These production increases, moreover, were only possible because of the discoveries which had been made earlier by the foreign companies. Between 1938 and 1944 Pemex drilled precisely three exploratory wells; it drilled only 126 wells in total during this period, which is well below the 480 drilled by the companies in the depression years 1932–7. This could not go on for ever; as it was, there were costs involved in the over-exploitation of particular fields[12] but at least they were there to be exploited. Without this abundant natural resource base, Pemex could hardly have survived its early crises. As it happened, Pemex began the 1950s in reasonable shape even if its financial position was somewhat unsteady. As the World Bank pointed out in 1953, 'for the Mexican economy as a whole . . . the petroleum problem is by no means insoluble or even especially difficult. It is in essence a matter of directing investment to petroleum from less urgent sectors.'[13]

The Bermúdez years 1950–8

The years 1950–8 saw the creation of a pattern of activity in the oil industry which was to remain substantially unchanged until 1973. Exploration activity recovered sharply; 93 exploration wells were drilled in 1956, compared with only 11 in 1946, while drilling continued to be fairly successful. Production increased more slowly than reserves largely as the result of marketing difficulties. Indeed, exploration seemed to pose remarkably little problem; the finding cost of crude reserves was calculated at $0.048 per barrel in 1952 and only $0.035 per barrel in 1956 since most of the drilling took place in areas which were known from the 1930s to be oil bearing.[14] More impressive was the development of refining; gasoline throughput almost doubled between 1948 and 1956 and output of kerosene and lubricants increased by even more. The Salamanca refinery came onstream in 1951, the pre-1938 Minatitlán refinery was completely rebuilt in 1956 and the Atzcapotzalco refinery was further expanded in the same year. By 1958 domestic supply to all areas except for the far north of the country had effectively ceased to be a problem. Moreover, Pemex began to develop the natural gas industry after about 1947, and this has continued to expand at a rate of at least 10% a year. While these successes were real enough, some of the constraints and limitations with which Pemex came to be associated also date from this period. These include the effective prohibition of exports, considerable overmanning and an unsatisfactory financial position. Each of these needs to be considered in turn.

Between 1945 and 1955 the attitude of the private sector towards Pemex underwent major change. In late 1944,

Right-wing media no longer considered it dangerous – in the sense of offensive to majority opinion – to state openly that it was necessary for foreign interests to return into the oil industry. In their opinion this was necessary in order to maintain an adequate level of oil production and not to damage the general economic position of the country; the state – they said – had failed as an administrator.[15]

During the Bermúdez years, however, this position changed. Pemex came to be seen as one, indeed the most important, of the many state enterprises which had been entrusted by Alemán with the task of providing the infrastructure and inputs to aid the import-substituting industrialisation with which Alemán's presidency was most closely associated.

Table 17.1 *Mexican oil production. Exports and wells drilled 1947–52*

	Crude production (m. barrels)	Oil exports (m. barrels)	Wells drilled (total)	Wells drilled (exploration)
1947	55.9	14.0	64	18
1948	59.8	13.0	83	38
1949	62.2	14.1	163	24
1950	73.9	23.6	219	17
1951	78.8	22.4	268	47
1952	78.9	15.4	307	101

Source: Pemex, *Annual Reports.*

We have already seen that domestic demand for oil products continued the rapid expansion that had been a feature in Mexico since around
1930. Moreover, there was an obvious political constituency for Pemex
if it continued to provide low-cost oil supplies to Mexican urban areas
and, more particularly, to Mexican industry. The question naturally
arose, therefore, whether by exporting such oil as it had available,
Pemex was not undermining its own ability to supply the domestic
market. For much of the Alemán period this was scarcely a problem,
but Pemex did increase its exports sharply at the end of the 1940s, as
can be seen from table 17.1. During this time, Pemex's official policy
was that

The adequate supplying of the national market is the main objective of Pemex.
Consequently, only surpluses are exported, despite the higher yield that can
be obtained from sales abroad.

   The company needs, on the other hand, to be able to increase its exports in
order to earn enough income to be able to buy materials and equipment which
are not produced within the country.[16]

In other words, it seems clear that Bermúdez was still aiming to export
enough to be able to recapitalise Pemex – a factor which was all the
more important now that it had become impossible to secure financing
from the USA. Since domestic prices were heavily subsidised, there was
no other option if Pemex's financial position was to remain strong.
Thus, in May 1951 the *Hispanic American Report* quoted Bermúdez as
saying that the Tabasco area of Mexico 'will soon be a second Venezuela' and that Mexican national production would quickly reach Venezuelan levels.

Signs soon developed, however, that there was serious opposition to this strategy. For one thing, the international market after around 1950 moved into a condition of surplus. Already in 1950 the US government was clearly concerned about the danger of cheap imports disturbing its domestic producers and it is likely that the matter was taken up informally with Mexico;[17] certainly Bermúdez explained the fall in exports in 1952 in terms of 'restriction in the export market'.[18]

At the same time, it appears that objections to this export policy were voiced within Mexico. In February 1952 the Mexican government set up a Ministry for Natural Resources to co-ordinate inputs for industrialisation. Moreover, in its report for that month the *Hispanic American Report* stated that

Pemex . . . has been expanding rapidly. The new field discovered at Ebano . . . and the investment last year of 225 million pesos (some $26.1m.) in the corporation's prize possession, the Poza Rica field, have led to such optimism that 500 million pesos will be invested by Pemex in 1952. The money will go to building refineries, gas conduits and plants to make by-products and aid refining. A note of warning, however, was sounded by the National Bank of Mexico. It stated that expansion and recognition of a growing foreign market must not blind oil men to the needs at home and must not crowd out plans for conservation of oil reserves for future use.

Although the policy of exporting 'surpluses' was not explicitly dropped, the new government of Ruiz Cortines (1952–8) no doubt made clear its objections to unrestricted exporting. In 1953 Bermúdez's *Director's Report* for the first time mentioned the fact that Pemex was maintaining as a matter of policy a 20-year reserve–production ratio.

Although the question was now largely settled and Pemex ceased to become a significant net exporter of oil, the issue was never completely forgotten. In July 1955 the *Hispanic American Report* stated that 'there are reports that the Mexican government is working to reduce and eventually eliminate the exportation of oil. Antonio J. Bermúdez, director general of Pemex, said that the goal is based on confidence in the expansion of domestic consumption.' Later in the same year Mexico's plan to sell limited quantities of natural gas to Texas Eastern of the USA, although carried through, was opposed by 'a group of nationalist industrialists in Mexico. This group, which is consistently in opposition to the sale of natural resources to the United States, advocates the conservation of Mexican mineral products for Mexican consumption.'[19] Bermúdez himself was quite happy to take this change on board. From around 1954 he defended the objective of net self-sufficiency, as he did in his memoirs:

Mexico is not a major exporter of petroleum and it is not the national policy that it should ever become one. It is illusory, and would be harmful, to pretend that petroleum produced and exported in large quantities could become the factotum of Mexico's economy, or the panacea for Mexico's economic ills. Mexico does not even wish to be forced to export such an indispensable energy and chemical resource.[20]

Tied up with this question was that of Pemex's finances. Pemex had now been denied both the possibility of extensive foreign credits and the opportunity of earning substantial foreign exchange by a policy of exporting. At the same time, its central function – that of producing and selling oil to stimulate Mexican industry – was becoming increasingly expensive. In real terms, Pemex's fixed investment more than trebled between 1952 and 1958, increasing at the same time from 11.26% of federal investment to 26.05%.[21] Nevertheless, as we can see from table 17.2, the price of domestic oil products continued to fall in real terms. Consequently, although Pemex's strategy was well in keeping with the industrialising direction of overall economic policy, the organisation increasingly had problems of its own. As the United Nations pointed out,

During the first twenty years of operation of the monopoly, Pemex appears to have made only a negligible contribution to investment programmes. Furthermore, Pemex could not meet its commitments to the state and owed considerable arrears of tax. On December 31 1958, the accumulated deficit totalled 215 million pesos [$17.2 million].

Assuming that the reserves were used solely to maintain the existing level of operation, it would seem that new investments were financed almost in their entirety by long-term or short-term loans and by arrears of debt to the state.[22]

Under these conditions, Bermúdez felt that financial rectitude was less important than maintaining the development of the organisation. Pemex began borrowing fairly heavily after around 1953, from whatever sources were available (including trade creditors), but eventually it became clear that Pemex could no longer meet its financial obligations. The growing financial difficulties of the 1950s created serious problems for Antonio Bermúdez, who recorded later that

Table 17.2 *Real prices of oil products 1938–58*
(*1938 levels* = 100)

	Gasoline	Kerosene	Diesel	Fuel oil
1938	100	100	100	100
1944	78	48	63	71
1948	67	37	61	100
1952	71	26	53	88
1956	60	22	53	112
1958	54	19	50	116

Source: Bermúdez, *The Mexican National Petroteum Industry*, tables 9–10.

that which in the *sexenio* of Ruiz Cortines checked the rate of development of the oil industry was his idea that Petróleos Mexicanos was the older and richer brother who ought to subsidise by means of low prices the other sectors of the economy . . .

The financial situation became critical after the devaluation of the peso in the month of April 1954. However, President Ruiz Cortines always opposed a price increase, despite being aware of the need for one, for reasons which he considered more important; my efforts to convince him, repeated and insistent though they were, proved futile. When the government came to its end, I decided to rectify the price level for the benefit of Pemex and its position in the national economy, since this measure was necessary, in the national interest, and could not be postponed; moreover, it would help the new President Adolfo López Mateos. I gave the orders on 30 November 1958, on the last day of the regime, and also of my tenure as Director General of Petróleos Mexicanos.[23]

Quite apart from this decision, Bermúdez was also willing to respond to Pemex's financial problems in other ways:

the first was of a general character; there were insufficient internal resources to be able to carry out the minimum investment programme which was necessary. I resolved to resort to credits, both from financiers and suppliers. Debt increased from 654 million [pesos] [$76.0m.] at the beginning of the *sexenio* to 3,886 million [$310.88m.] at the end of it. But subsoil reserves increased at a very satisfactory rate, as in no other period, production increased and the programme of structural change in the oil industry was virtually completed; now it was possible to supply satisfactorily the whole national market. The other decision was specific, if well within the general policy orientation of the first. In 1955 the expansion of the capacity of the Atzcapotzalco refinery was indispensable in order to meet domestic demand. Because of the lack of resources, the Council of Administration, in which various Secretaries and Subsecretaries of State were present, ordered the suspension of the work. If this had been done, it would have quickly brought about a fatal shortage of products which would have had to be rationed in the centre of the Republic, thus constituting a grave political and economic problem. My position as Director was in peril. I took the decision not to stop the project and my colleagues responded with enthusiasm.[24]

Bermúdez's words should be considered carefully by all those interested in the question of presidential power in Mexico.

The third area in which Pemex needed to resolve real problems was that of labour relations. We have already seen that Bermúdez was able to put an end to the threat of polarisation between the labour movement and Alemán during the stormy years 1947–8. Consequently, labour unrest within the enterprise was considerably reduced and payments to labour fell from 32.2% of Pemex's total income in 1946 to 16.1% in 1950 rising only to 22.1% in 1958, in which year Pemex's income was held back considerably by the low domestic prices. Thus, although wages, salaries and employment continued to increase in real terms during this period, they did so no more rapidly than Pemex's own income.[25]

However, there was a price to be paid for the acquiescence of the labour force; this was official tolerance of a union structure which was efficient at preventing disruption, but also increasingly corrupt and willing to resort to illegal measures. Union leaders were able to enrich themselves by taking full advantage of first preference for Pemex contracts, often farming them out to favoured suppliers in return for a percentage. They were able to keep the workforce in line by playing on the distinction between permanent workers and the increasing number of workers with only temporary positions. As part of the price for their support, moreover, Pemex's management had to agree to employ far more workers than necessary; the total workforce rose from 16,000 in 1938 to 29,100 in 1948 and 45,500 in 1958.

It was not this, however, which seems to have been most worrying to the federal government. Rather, its main concern appeared to be at signs of a militant reaction against these union leaders on the part of at any rate some of Pemex's workers. As in 1947–8, this seems to have been part of a more general trend of worker unrest which the incoming President López Mateos tried first to co-opt and later decided to repress. As a consequence of this, the López Mateos government revealed a number of practices which apparently became institutionalised under Bermúdez but which were not greatly different under his successors. Thus, in 1959 *Hispanic American Report* reported that Pemex's new press secretary (under the incoming López Mateos) 'told of corrupt Tampico employees who allowed new machinery to rust and then sold it to their friends for scrap'.[26] He claimed that overmanning had been deliberately permitted by the Pemex authorities in order to win the support of union officials and he allowed it to be hinted that Cárdenas had played a part in this.[27] For the next year or so, revelations continued to be made; for example:

the 'caudillo' of Poza Rica controlled water and electric power in his region, which he utilised for his own benefit through his position with Pemex, and he also installed his supporters in key positions in labour and welfare organisations. Fuel losses, which averaged around 10% at other installations throughout the nation, were listed at 30% at Poza Rica and investigators found proof that missing gasoline had gone to service stations owned by relatives of the former superintendent.[28]

Changes did take place in 1959, from which date the federal government embarked upon a long and ultimately unsuccessful attempt to place its own nominees in key posts of the oil-workers' union.

Progress and problems 1958–73

By 1958 Pemex had largely settled down to the existence which subsequently came to be regarded as typical. It now had the support of the Mexican business community which was promoting rapid industrialisation with the help of cheap oil. Given Mexico's apparent abundance of crude oil, it appeared that the domestic market could be supplied without great difficulty while the downstream sector gave the company at least a certain dynamism. After 1958 the dynamic sector came to be petrochemicals rather than refining, which now needed only to increase in line with the growth of demand. As long as Pemex steered carefully between the Scylla of *entreguismo* and the Charybdis of insolvency, it would maintain its basic viability without needing major new departures. Politically, the years after 1958 were also quieter. As we have seen, Bermúdez had been exceptionally powerful, both as a personality and a director general, and had played perhaps the major role in building up the company. The directors between 1958 and 1976 were quieter figures who did not find it necessary to depart from the normal pattern of following presidential leadership and in some cases had difficulty in asserting control over Pemex itself. These points will become clear after a more detailed examination of the period.

The major departure of Pemex under the presidency of López Mateos was the development of petrochemicals. 'Basic' petrochemicals had been reserved for Mexicans as early as the law of 1941, but the crucial legislation was passed in December 1958 as one of the last acts of the outgoing Ruiz Cortines Administration. According to Bermúdez, 'the new oil law enforced Article 27 of the Constitution; it conformed to the proposal which, when I was Director of Pemex, was prepared under my instructions; President Ruiz Cortines converted this proposal into a law and this was approved by Congress'.[29] This decision, according to *World Oil*, 'marks the end of a long and angry struggle behind the scenes. Private enterprise in a number of countries, particularly Italy, was hopeful that Pemex would leave that facet of the industry to private capital.'[30] Indeed, as early as 1953 Bermúdez had discussed petrochemicals in his *Director's Report* and commented that 'Pemex considers it a duty to promote its development.'[31]

A great deal followed from this decision. For one thing, basic petrochemicals is an industry with high capital costs. It was out of the question for Pemex to finance major petrochemical projects internally and, until the financial reorganisation of the agency which took place in early 1959, borrowing abroad was similarly out of the question. Pemex's room for manoeuvre was further limited by the Ruiz Cortines government's decision, in 1958, not to allow Pemex to seek loans from foreign government agencies, even though it was by no means clear that such loans were available.

Subsequently, López Mateos did permit Pemex to contract loans from private foreign sources even though 'Mexican nationalists and Communists were highly critical of these loans and accused the oil industry of selling out to foreigners.'[32] This opposition led to a congressional committee of inquiry which, not surprisingly, supported the government's position. Later in 1959 Mexico apparently rejected a Soviet offer of trade credits tied to the purchase of petroleum equipment.[33]

Moreover, the large size of petrochemical investments and the eagerness with which Pemex rushed to carry them out contributed to new financial difficulties for the organisation. Following the near bankruptcy of Pemex at the end of 1958, Pemex's debt to the state was converted in 1959 into 99-year 8% bonds. In 1960, however, despite the higher prices now prevailing on the domestic market (set by Bermúdez in 1958 and confirmed and extended by the incoming regime), Pemex still had to request a moratorium on its debts to the government. In that year 'Pemex was still covering almost 70 percent of its investments by loans'[34] and

by the spring of 1961, Pemex seems to have become badly overextended. Supplier credits were being cancelled wholesale, United States credit sources were drawing back from further commitments; and the director of the company was shopping in Europe for new sources of credit. It took nearly a year to bring the Pemex finances back under control, partly through a funding of short-term liabilities.[35]

The immediate cause of the problem was the temporary closing of the US market while a new export arrangement was negotiated; Pemex's exports fell from $29m. in 1959 to $18.3m. in 1960 before rising again to $34.8m. in 1961. Pemex was also accused by Bermúdez, obviously a hostile critic but undoubtedly a well-informed one, of a loss of financial control:

It is a fact that they [the new administration] simultaneously began many new projects in order to attract the maximum of finance, although without being certain of being able to finish them. For two and a half years, between 1960 and 1963, construction of the new refinery at Ciudad Madero was suspended without the suspension of purchases financed on credit or the shipments of goods imported for this project. For a long time, material and equipment were abandoned and left subject to deterioration over time. A similar situation took place with the project to expand the refinery and petrochemical plants at Minatitlán. Work stopped but payment of interest continued.[36]

Pemex tried to cover its costs by contracting out the provision of various services; again, as we shall see, Bermúdez was critical but there is no independent evidence on the results of this venture.

The financial squeeze, coupled with the importance attributed by Pemex to its petrochemicals programme, led to some reconsideration of the policy of leaving basic petrochemicals exclusively to Pemex. López Mateos's press secretary had, during the presidential campaign, floated the idea of liberalising this regime but the idea was dropped in the face of strong nationalist attack.[37] Subsequently, Pemex formed a joint venture with Du Pont for an $80m. polyethylene plant arguing that polyethylene was not a primary petrochemical industry;[38] this project again proved controversial and was finally cancelled during the presidency of Díaz Ordaz.

In fact it appears that Gutiérrez Roldán's administration was more concerned with financial balance (which clearly improved after 1958, despite the setback described above) and less with the long-term structure of the oil industry itself. Perhaps it was inevitable, however, that a weaker man following in Bermúdez's footsteps would encounter serious problems, and it certainly appears that the directorate lost control of Pemex's spending after 1959 (thus encouraging this degree of overextension). Thus, it was partly as a result of Pemex's experiences that Vernon drew the conclusion that

the process of investment and the expectation of continued investment in these sectors were so thoroughly institutionalised that presidents who sought from time to time to retrench in these fields were not always successful in their efforts. The momentum of the bureaucracy in these decentralised activities was sometimes so strong that directives from the center were not sufficient to stem the continued inflow of capital funds.[39]

However, a history of near insolvency and a desire to break with the Bermúdez legacy at nearly any cost did nothing for Pemex's self-restraint.

Pemex's petrochemicals programme eventually provided a useful magnet for attracting foreign loans to the agency, and these allowed a number of ambitious projects to go ahead. Thus, according to Bullard,

financial difficulties delayed the construction schedule during 1960–61, although the two ammonia plants at Minatitlán and Salamanca were completed only slightly later than planned. Pemex's investment problems have been ameliorated considerably by the new United States private loan of $50 million which was to be spent, in large measure, to expedite the petrochemical projects' construction programme. More recently, Mexico's developing petrochemical industry has attracted investment capital from several European nations. A turning point in the financial position of Pemex and its nascent petrochemical industry was achieved by the negotiation in 1963 of a US $110m. line of credit with the French government and a group of French banks, on terms favourable to the developing industry.[40]

It is highly probable that the petrochemicals industry, which was free from the labour constraints of oil production, was favoured by the technocrats of Pemex precisely for these reasons. Moreover, the self-sufficiency target for Mexico stimulated investment rather than holding it back. Already by 1963 Mexican petrochemicals growth was described as 'spectacular',[41] and between 1965 and 1970 28% of Pemex's total investment was in petrochemicals which in 1970 pro-

Table 17.3 *Comparative price changes in Mexico 1960–72*
(*Index: 1960 = 100*)

	Agriculture, fishing, etc.	Oil production and refining	Basic petrochemicals	Construction
1960	100.0	100.0	100.0	100.0
1963	114.9	110.4	96.0	112.4
1966	120.9	112.5	96.5	130.7
1969	131.1	109.1	91.2	146.8
1972	149.4	106.2	89.5	175.5

Source: T. Gutiérrez, 'La intervenión del estado mexicano' (*licenciatura* thesis, Instituto Politécnico Nacional, 1978), p. 87.

vided 10% of Pemex's total income. Although Pemex encountered criticism for unduly emphasising petrochemicals at the expense of other sectors,[42] this development did represent an important achievement. There was no market constraint on Pemex's expansion; the government simply prohibited imports of those products which Pemex produced. However, in order to avoid conflict with the private sector, Pemex adopted a policy of pricing its output at international prices. As can be seen from table 17.3, this was good for consumers but must have done nothing to strengthen Pemex's own financial position.

Finally, Pemex's development of petrochemicals tied the company in even more closely with the private sector, which was allowed to invest in secondary petrochemicals (with foreign interests allowed a maximum of 40% in any venture). It is likely that this connection provided a further reason for Pemex to invest heavily in petrochemicals since the secondary sector, which had been defined as a national priority, also grew rapidly during this period. Thus, in 1965, the Director of Pemex reported that 'we have to admit honestly that up to now the basic petrochemicals industry is behind the derivative one and we must increase production in order to supply existing demands. There are derivative petrochemical industries which up to this moment are supplied from abroad.'[43] Moreover, Pemex's own investment further stimulated investment in the private sector despite occasional recriminations from both sides to the effect that the other was holding it back through non-fulfilment of particular plans.[44] This lack of balance undoubtedly caused a certain mutual irritation between Pemex and the private sector, but it almost certainly accelerated the growth of the petrochemicals sector; how far it diverted Pemex's investment from oil exploration is another question. The official answer to this question was that the petrochemicals sector was financed out of profits from refining rather than from production;[45] but, as we shall see, the problem of exploration was not so easily resolved.

One of Pemex's major successes during this period was the setting up of the Mexican Petroleum Institute (IMP) which was created on 26 August 1965. Up until then the diffusion of technology within the organisation tended to be informal and was not fully satisfactory.[46] A few Mexican technicians were sent abroad, and upon their return were expected to share their knowledge with their colleagues; at the same time, Pemex remained very dependent on foreign help with respect to the major construction projects. In 1966, the Director of Pemex reported that 'Petróleos Mexicanos has spent abroad for project engineering 300 million pesos [$24m.] since 1958 and for consulting engineering and technical assistance and services 600 million pesos [$48m.].'[47] IMP, therefore, was set up in order to institutionalise the transfer of technology.

At first the objectives set for the agency were not particularly ambitious. Reyes Heroles set out some of IMP's advantages in 1968: 'the petrochemical world is not mysterious. Licences and patents are easily available for reasonable royalties. It is not convenient, however, to be absolutely dependent on them. Technological knowledge will enable us to select between alternatives, to negotiate more effectively, and to choose those which are better given the composition of our raw materials and the likely size of the market.'[48] Two years later the IMP went even further:

on the tenth of March of this year, an agreement was drawn up with the firm Universal Oil Products Company, that holds numerous licences in the fields of refining and petrochemicals, in order to carry out process research jointly in this area. This agreement, with a duration of five years, establishes that each year the parties will work jointly in two projects, one proposed by the Institute and the other by Universal Oil, and the royalties obtained from the licences of the jointly developed processes will be distributed in the following manner: in Mexico, the IMP will receive 60 percent and Universal Oil 40 percent; in the remainder of the world, the Institute will receive 40 percent and Universal Oil will receive 60%.[49]

By 1976, the IMP had succeeded in establishing itself as a major influence in Latin America as well as in Mexico. It had carried out feasibility studies for a pipeline system for the Ecuadorian State Oil

Company and was even given a design and engineering contract by the government of Jamaica for an 80,000 b/d refinery. During 1976 '34 contracts were concluded with Petróleos Mexicanos, three agreements with national private firms and eight with foreign firms'.[50] By the end of the 1970s the IMP, with its 4,000 employees, had become a major source of strength to the Mexican oil industry.

While Pemex was continuing to develop 'downstream', however, its oil discoveries and reserves were increasingly being overtaken by demand. This situation can be traced back to the decision, made early in the 1950s, to abandon any effort to become a significant net exporter of oil. As we have seen, this gave rise to various financial constraints and Bermúdez put more emphasis on the need to maintain the supply of oil to the cities than on a continuing high rate of exploration. As the Levy Report made clear, during the 1955–9 period 'the refinery program was accelerated; total drilling tended to level off; and exploration activity yielded to development'.[51] Bermúdez himself, however, argued, with some justification, that this levelling off was a response to financial necessity. Later it appeared to result from a deliberate decision to put more emphasis on other aspects of the industry. Bermúdez himself was particularly critical of the López Mateos Administration:

Another example of Pemex's over-concern with matters of finance and its inability to understand priorities combined, in this case, with bad administration, was the policy of contract drilling initiated during the 1959–64 *sexenio* and fortunately changed in the next *sexenio*. Although the amount of drilling increased considerably in these six years, this was exclusively because of more development drilling, while the number of exploration wells remained roughly the same as in the previous six years, despite the considerable increase in income which stemmed from the price increases I ordered on 30 November 1958. The policy of drilling by contract, begun on the pretext that it would be cheaper than keeping the task within the organisation, produced exactly the opposite result; drilling costs increased considerably. Moreover, there were other disadvantages; although some were capable organisers, other contractors were chosen who lacked technical and financial capacity . . . these were then allowed to hire the best drilling and technical personnel from Pemex so that it was the contractors who benefited from the very expensive training that these people had received from Pemex.[52]

In fact, exploration drilling increased only from 527 wells between 1953 and 1958 to 570 between 1959 and 1964, although, to be fair, this did not seem to be much of a problem at the time.

Table 17.4 *Oil reserves and production 1946–73*
(*percentage change for oil and gas*)

	Oil				Gas			
	Reserves (including condensates) (million barrels)	Percentage change	Production	Percentage change	Reserves (million barrels of oil equivalent)	Percentage change	Production	Percentage change
1946	1,065.5		49.5		371.8		5.2	
1952	1,647.1	+54.6	78.9	+59.4	593.5	+59.6	18.7	+259.6
1952	1,647.1		78.9		593.5		18.7	
1958	2,512.1	+52.6	100.6	+27.6	1,558.1	+162.5	52.5	+180.7
1958	2,512.1		100.6		1,558.1		52.5	
1964	2,925.3	+16.5	129.5	+28.7	2,302.0	+47.7	97.0	+84.8
1964	2,925.3		129.5		2,302.0		97.0	
1970	3,288.4	+12.4	177.6	+37.1	2,279.1	−1.0	133.0	+37.1
1970	3,288.4		177.6		2,279.1		133.0	
1973	3,269.4	−0.6	191.5	+7.8	2,162.3	−5.1	135.4	+1.8

Source: Bermúdez, *La política petrolera*, p. 76.

Under Díaz Ordaz and Reyes Heroles, in contrast, exploration was given a far higher priority, although it was during this *sexenio* that serious problems became apparent. Although the position is not easy to evaluate, these problems were not, at least at first, primarily due to a lack of resources or a lack of political will. It is true that the idea had been floated during the López Mateos presidency that the low international prices then prevailing made it rational to de-emphasise oil exploration and to concentrate on elaborating cheap imported crude oil,[53] but this never became official policy and was vigorously rejected by Reyes Heroles after 1964. It might seem, however, that the force of his rhetoric was related to the persistence of the opposition to his position. In any case, the arguments which he put forward are interesting:

Present surpluses, world over-production and low prices of crude oil will not alter our present policy, as it is impossible to predict the future, even during the short run . . . Naturally, in other parts of the world the cost per barrel is very much lower than in Mexico. This does not convince us; other producers are at a stage when oil extraction is easy, and in some cases their workers work long hours for low wages . . . it is important for us to intensify exploration. Exploration is risky and apparently barely profitable, but it is the basis of any petroleum industry.[54]

Reyes Heroles returned to this theme in 1968:

Our petroleum policy has become a matter of controversy. It has been argued that we should import oil, since costs abroad are lower than costs here. Strictly speaking, our costs are higher . . . because of the difficult extraction problems of our industry. However, if we were to import crude oil we would damage our balance of payments and would expose ourselves, in the future, to a dangerous dependency.[55]

On the other hand, in 1970, when world oil prices were still lower, Reyes Heroles used very different arguments:

Only the ill-informed can maintain the theory that it is to our advantage to import cheap oil. The lowest priced crude oil that we could get, in accordance with international prices, and have delivered to our ports and industrial locations, would be more than 20% above the approximate average cost of Mexican crude, which with new discoveries is bound to fall, or at worst to remain constant, since the average output per well in Mexico has been increasing and will surely continue to increase.[56]

One possible explanation for this apparent contradiction came in the same report: 'Our accounting problems mean that we only have avail-

able gross information on costs, in some cases of limited dependabil-
ity.'[57]

Indeed, one of the consistent themes running through commentaries
on Pemex has concerned the difficulties of extracting information, even
from within the organisation.[58] Thus, in 1966 it was with pride that
Reyes Heroles pointed out that:

For the first time, those who delivered crude oil and those who received it
were in agreement on the figure which we reveal today. The contradictions
which previously existed made it appear that there was a substantial difference
in the amount of crude delivered according to whether one accepted the figure
given by those who received it in refineries, or the one by those who sent it
from the fields; this no longer occurs.[59]

Even given the clear difficulties which the Pemex management
encountered in costing its own operations, it is possible to come to
some reasonably clear conclusions about the economics of oil exploration during this time. First, some rather rough studies of Pemex's oil
exploration have been made which have worked out the ratio of government spending on oil exploration and development to additions to
new reserves. One of these shows that the average cost of finding a
barrel of oil (at 1960 prices) increased steadily from $0.053 in 1957 to
$0.094 in 1960, $0.206 in 1963, $0.197 in 1966 and $0.438 in 1969
before dropping sharply after the major discoveries made after 1972.
In 1976 the figure was only around $0.02.[60] Even this is not the whole
story. New reserves are far cheaper to find from existing fields than
from new fields; the Poza Rica field, which was discovered by El Aguila
in 1932, was still producing a large part of Pemex's oil in 1972.
Indeed, at the end of 1972 the Poza Rica district accounted for 1.6
billion barrels of total Mexican oil reserves of 2.8 billion barrels, that
is, for 57.86% of the total. To that extent, Pemex had been living off
its underground capital. It was only in 1972 that Pemex made a major
discovery completely on its own initiative. Secondly, as Adelman
pointed out, *ex post* finding costs of oil are 'often unknowable, usually
unknown and always uninteresting'.[61] The real point, from the position of Pemex, was not so much the 'cost of production', except in as
far as this dictated its availability of funds, but rather the increasing
length of time without a major new oil discovery. It is probable that
Pemex was able to make a small profit on the development of its existing finds as opposed to importing, and quite certain that it could have
made a substantial profit on this operation were it not for the high

manning levels maintained most of all in the older oilfields.[62] Genuine exploration drilling, however, as Reyes Heroles frequently pointed out, now needed to take place at higher cost in less accessible locations – deeper into the subsoil or offshore. The real problem was the absolute level of new oil finds and not so much the relative cost. It was on this basis that the Pemex management showed increasing signs of alarm as the 1960s wore on. This changing position was fully recognised within the organisation. In 1968, for example, Reyes Heroles asked the exploration and production department to draw up a ten-year plan; until that point, the time horizon had never been more than two or three years.[63] Moreover, in the *Director's Report* in 1970, Reyes Heroles added for the first time to the proven reserve figures (which, as we have seen, had not increased very much during the entire *sexenio*) a figure of probable reserves which he put at 1.8 billion barrels. This ran directly counter to his position in 1966, which was that: 'If we should give figures on probable reserves, we might be able to inspire a great wave of optimism. But we prefer to confine our estimates of what we have available to proved reserves, making it plain at the same time that in determining these we have applied extremely conservative methods.'[64] When, at the end of the 1960s, these exploration worries were exacerbated by financial difficulties, the organisation began to experience real problems.

These financial difficulties stemmed from the fact that there had been no general increase in domestic oil prices after 1958. During the 1960s Pemex was able to maintain its investments at the desired level, even though it needed to borrow on an increasing scale. In 1969, for example, Pemex needed to borrow 41% of its investment budget.[65] This figure did not include the use of revolving credits which were paid back within the year. By 1972, however, the price level was influencing not only Pemex's financial structure, but also the extent to which it could continue with essential investments. Among the most important of these was the maintenance of an effective drilling programme now that exploration wells needed to be deeper and were therefore higher cost. This was pointed out in the *Director's Report* of 1972:

Exploration projects form a part of the Pemex programs, but the intensity of its development will depend on the resources available.

The economic justification of the large investments required is assured as long as we maintain low costs and autonomy in production. In that respect we believe that the main financial support of industrial expansion should be generated from our own resources. It would not be justified, for the sake of national economic development, if we were to maintain indefinitely prices on our products below world levels, at the expense of dangerously jeopardizing the sound growth of the industry, making it depend on a high proportion of internal and external debts. We hope that public opinion will support this attitude . . . the shallow petroleum deposits have been exhausted in provinces already known; we are now searching at depths of more than 5,000 metres and in the ocean many kilometres offshore, which raises the cost and lengthens the time needed for discovery. To compensate for that, we make use of the most modern geophysical techniques . . . It is worth mentioning that the cost of our crude oil and its derivatives is still lower than the prices on the world market.[66]

In March 1973, with net imports now mounting seriously, Dovali Jaime was even more outspoken:

For the time being, hydrocarbon consumption has overtaken the industry's supplying capacity; this is due to economic conditions which have restricted the resources that could be applied to timely exploration and refining projects.

This does not mean that Mexico lacks the resources and potential to cover this deficit. The implication is that we need to invest in order to discover, exploit and market our hydrocarbon wealth . . .

The difference in cost between domestic and imported crude is considerably in favour of national supply. Moreover, imports lead to the allocation of a part of our resources for the benefit of foreign economies to the detriment of our own and help to damage the balance of payments. Moreover, the imports of gasoline, diesel fuel and liquified gas are made at a loss because they are sold at prices below the purchasing price to which must be added the transportation cost; this causes serious damage to the industry's investment capacity.[67]

Now Pemex was caught in a vicious circle. Imports on a significant scale began in 1972, when the world price was already considerably higher than it had been a few years earlier, and the resulting outflow of funds aggravated Pemex's difficulties in funding new investments. The position would have been yet more serious but for two major changes: the discovery of the Reforma field in 1972 and the major increases in the domestic price level put into effect in December 1973.

The transformation of Pemex 1973–9

It would be difficult to exaggerate the effect of the oil finds made in the Tabasco and Chiapas area (the Reforma field) in and after 1972. By early 1979, official figures gave proved hydrocarbon reserves at 40.8 billion barrels, as against 3.2 billion at the end of 1972. Potential reserves were put at over 200 billion barrels – around 25% of proven world reserves. Although new finds were made after 1972, the southern finds made during that year were decisive in the complete transformation of Pemex's position in the Mexican economy. Moreover, not only were the finds extremely large, they were also relatively low cost, for although the wells were deep they were both onshore and prolific. Indeed, as was pointed out in 1977:

it is a remarkable fact that within four years of their discovery, the fields of the Reforma–Tabasco zone were producing half the country's crude oil; the average yield per well is 5,500 barrels a day, and some wells have a daily potential of 30,000 barrels. These figures compare with a national average which Pemex recently declared to be as low as 120 barrels.[68]

Moreover, according to Pemex, 'We know about the existence of considerable volumes of oil and gas in Chiapas and Tabasco; we believe that they can also be found in other sites, we are sure that the crude can be produced at a cost of one fifth the price that is now being demanded on the international market.'[69]

With these changes went a major change in Pemex's financial position. The transformation of Mexico's oil balance of payments was shown in table 5.3 above, and its investments during this period can be seen in table 17.5. At least two points are clear from this. First, overall investment increased very rapidly – some would say spectacularly – and brought about a qualitative leap in Pemex's importance to the Mexican economy. Secondly, up until 1977 the most rapid increases took place in the downstream sectors. Investment in refining grew nearly eight times during the 1972–7 period, while petrochemical investment similarly increased just over sixfold. The reasons why investment in exploration and production did not grow still more rapidly will be considered further below, but it is worth pointing out here that the Echeverría government responded to the major oil discoveries by making a bold and probably successful effort to turn Mexico into a major international refiner of oil and producer of petrochemicals.

This transformation was in keeping with an ideology of economic development according to which it is always better to export manufactured products than raw materials. There were also more pragmatic grounds for the Mexican decision. For one thing, there was the opportunity of taking full advantage of scale economies – notably in the petrochemicals sector – to lower domestic costs, which were in any case to be held down deliberately in order to stimulate domestic industry.

Exports were to be restricted to the surplus once domestic demand had been filled. For another, petrochemical development would provide a further stimulus to Mexican technical capacity. As one internal document pointed out, 'the petrochemicals industry is the only high technology industry which has been successfully developed within the country'.[70] Further, when world market conditions were difficult, the Mexican refining and petrochemicals industry would be able to be certain of a steady supply of crude oil at a predictable price. The same could not necessarily be said of industries where the feedstock had to be imported. Finally, access to almost limitless supplies of low-cost crude oil would give Pemex a considerable competitive advantage in an oligopolistic international market.

These various changes had major political implications, the most important of which came to be tied up with the question of how far the discoveries would permit Pemex to become a net exporter of oil and gas and with what result. This, in turn, came to be related to the issue of how much oil Mexico really possessed. One important complicating factor in this respect was pressure from the USA, which appears to have developed at a very early stage. At the end of 1972 the *Oil and Gas Journal* pointed out the potential importance of the Mexican discoveries,[71] and as early as March 1973 Dovali Jaime declared:

We have had offers for technical advice in exploration and drilling matters, as well as loan proposals to support those activities and to finance the necessary production and transportation facilities. All of them include, as a basic condition, payment for services offered, or amortisation of credits and interest, with a share of Mexican production . . .

Fortunately, Mexico is now in a more advantageous position than that of years ago . . . [this] provides support to the irrevocable decision of the President of Mexico not to accept such offers . . . The national oil resources should be destined only to the satisfaction of our needs, no matter how seductive the offers from abroad may look, nor how strong may be the pressure to make us accept them.[72]

This was the last time that such uncompromising language was heard. US pressure on Mexico intensified in October 1974 when, as we have seen in chapter 5, the *New York Times* reported on Mexican oil discoveries.[73]

Within Mexico itself, some of the most determined conservationists were to be found within the exploration department of Pemex. It is not fully clear how far attitudes there reflected genuine doubts about the extent of Pemex's discoveries and how far they were due to an

Table 17.5 *Pemex's investment by sector 1972–8*
(dollars)

	1972	1973	1974	1975	1976	1977	1978
Exploration	38.7	39.2	46.1	72.0	112.4	80.8	115.5
Exploration drilling	98.6	88.6	110.1	122.6	130.2	142.1	209.0
Development drilling	99.6	116.2	148.6	183.9	191.4	175.6	365.0
Production	46.7	96.1	118.1	144.8	256.3	279.8	527.7
Refining	44.9	62.3	96.6	259.2	270.1	356.2	464.3
Petrochemicals	44.8	77.9	96.1	146.0	258.1	271.0	493.2
Transport and marketing	90.4	136.7	94.8	163.9	222.0	175.7	598.0
Other	5.3	11.5	10.7	3.0	3.2	35.9	132.5
Total	468.9	628.6	721.0	1,095.4	1,443.7	1,517.1	2,905.1

Source: Pemex, *Annual Reports,* and *Petroleum Economist,* March 1979.

unwillingness to export as a matter of policy. Although the former reason was certainly important, there are good reasons for believing the latter to have been significant as well. One of the geologists involved in making the Reforma discovery later told me: 'I said to my superior "We have found enough oil to meet all of Mexico's needs." I did not dare to say anything about exporting.'[74] Moreover, it is striking that, after the Reforma discovery and even after the price increases of December 1973, the number of wells drilled by Pemex actually fell. Thus, in 1972 Pemex drilled 143 exploration and 280 development wells; in 1973 the numbers were 103 and 319; in 1974, 100 and 309, and in 1976 only 79 and 257. Although more was actually spent upstream, the bulk of the new investment was spent on development drilling (table 17.5) in order to get the existing fields onstream as quickly as possible. From these figures and from various interview sources it is clear that the top management of the exploration–production division of Pemex regarded the idea of exporting crude oil with a marked lack of enthusiasm. In doing this, it was only repeating on a larger scale its earlier policies. Thus, when considering the pre-1976 period, Mega-delli wrote that 'Generally speaking, Pemex slows down its exploration activity and decreases expenditures as soon as a sufficient number of discoveries are made in a given year. It does this in order to direct investment toward development.'[75] While this may be true, it is most unlikely that this division went so far that President Echeverría was not properly informed about the magnitude of the reserves, although even this assertion has sometimes been made.[76]

However, the strictly technical dimension must also be stressed; the traditional exploration and production managers in Pemex were not well equipped to evaluate fully the completely new structures which had been discovered at Reforma. Díaz Serrano, himself a technical expert on drilling, later stated that in 1973

there were discovered the first fields . . . of the Cretaceous in the Reforma area of Chiapas–Tabasco, but due mainly to the inertia of a technical approach which had been formed during a long history of oil development, based on a daily average of 120 barrels daily per well, the real possibilities of this new productive horizon were not immediately detected . . . And not only was it not detected but it was underestimated in both its size and its potential . . .

At the beginning of the presidential campaign of Lic. José López Portillo, a group of engineers from the institution [Pemex] presented a document to him in which it was said that there was real danger that, in the course of four years, Mexico would lose its ability to produce hydrocarbons in sufficient quantity for the nation and that, from 1980, it would be necessary to import, at any rate unless new major deposits were found.[77]

In any case, the Mexican government, near the end of its term of office and caught between the conflicting pressures of the USA and Pemex itself, took care not to commit itself irrevocably to any position. Dovali Jaime stressed conservation rather than expansion and agreed that the new reserves would first be used to allow Pemex to operate at a 20-year reserve–production ratio and not the 16-year ratio that existed previously. This was more significant than it seemed, for the official reserve figures were kept down at an unrealistically low level. At the end of 1976 the official figures were still no more than 6 billion barrels. This attitude of caution was well expressed in the *Director's Report* of 1975:

For the time being, the policy of exporting oil and product surpluses, defined by the President of Mexico, aims to balance, within a reasonable margin of safety, the cost of imports of other crude derivatives, of those petrochemicals in which we are in deficit, and of materials, equipment and parts for the plants, that in some cases cannot be supplied by national manufacturers. Exports in quantities greater than the amount necessary to meet the value of the imports required will depend, finally, on a more accurate knowledge of proven reserves.

The major change in Pemex's position came with the transfer of the presidency from Echeverría to López Portillo in December 1976. López Portillo named Díaz Serrano as the new Director of Pemex and he, in his first statement in office, sharply upgraded Mexican proven reserves from 6 billion barrels to 11 billion. Soon afterwards, the *Financial Times* reported that 'the controversy over whether the reserves should be exploited quickly or preserved for future generations has unavoidably been resolved by the need for a rapid increase in exports'.[78] Broadly speaking, there were two main reasons for the change; these will need to be considered in turn.

The first of these reasons was technical and organisational. With the replacement of Dovali Jaime by Díaz Serrano, Pemex acquired its strongest director since Bermúdez, in terms of both his own personality and his access to the new president. Díaz Serrano showed a marked lack of sympathy for the conservationists in Pemex, who were weakened by the normal retirements and replacements resulting from a new *sexenio*. Díaz Serrano, moreover, was the leader of a group of technical experts who, under the instructions of López Portillo, carried out a review of the oil industry in 1976. He concluded:

> For many years, the Mexican oilfields were developed through drilling at short distances around the discovery well, 200 or 300 metres apart and expanding in a circular direction . . . This type of development led to very slow progress, with the expensive investment of a large number of wells and with a doubling or trebling of necessary surface installations such as tubes, separators and tanks, all of them small and in large quantity. All of this led, fundamentally, to oil operations taking place on the basis of low estimates while the real magnitudes were very large. This expensive and slow process led to the issuing of initial estimates of very small reserves while the full extent of the reserves would be known ten or more years afterwards, after the unnecessary drilling of a large number of wells at a short distance from each other . . .
> The Committee set up under López Portillo to study the oil question at the beginning of 1976 studied the reserves of the country using more modern techniques. It was for this reason that we were able to inform the Mexican people on 22 December 1976 that proved reserves of oil, natural gas and gas liquids had increased from 6,300 million barrels to 11,200 million barrels.[79]

The second major reason for the change in Pemex's position lay in the Mexican economy itself. For various reasons the progress of the Mexican economy, impressive enough until the late 1960s, began to run into trouble. The private sector began to show increasing caution about investment while the public sector reacted by expanding its role and pushing ahead with a number of major projects. Some of these proved to be ill planned and poorly organised, however, and Mexican foreign debt increased sharply, notably under Echeverría, without a corresponding increase in the capacity of the country to repay. The effect of these changes was aggravated by heavy capital flight, particularly in 1975 and 1976, and the whole process culminated in a devaluation of the peso by nearly 50% in 1976. By then, Mexican foreign debt had reached the historically high figure of $22 billion and private investment had practically dried up. The effect of this economic crisis was further aggravated by a tendency towards political polarisation in Echeverría's last year in office, with capital flight on the part of the wealthy and radicalisation on the part of the regime feeding upon each other. By the time that Echeverría handed over power to López Portillo, rumours were even circulating about an impending military coup.

When López Portillo took office, therefore, his first objective was to try to restore the confidence of the private sector in the government while dealing with the IMF and the international financial organisations on whatever terms were available. Under these circumstances, the 'oil card' was one of the very few which he still possessed and he needed to use it.[80] Indeed, the dramatic improvement in the Mexican trade balance that followed the crisis years of the mid-1970s was almost exclusively due to oil; after being a significant net importer of oil in 1972–3, Mexico exported (net) around $800m. worth of hydrocarbons in 1977, $1,800m. in 1978, $3,986m. in 1979 and around $10,402m. in 1980; the figure for 1981 was expected to be around $17,000m. Moreover, as we saw above (p. 126), oil production roughly doubled between 1973 and 1976 and increased by a further 60% up until the end of 1978, at that time reaching a total of 1,500,000 b/d. By March 1981 the rate was over 2,500,000 b/d and was still increasing rapidly.

During the presidency of López Portillo, therefore, rapid expansion became the keynote. In 1977 Pemex published its *Plan sexenal,* which provided for an investment of around $15,500m. during the period in order to increase oil production from around 1,100,000 b/d at the beginning of 1977 to some 2,200,000 b/d by the end of 1982, while major investments were also planned in refining and petrochemicals. For the first time Pemex was due to become a major exporter of refined oil products and certain basic petrochemicals.

This programme of expansion was also welcome to the Pemex unions. Although the processes of Pemex's union politics are always obscure, it is clear that the union leadership had lost little of its power after 1958, despite the efforts of several governments to select their own, more pliable, nominees for the crucial positions. Around 1972, however, government policy changed as Echeverría became increasingly concerned to win support from the existing Pemex union leadership. The total workforce, which had already expanded from 45,500 in 1958 to 71,737 in 1970, was allowed to expand further to 77,336 in 1973, 94,500 in 1976 and some 98,000 in 1977. Moreover, towards the end of his term of office, Echeverría greatly reduced the power of management over appointments and manning levels by cutting back considerably on the number of *de confianza* posts which, according to Pemex tradition, were filled by management with men who did not need union affiliation. All other posts, whose number was now greatly expanded, were in the hands of union appointees. Partly because of these new appointments, and partly because of increases in wages and fringe benefits, the total Pemex wage bill rose at an average of 15% a year between 1970 and 1973 and 30% a year between 1974 and 1977.[81]

In order to avoid possible retrenchment after 1976, the unions were happy to support a policy of very rapid growth in Pemex's total activities, which also offered the management possibilities of increasing efficiency by moving labour within the company to more productive positions. Nobody was therefore greatly surprised when Díaz Serrano announced in 1977 that he had discussed the expansion programme with the unions, and that 'The company is very satisfied with the climate of cordiality, the spirit of understanding and patriotism which were present in these discussions . . . I am sure that these signs will be transformed into productive realities, because this programme signifies work for many people.'[82] This labour support certainly did nothing to reduce the power of the unions, but it did provide major backing for Díaz Serrano's objectives. At the same time, management was able to regain a certain flexibility. This, however, should not be exaggerated; according to one journalist, reporting in 1977:

Managers admit the corporation is overmanned. The worst featherbedding goes on in areas of declining production, where wells yielding only a trickle of oil are often staffed as if they were gushers. Pemex is hoping that by moving these workers to the south, and hiring the minimum of new staff, it can win back higher productivity. But the cautious approach of top management to any assessment of manning levels shows how far the initiative has been taken out of their hands. 'The general policy of Pemex', comments Gregorio Hernández of the planning department, 'is to slow down the increase in the workforce as much as possible.' Expansion allows the company to make a virtue out of an uncomfortable necessity. Díaz Serrano notes that overmanning 'came in very handy now that we have such a demand for labour'.[83]

It should be emphasised, therefore, that the rapid expansion of Pemex in 1977–8 and the even more ambitious projects planned for later in the *sexenio* were not the result simply of technical changes (important though these were) or of an increase in the power of the Pemex management, although this was also a factor. The support for expansion was fairly wide; it came from the Pemex unions, from the Finance Ministry and those concerned directly with the running of the economy and, most important of all, it came from the president himself, who badly wanted the breathing space that increasing oil revenues and reserves would provide.

Consequently, development moved ahead on all fronts and the targets of the *Plan* were in many respects exceeded. Oil production, targeted to reach 2,200,000 b/d at the end of 1982, had reached 2,550,000 b/d by March 1981 and was still increasing. The gas pipeline to the USA, which was not envisaged at all in the *Plan,* was exporting 300 million cubic feet daily, while prodigious strides were also being made to increase consumption of natural gas within Mexico. More dramatically still, Mexico's proven hydrocarbon reserves, estimated at 11 billion barrels in December 1976, were adjudged to have reached 67 billion barrels in March 1981 out of a notional total of 250 billion barrels of potential reserves. Neither Díaz Serrano nor López Portillo was inhibited by international considerations from issuing figures of this magnitude.

Almost as impressive as the quantity of Mexican oil has been its subterranean distribution. According to an official government study, 72% of Mexican territory (including its Continental Shelf), of which only 10% had been carefully explored by the end of 1980, is potentially oil bearing.[84] The most prolific field was Campeche, an offshore field where production reached 888,000 b/d in October 1980, even though production did not begin until June 1979. The field is truly remarkable; one well, the 'Akal', produced 42,000 b/d at its peak, a world record. In 1980 the largest producing field was the Reforma (Chiapas–Tabasco) which yielded 998,519 b/d. The field with the largest potential is the onshore Chicontepec find, with recoverable reserves estimated at 17.6 billion barrels. This field, however, is highly fractured and will require a great deal of drilling if it is to yield its full potential.[85] This outstanding resource base was clearly essential to Pemex's strategy of expansion.

Despite this expansion, however, it remains clear that Pemex is under firm political control. The agency has been pressing for several years for an increase in the domestic price of oil products; there have indeed been limited increases, but they have fallen far short of those the agency would have preferred to see. Moreover, despite the vast increase in Pemex's revenue, the government has adopted a deliberate strategy of taxing away the agency's surplus and the company has thus been increasing its international indebtedness, to over $8,000m. in 1981. Thus, in 1980 Pemex increased its net borrowing by $2,700m. while paying taxes of $7,060m.[86] The government has adopted this strategy (which runs counter to that outlined in the 1976–82 *Plan*) both to take advantage of Pemex's international creditworthiness and ability to borrow on favourable terms and to prevent the company from enjoying too much financial independence. The government also argues that it was necessary to keep the profit share automatically paid out to the oil-workers under national profit-sharing legislation within reasonable bounds. Finally Pemex, despite a few indications that it wished to do so,[87] has not been allowed to enter any new economic areas, although it has certainly invested very heavily within its traditional ambit. All of this suggests that the oil discoveries and the qualitative change in the size and importance of Pemex have not fundamentally altered its traditional relationship with the Mexican government.

There is a final point of great importance which is somewhat beyond the scope of this book, concerning the effect of oil wealth upon the Mexican economy. During the López Portillo *sexenio* voices were often heard from Mexicans who worried about the possible effect of a flood of oil wealth upon the Mexican economy.[88] It was argued that the 'petrolisation' of the economy would damage Mexican manufacturing and create an unhealthy form of economic dependence, that it would lead to inflation, rising expectations and intense social conflict, and that it would turn international (and particularly US) attention on Mexico and so compromise Mexican independence. Some of these fears were probably justified, others perhaps exaggerated, but there can be no doubt that Mexico is in the process of becoming a major oil-exporting country. This is perhaps the most momentous economic change in the history of Mexico since Alemán committed it to a policy of conservative industrialisation just after the Second World War.

Concluding reflections

Oil exploration has often been regarded as the Achilles' heel of state companies. Control of the market, it is argued, can guarantee the viability of refining and marketing operations even if there is some budgetary cost attached, but there are no guarantees in the field of oil exploration and no government will tolerate the spending of scarce capital on repeated failures. If this argument is taken seriously, then Pemex did not come of age until 1972. Before that time, although it had clearly made significant finds of its own, it continued to rely for much of its oil on the discoveries made by El Aguila in the 1930s. The Reforma find, however, dramatically changed this picture. Indeed, this find seems to have been the most significant ever to have been made by a state oil company.

There was perhaps good fortune in Pemex's ability to find such a field at such a time, although it was the culmination of a number of years of extensive searching. However, the Reforma find clearly shows the narrowness of the margin between failure and success in oil exploration; if Pemex's imports had continued to rise after 1973 as they had in the preceding two years there can be no doubt that the Mexican government would have faced severe problems, and perhaps even pressures to allow the return of foreign investment. Whatever the final outcome, such a situation would have been a major political defeat for the Mexican Revolution. As things turned out, however, Pemex has come to be regarded as a major success and the income which it is now generating is playing a major part in rescuing the Mexican economy from one of its most serious post-war crises. Moreover, given the massive appetite of the USA for oil and Mexico's own vulnerability to US pressure, public ownership of Mexican oil is likely to prove crucial in the difficult geo-political and economic conjuncture which undoubtedly lies ahead. For a state oil company, geology is often destiny.

Despite these uncertainties, Pemex's own strategy has generally tied in closely with the overall direction of Mexican development. In the period after 1938 it transformed the pattern of the industry from an export-oriented crude oil producer to a low-cost supplier of Mexico's import-substituting industrialisation. Subsequently it helped the growth of this industrialisation by moving into petrochemicals and by building up a centre of Mexican petroleum technology. Finally, when the ISI model ran into crisis, Pemex almost single-handedly generated the export income and capital goods market which have helped to promote economic recovery. During all of this time, moreover, the oil sector was sacrificed to a greater or lesser extent for the benefit of the rest of the economy. Despite the generally high profitability of the oil industry, Pemex has several times found itself in severe economic difficulty. In general, its position has been sustainable, but good investments did have to be delayed in the early 1970s because of a lack of financial resources; conversely, urban Mexico has benefited greatly from 40 years of cheap oil and, consequently, lower industrial costs than would otherwise have been the case.

All of this might suggest that Pemex was an obedient servant of the Mexican state. Interestingly enough, however, this overall coherence between the policies of Pemex and the objectives of successive Mexican governments has not prevented considerable conflict in matters of detail, while there have been times when the Pemex management has seemed to lead rather than follow the processes of official decision making. This seeming paradox has been explored in this chapter and it remains to put forward an explanation.

Pemex is not, and has never been, a hierarchical, rational and disciplined agency on the Weberian model. It is, rather, a technically talented but administratively chaotic institution which badly needs strong, perhaps even charismatic, leadership. When such leadership is strong (as was the case with Bermúdez, and appears to be with Díaz Serrano), some decisions will be made by the head of Pemex which are unwelcome to the political authorities; indeed, as we have seen, Bermúdez's independence at times came close to open insubordination. Moreover, where the political conjuncture permits, a strong head of Pemex will look for, and probably find, influential support from outside the organisation for his own chosen policies. Thus, Díaz Serrano's ability to win the support of the Pemex unions for the expansion proposals has been an important factor in recent years.

Nevertheless, given the nature of the Mexican political system, the most important factor in the strength of any director of Pemex has been his access to the President of the Republic. Mexican presidents generally exert power over the bureaucracy by selecting men and determining priorities rather than by detailed policymaking. Naturally this leaves a great deal to senior administrators. However, really important policymaking generally requires some degree of control over questions that normally fall within the presidential sphere – if only because they involve a balance of interests and not simply those within a single agency – and it is here that a 'strong' director-general needs to prevail for at least a part of the time. At least half of the job of the Director of Pemex, therefore, is to act as a successful politician. Naturally the inherent importance of Pemex will give his position considerable weight, but the most effective directors have been able to add something to this. Conversely, this same structure has enabled successive Mexican presidents to keep control over Pemex and to guide its policies in the direction felt to be necessary for the overall development of the Mexican economy.

Thus, even strong figures are by no means omnipotent. Both Bermúdez (on the prices question) and Díaz Serrano (on the volume of production) had to respect presidential decisions on important matters about which they clearly disagreed. Just as important, however, were the limits of their power within the organisation. Sandeman detailed some of the problems facing Díaz Serrano:

> Too much centralisation, and not enough contact between departments, are problems endemic to organisations in Mexico. Because all five major departments in Pemex – covering exploration, production, petrochemicals, sales and finance – behave like feudal fiefdoms, communication between departments tends to go through the top . . . the bad old habits die hard. Although the co-ordination and planning office has doubled its staff, the corporate planners admit that they just cannot get the information they need to start improving communications.[89]

With weaker leadership, crucial information did not always find its way to the top. We have already seen the difficulties facing Reyes Heroles (not by any means a weak director himself) in trying to calculate the cost of domestic oil production.

When leadership is less strong, in fact, power tends to move downwards rather than up. Crucial decisions made at lower levels are not co-ordinated, let alone effectively checked, higher up. A good example was the way in which the Pemex exploration department was able to keep the extent of the Reforma find to itself; this ability to retain secrecy would have probably been even greater had it not been for articles in the international press. Another was the way in which Gutiérrez Roldán, although himself a financial expert, was unable to keep effective track of overspending on petrochemical and other projects which caused such difficulties in 1960–1. Indeed, it appears to have been these events, rather than the iron rule of Bermúdez, which led Vernon to his conclusions about the power of public sector *técnicos* and Wionczek to remark that, 'though political power is highly centralised in the office of the president in Mexico, public enterprises have always shown an incredible ability to escape effective federal control'.[90] If the Director of Pemex is not effectively in control, the President of the Republic has very little chance.

The position of any director of Pemex is naturally influenced to a great extent by the senior management immediately below him. A fascinating recent study shows how this has evolved since 1938.[91] In general, only around half of the senior management changes every *sexenio* so that a significant corps remains to add continuity. There has, however, been a significant shift in the character of Pemex's senior managers since nationalisation. At the beginning, the senior managers were all oil specialists who retained such expertise as was available to Mexico following the expulsion of the private companies. They were in no sense political figures and their intense loyalty to the organisation prevented them from seeking their fortunes in the private sector. In the 1950s the senior managers were also for the most part oil specialists but this generation proved increasingly willing to move from Pemex to lucrative private sector positions. It is likely that Pemex's own policies of relying increasingly on contracted services (see above, p. 343) played a part in this, as did the increasing sophistication of the private sector's own oil-related activities, but one must also mention that the 'heroic' period for Pemex ended around the mid-1950s for reasons already discussed in this chapter. This change no doubt weakened loyalties within Pemex. After around 1964 the position changed again. Senior figures within Pemex were less often oil specialists and more often general economists and administrators. Many of these went on to fill senior government positions in areas other than oil (Reyes Heroles, Espinoza de los Reyes and de la Madrid Hurtado may serve as examples). This may have led to a certain amount of administrative padding (a fact of which Bermúdez complained strongly)[92] but it also increased Pemex's flexibility and its responsiveness to directives from above. Meanwhile, the connections between Pemex and the private sector appear, if anything, to have become still closer.

These patterns of managerial recruitment tie in closely both with the economic position of Pemex and with the nature of its relationship to the central government. During the ten years after nationalisation, managerial control over Pemex was generally weak. The unions retained a great deal of power and in any case Pemex was more concerned to keep going and ward off political attack than to take any important new initiatives for which tighter managerial control would have been necessary. The main political link between Pemex and the government was provided by the union leaders, whose good relations with Lombardo Toledano and Cárdenas himself were sufficient to protect the agency politically. At that time the political attack on Pemex was quite strong. It came from across the border (and from Britain) first through the company-sponsored boycott of Mexican oil and later from the more subtle pressures of the US State Department. It also came from domestic conservatives who preferred efficient service to national control and were not yet aware that it was possible to have both. Pemex's main line of political defence, the link between the oil-workers and the left wing of the PRI, sharply constrained the actual conduct of management.

During the next ten years (1948–58), the government's main connection with Pemex came from Bermúdez and a small group of top managers. This change was partly the result of a transformation within the PRI and the Mexican government which, its last vestiges of *cardenista* labourism gone, moved decisively to the right. In a typically Mexican compromise, the government held back from readmitting foreign investment but nevertheless broke the power of the Pemex unions and asserted managerial control. Moreover, as industrial capitalism developed more strongly, Pemex was given the task of supplying the domestic market and its exporting function was largely eliminated. Bermúdez himself was a charismatic figure who was given considerable freedom to manoeuvre within these fairly broad limits. Although undoubtedly relying to some extent upon corrupt influences within the union bureaucracy, Bermúdez also made his own task easier by his outspoken nationalism and promotion of Pemex. He was also allowed a freedom from financial and political control which has never been granted to his successors. The carefully cultivated Pemex mystique and Pemex's undoubted success in supplying an expanding domestic market were enough for Mexicans to overlook the increasing evidence of labour corruption and financial chaos.

The period since 1958 has seen the increasing organisational, technological and political maturing of Pemex. The Bermúdez period had been successful in integrating Pemex into Mexico's increasingly institutionalised political system and securing its acceptance by the Mexican private sector. After 1958 it became increasingly necessary to extend Pemex's activities into other fields and to increase its technical sophistication. Pemex's own expansion also made it increasingly important to run the organisation through economic and administrative rather than purely technical skills. For all of these reasons, oil specialists and Pemex loyalists increasingly gave way to upwardly mobile technocrats and to oilmen mobile between the private and the public sector. These changes have been beneficial in terms of increasing both Pemex's political flexibility and its technical sophistication. Although some of the early rigidity undoubtedly remains, Pemex's remarkably successful record since the Reforma discoveries bears witness to these changes.

18

The development of Petrobrás: oil company to conglomerate?

Petrobrás was not set up completely from scratch; by 1954 the CNP's total investments amounted to some $165m. and a major refinery, with a capacity of 45,000 b/d, was under construction at Cubatão. These assets were then passed over to Petrobrás. Nevertheless, the agency was still small and inexperienced when compared with what it had been set to do, which was to produce and refine enough oil to make Brazil self-sufficient with only the limited help of two small privately owned refineries. The first President of Petrobrás, Juraci Magalhães, later recalled that 'the state company began as a real "encampment". Everybody installed himself where he could, and the desk which he [Juraci] began using had been bought from an engineer who worked in the same office block in which Petrobrás had been installed.'[1] Nevertheless, the agency began with many opportunities in the most important areas: those relating to the formation of financial, human and political capital. For the first seven years, these were generally used to advantage.

Petrobrás 1954–61: the enterprise matures

Looking back on the period 1954–60, W. J. Levy concluded that, while Petrobrás had certainly not faced serious financial problems, 'it is clear that a major part of Petrobrás' profitability cannot be regarded simply as earnings from operations. Behind it is a deliberate policy of public support.'[2] It was not difficult to find evidence for this assertion. For the six years up until the end of 1959, fully 39.4% of Petrobrás's funds had stemmed from tax exemptions and earmarked sources of revenue. Moreover, in 1959 over 40% of Petrobrás's profits came from direct government protection of the refining sector, calculated as the difference between import duties on refined products (then still imported by the private distribution companies) and taxes levied on

Table 18.1 *Financing of Petrobrás 1955–60*
(*m. cruzeiros*)

	1955	1956	1957	1958	1959	1960
Sales income						
(less cost)	1,021	2,817	4,705	7,766	13,333	15,477
Reinvested profits[a]	n.a.	166	1,577	3,492	4,687	7,522
Earmarked taxes	936	1,300	2,557	3,042	4,575	6,118
Vehicle levy	446	472	416	7	11	2
Total	2,403	4,755	9,255	14,307	22,606	29,119

[a] Previous year
Source: Petrobrás, *Annual Report for 1960.*

refining. As a consequence of these fiscal advantages, Petrobrás's financial position was extremely strong. The future also looked promising since after around 1960 depreciation and amortisation provisions, which up until then had accounted for only 4.1% of Petrobrás's funds, would, as a result of the oil industry's highly conservative accounting provisions, increasingly provide a safety cushion if Petrobrás's profits lagged. Moreover, the level of direct fiscal subsidy became increasingly unimportant as Petrobrás's own business grew, as can be seen from table 18.1.

These *ex post* evaluations, however, while certainly important, should not conceal the early financial uncertainties of Petrobrás's operations. At the beginning, there were serious problems with exchange controls; the Financial Director later recalled that:

The major difficulties were in the financial and exchange field. It was a struggle, for example, to finish Cubatão. Every dollar had to be extracted from the Banco do Brasil with great effort. When Cubatão began operating, I received every day a bulletin of production statistics and, comparing these with the cost statistics, I came to the conclusion that it was going to make losses. Like the refinery, the oil fleet was set to make losses.[3]

The position only changed in 1955 when the government increased domestic prices.

Profitability was, however, a crucial objective for the senior management of Petrobrás for, as Getúlio Carvalho explains, it was essential for them to secure the company's independence from its congressional critics.[4] By 1960 this objective seemed largely to have been secured.

Petrobrás certainly appeared to make good use of its independence in its policies of technical training and hiring of foreign experts. In 1954 Petrobrás signed a contract for technical assistance with Creole, the Jersey Standard subsidiary in Venezuela, and, as Hilnor Canguçu da Mesquita recalled, 'We were able to rely on the full-time collaboration of two employees of Esso's Venezuela subsidiary, who were contracted especially to advise us in the operational and technical training fields.'[5] Moreover, both Creole and McKee (one of Creole's specialist contracting companies) agreed to take for training a number of Petrobrás employees.[6] Petrobrás was also willing to recruit internationally. Soares Pereira pointed out that:

It was necessary to look abroad and attract capable people. Our contracting of several Mexican technicians provoked some friction between the governments of our two countries. Perón, who had established a salary structure which penalised qualified Argentine personnel, facilitated the arrival of a number of qualified engineers in Brazil. The same was true of Colombia, at that time passing through a major salary crisis. Since many Indonesian technicians had been forced out by the war, it was possible to contract some of them in Europe. Thus, the company began to look like a kind of United Nations.[7]

The most controversial and important of all the appointments, however, was that of Walter Link. Link was at that time an employee of Jersey Standard and was said to be one of the foremost geologists in the world. Link himself evidently shared this evaluation since he agreed to work for Petrobrás as head of the exploration department for the modest salary of $100,000 a year. Some influential members of the 1954–5 Brazilian government were unwilling to pay this amount, and it is said that the transfer of cruzeiros to dollars necessary to make the required payment went through the army after the Finance Minister had refused to provide the foreign exchange. Nevertheless, Link was hired.

Link was given considerable autonomy in setting up the exploration department, Depex. He began work with the declaration that 'since Petrobrás is in its infancy, struggling to get on its feet and become self-sufficient, we must explore the regions that offer the best prospect and are easiest of access'.[8] The department was then organised geographically. Pedro de Moura, a former Petrobrás geologist, wrote:

The district managers analysed and discussed the geological findings presented by the heads of the survey teams with their advisers, themselves contracted geologists; they sent their reports back to Depex in Rio de Janeiro where they were studied and analysed again by the sector chiefs, who, finally, passed them to the chief geologist, Luis G. Morales, for examination and decision by the *superintendencia*.

The exploration strategy of Link was centred around two key points. To develop exploration at Bahia and survey the largest sedimentary basins in Brazil, in which it appeared almost certain that new oilfields would be discovered with reserves of at least 100 million barrels. Sights were set principally on the Amazon and Paraná basins, both because of their size and because of their geographical and economic relevance.[9]

It was only when Link reported his findings that controversy began.

Until the early 1960s Petrobrás had the political strength born of a sense of purpose. The company had been set up to refine oil profitably and to use the money thus earned to mount a major exploration campaign. The early Petrobrás management showed no interest in extending the role of the company beyond these boundaries. Thus, in 1956

Petrobrás was asked to give an opinion about a bill, being discussed in Congress, which among other things would give the company a monopoly of distribution of refined products in the country. In the statement made to the Chamber of Deputies, the president of the company provided the studies and information according to which Petrobrás made its decision not to recommend, for the moment, the extension of the state monopoly into the distribution of refined products.[10]

Petrobrás was given the legal right in 1957 to enter the petrochemicals industry should it choose to do so, but no effort was made in this direction until after 1960.

The question of whether foreign investment should be allowed to explore for oil in Brazil was altogether more sensitive. Although Juarez Távora, who had been one of the most prominent opponents of oil nationalism in Brazil, declared in October 1954 that he accepted the state monopoly, the issue was by no means completely closed. In April 1956 the *Hispanic American Report* quoted Tad Szulc to the effect that 'Key members of the administration acknowledge that foreign help is essential, but they mention that a careful educational process is necessary to convince the nation that this can be had without jeopardising Brazil's sovereignty.' Moreover, although President Kubitshek (1956–60) quickly discovered the value of asserting his own commitment to nationalism, largely, it appears, under prodding from his Minister of War, General Lott, the matter still did not appear completely closed. The US government continued to press hard for its foreign companies to be allowed to explore for oil in Brazil and the matter was still dis-

Table 18.2 *Wells drilled by Petrobrás 1955–61*

	1955	1956	1957	1958	1959	1960	1961
Exploration	14	7	35	58	90	95	78
Development	39	40	53	81	137	140	170
Total	53	47	88	139	227	235	248

See also table 18.8.
Source: Petrobrás, *Annual Report for 1963.*

cussed within sections of the government. For example, Lima Rocha remembered an occasion (which must have been between 1956 and 1958) when

The Chancellor Negrão de Lima and his aides discussed the problem and gave their opinion that the solution for Brazil was to adopt exploration contracts. Janari [Nunes] [head of Petrobrás 1956–8] spoke, defending on behalf of Petrobrás the policy already in existence and said that it could not be modified. He asked my opinion and I asked the President whether political conditions existed which would permit the monopoly to be altered. He did not reply, changed the subject and the matter remained there.[11]

However, Petrobrás's objective of discovering enough oil to make Brazil self-sufficient soon appeared to be threatened from another direction, as doubts came to be raised about whether sufficient oil could ever be found. Certainly Petrobrás tried hard. As can be seen from table 18.2, its drilling continued to increase, and there was a growth in oil production from 2,721 b/d in 1954 to 80,910 b/d in 1960. This was not spectacular when set against Brazilian consumption in 1960 of 263,844 b/d. However, until the publication of what came to be known as the 'Link Report' in 1960, few Brazilians doubted that the necessary oil could be found and produced.

Link had apparently been unhappy for some time about the extent to which Petrobrás was exploring in the Amazon as against the known and lower-cost oil-producing areas in the Brazilian north-east. According to Soares Pereira:

More than once he [Link] suggested to the administration of the enterprise, especially at the time of Janari Nunes (1956–8), that it should spend less in the Amazon and devote greater effort to Bahia and Sergipe, which he denoted as areas worthy of greater consideration . . . This point of view of Mr Link clashed with the existing climate in Petrobrás, where several technicians that I knew reacted very emotionally. They said that the 'gringo' was trying to hold back exploration and that the Amazon was a sea of oil. Evidently this was not so.[12]

Certainly Link's findings triggered an emotional response. The initial document, the Link Report, stated that in the whole of Brazil only three north-eastern basins (in Bahia and Sergipe) were really promising, whereas the Amazon was disappointing and also excessively high cost for a company of Petrobrás's resources. If Petrobrás really wanted to find more oil, it should look offshore and overseas.

Politics and crisis 1961–4

With hindsight, it is not surprising that such a report, issued in the name of a highly paid US geologist (even if signed by thirteen other top geologists, six of them native Brazilians), would, if it ever became public, create an outcry. Brazilians had long been used to the idea that the country contained an abundance of all kinds of raw materials, including oil, and that Petrobrás was necessary because the 'trusts' had no interest in producing it.[13] It was but a short step for Brazilians with a suspicious turn of mind, or with a political axe to grind, to conclude that Link was in league with the 'trusts' in order to discourage Brazilian exploration. Ironically, however, the 'trusts' generally did believe the Link Report and foreign company interest in exploring in Brazil practically disappeared for another decade.

The Link Report also highlighted what was becoming another problem with Petrobrás – the nature of its political involvements. As we have seen, the creation of Petrobrás was a response to a mixture of political and technocratic pressures. Then, in order to take some of the political heat away from the organisation, both Vargas and Café Filho (President 1954–5) appointed relatively conservative administrators to run the agency (Juraci Magalhães and Arthur Levy respectively). Kubitshek appeared to be following in the same direction when he appointed Colonel Janari Nunes to the head of the agency. Nunes had been governor of the Territory of Amape and had shown himself to be something of an economic liberal in this position. Consequently, 'the nationalists thought that he was about to negotiate with foreign capital and weaken the monopoly. I think that, for this reason, he felt it necessary to give many explanations. He travelled all over the country, visiting the areas in which the company operated and everywhere gave press conferences that practically turned into election meetings.'[14] Nunes's personal style of campaigning did not please everybody; at least some military officers believed that he was directly involved in financing the nationalist slate in the Military Club elections of 1958.[15] Moreover, in the same year he clashed strongly with Colonel Bittencourt who had been appointed to head the government's regulatory agency, the Conselho Nacional do Petróleo. As a consequence of the conflict, both men were forced to resign, but the institutional battle resulted in success for Petrobrás which at that time showed itself to be outside effective ministerial control.[16]

Nunes's adventures and, subsequently, the Link Report hastened the politicisation of Petrobrás, although this was perhaps inevitable in the face of changes that were taking place in national politics at that time. At the risk of some oversimplification, it may be said that these changes amounted to a growing crisis in the way in which Brazil was governed. No political organisation had been very effective in capturing the support of the new political groups which were being thrown up by the very rapid process of industrialisation and by the urbanisation that had taken place in Brazil after the 1930s. Presidents Dutra, Vargas and Kubitshek had, however, been able to rely with some success upon the essentially corporatist mechanisms of labour control set up by Vargas in 1943. As time went on this control became more difficult and the political left, whose undoubted potential for popular support was undermined by these mechanisms, became increasingly aggressive, militant and disruptive, particularly after the Cuban Revolution in 1959.[17] Any attempt to exert tougher political control, however, would play into the hands of the political right, where there remained throughout this period a military veto and, ultimately, a capacity to impose military dictatorship. Until 1964, however, the military nationalists held the crucial balance and provided essential, although only conditional, support for President Kubitshek (1956–60) and for Goulart (1961–4) until they largely deserted him during the political crisis of 1964. Successive presidents, therefore, remained in office by playing off rival groups and trying to see to it that political issues were never too well defined. Naturally these attitudes encouraged further militancy on the left and more obstinate intransigence on the right, and the political balancing act became increasingly difficult, particularly in the face of growing economic difficulties after 1961. Although President Goulart did not finally fall from the tightrope until 1964, it had for some time previously become necessary for most of those with executive power in the state enterprises to replace technocratic modes of leadership with the building up of political coalitions, themselves in varying degrees unstable.

It is difficult to point to the exact date when the politicisation of Petrobrás began, if by politicisation is meant not the deliberate creation by the Petrobrás management of a political constituency (which began with Nunes), but rather the search by Petrobrás managers and workers for a political base outside the organisation as a weapon in internal political conflicts, and the consequent substitution of political for organisational criteria in internal decision making. One early indication lay in November 1960 when General Sardenberg, the head of Petrobrás, in a presentation to Congress specifically attacked Link and the Link Report in terms which had to do with political propaganda rather than reasoned analysis.[18] In late 1960, press reports for the first time carried stories of internal conflicts within Petrobrás.[19] Moreover, during the seven-month presidency of Janio Quadros in 1961, Geonísio Barroso was selected as head of Petrobrás. According to P. S. Smith, 'Barroso was chosen in response to pressure from the Bahia oilworkers union: labour in Petrobrás' Bahia installation had not been organised until 1958: to have had such power by 1961, indicates the degree to which Petrobrás had become politicised'.[20]

In the jockeying for position which followed, the extreme nationalists within and outside the organisation pressed for the extension of Petrobrás's control into other areas. In 1960, General Sardenberg himself called for the extension of Petrobrás's control over the whole of the oil industry, arguing that while 'the high-cost, small-profit exploration and exploitation phases of the industry were exclusively the responsibility of Petrobrás, the lucrative distribution end was in the hands of private capital'.[21] As we have seen above, it is extremely difficult to reconcile Sardenberg's assertions with any plausible reading of the facts; the small element of truth in them relates to the difficulties which Petrobrás was encountering in its oil exploration – difficulties implicitly denied by the nature of Sardenberg's attack on Link. As for the question of distribution, Petrobrás did begin a limited service after 1961. However, 'by August 1963 federal agencies owed Petrobrás Cr$16 billion (almost US$27 million) and the total was steadily rising. The private distributing companies had had the same problem with the Brazilian bureaucracy but had always paid Petrobrás in thirty days.'[22] The profitability of this sector does not appear to have been exciting.

It is in fact likely that the pressure for the expansion of Petrobrás's activities, the move into distribution, the expropriation of the two small existing private refineries and the development of exploration in the Amazon came from within the organisation itself – certainly from the trade unions and their largely Communist leadership, and perhaps also from the technical staff. While it is clear that the question of Petrobrás's expansion came to be tied up with the question of the over-all control of the enterprise, the fact remains that the pressure within Petrobrás for diversification remained well after these particular polit-ical conflicts were resolved and the expansionists clearly had a far wider constituency than the Petrobrás unions and the radical left.

Indeed, it is interesting that many of the decisions to expand taken by Petrobrás after 1964 were presaged by discussions during the 1960–4 period. Hector Lima Rocha, Finance Director of Petrobrás until his enforced resignation in 1962, made two suggestions:

First, the internationalisation of Petrobrás, without prejudice to its internal exploration activities. The timing was favourable and I had made several con-tacts . . . We had a proposal to associate with ENI and other companies because we had an asset, which was our market . . . I explained this in Petro-brás; everybody agreed, but they all were aware of the repercussions upon public opinion.[23]

Clearly the problem was tied up with the Link Report; exploration abroad might have been construed as a tacit admission that Brazil could not expect to be self-sufficient on the basis of its own reserves.

Lima Rocha's second suggestion

was the following; Petrobrás had hundreds of proposals from foreign petro-chemicals companies which wanted to set up joint-ventures, or associated industries, or whatever. Association with Petrobrás would be difficult because Petrobrás was already involved in exploration, refining, etc. I therefore sug-gested that Petrobrás should create a few subsidiary companies which would associate themselves with private capital in order to develop the petrochemi-cals industry.[24]

According to Lima Rocha, it was the leaking of these proposals that led to his enforced resignation. However, the main point is that both of these proposals – from a relatively conservative technocrat – implied the expansion of Petrobrás itself. In that respect at least there was a similarity between the position of the extreme nationalists, who effec-tively controlled the Petrobrás unions, and the more conservative

Petrobrás technicians. This had become something of an orthodoxy shared by those of radically different political persuasions and attitudes on other questions.

The promise of expansion alone, however, was insufficient to resolve the growing tension between the Petrobrás technicians and trade unions, which spilled over into open hostility in 1962–3. Since the conflicts within Petrobrás during this period have been discussed in detail by P. S. Smith,[25] only a few points will be made here. Essentially, the Petrobrás unions, in which the Communist Party was strongly placed, were able to gain an increasing degree of control over the running of the organisation by aligning themselves with President Goulart and, even more so, with the radical left outside Petrobrás. The technical and administrative staff resisted this process, but theirs was a defensive struggle until their position was vindicated by the right-wing military coup of 1964. Although the nationalists' proposal to take over the remaining private oil refineries was controversial, it is clear that the main conflict concerned the question of who should control Petrobrás rather than what its role should be. As well as moving tentatively into distribution, Petrobrás was in fact given a complete monopoly over oil imports in December 1963 and, in one of his last acts in office, President Goulart responded to union pressures (which had included strikes) and finally decreed the nationalisation of the remaining private refineries.

Consolidation and expansion 1964–73

In retrospect, it is clear that the 1964 coup was technocratic rather than economically liberal at least in terms of its effects upon Petrobrás. There was a limited amount of purging and the relatively stable and authoritarian political climate discouraged disgruntled Petrobrás employees from pressing their grievances through political action. However, the economic liberals, who had been prominent in fomenting the 1964 coup, made very little progress in changing the structure of the oil industry. The new president of Petrobrás, General Ademar de Queiros, was able to maintain the company's monopoly over the import of crude oil and even tried, unsuccessfully, to retain the nationalised oil refineries; the government proved willing to hold them, but the Supreme Court ruled that Goulart's last actions had been illegal. As far as exploration was concerned, Stepan stated that

Some but not all members of the Cabinet wanted to allow private and foreign capital a role in the development of oil, traditionally the exclusive domain of the nationalised oil monopoly Petrobrás. Nationalist sentiment in Brazil and in the Armed Forces was so strong, however, that the government eventually decided not to push the matter but left it an open question for future consideration.[26]

As well as keeping all of its old functions, the Petrobrás 'technostructure' also benefited from the suppression of trade union activity and the easing of foreign exchange controls which had created bureaucratic problems for the company in the past.

The creation of Petroquisa in 1967, which expanded Petrobrás's authority into the field of petrochemicals, was the first major development after 1964. As we have seen, the idea of setting up a Petrobrás subsidiary to move into petrochemicals on a joint venture basis was mooted by Lima Rocha in 1962 but was then blocked for political reasons. The incoming military government, however, quickly recognised the importance of developing this field; in May 1964 two senior Petrobrás technocrats told the press that 'The petrochemical programme is, in fact, well behind. They said that the company planned to develop a ten-year plan for the sector but that to do this it would be necessary to have a discussion with potential consumers, which was now being done.'[27] The private sector was also interested in petrochemicals development. In 1965 Union Carbide went to the government and proposed a joint venture with Petrobrás in a major petrochemicals development. At almost the same time a group of local businessmen, the Capuava group, put forward the idea of a project and looked for involvement on the part of foreign companies. They enlisted Phillips Petroleum and some other local capital. Thus, when Petroquisa was set up (51% owned by Petrobrás, 49% by private interests) it could move quickly to create a new and dramatically expanding Brazilian industry.[28]

The setting up of Petroquisa presaged, although it did not by itself determine, the huge expansion of Petrobrás's activities which took place after 1969. There had been some behind-the-scenes conflict over the question, and President Costa e Silva tried to meet liberal objections by giving 49% of Petroquisa to the private sector.[29] Nevertheless, the effect of the move was to make the role of the state central to the development of a new and dynamic industry.[30]

The period 1969–73 was perhaps the most important, and certainly the most controversial, in the entire history of Petrobrás. In national

Table 18.3 *Petrobrás income 1970–8*
($m.)

	1970	1971	1972	1973	1974	1975	1976	1977	1978
Net sales	840	1,047	1,538	2,337	5,033	6,270	7,320	8,253	9,126
Gross profit	319	406	514	738	1,487	1,914	2,199	2,400	2,376
Net income[a]	127	190	260	302	508	636	816	958	1,049

[a] After depreciation and amortisation, taxes and various expenses.
Source: Petrobrás News (March 1979), p. 5.

politics this period – the government of General Medici – was one of unusual authoritarianism in which press freedom as well as political organisation were sharply restricted. Within Petrobrás itself, the new president, General Ernesto Geisel, was not only a man of very strong character but was also the brother of the army minister and one of the most powerful officers in the Brazilian army; he did, in fact, become President of Brazil in 1974. Two journalists, Stumpf and Pereira, described Geisel's accession as follows:

General Geisel had expected to enjoy a tranquil life in STM, the Superior Military Tribunal, until August 1968. It was he who said to Figueiredo: 'In Petrobrás I may remain four years, four months or four days.'
Figueiredo [who told him of the new posting] insisted and guaranteed that this was the desire of President Emilio Garrastazú Medici. Geisel agreed, on one condition: his administration of Petrobrás would be completely autonomous, free from any subordination to the Minister of Mines and Energy. Professor Antonio Dias Leite Figueiredo carried this request to Medici, who agreed. Geisel took up the presidency of Petrobrás and carried out the second part of his request; he changed the entire directorate.[31]

These factors explain much of Petrobrás's new importance, but there is another consideration as well: in the years after 1969 Petrobrás became vastly profitable and increasingly capable of internally financing its rapid expansion. This can be seen from table 18.3.

One of the main reasons for this financial transformation was unintended. After the Supreme Court had annulled Goulart's nationalisation of the private oil refineries, Petrobrás had to share the market with two small and essentially uneconomic private sector refineries which were prevented from expanding further; consequently the latter needed to be given a set of prices for refining which, when applied to Petro-

Table 18.4 *Source and c.i.f. price of Brazilian oil imports 1961–70*

	W. hemisphere (percentage)	Africa (percentage)	Middle East (percentage)	Europe[a] (percentage)	Cost of crude imports ($ barrel)
1961	54	0	42	4	2.41
1963	49	9	39	3	2.31
1965	39	1	38	22	2.07
1967	21	7	67	5	n.a.
1968	19	14	64	3	2.15
1969	18	21	60	1	2.07
1970	17	27	56	0	2.11

[a] Mainly USSR.
Note: The table shows current dollars; the price in real terms fell by even more.
Source: Petrobrás, *Annual Reports.*

brás's own more modern and larger refineries, guaranteed high profit-ability.[32] Thus, as Horta Barbosa had anticipated, although for rather different reasons, refining provided the backbone of Petrobrás's finan-cial strength during this period. Petrobrás continued to progress smoothly by expanding old or building new refineries as the needs of the market required. Refining capacity increased from 365,000 b/d in 1965 to 501,600 b/d in 1969 and 986,000 b/d in 1975 although, as we shall see, refining policy ran into difficulty in the late 1970s.

Another reason for Petrobrás's growing financial strength dated back to before 1964. From the early 1960s there developed a situation in which the world oil market was in oversupply but in which a reduction in the official 'posted price' of oil was impossible for political reasons. Consequently, international companies became increasingly willing to offer discounts on posted prices, essentially on an *ad hoc* basis, to buyers able and willing to shop around; in the mid-1960s there was a saying that 'only fools and affiliates pay posted prices'. The oil import monop-oly decreed in December 1963 gave Petrobrás considerable leverage, which successive governments used to force down the import price while, incidentally, shifting Brazil's main source of supply from Ven-ezuela to North Africa and the Middle East (table 18.4). This transi-tion was also helped by a fall in tanker costs and Petrobrás also took advantage of this situation to build up its own fleet of very large tank-ers which carried an increasing proportion of Brazilian oil imports.

The Geisel Administration also greatly expanded Petrobrás's participation in the distribution sector. As we have seen, some tentative moves were made in the early 1960s to expand Petrobrás's distribution facilities, but by 1964 almost all of its sales to final consumers were to government agencies; the private distributors were not unhappy at this turn of events since government agencies were not punctual with their payments. After 1970, however, Petrobrás moved aggressively into all parts of the distribution market and its distribution subsidiary, Distribuidora, was set up in 1971. One justification put forward for this move was that of security. There was some feeling that those private companies which until then controlled the distribution trade could not necessarily be trusted to supply oil products to areas where profit margins were low even if social needs were high. Nevertheless, the most important reason was probably a belief that distribution was highly profitable (which turned out not to be the case) and it was also considered that the Petrobrás sign over gasoline outlets would be good public relations. Thus, Petrobrás's final market share increased from 10.4% in 1965 to 15.2% in 1970, 22.1% in 1971 and 27.5% in 1973.[33]

The most controversial aspect of Geisel's presidency of Petrobrás, however, concerned oil exploration. In discussing this, one needs first to examine the many criticisms made of the agency during this period to the effect that it effectively abandoned domestic oil exploration while preventing foreign companies from themselves entering to explore. Of the second point, at any rate, there can be no doubt. On 22 May 1977, *O estado de São Paulo* described in detail a decision that was taken in 1970. By 1970 the Brazilian government was becoming increasingly conscious of its dependence upon the Middle East for its sources of oil. Dias Leite, then Minister of Mines and Energy, presented a set of estimates for the years 1970–80 which were extremely pessimistic about the oil situation. Despite being unable to obtain satisfactory information from Petrobrás, Dias Leite came to the conclusion that some foreign investment in oil exploration was necessary and proposed to a Cabinet meeting of 9 August 1970 that Petrobrás should sign service contracts with foreign companies for exploration within Brazil. According to the Minister, this could be done without making any revision to the 1953 law whereby Petrobrás had been created. Occidental Petroleum had expressed interest in the proposal. Occidental had agreed to accept a fee of $0.37 a barrel for any oil which it discovered and to turn all such discoveries over to Petrobrás for development.[34] However, although Dias Leite received some governmental support for his proposals, they were effectively blocked by General Geisel.

One of Dias Leite's other proposals was accepted. This was to set up an overseas exploration subsidiary of Petrobrás, Braspetro, to find oil for importation into Brazil. As we have seen, Lima Rocha had argued for this change in the early 1960s and the call had been repeated in an article by Roberto Campos in 1968.[35] Campos argued that, since the geological opportunities were greater in the Middle East, returns per dollar spent would be greater and Petrobrás should therefore locate some of its exploration investment overseas. Although less momentous than a decision to admit foreign oil investment would have been, the setting up of Braspetro amounted to a tacit admission that the government had abandoned the objective of making Brazil self-sufficient in oil. Indeed, rather more explicit statements were made on the same lines. As late as 1967 the Mines and Energy Ministry had asserted that 'The primary objective of Brazilian oil policy is the discovery in the shortest possible time of reserves which will allow production to meet national requirements through the intensification and improvement of exploration and production.[36] However, in July 1970 Geisel argued that 'It would not be a great national catastrophe if Brazil did not become either self-sufficient or a great international oil power.'[37]

This change had major implications. Petrobrás had originally been set up to refine imported oil in order to generate the funds necessary to achieve self-sufficiency for oil in Brazil. It was therefore given a specific role to play in Brazilian import-substituting industrialisation. The Petrobrás technocrats, like most Brazilians, preferred to ignore Link's warning that self-sufficiency might not be possible but, as the 1960s wore on, it became increasingly clear that Link might have been right. Self-sufficiency, if possible at all, could be reached only with massive investments that would have been quite disproportionate in a world where crude oil was selling below $2 a barrel. But if self-sufficiency was abandoned, what then should Petrobrás's objectives be? There had already been pressure from within the organisation and sometimes outside it to move away from exclusive concern with oil refining and exploration and to diversify into marketing, petrochemicals and oil exploration overseas. Certainly if Petrobrás were to move downstream by taking minority or even majority holdings in industries only tenuously connected with oil exploration and refining, and if, as Dias Leite had proposed, it were to allow private companies to explore for oil within Brazil, then it would become something very different from a simple state oil monopoly. Moreover, if self-sufficiency in oil were abandoned as a target, there needed to be some new criterion for Petro-

Table 18.5 *Production and consumption of oil in Brazil 1960–9*
(000 b/d)

	Production	Consumption		Production	Consumption
1960	81	264	1965	94	350
1961	95	300	1966	116	370
1962	93	325	1967	147	384
1963	98	345	1968	164	415
1964	91	370	1969	179	475

Source: Compiled from G. Balestrini Contreras, *La industria petrolera en América Latina* (Universidad Central de Venezuela, 1971).

brás's investment, and profitability appeared to some to be the obvious choice.

It is less clear how far these changes responded to a conscious change of direction on the part of Geisel and his influential Finance Director, Ueki, and how far they amounted to a recognition of the inevitable. By the end of the 1960s the Bahia fields were in full production, almost all of the onshore sedimentary basins had been explored and, as can be seen from table 18.5, Brazil was still very far short of self-sufficiency. As Link had warned, the Amazon had not yielded very much and attention therefore shifted to the Continental Shelf. The technology of off-shore oil production developed rapidly after around 1967 but by any standards the Brazilian offshore, while promising geologically, was extremely high cost.

There were, therefore, powerful bureaucratic and geological reasons for Petrobrás to hold back on oil exploration. It was difficult to justify, particularly in a state company, heavy spending on oil production, perhaps at a cost two or three times higher than that at which it could be purchased internationally. Petrobrás did begin offshore work in 1967 and some investment took place on terms that could not be justified by purely commercial criteria. Nevertheless, even if Petrobrás managers expected that the price of oil would rise considerably, it was difficult for them to invest on the basis of hypothetical estimates when real prices remained low. The magnitude of the world price increases in and after 1973 took Brazil, like the rest of the world, by surprise. Ueki later explained some of the problems:

Let me give an example: when we found oil in Guaricema, a small reserve, we concluded at the time that the cost of production would be three or four times the market price, I think around US $3.60 or 3.70 a barrel. The Council of Administration in Petrobrás asked the question: if oil could be imported at $1.20, why spend $3.60 to produce oil in Guaricema? . . . Geisel said that even if the oil cost three times as much, we had to invest for two reasons: first, in order to learn to produce oil in deep water, for Guaricema was in 20 metres of water, and because on land the possibilities are fewer, and secondly because the world price will tend to rise.[38]

However, the number of such decisions that could be taken was clearly limited and, as can be seen in table 18.8, investment in exploration and production remained relatively flat between 1964 and 1972.

Ueki, who remained an ouspoken defender of Petrobrás policy during this period, pointed out that the Petrobrás technicians themselves were extremely cautious about their evaluations offshore.

Exploration and drilling activity must obey certain rules and there is no point in throwing money out of the window. A petroleum geologist is a scientist whom we must obey when we decide on location and drilling. However, throughout this period the exploration and production departments of Petrobrás were never denied the resources which they asked for during this time. It was the only department that did not suffer spending cuts.[39]

There were also problems associated with training enough technicians sufficiently quickly for them to play a role in this new area of oil exploration. Moreover, we have already seen that the Brazilian offshore was (and still is) one of the most difficult and high-cost areas of the world and time-lags were, and have continued to be, considerable. As a geologist sympathetic to Petrobrás pointed out, 'oil exploration has its own rhythm and one cannot speed up an exploration programme by putting more money on the table, with the same velocity as one could, for example, speed up car production from a given factory'.

Over all, therefore, while it is likely that there was some deliberate shift of perspective during the Geisel and Ueki period, it is clear that this was largely in harmony with the technical, economic and bureaucratic logic of the time. Certainly it is possible to say with the benefit of hindsight that exploration within Brazil was too much neglected, but this was by no means irrational in terms of what might reasonably have been expected at the time. Even so, the policy met criticism from those who believed that Petrobrás was sacrificing oil production to the pursuit of profitability. Certainly Ueki confirmed the worst fears of both the nationalist left and the neo-liberal right when he remarked on

28 June 1974 that 'We must transform Petrobrás into the eighth sister.'[40]

Petrobrás and its critics 1974–79

By 1974 Petrobrás had undoubtedly reached a certain level of maturity. The military officers, who had assumed prominent positions throughout the company in the 1950s, had largely been replaced by civilian technical specialists. Most senior positions, up to and including the board of directors, were filled by specialists from within the organisation. Petrobrás was organised into departments with strong internal loyalties and between which there was relatively little co-ordination. The company was acquiring certain features which are typical of large-scale organisations; it tended to be secretive, risk-averse and rather conservative. It could carry a weak president and conceal his limitations, but only a very strong and well-informed one could really influence the internal workings of the organisation. Even Geisel, by far the most powerful president Petrobrás ever had, occasionally expressed his frustration: 'I am not President of anything. Here everybody is the boss. This creates problems in everything and Petrobrás has to pay for it all. I am reputed to have a great deal of power. But, as with notices of new oil discoveries, information is always exaggerated, or news is concealed, or information is too optimistic or too pessimistic.'[41]

Petrobrás had also acquired the reputation of being very inward-looking. Certainly the company had flourished best in a political climate that was either authoritarian (1964–68) or extremely so (1969–73). During this period it took very little trouble to keep the rest of Brazil informed of its activities. It did not even bother to set up a public relations department until it had over 40,000 employees. This attitude left the company relatively ill equipped to deal with a political environment which opened up, at first gradually and then quite rapidly, after 1974. For these reasons, Petrobrás did not make many friends outside the organisation itself. Moreover, Petrobrás's relations with the private sector were made still more difficult by the changing role of the agency itself. Economic liberals who had once opposed the creation of a state monopoly could at least reconcile themselves to the existence of a company that found oil and restricted itself to refining it. A company which imported oil, made high profits and diversified freely into non-oil matters was altogether a more awkward bedfellow.

However, the logic of Petrobrás's expansion had, as we shall see, much to do with the specific nature and evolution of Brazilian capitalism.

Certainly a part of the reason for Petrobrás's diversification lay, as we have seen, in the desire of the technocrats themselves to control related activities and to compensate for the high risk inherent in oil exploration (particularly in Brazil) by finding secure sources of profit in other areas. However, some of Petrobrás's new ventures were encouraged and promoted from within the government where ministers found it easier to rely on Petrobrás's financial and technical strengths than to try to co-ordinate the lesser resources of even the largest private sector companies.

This was particularly true of the period after 1969. From 1964 to 1968 government policy was substantially influenced, even if not quite dominated, by ideas of orthodox economic liberalism and counter-inflationary policy. After 1969 financial discipline was relaxed in a headlong dash for growth (particularly during 1969–74, the years of the 'Brazilian miracle') and was tightened significantly only in 1979. In the context of a highly expansionary overall policy, the growth of Petrobrás was largely encouraged by the government. Indeed, once central government takes upon itself the function of pressing for economic development, there is likely to be a general tendency towards an extension of state control in gap-filling and bottleneck-breaking areas until almost all of the main sources of economic power are partly or totally in the hands of the state.[42] Thus, for example, Petrobrás set up a subsidiary to develop the fertiliser industry in 1976. The initiative for its creation came from the Planning Minister of the Medici government after it had become apparent that there was going to be a shortage of domestically produced mineral fertilisers. Under these circumstances, it was far easier to persuade Petrobrás to find $200m. for a major investment than it would have been to interest the private sector and put together a consortium.[43] Nevertheless, *O estado de São Paulo* complained on this issue that 'If the government, through BNDE [the National Development Bank] would approve all of Petrobrás's projects rapidly and offer it every support, including financial help, why could it not do the same for Brazilian entrepreneurs who might have been interested in the project?'[44] The economies seem to have been administrative and organisational as well as simply financial.

Indeed, the creation of subsidiaries and their expansion was an almost constant feature of Petrobrás's behaviour after 1964. Petroquisa had been set up in 1967 and was followed during the 1969–73 period by

Braspetro and Distribuidora. During the Geisel presidency (1974–9), Petromín (later called Petromisa) was set up in 1977 in order to prospect for, develop and market minerals. The minerals involved were to be those discovered by Petrobrás in the course of prospecting for oil; by the end of 1978 plans were already underway for the development of potassium and sulphur reserves in Sergipe. By 1980 a potassium project was under construction and due on stream in 1983. Interbrás was set up in 1976 with the objective of trading with the Middle Eastern and African countries from which Brazil bought its oil. The idea was to take advantage of any possibilities for barter arrangements and thus develop Brazilian export capacities. In the following years Interbrás undertook such activities as exporting frozen chickens to the Middle East and buying coffee from Angola in order to support the international market price. This again appears to have had government support. *O estado de São Paulo* commented that 'Various economics ministers allowed Petrobrás to intervene in this, insisting on the need to tie exports to imports as part of the traditional strategy of protectionism.'[45] Petrobrás in particular exercised considerable power over the private sector. In 1978–9 Petrobrás also tried to take some form of control over the fuel alcohol programme but this time the political opposition proved too great and its proposals were rejected. This did not prevent Petrobrás contracting in 1981 to set up a joint venture to export fuel alcohol. The technology was to be imported for a large plant in Piauí in north-east Brazil. Other private companies were reported to be interested in signing similar contracts.[46] While it is impossible to discuss in more detail the new, rapidly growing and potentially highly important fuel alcohol industry in Brazil, it is likely that Petrobrás will continue to show an active interest here. Petrobrás is also stepping up its investment in developing oil shale in southern Brazil.

In some respects this expansion itself created problems. This was particularly true in the refining and tanker sectors. Between 1968 and 1974 the Brazilian economy, which had already shown considerable dynamism, underwent a period of extremely rapid growth averaging over 10% a year. Oil consumption increased even more rapidly from 415,000 b/d in 1968 to 816,780 b/d in 1974. Since then, however, the economic growth rate has fallen somewhat, to around 6–8% a year, and oil consumption also slowed down under the impact of high prices. Oil consumption in 1980 was still only around 1,100,000 b/d. In the meantime, Petrobrás made its investment decisions on the assumption

Table 18.6 *Source of oil imports into Brazil*
(percentages)

	Western hemisphere	Africa	Asia and Middle East	Europe[a]
1971	12	23	63	n.a.
1972	8	15	76	n.a.
1973	6	6	86	n.a.
1974	4	15	79	2
1975	3	10	86	1
1976	3	10	87	0
1977	2	9	89	0
1978	2	8	90	0

[a] Mainly USSR.
Source: Petrobrás, *Annual Reports.*

that oil consumption would continue to increase rapidly. Thus, in 1973 a Petrobrás plan was drawn up which projected an increase in oil demand of 8.5% a year, but Admiral Faria Lima, who took office as head of Petrobrás in July 1973, insisted that this figure be increased to 16%.[47] Consequently, Petrobrás invested heavily in refining, which took 38.8% of its total investment in 1974 and 30.9% as late as 1976. It could certainly be said that planning requirements and long lead times made it difficult for Petrobrás to cut back quickly, but the fact remains that in 1980 Petrobrás had acquired a refining capacity of 1,300,000 b/d to service a domestic market whose total demand was some 200,000 b/d less. Some efforts were made to export gasoline but these could not offset the refining over-capacity.[48] Petrobrás also responded to the 1973 oil crisis by stepping up its purchasing and contracting of tankers and, for the same reason, suffered financial losses as a result.

Brazil was also slow to change its international purchasing policy as a result of the oil market revolution. Instead, it preferred to change its foreign policy. As can be seen from table 18.6, Brazilian dependence on the Middle East continued to increase. Even after the Iranian Revolution, Brazilian policy aimed at persuading Iraq to make up the loss of supplies from Iran. The outbreak of the Iraq–Iran conflict in September 1980 demonstrated the difficulties of this approach. Petrobrás defended its policy by saying that there remained a small price advantage in Middle Eastern production, especially allowing for the fact that

Table 18.7 *The cost of oil imports to Brazil 1971–80*

	Average per barrel cost ($,f.o.b.)	Total cost of oil imports ($m.)	Total imports ($.m.)	Oil as percentage of imports
1971	1.88	377.0	3,247.4	11.6
1972	1.99	469.4	4,232.3	11.1
1973	2.79	769.4	6,192.2	12.4
1974	11.11	2,894.8	12,641.3	22.9
1975	10.49	3,073.5	12,210.3	25.2
1976	11.50	3,826.9	12,383.0	30.9
1977	12.30	4,068.8	12,023.4	33.8
1978	12.44	4,485.1	13,683.1	32.8
1979	17.11	6,697.8	17,961.3	37.3
1980	30.60[a]	n.a.	n.a.	46.3[b]

[a] Estimated figure given by Minister of Energy Ernane Galvêas in July 1980. In fact, because of the Iran–Iraq war, the real figure may be slightly higher.
[b] On the basis of figures from January to May 1980.
Source: Tamer, *Petróleo,* pp. 296 and 298.

Brazilian super-tankers could use deep water Middle Eastern ports. Moreover, it was hoped to use Interbrás (Petrobrás's trading subsidiary) in order to find ways of exporting to Africa and the Middle East and thus to reduce Brazil's commercial deficit with its oil suppliers.

In fact, Brazil after 1974 increasingly resorted to government diplomacy in order to try to safeguard its oil supplies. During 1974 Brazil moved away from its previous support for US diplomacy and tilted considerably towards the Arab position on Israel and other Third World issues. In 1975 it went further and officially recognised the MPLA government in Angola against the wishes of the USA, which was still concerned to prevent MPLA from coming to power. In 1979, continuing this policy, Brazil permitted the Palestine Liberation Organisation to set up an office in Brasilia after coming under pressure on this point from Iraq.[49] Even so, this strategy was by no means wholly successful; there was a modest increase in Brazilian exports to the oil-exporting countries but, as can be seen from table 18.7, the country gained almost no advantage in terms of the price to be paid for its oil.

Petrobrás also seemed to its critics to be very slow to expand its exploration activities despite the sharp increase in the cost of Brazilian oil imports in and after 1973. According to inside sources, oil exploration did pick up from a low point in the early 1970s, but the time-lags were such that little difference could be detected for several more years. Clearly it was necessary to do a certain amount of basic work before serious exploration drilling, let alone development drilling, could get underway. Nevertheless, for some time Petrobrás showed little sign of urgency, preferring to proceed 'with all *deliberate* speed' rather than at a rate which the situation required. Again, much of the reason for this appears to have been organisational. Petrobrás has always been a highly departmentalised agency and if it is, indeed, as it has often been described, a state within a state, then its exploration and production department could perhaps be described as a state within a state within a state. *O estado de São Paulo* spoke for many when it complained that

Petrobrás's production department is closed; its technicians, convinced of the correctness of their own judgement, do not reveal anything and, as far as possible, keep things secret. Even the directors of the agency do not know what is happening in this sector. Two former directors informed us that they never got a reply when they asked why secondary or tertiary recovery processes were not used more in the depleted Bahian fields.[50]

As can be seen in table 18.8, however, investment in exploration and development (the only figures available) did build up rapidly after about 1975. In 1978, in an attempt to speed up the exploration activity, the Petrobrás exploration department was given a specific drilling target for the first time: it had to drill 300 onshore and 350 offshore wells over the next four years at an expected cost of $2,500m. By 1979 Petrobrás had clearly come to devote its major attention to oil exploration and development, but its critics could certainly argue that the hour was rather late.

Petrobrás did make a major oil find in deep water at Campos, off-shore Rio de Janeiro, in 1974 and later in the decade encountered other promising structures in various offshore locations. According to the official and deliberately conservative estimates of reserve levels issued for mid-1979, the Campos basin had reserves of 540.3 million barrels, whereas the total offshore reserves were 637.1 million barrels and total reserves 1,244 million barrels. This compared with a total of 983 million barrels, almost all onshore, at the end of 1975.[51] It seems probable that oil production should rather more than double – to some 500,000 b/d – by 1985. This will still, however, leave Brazil as a large-scale importer of oil.

While the full story of the Campos discovery and development is not

Table 18.8 *Petrobrás's investment in oil exploration and production 1954–79*[a]
(*$m. (at constant 1979 prices)*)

	Amount	Percentage of total investment
1954	6.04	15.9
1955	21.25	43.1
1956	37.00	54.0
1957	73.45	70.4
1958	103.71	62.0
1959	83.20	40.9
1960	85.58	27.0
1961	115.20	36.9
1962	137.62	42.8
1963	150.76	46.3
1964	156.25	45.7
1965	183.63	48.3
1966	183.66	47.1
1967	187.49	52.6
1968	184.21	50.6
1969	200.55	50.1
1970	237.81	39.5
1971	201.63	24.5
1972	242.18	29.9
1973	284.05	29.5
1974	366.28	26.9
1975	500.31	27.8
1976	622.61	36.3
1977	701.40	40.0
1978	833.45	46.9
1979	1,144.60[b]	53.8

[a] These figures were issued by Petrobrás in *Petrobrás News*, December 1980. As such they are clearly the best available although even Petrobrás may have had some difficulties making precise estimates in particular years. I have converted from constant cruzeiros (May 1979 prices) into dollars using the exchange rate ($1 = Cr$25.65) prevailing in May 1979, which is when this table first appears to have been drawn up.
[b] Estimated as in May 1979.
Source: *Petrobrás News* (March 1981).

widely known, such information as is available does illustrate some of the difficulties faced by Petrobrás. Oil is still an emotive subject in Brazil; there is much truth in Santiago Dantas's remark that 'Oil is a substance which has the unique property of not permitting calm discussion about itself.'[52] Moreover, where oil discoveries are concerned, expectations tend to fluctuate wildly. Thus, in late 1974 Petrobrás announced a significant oil discovery at Campos and excitement quickly mounted among outside sources (including the press) to such an extent that the question was even raised of whether Brazil ought to join OPEC. When these expectations, which were raised by the press and by political figures rather than by the agency itself, came to be seen as clearly exaggerated, the ensuing disappointment rebounded to some extent upon Petrobrás. After this, the agency's natural secretiveness with regard to oil reserves intensified to the point where official figures failed to give any real indication of Brazil's true oil potential.[53] Later, Petrobrás strenuously resisted suggestions made by outsiders, who apparently included Ueki as Minister of Mines and Energy under Geisel, that the development of the Campos basin should be contracted out to the private sector.[54] The decision to keep overall control of Campos development within Petrobrás, while by no means self-evidently mistaken, did have the effect of sacrificing speed for experience. Although the experience will doubtless be of long-term value for Petrobrás, the series of postponements of the start-up date of the Campos complex (postponements by no means unknown in other parts of the world) and real or suspected mistakes in the development inflicted further public relations damage upon Petrobrás, whose critics were once more able to argue that the interests of the agency (in gaining experience) were allowed to take priority over the urgent national need for short-term oil production and thus balance of payments relief.

The government did, however, undertake a major change of policy in 1975 when it declared that it would sign 'risk contracts' with foreign oil companies. This would permit direct foreign investment in oil exploration in a manner which compromised Petrobrás's position as little as possible. The question had been pending at least since 1970 when the issue was blocked – but not killed – by the opposition of Ernesto Geisel. The 1975 decision followed a considerable amount of manoeuvring behind the scenes.[55] However, changes in the institutional balance of power appear to have been less significant in this respect than was a growing realisation among senior military and government figures – not least Ernesto Geisel himself – that a step of this kind was necessary in view of Brazil's growing oil deficit and, not less important, growing foreign debt. While journalistic accounts of this decision differ slightly, they were essentially agreed on the fact that Ueki (Minister of Mines and Energy under Geisel) and Mario Henrique Simonsen, the Finance Minister, were the most powerful defenders of the 'risk contracts', whereas these were opposed by certain traditionally nationalist government ministers and many of Petrobrás's own technocrats. It was one of the few cases in which the operations of Petrobrás were affected in a serious way by a decision made in the central government and over which the company had little real influence.

Once the decision was made, Petrobrás itself maintained control of the contract negotiations. Its handling of the question prompted accusations from economic liberals that the process was being slowed down unnecessarily by officials who were themselves unsympathetic to the idea of foreign oil investment. It is certainly true that there were good organisational reasons for Petrobrás to go slowly and there was, no doubt, some anxiety within Petrobrás lest the private companies find oil on a large scale within a few years of operation. As the difficulties surrounding oil exploration in Brazil (which faced the private sector just as much as Petrobrás) became increasingly apparent, so the reluctance of executives within Petrobrás to sign contracts diminished. By the end of August 1979 27 risk contracts had been signed.

Important changes were also taking place in the Brazilian political climate after around 1973. The Medici government (1969–73) had been a period of tight political control and very rapid economic growth, in which state companies, including Petrobrás, had played a major part. In this respect, the history of Petrobrás was archetypal of this period: a large, effectively autonomous state company which moved aggressively into areas which had previously been regarded as the preserve of the private sector. While there is some dispute over exactly how far real state control expanded during the period, there is no doubt that the trend was perceived with alarm by influential spokesmen for the private sector, and the easing of press censorship after Ernesto Geisel became President in 1974 was followed by a campaign in a number of newspapers, notably *O estado de São Paulo,* against *estatização* – excessive state direction of the economy. Petrobrás, because of both its size and its inability to shield Brazil from the full effects of the oil crisis, was vulnerable to such criticism, and the press attack began in earnest with a series of critical and extremely informative articles in *O estado de São Paulo* (many of which have been quoted above) in May and June

1977. Petrobrás responded by calling a press conference in August which was also very informative but did not halt the criticism of the company.

It is clear that the Figueiredo government, which took office in early 1979, was of the opinion that energy policymaking needed to be centralised and that Petrobrás would necessarily have to become less influential over energy matters than before. The incoming government set up a national energy council under the Vice-President of Brazil, Chavez de Mendonça, with the purpose of advising and encouraging the development of all forms of energy in Brazil. It is true that a good deal of effort had gone into developing new energy sources under Geisel as well as under Figueiredo, but this degree of centralisation was certainly a new element in policy. There were also important new policy initiatives on alcohol production (a new industry from which Petrobrás was excluded).

Another major change lay in the increasing availability of territory and easing of terms for the signing of risk contracts. While Petrobrás kept overall control of these negotiations, there could be no doubt that its new more open approach represented policy preferences in Brasilia as well as changing circumstances brought about by the Iranian Revolution.[56] Thus, in August 1979 Exxon was given a bloc where, unlike those offered previously, no seismic work had been done, and the company was allowed to do its own surveying before deciding whether to continue exploration or to return the acreage. In the same month, Shell was given an onshore contract in the Amazon – the first onshore contract to be signed. In September Petrobrás went further and offered a total of 123 blocs for its fourth round of bidding, 74 of which were in São Paulo. This total compared with 10 blocs offered in the first round (1976), 15 in the second round (in 1977) and 42 in the third round (in 1978).

The specific inclusion of so many blocs in São Paulo was Petrobrás's response to a conflict with the ambitious São Paulo governor, Maluf, who was interested in involving the state government directly in oil exploration. It is not clear how far his aims were political and concerned with putting further pressure on Petrobrás to open up Brazil to private exploration and how far they represented a real effort on the part of the São Paulo business community to mount an exploration campaign; no doubt time will tell, but it is interesting that São Paulo state organisations contracted 17 exploration blocs at the end of 1979. In any case, at the end of 1979 the decision was taken to open practically the whole country except for territory currently being explored by Petrobrás to private investment; bidding for this 'Fifth Round' would take place in 1981 and 1982. By the end of 1979 the almost complete lack of success in finding oil encountered by the private companies had both raised fears of a wholesale withdrawal of foreign company interest in Brazilian exploration and partially vindicated Petrobrás, whose own record of oil discovery was beginning to appear extremely respectable.

Meanwhile, Petrobrás itself was continuing to develop its Campos complex and made a further encouraging discovery in the mouth of the Amazon. By the beginning of 1980 output had begun to increase significantly from its low point (reaching 200,000 b/d in mid-1980) and it was planned to rise to around 500,000 b/d by 1985, or rather less than one half of total Brazilian consumption. There was some confidence that Brazilian oil imports had peaked in volume terms, even if not in terms of value.

On the other hand, the state company continued to be active downstream. Braspetro did make one major retreat, in Iraq, where it sold its share in its one major offshore oil discovery after a number of fears had been expressed within Brazil that the company might decide to commit heavy expenditures to developing the field only to be expropriated later.[57] Against this, Braspetro in 1980 signed a contract to develop oil in Angola. On the other hand, Ueki's earlier idea – put forward in 1978 before his appointment to the presidency of Petrobrás – that the profitable sectors of Petrobrás should be hived off to the private sector was quietly dropped.[58]

Even if Petrobrás is unlikely to be reduced significantly in size, however, it is likely to remain under fairly tight political control for as long as the balance of payments problem is seen as more important than a low rate of economic growth. It is notable that in October 1979 the new Planning Minister, Delfim Netto, was given power to control the foreign debt of all public enterprises and made it clear that he would take a more active role in oil policy than had any of his predecessors, even touring the Middle East in an effort to get favourable terms from Brazil's major oil suppliers.

Conclusions

The *estatização* debate in Brazil drew attention to the extent to which Petrobrás, like other big public sector companies, had lost its traditional support on the political left while continuing to draw criticism from its old opponents on the neoliberal right. From both perspectives, Petrobrás has seemed to exemplify the ugly face of Brazilian industrialisation, speculationist, opportunistic and in the true sense of the word, irresponsible. According to Peter Evans, a critic from the left,

The men of Petrobrás are archetypal of this [state capitalist] group. They combine technical training, like engineering, with long managerial experience. They consider themselves administrators, not entrepreneurs, regardless of the entrepreneurial values that they instigate and direct. They share a culture and a set of values with the multinational managers . . . The largest and most successful of the local corporations are also staffed by men of this type, men with long training in large organisations, private and public. The consensus among these men is thoroughgoing. If anything, the structure that has been created in Brazil is more tightly knit and closely interconnected than equivalent structures in the United States or other developed countries.[59]

In other words, an organisation which was created to do battle with the major oil and chemical companies in the name of nationalist values has largely forgotten its birthright and become just another big company.[60] Alberto Tamer, an economic liberal and journalist for *O estado de São Paulo,* attacked from a different standpoint:

In its 23 years of existence, Petrobrás has not even found enough oil to meet 20% of internal demand, but has transformed itself into the richest and most powerful national company, dominated innumerable basic industries in Brazil, chosen to make money rather than take risks and invested massively in profitable sectors, particularly those in the 'open market' where it has spent $260m. in the first four months of this year [1977] alone. Above all, it has shown itself to be insensitive to the grave energy problems of the nation.[61]

These critics do direct themselves to a genuine reality, but one which owes much to the structures of Brazilian capitalism itself (as Evans indeed argues) as well as to the specific characteristics of Petrobrás. Although Petrobrás has undoubtedly made high profits, it would be wrong to assert that its interests were guided solely by profit. As we have seen, Petrobrás's expansion has at times resulted from governmental and even private sector pressure (for example the formation of Petroquisa) as well as from the desire of the Petrobrás technostructure itself to expand into new areas. There is no single pattern according to which decisions have been made to expand Petrobrás's functions, although almost every presidential term in Brazil has seen the acquisition of important new powers by the agency. Moreover, while it is certainly not difficult to find examples of what can only be described as speculationist attitudes on the part of some Petrobrás officials,[62] the link between profitability and diversification is not simple. Most of Petrobrás's profits throughout the 1970s came from the refining sector, the area where the company was initially granted its monopoly. Petrochemicals have certainly proved profitable, which is not surprising since, as liberal critics have pointed out, the government has sufficient power over pricing to assure Petrobrás a profit in this sector; nevertheless, in 1978 only 5.8% of Petrobrás's net sales, and 11.4% of its net profits, came from the petrochemicals sector.[63] The figures for distribution were 24.6% and only 5.4% respectively, although it is likely that Petrobrás originally expected to make a higher profit on distribution than in fact proved to be the case. Braspetro and the subsidiaries set up after 1974 have made only negligible, or even negative, contributions to Petrobrás's profitability. Nor is it true that Petrobrás's main investment decisions were made on purely commercial criteria; Petrobrás executives acknowledge that money does play a part in investment decisions, but there are too many pressures of other kinds, including political pressures, and too many uncertainties for profit to play a major part in company calculations.[64]

One key to the understanding of Petrobrás, therefore, is the nature of Brazilian economic growth over the past 50 years. As has been pointed out by Werner Baer, among others,[65] there has been a historical trend towards the expansion of the economic role of the state in Brazil, motivated very little by policy preference for state control but far more by the perceived needs of Brazilian industrialisation and economic development. A company such as Petrobrás, with the capital and technology necessary to enable it to move quickly into gaps and to break bottlenecks, would almost of necessity prove to be a chosen instrument of growth-maximising government. The private sector would be too unpredictable, too free of government control and, above all, individually too small scale to be capable of carrying out the required kind of investments at the right time. Where private companies entered such sectors as petrochemicals, they often burnt their fingers and came to rely upon the support of Petrobrás itself.[66] Inevitably the existence of such powerful state companies as Petrobrás creates concern within the private sector, but it is only fair to point out that the Brazilian pattern of development, in which state companies have played so prominent a role, has had its successes as well as its drawbacks.

A second perspective is to see Petrobrás as a large Brazilian public sector bureaucracy, with many of the characteristics of its type.[67] Essentially this perspective is concerned with the elitist mentality of the agency, its preference for expansion and its resistance to change. Regarding the former, there is no real evidence that Petrobrás managers self-consciously consider themselves to be members of a state elite,[68] but there can be little doubt that there is a strong identification with the agency and a feeling that 'what is good for Petrobrás is good for Brazil'. However, while outsiders may find this irritating, an *esprit de corps* of this kind may well be essential to the effective functioning of a large organisation and an important barrier against extremes of politicisation such as were encountered in the early 1960s. As far as preference for expansion and resistance to change are concerned, there is little doubt that Petrobrás's behaviour conforms to the behaviour of other public sector bureaucracies.

To illustrate the question of overall political control, it might be useful to compare Petrobrás with the Brazilian state power company CEMIG, as described in Tendler's excellent study. For example:

One of CEMIG's managers . . . specifically wanted *not* to be president of the company. He preferred to see a politician as company president . . . the less this politician–president knew about engineering the better. Having a politician in the company who knew nothing about electric power and at the same time occupied the managerial position most sensitive to political pressure was a kind of pre-emptive manoeuvre. The company became politically well-connected and at the same time ensured that it could not be meddled with. The new enterprise might feel safer with the politicians in its midst rather than on the outside.[69]

This 'ambassadorial' role for the president of the company is strikingly similar to that claimed by João Barreto, the second president of the old CNP, as long ago as 1945:

The fact that I have been chosen by the President of the Republic to take on the position of President of this organisation . . . does not automatically make me an oil technician. I am not concerned with the problems of exploration and production of oil in the country, which is an important part of our work; since you yourselves are responsible for this problem, I will act . . . as intermediary between yourselves and the government.[70]

One oil executive was even blunter: 'Who cares about the President? – he doesn't know how to drill an oil well.'[71]

This system works well when there is reasonable harmony *within* the organisation, and when there is no perceived conflict between the functions of the agency and the national interest. The arrangement ran into crisis when, in the early 1960s, successive presidents of Petrobrás had to rely upon limited power bases within the organisation and to use their access to the media and the government to try to reinforce their hold over it. Once managerial norms were restored after the 1964 coup, the agency again appeared to flourish, but difficulties of a different kind reasserted themselves after 1974. The limited political opening and the sharply rising oil import bill both encouraged critics of the company and eventually persuaded the government that it would be necessary to impose tighter political control over the agency. Under Figueiredo, Ueki has become something of an ambassador in reverse, using his position as President to try to force changes through Petrobrás and upon Petrobrás – notably an increased role for private enterprise in oil exploration – which were by no means uniformly welcomed.

Tendler also shows, however, that CEMIG was not a particularly commercially minded company, a conclusion that might contrast with some of the things said about Petrobrás. We have already seen that it would be over-simple to regard Petrobrás as just a money-making organisation, but there is a point here that needs more detailed examination. This relates to the nature of the oil industry itself.

The third perspective on Petrobrás is to consider the structure of the Brazilian oil industry. It would be unkind to describe Petrobrás as 'an oil company without oil', but certain parallels with the Italian ENI – which initially attracted this description – are instructive. In both cases there was a tendency to link backward into overseas exploration and forward into chemicals and distribution. Petrobrás had initially been set up to discover sufficient oil to make Brazil self-sufficient; the question of what would happen if sufficient oil was not discovered was never seriously considered. Most Brazilians believed implicitly that oil did exist and reacted emotionally against anybody who cast doubt on this belief. Nevertheless, proposals for Petrobrás's expansion, into petrochemicals, overseas exploration and distribution, began to be made seriously just after the publication of the Link Report, when the abundance of Brazilian oil reserves was first seriously called into question. The proposal for overseas exploration was a 'natural' response to the difficulty of finding oil in Brazil. Moreover, the most important period for actual diversification – 1969–1973 – coincided with the completion by Petrobrás of initial exploration of the main onshore sedimentary basins and with the peaking of production from the Bahia fields.

Once such diversification began, it took on a momentum of its own. Braspetro generated Interbrás, and the move from petrochemicals into fertilisers, fertilisers into minerals, was similarly easy enough to understand. It should not be forgotten, however, that even in 1978 fully 86.5% of Petrobrás's sales and 82% of its profits came from the traditional activities of production, transport and refining.[72] The remainder may be considered as no more than a protection against the high financial risks associated with oil exploration in Brazil and in terms of an alternative role should oil exploration prove unrewarding. During a period when oil was relatively cheap, this kind of structure was easy to justify, but when the price rose sharply in 1973–4 and then again in 1978–9 it appeared evident that overriding priority should be given to oil exploration and development at almost any cost. Very recently Petrobrás has been moving in this new direction.

19

YPF 1932–1979: public enterprise or bureaucracy?

Unlike Pemex and Petrobrás, which have operated as largely autonomous public enterprises, YPF has generally been identified much more closely with the Argentine government. A large part of the reason for this has stemmed from the fact that there was never a real base for public enterprise *desarrollismo* in Argentina. Indeed, there has been little political continuity of any kind in that country and YPF has suffered many of the consequences of frequent political upheaval. While the effects of these political upheavals upon policymaking were by no means confined to YPF,[1] the development of the state oil company was particularly difficult as a result of the early politics concerning oil in Argentina. As we have seen, the Radical Party was unable to consummate its relationship with oil nationalism in the 1920s, but instead retained its visions of a romantic past during later years when both the party and the issue had shown signs of age. For much of their period in office the Peronists, who replaced the Radicals as the most popular party in Argentina, were committed to 'redistribution of income without growth, participation without social restraint and nationalism without efficiency'.[2] Such policies, not surprisingly, were unhelpful to YPF. For Argentine conservatives, on the other hand, YPF was an embarrassment – an illegitimate offspring which had to be maintained in some fashion but which could not be allowed independence and still less a real part in national politics.

YPF ignored 1935–58

In the 1930s successive conservative governments in Argentina sought to depoliticise oil by downgrading it. While the private companies were barred from future expansion and made to share the market with YPF, the latter was also strongly discouraged from any show of independence. General Mosconi, who had done most to develop the agency in the 1920s, was denied significant government office in the 1930s,[3] and even the day-to-day workings of the state company came under close governmental supervision to the obvious detriment of its efficiency. In 1932 a law was passed which gave the central government control of almost every aspect of YPF's day-to-day activity – control which it did not hesitate to exercise in a highly bureaucratic manner. Thus, in his *Annual Report for 1934,* the head of YPF complained:

It is incredible how much time is lost in inconvenient procedures. It often happens that tenders are annulled, renewed and annulled again before it is possible to do what should have been done originally; that is to say, the direct acquisition of needed materials . . .

Experience shows the difficulty of developing production plans when these are interrupted by inevitable delays in the supply of materials. These delays in offices, where requests gather dust and age, are passed on to the oilfields and hold up work, disorganise the workforce and lead to financial losses.

The bureaucratic structure which had been created by the 1932 law did, however, have the advantage of keeping YPF under tight political control.

The economic situation also made it difficult for YPF to expand. Although continuing to be profitable despite falling retail price levels, YPF was unable to borrow significantly after 1930 (despite the success of the La Plata venture in the 1920s) and at no time between 1936 and 1945 was debt above 10% of YPF's assets. Moreover, under the 1932 law, YPF was subjected to a 10% tax on its own profits. Furthermore, the mere acquisition of equipment from abroad was made difficult by foreign exchange controls which, implemented by the Central Bank, 'made more difficult and delayed purchases of imported goods which were indispensable for all aspects of the oil industry'.[4]

Despite these obstacles YPF did manage to increase its oil production from 5,675,184 barrels in 1932 to 12,474,655 barrels in 1940 and tripled its oil reserves during the decade. Together with the continuing expansion of refining facilities, this was a reasonably good record, which strongly suggests that YPF's technical personnel were as good as the majority of those operating in the world at that time.[5] With the Second World War, however, the situation changed. At first the difficulties seemed purely technical and temporary; YPF and the private companies found it almost impossible to import equipment, with the result that their existing capital stock became increasingly obsolescent. This indicated that YPF's equipment needs would be heavy after the war came to an end, although it appeared that Argentina would have the foreign currency reserves to make the necessary payments.

After the GOU coup of 1943 and still more after the election of Perón in 1945, however, YPF became politicised. Until that time, its role had been restricted by various controls but the agency had at least benefited from the conservative governments' low-key approach to the politics of oil. Ingeniero Ricardo Silveyra had remained as head of YPF for 11 years and political considerations had not been important to the internal running of the enterprise. After 1943, however, loyalty appeared to replace knowledge of the industry as a criterion for appointment. As Canessa, himself at one time head of YPF, pointed out:

Between 1943 and 1946 Yacimientos Petrolíferos Fiscales, for reasons of political intolerance, lost 70% of its senior personnel; later, as a result of the contract with Standard Oil of California, the most determined opponents of this policy lost their jobs and after the Revolution of 16 September 1955, senior technicians and skilled workers who were believed to be supporters of the previous government were also removed from their positions.[6]

Largely as a consequence of these changes,

the personnel who remained in YPF suffered directly or indirectly from the anarchy and corruption which was rampant. The senior managers were not respected and lacked all capacity. Nobody would take any responsibility. Studies and plans were carried through with neither thoroughness nor depth, often for public relations purposes or in order to boost morale. Work was begun without a proper study of the available material, without proper budgeting and without fixed dates for completion. Orders were carried out without thoroughness; valuable materials were not stored, protected or used rationally.[7]

In short, much of YPF's later reputation for inefficiency was earned under Perón, particularly in the period 1945–9. The technical library was destroyed, technical information was suppressed, and training abroad was cancelled.[8] In the economical words of Villa and Canepa, 'YPF as a state enterprise suffered in marked form the damaging effects of the government's demagogic policy.'[9]

The Peronist government also destroyed much of the financial as well as the human capital of YPF, although it is difficult to be precise on this point since the relevant information was simply not released. Nevertheless, it is not difficult to find indications of what occurred. Domestic prices had been deliberately kept low in the 1930s, and this policy was accentuated during the 1940s and its effects aggravated by the unionisation and wage increases encouraged by Perón. Moreover, between 1939 and 1956 gasoline taxes rose from 22% to 62% of the final price. Furthermore, exchange controls – which were tightened under Perón – posed exceptional difficulties for YPF, which needed to wait in line for such foreign exchange as was available.

This damaging policy towards YPF can probably be explained in large part by the Peronist government's lack of confidence in the agency's capacity. The regime consistently gave priority to the development of Argentina's hydroelectric resources. Moreover, the notorious contract Perón signed with Standard Oil of California was only the last of a number of efforts he made to attract some form of foreign investment into oil exploration. Until 1955, however, he proved unwilling to take the political risks that such a policy would have required.

As early as 1946 Perón indicated to US Ambassador Messersmith that he was interested in attracting new foreign investment in oil exploration.[10] Following this, he began serious negotiations with the local manager of Jersey Standard. Perón showed serious interest in the company proposal, which would have involved a joint venture arrangement giving the government genuine power to veto any major decisions. Unfortunately the local representative had not cleared the plan with his head office, which was unhappy with the degree of power-sharing involved and insisted on modifications which would have 'reduced the mixed company from a joint venture to a barely disguised direct concession to Standard Oil'.[11] The new proposal would also have involved changes in the 1935 law and so required congressional approval. This was too much, and negotiations were abandoned.

After these negotiations aborted a group of Peronist ministers began to press for a reversal of policy and full-scale nationalisation of oil. After the matter was actively debated in two Cabinet meetings in December 1947, this plan was also dropped.[12] Instead Perón decided, for the moment at least, to maintain the status quo. In 1949 the oil issue surfaced again, but policy appeared to move in two different directions at once and the end result was inconclusive. On the one hand, according to Gómez Morales, who was Perón's Minister of Economic Affairs,

an exploration contract was suggested to Esso and Shell and was rejected on the grounds that to accept such a contract would leave them open to similar

Table 19.1 *Exploration wells drilled by* YPF *1946–55*

1946	22	1951	31
1947	12	1952	47
1948	19	1953	58
1949	27	1954	54
1950	29	1955	49

Note: Pemex's average for 1951–4 was 122 exploration wells annually. In 1926 YPF drilled a total of 141 wells of all kinds.

restrictions by other nations. A number of Argentine officials were assigned to study Mexican oil policy; as a result of these studies, Argentina began negotiations with more than twenty smaller oil firms.[13]

These negotiations similarly proved indecisive.[14]

Against this, however, YPF, after the appointment of oil nationalist Julio Canessa to the presidency in May 1949, began to attack the marketing position of the companies. Until then, YPF's market position was restricted because its marketing and refining network had to be based exclusively on its domestic production. In 1947 Perón, no doubt in order to soften his decision not to carry out a full-scale expropriation, deprived the private companies of their previously exclusive right to import oil. Instead YPF was given a nominal import monopoly but this at first made no practical difference. In 1949, however, YPF tendered for a cargo of imported crude oil and began to challenge the companies directly.[15] Eventually YPF's offensive was blunted and then reversed, largely, it appears, as a consequence of Argentina's weak international trading position.[16]

Perón's apparent keenness to attract foreign investment into oil exploration rather obscured the fact that there was, at this time, no real shortage of oil reserves in Argentina. Although exploration drilling certainly fell away in the late 1940s (see table 19.1), reserve: production ratios were never less than adequate – especially when one takes into account the fact that secondary recovery techniques, particularly valuable for older oil fields such as Rivadavia, were unknown to Argentina prior to 1955. Indeed, as can be seen from table 19.2, after a limited recapitalisation of YPF was undertaken in the early 1950s, YPF's geologists quickly made some major discoveries, particularly in Salta, where the Campo Durán and Madrejones finds were made in

Table 19.2 *Proven oil reserves in Argentina 1946–55*
(*m. metric tons*)

	Rivadavia (Chubut)	Huincul (Neuquén)	Mendoza	Salta	Total	Reserve: production ratio
1946	32.5	4.5	10.5	0.6	48.1	21
1947	33.6	5.2	15.0	0.7	54.5	21.5
1948	39.7	5.5	15.5	0.6	61.3	22
1949	37.1	5.7	11.7	0.7	55.2	21
1950	35.2	4.6	11.7	0.5	52.0	19
1951	39.9	4.9	12.8	4.5	62.1	21
1952	39.0	8.2	16.5	6.7	70.4	22.5
1953	44.4	10.7	15.2	10.8	81.1	22
1954	49.0	9.0	21.0	15.0	94.0	23.5
1955	52.0	10.5	23.5	17.5	103.5	25

Source: Villa and Canepa, 'El petróleo argentino'.

1951 and 1953 respectively. The real bottleneck for YPF, in fact, was not exploration drilling but development, and here the problems were a lack of co-ordination within YPF (the result of bureaucratisation and political purging) and a lack of capital. Nevertheless, following the reorganisation of YPF in 1949, one can detect some improvement in the company's performance (see table 19.3), but this only brought into relief the transportation bottlenecks which prevented the growth of production from keeping pace with the increase in reserves. Thus in 1955 oil production was being held back in Rivadavia (Chubut) by a lack of gas compressors, which meant that any increase in oil production would have to be accompanied by large-scale flaring of gas. In Neuquén there was a railway bottleneck which could most effectively be broken by construction of an oil pipeline, and the same was also true of Mendoza, while the Salta finds, potentially of major significance, were still shut in because of the absence of reliable transport. Bids had been called for oil and gas pipelines from Salta in 1953 but the tender had proved abortive, largely because of the ineptitude of the bureaucrats involved.

Meanwhile, after 1949 Argentina's balance of payments situation, which had been extremely favourable in the immediate post-war period, was becoming increasingly difficult. In response, Perón became increasingly orthodox in his economic policies. Domestic oil prices rose

Table 19.3 *Drilling activity by* YPF *1939–55*

	Average active rigs in service	Wells drilled	Metres	Wells per rig per year	Metres per rig per year
1939–43	40.95	940	1,142,213	4.60	5.58
1946–50	36.26	637	877,140	3.38	4.84
1951–55	53.97	1,207	1,850,765	4.47	6.89

Source: Ibid.

Table 19.4 *Argentina's oil balance 1925–55*
(000 *cubic metres*)

	Production (gross)	Imports (gross)	Consumption (net)	Percentage imported
1925–9	1,330	1,210	2,190	47.7
1930–4	2,070	1,260	3,100	37.8
1935–9	2,740	1,780	4,120	22.8
1940–4	3,780	1,110	4,470	16.4
1945–9	3,630	3,400	6,340	48.3
1950–4	4,990	5,440	9,460	52.2
1955	5,000	7,560	11,450	60.2

Source: UN, ECLA, *Análisis y proyecciones del desarrollo económico.* Vol. 5, *El desarrollo económico de la Argentina,* p. 36.

sharply in 1951 and Perón showed increasing willingness to rely upon foreign capital for oil exploration. Given the international circumstances of the time, there were few alternatives to the major oil companies in this respect. In 1952 Argentina did sign a trade pact with the USSR in which the provision of oil equipment was discussed, but some years later 'Journalists recalled that in 1952 Argentine state oilmen went to the Soviet Union to inspect preferred drilling equipment, but found it clumsy and not interchangeable with the US oil rigs in use.'[17] Subsequently Perón once again looked for an agreement with the international oil companies. In 1953 he again approached Shell (which sent a group of senior officials to Argentina in October in order to negotiate with Perón) and Standard Oil of New Jersey, but neither seemed particularly interested. In April 1954, the *Hispanic American Report* stated:

so far, Standard Oil of New Jersey, whom the government has been attempting to interest in exploiting Argentine petroleum, has repeatedly hesitated to
accept the conditions offered. *La Opinión* of Los Angeles reports, on the other
hand, that an unspecified US company has now agreed to invest US $100m. in
the installation of drilling machinery and the exploitation of new deposits.

This 'unspecified company' turned out to be Standard Oil of California
(Socal), which in 1954 submitted its own proposals to the government.

After some further negotiation, the Socal contract was finally signed
on 26 April 1955. Under its terms, the company had agreed to invest
a minimum amount in its exploration area (which was in Patagonia)
and profits tax was set at 50%; against this, however, Socal was given
extensive freedom to operate and few legal obligations other than
strictly financial ones.[18] At the time, it was expected that this contract
would be only the first of a number of similar arrangements with foreign companies.[19]

The Socal contract brought oil policy back to the centre of the political stage. The Radical Party, which had earlier lost its position as the
largest party in Argentina as a result of Perón's alliance with the trade
unions and working class, had continued to call for the full nationalisation of oil throughout Perón's regime. The Socal contract gave it an
opportunity to go over to the attack. There was also a tradition of oil
nationalism within the army, although this was by no means a unifying
force in a very divided institution. In 1955 the most important political factor was not so much this specific opposition but rather the fact
that the Socal contract provided an issue upon which opponents of the
Peronist regime could mobilise at a time when the government already
seemed to be in a weak position. The Argentine economic elite was
quite unwilling to be won over by Perón's hesitant moves towards
economic orthodoxy in the early 1950s, while many of Perón's own
supporters were dismayed by Argentina's economic difficulties, by
Perón's conflict with the Church (which broke out in 1954) and now
by the Socal contract, which appeared to contradict his earlier (at any
rate public) nationalism. Under these circumstances, rumour and exaggeration compounded the damage done to Perón's position by the
announcement of the contract itself. In its report for July 1955, the
HAR stated that 'objections to the contract became so strong that by
the end of the month Minister of Industry Orlando Santos admitted
that he had started renegotiations'. While it is difficult to know exactly
how much weight to give to the oil question in the overthrow of Perón

on 19 September 1955, incoming President Lonardi entered Buenos Aires on 23 September and was welcomed by crowds with the chant '¡Petróleo sí! ¡California no!'. The Socal contract was allowed to lapse.

Cancellation of this contract, however, did not tackle Argentina's main problem: how to develop the oil industry in view of the country's by now chronic lack of foreign exchange. This question was discussed within the government and it was agreed that further efforts would be made to improve YPF's performance in the expectation that existing reserves would permit a large increase in YPF's production. Villa and Canepa, who acted as advisers to President Aramburu (who took over from Lonardi in 1955), estimated that existing oil reserves would permit a level of output of 9,000,000 cubic metres a year (155,096 b/d) as against YPF's 1955 production of a little over 4,000,000 cubic metres (68,932 b/d). This was still some way short of self-sufficiency, but it would have represented a major advance.

Nevertheless, little progress was made in this direction in the three following years, although YPF did draw up a 'Plan de reactivación' in 1956 on the basis of which further investments were to be made. Despite the government's promise to recapitalise YPF, the latter's position, if anything, worsened during this period.[20] In 1962 the United Nations reported:

It is true that until [1958] public funds from the Treasury and National Energy Fund, and miscellaneous contributions and appropriations for the YPF 'expansion plan' had, to judge from the balance sheet of 31 December 1958, provided a very high proportion of YPF's capital requirements. Relatively little came from its own resources or outside contributions.[21]

There is evidence that financial difficulties did interfere directly with YPF's operating plans. Thus, in 1957 ECLA reported that 'the greatest difficulty confronting YPF is the financing of its programme'.[22] In that year YPF floated two bond issues but did not raise enough to make a major difference to its finances.

The Aramburu regime added to YPF's difficulties by abolishing the 1949 constitution which had federalised all oil reserves and instead returned jurisdiction over oil matters to the provinces. However, since YPF retained its effective monopoly of fresh oil exploration, the result of this was merely to create friction between the oil provinces of Salta and Mendoza and the government in Buenos Aires.[23] Private refineries were, however, permitted to invest and did so; private refining capacity expanded from 56,000 b/d in 1955 to 92,000 b/d in 1958.

As far as exploration and development were concerned, YPF sought to resolve its problems by seeking long-term credits in a programme of competitive bidding for development programmes, but no foreign firm was willing to offer more than five years of credit, which was not enough for YPF. Further increases in consumer prices in January 1956, which raised the price of oil products threefold, similarly did little to improve YPF's finances since these had now come to depend heavily on direct government aid. When this aid was cut in 1956 as a result of Argentina's balance of payments difficulties, YPF was seriously affected. Moreover, despite some restructuring of YPF, many of the problems of bureaucratisation remained: YPF still faced major problems in getting dollars from the Central Bank, and resignations of senior technical staff continued because of low pay.[24] Despite the fierce nationalist criticism of Perón's contract with Socal, therefore, demands again began to be heard for a return to a policy of encouraging foreign investment in oil exploration. In April 1957 the *Hispanic American Report* reported:

Ex-Industry Minister Alvaro C. Alsogaray, a spokesman for the growing group of Argentine industrialists who believe that petroleum must be opened to private exploitation, advocated parallel YPF–private enterprise development . . . It was doubtful that Alsogaray's views were shared in official circles, but they appeared to be gaining support among industrial interests whose productivity was being curtailed by fuel shortages and whose profits were being reduced by rising fuel costs.

And so matters remained until 1958.

The Frondizi period 1958–62

In the elections of 1958 Arturo Frondizi, although nominally a Radical, appeared to be offering a kind of Peronism without Perón. He had successfully attracted a number of Peronist votes through a pact with Perón, who himself had been barred from taking part in the election, and his economic approach was essentially technocratic. He planned to strengthen Argentina's industrialisation by breaking the balance of payments bottlenecks, which, he argued, centred on steel, petrochemicals and, above all, oil.

Moreover, Frondizi, who had been an outspoken oil nationalist during the Peronist period, had become increasingly convinced of the need for foreign capital in oil exploration in order to supplement YPF's own resources and reduce the balance of payments cost of oil imports, which in 1957 had been $271m., or around 21% of all Argentine imports. While Frondizi played down his approach to oil policy during the election, the question assumed central importance subsequently. It should be pointed out, however, that technocratic economic policies such as those proposed by Frondizi by no means reflected a simple conservatism. On the contrary:

the economic theory of development put forward by Frondizi and Frigerio drew on a deep running ideological well within Argentine nationalism and society which had its roots in the 1930s and the analysis of Argentine reality first put forward by Forja and later developed under Peronism. This ideological current had posited that the chief obstacle to Argentina's economic development was an outmoded economic structure dominated by British imperialism and the landowning class which exported to Britain . . . In opposition to these forces was a whole spectrum of social groups from workers through to industrialists who had a common interest in achieving *un gran país soberano e independiente* [a great, independent and sovereign country].[25]

There was some reason to believe, therefore, that if Frondizi were able to implement such policies and to remain in office until the economic benefits became clear, he might find a strong political base for the developmentalist policies being pursued.

Once elected, Frondizi, with the direct assistance of his ally Frigerio, and Arturo Sabato, who was appointed to head YPF, moved very quickly to sign contracts with various private companies. These were of three kinds. The first and most controversial group of contracts, signed with Amoco, Cities Service and Tennessee Gas, provided for the drilling of wells in areas in which oil had already been discovered and in some cases partially developed by YPF. These companies were to be paid cash for oil produced, at prices significantly below international levels, partly in Argentine pesos and partly in foreign currency. The second type were specifically drilling contracts with payment per metre drilled and/or per hour spent drilling in areas selected by YPF. Finally, pure exploration contracts were signed with Esso, Shell and Union Oil, with payment also to be in cash per cubic metre of oil or gas discovered, with the exception of the Shell contract which was of the more conventional profit-sharing kind. No doubt assisted by the fact that these contracts had been signed, the government was also able to secure a $100m. loan from the Export–Import Bank and a number of largely untied credits from Europe which were to be used by YPF itself.

The economic consequences of these contracts were and, indeed, still are extremely controversial within Argentina and it is therefore neces-

Table 19.5 *Reserve levels, drilling and oil output, 1958–63*

| | Reserves (proved) | Wells drilled | Output (m. cubic metres) | | | |
			YPF	Contractors	Concessions	Total
1958	390	392	5.0	0	0.7	5.7
1959	n.a.	565	6.1	0.3	0.7	7.1
1960	n.a.	1,184	7.1	2.5	0.6	10.2
1961	580	1,613	9.1	3.8	0.5	13.4
1962	n.a.	1,295	10.4	4.7	0.5	15.6
1963	n.a.	804	10.3	4.7	0.4	15.4

Source: A. Sabato, *Petróleo: ¿dependencia o liberación?* (Buenos Aires, 1974), pp. 26, 36 and 80.

sary to be careful about the conclusions to be drawn. It is, however, inescapably true that Frondizi's policies proved to be highly successful in their primary objective, which was to get the oil industry moving again. As can be seen from table 19.5, output almost tripled in five years and by 1962 Argentina was effectively self-sufficient. This had been achieved without any reduction in proven reserve levels. Secondly, it should be noted that most of the increased production came from YPF itself; the contracts for development drilling, while important, were secondary in economic terms although politically they were the most controversial. Thirdly, it is clear that these contractors made far better use of the areas concerned than YPF had made at any time in the past. Thus, although Tennessee Gas took over an area which had been discovered by YPF as early as 1938, the US company produced 2,600,000 cubic metres from this area at the end of five years of operation, whereas the state company had produced only 54,069 cubic metres in the preceding 20 years. Amoco took over from YPF an area producing 29,000 cubic metres after 26 years of commercial operation, and after a further year was producing 100,000 cubic metres. Cities Service, which had been given an area that in 1958 contained 17% of proved reserves in Mendoza, was up until 1963 able to produce more than half of the oil output of the province.

Although these factors might have been expected to indicate that Frondizi's policy had proved its worth, this conclusion was by no means universally shared. Some of the objections raised were limited and technical. Without inside information, for example, it is very difficult to know whether there is any justification in the charge that some of the drilling contractors overdrilled in particular areas,[26] or that YPF de-emphasised exploration in the interests of rapid oil development,[27] although proved oil reserves increased during the period so that it would be difficult to argue that either of these things was true of Argentina as a whole. Similarly, it may be true that YPF was excessively generous in the price paid to some of its contractors (one never knows whether it *might* have got away with less) but clearly untrue that it was more expensive to pay for contract oil than to import.[28]

Essentially, however, the objections to Frondizi's policies were political. In some cases these were tactical and opportunistic, but it should nevertheless be recorded that many Argentines, particularly those in the Radical Party, were acutely frustrated by Frondizi's measures and felt that a great opportunity had been wasted. According to this view, the main problem with oil nationalism was that it had not been tried; YPF had always found its interests subjected to those of other agencies or social groups, with the result that its full potential had not been realised. A policy of 'nationalism with efficiency' would, in this view, have been more successful in the long term as well as being desirable on the grounds of national sovereignty and Argentine history. Frondizi had, after all, taken a similar view himself in a book published as recently as 1956 and, instead of taking time and trying to convince his erstwhile nationalist friends that changes were necessary, he had moved quickly and secretively in an unexpected direction. Indeed, his political approach, or rather his lack of it, seemed almost calculated to make enemies of his former colleagues. His criterion was speed rather than political acceptability; as Arturo Sabato put it in an interview in September 1979, 'We didn't want things put off until tomorrow, we wanted them done yesterday!'

Some opposition came from within YPF itself. To some extent this was predictable. The management and technical staff of YPF had no responsibility at all for the various oil contracts which were negotiated exclusively by Sabato, Frigerio and Frondizi, and no doubt resented their exclusion. YPF was also displaced from certain areas which it had already – even if not very effectively – worked, and it had to contend with the direct comparisons which would now be possible between the efficiency of the contracting companies and that of YPF. These comparisons would be unlikely to favour the latter. Moreover, quite apart from the contracts themselves, the Frondizi government proposed to carry out a reorganisation of YPF.[29] Consequently, 'as early as June

1958, YPF professional personnel began organising to protest the contracts and ask for their annulment or modification. Failing to obtain their ends, many prominent persons in YPF resigned.'[30] Despite these resignations, however, many senior figures opposed to the contracts remained in their positions.

Certainly there was some truth in Arturo Sabato's assertion:

> YPF was debated from two extreme positions. On the one side, there was a group of devotees whose centre of gravity lay in the institution . . . Through a kind of professional bias, these had ended by convincing themselves, with total sincerity, that YPF was the national saviour or, at least, the national emblem. Thus they had inverted the true relationship and come to believe that the country ought to be at the service of YPF rather than the other way around. They defended the state monopoly and asserted that all the stages of exploration, development, refining, distribution and sales ought to be the responsibility of YPF, without any foreign collaboration. At the other extreme there were those critics of YPF who themselves made no compromises. For them, the problem was not the state monopoly, but the very existence of a state company.[31]

It is also true, however, that the Frondizi government was the first since Yrigoyen to treat oil as a major priority. Between 1930 and 1958 Argentina had the benefit neither of determined laissez-faire solutions, nor of consistently and determinedly pursued nationalist ones, nor even of the kind of ingenious compromise produced by Frondizi. After a long period of indecision and neglect of oil policy, determined action of any kind was certain to be controversial, particularly if it was the result of decisions taken quickly and in secret and then presented without any real debate as *faits accomplis*. Supporters of Frondizi's approach still argue that the policy was justified by its results, but it is certainly not difficult to understand the political opposition which it aroused.

It is nevertheless interesting that the centre of opposition to Frondizi lay in the orthodox Radical Party (the UCRP) and in YPF itself, rather than in the major centres of political power at that time – the Peronist movement and the military. Although Frondizi remained in power only so long as he was tolerated by the army, his oil policy was a matter of very little concern to most military officers. Although Frondizi received no fewer than 36 *planteos* – or political demands – from the military up until his final overthrow in 1962, not one of these was related to oil policy; the only factual enquiry received on this matter came from the army company Fabricaciones Militares, and this was a relatively straightforward question to deal with.[32]

The Peronist position was more complicated, but it was essentially tactical and motivated by general political considerations rather than by oil *per se*. Essentially, the Peronists were concerned to play off Frondizi against the army; keen to prevent a military coup, they were also determined to prevent Frondizi from becoming too powerful and independent. This can be seen from Peronist attitudes towards an all-out strike declared by the Communists against the oil contracts in the province of Mendoza for early November 1958.[33] This strike, as James recounts,

> had broken out in the Mendoza field at the end of October and was led by a coalition of Radical Party and Communist activists. The union (SUPE) . . . had not yet had new elections and hence there was no centralised dominant leadership of any one tendency. The Peronist union grouping, the *Junta de Petroleros 13 de diciembre,* whilst claiming the support of the majority of petrol workers, had not been able to translate this into effective control of the union apparatus. Its two key leaders from the Peronist epoch . . . had both been banned from activity by the military government. The first response of the Peronists to the strike was a communiqué issued by the *Junta de Petroleros* on October 31st warning the Peronist workers in YPF of the political nature of the strike led by the Communists and Radicals and calling on them to continue working. On the 2nd November the *Consejo Coordinador y Supervisor del Peronismo* came out in support of this position. On the 4th *Linea Dura,* the semi-official organ of the movement in referring to the opponents of the contracts, spoke of the 'anti-national front promoting a confrontation between the workers of YPF and the need for self-sufficiency in petrol which the nation so desperately needs'.[34]

In fact, Peronist attitudes were rather ambiguous and complicated. On the one hand, they had no objection to making political capital out of the oil contracts if this could be done (it was, after all, no more than Frondizi had himself done in 1955), but on the other, they were unwilling either to follow a movement led predominantly by non-Peronists or to abandon their own *desarrollista* economic ideas for the banner of oil nationalism. Thus, in mid-1958, when the question of the oil contracts first came on to the political agenda, the Coordinating Council of the Peronist unions (the '62') made a statement denouncing 'certain elements using supposedly nationalistic banners' since even 'these elements know perfectly well that only to the extent that we build up an economic order freeing ourselves from imports of things such as petrol will we have broken the bonds of colonial domination'.[35] Frondizi might have said the same himself.

By November 1958, however, Perón, 'who had been increasingly worried at the leeway given Frondizi by the movement in Argentina, sent strict instructions ordering a denunciation of the contracts'.[36] The Peronists' objective, therefore, was purely tactical and Peronist unions joined the Communists on strike. At this point it appeared that the Peronists were moving openly into opposition, but their unwillingness to join a broad nationalist front became clear a few days after the strike when it became known that Vice-President Gómez, a Radical, disagreed with the contracts and it was rumoured that he was talking to military officers. Again the Peronist unions retreated and Gómez, who found no support in the army, was forced to resign.

Illia and the cancellation of the contracts 1963–6

The removal of Frondizi by the military in March 1962 had nothing to do with the oil issue. However, the elections which were promised in 1963 provided a new opportunity for the nationalist UCRP to win office and carry out its promises to repudiate the contracts which Frondizi had signed. During the military interregnum of 1962–3, there took place a major debate within YPF over whether or not to annul the contracts. The movement to annul failed only narrowly, by a vote of 6 to 5 on the board of directors and, although the government took no immediate action, it was certain that the issue would surface again. It did so when Illia won the 1963 elections for the UCRP and annulled the contracts in November.

The reasons for the cancellation were not primarily economic. According to an electoral survey carried out in 1963, the UCRP drew its support from voters whose 'habits had relatively little to do with political or economic considerations and were chiefly determined by reference to the traditional moral values represented by the party and its leaders'.[37] Traditional moral and political values, and the Radical Party's historical commitment to a policy of oil nationalism, also explain the attitude of the Radical Party leadership which won the 1963 elections with 25.4% of the votes – an identical proportion to that which it had received in the 1958 elections when Peronist support had enabled Frondizi to win.

There is a sense in which the annulment was well timed. The work that had been carried out under Frondizi was irreversible and Argentina was now within range of self-sufficiency; even if it slipped back a little and imports increased, this was no great problem at a time when world

Table 19.6 *Production, drilling and oil imports in Argentina 1961–66*

	Output (m. cubic metres)	Wells drilled	Cost of Imports ($m.)
1961	13.42	1,639	106.9
1962	15.61	1,289	65.9
1963	15.44	803	30.9
1964	15.94	506	68.1
1965	15.62	555	94.6
1966	16.64	714	79.6

Source: Juan Sabato, p. 17 of Fundación Eugenio Blanco, *El Ministro Eugenio A. Blanco y la anulación de los contratos de petróleo* (Buenos Aires, 1969).

oil prices were low and tending to fall further. Moreover, Argentina had considerable bargaining power when dealing with companies supplying only the domestic market and was in many cases able to strike excellent bargains with the expropriated companies. Certainly the cycle of contract and annulment proved to be far from catastrophic in the long run.

When the contracts were annulled, the companies were not actually taken over. Within the Illia government there were some who were willing to settle for little more than a renegotiation of at any rate the less controversial of the contracts perhaps involving new bidding. There were others, however, who argued that the companies had to be seen to be nationalised. When government policy was finally settled, it was clear that the hard-liners had enjoyed the better of the argument.[38] The government declared itself willing to offer a formula of 'money back plus interest' to the companies, although this was not immediately acceptable to them. Only Marathon, which had found no oil and expected no payment, and Astra, which accepted the formula together with a notional 15% return on capital invested, had settled by the end of 1964. After further negotiations, the principle was generally accepted that the government would return money, interest and an allowance for the rate of return on capital. Considering the work that some of the companies had put in, this represented an excellent bargain for Argentina.

One of the first major settlements, with Tennessee Gas, was signed in April 1965. The company, which had already received $22.7m. as payment for its crude oil from YPF, now received a further $42.3m., as a result of which YPF received the oil and gas *in situ* at a far lower cost than would have occurred had the contract remained in force. Shell, which settled for $22.5m. in March 1965, had discovered oil and gas *in situ* which, according to Juan Sabato, could be extracted by YPF at a cost of $21m. and would sell for $63m. at world prices. Esso also settled fairly cheaply, for a combination of $28.2m. and 109m. pesos. At the time of the 1966 coup, negotiations with Cities Service and Amoco were still continuing.

None of these changes did a great deal to improve the efficiency of YPF. Although the Illia government did redirect some of the state company's activities toward exploration, in order to make up for the activity which was no longer being carried out by the contractors,[39] the organisation's financial problems remained and, if anything, seem to have become worse. Under Frondizi YPF had been able to make limited profits on current sales but almost all of the company's investments had to be paid for by borrowing, with the result that YPF's internal debt rose from 13,000m. pesos in 1958 to 61,000m. when Illia was inaugurated. At least YPF had an increase in real output and activity to show for it. After 1962 the latent chaos in Argentine public finance reasserted itself even more strongly; thus, for example:

In June 1964 it was reported that the state coal enterprise owed YPF US$236.8 million for the supply of liquid fuel and that an agreement had been reached whereby the state coal agency would pay US$40 million in debt cancellation certificates (usable only for discharging intergovernmental debts) and the balance in monthly installments of 10 percent.[40]

It is unlikely that the railways were as forthcoming.

Chaos was compounded by YPF's own traditional reluctance to take account of financial constraints when making its own plans. As Edwards pointed out:

First of all, YPF was attempting to fulfill its obligations under the so-called Plan of Reactivation which had been approved by the government in 1956 and for which the Treasury had found it impossible to supply sufficient funds. In the second place, YPF had made its plans without regard to its own resources, always relying on state aid to come to the rescue.[41]

One might also add that YPF was structured in such a way as to make internal cost accounting extremely difficult, a point to which we shall return below.

Nevertheless, the oil industry under the Illia regime stagnated rather than collapsed and the government did take over large quantities of oil and gas reserves from the private sector at fairly low cost. At the same time YPF made plans for a considerable expansion of its refining capacity, relying in this field on foreign help both for the design and engineering stages and for the actual construction projects.[42] This help was not affected by the nationalisations. Internal calculations suggested that these projects would prove highly profitable, although it is likely that profitability depended upon YPF using its market and if necessary legal power to ensure that these refineries worked at full capacity even if crude oil had to be diverted away from the private sector refineries in the process. This point was later to become important. In any case, a firm contract was signed for the expansion of the La Plata refinery in late 1965, while design and engineering studies were invited in the same year for the expansion of the refinery at Luján de Cuyo and preparations at an earlier stage were in progress for the expansion of the San Lorenzo refinery.

The expansion of the state refining sector may well have been designed in the long term to facilitate the nationalisation of the existing privately owned refineries. Certainly the government intended to move from its annulment of Frondizi's contracts to an overall nationalisation of the oil industry. Thus, as Juan Sabato recalled: 'It was our firm proposal, during the Illia government, to give legal force to the offering of future marketing outlets only to YPF . . . In March 1966 a decree was ready which would have regulated the marketing of oil products but its promulgation was delayed by the sickness and subsequent death of the then Secretary of Energy Antulio Pozzio.[43] Before alternative arrangements could be made there was a military coup at the end of June 1966.

Onganía and after: 1966–79

General Onganía's coup of 1966, while originally supported by a variety of political tendencies, essentially proved to be a victory for economic liberalism. The new government introduced a new oil law in 1967 which gave the government the right to offer oil concessions on fairly traditional terms if it wished to do so. Although the new law was defended on the ground that it did not make the granting of concessions compulsory and that therefore policy could be changed without further changes in the law (as indeed later happened), it also ended any attempt to find, through the use of contracts, some middle ground between the nationalists and the liberals. This policy was, not surprisingly, attacked by Arturo Sabato speaking for the *frondicistas* as well as by the left and by some right-wing nationalists (notably the magazine *Azul y blanco*). As *Latin America* remarked, 'with normal political life frozen since General Onganía's regime banned existing parties after last year's takeover, the much disputed feature of the oil industry is providing an arena for the exertion of opposition pressure against the government'.[44] In November 1967 *Azul y blanco* was closed when it tried to organise a 'March of Sovereignty'. In any case the legislation went through, with little opposition from within the government or the officer corps, showing once again that the army as a whole was not greatly interested in the oil question.[45]

A number of concession contracts were then signed, while Amoco (which had not settled compensation terms with the Illia government) was persuaded to remain in Argentina.[46] However, unlike previous exploration campaigns, most of the private exploration investment after 1966 – including all of the offshore, where 32 wells were drilled – proved to be unsuccessful. Nevertheless, output increased quite quickly during the period, partly as a result of secondary recovery work undertaken on a large scale for the first time, mainly by private Argentine companies under contract to YPF. However, as can be seen from table 19.7, exploration success did not increase proportionately with increased production and the reserve:production ratio began to decline. By 1970 this decline was beginning to concern government ministers.

Meanwhile, the incoming administration of YPF, headed by Daniel Brunella, was not over-impressed by the working of the state company. Many of Brunella's complaints, however, were similar to those which had been made by Silveyra in the 1930s and Villa and Canepa in the 1950s and which were to be made again by Ondarts in the 1970s. In general 'YPF was managed like another branch of public administration, with financial budgets rather than useful accounts, without any analysis of real costs and, above all, with the pervasive bureaucratic mentality of public employment on the part of the personnel.'[47] This mentality 'could be summed up as a refusal to assume responsibilities, and apathy brought about by the fact of equivalent treatment for all, which took no account of differing abilities and tasks'.[48] The internal structure of YPF also showed the scars of the earlier politicisation of the enterprise: some manifestly unsuitable people had been appointed to senior positions, while outsiders who had earlier been purged were eager to get back their old jobs and pressurised incoming governments

Table 19.7 *Oil output, reserves and drilling 1965–70*

	YPF output (000 cubic metres)	Contractors' and concessionaires output (000 cubic metres)	Oil imports (000 cubic metres)	Oil reserves (m. cubic metres)	YPF drilling (000 metres)	Contractors drilling (000 metres)
1965	10,198	5,113	4,203	439.8	833	6
1966	12,164	4,198	4,122	423.0	818	331
1967	13,772	4,192	2,915	400.0	667	410
1968	15,114	4,599	2,351	320.0	605	169
1969	14,876	5,595	2,668	250.0	524	71
1970	15,380	7,221	1,684	n.a.	679	178

Source: Argentina, Ministerio de Economía, *Serie histórica de estados de fuentes y usos de fondos y balances generales* (August 1978), vol. 2, table 15.

to this effect. Moreover, the weakness of the channels of information within the agency meant that, even when political criteria were not used, there was little alternative to promotion based purely on seniority. Finally, YPF lacked autonomy: in the past it had frequently suffered from the central government's balance of payments or counter-inflationary policies and was often either starved of funds or forced to hold its prices unrealistically low or both. Even YPF's budget, which needed prior governmental approval, was rigidly enforced, with the result that a certain amount of unnecessary equipment was bought with leftover funds that needed to be spent in the year of approval, while the impossibility of securing quick approval for unexpected purchases encouraged managers to carry an excessive number of spare parts and stocks, tying up capital which might have been better used elsewhere.

Although Brunella did make an effort to improve the efficiency of YPF, his achievements were more than nullified by the results of the increasingly chaotic political situation of the 1970s. Nevertheless, many of his reforms were similar to those attempted after 1976: an attempt was made to decentralise the agency by substitution of financial aid for direct operational control after efforts had been made to find out what the real costs of the enterprise actually were. Manning was reduced from 40,779 in 1966 to 33,615 in 1970 and there was also some improvement in YPF's financial position.

By 1970, however, the mood of the military had changed. The neo-liberal economic policies of the Onganía regime had proved to be conspicuously unpopular and, after his overthrow in that year, successive military regimes pursued policies first of 'Peronism without Perón', and second of trying to win Perón's support for their own objectives and, failing this, to secure the return of Peronism on acceptable terms. Although oil policy was by no means the foremost concern of this period, the Levingston government (1970–1) appointed oil nationalists to the key positions which related to this question. Consequently, the granting of new concessions to foreign oil companies ended.

The main policy change, however, concerned the refining sector. Under the Onganía regime both the private companies and YPF expanded their refining capacity so that there was a temporary surplus, at any rate if one considered some of the older equipment still in the hands of YPF. Up until then, the market had been shared out according to an informal quota system, which gave YPF around 60% of the domestic market while the private sector retained the other 40%. However, in 1971 YPF was given exclusive rights to import crude and to take enough to cover its own marketing requirements before allocating the balance to the private companies, and it was made clear that YPF would use this power to run its refineries at full capacity and leave the companies to face the full effect of the temporary surplus. It appears that full-scale nationalisation was also briefly considered, but any such ideas were aborted by the Lanusse coup of 1971.

It would be difficult to say that any Argentine government between 1971 and 1976 had any oil policy. Although the five governments in power during this period (Lanusse, Campora, Lastiri, Perón and Isabel Perón) were all in some sense nationalist, YPF was allowed to deteriorate sharply. Personnel increased from 33,615 in 1970 to 37,474 by 1972, 50,555 at the end of 1975 and some 53,000 at the time of the coup of April 1976. YPF's accounts had become so unreliable that the Economics Ministry's own statistics for YPF in 1975 and 1976 had to be qualified with the remark that 'the financial balances do not provide a reasonable reflection of the economic, financial and capital situation of the company'.[49] Meanwhile, oil production reached a peak in 1972 and then there began a gradual decline, largely because of the lack of effective recovery techniques, while little oil exploration took place and no new oilfields were discovered. YPF did try to move into new areas, signing an exploration contract in Ecuador in 1974, but with little positive result. Some half-hearted efforts were made to attract the return of foreign investment into exploration, but these also proved abortive.

The Lanusse government dropped the Levingston government's apparent policy of gradual nationalisation of the oil industry and, indeed, in 1972 offered a new set of exploration concessions, but these did not attract any response. The *Petroleum Press Service* reported that 'the companies might have responded to the call for exploration, except that their position in Argentina has been made very difficult by the government's policy to advance YPF's control over the local market at their expense'.[50] With the return of the Peronists in 1973 a somewhat reluctant government went further in a nationalist direction, largely as a result of pressure from the oil-workers' union, SUPE. According to Juan Sabato, himself a confirmed oil nationalist:

The draft oil law which the government sent to the Chamber of Deputies on 24 July 1974 caused great disappointment and resulted in a negative reaction on the part of certain groups close to the government, and especially from the oil-workers' union SUPE. The demand made by SUPE, which enjoyed the support of the CGT, was aimed particularly at the modification of Article 5, which did not change the position of the private companies, particularly Esso and Shell, in the marketing sector, to the detriment of YPF; there were meetings in the Secretaría de Energía, whose employees supported the position taken by SUPE; Gómez Morales, the Economics Minister, participated in some of these meetings and there were serious disagreements.[51]

Finally, in August 1974 the incoming government of Isabel Perón carried out an 'intervention' of private sector marketing outlets, which amounted to nationalisation without the intention of offering compensation. At this point Shell was apparently considering complete withdrawal from Argentina.[52]

Under Isabel Perón, however, there were discussions about the possibility of new exploration contracts with foreign companies, but the government was by this stage too insecure to be able to carry out any effective policy. By 1975 Argentina was in a state of practical civil war, hyperinflation and near international bankruptcy and, although the geological prospects of the Argentine offshore appeared far better as a consequence of the world price increases, no company would undertake major new investments under such circumstances. YPF's own efforts to explore the offshore, however, proved spectacularly unsuccessful and reached some kind of nadir when an offshore drilling rig, which had been unwisely purchased and the subject of many delays, sank in the Gulf of Mexico on its way to Argentina; the rig had not been insured.

The military coup of April 1976 was, in the economic sphere, a qualified victory for neoliberalism. In the oil industry, marketing outlets were returned to the private companies and the incoming regime sought to attract private investment into the industry to the greatest extent possible. By the middle of 1979 three major oil exploration contracts had been signed for the offshore area – two with Shell and one with a group including Bridas, Total and Deminex. Onshore, YPF placed increasing emphasis on contracting out work: 'In 1977 the Government started out on a very ambitious plan which proved productive, by relieving YPF from the burden of carrying out all the secondary recovery or waterflood activity and invited private companies to participate in this task.'[53] Eleven areas were temporarily retained by YPF but a further 21 were contracted to the (mainly domestic) private sector. Downstream there was even talk of the possibility of allowing another refinery to be built by the private sector.[54] Over all, the government hoped that, by 1985, around 30% of the industry's entire investment

Table 19.8 *Oil production and drilling 1971–7*

	YPF output (000 cubic metres)	Other Argentine output (000 cubic metres)	Imports (000 cubic metres)	YPF drilling (000 metres)	Contractors (000 metres)
1971	16,939	7,440	2,540	734	143
1972	17,583	7,429	1,736	731	332
1973	17,326	6,950	3,395	655	419
1974	17,062	6,805	3,424	723	450
1975	16,277	6,723	2,485	617	454
1976	17,090	5,866	3,524	679	542
1977	18,786	6,063	3,360	729	486

Source: Ministerio de Economía, *Síntesis estadística,* table 15.

would come from the private sector and the intention was to increase the level of private investment to the maximum possible but without imparting any major new shocks to the system.

Although YPF's area of activity was considerably curtailed (it largely pulled out of offshore exploration, for example) it was able to increase output considerably from the levels to which it had fallen under Isabel Perón. While the agency was streamlined, with the number of employees falling from some 53,000 at the time of the coup to 35,900 in mid-1979, no attempt was made to curtail its role drastically or to relegate it to a backwater. Again, shock treatment was ruled out. On the contrary, major training schemes were announced for YPF personnel, and an effort was made, as it had been in the 1960s, to improve the quality of the staff and to improve YPF's internal financial accountability. According to Raúl Ondarts (head of YPF until his death in a helicopter crash in December 1979), prior to 1976 the agency's 'statistics were completely absurd' and subsequently efforts had to be made to discover what YPF's costs really were.[55] Nevertheless, despite some undoubted organisational improvements, it was less clear that YPF's autonomy increased significantly after 1976, for the central government still vetted YPF's budget in detail and in 1979 insisted upon curtailment of some of YPF's investments as part of its counter-inflationary strategy. For as long as the agency continues to depend upon the public sector bureaucracy, there will always be limits on the extent to which YPF's own tendency to bureaucratisation can be checked.

Conclusions

The case of YPF shows clearly that considerations of geography and geology, while setting limits to what is possible, do not of themselves determine the performance of state oil companies. Argentina, while not oil-abundant in the Middle Eastern sense, should have had few difficulties in reaching self-sufficiency in oil at any rate after the Second World War, when the outstanding political and policymaking questions appeared for a time to have been settled. Argentina discovered a huge oilfield, in an excellent location near the sea, as early as 1907; even today this field produces a significant proportion of Argentina's oil. YPF also successfully made some major oil discoveries in the early 1950s in Salta, using techniques which were not available to the private companies which explored the area in the 1930s. Moreover, Argentina had a ready market for any oil discovered, large enough to permit economies of scale in refineries and transportation facilities, but small enough for self-sufficiency to seem a feasible task given Argentina's resource base.

It is true that Argentina has been very nearly self-sufficient in oil since the early 1960s, but this was despite rather than because of the performance of YPF. This performance was in no way related to the technical competence of Argentine engineers; rather, as Arturo Sabato pointed out in the early 1970s, 'as well as lacking a clear and workable policy of oil development, there are faults of an administrative kind which lead to the employment of a far larger number of people than is necessary'.[56] More brutally, A. H. Hanson wrote in the 1960s: 'Argentina offers an example of the proposed disintegration of an enterprise, the Yacimientos Petroliferos Fiscales, which has ramified in a manner such as to give rise to what some observers consider unnecessary and harmful organisational complexity.'[57] While there is nothing inevitable in this state of affairs, and it is to be hoped that the improvement in YPF's performance since 1976 is continued, it is perhaps worth enquiring further into the causes of YPF's difficulties.

The problem certainly did not lie in a lack of perception on the part of well placed Argentines. Silveyra in the 1930s, Canessa in the 1940s, Canepa and Villa and later Frondizi in the 1950s, Brunella in the 1960s and Ondarts in the 1970s were all well informed – indeed informative – about YPF's organisational problems and all made efforts to solve them. Nor did it lie in the pursuit of a rigid, inflexible and mistaken policy. Almost everything has been tried since 1935 but only the Frondizi government could be counted as successful in its oil policy, although some of the others – Onganía and, from a very different perspective, Illia – did achieve some success. Nor could the mere fact of fluctuating policy explain the difficulties, for Argentine oil policy was rather more successful in the 21 years since 1958 than it had been in the preceding 21 years, which were a period of quasi-monopoly on the part of the state. Certainly the political breakdown of the mid-1970s had serious repercussions, as it was bound to do, upon YPF, but this clearly did not mark the beginning of its failures. Even if some of the blame is placed on the first Peronist Administration, the puzzle remains: why did a government which was ostensibly committed to industrialisation and economic progress pay so little attention to the needs of YPF and, by extension, to the needs of the Argentine oil industry?

Essentially the problem appears to have been political in the sense of concerning priorities. For every Argentine government since 1930, the needs of YPF were considered to be at best secondary to other political or economic objectives. The liberal-conservative governments were essentially concerned with the welfare of the private sector and the role of YPF was restricted either deliberately (as before 1943) or in consequence. The latter strategy, provided that YPF was given and allowed to fulfil a significant role within the overall system, was not necessarily either undesirable or doomed to failure, but few *desarrollista* governments in Argentina (the only real exception being Frondizi) have remained in office for long enough to bring lasting change to the oil industry. Nationalist governments, even less permanent, were generally more concerned with ownership *per se* than with the efficiency of what passed into the hands of the state, with the result that the concept of state ownership subsequently became discredited along with these governments themselves.

Observers have often commented on the essentially conflictive nature of Argentine political society and the consequent difficulty of establishing any kind of common ground on which continuity of policy could be based. This proposition is no less true for being widely asserted. No doubt this could be explained in part by the fact of Argentina's relatively early economic development compared with that of other parts of Latin America. Economic liberalism was well entrenched throughout Latin America prior to 1930 but only in Argentina did it appear to have brought results; it was therefore more difficult for a *desarrollista* orthodoxy to take root and find support across the political spectrum.

Opposition came from the right in the name of laissez-faire, while the political left and the Peronists were not so much concerned with the achievement of economic development as with the redistribution of income.

Moreover, the dramatic nationalisations of oil in Brazil and Mexico effectively ruled out, at any rate for a long time, any return to private investment in oil exploration and refining. The Argentine experience prior to 1935, however, did not so much rule out future policy options as convince the military–political leadership of the time that oil needed to be kept out of politics as far as possible. As a consequence, YPF was never able to develop a real political constituency, with the exception of a few voices in the Radical Party, and could be sent to the end of the queue, or its workings interfered with, when other political priorities seemed more pressing. The Frondizi government subsequently established the primacy of oil policy but did so in large part by relying on contractors from the domestic and international private sector. This ensured that, to many, ownership of oil appeared more important than the development of the industry, and policy fluctuated according to the preferences of the government of the day. Under these circumstances, the efficiency of YPF was again frequently neglected. Considering the period as a whole, in the jargon of political science, YPF was unable to maintain its boundaries until the time came when these seemed hardly worth protecting.

It should be noted, however, that the consequences of YPF's difficulties were partially offset by the activities of private investment. Argentina's large domestic market played an important part in persuading foreign companies to enter under a variety of contract terms under Frondizi and, more recently, its promising offshore geology has led to renewed interest from several foreign companies. Even more important has been the role played by several domestic Argentine companies, notably Pérez Companc and Bridas, which moved into oil development after generating the needed resources from the capital goods industry. YPF's difficulties made it easier for these companies to hire trained technologists from the public sector and, at any rate since the Frondizi period, government policy has been at least sporadically sympathetic to ventures of this kind. The weakness of YPF, therefore, did a considerable amount to encourage the development of domestic capitalist interest in oil. This is greater in Argentina than in most other parts of Latin America.

20

Petroperú 1968–80: achievements and hard lessons

The case of Petroperú well illustrates the difficulties inherent in setting up a model in which development is led by an autonomous and efficient state enterprise sector linking effectively with international technology and the world market. The difficulties in the Peruvian case were essentially political and managerial, although Petroperú suffered to some considerable extent from the vagaries of Peruvian geology. One conclusion may be that, whereas state enterprise is a feasible solution in countries where oil reserves are known to be abundant (Mexico) or where the domestic market is more important than domestic oil production (Brazil), state oil companies are not equipped to take major risks unless these are restricted to a minor part of their overall activity. Even more central is the fact that the creation of a successful state oil company is a difficult matter which requires a considerable degree of political as well as technical sophistication. Problems of economic policymaking do not disappear when foreign companies are nationalised.

The early politics of Petroperú 1969–71

After the expropriation of IPC in 1968–9 by the incoming military government, the state company Petróleos del Perú (Petroperú) appeared to have a considerable number of initial advantages. These stemmed from several different factors. One of the most important of these was the enormous amount of emotional capital invested in Petroperú. During the whole course of the debate on IPC, a main argument used by the opponents of nationalisation was the incompetence of state enterprise in Latin America. Once IPC had been turned into a major political issue and finally expropriated in dramatic style (see chapter 12), the Peruvian military government simply had to make a success of the petroleum industry. Petroperú's initial successes were therefore seen as a great symbolic victory for Peruvian nationalism; as one of

Peru's leading daily newspapers asserted, 'Peru has successfully constructed a national company of the first rank . . . Petroperú is a syn-
thesis, a symbol and an emblem.'[1]

This initial position allowed the development of a new Peruvian
ideology of state enterprise activity which was shared by the head of
Petroperú and much of the central government. The nature of this can
clearly be seen from a speech made by General Fernández Baca, the
President of Petroperú from 1968 to 1974, on behalf of the government at the annual meeting of industrialists at CADE in November
1969:

Public enterprise should emerge as a natural counterweight to the excessive
economic penetration of the great foreign companies . . . In order that public
enterprise should fulfil this mission, its organisation and administration
should use the techniques and procedures that are used by the large American
companies.

In this country, there have been many attempts to disparage public enterprise. It is said that the state was a poor administrator. This is not our view
and we are proving our case by the results that we have obtained from EPF
formerly and now Petroperú.

It cannot be denied that the maintenance of state enterprises under the same
norms as those prevailing in the branches of the central government regarding
personnel, cost control, methods of payment, systems of promotion and general administration – methods less satisfactory in a commercial organisation
than a political one – would tend to drag down efficiency in its administration.
But when state companies are organised as autonomous entities, there is no
reason why the directors or advisers in the administration should not be men
as competent as those in the big companies; and, as for technicians, there is
no difference between public and private enterprise.

Public enterprises also provide an excellent school for the study of social
and economic problems . . . They permit the prices and profits of the private
companies involved in the same activity to be monitored and policy moulded
to meet the needs of the situation. Because of its public responsibilities, this
kind of enterprise cannot and should not aim primarily at 'profit maximisation' but should aim to break even.[2]

A second major source of initial strength was Petroperú's financial
position. Having taken over IPC's assets at a time when that company
was still profitable and also benefiting from the opening of the La Pampilla refinery by EPF at the end of 1967, Petroperú was at first able to
reinvest substantially from its own resources. Although the total
amount was not spectacular (see table 20.1), it was able to commit
itself to certain investment projects for which heavy additional financing would be needed but which would be difficult to call off at a later,

Table 20.1 *Petroperú's gross income and cash requirement 1970–2*
($m., at 40 soles to $1)

	1970	1971	1972
Gross income	117.7	125.1	145.3
Post tax income	10.7	4.9	9.4
Investment[a]	25.9	37.8	44.7
Re-investable surplus[b]	24.3	21.3	29.8
Cash requirement[c]	1.6	16.5	14.9

[a] Including repayment of loans (principal).
[b] Includes amortisation, depreciation provisions and social security contributions that were not paid out, but does not include taxes (accounted or paid), loans or royalties.
[c] I.e. decline in working capital, plus subsidies from the government and loans contracted from elsewhere. (Investment minus reinvestable surplus.)
Source: Philip, 'Policymaking in the Peruvian Oil Industry', p. 352.

more financially sensitive, stage.[3] This is, in fact, what happened. Thus, Petroperú's jungle exploration programme was a major step for Peru and made a number of subsequent decisions almost inevitable, but the company was able to take it without reference to the rest of the government.

Thirdly, there was the question of internal cohesion. In order to secure to the maximum the 'normal' public enterprise advantages of information control and expertise, it is necessary for an agency to prevent officials within it from building alliances with groups outside it. To some extent military discipline may help to limit the tendency for the formation of 'cross currents' but it did not always do so in Peru, where political loyalties were often strong. It was all the more important, therefore, that Petroperú inherited an *esprit de corps* which stemmed from the fact that it inherited IPC's organisation and most of its men.

Moreover, the political weight of Petroperú's leadership was greatly increased by the military appointments to its senior executive positions. The President of the organisation, General Fernández Baca, was a full general and so the military superior of many members of the Council of Ministers. He was also a long-standing personal friend of Velasco and his promotion to full general was a mark of unusual respect for a man who had spent most of his career in staff positions. He had four military subordinates on the agency, at least one of whom – General Carlos Bobbio – was a senior military figure in his own right.

Although Petroperú was strong, however, it was by no means invincible. The very lack of political definition which helped Petroperú so

much at the beginning ensured that things could go badly wrong if
the political balance shifted. Moreover, Petroperú itself came to
acquire a reputation, whether justified or not, for arrogance; this reputation redoubled the determination of other government agencies to
keep it in check.[4] The Mines and Energy Ministry, which was Petroperú's nominal superior, did not have sufficient expertise to challenge
Petroperú's technical judgements, but it could – and eventually did –
set up legal and bureaucratic obstacles in order to create problems for
the agency. Moreover, the Mines and Energy Minister, General Jorge
Fernández Maldonado, was a determined radical and nationalist. He
was a key member of the radical faction of the Velasco government,
who regarded Petroperú's various international contacts with grave suspicion.

It is perhaps generally true that, in any strongly nationalist government, any branch of government responsible for dealing with foreign
companies might expect to find that a certain amount of suspicion
rubbed off on itself. Petroperú had additional problems, however, in
that most of its staff originally worked for IPC. The ex-IPC nucleus was
crucial to the effective operational functioning of the company, and
even so it was by no means clear that Petroperú had the depth of expertise required to tackle its very ambitious programme. This nucleus,
however, had some difficulty in settling down under the new arrangements prevailing after the nationalisation. This was partly a matter of
political sensitivity. While many of its executives strongly welcomed
the nationalisation of IPC, it is possible that others did not. Moreover,
the 'IPC connection' provided a useful debating weapon for any nationalistic opponents of the company. There was also the problem of transition from a multinational enterprise with a very decentralised structure (too decentralised, in some ways, for Exxon's own benefit) to a
tighter command structure presided over by military officers with little
knowledge of the oil industry and no previous experience of commercial management. It was perhaps not surprising, therefore, that after
1972 Petroperú was seriously hurt by the fact that a fairly large number
of its executives (including several from the contracts division) took up
jobs with private contracting oil companies.

Exploration of the Selva 1970–4

The Peruvian oil industry in 1968 was undergoing a period of relative
decline. This was not true of refining and marketing since domestic

consumption, boosted by low domestic prices, had been expanding quite quickly. Production, however, had been stagnant or only slowly rising for the previous thirty years (see chapter 12) and Peru, which had been a significant exporter of oil until the Second World War, had now become a significant net importer. Prior to 1968 nationalists had blamed IPC's inactivity for the declining level of oil production in Peru and assumed that expropriation of the company would solve this problem. In fact, EPF—Petroperú worked hard at the beginning to try to increase output from the north-west fields, or at least to stem their rate of decline, but was not successful.

Simple 'hit and miss' tables do not tell the full story of Petroperú's difficulties in this area. Although the number of wells drilled by Petroperú was no higher than the number drilled by IPC itself, the work was held back by the unpromising nature of the geology. Moreover, the size of the finds made became less and less significant. Thus in its *Annual Report of 1970,* Petroperú calculated:

In La Brea, 17 development wells struck oil but averaged only 63 b/d; 13 of these averaged only 13 b/d although the other four were relatively productive.

Although four exploration wells struck oil in La Brea and Los Organos, none of these finds was significant.

In the Lima field, 45 development wells were successful and averaged 184 b/d, but even here 38 wells averaged only 45 b/d and the overall average was lifted by seven quite large finds.

There were six successful exploration wells in the Lima field; of these five were of very limited value, averaging 14 b/d, although the sixth was larger (182 b/d).

The report concluded that it was 'more and more difficult to find new reserves. This is why during this year 34 development wells fewer than in 1969 were drilled, despite the effort made to encounter new productive areas.'

Thus, Petroperú decided to look elsewhere for exploration sites. One possibility was the offshore area, but this was not a very promising prospect either. The geology was similar to that onshore – fractured and complicated – while the Pacific Ocean quickly became too deep for effective commercial exploration (at least until several years later). Petroperú therefore became increasingly interested in the Selva.[5] The geological structure here was interesting; structures were large and simple, and recent successes in Ecuador suggested the probability that there would be large-scale deposits of oil. In fact, IPC had shown some interest in the Selva prior to the coup and its former employees, who

Table 20.2 *Drilling and output in the north-west of Peru 1966–70*

	Output (000 b/d)	Percentage change	Wells drilled	Exploration wells	Dry holes
La Brea					
1966	6,715	100.0	36	13	13
1967	6,974	103.9	28	12	9
1968	5,564	82.8	11	0	1
1969	4,950	73.7	41	4	9
1970	4,373	65.1	25	7	6
Lima					
1966	10,883	100.0	62	4	4
1967	10,798	99.2	72	19	8
1968	10,994	101.0	71	9	9
1969	10,320	94.8	52	3	5
1970	10,180	93.5	59	9	8
Los Organos					
1966	2,349	100.0	45	n.a.	n.a.
1967	2,342	96.0	12	n.a.	3
1968	2,028	83.1	16	3	2
1969	1,682	69.0	23	7	9
1970	1,042	42.7	5	3	1

Source: Ministerio de Minas y Energía, *Estadística petrolera,* 1966–70.

had long understood the situation in the north-west, began to look seriously at a Selva campaign from the beginning of 1969.[6]

The decision to mount an exploration campaign in the Selva was momentous for a number of reasons. First, there was the sheer scale of the enterprise. When exploring 50 million hectares of jungle, there was no point in a small-scale operation. Table 20.3 shows Petroperú's own calculations of the cost of exploring a 1 million hectare bloc. It was estimated that of the $877m. cost of this operation, some $617m. could be financed out of reinvested income but $260m. had to be committed before any return could be expected.

Thus, Petroperú, even if it limited the scale of operations to 2% of the possible oil-bearing area, and even if its expedition was successful, would still have to find $260m. This was more than the entire worth of the company, which in 1971 was approximately $73.3m. Clearly Petroperú could not have raised this kind of money out of retained earnings or borrowings and to raise it out of government revenue would have involved heavy sacrifices of other projects.

Table 20.3 *Estimated cost of successfully exploring 1 million hectares of Selva, and developing 125,000 b/d.*

Item	Cost ($m.)	Comments
Geological survey	8	
Exploratory drilling	66	Assuming that 60 holes were drilled and that 12 found oil.
Development drilling	185	Assuming the drilling of 218 wells and
Tanks and storage	20	success in 167.
Pipeline	200	
Running costs	308	
Cost of running pipeline	90	
TOTAL	877	

Source: Colonel Bobbio's speech to CADE, 1970.

Moreover, there was the question of risk. Risk is in inverse proportion to the amount of activity undertaken. An observer in 1970 could be almost certain that there was oil to be found somewhere in the jungle but the total area was 50 million hectares and if only a small area were selected, it might have proved a bad choice. Up until 1970 there had been around 30 dry holes drilled in the Peruvian Selva as well as a gas find which was at that time uncommercial. The cost of covering the whole area, however, would be astronomical and if Petroperú were to do it all alone it would take centuries. These economies of scale also applied to transportation, given the high costs of pipeline construction; the greater the amount of oil found, the greater the possible size of the pipeline and the lower the throughput costs.

Finally, there was the problem of technical capacity. At the end of 1965 the previous state oil company, EPF, was by any standards a small company with a fixed investment of some $27m. The opening of the La Pampilla oil refinery at the end of 1967 changed this substantially and EPF's fixed investment rose to around $39.5m. After the IPC nationalisation, the book value of the state company's fixed investment rose further and stood at around $73.3m. at the end of 1971. Even this, however, was extremely small by the standards of most private oil companies. Amerada Hess in 1973 was ranked nineteenth largest of all the US oil companies, with capital of $1,460m.[7] Moreover, as Stepan pointed out:

IPC provided a valuable core for Petroperú, but not one foreign geological or petroleum engineer stayed with the company. In addition, since IPC had been engaged in a bitter conflict with the Peruvian government throughout the 1960s, it had not expanded the training of high-level Peruvian oil exploration and managerial professionals. Peru's national educational system was not capable of filling the gap by training oil engineers at home.[8]

Thus, Petroperú came to be faced by a set of choices. One option would have been to do nothing and allow ouput to continue to fall in the north-west. This would turn Peru into an importer on an ever increasing scale and slow down Peru's growth. On the other hand, it would avoid the need to commit resources heavily to a highly capital-intensive project of long gestation and high risk. A second option would be to bring in foreign investment to explore the Selva while Petroperú confined its own activities to the coast. This might generate investment activity and output and would free Peru's own resources for other high priority areas which perhaps offered more tangible returns. A third option would be to go it alone in the jungle, perhaps with a heavy fixed-interest loan from abroad such as might well have been obtainable from Japan. Given the scale at which Petroperú could operate, this would have involved a gamble on a quick success which, in view of past unsuccessful exploration campaigns, would be unlikely to succeed. If the gamble failed, Petroperú would forgo any chance of contributing to Peru's economic development in the foreseeable future and would tie up large quantities of capital for a long time.

The final option, and the one actually chosen, was to maximise the resources for jungle exploration by joining forces with private investors entering under contract. This had the advantage of mobilising resources into oil exploration on a large scale and left open the possibility that Petroperú's own future would be secured by major exploration successes. On the other hand, as became clearer over time, there were also major drawbacks. It is likely that there would have been difficulties had Petroperú proved less successful in discovering oil than the foreign contractors. Conversely, as actually did happen, Petroperú and, even more so, the whole Peruvian government, became over-optimistic as a result of several quick successes and the agency consequently became greatly over-extended. Moreover, there was a problem with the contracts themselves: the 1970s was a decade of dramatic change in the oil industry and contract terms which seemed reasonable in 1971 came to appear over-generous in 1974–5 and over-rigid by 1977. This, however, is to anticipate events.

At first, Petroperú's venture appeared to be crowned with success. Negotiations with Occidental Petroleum over the terms of a new, crude-oil-sharing, 'Peruvian model' contract were concluded in June 1971 and this contract was followed by a number of others in the years 1971–3.[9] By mid-1973, contracts had been signed for the exploration of sixteen 1-million-hectare blocs in the Selva and a further two off-shore. Moreover, Petroperú's initial oil explorations proved quite remarkably successful. Petroperú struck oil with its first well in November 1971 and again in February and June 1972.

These initial successes led to a wave of euphoria throughout Peru. As early as 12 December 1971, the *New York Times* correspondent reported 'a glow of optimism in official circles', and on 9 June 1972 the *Guardian* reported that 'flag waving Peruvians paraded in the streets of Lima on May 24, following reports that Petroperú had struck oil in its third test well near the tiny Indian village of Pavayacu'. Exploration came to look easier and success more certain than it had before or has done since. During the period before its first drilling, Petroperú had wisely stressed the difficulty and uncertainty attached to oil exploration as insurance against possible failure. G. Bischoff, a German geologist working under contract with Petroperú, noted in a Petroperú handout: 'if our first well achieves a positive result, we shall be very lucky. The world average success ratio is only one hole in nine. But a dry hole is not a wasted effort.'[10]

This abrupt change in mood was deliberately played up by certain members of the military government. Certainly the regime was only too keen to make the most of a genuinely important economic success but there may have been another motive as well. The collapse of the fishmeal industry, which took place in 1972, must seriously have worried the regime and threatened its access to external financial markets at a time when credit was being sought for a number of other major projects. Emphasis on oil must have seemed a natural response. In any case, by mid-1972, before there had been a single oil find of guaranteed commercial value, General Fernández Maldonado, the Minister of Mines and Energy, was issuing detailed estimates of future oil production as if they were certainties. Petroperú's former exploration manager later recalled: 'One reason why I left Petroperú was that I think the whole Peruvian oil play is extremely exaggerated for political reasons.'[11]

When the oil play did indeed prove to be 'extremely exaggerated for political reasons' subsequent disappointment was bitter. Petroperú, which in April 1974 was confident that it already had the capacity to produce 38,000 b/d from the Selva,[12] was in mid-1978 producing only 28,000 b/d from a potential capacity of 40,000 b/d. All but one of the Selva contractors had pulled out after failing to discover commercial quantities of oil and, were it not for the significant discoveries made by Occidental Petroleum, the whole exploration campaign would have become an utter fiasco. As it was, Petroperú had in mid-1978 already spent some $900m. on a trans-Andean pipeline which would, for some time at least, only be used at around 50% of capacity, and a further $500m. on exploration and development which would yield only a modest return. With the country as a whole in a confused and unsatisfactory financial situation in the years 1975–9, Petroperú's economic failures stood out – the major symbol of the shambles which the 'Peruvian Revolution' had become. Why had the outcome proved so bitter?

Petroperú in crisis 1975–9

A part of the reason, but only a part, lay in the disappointment of Amazonian geology, which flattered only to deceive. Petroperú found only one new commercially viable oil structure between 1974 and 1978 and the vast majority of the private contractors pulled out without finding commercial quantities of oil. All in all, some $300m. was spent by unsuccessful private contractors; only Occidental found commercial quantities of oil in the Selva and only Belco continued to be successful offshore. Against this, however, it should be noted that by mid-1978 Petroperú had itself found five commercially exploitable oilfields with a potential capacity of over 40,000 b/d, that Occidental had achieved a potential capacity of 120,000 b/d and was continuing with its investments and that much of the northern Selva remained largely unexplored.[13] Although the many failures in the area were certainly a disappointment, the full story of Petroperú's difficulties is much more complicated.

The other major 'single factor' explanation put forward for Petroperú's difficulties concerned the trans-Andean pipeline which, it was said, was far too costly to be justifed by the extra oil production which made it desirable. However, although this was certainly a bungled and expensive project, it also represents only a part of the real story. The decision to build the trans-Andean pipeline was apparently taken very quickly. As early as 6 June 1972, Decree Law 19435 declared that construction of a pipeline across the Andes was a national priority. It appears that the initial decision came from Petroperú itself,[14] which calculated that a pipeline across the Andes would not only be cheaper than exporting down the Amazon and to the main Brazilian population centres, but also that the latter was only feasible for very small-scale production. Although there was certainly some unwillingness to become too closely associated with Brazil,[15] it appears that there was no real alternative to a trans-Andean pipeline if production was to be undertaken seriously. Nevertheless, there were distinct signs of over-optimism in the pipeline plans; the earliest estimates put the 'break-even' point for a trans-Andean pipeline at the suspiciously low level of 70,000 b/d.

Moreover, there can be no doubt that the prospect of a trans-Andean pipeline was regarded with enthusiasm by the military itself and that the matter was subsequently largely taken out of the hands of Petroperú. As Stepan points out:

In informal conversations, various military officers stressed geopolitical reasons for wanting to invest heavily in the Amazon region: it was a nearly unin-habited area of Peru with borders with Ecuador, from whom Peru had won territory in 1941, and with Brazil, who, Peru feared, harbored expansionist intentions. Development of oil would bring people, roads and, because of the rough terrain, extensive use of helicopters. Since the state could give the Peruvian air force a virtual monopoly of helicopter transportation this would subsidize the expansion of Peru's helicopter force. Peru's air force helicopter squadrons in the Amazon increased from one to five from 1971 to 1974 and a Bell helicopter representative estimated that the Peruvian air force (even before a planned $30 million of scheduled investment) was already the 'world's fourth or fifth largest commercial helicopter operator'.[16]

While the pipeline itself will be discussed again below, this last point comes close to the most important reason for Petroperú's difficulties after 1973–4. The agency itself was increasingly losing its indepen-dence and was more and more required to accommodate itself to var-ious demands put forward by other interests which, in the long run at least, were very damaging to the operation of efficient public enter-prise. One of the first examples of this came in 1973, when the Peru-vian air force was given the right to provide inefficient helicopter 'ser-vice' for the various private companies (as well as for Petroperú) or to take a 10% cut if it gave permission to the contracting companies to make their own arrangements.[17]

Given the pervading secrecy of the Peruvian government, it is dif-ficult to trace in detail the decline of Petroperú's position after 1974. Nevertheless, an important clue is provided by the report of a working

committee on nationalised industries whose findings on Petroperú were
sent to the rest of the government in December 1976. According to
this, the agency suffered from delays in getting import permits from
the Ministry of Mines and Energy, and similar delays in securing permission to go ahead with any projects. There were also delays in getting permission to hire qualified personnel, and Petroperú's budget
could no longer be modified without the consent of the Planning Institute and the Finance Ministry. Petroperú's managers were tied down
for long periods in trying to satisfy the voracious demands for information that came from the rest of the government. The division of
responsibility within the agency was unsatisfactory; relations between
the directorate and the management were ill defined and the directors
were rotated after a year in nearly every case.[18] Moreover, given the
management's lack of control over personnel or salaries, it had no way
of motivating the workforce. Salaries were fixed by the government
with ceilings which were determined bureaucratically and set too low
to attract real talent. Overmanning was estimated at around 20–30%
and, as a result of almost total job security, 'there are signs of careless-
ness and a lack of responsibility among the workforce'.[19] To all of these
obstacles must be added that of a financial position that was extremely
unsatisfactory. Given this severe and all-pervading set of difficulties,
one major explanation emerges for the failures of Petroperú: the government as a whole had largely ceased to care whether or not this, or
the other state industries, were successful or not. The political reasons
for this will be discussed further below; first it will be helpful to discuss
the consequences.[20]

If we assume that the operating efficiency of a company is low, then
any discussion of its problems in purely financial terms may be of limited value. This is because *ex post* measurements of cost will reflect
inefficiency as much as bad commercial judgement. For this reason,
some of the criticism of Petroperú's trans-Andean pipeline may be mis-
placed. Construction costs were probably higher than necessary and it
is certain that the subsidiary projects (feeder lines, etc.) were badly
timed, with the result that in its early stages throughput was far less
than might have been achieved. For example, as late as January 1980
Petroperú was producing only 28,000 b/d from its jungle fields
although this could have been raised to 41,000 b/d from existing discoveries had drilling not been delayed by lack of funds. However, a
lack of funds may indicate operational inefficiency as much as financial starvation.

Even bearing these qualifications in mind, however, we must conclude that Petroperú's financial environment was allowed to deteriorate to such an extent during the 1974–8 period that many of its difficulties could be measured in these terms alone. To examine the full extent of this we need to go beyond Petroperú's accounts (which are not audited externally) and consider broader evidence.[21] To begin with, there is the question of price. As we saw in chapter 12, retail gasoline prices in Peru had long been kept at low levels and this policy was continued after the IPC takeover. At first, the low and declining world price appeared to make this a feasible proposition, but the 1970–3 world price increases put Petroperú's finances under increasing strain. As early as 26 March 1973, one Peruvian observer pointed out that 'the fact is that this circle according to which petroleum subsidies increase year after year is one of our most important economic irrationalities. In a country in which inflation is running at or around ten per cent per annum, the oil industry is keeping its prices at 1959 levels.'[22] At the end of 1973 Petroperú's application for permission to increase domestic prices was rejected and a rather half-baked rationing scheme was substituted. The Velasco regime was too concerned by the need to avoid antagonising its supporters in the Lima lower middle and working classes to allow so unpopular a measure to go through.[23]

Gasoline prices were not increased until mid-1975, after which the price changes were sharp and dramatic. Between July 1975 and the same month in 1976, premium gasoline prices more than quintupled in local currency terms and they doubled again in the following year. In international terms, prices also increased but by less, because of the devaluations into which the government was forced during this period. In October 1976, however, Petroperú complained that it was still selling locally at a loss.[24] By this time Petroperú's financial situation was so chaotic and its operating efficiency so low that even major new price increases were barely sufficient to solve the problems.[25] The *Andean Report* in July 1978 could quote a government official as saying that 'We need a gasoline price of S/250 a gallon [present price S/125] to wipe that [deficit] out. Petroperú is a major problem. It is incredibly inefficient. It's our local version of the Argentine railways.' As late as June 1975 the domestic price had been S/10 a gallon.

Petroperú, on the other hand, put much of the blame for this state of affairs on taxation provisions. In 1976 it had complained that 'Petroperú is subject to a series of fiscal regulations which daily complicate its activities, especially given the lack of definition which exists between the application of these regulations and the Oil Law 11780.'[26] The crowning illogicality in Petroperú's tax structure lay in the way it was taxed over and above its income from the private contractor companies. According to the contracts signed with Occidental and Belco, Petroperú would pay taxes for both parties in return for a share of the crude oil produced. As a result of a ruling made within the Peruvian government in 1974, the government defined Petroperú's tax liability in such a way that it became liable for tax both on behalf of the private companies and on the crude oil it received from the companies; in other words, it was taxed at over 100%. The eventual rate, in fact, turned out to be around 130%. Even this, however, was not a complete explanation of the problem. There was also the fact that during the years in which the domestic price of gasoline was held down 1974–6, Petroperú theoretically received monetary compensation from the government for its loss of income. This money was in fact never paid and Petroperú attempted to resolve the situation by short-term borrowing on the international market.

By mid-1978, therefore, Petroperú's financial position was bordering on the hopeless. In August the *Andean Report* stated that the company owed some $26m. in taxes and had well over $400m. of short-term debt, 'some of which has been confused into the Banco de la Nación accounts'. In March 1979 it had become clear that Petroperú's foreign debt was around $1,000m. to some 250 different foreign banks.[27] In that month Petroperú's cheques were finally 'bounced' by the Banco de la Nación, and the *Andean Report* commented:

Every major entity involved gives a different version of events, often diametrically opposed to each other, but it is certain that the corporation's chaotic finances have already seriously affected output in the jungle, with the loss of tens of millions of dollars worth of production, a three-year delay – at least – in badly needed new exploration, and millions of dollars more in extra financing charges.[28]

Finally, in May 1979, most of Petroperú's debts were written off by the central government.

It can be seen that Petroperú's problems stemmed from general ineptitude on the part of both the agency and the government as a whole rather than from any single, specific blunder. The Amazon venture may have been the occasion for the near-collapse of the company, but it was hardly its cause. Indeed, according to an estimate in the *Andean Report* in April 1977, Petroperú's Amazon venture should have proved at least marginally profitable. By this time, the trans-Andean pipeline had been completed at a cost of around $900m. and a further $400m. had been spent on feeder lines and general exploration. Against this, the company had discovered 260 million barrels of oil in its own bloc and had a right to half of Occidental's discovery of 160 million barrels, to make a total of 340 million. The cost, at $3.82 a barrel, was well below the world price and, even allowing for borrowing costs, should have allowed some profit. Moreover, as the article did not point out, around $150m. toward the pipeline cost would have been met by the tariff for moving Occidental's own oil. Admittedly Petroperú's estimates of mid-1979 looked less sanguine. It put its 'proven reserves' at only 174.2 million barrels (having already produced around 25 million) and Occidental's at 246.9 million (of which Petroperú had half, or 123.4 million), leaving 297.6 million still to be produced.[29] Nevertheless, there could be little doubt that there was more oil still to be found in the area.

Moreover, since the thrust of this argument is that Petroperú's problems stemmed from its inefficiency due, in turn, mainly to bureaucratic interference rather than to any single mistake or piece of bad luck, there is no reason to regard *ex post facto* costs unambiguously. Much the same can be said about the costs of supplying gasoline and other products to the domestic market at very low prices until mid-1975. The real reasons for these handicaps were political rather than geological or even economic. For one thing, between the illness of President Velasco in February 1973 and the holding of Constituent Assembly elections in June 1978, the state apparatus served more as a battleground over which rival factions competed than as an instrument devoted to a common purpose. Between 1973 and Velasco's overthrow by Morales Bermúdez in August 1975 there was a struggle for the succession in which the goals of economic management were largely submerged by the rivalry of competing groups. There was also a connected political crisis following the failure of the regime's earlier efforts to stimulate the desired form of popular participation. Moreover, after damaging anti-regime riots in the south of Peru in November 1973, the government was in no mood to risk a still more damaging series of riots in Lima of a kind frequently triggered off by increases in gasoline prices. It also appears that the Finance Ministry largely lost its grip on the bureaucracy after the departure of Morales Bermúdez at the end of 1973. Borrowing was already a central part of the government's strategy and, after this, a large number of loans came to be contracted, more or less irresponsibly, by a large number of government agencies, of which Petroperú was the most important.[30] With the accession to power of Morales Bermúdez, some reform appeared likely but effective changes were held back for a long time both by the growing economic crisis (in evidence after the middle of 1975) and by the insecurities of the President's own position, which were only gradually resolved.[31]

There is also a further set of political factors which are of a longer-term nature. Until 1968 there was very little state enterprise in Peru. With the exception of a few instances, which were quickly reversed, the economic history of Peru has been a story of private enterprise.[32] The Velasco government, therefore, which by September 1976 had set up 48 wholly state-owned companies, of which Petroperú was clearly the largest, marked an almost complete break with tradition. State enterprise was now to be the new engine of Peruvian growth. But with so little experience, it was by no means clear how this was to work out in practice. At first, as we have seen, the government adopted a policy which allowed a wide range of autonomy for public sector companies and Petroperú, which had taken over IPC's assets and organisation, was well placed to make the most of its freedom. It was further encouraged to do so by its initial profitability and, later, by the ease with which Peru could secure external financing. However, this experiment with public enterprise autonomy was not an unqualified success, particularly in the case of organisations which were less well prepared than Petroperú. As the *Andean Report* reflected, 'Between 1971 and 1973 there tended to be more money available than there were properly prepared projects to spend it on . . . [Consequently] big ministry buildings were especially in vogue despite specific overall planning instructions to the contrary.'[33] Those projects which did go ahead, notably the Amazon oil exploration venture, did so largely because the enterprises involved were the best organised and not because the projects were of the highest priority. Indeed, as we have seen, Petroperú did not even seek overall government approval before beginning its exploration in the area. Conversely, other projects which might have provided more evident benefit for the Peruvian economy were held back because the various enterprises involved were not yet prepared to carry them out.

In 1972 the Council of Ministers considered a proposal from the Finance Ministry and the Planning Institute to establish a much more centralised form of control over the economy, but this was eventually rejected.[34] Even so, however, Petroperú did find itself in conflict with the Finance Ministry over some issues, notably over how far it was free to raise loans internationally. Even more important, the Ministry began to take advantage of various opportunities to exert control over Petroperú and relations between the two deteriorated quite sharply. Petroperú began to lose out in important inter-bureaucratic conflicts with consequences which became clear in the 1976 government report. In a sense the company had the worst of both worlds; rather than face a strong and effective planning agency, it lost its effectiveness through a series of *ad hoc* decisions made in different parts of the bureaucracy.

In 1974 Peruvian public enterprises were badly shaken by the government's attack on EPSA (Empresa Pública de Servicios Agropecuarios, the state food marketing agency). After an alleged corruption scandal, which appears to have involved financial incompetence rather than criminal behaviour, the agency suffered a police raid and wholesale arrests. Although this case did not relate directly to the oil industry, Cleaves and Scurrah note that

a nervous disorder dubbed *epsitis* spread through all public enterprises. The symptoms of this disease were excessive prudence and unwillingness to take risks, inflexibility and demands for legal justification for even the most trivial decisions, and in general a reinforcement of the conservative attitudes associated with the traditional ministries.[35]

During the same period Petroperú appeared to be losing control over some of the functions which it had exercised previously. There is evidence that the Planning Institute and other sections within the government were preparing to renegotiate the exploration contracts which Petroperú had already signed with the companies. These contracts came to seem unnecessarily generous.[36] Yet this new control unfortunately turned out to be 'bureaucratic' only in the worst sense of the word. It is striking that, at a time when Petroperú faced major delays in getting import permits for the capital goods required for its investment programme, it was able to run up hundreds of millions of dollars of short-term credits on imports of oil itself. Such government control as existed came to reflect political conflict and empire-building within the bureaucracy rather than any clear perception of governmental priorities.

While the balance of power within the government may have shifted excessively towards the nationalised industries in the years after the coup, therefore, it shifted at least as far in the other direction in the years after 1974. By 1976 it had clearly come to be recognised within the government that the move had gone too far. In that year President Morales Bermúdez was again telling CADE that:

Public enterprises need to demonstrate their efficiency and intensify their efforts towards achieving their best results. Executives and workers together need to assume the responsibility of showing the capacity of nationalised industry and should act according to the same criteria of profitability as prevails in the private sector.

A public enterprise must not become an administrative and bureaucratic entity, but should be a dynamic and aggressive organisation which has the ability to intervene actively in the market and compete successfully against other enterprises.[37]

Unfortunately, vested interests and red tape had, by this time, become so entrenched within the bureaucracy that it took almost another two years before these words were followed by action.

Occidental Petroleum and the private sector

As we have seen, 15 of the foreign oil contractors exploring the Amazon spent over $300m. between them and found nothing of commercial value. On the other hand, Occidental Petroleum encountered a number of important successes and by 1979 was able to produce oil at an average of 120,000 b/d. Moreover, Occidental's position in Peru was extremely profitable. The 1971 contract under which it had entered Peru specified that any crude oil found should be split 50–50 between Occidental and Petroperú, with Occidental's share being tax free. These terms seemed quite favourable to Peru in 1971, but as the world price increased, so the balance came to favour the company. Thus, in 1979 Occidental's annual profits were reported in the authoritative *Andean Report* at $207.5m. on an investment which, at the end of 1978, was reported by the company to have reached $327.6m.[38] There can be no doubt that Occidental had been able to recoup its initial investment very quickly indeed.

One consequence of this was that Occidental was increasingly willing to expand its activities in Peru. As early as 1973 it had shown an interest in extending its exploration area, but its offer was rejected by Petroperú.[39] In mid-1976 Occidental again approached the Peruvian government and declared itself interested in exploring further one of the contract areas abandoned by another company, Union Oil. Occidental believed that the heavy oil which the Union consortium had found but believed to be uncommercial could be mixed with the lighter crude of Occidental's own bloc and then extracted. A contract was signed in April 1978. Occidental seems to have been given the terms which it sought – easier than those which applied to its own bloc – and promised to invest $150m. in the area over a period of four years. A successful discovery early in 1979, which included light as well as heavy oil, suggests that this contract may be of considerable significance. Moreover, Occidental also formed a partnership with Bridas of Argentina (84% Occidental, 16% Bridas) and signed a contract with Petroperú in April 1978 for a secondary recovery project in the coastal oilfields (with the exception of La Brea); the consortium agreed to invest at least $150m.

Occidental's unique position within Peru gave the company considerable bargaining power. Even more important, the renegotiation of terms that might well have been expected under these circumstances was delayed by two main factors. The first was the demoralisation of Petroperú, for reasons which we have already considered. As one well placed observer put it, Petroperú wanted to alter the terms but 'they can't tell a good deal from a bad deal and don't know how to negotiate'. The second was the extremely difficult position of the Peruvian economy as a whole in 1977–9. During this time, the Peruvian government's overall financial position was little short of desperate. Peru was preserved from a technical default on its foreign debt in early 1978 only by an advance on its taxes from Occidental. Under such circumstances the government could not afford even the slightest disruption to its oil production and could therefore not easily renegotiate terms.

There was, however, some advantage for Peru in the decision made in 1978 by the US revenue authorities that the crude-oil-sharing agreements between Peru and Occidental and Belco Petroleum (which had a small offshore oil operation) did not permit full tax relief from the US government. When, in late 1979, the Peruvian government seriously began its efforts at renegotiation, the companies were in a mood to compromise provided that any new arrangements made them eligible for such relief. By then, increased oil production and a general recovery of international mineral prices had brought about something of a recovery in Peru's foreign exchange position. Meanwhile, the military government was anxious (as, for that matter, were the private companies) to prevent the oil contracts from becoming an issue in the presidential elections scheduled for May 1980. As a result, Silva Ruete, the Eco-

nomics and Finance Minister, and Manuel Moreyra and Alonso Polar
of the Central Bank began renegotiation with the companies in late
1979. In March 1980 arrangements were more or less imposed upon
the companies which subjected them to profits taxes as well as the
existing 50% share of their crude oil production.[40] The incoming government of Fernando Belaúnde (who took power in July 1980) felt that
these terms were too severe and would inhibit future investment.
Thus, in December 1980 further legal changes (Decree Law 23231)
were made offering tax credits to companies which stepped up their
investment in oil exploration. In March 1981 an exploration contract
was signed with Superior Oil and it had become clear that a further
significant increase in private foreign investment was about to take
place.

Concluding reflections

There was a limited recovery in Petroperú's financial position after
1979. There was a major debt rescheduling exercise in 1979–80 and
Petroperú benefited further from a World Bank loan in 1980 and from
the effects of the contract renegotiations of the same year which
removed some of its own tax burden. Moreover, as can be seen from
table 20.4, Peru's oil pricing system was rationalised as other oil product prices were increased in real terms so as to catch up with the very
heavy gasoline price increases of 1975–7. Even so, however, the World
Bank in March 1981 calculated that Peruvian domestic prices were
only around one half of their international equivalents, involving a
total subsidy of $1,000m. a year, or around 4.5% of Peruvian GNP.[41]

After around 1979, when the worst of the economic crisis had
passed, Peruvian governments also began to turn their attention to
improving the level of technical knowledge within Petroperú. A 1978
law increasing managerial freedom to pay high salaries to maintain staff
was largely frustrated by the dreadful economic situation in Peru as a
whole which led to a considerable brain drain, notably to Venezuela.
The *Andean Report* later noted that Petroperú had lost most of its best
technical staff during this period.[42] Under these circumstances, governments began to plan joint venture arrangements which would
enable Petroperú to acquire technical expertise from private sector partners. In 1980 the secondary recovery project covering the north-
western oilfields (originally signed with Occidental and Bridas in
1978) was renegotiated as a joint venture and the Peruvian government

Table 20.4 *Prices of selected petroleum derivatives 1977–81*
(US *cents per gallon*)

	June 1977	June 1978	June 1979	June 1980	March 1981
Gasoline (95 octane)	137.7	93.9	86.6	91.5	108.6
Gasoline (84 octane)	93.9	81.0	75.5	75.6	87.9
Kerosene (domestic)	12.5	9.7	8.9	10.6	17.1
Diesel oil	21.3	32.4	35.5	40.3	53.0
Residual fuel oil	13.8	24.0	24.4	27.4	33.0

Source: IMF, 'Peru: Staff Report for the 1980 Article IV Constitution' (April, 1981), p. 25.

also negotiated, this time unsuccessfully, to take a minority share of the Superior Oil bloc. In 1981 Petroperú was turned into a legal liability company which further increased its freedom to recruit and maintain the best technical staff.

These steps, as well as the 1980 contract renegotiations, went some way to offsetting the setbacks received by the Peruvian oil industry during the mid-1970s. Moreover, by 1981 Peru was an oil-exporting country with every chance of increasing its oil production well above the 200,000 b/d level reached at the time. Oil was now Peru's main export and the vast majority of the surplus generated by oil production remained in the country. Moreover, much of the estimated $3,000m. invested in Amazonian oil exploration and development has yielded a return in technical knowledge and physical assets which will lower the cost of future oil development.

Even so, however, the period as a whole could hardly be regarded as a success for Peru when set against what might have been possible. It is worth discussing why this was so. At a subjective level, it is necessary to emphasise the inexperience and over-confidence of the Peruvian policymakers. The decision to undertake exploration in the Amazon was probably justified on balance, but there could be no real defence for the government's persistent over-optimism regarding the oil finds, for its policy of continuing to subsidise gasoline at almost ruinous cost to Petroperú, for its infliction on Petroperú of one bureaucratic control after another until its most talented staff had either left or been reduced to powerlessness, and for its general lack of financial prudence – in short, for its failure to consider seriously what the needs of an efficient state company might be. Moreover, its distrust of foreign companies in the early 1970s led, not to policies of determined nationalism, but to indecision and eventually to dependence upon the one significant foreign oil company willing to brave the political conditions and invest substantially in Amazonia.

At another level, there was conflict between political will and economic capacity. In political and diplomatic terms, the Peruvian government's nationalisation of IPC was a clear success, as was its nationalistic approach to a number of other issues. Short-term political considerations, however, were not a subsitute for – and often operated against – the long-term needs of any effective alternative to the almost extreme laissez-faire policies which had prevailed in the past. Moreover, the fact that the setting up of Petroperú, and a greatly expanded state sector in general, marked a sharp break with previous tradition and not (as had been the case with Petrobrás in Brazil) a gradual evolution of an existing pattern of state control, added to the problems. Having perhaps overestimated the political problems associated with 'changing the structures' of the pre-1968 economy, the government became over-confident and careless of the problems of building up new enterprises. In the resulting political vacuum, it became inevitable that normal bureaucratic vices – red tape, unwillingness to assume responsibility, and lack of internal co-ordination – flourished.

It remains true, however, that these attributes were seen at their worst in the context of Petroperú's Amazon venture. The Amazon basin might almost have been set as a trap for the unwary; geological structures were flattering, early discoveries were promising and a number of exploring companies – by no means only Petroperú – were expensively deceived.[43] If the early promises of oil abundance had been realised, it is possible that Petroperú might have taken on board all the difficulties that were instead to lead it to crisis. Pemex, after all, has always sold its domestic oil cheaply and survived some very difficult early years on the basis of its oil wealth, and Petrobrás, with its strength downstream, survived an extremely difficult period in the early 1960s. One might argue that environmental conditions both punished more severely and contributed significantly toward those faults which existed in Petroperú but which could also be found in some measure in most other state (and even private) oil companies. Neither radical over-optimism nor extreme disillusionment make for efficient economic management.

21

YPFB and the development of oil in Bolivia

YPFB came into existence following a decree law issued by General Toro in 1936 and took on real importance with the nationalisation of Standard Oil in the following year. For the next 20 years it achieved slow but steady growth until, by the mid-1950s, it had become an important prop to the Bolivian economy, although its scale of operation was still insignificant by international standards. In the next decade, the company suffered from the consequences of Bolivia's dependence on the USA and from competition with Gulf Oil. In 1969, however, YPFB underwent a major expansion with the nationalisation of Gulf and it thus became a significant earner of foreign exchange for the first time. Its economic importance increased further with the completion of a natural gas export pipeline to Argentina in 1972 and with the world price increases of 1973–4. Continuing financial difficulties, however, and the vagaries of Bolivian geology contributed to an increase in problems for the agency. Serious difficulties became apparent in 1977 and have since become increasingly pressing. It is possible that YPFB is once more heading for crisis.

During the whole period YPFB has had to operate in a political environment that could best be described as difficult. Bolivia could never be described as genuinely politically stable for, even when there was continuity in La Paz, there were frequent upheavals in the provinces and severe constraints on many forms of economic policymaking. At times, moreover, turnover of government in La Paz was high and unpredictable; there were, for example, five different presidents of Bolivia in the years 1969–71. At almost all times, therefore, it may be said that the conduct of government in Bolivia was largely dictated by short-term political considerations and there was little opportunity for a long-term strategy to emerge. Thus, YPFB's own objectives were frequently frustrated by unpredictable government and there were times when the agency itself became involved in politics.

451

It is also true that the Bolivian economy has often, although not always, severely limited the resources available to YPFB, although there have been some important recent changes in this respect. Although the unsatisfactory nature of many Bolivian statistics makes evaluation difficult, it may be said that between 1936 and 1952 the economy was basically stagnant, though with considerable fluctuation depending on the world market price of tin, which was Bolivia's single main export. Between 1952 and 1964 this position did not change significantly, although heavy aid from Washington partly compensated for serious problems in the tin mines and the revolution significantly improved the distribution of income. In the years after 1964, however, there has been an uneven but unmistakable increase in Bolivian prosperity based on rising world prices for Bolivia's two major exports, tin and (since 1966) hydrocarbons and on the development of the province of Santa Cruz. Consequently, in the middle 1970s the country enjoyed several years of considerable real growth and took on some appearance of prosperity, although the fragility of the economy is very apparent.

The Bolivian hydrocarbons industry could be described as moderately promising by international standards. Certainly Bolivian oil and gas are not of Mexican or Venezuelan, let alone of Middle Eastern, proportions, but Bolivia has for a long time been believed to have export potential, if only because of the smallness of its domestic market. Conversely, the small size of the domestic market has posed problems, both by raising the question of scale economies in acute form and by preventing a state company historically based on supplying the home market from generating the resources necessary for large-scale exploration. Indeed, it may be said that whereas until the mid-1950s the main obstacle to the development of Bolivia's petroleum potential was inadequate transportation, since then it has been insufficient discovery of new oil.

The emergence of YPFB 1936–52

YPFB's infancy was very long and its growth very slow. Standard Oil of Bolivia, which was nationalised in 1937, was barely a going concern at that time since its production was minimal and its transportation facilities practically non-existent. However, while Bolivian oil production did not decline with the nationalisation, neither did it expand rapidly. Some progress was made, particularly after Standard Oil turned over its maps and geological data to Bolivia as part of the 1941 compensation agreement, and production of crude oil doubled between 1936 and 1948; in the latter year, however, it reached only just over 1,250 b/d.

Serious development began when Washington, as part of the compensation agreement of 1941, offered a loan to Bolivia, a part of which was to be allocated to the petroleum industry once La Paz had agreed to support the return of foreign investment into oil exploration. YPFB's original plan was then modified to fit in with the government's overall objective of developing the Santa Cruz area. Nevertheless, although implementation was delayed by the war and by various political factors, the plan was put into effect by the late 1940s. Its main features were the construction of a small oil refinery at Cochabamba at a cost of just over $4m., and of a pipeline to link Cochabamba with the Camiri oilfield (at a cost of $6.55m.). The need for further drilling and other minor items brought the full cost of the programme to $14.15m.,[1] of which the Export–Import Bank was to provide $8.5m., the Bolivian Central Bank a further $5m. and Williams Bros. $0.65m. in trade credits.

This programme was put into effect (the pipeline was built by Williams Bros. and the refineries by Foster Wheeler) but was modified by the government in 1947. For political reasons, a small refinery was constructed at Sucre. This was only the first of many political pressures on the agency; it raised the cost of the programme to $20m., with proportionate damage to YPFB's accounts, and also forced upon the company an unusable refinery, which could not be moved (because of local political pressure) until the 1950s.

Partly as a result of this, and also because of low domestic oil prices, YPFB soon found itself in what was to be a characteristic position of technical adequacy but financial near-bankruptcy. As early as 1947 the British Ambassador reported of his visit to the oilfields: 'I readily admit that I was agreeably surprised by the conditions prevailing at the Bolivian oilfields at Camiri and Sanandita. Organisation seems to be very satisfactory and the young engineers in charge gave me the impression of knowing their job, while there was no doubt as to their keenness in regard thereto.'[2] Nevertheless, YPFB's financial position continued to be difficult.[3]

This considerable gap between technical and financial capacity was also pointed out by Eder. He reported (of the mid-1950s) that YPFB's technical abilities generally stemmed from the fact that it retained many of Standard Oil's old employees, including the American-trained exploration manager, Hinojosa. Indeed, Standard's 'value to the YPFB is demonstrated by the fact that there is not a single area that has been brought into production by YPFB up to [1956] . . . that has not previously been laid out for drilling, or drilled, by Standard Oil. Modern drilling and production methods account for the rise in production since 1954.'[4] However, according to Eder, YPFB was simply too small to generate an adequate base for financial expansion. YPFB's barter treaties with Brazil and Argentina, signed in 1938 to enable it to export its oil from Santa Cruz (see chapter 9), later appeared highly disadvantageous: 'pipelines were purchased from Brazil at prices higher than they could have been bought elsewhere, the cost being disguised by the exchange rate, and by arrangements for the purchase of Bolivian oil in "treaty dollars" that could only be exchanged for Brazilian goods at exorbitant prices'.[5] And, as for Argentina, exports were 'payable in treaty dollars so that this trade must be looked upon as a subtraction from the nation's wealth rather than as a source of income'.[6] These judgements may be unduly harsh, considering that until the mid-1950s Bolivia had few other sources of disposal for its oil and transportation costs were high, but it is clear that these export markets were far less advantageous to Bolivia than open-market trade would have been.

Ever since 1946 the Bolivian government had been in favour of bringing direct foreign investment back into oil exploration.[7] It had high hopes of future oil production, as a YPFB memorandum of 1947 made clear:

The development of the petroleum resources of Bolivia appears to be of principal importance in the immediate salvation of the economy of the country. It is believed that Bolivia is now in a position to embark upon a new economic cycle which may be called the Petroleum Cycle . . . geological structures containing vast deposits of petroleum consist of a wide band of the eastern slope of the Cordilleras.[8]

However, actual foreign investment was not so easy to attract. In 1947 the government approved new legislation providing for the setting up of mixed government – company operations and this law, approved by the Chamber, finally cleared the Senate in 1950. According to *World Oil* in 1952, however, 'preliminary talks have taken place between YPFB officials and US companies but without result'.[9] Nor did the Bolivian authorities have a great deal of success with their other objective, which was to secure a further loan from the Export–Import

Bank.[10] Further developments in this area were then cut short by the Bolivian Revolution of 1952.

The rise and decline of YPFB 1952–69

At the time of the 1952 revolution, YPFB had set up what was technically a reasonably successful oil company. Its exploration expertise was adequate to increase production considerably without the assistance of foreign technicians.[11] It had two modern, although small, refineries: Sucre, which had come onstream in 1949 at a final cost of $4.7m., and Cochabamba, which had come onstream in 1951 at a cost of $6.6m. During the 1950s it completed a fairly extensive pipeline network which linked Cochabamba with La Paz and the Camiri oilfield with Santa Cruz, thus finally connecting the producing areas of the southeast to the main centres of Bolivian consumption.

Financially, the revolution and the consequent hyperinflation let YPFB off the hook. In an unstable financial environment, YPFB was in a favoured position since it could borrow dollars from the Central Bank at the highly over-valued official rate. Thus, 'as an example of unrealistic accounting, in 1955 YPFB bought 20 tank cars, worth over US $15,000 each, and paid for them through the Central Bank at the *boliviano* equivalent of US $675 each'.[12]

Consequently, YPFB's real output increased sharply between 1952 and 1956. In fact, YPFB drilled six wells in 1948, five in 1949, five in 1950, three in 1951, but nine in 1953 and thirteen in 1954. During the early 1950s output rose sixfold (from 1,441 b/d in 1952 to 8,758 b/d in 1956) and Bolivia achieved self-sufficiency in 1955, despite the considerable increase in consumption brought about by price controls. At the same time, YPFB's employees grew in number from 2,489 in 1952 to 4,349 in 1956. Moreover, during this period YPFB's geology department was reorganised and it began, for the first time, to make a general survey of the whole of Bolivia.[13]

Despite this success, however, there appears to have been no hesitation on the part of the MNR leaders in deciding to bring back foreign investment into oil. This was clear from the MNR plan of 1953 and stemmed from President Paz's concern for rapid economic growth and his desire to diversify the Bolivian economy away from tin, over which the central government had largely lost control after the revolution. Moreover, the American Embassy was a powerful advocate of a liberal oil code (see chapter 3), which in any case stemmed from the logic of the situation. YPFB had invested heavily by Bolivian standards and had achieved some success, but it was still leagues away from the scale of operation that might have been expected from a multinational.

It has been reported that this favourable attitude to foreign investment was reflected within YPFB itself.[14] In fact, Mariaca suggests that there was always some opposition to the terms of the 1955 code (mainly with regard to the territory opened up) within the technical sector of YPFB. However, with the President's brother in charge of the organisation and in secure control at that time, it would have been very difficult for any such opposition to have been effective.

Under the terms of the code, concessions were given to a number of companies, including Gulf, Shell and a number of independents. However, of these only Gulf was successful. Indeed, there was a great deal of private exploration and considerable losses were sustained by particular companies. Thus, the argument heard subsequently from YPFB, that the private contractors had taken all the best areas in Bolivia, while understandable, does not seem to have been heard a great deal at the time. There was, however, one exception. This concerned the Madrejones area, where, according to YPFB, it was necessary to contract out the area as the result of a lack of revenue.[15] This contract proved to have little economic significance.

In the 1950s critics of the oil code (notably Almaraz)[16] fastened onto the Madrejones contract as being the one which, since it involved yielding territory which YPFB had already explored, would do the most damage to the state company. However, it is interesting that Mariaca Bilbao, when on the board of YPFB, was willing to inaugurate the Madrejones well and defend the contract terms in public.[17]

There is evidence that YPFB's attitude towards the government was changed less by the oil code than by the economic stabilisation programme which was put into force in 1956. Until then, as we have seen, YPFB was in a relatively privileged position and George Jackson Eder (the American representative on the Stabilisation Council) set out to restrict its spending, along with that of the rest of the government. According to Eder's own account, YPFB came to the Stabilisation Council in 1956 with two proposals for the fiscal year 1957: the high estimate of YPFB's necessary expenditure was $25m., and the lower estimate, 'pared to the bone', was $14m. YPFB was given $10.8m., and a further $1.8m. to import Aviation Gasoline for the national airline.[18]

There is no doubt that YPFB resisted these restrictions whatever way it could, sometimes with the connivance of members of the government. Thus, at different times, YPFB sent a formal note to the Council stating that it was not responsible for the consequences of its budgetary curtailment, it contracted 'one of its largest suppliers' to offer five-year credit terms on its purchases, it refused to rationalise its accounting procedures[19] and it sought presidential support for an arrangement that would earmark to the company the money earned by the government from the sale of concession rights to private companies. When Eder complained to Siles Zuazo (President, 1956–60) about this arrangement, the latter told him that he had wanted to keep these payments secret, but could not avoid making them 'for political reasons'.[20]

However, despite its struggles, YPFB's position worsened sharply. It suffered not only from the Stabilisation Council's measures but also because the government dared not pass all of these on to the consumer in full and consequently used YPFB as a kind of buffer. Price increases which had been accepted by the Council were not put through as a result of trade union opposition. At the end of 1956:

YPFB had been instructed by the President (without consultation with the Council) that it would be permissible to raise gasoline prices, but not prices for kerosene or fuel oil. YPFB was consequently trying to work out new price scales and estimates in the hope that it could balance its budget under these conditions. Later, President Siles gave orders that kerosene prices must actually be cut Bs 50 a liter.[21]

Moreover, in 1957:

the Council had agreed to a single 3 per cent tax on all gasoline and fuel oil sales, eliminating the prior myriad taxes earmarked for political cells, labour unions and other purposes. In point of fact, the YPFB people stated, the earmarked taxes had not been abolished and YPFB's taxes were running at the rate of Bs 2,591 millions per annum instead of the Bs 1,080 million budgeted. The government would not permit YPFB to pass the taxes on to the consumers.[22]

YPFB also suffered from the fact that certain other state agencies, notably the mines, were frequently behind in their payments.

Splits within YPFB could be seen clearly for the first time over the question of the Arica pipeline. This was an export pipeline built from the south of Bolivia to the Pacific coast of Chile. It was to be built by YPFB to provide a new outlet for Bolivian oil production, although Bolivia did not have the oil reserves to fill it. The original pipeline cost $11m. and was partially financed by a $5m. loan from Gulf Oil. Gulf, however, would not only earn interest on the loan (8–9% p.a.) but would also have the right to use the completed line at a fairly low price as and when its discoveries permitted. It is easy to see why Gulf was interested in the arrangement, but not so easy to see YPFB's motives for agreement. Here, the fullest account is provided by Mariaca.

According to Mariaca, the idea for the pipeline was originally Gulf's, and the government accepted its proposals with modifications.[23] They were then apparently put to the YPFB board of directors and accepted, although Mariaca asserts that the technical section of the company opposed the project. He suggests that the government, which wanted to free itself from dependence on Argentina and Brazil and to promote oil exports as a substitute for tin, induced YPFB to go ahead. In any case, the story suggests a division within YPFB between the management and those (who seemed to be connected with the technical side) whose main priority was to build up the level of reserves in order to encourage greater output in the future. The latter group, which included Mariaca, saw no objection to increasing exports to Brazil and Argentina, who paid in 'treaty dollars', rather than investing heavily in alternative outlets which the company might not be able to fill. The other section, which was dominant and which included José Paz, the President of YPFB and brother of the MNR leader, was eager to expand the oil industry by all means available.[24]

The problem with the expansionist strategy, however, was that YPFB was not able to discover the required quantities of oil. The increases in production in the 1950s were based on more modern and intensive development drilling rather than on exploration success. As we have seen, in 1954 YPFB did embark on an ambitious exploration effort, but this was largely aborted by the stabilisation measures and YPFB's consequent shortage of funds. This can be seen from table 21.1.

There was, perhaps, no answer to this dilemma. In a country geologically as difficult as Bolivia, YPFB was simply not big enough to be viable. It had been able to develop Standard Oil's initial discoveries and to use the resulting revenue to install pipelines and refineries to serve the domestic market, but even the Bolivian market would soon absorb enough oil to make further exploration work necessary; this YPFB would find difficult to afford. The expansion of 1952–6 had, after all, been possible only under exceptionally favourable financial circumstances. Moreover, it would have been highly expensive for YPFB to explore seriously without establishing proper export outlets. Cut-price supplies to Brazil and Argentina or small-scale production for the local

Table 21.1 YPFB's *income 1952–62*
(*m. current dollars*)

1952	5.3	1957	6.0
1953	6.2	1958	5.8
1954	6.0	1959	3.5
1955	11.2	1960	3.8
1956	11.8	1961	0.6
		1962	4.5
TOTAL	40.2	TOTAL	24.5

Source: Mariaca, *Mito y realidad,* p. 242.

market would hardly justify heavy exploration and development costs. The Arica pipeline was expensive and made scale economies even more important, but scale was exactly what YPFB lacked. As a result of these problems and Eder's financial squeeze, YPFB in the late 1950s went into decline.

The political consequences of this decline have been discussed elsewhere (chapters 4 and 13), and will not be analysed again here. By 1960 Washington became so concerned about nationalist feeling in Bolivia that the IDB agreed to grant limited quantities of aid to YPFB. Before administering this aid, the ICA sent De Golyer and McNaughton to report on the state of the oil industry in Bolivia. While this report was not wholly negative, it did criticise YPFB for an excess of exploration drilling, stating that: 'YPFB has had little success in its exploratory efforts to date . . . there are just not enough trained geologists in YPFB . . . this reflects on the efficiency of the wildcat drilling programme, and more exploratory wells are being drilled annually than can properly be justified.'[25] Possibly because of this report, YPFB in 1962 contracted Schlumberger (a French specialist oil company) for its secondary recovery programme, which did help to raise output from the Camiri fields. The report was in any case approved by the ICA in December 1961 and YPFB was offered $10.5m. in technical help.

While nationalist pressure continued, Gulf Oil made its first major find in 1961 and began to produce oil in 1962, selling small quantities to YPFB for domestic marketing at the fairly low price of $1.65 a barrel. In 1962 Gulf went further and asked the government for permission to supply gas to the local consumers of Santa Cruz. Although this proposal was not acted upon, it did provide the issue over which Mariaca (who had been outmanoeuvred on the question of accepting aid from the USSR) resigned. After that, YPFB ceased to be a centre of nationalist opposition, even though it continued to press hard on matters which directly concerned its own organisational interest.[26]

Between 1964 and 1969 YPFB became something of a client of Gulf Oil. Both René Barrientos (President, 1964–9) and Gulf Oil sought to find ways of taking the edge off YPFB's political discontent, which was perceived (rightly) as being politically dangerous. However, these initiatives tied YPFB even more closely to Gulf itself. Thus, for example, YPFB shared ownership of the gas export pipeline to Argentina with Gulf Oil. This was initiated in 1968, and YPFB and Gulf Oil also shared a joint venture in exploration of the Bolivian Altiplano, although this proved unsuccessful. Consequently YPFB, although saved from actual collapse, had now become a Cinderella beside the large and expanding Gulf Oil. Thus, in December 1968 YPFB's oil reserves were 33 million barrels and Gulf's were 187 million. Gulf Oil had invested $120m. in exploration over a period in which YPFB had invested $38m. on all aspects of its activities. In 1968, moreover, YPFB produced some 8,000 b/d (less than in 1956 and not enough to supply the domestic market), while Gulf Oil produced some 33,000 b/d.[27] Moreover, given its client status, YPFB faced few pressures to modernise or develop and instead became a convenient depository for projects which nobody else wished to carry out. Thus, according to one Bolivian technocrat, YPFB 'is used by the Central Government in order to finance projects which are totally alien to the commercial nature of the agency (transfers to public pension-holders and war veterans, covering of certain of the Central Government's deficits, etc.) without mentioning the employment of personnel for political reasons'.[28] Moreover, a combination of political pressures and labour militancy had prevented YPFB from reducing the number of staff from the high levels of the early 1950s; in 1968 YPFB employed 4,200 as against 200 employed by Gulf Oil.

Expansion and its aftermath 1969–78

The events of 1969–71 are not always easy to follow as a result of partial press censorship and the general political upheaval. The period was an extremely eventful one for YPFB. For one thing, there was the nationalisation of Gulf Oil and the consequences thereof; these were discussed in chapter 4 and it need only be said here that compensation arrangements were not finally settled until 1971. Secondly, there appear to have been severe conflicts between left-wing officials appointed by Presidents Siles, Ovando and Torres and the older *barrientista* officials who were partially or completely brushed aside. This conflict of personnel appears also to have been complicated by the compensation arrangements, since Gulf Oil, the World Bank and the USA appeared to make little secret of their preference for certain individuals, notably Ingeniero Roberto Capriles, whom successive Bolivian governments found it expedient to retain. Finally, in 1970–1 there were conflicts directly involving the YPFB labour force, its technical staff and the central government.

It is not possible to provide a full account of the period, but serious organisational difficulties were clear as early as April 1970, when Quiroga Santa Cruz resigned as Minister of Energy after a clash with Patino Ayoroa, who was head of YPFB and brother of the Minister of the Interior. After this, the directorate of YPFB was abolished and the President was given complete control of the organisation. With the Torres coup of September 1970, however, the new Energy Minister, Mariaca Bilbao, began to look for ways of re-establishing control over YPFB. In doing so, however, he clashed with Rolando Prada, who was Patino Ayoroa's successor as head of YPFB and the brother-in-law of the right-wing General Banzer. When Rolando Prada was demoted at the end of 1970, the oil-workers' union struck in protest. Its leaders explained: 'We are not defending Rolando Prada, we are simply opposed to YPFB being transformed into an agency which obeys political directives. Unfortunately, ministers change constantly and each of them brings in his own people to "work"; this situation means that YPFB does not have sufficient continuity to operate.'[29] Despite this strike, however, the government appointed a new directorate to YPFB, which met for the first time in February 1971.

This conflict appears to have been only the tip of the iceberg. At the beginning of 1971 YPFB also faced serious difficulties in Camiri, where the workforce threatened to strike if the company moved its drilling equipment out of the area into more geologically promising places. YPFB was forced to yield to the demands of the strikers, as it had earlier in Sucre. Moreover, a new strike of oil-workers took place in Santa Cruz in April 1971[30] and escalated in May, when the board of YPFB came out in open opposition to the regime. In May the General Manager of YPFB was sacked by the President, and the whole organisation struck in sympathy. Consequently, on 19 May President Torres

declared that 'anti-national interests' had 'infiltrated the high bureaucracy of the state companies and tried to hinder the execution of the
new revolutionary policy'.[31] Torres then reorganised YPFB, appointing
three workers and three ministerial representatives to the board
together with Torres himself as President of YPFB. Thus, the permanent executives of YPFB were denied membership of the board of directors (the General Manager was given voice but no vote), and the structure was also decentralised.

Although not everything is clear about the policies or motives of
those in conflict, these were certainly serious internal disputes which
must have disrupted the work of YPFB. Certainly, things appeared that
way to the YPFB management which took power after Banzer's coup of
August 1971. YPFB's *Annual Report for 1971* reported that 'with the
ending of anarchy and the reassertion of the principle of authority,
YPFB has carried out a change in the technical and administrative systems which have benefited both the agency and the country'.

The Banzer coup did for a time effectively remove YPFB from the
political stage, although the company continued to be subject to various political constraints. Banzer reappointed Rolando Prada as head of
YPFB and allowed the company a certain operating autonomy. Thus,
for example, YPFB was empowered to borrow abroad with the approval
only of the Central Bank and not of the government as a whole,[32]
although its personnel were still subject to centrally determined pay
restrictions, with the result that YPFB continued to lose many trained
technicians.[33]

In the period 1971–6 YPFB enjoyed a fairly good financial position,
largely as a result of the opening of the gas pipeline to Argentina in
1972 and of the sharp increase in world oil prices in 1973–4. At the
same time, YPFB became an increasingly important source of revenue
for various government authorities. It is significant that, despite the
sharp change in the price of oil and thus in the relative position of the
oil provinces, the government made no effort either to capture more of
the surplus for itself or to recapitalise YPFB. Indeed, in September 1977
the government turned down a proposal from the Minister of Energy
to limit the royalty payments to Santa Cruz; the political implications
of such a move were unacceptable.[34] As a consequence, it is clear that
a large proportion of the oil revenue went to the province that needed
it least. In 1977, the *Financial Times* reported that the Santa Cruz
public works committee 'has never had to fork out a penny for an oil
well, pipeline or refinery. Of this year's $40m. budget, $25m. – or as

Table 21.2 YPFB's *financial position* 1970–6
($m.)

	1970	1971	1972[a]	1973	1974	1975	1976
Export sales	13.07	23.70	32.12	64.54	175.90	140.6	154.8
Internal sales	31.03	33.09	22.01	29.55	34.36	44.3	64.3
TOTAL							
INCOME	44.10	56.79	54.13	94.09	210.26	184.9	219.2
Gross profit	18.29	23.86	23.83	38.28	92.16	69.9	96.4
Net profit[b]	4.77	10.05	12.64	25.99	67.30	32.7	52.0

[a] 1972 was a devaluation year, with the $b. devalued from 12 to the dollar to 20. I have followed YPFB's accounting practices and calculated these accounts as if the devaluation had taken place at midnight on 31 December 1971. This causes the figures for 1972 to be slightly underestimated.
[b] After tax but before investment.
Source: YPFB, *Annual Reports.*

Table 21.3 YPFB's *financial contribution to the Bolivian authorities* 1970–6
($m.)

	1970	1971	1972	1973	1974	1975	1976
19% profits tax	3.39	5.06	5.49	14.51	51.39	42.7	46.9
Export taxes	n.a.	n.a.	1.70	3.31	17.35	13.3	12.7
Contribution to La Paz	3.39	5.06	7.19	17.82	68.74	56.0	59.6
Royalties: TOTAL	2.13	3.47	4.95	8.24	28.7	24.8	27.1
to Santa Cruz	n.a.	2.61	3.88	6.52	21.0	18.6	n.a.
to Chuquisaca	n.a.	0.82	1.00	1.44	4.8	3.6	n.a.
to Tarija	n.a.	0.04	0.07	0.28	2.9	2.6	n.a.

Source: YPFB, *Annual Reports.*

much as the total 1976 budget – comes from oil and gas and the rest, apart from a few odd taxes such as on beer and spirits, from external loans'.[35]

However, even these taxes do not explain YPFB's financial difficulties that became apparent after 1977. The biggest imposition of all was the low domestic price of oil, which encouraged a rapid rise in domestic consumption (which has included a measure of smuggling into other counties where oil was more expensive). Domestic consumption increased from 12,000 b/d in 1972 to 19,000 b/d in 1976 and some

25,000 b/d at the end of 1978.[36] The financial effect of this can be seen from the fact that in 1976 YPFB, according to its own accounts, exported 8,000,000 barrels of crude oil for an income of $112.5m. while it marketed domestically 6,600,000 barrels of oil products for an income of $64.3m. This $64.3m. was inadequate to cover the cost of transportation, refining and marketing together with the royalty which had to be paid and was levied on the national export price of this production. By mid-1977 YPFB calculated that its domestic marketing side was running at a loss and in 1978 falling production and rising consumption led to a complete suspension of oil exports.

As a consequence of this worsening financial situation, YPFB moved increasingly into debt in order to maintain a fairly ambitious investment programme. According to its own figures, YPFB's investment increased sharply in the mid-1970s and reached $114m. in 1976 and around $160m. in 1977.[37] Consequently, an increasing proportion of the investment budget needed to be borrowed and some of the lending was on commercial terms; in 1977, for example, YPFB borrowed $75m. from the Bank of America. This loan, and the general increase in YPFB's indebtedness, became the subject of considerable press criticism.[38]

Even more serious was the fact that YPFB faced increasing difficulties on the physical side. These were partly the result of, and partly the cause of, YPFB's increasing financial weakness, but there were other considerations of equal importance. For one thing, there was the nature of Bolivian geology itself. Oil production reached its highest point in 1973 and then began a gradual decline, despite the fact that YPFB and various private companies had together spent a total of some $120m. in oil exploration in the 1971–7 period. During this time only around 20 million barrels of oil and 50 billion cubic feet of gas had been discovered.[39] By the late 1970s the discoveries made by Gulf Oil during the 1960s – Río Grande and Caranda – and YPFB's own Monteagudo find (of 1969) were beginning to become depleted and there was very little else to take their place.[40] Consequently, although Bolivia's 1976–80 *Plan nacional* contained an output target of 180,000 b/d for 1980, production fell from an average of just over 40,000 b/d for 1975 to around 32,000 b/d at the beginning of 1979 and under 30,000 b/d in 1980.

A third major problem may be regarded as geopolitical. Bolivia is undoubtedly rich in natural gas and sold increasing quantities to Argentina after 1972. Moreover, from as long ago as 1973 the Bolivian government planned to construct a gas pipeline to Brazil which would have provided a further outlet for Bolivia's gas reserves and an escape from exclusive reliance on the Argentine market. However, although a letter of intent was signed in 1973, no final agreement has yet been made. It would not be easy to finance the project (although the World Bank was believed to be interested), but the major obstacles were provided by internal political opposition to a project which would link Bolivia closely with its most powerful and ambitious neighbour. Moreover, despite the small size of Bolivia's internal market, objections were raised to the proposed pipeline on the ground that 'the volume of future gas sales will prove to be a serious handicap to Bolivia's eventual internal development.'[41] It was certainly true that YPFB had done little to develop the internal market for gas, but this was essentially because of the very low domestic price prevailing for the product.[42]

Finally, the management of YPFB made a controversial decision during this period to spend less on exploration and to concentrate instead on a complete modernisation of Bolivian refining capacity. At a total cost of around $160m., YPFB installed a completely new refinery at Santa Cruz, while modernising and expanding the refinery at Cochabamba, where a lubricants plant was also installed. Together these provided refinery capacity of around 70,000 b/d – a figure which might be thought extravagant when compared with Bolivian consumption of around 25,000 b/d during 1978. The refinery project was partially financed by a $46m. loan from the IDB. At the same time, YPFB's investment in exploration, which did increase in the mid-1970s, subsequently appears to have dropped considerably. In October 1978, Luis Salinas, former Exploration Manager of YPFB, said that five exploration teams under contract to YPFB had stopped work because the state agency was far behind on its payments.

Another of the policies of the Banzer government was to open some parts of Bolivia once again to foreign investment. In March 1972 a new oil law was issued allowing foreign companies to return to Bolivia under contract. YPFB wanted to model all operating contracts on the type which had been devised by Petroperú in 1971 and hired an executive from that company to advise them on their negotiating strategy.[43] Negotiations with the first company, Union Oil, lasted for almost a year and the contract was finally signed in April 1973. This was followed by about 14 others. The contracts were devised according to a crude-oil-sharing formula, with the early contractors agreeing to a 50–50 split with the government and the later ones paying up to

57%. However, although a considerable amount of exploration did take place, the results were generally disappointing and by the end of 1979 only Occidental and Tesoro Petroleum had found commercial quantities of hydrocarbons, although Occidental's Tita find was about to come onstream.

There were signs that Occidental was coming to play a major part in the Bolivian oil industry. As the other companies pulled out, Occidental's bargaining power increased. In 1978:

President Juan Pareda went to Santa Cruz in mid-September to talk to Joseph Baird, an executive of Occidental Petroleum, which is exploiting a small oil field in Tarija; he assured him that his government would give full guarantees for investments of this kind. These talks followed the publication of an official document which said that the government intended to offer guarantees against nationalisation to oil companies wishing to operate in the country.[44]

As a consequence, there were signs that some form of nationalist backlash was again brewing, this time against Occidental Petroleum. At the beginning of 1979 *Latin America* reported a speech by a former manager of YPFB to the effect that:

YPFB itself discovered the Tita oil deposits but went ahead to grant the area to Occidental for exploration. The pipeline from the Tita field down to Santa Cruz built by YPFB has a capacity for 30,000 b/d but production from the field has never been expected to be more than 5,000 b/d. The massive excessive capacity, Suárez suggested, was no doubt related to a dubious practice of paying a proportional commission to YPFB directors on the completion of construction projects.[45]

Indeed, there are signs that another phase in the history of YPFB is coming to an end. The increasing difficulties facing YPFB coincided with an unexpected change in the political environment, with six presidents between 1978 and 1981. This changing political climate helped destroy the apparent unity of YPFB and a number of accusations and counter-accusations began to be made by existing and former YPFB officials. At the same time, the uncertain political climate has led to further postponement of the rise in domestic oil prices which will be necessary if YPFB is to be recapitalised. It is too early to say how these new developments will influence Bolivian oil policy.

Conclusion

Any overall judgement on YPFB must be mixed. On the one hand, it provides almost a textbook example of the difficulties that may be faced by a state oil company in a small, poor and politically unstable country. On the other hand, when the difficulties are taken into account, Bolivian oil policy over the last 40 years must in many ways be accounted a success, even if a somewhat irregular one.

To consider the difficulties first: Bolivia's oil market has been too small for ambitious downstream projects, and international co-operation, which might have extended YPFB's effective market, has been limited. It is only very recently, for example, that modern large refineries have been built in Bolivia (the small refineries built in the 1940s were far simpler than the more advanced and larger units available at the time) and even now the capacity is vastly greater than the size of the Bolivian market. Moreover, given Bolivia's low population density and large size, the internal distribution network has had to be built on an expensive system of pipelines. Bolivia's international position has also proved difficult in view of its poverty and landlocked status; its export pipelines have frequently tied it in with powerful purchasers who have been able to force down the effective price of its oil and gas. At other times Bolivian projects have been held back by the reluctance of its neighbours or by the fear of becoming too dependent upon them.

Oil exploration in Bolivia is difficult and expensive – too much so for YPFB. The company achieved some success in the early 1950s, basically on the foundations laid by Standard Oil, but Bolivia's real discoveries have been made in three waves of private investment. In the first, Standard Oil of Bolivia found oil in Santa Cruz; the bottleneck to its development stemmed from transportation difficulties rather than from problems with the oil itself. Subsequently, Gulf invested heavily in the 1950s and 1960s and vastly expanded Bolivia's oil reserves. Most recently, the companies which entered Bolivia under the latest contract arrangements have made at least some commercial discoveries. Their precise nature and extent is by no means clear but it is likely that Occidental Petroleum will continue to invest in exploration for some time to come if it is permitted to do so. It was in keeping with Bolivian history that the Cabinet Minister commented on the most recent oil search in Bolivia: 'I don't know what the nature of foreign companies in Bolivia will be, but for the moment their activities are finding us a lot of new assets which will be ours after they have gone.'[46]

Thirdly, other than during a few exceptional periods, YPFB has suffered from real, sometimes severe, financial constraints. The 1952–6 period, which saw a loss of budgetary control by central government, and the 1971–6 period, which saw a number of windfall gains (the

Gulf nationalisation, the gas pipeline to Argentina and the vast increase in oil export prices), were by no means typical and, at the time of writing, it is clear that YPFB is in another period of financial difficulty. During the 'lean' periods, YPFB was largely kept afloat by outside help: the Export–Import Bank loan in the 1940s and the ICA loan and several loans from Gulf in the late 1950s and early 1960s. A World Bank Loan for YPFB in 1979 and further World Bank finance in the future may be seen as part of this pattern.

Finally, YPFB has faced constant, and sometimes severe, political problems. The organisational disruptions caused by the political infighting of the 1969–71 period were not typical, but there has been a whole series of less serious but nevertheless irksome problems caused by the demands of the central government. Pay restrictions have made it extremely difficult for YPFB to keep qualified middle managers who could easily earn more in the private sector; this has added to the centralisation of the organisation. Moreover, YPFB has frequently been made to undertake unwanted or barely profitable projects at the behest of the central government (the refinery at Sucre, the Arica pipeline), and there has been the almost permanent problem of low domestic prices which have been kept down by successive governments in order to avoid political disruption.

Against these difficulties, however, it is necessary to set a number of important achievements. Between 1940 and 1972 Bolivian oil production increased from 280,000 barrels to 15,970,000 barrels, a compound growth rate of around 12% a year. Consumption, meanwhile, grew at a compound rate of around 7.5% a year (roughly the world average). Moreover, by the mid-1970s, even though oil production was again falling, Bolivia was a substantial exporter of natural gas, it had installed a set of modern oil refineries and it had created a nationwide distribution system from virtually nothing. Thus, despite the geological difficulties, the political and financial constraints and the unpredictable changes in policy, YPFB has shown considerable resilience. It is, after all, easier for an incoming government following a period of political uncertainty to reorganise and recapitalise a state company than to carry out a major and successful change of policy *vis-à-vis* a large multinational or foreign investment in general. Bolivia's various problems have hindered the development of YPFB but they have also made the agency indispensable.

22

Petrovén: the birth of a giant

By the beginning of 1976, when Petrovén formally came into being, the Venezuelan oil industry was in a technical sense already showing signs of age. In 1970, 2.7 of the 3.7 million daily barrels of oil produced came from six fields. These were Lagunillas, Tía Juana, Bachaquero, Lama, Lamar and Centro, discovered in 1926, 1928, 1930, 1937, 1938 and 1959 respectively. All of these were in the area of Lake Maracaibo and all were onshore; there was significant oil production from the east of the country but offshore work had hardly begun. Until large-scale new oil discoveries could be made, it was the job of the new state company to keep the oil flowing from these fields for as long as possible. This required increasingly sophisticated recovery work and, thus, some continuing reliance on the main international centres of technology.

At the same time, the nationalisation took place when the international balance of oil power was moving sharply away from the companies and consumer interests to the governments of oil-exporting countries. Naturally there were advantages for Venezuela in this process. There were also important policy decisions to be made as Venezuela moved away from the protective shelter of technical and marketing agreements with the foreign companies which had been carefully constructed as part of the nationalisation. The nationalisation also raised political questions: how would the creation of a public enterprise of such size and economic power affect Venezuelan democracy?

The initial takeover process was smooth. The nationalisation was carried through by a close-knit political elite, essentially consisting of the high command of Acción Democrática, without a great deal of open public debate; oil policy was always intended to be a matter for the elite. The expropriation was ceremonial rather than bitterly contested and, as critics of the left have argued, the political importance of the act was thereby greatly diminished.[1]

Petrovén's economic activity 1976–80

Although conceptions of national sovereignty were involved in the nationalisation, one of its main objectives was to increase activity in the oil industry which had fallen off considerably in the preceding years. In the first year after the nationalisation, the tax structure was changed so as to give Petrovén the economic freedom to reinvest. As we shall see, this had important implications for Petrovén's role in the political system, but it should first be noted that the company has stepped up its level of activity very substantially from prenationalisation levels; this can be seen from table 22.1. At the end of 1975 the state company, with its subsidiaries, took over an industry with a book value of around $1,000m. but a replacement value of perhaps 20 times this amount. The companies had, as we have seen, consistently run down the value of their investments in exploration and production since the late 1950s and the industry was now in absolute decline. Private investment in all aspects of the oil industry had amounted to no more than $220m. in 1972 and $320m. in 1975.

Petrovén began cautiously, investing only $323.5m. in 1976 but, as can be seen from table 22.1, this total soon increased and was followed by several years of rapid expansion. The first aim was to maintain a constant level of proven oil reserves and production capacity. As one journalist put it, it was necessary for Petrovén to run as fast as it could in order to stand still; to make any progress it would have to run even faster.[2] Apart from the fact that there had been few major discoveries in the years prior to the nationalisation and that increases in Venezuela's oil reserves had stemmed either from more intensive working of existing deposits or from changed economic logic stemming from increasing world prices, there was also the question of the distribution of the oil reserves. In 1976 approximately 3 billion barrels were of light oil but 5 billion were of medium and 10 billion were of heavy. Not only was heavy oil of lower value, it was also harder to sell on world markets. In 1976 35% of Venezuela's oil production was light oil, 38% was medium and 27% was heavy, a proportion which has not changed much in subsequent years. It was believed that, unless new discoveries could be made, serious problems would result from this distribution as early as 1980. To the extent that the position could be remedied by the application of increasingly sophisticated recovery techniques, the Venezuelan oil industry would become increasingly high cost and less able to transfer income to the rest of the economy. Finally,

Table 22.1 *Investment, employment and reserves in the Venezuelan state oil industry* 1976–80

	1980	1979	1978	1977	1976
Capital spending ($m.)					
TOTAL	2,270.0	1,515.3	1,010.2	526.1	323.5
Exploration	510.2	320.9	181.6	96.1	93.7
Production	959.8	726.5	506.5	341.9	203.0
Refining	686.5	423.3	172.1	37.9	6.5
Internal marketing	64.4	27.2	21.4	17.7	4.9
Other	49.0	17.4	128.6	32.6	15.3
Proven reserves (end of year)					
Oil (m. barrels)	19,666	18,515	18,228	18,039	18,228
Gas (000 billion cubic metres)	1,330	1,249	1,211	1,185	1,180
Number employed by Petrovén	37,699	33,242[a]	29,822[a]	25,223	23,668

[a] As a result of ownership transfer, Petrovén took control of the petrochemical industry in 1978 and thus took on its former employees.
Source: Petrovén, *Annual Reports.*

as General Ravard, the head of Petrovén, pointed out in 1977, there was also a problem with human capital. In the late 1950s there were more than 800 geologists actively working in Venezuela; in 1976 there were only 160.[3] Consequently, before any serious exploration could take place, it was necessary to build up and co-ordinate the exploration departments of Petrovén's various affiliates.

Exploration spending picked up considerably after 1977 and in 1979 serious offshore drilling began. The aim was to drill in as many areas as possible in order to acquire the maximum of geological information on which future plans could be based rather than to aim for quick development of any discoveries made. A number of encouraging gas finds were made and Petrovén's *Annual Report* stated that 'Almost all wells drilled in completely new areas have provided favourable indications about the possibility of finding hydrocarbons in the respective sedimentary basins.'[4] There were three significant finds and during that year 406 million barrels of oil were discovered, compared with

196 million barrels in 1978 and only 168 million barrels in 1977. Moreover, better recovery techniques enabled a total of 1,147 million barrels to be added to reserves in 1979 as compared with 973 million barrels in 1978. As can be seen from table 22.1, the level of proven reserves has been increasing since 1977 and will certainly increase during 1980 if only because rising oil prices have made some older deposits commercially worth extracting. On the basis of existing discoveries it is estimated that perhaps 30–40 billion barrels could ultimately be recovered, but costs would be high and most of the crude oil thus produced would be low grade and difficult to market internationally.

Petrovén also began a serious effort to develop oil from the Orinoco Oil Belt. This was a belt of extremely heavy oil whose existence had been known for a long time but from which production depended on high international prices and considerable advance in the technology of extraction. In the 1960s Shell made a tentative proposal to develop the belt but this was rejected by Leoni. In 1972 the USA became interested and James Atkins of the State Department proposed to the Venezuelan government that US companies be allowed to carry out an intensive study of the belt in order to determine its commercial possibilities. If commercial production could be developed, the US companies would receive guarantees to make it worthwhile for them to undertake it. Atkins's offer was also rejected by the Venezuelan government, which was at that time moving toward the nationalisation of the oil industry. When Petrovén began to consider the oil belt, it found that potential reserves were vast; in 1980 the Venezuelan government announced that 500 billion barrels of oil could eventually be recovered. The oil, however, was extremely heavy and metallic. There would be difficulties with the extraction of the oil, which would involve highly sophisticated techniques and very high costs, and also with the purification of the oil produced. The financial and technical questions thus raised also had an important political dimension: how fast should the oil be produced and how far should foreign technology be used in extracting it?

Following a government decision made in 1977, Petrovén set up a special Orinoco Belt Department in 1978 in order to carry out a survey. This was finished in 1979 and recommended that serious efforts should be made to develop the belt during the 1980s. The belt area was then divided up among the main subsidiary companies of Petrovén and serious work began. A Plan was put together which called for an $850m. evaluation of the belt to be carried out between 1980 and

1983 and work has been continuing. The first major step in developing the belt, the signing in March 1981 of a contract of technical association between Lagovén, the US company Lummus and the Venezuelan company Vepica, illustrates clearly some of the political and administrative problems that must be tackled if the project is to be developed. It was originally reported that a large US concern would get a 'turnkey' contract to provide a recovery plant capable of producing up to 125,000 b/d from the Orinoco Belt by 1988. This suggestion met opposition from many Venezuelans who felt that development tasks should not simply be handed over to foreign technologists and that a slower pattern of growth, which involved Venezuelan companies more directly in developments, was more desirable. After showing lack of interest over a long period, some large Venezuelan companies became increasingly interested in oil-related projects when the industry began to be reactivated following the nationalisation. Thus, rather than offering an all-inclusive contract of the kind earlier suggested, Lagovén instead signed a more limited (but still extensive) contract with a US–Venezuelan consortium, excluding some other contenders apparently because of their less satisfactory record in employing and sharing technology with Venezuelans.

Although the upstream end of the oil industry was crucial, Petrovén, as can be seen from table 22.1, built up its investment much more rapidly in oil refining. The largest refineries in Venezuela were built in the late 1940s under the tax incentives offered in the 1943 law. The companies found very large and simple refineries to be the most profitable, partly because tax concessions were offered on the quantity of oil refined rather than on the sophistication of the refining process, but also because large quantities of heavy fuel oil could be marketed conveniently on the US east coast alongside the lighter oils produced and refined within the USA. Moreover, these refineries were built at a time when Venezuela's crude oil was lighter, on the average, than it became later. In order to produce even the same output combination from heavier crudes, it was necessary to modify them. Finally, the increasing demand for gasoline within Venezuela itself ensured that the output 'mix' of the old Venezuelan refineries could not satisfy the domestic market without creating other problems. The *Annual Report for 1978* complained of 'the inflexibility imposed on the country's refining industry by the need to satisfy increasing domestic demand for refined products – especially gasoline. To meet this domestic demand,

Venezuela had to produce large volumes of residual fuel oil which it was then necessary to place on the international market at a time when demand was already weak.'[5]

The two main projects undertaken during the 1970s were the expansion and addition of new units to the refineries at Amuay and El Palito; similar work on the Puerto la Cruz refinery was scheduled for the early 1980s. The catalytic cracker at the Cardón refinery was also modernised in 1978. While these changes were being put into effect, Shell agreed to lease part of its Curaçao refinery to Venezuela for the purposes of producing gasoline for the domestic market. There were some negotiations regarding the possible sale to Venezuela of part of this refinery but these proved abortive, apparently because Shell changed its mind.

The trouble-ridden Venezuelan petrochemical industry was also put under the control of Petrovén in March 1978. The former IVP (later known as Pequivén) was financially and organisationally restructured by the Mines and Energy Ministry during 1977. Subsequently foreign technical help was sought to improve the quality of the existing plants. These were still running at a loss throughout 1979, even despite some continuing investment, but Petrovén officially expressed the hope that its financial situation would improve relatively quickly.

Petrovén followed the tradition of the private companies by continuing to lose money on the domestic market. While prices were held down, demand boomed, reaching 283,000 b/d in 1978 and 317,000 b/d in 1979. Of the latter figure, just over 150,000 b/d was demand for gasoline. The government tried to limit the growth of gasoline consumption by several administrative measures but remained unwilling to undertake any serious revision of the old price. Certainly the expropriation did not make it any easier to take such a step for, as *Business Venezuela* pointed out, 'historical experience has shown that any crisis in Venezuela's tenuous public transport system is explosive. An example was the transport strike that jolted the country in the early 1960s, leaving more than a score dead in nationwide clashes.'[6] Distribution facilities soaked up a certain amount of Petrovén's investment but the main cost to the state company lay in the burdens placed upon its refining capacity and the lost opportunity of international sales.

Petrovén and the foreign companies

Petrovén's various investment plans implied a need, in the short term at least, to rely more heavily upon foreign expertise than had earlier been anticipated. As part of the original nationalisation agreement, the foreign oil companies contracted to supply technical services to the various operating companies which took over from them in return for a per barrel fee plus the actual cost of supplying the technical specialists. The per barrel fee – around $0.16 for Shell and $0.19 for Jersey Standard – was criticised within Venezuela for being too high and it was widely believed that a somewhat inflated technical services fee was a *quid pro quo* for company acceptance of nationalisation terms which provided compensation only at book value. Nevertheless, the technical experts provided by the companies were undoubtedly needed and demand for these proved to be greater than expected. On 30 November 1979 the *Latin America Regional Report* stated that 'about 500 key personnel' were on loan from the multinationals. These technical service contracts were to be renegotiated after four years and discussions went on through 1979 until agreement on new terms was finally reached. The *Latin America Weekly Report* summarised the outcome:

The per barrel fee has been eliminated and replaced by payment for actual services rendered. Annual technology payments will fall from the previous Bs. 700m. ($163m.) but not by as much as Calderón [the Venezuelan Oil Minister] had wanted. The confidentiality clause, under which data produced to one of PVDSA's [Petrovén's] operating subsidiaries could not be shared amongst the others, has also been removed. There are five principal contracts – with Exxon, Shell, Gulf, British Petroleum (new) and Phillips (for the petrochemicals industry) running for a maximum of two years.[7]

There were also marketing contracts signed with the recently expropriated companies. The rather specific nature of Venezuela's output of refined oil, and the high proportion of Venezuela's oil which was exported after being refined (around one third of total exports), gave a short-run advantage to the companies in marketing negotiations. At the beginning the marketing arrangements entered into between Petrovén and the private companies, although subject to revision every three months, provided further evidence of Venezuela's policy of maintaining continuity with the pre-nationalisation status quo. As we have seen (chapter 5), during the immediate post-nationalisation negotiations (in rather a depressed international market) the oil companies bargained by threatening to refuse to take Venezuelan oil in large quantity unless the price was right. If the companies took less and the Venezuelan government had no alternative markets, then less could be produced and export revenues would suffer in consequence. During the following years, however, Venezuela worked quietly to disengage itself from this pattern by finding new markets, and the amount of oil sold to 'non-traditional customers' grew steadily, from 26% in 1977 to 37% in 1978 and 42% in 1979. A figure of around 50% was expected for 1980. This transformation was greatly helped by the sellers' market prevailing in 1979 and early 1980 following the Iranian Revolution. When sales contracts were renegotiated in 1979, therefore, Venezuela found itself in a very strong position. It eventually agreed to continue selling to the multinationals but on terms that could be changed at only one month's notice and with a clause giving Venezuela the right to decide on who final consumers should be. This raised the possibility of oil supply being used for foreign policy purposes. In fact in 1980 Venezuela, together with Mexico, agreed to supply oil to Central American and Caribbean countries at a special low price, with the difference between this and the world price being put into a special fund to be lent back to these countries for development projects.

Although the technical services and sales contracts were highly acceptable to the oil companies, there remained a serious problem over payment of compensation. Following a law passed in 1971 the oil companies were ordered to post a bond with the Venezuelan government to ensure that their property was handed over in good condition once the actual nationalisation took place. Before this could be handed back to the companies, a Venezuelan politician challenged the companies in the courts, claiming that the companies owed backtaxes for underproducing oil in 1971. Although both the Pérez (1974–9) and Herrera Campíns (1979–) governments believed that this money should in fact be paid, there were a number of legal difficulties involved and the matter is still unresolved.

Political organisation of Petrovén

It is clear that a great deal of thought lay behind the structuring of Petrovén. It was important both to remove the oil industry from the more damaging kinds of political interference and to ensure that control over the state company did not become a weapon in domestic political disputes. The appointment of a military man as head of Petrovén – General Ravard – was typical of this determination. So also were the financial arrangements that were made; General Ravard later told an interviewer that from the outset, the Mines Ministry and Petrovén rejected the idea of being dependent on allocations from the national budget. They believed that the industry would have to stand in the queue with other government agencies such as the Social Security Ministry . . . [instead] it was decided to try to self-finance day-to-day activities and borrow to finance really major projects in the same way as the big multinationals.[8]

A few months later he was even more emphatic: 'financial autonomy is an indispensable condition for guaranteeing the operational efficiency and expansion of the industry. The day on which it is necessary to go to the Executive or Legislature in search of extra finance will be the day on which it may be said that Petrovén has lost its freedom of action.'[9]

The same strategy lay behind the government's decision to keep, as far as possible, to the same industrial structure as had existed prior to 1976. Petrovén itself, given overall responsibility for the industry, was no more than a holding company with some 70 employees 'from managing director to office boy'. Thus, the government abandoned an earlier idea of using the small state company, CVP, to take over the running of the industry. The CVP had been set up in 1960 with this objective in mind but, although not badly managed and certainly more efficient and successful than some other Venezuelan state companies, it was still in a completely different league from the majors in terms of both size and technical capacity. Consequently, CVP was given some new functions and made subordinate to Petrovén.

Thus, instead of centralising the oil industry structure completely, the government kept the old organisational structure, many former oil company personnel and many of the links which previously existed with parent companies. Thus, Shell was contracted to advise its former subsidiary Maravén and Jersey Standard advised Lagovén. The large companies survived this transformation fairly successfully; they had long been used to a high degree of effective independence and were happy to retain it. The arrangement also had the advantage of creating a climate of confidence among senior executives and technical experts who had earlier expressed considerable anxiety about their conditions of work in a nationalised enterprise. While the largest affiliates survived this tranformation fairly successfully, however, there remained problems with the smaller ones. These had often been highly dependent on their parent companies and were relatively short of technical expertise. Consequently, they were gradually amalgamated during 1977 and 1978 until Petrovén was left with only four affiliates: Lagovén (formerly Jersey Standard), Maravén (formerly Shell),

Menevén (Gulf plus a few small acquisitions) and Corpovén (CVP plus a number of smaller companies).

The structure set up was very much an experimental one and was designed to avoid obvious dangers rather than to conform to a particular strategy. As one observer pointed out, 'the government knew what it didn't want, not what it wanted'. At the beginning, the emphasis was on decentralisation. Petrovén, as noted above, was deliberately kept small. Moreover, the Energy and Mines Ministry lost an important inter-bureaucratic battle in 1976 over Petrovén's sales policy; the Ministry tried to impose rigid rules on oil production but was prevented from doing so by President Pérez and those most responsible were demoted for trying to restrict Petrovén's production from within the Ministry. During Pérez's presidency, the Oil Minister, Valentín Hernández, did not involve himself particularly closely in the running of the industry.

After a few years, however, and particularly after Herrera Campíns took over as President early in 1979, perspectives changed somewhat and the policymaking elite swung round to the opinion that decentralisation could go too far. One journalist summed up the 1976–8 period by saying that Valentín Hernández had concentrated too much on international oil policy and that 'critics claim that because of this, PDVSA [Petrovén] acquired unwarranted powers of decision yet, nevertheless, was unable to control its four operating units – Lagovén, Maravén and Menevén and Corpovén. This situation caused bitter confrontation between the Energy Ministry, PDVSA and operating company executives.'[10] Calderón Berti, appointed Oil Minister by the incoming COPEI government, pointedly remarked upon taking office that 'There are not two oil industries, just a single one which is governed by the Ministry of Energy and Mines, the entity that guides and formulates the policy that Petróleos de Venezuela and the operating companies must execute.'[11] It appears that one means of ensuring greater centralisation was the bringing of Intevep (the Venezuelan Technological Institute) into much more of a key position at the centre of policymaking. In 1979 Intevep, formerly an independent foundation, was formally integrated into Petrovén and given a considerable role in planning the development of Orinoco oil and organising the operation of crude recovery techniques. Its pay-roll increased from 386 at the end of 1978 to 565 at the end of 1979 and 750 in early 1981 (of whom 67 are foreigners under contract), making it considerably larger than Petrovén itself. Its importance will have been increased by the renegotiation of the technical service contracts that enabled an unprecedented centralisation of Venezuela's research effort.

It is clear that, as a result of the overwhelming importance of oil to Venezuela, the management of Petrovén has had to be treated with great respect and its organisation somewhat set apart from the rest of Venezuelan society. As General Ravard put it,

> there has emerged in this industry, more than anywhere else, the figure of the professional manager . . . If you analyse the development of the Venezuelan industrial sector, you will find that almost all companies have a familial origin, in which the head and his immediate colleagues were or are members of a family nucleus. The oil industry has needed to rely on a technical nucleus which devotes its talent and dedication to the success of the enterprise in return for guarantees of good pay, good treatment and security.[12]

The initially decentralised structure of Petrovén was aimed in large part at protecting the position of the professional technician and keeping him in the industry despite the great international opportunities for qualified men of this kind. At the time of the takeover, fears were expressed that 'the industry may eventually become politicised. If so, this would lead not only to organisational strains, but to an exodus of high-powered talent from the industry at a time when qualified personnel is lacking.'[13] This was the first problem to be avoided.

Over time, however, there was growing awareness that the oil industry must remain under ultimate political control, if only in the interests of co-ordination and communication. Thus, there seems to be something of a learning process underway in which the government began by decentralising the industry in order to avert fears of 'politicisation' and is now trying to re-emphasise the importance of central control of a less damaging kind. It is still early days, however, and the institutional character of the Venezuelan oil industry is by no means fully established.

Petrovén has also been fortunate in having been able to establish itself under extremely favourable international conditions. Just as the decline in oil production in the years prior to the oil nationalisation was offset by the sharply rising oil prices of 1970–4, so the commitment by Petrovén of increasing resources into the recapitalisation of the Venezuelan oil industry has been rendered painless by the oil price increases of 1979–80. Thus, there have been no sharp choices to be made. It has been possible for Petrovén to build up its investment rapidly while continuing to provide the Venezuelan public with very cheap oil and continually increasing its payment to the central government ($5.7 billion in 1978, $8.9 billion in 1979 and around $12 billion in 1980).

It nevertheless remains clear that the Venezuelan oil industry may face serious problems in the longer term. According to Petrovén's own figures, the margin of Venezuela's exportable oil surplus, which has been falling constantly since around 1970, is likely to continue to fall. The company estimates that production may reach 2.8 million barrels daily by the year 2000, of which 1.3 million will come from existing fields, 0.5 million from yet-to-be-discovered conventional oilfields and 1 million from the Orinoco. This oil will be much more expensive to produce than is presently the case as both development costs and secondary recovery costs rise. Against this, demand will have reached at least 600,000 b/d and possibly as much as 1,600,000 b/d. A median estimate of 1,100,000 b/d would cut the potential export surplus to 1.7 million b/d. It may of course be that real oil export income will rise, as happened in the decade prior to 1981, and so offset any fall in production, but this cannot be regarded as certain. What is more certain, however, is that Venezuela will continue to be highly dependent on oil exports for the foreseeable future.

Apart from simply maintaining production, Petrovén is likely to face the important but perhaps difficult task of integrating local companies into the area of oil-related activities. It is becoming increasingly less realistic to discuss relations between the state company and the multinationals without taking local Venezuelan capitalists into account. These will certainly be able to exercise a degree of political 'pull' out of proportion to their real economic importance and are likely to use this to slow down projects in order to get a share of what is on offer. They may also compete with Petrovén for the services of key technical men which no state company can afford to lose. It will be necessary, but not easy, to reach a compromise which brings in local capital to a far greater degree than before without holding back overall development in a way that may prejudice the Venezuelan balance of payments.

23

State oil companies in Latin America

In the oil industry, as in many other areas, state enterprise in Latin America has developed as an alternative to foreign investment. Such an alternative suggests an obvious point of comparison. This chapter will therefore begin by considering those areas in which the foreign companies might be thought to possess an advantage – scale economies, access to technology and finance, and experience of diversity – and will go on to examine the extent to which state companies can be given greater freedom in pricing and investment decisions. Finally, it will go on to consider the less tangible but perhaps even more important question of political control.

In order to evaluate these questions, it will be useful to look again at the activities of the main state oil companies and the position of their oil industries. It can be seen from table 23.1 that two state companies (Pemex and Petrovén) which already control very extensive hydrocarbon reserves are the only ones to have maintained a completely unqualified state monopoly upstream. It is much more common, however, for state oil companies to maintain a monopoly of refining and of the marketing of natural gas; of the six companies already considered, only YPF allows private refineries to operate and there is evidence that this policy has inflicted significant extra costs upon the state enterprise.[1] Finally, within the petrochemicals sector, state participation but not state monopoly has been the rule; the state either takes a sector of the industry or it shares with private national and foreign capital at several different stages.

It is clear that the argument for admitting private capital is more pressing in the exploration–development sector of the industry than it is downstream. There are good intellectual reasons for this. As has been pointed out many times,[2] exploration is inherently a high risk activity. An unsuccessful exploration venture might lead to the waste of tens, or even hundreds, of millions of dollars. Moreover, geology is not an

Table 23.1 *State oil companies in Latin America: participation or monopoly by sector*

	Exploration drilling	Oil production	Refining	Marketing		Petrochemicals	
				Oil	Gas	Primary	Secondary
Pemex	M	M	M	M	M	M	X
Petrobrás[a]	P	M	M	P	—	P	P
Petrovén	M	M	M	M	M	M	P
YPF	P	P	P	P	X[b]	M	P
YPFB	P	P	M	M	M	—	—
Petroperú	P	P	M	M	—	M	—
ENAP	P	M[c]	M	P	M	P	P
CEPE	P	P	P	P	M	—	—
Ecopetrol	P	P	P	P	M	P	P
ANCAP	P	—	M	P	—	—	—

M = monopoly

P = participation

X = exclusion from sector

— = sector not economically significant

Note: Arrangements do not vary considerably over time. This table is correct at 31 December 1980.

[a] Petrobrás participates in many more sectors than are shown here.

[b] The job of Gas del Estado, also a state company.

[c] This will be altered as and when private companies discover oil; it exists only *de facto*, not *de jure*.

exact science. An element of hunch, or at any rate judgement, is crucial in oil exploration and it often happens that one company finds oil where others fail. The greater the number of companies searching for oil in a given area, the more likely it is that oil will be found. The larger privately owned oil companies will have the experience of searching in a variety of international conditions and may be better able for this reason to evaluate particular cases. They will also, because of their world-wide operations, be able to 'insure' against failure by setting potential losses in some countries against finds already made in others.

There may also be good reasons for a state company to invest in oil exploration. For one thing, prior to around 1970 it was difficult for Latin American governments to attract foreign oil investment on a substantial scale on terms which made it inevitable that substantial exploration would in fact take place. Rather, as we have seen in some earlier chapters, it was necessary for host governments to give up effective control over oil activity by signing a concession contract. However, it would be wrong to regard state investment in oil exploration purely as a response to lack of interest on the part of international companies. On the contrary, there are both economic and political reasons for the upstream activities of state oil companies. Economically, it is not clear why it is wrong for a 'developmentalist' state to risk a limited amount of money in oil exploration if the geology is promising and the potential rewards great.[3] Certainly state oil companies, most spectacularly but not only Pemex, have succeeded in making very significant oil discoveries in Latin America. Once a state company has succeeded in finding oil, it is highly likely that it will continue with at least some exploration activity.

During the 1970s ownership became a less divisive issue within the oil exploration and production sectors. Countries with long established monopoly policies, notably Brazil and Chile, brought foreign investment back into oil exploration, although so far without this leading to the discovery of major new reserves. Other countries with a policy of allowing private sector companies to explore for oil somewhat strengthened the incentives encouraging such exploration. Only Mexico, where the state company made a series of massive discoveries during the 1970s, and Venezuela, where the oil industry was nationalised and recapitalised by the state company, maintained their existing monopolies.

In the downstream sectors, the argument for private direct investment is partly a matter of scale and partly a matter of guaranteeing the transfer of technology. For host governments, the main concern has generally been strategic control of the industry. It is for this reason that refining has been of such importance to state companies even though private investment has in many cases been allowed to remain in the marketing sector. All of the countries considered here have passed the stage where oil refining presents problems of scale, and in any case international technology during the 1950s and later became increasingly responsive to government demands for relatively small state-owned refineries.[4] In petrochemicals, however, state companies have generally preferred joint ventures with a combination of local and foreign capital. Financing requirements provide a part of the reason for this, particularly since the IDB (in the 1960s) and the international banks (in the 1970s) preferred to lend to joint ventures. Perhaps more important, however, is the fact that international chemical companies are willing to accept joint ventures since these allow the spread of research and development costs across the globe. Such companies are relatively uninterested in construction and production decisions. The government can directly control the investment while using its credit and tariff policies to guarantee that the investment remains profitable. Private local capital can extend political protection to both parties.

Over all, therefore, state oil companies in Latin America have generally been 'rational' in the sense that the extent of their activity has corresponded, at any rate in most cases, to some form of easily understandable economic logic. This is not to deny the importance of political choice, for we have certainly seen that oil policy is often a political matter, but only to suggest that at least in the long term political decisions have generally respected the technical options available.

This essentially 'micro' logic also points to two striking conclusions of this study: that throughout the century the market has remained open to specialist technology and that credit has been relatively easily available. These features also stem from the logic of the oil industry. Economic power has traditionally stemmed from control over oil reserves or from control over market outlets; the major oil companies therefore concerned themselves mainly with these matters and were willing to contract out the production of technically sophisticated capital goods to competitive specialist companies. These then became available to fill the needs of state oil companies. As a result there have always been specialist construction companies for refineries, pipelines, transport terminals and petrochemicals plants, and technical innovations within the industry have almost invariably led either to the adaptation of existing companies or to the creation of new ones. The way that both state and large private companies in Latin America have developed their expertise in the oil industry attests to the relative openness of the market to technology.

The market for credit to the oil industry has generally reflected the overall state of world capital markets; these were relatively tight in the years 1930–60 but much easier both before this and after. During 1930–60 the US government tried to avoid offering credits, or allowing the international lending agencies to do so, on conditions which could undermine the position of its multinationals. Nevertheless, some loans were made available for foreign policy reasons and contractors might in any case offer a limited amount of private credit. Frozen European credits could also sometimes be used to purchase equipment. After 1960 the credit position gradually became easier and access to finance has never been a general problem since then. Indeed, it is now often the case that state oil companies are among the biggest international borrowers.[5]

Technology, pricing and investment

While it is true that technology and finance are generally available internationally, it by no means follows that domestic supply is unimportant. On the contrary, two of the most important indicators of the performance of a state oil company are its technological abilities and its financial position. This is both because of the intrinsic importance of these two factors and because government policies which do not respect them are likely to be damaging in other ways as well.

As noted above, the market for technology and technical services is an open one. Some state companies in Latin America have been willing to go so far as to hire key technical staff from the foreign private sector. Petrovén has, since 1976, made arrangements directly with large foreign companies for the right to contract technical advisers in return for a fee. Petrobrás in the 1950s, and several other companies since then, have simply hired prominent geologists at the salaries they required. In other cases, particularly with established and technologically fairly advanced state companies, specialised research institutes have been set up in order both to supervise internal technological requirements and to liaise internationally with suppliers of technology. The IMP in Mexico has collaborated directly with smaller specialised US companies and has helped cover its costs by exporting its expertise to third countries. There are signs that Intevep in Venezuela is beginning to play the same role. However, even though the transfer of technology is not a particularly difficult matter for a well-organised state oil company, nothing is easier than for an inept management or an unstable or unsympathetic government to destroy the technical capacity of an agency for a good many years. This is a point to which we shall return.

State oil companies are also sensitive to the level of domestic prices. Within Latin America there are now only three countries which export more oil than they sell domestically; these are Mexico, Venezuela and Ecuador. Even here a heavily subsidised domestic price can be expensive; in Mexico it was calculated that had Pemex in 1979 sold its domestic products at full international prices, it would have earned an extra $16,000m. on top of its export sales of $3,987m. and domestic market sales of $3,240m.[6] However, political pressures in these countries to follow a low-price policy are overwhelming. A second group of countries, including, notably, Brazil and Chile, have a tradition of importing oil and a history of high domestic prices. In these countries prices have been kept high and, if anything, increased since 1973 in an effort to choke off increases in demand. Finally, there are a number of countries (Peru, Bolivia, Argentina and Colombia) in which hydrocarbon production and demand roughly balance. Here political pressures for low domestic prices are very considerable but so also are the costs of such a policy which, as we have seen in chapters 20 and 21, can inflict real damage on state companies.

It is of course quite reasonable to price oil products more cheaply in oil-exporting countries than in countries which import oil. In the former the export price may to some extent be sensitive to the amount sold and it may therefore be rational to price domestic products so as to increase domestic consumption a little and to shave the exportable surplus. In oil-importing countries, on the other hand, it may well be rational to assume that the real price of oil and gas will increase over time (Brazil has explicitly made this assumption since the Iranian Revolution) and thus to seek to discourage oil use. Both sides may reasonably be risk-averse in relation to future price expectations; this attitude will lead exporting countries to expand their domestic consumption and importing countries to reduce theirs.

A far more important factor than price expectation, however, is income distribution. Latin American populists, and some radical social scientists, have argued for low domestic energy prices on the grounds that these favour the poor and encourage industrialisation. It is obvious, however, that those who benefit most from cheap energy are those who consume most of it. Since there is a fairly direct relationship throughout the world between income level and energy use, it is clear that the rich use more energy than the poor and that the distributional effects of cheap energy are regressive. Latin American governments have sometimes sought to minimise or even reverse this regressive effect by manipulating the relative prices of the various oil subsidies. Domestic kerosene, used in poor urban households for cooking and heating, has generally been kept very cheap throughout Spanish America. In rather a different way, Brazilian policymakers since 1973 have sought to curb domestic rather than industrial use of oil products by deliberately overpricing gasoline relative to diesel oil. There are, however, problems with such a policy since, no matter how inelastic total demand for energy may be, the demand for any particular oil product is very elastic and there is very little that governments can do to prevent 'unauthorised' switching of demand into particular products. Moreover, such a major shift in the pattern of demand can create serious problems for oil refineries given that crude oil yields joint products with only a limited margin for substitution. Thus Brazil, as a result of the pricing policy mentioned above, was left with a surplus of gasoline, after demand for diesel oil had been met, which had to be exported at very low international prices. An alternative way of tackling this problem is to supplement the price mechanism with administrative controls. In some cases, notably when the state oil company sells to other state companies, this can be quite effective. In Mexico, for example, the state electricity industry was ordered to use natural gas rather than oil products even though the conversion plus purchasing cost was higher. Nevertheless, even if this works for the industrial uses of oil, it does nothing to remove one of the most striking features of a number of Latin American countries: very low gasoline prices.

Pricing policies also relate to the capitalisation of the industry. There is nothing in principle to prevent a government adopting a deliberate policy of low prices for oil-product consumers and high investment for the state oil company, with the financial balance being provided through direct government subsidy. In practice, however, such arrangements are usually unstable. As a matter of historical experience, except for brief periods of hyperinflation such as that prevailing in Bolivia in 1952–6, a large element of self-financing has been essential to the working of successful state oil companies. The main reason for this is probably that all Latin American governments face major claims for expenditure from a variety of domestic groups. Some of these will be based on social need although the most pressing will be based on possession of political power. Government resources are always likely to be under considerable pressure and the claims of a state oil company will not rank high in a competitive struggle. General Ravard correctly perceived this when he demanded in 1975, as a matter of the highest priority, that Petrovén should be essentially self-financing. In fact, taken as a whole, Latin American oil companies seem to have been reasonably successful in financing investment internally but, as we have seen, there are some very important variations between countries.[7]

The cost of resource misallocation as a result of low oil-product prices has often been compounded by attempts to disguise the effect of such a policy. For example, in Peru in the mid-1970s not only were domestic prices kept low but subsidies were not made available by the central government. As a result, Petroperú had to borrow abroad at positive real rates of interest that compounded the loss of real resources. Another consequence was that Petroperú had insufficient cash to continue developing its Amazonian reserves even though it was obvious to all concerned that a significant increase in oil production would have followed very quickly from such development, thus helping to alleviate Petroperú's financial difficulties. When the position eventually became impossible, domestic oil product prices had to be raised very sharply indeed.

In Argentina the damage went deeper still. The problem here has been not simply a low-price policy but an intense suspicion, both within YPF and on the part of certain governments, of any kind of financial orthodoxy. This was in part the result of an over-protected economy. Its effect, however, was not simply a misallocation of resources; it also led to the development of a cumbersome system of physical controls which greatly restricted managerial initiative and which also contributed, in no small part, to overmanning within the agency. Once an apparatus and a mentality of physical rather than financial control develops within an agency, reform will be costly, slow and difficult.

It is evident that throughout Latin America gasoline prices are a major focal point for political unrest. Price increases involve opposition from a powerful urban lobby of professional drivers, car users and bus passengers which contains just enough poor people to convey a populist appeal. Consequently, one might almost be able to compose an index of governmental repressiveness based on the domestic gasoline price; repressive governments raise prices while popular governments keep them low. It would, however, be unfortunate if repressive governments were able to claim a monopoly of economic rationality or if a sincere concern with the people led radical governments to squander their resources on policies of negative income redistribution.[8]

There is, as we have seen, a close connection between pricing and investment policies within the Latin American state oil industry. Lack of finance has undoubtedly constrained some investment plans and complicated others. However, the main inducements to invest have generally come either from the specific requirements of the industry or from political pressure. Very often state oil companies have been given specific objectives such as to discover enough oil to achieve self-sufficiency or to refine and market enough oil for domestic consumption. In some cases, however (notably Petrobrás), state companies have wished or been encouraged to move into sectors which had little intrinsically to do with oil. The government could count on a quick and certain response from Petrobrás in a way that it could not had it tried to deal with the private sector, and Petrobrás's own size and technical sophistication more or less guaranteed that it would carry out its new responsibilities reasonably well. Such a policy did, however, lead to opposition from the private sector, which feared that state control over the economy might go too far, and also from critics on the left, who felt that Petrobrás was sacrificing its identity and becoming just another conglomerate company. Nevertheless in general, the high capital-intensity of the oil industry and the internationally-traded nature of oil production have ensured that 'social obligations' are generally less important in the case of oil than in most other sectors.

Latin American state oil companies do face one other 'social' consideration of great significance. Whereas physical assets are important to their operation, the most important determinant of their success is the quality of their 'human capital'. A successful oil company is dependent on the services of highly trained and highly mobile men who are able to command very large salaries internationally. Unless state companies pay such salaries, they will not retain their best technicians and their quality will suffer greatly – witness YPF between 1946 and 1966. Similarly, a high salary policy can attract many talented foreign professionals into employment, as Petrobrás found in the 1950s. The danger of losing such staff is even greater when, as is now the case in the more industrialised countries of Latin America, there is a sophisticated local capital goods and oil-related industry. Naturally some interchange between public and private sector oil companies may be mutually desirable but the exchange may easily become an unequal one. Moreover, the 'politicisation' of an agency may be even more damaging than a low salary policy both because it embitters those who suffer from it and because it leads to a failure to appreciate the quality of their information; Brazil paid dearly for its over-emotional rejection of the Link Report both through misdirecting its exploration effort during the 1960s and through the loss of good technical staff from the agency. This brings us to more directly political factors.

Some political factors

It is generally true that conflict between the commercial operations of state (and private) oil companies and political sensitivities is often acute. To mention only the more evident factors, conflict may stem from the level of domestic prices, the location of investment by region, its allocation by sector, the nature of oil company funding or the relations between the state company and foreign suppliers, purchasers or bankers. Moreover, the oil industry in most Latin American countries is of great economic importance and is therefore likely to attract a good deal of political attention. There is always a danger, then, that the state oil company will attract political attention of a kind that will make its tasks more difficult.

One of the most serious problems facing some state companies has been the lack of day-to-day freedom from the attentions of an unsympathetic or uncomprehending government bureaucracy. There are many stories, in particular from YPF and Petroperú, concerning excessive centralisation in decision making, the development of bureaucratic practices damaging to the exercise of rational judgement, capricious or politically expedient intervention from the senior authorities and so forth. Such features may reflect a lack of understanding of the oil industry and bewilderment in the face of its many technical complexities.[9] They may also reflect an over-emphasis on the importance of formal status as against possession of expertise or a lack of trust on the part of senior authorities of their nominal subordinates. There may also be an excessive fear of failure regarding the organisation as a whole. At least at a psychological level these characteristics are likely to be strengthened further by bad results and suggest the possibility of some kind of vicious circle in the operation of the less successful companies.

Excessive centralisation is likely to be particularly damaging to an oil company in view of the variety of expertise, the multiplicity of judgements and the close co-ordination that must be involved in any successful project. At the same time, the extreme uncertainties associated with oil exploration may also lead over-cautious managers to seek an excessive degree of centralisation. As the local manager of one of the oil majors pointed out:

there is a tendency in all companies of this kind to push the level of responsibility upward. It is the job of people at the top to make sure that decisions are taken lower down and, if necessary, to insist on this.

When I was a young man who had just joined the company, I made several expensive mistakes which cost the company tens of thousands of dollars. I half-expected to be fired. On the contrary, my superiors continued to show confidence in me and insisted that I keep making my own decisions. Gradually I improved and, although I still frequently make mistakes, they are now fewer.

With the state company here, however, even senior officials are afraid of dismissal, press criticism or even prison if they make a serious mistake. So of course every decision is referred upwards, and passed around from section to section, and nothing gets done.[10]

An executive from a different private company but in the same country (not one of the six discussed above) told me of the time when the state oil company appointed a new managing director, a general. 'We knew he was no good when, in his first week in office, he personally sent us a directive complaining about a tap which had broken on one of our offshore loading jetties.'

It is not difficult to find examples of what can go wrong with state enterprise. Latin America has so far avoided some of the really spectacular disasters which have struck companies in other parts of the Third World.[11] Some Latin American companies have, however, been relatively unsuccessful if not quite disastrous, whereas others have records worthy of genuine pride. One important difference between the more and less successful state companies relates to the presence or absence of sense of direction on the part of their managements. In general this can be related to the nature of the original nationalisation. Essentially, foreign oil companies are excluded or expropriated from a mixture of two motives. The first, which may be called defensive, stems from a simple desire to 'keep the foreigners out'. The second, which may be called strategic, stems from a desire to bring about certain changes for which it seemed unsatisfactory to rely on foreign investment. There is some evidence for the hypothesis that state oil companies have been more successful when the motivation for nationalisation has been mainly strategic than when it has been mainly defensive, although as it stands this formulation is still too crude and does not work for Mexico or Argentina.

With a slight modification, however, a connection can be made between motivation and success rate. The more successful state companies were set up for a positive purpose by a political elite which was able to keep control during their formation and early years, or, alternatively, they were taken over and remodelled over a substantial period by such an elite. Conversely, when nationalisation took place as a response to excessive foreign influence (as in Mexico, Peru and Bolivia), the early years of the state company were difficult largely because of the lack of preparation and absence of a coherent strategy for public enterprise management. As Rosemary Thorp has pointed out for the case of Velasco's Peru (although she is referring here to the overall strategy), 'there is a definite "learning process" which operates in this area and Peru has never embarked very seriously upon it. This has the undoubted consequence that in the short term such policies either do not appear to be an option or else are seriously mishandled.'[12]

If a state oil company is to be 'turned round' after an unpromising start, it is crucial that it should be provided with a series of objectives which are both politically acceptable and within its operational capacity. When its objectives are not clear, a state company is likely to lose out in the inevitable 'boundary disputes' with other state agencies and be sent to the back of the queue for such things as access to scarce foreign exchange or other funds or for control over key parts of its programme. Something of the kind happened to YPF between 1935 and 1955. Once a government agency has been confined to the status of a Cinderella there will be considerable resistance on the part of others to any attempt to improve its position, because such improvement will involve the diversification of financial or political resources away from themselves. On the other hand its claims for better treatment will be prejudiced by its previously poor performance. Only a change of government and/or senior management is likely to bring about the required change of attitude.

Purely managerial reorganisations, however, will not put an end to deeper structural and political problems, such as the lack of any national consensus on the purpose of the agency or the lack of realistic appreciation of what can be expected from it. It is also true that there are other factors making for a vicious circle in poorly run state companies. Technically skilled workers are likely to leave a badly run organisation and may be difficult to bring back later, partly because they may not wish to return and partly because the less highly qualified men who have taken their place will not be eager to move over and make room. Appointment on the basis of political loyalty also opens the door to purging and counter-purging. Economic failure will further damage morale within an agency since it will stimulate the creation of a hostile political climate where any blunder will be eagerly seized upon and those inside the agency will become afraid of failure or individual blame rather than eager to innovate. Dogmatism or indecisiveness will tend to replace the use of judgement.

All of these considerations suggest that there are important pitfalls as well as advantages associated with state oil companies. However, it would be a mistake to end without emphasising that some state oil companies have proved to be very successful. Moreover, even though there is no simple 'one best way' of managing a state oil company, it is possible to suggest, at a high level of abstraction, what some of the best conditions for success might be. Clearly one must begin by mentioning a degree of political consensus and stability. This need not (or should not) imply simple conformity or atrophy and is in no way incompatible with active political competition. What is required, however, is at least a basic mutual trust between the oil company 'technostructure' and the government. This will not be achieved if the 'technostructure' is engulfed in political conflict. This trust and confidence will also be helped if the state company is given a role which is both clear and within its capacity to perform. Again, there will remain legitimate differences of opinion on what such a role should be, but clearly it does not help if demands are made on the agency which reflect a false view of the country's hydrocarbon resources or of the financial and technical attributes of the state company. Finally, it is necessary to respect the technical and organisational needs of state companies; these put severe limits on the extent to which 'social' criteria can be imposed upon state company management without serious side-effects. Growing awareness of these constraints has led some Latin American radicals into disillusionment with nationalisation and with the emergence of public sector technocracy. While it is likely, however, that some of the hopes which lay behind the creation of state oil companies could never be fulfilled, it remains true that in the right circumstances a state oil company will prove a valuable instrument in the hands of a government that has a clear and realistic idea of its strategic objectives.

24

Concluding reflections

Much of the economic history of the twentieth century could be written around the oil industry. In 1896 the world produced 114.2 million barrels of oil; in 1974 the figure was 20,338 million. Apart from the major changes in the industrial and political geography of oil extraction, the availability of oil has been essential to the development of aviation, automobiles and the vast chemical industry. The century has also seen major technical changes within the oil industry itself. To mention only the more striking developments, drilling techniques were revolutionised during the 1920s, catalytic cracking was introduced into refining in the 1930s and the natural gas industry was developed within the USA. Petrochemical and pipeline developments followed the Second World War, as did the increasing sophistication of crude oil recovery techniques, while serious offshore exploration began in the 1960s.

It is worth mentioning all of this in order to make the point that oil wealth and the value of crude oil reserves did not simply exist but had to be created by the development of oil-consuming industry, by world economic growth and by the development of increasingly sophisticated techniques to extract and transport oil and gas. These developments created the conditions which allowed the oil-producing countries to transform the international market to such an extent after 1970.

Thus, in the years before 1928 the oil companies were clearly engines of growth and were welcomed throughout Latin America, despite their occasional barbarities and general lack of sympathy for the aspirations of poor countries. They opened much of the continent to serious oil exploration and created conditions which would later enable at least some of these countries to turn the management of their industry to national advantage.

After 1928, however, under the impact of the depression and subsequent war, the largest companies lost much of their buccaneering character and became mature, bureaucratic enterprises. Daunted by the prospect of world oil surpluses and falling prices, they collaborated in order to restrain and slow down growth. Output continued to rise, profits were distributed more equitably between companies and governments and the companies still made many key decisions, but the companies gradually ceased to be indispensable or even capable of protecting their own interests. At first reluctantly and with misgiving, later with growing confidence, host governments began to attack and erode the position of the companies. When oil was in surplus oil-importing countries made most of the running, and when the prospect of shortage loomed the oil exporters took advantage of the situation. The parent governments, seeing the position of their companies eroded, their economies damaged by price increases and their oil supplies called into question, did not fully understand the situation and, as they were in any case only lukewarm imperialists, were unwilling or unable to shore up a disintegrating position with force. Thus the oil exporters, with a very clear common interest and a common producer ideology, were able to take advantage of their market strength and force irreversible changes on the world oil system.

Latin America played its part in this transformation. Two Latin American countries (Mexico and Venezuela) have possessed sufficient oil reserves to allow them to participate significantly in world oil politics. Although there is always a problem of defining oil reserves (definitions being either vague and uncertain or precise but misleading), there has been a surprising continuity in Latin American resource positions. Mexico has always been an important potential supplier of oil and is now much more important than ever. The same was true of Venezuela, although the Venezuelan industry has been contracting slowly since 1970: it may well begin to expand again after around 1985 (see chapter 22). There are several other Latin American countries with oil-producing industries which, although not great by world standards, are nevertheless crucially important in domestic terms: these countries were discussed in more detail in chapter 6.

Very little can usefully be said about the amount of oil which may eventually be recoverable from the world. Existing proven oil reserves say almost as much about the history of oil exploration and the state of oil recovery technology as they do about ultimate capacity. Certainly there are areas of the world in which there is no real chance of finding any oil, but there are large areas – including most of Latin America – where much of the work is still to be done. Prior to 1928 many of

these areas, particularly those in Latin America, were explored energetically by foreign companies. The Mexican boom went sour (for reasons considered in chapters 1 and 10) but Venezuela, under a modernising military dictator, established itself as a major oil producer.
Contemporary critics saw Venezuela as a 'petroleum factory' from
which local citizens achieved little return, but the way was at least
open for Gómez's successors to seek an improvement in these conditions.

In the years between 1928 and 1970 some foreign investment was
still available to Latin American governments. However, these were
the years in which attention shifted from Latin America to the Middle
East, while the industry was for most of this period in potential surplus. Thus the major companies were generally unwilling to invest
aggressively in oil exploration in Latin America, except perhaps in
Venezuela during the 1940s. Moreover, seeking to protect their positions in the Middle East, the majors insisted on concession contract
terms if they were to invest at all; these were designed to give the
investing companies almost complete freedom of manoeuvre. In several
cases, notably in Brazil, Argentina and Chile, these terms were unacceptable to host governments which might have been willing to permit
foreign investment under less restrictive conditions. Independent companies, generally more flexible in the terms they would accept, played
important roles in Venezuela in 1956 and Argentina after 1958 but
achieved prominence throughout the continent only after 1970. Thus,
in many Latin American countries, exploration was left to the state. At
times, as in Brazil (see chapter 11), state companies began serious work
only after political debates that lasted a decade or more. In other countries, notably Mexico, (chapters 10 and 17), the state companies came
into existence via expropriation on terms which guaranteed a few difficult years for the host government. State companies faced few insu-
perable technical problems although there was a significant financial
constraint during the dollar-scarce post-war years; by about 1960,
however, this had all but disappeared. Fundamentally, the successful
state companies were able to create, or take advantage of, a political
climate in which they could flourish; the less successful ones became
prisoners of political conflicts not of their own making.

During the 1970s state companies clearly became the dominant
force throughout Latin America. There were nationalisations in Ecuador and Venezuela and a major exploration success in Mexico which
raised Pemex to a position of world standing. In almost all oil-produc-

ing countries in Latin America the state exploration budget is greater than that of the private sector. Foreign investment is still available, and even the major companies will now consider terms which they would have rejected before 1970, but it is not always eager to commit itself; private oil companies have generally shown a disproportionate interest in the politically safest areas. International agencies, notably the World Bank, are showing a new interest in the finding and development of oil, and although their overall role has been small so far, they may come to play an increasingly important part in both financing projects and promoting various kinds of joint venture.

There remain areas in Latin America where it is likely that foreign companies can achieve some large-scale exploration success; offshore areas in Argentina and Brazil come immediately to mind. Nevertheless, it is now generally true that the main responsibility for finding oil lies with the state oil company. Some state companies (such as Pemex) have been remarkably successful and others (such as Petrobrás) have done reasonably well in difficult circumstances. It would be misleading to suggest, however, that all state companies have the ability to discover and develop such oil as may be in place, particularly in difficult offshore or otherwise remote parts of the country. In many cases host governments will find that a mixture of state and private investment will best suit their interests; much will depend upon the foreign companies' ability to maintain a flexible and diplomatic approach. International agencies such as the World Bank as well as parent governments may also help facilitate this process; crude pressure tactics will almost certainly fail, but other options remain.

Private Latin American capital is also likely to play an increasingly important part in the oil industry. In the period before 1930 the Latin American bourgeoisie, such as it then was, showed very little interest in oil and it was left to a comprador class to mediate between foreign capital and the weak Latin American state. From around the mid-1950s, however, the larger Latin American countries (Mexico, Argentina and Brazil) increasingly found local capitalists eager to move into oil-related activities; decades of industrial growth had allowed the creation of increasingly powerful local entrepreneurial groups who, though still willing to mediate between the state and international capital when it suited their purposes to do so, were increasingly willing to take a direct role in actual production. More recently, this trend has spread to countries such as Venezuela where for generations the oil industry had been left to the state and the multinationals. It remains improbable that local capital will play a major role in actual wildcatting but it may well move into oil development on an increasing scale, while continuing to play a significant role in providing technical services and producing petrochemicals.

Latin American countries have also participated in the world oil system through their domestic markets. As we saw in chapters 2 and 3, increasing market size did a great deal to determine the oil policies of a number of Latin American governments. State companies in Brazil, Chile and Uruguay all built their first refineries between 1935 and 1955, while Pemex re-oriented its oil policy away from a concern for export-led growth towards the objective of satisfying the domestic market. These projects and strategies would not have been possible earlier; had they been left until later they might well have been pre-empted. Argentina, with the largest home market in the 1920s, developed the first worthwhile state oil company, whereas Ecuador, with one of the smallest markets, was one of the last to do so. Increasing market size also played a central part in the decision of most Latin American countries to set up local petrochemicals industries and permitted the massive growth of this industry in Brazil and Mexico. Mexico is now planning to become an exporter of petrochemicals, a step that has been made possible only by the large size and rapid growth of its home market.

As well as making scale economies possible, market size also had the effect of increasing the balance of payments cost of oil imports. It is notable that oil-importing countries generally set up state oil companies before countries that exported oil; the effect of the depression, in which oil supplies became scarce because the governments could not easily afford to pay for imports, proved crucial for Chile and Uruguay. In a more long-term sense, the depression focussed attention within Latin America upon the balance of payments and stimulated the doctrine of import-substituting industrialisation. According to this doctrine, foreign exchange was naturally scarce and needed to be protected by tariffs and state investment in strategic areas. A state oil company exploring domestically became a natural part of an industrialising state. With the exception of Pemex, such state oil companies were set up more to promote state investment in oil than to restrict foreign investment. Between 1955 and the early 1970s, the gradual fall in world oil prices and the increasing availability of foreign credit reduced the pressure on oil policy and state companies in importing countries. Following the world oil revolution, however, acute balance of payments

problems had much to do with the decision to readmit foreign investment into oil exploration in Brazil, Chile and Uruguay, although a
change in the intellectual climate was also an important factor.

In the case of Brazil, the largest importer of oil in Latin America,
balance of payments considerations were paramount in a whole series
of policies adopted in the energy sector after 1970. In 1970 Braspetro
was set up to explore internationally and repatriate any profits to Brazil. In 1975 foreign companies were allowed for the first time to
explore directly for oil in Brazil; since then the amount of territory
open to such companies has been steadily extended. Petrobrás itself
undertook a major reallocation of investment into domestic exploration
and development. Outside the oil sector itself, Brazil has been investing very heavily in hydroelectricity and has also pioneered the substitution of alcohol for oil products in gasoline. This substitution programme could take on very great importance in the 1980s. Moreover,
the direction of Brazilian foreign policy has been influenced perceptibly
by the need to protect its oil supplies in the years after 1974.

A major problem for almost all Latin American governments has
been the level of domestic prices. Brazil and Chile, with military governments promoting liberal economic doctrines and with a history of
importing oil, have been able to raise their domestic prices to near
world levels and thus to hold back increases in domestic consumption.
Other countries have faced difficulties. Traditional exporting countries, eager to spread the benefits from oil by a policy of low domestic
prices and mindful of the political upheavals that might result from
high gasoline prices, have been reluctant to make changes in response
to changing world conditions. In some cases (notably in Venezuela,
Mexico and Ecuador) this has resulted in extremely low domestic price
levels which eat severely into potential oil export income and encourage
the international smuggling of oil products. In others (notably in Peru
since 1975) policies have finally been changed after major budgetary
crises but at high political price. Some countries that are not quite self-
sufficient have continued with a damaging low-price policy while governments, in many cases unhappy with this position, lacked the political courage to change it.

A third way in which Latin American countries are just beginning
to become internationally important lies in their marketing or purchasing policies. For importing countries the problem is easy to state
although difficult to resolve: how to make the best of changing world
realities. Not surprisingly, the foreign policies of at least the largest

importing countries have shown a marked tilt towards their oil suppliers. Exporting countries have had to consider a wider range of issues; exporting decisions have tended to reflect the income needs of the domestic population, the state of the world oil market and the foreign policy preferences of the country in question. Until the 1970s most oil production decisions of international importance were taken by private companies interested in global balance rather than in the needs of the particular country in which they operated. Since then state companies and host governments have played a more important role and have, naturally enough, taken into consideration the absorptive capacity of their own populations in relation to potential export earnings. Smaller countries have sought to lower their output, larger countries have sought to increase theirs or at least to maintain it, although since the Iranian Revolution all governments have been wary of the political effects of an uncontrolled flood of oil income. The main Latin American oil-exporting countries have comparatively large populations with a high propensity to import; even so, the Mexican government will reflect carefully in the future on how much oil revenue its economy can usefully absorb. International market conditions remain unpredictable but it is likely that both Mexico and Venezuela will cut back their levels of production if the position of OPEC or the world price level are seriously threatened. Regarding foreign policy, the elites of the main Latin American oil producers face something of a conflict between their historically close relationship with the USA and the new financial and economic power of the main Middle Eastern oil exporters. Both Mexico and Venezuela (and for a very short period Ecuador) played leading roles in asserting oil nationalist policies in the past, but from the mid-1970s they have increasingly taken a back seat to Middle Eastern countries, whose preoccupations with the state of Israel and with fundamentalist Islam are specific to that region. Thus, Latin American exporters have attempted to play a moderating and mediating role. Venezuela has pressed for high prices but always maintained continuity of supply. Mexico has sought to diversify its markets away from the USA but has not joined OPEC; it remains to be seen how far its future production decisions are made with foreign policy considerations in mind. The Mexican–Venezuelan agreement to provide cheaper oil to Central America and the Caribbean countries has been regarded as an imaginative contribution to relieving Third World poverty as well as creating new foreign policy concerns for those countries. Mexico's oil trade with Cuba, or the lack of it, will also become the subject of international scrutiny.

Whatever detailed policies may be, however, state companies have played a central role in the international oil system during the past decade. This has been no more than the culmination of a series of tendencies whose historical roots are at least as old as the century. The twentieth century has been one of increasing state control over oil, a trend which has been clear in Latin America as elsewhere. It is likely to continue.

Notes and bibliography

Notes

Introduction: The politics of oil in twentieth-century Latin America

1 'The devil's excrement'.

1 The corporate ascendancy 1890–1927

1 Quoted in H. F. Williamson *et al.*, *The American Petroleum Industry: the Age of Energy 1899–1959* (Seattle, 1963), p. 242.

2 M. Wilkins, *The Emergence of Multinational Enterprise: American Business Abroad from the Colonial Era to 1914* (Cambridge, Mass., 1970), p. 64.

3 John De Novo, 'The Movement for an Aggressive Oil Policy Abroad 1918–20', *American Historical Review*, vol. 62 (1956), pp. 854–76.

4 *Annual Report for 1920*.

5 R. Hidy and M. Hidy, *Pioneering in Big Business 1882–1911: History of Standard Oil New Jersey* (New York, 1956), p. 258.

6 Wilkins, *The Emergence of Multinational Enterprise*, pp. 185–6.

7 Pearson Collection at the London Science Museum, box c26, Cowdray to Murray, 17 June 1913. As we shall see, however, Cowdray had not always followed his own advice.

8 *Annual Reports for 1920–9*.

9 M. Wilkins, *The Maturing of Multinational Enterprise: American Business Abroad from 1914 to 1970* (Cambridge, Mass., 1974), pp. 61–2.

10 *Petroleum Press Service* (1950). I have converted the figures from metric tons to daily barrels.

11 C. Gerretson, *Geschiedenis der 'Koninlijke'*, vol. 5 (The Hague, n.d.) p. 318. At this time, Chile's main import was fuel oil (purchased as crude oil), which competed with coal in the nitrate mines. Demand for gasoline 'took off' only after the First World War. Fuel oil demand rose from 368 b/d in 1906 to 8,280 b/d in 1914.

12 Pearson Collection, box c 44, file 1, memo by Cowdray, 13 August 1912.

13 G. Gibb and H. Knowlton, *The Resurgent Years 1911–27: History of Standard Oil Company, New Jersey* (New York, 1956), pp. 566–7.

14 R. Miller, 'British Business in Peru 1883–1930' (PhD thesis, Cambridge, 1979), p. 168.

15 *Ibid.* p. 173. In fact, as Miller points out, up until 1914 the main problem was to find a market for the product. See also Cowdray's comments (n. 7, above).

16 Capital values for these years are provided by Gibb and Knowlton, *The Resurgent Years,* p. 377.

17 J. Herbert Sawyer, 'Exploration in Latin America', p. 962, in E. Wesley Owen (ed.), *Trek of the Oil Finders: A History of Exploration for Petroleum* (Tulsa, 1975).

18 FO 371, A 2629/1166/26, 4 April 1934.

19 N. Stephen Kane, 'Corporate Power and Foreign Policy: Efforts of American Oil Companies to Influence United States relations with Mexico', *Diplomatic History,* vol. 1, (1977), pp. 170–98, p. 174).

20 Pearson Collection, box C 44, file 3, Cowdray to Cadman, 8 May 1919.

21 *Ibid.* 22 May 1919.

22 Gibb and Knowlton, *The Resurgent Years,* p. 361.

23 *Ibid.* p. 365.

24 Quoted in *ibid.*

25 Brian McBeth, 'Venezuelan Oil' (mimeo, London, 1979).

26 Henrietta Larson, K. Knowlton and C. Pople, *New Horizons 1927–50: History of the Standard Oil Company, New Jersey* (New York, 1971), p. 128.

27 FO 371 A 694/410/54, 27 January 1938.

28 On which, see Rory Miller, 'The Forgotten Firm: Lobitos Oilfields Limited and the Early Development of the Peruvian Petroleum Industry' (mimeo, Liverpool, 1979).

29 R. Thorp and G. Bertram, *Peru 1890–1977: Growth and Policy in an Export Economy* (London, 1978), p. 103.

30 See Miller, 'The Forgotten Firm', and Thorp and Bertram, *Peru 1890–1977.*

31 McBeth, 'Venezuelan Oil', p. 12.

32 Pearson Collection, box C 29, Masters to Cowdray, 6 May 1913.

33 Gerretson, *Der 'Koninlijke',* vol. 5, Deterding to Plyte, 5 January 1915.

34 L. Meyer, *México y los Estados Unidos en el conflicto petrolero 1917–42,* 2nd edn (Mexico City, 1972), p. 38.

35 Miller, 'The Forgotten Firm', p. 5.

36 Larson, Knowlton and Pople, *New Horizons,* p. 134.

37 Peruvian Corporation Archive, University College, London. Thurlow to Cooper, 17 August 1923. The Peruvian Corporation later pulled out on the advice of Deterding himself.

38 Miller, 'British Business in Peru', pp. 175–6.

39 *Ibid.*

40 Quoted in B. McBeth, 'Juan Vicente Gómez and the Venezuelan Oil Industry' (B. Phil. thesis, Oxford, 1975), p. 69.

41 For similar conclusions on Mexico see Meyer, *México y los Estados Unidos,* p. 45, and on Bolivia see H. Klein, *Parties and Political Change in Bolivia 1880–1952* (Cambridge, 1969), pp. 77–8.

42 Pearson Collection, box C 27, letter from Pérez, 7 September 1914.

43 FO 371 A 521/38/26, 20 January 1928.

44 Meyer, *México y los Estados Unidos,* p. 36, quotes a figure for El Aguila of only $1.1m.–1.25m. per year, and goes on to quote a number of other specific cases where royalties were very low indeed. These latter figures appear to have been taken from Josephus Daniels, *Shirt-sleeved Diplomat* (Chapel Hill, 1947). These, however, were provided by landowners who had complained about how little they

received (some such complaints were successful) and cannot be regarded as representative. According to Gibb and Knowlton, *The Resurgent Years,* p. 363, Jersey Standard estimated in 1922 that its average royalty was 5c a barrel – not a trivial sum but less than that implied by El Aguila's £30m. In July 1980 a secret archive of Huasteca Petroleum was discovered in Mexico; once it has been investigated, the question will probably be answered.

45 Argentina is discussed again in chapter 8. The best study of the politics of oil concessions during the period is that of J. Buchanan, 'Politics and Petroleum Development in Argentina 1916–30' (PhD thesis, Univ. of Massachusetts, 1973).

46 C. Mayo *et al., Diplomacia, política y petróleo en la Argentina 1927–30* (Buenos Aires, 1976), p. 21. This very useful study is wider than its title implies. The Colombian position was rather similar; see J. Villegas, *Petróleo, oligarquía e imperio* (Bogotá, 1975), p. 115. In Chile, Shell found that in 1913 the potential oil-bearing territory was covered by no fewer than 3,471 prospecting licences; see Gerretson, *Der 'Koninlijke',* vol. 5, ch. 10.

47 Quoted in C. Solberg, *Oil and Nationalism in Argentina: a History* (Stanford, 1979), p. 38.

48 E. Mosconi, *El petróleo argentino* (Buenos Aires, 1936), p. 115.

49 Pearson Collection, box C 26, file 1, Ribon to Cowdray, 25 March 1913.

50 I. G. Bertram, 'Development Problems in an Export Economy: a Study of Domestic Capitalists, Foreign Firms and Government in Peru', (DPhil thesis, Oxford, 1974), p. 258.

51 Lobitos, like IPC, was willing to lend money to President Leguía in return for specific favours. Royal Dutch/Shell originally helped to finance Leguía's coup of 1919 but, after abortive negotiations for a concession, finally pulled out in November 1921 after Leguía asked for a further $100,000. See Gerretson, *Der 'Koninlijke',* Murray to Anglo-Saxon Petroleum 9 November 1921.

52 FO 371 A 2334/2334/55, *Annual Report for Bolivia 1930.*

53 *Ibid.* A 3165/2547/5 25, June 1924. Things might perhaps have been different if Bolivia had been more central to Jersey Standard's designs. However, as Corwin wrote to Teagle in 1920, 'the whole interest in such fields is the assurance gained by holding large areas available for production in the distant future when the fields now in sight will either diminish or fail to supply the increased consumption'. Quoted in Gibb and Knowlton, *The Resurgent Years,* p. 362.

54 One British company, sincerely shocked by the suggestion that a British company should pay bribes in Bolivia, set up a Chilean subsidiary for the purpose.

55 See E. Lieuwen, *Petroleum in Venezuela: a History* (Stanford, 1954), and Brian McBeth, 'Juan Vicente Gómez and the Venezuelan Oil Industry' (DPhil thesis, Oxford, 1980).

56 Pearson Collection, box C 25, Field to Ryder, 25 January 1923.

57 *Ibid.*

58 Ribon to Murray, 25 January 1914, and to Cowdray, 25 March 1913.

59 Pena Herrera to Lucian Jerome, 15 September 1913.

60 S. J. Randall, *The Diplomacy of Modernization: Colombian–American Relations 1920–40* (Toronto, 1977), p. 91.

61 Shell did briefly offer a joint venture arrangement to Peru in 1921, mainly because it wanted the Peruvian government to put up some of the capital, take some of the

risk and protect the company from local landowners and other extortionists. The company was well aware that, as Murray pointed out, the government knew next to nothing about petroleum and was having difficulty in finding the cash to pay its own civil servants. See Gerretson, *Der 'Koninlijke'*, vol. 5.

62 Mayo *et al.*, *Diplomacia*, p. 185.

63 Randall, *Diplomacy of Modernization*, pp. 98–9.

64 N. Stephen Kane, 'Corporate Power', p. 196. This conclusion runs counter to that of Meyer, who provides the best available blow-by-blow account of the 1925–7 conflict in *México y los Estados Unidos*, pp. 233–89. Meyer's perspective is broadly shared by R. F. Smith, *The United States and Revolutionary Nationalism in Mexico 1916–32* (Chicago, 1972).

65 The belief, held by the Wilson administration in Washington and by some later historians, that British policy toward Huerta and Carranza was entirely dominated by oil considerations, has been discredited by Peter Calvert, *The Mexican Revolution 1910–14: the Diplomacy of Anglo-American Conflict* (Cambridge, 1968). But see also E. Durán de Seade, 'Mexico's Relations with the Great Powers during the Great War', (DPhil thesis Oxford, 1980). The author shows that British interests were active in defence of their oil properties.

66 Quoted in Smith, *The United States and Revolutionary Nationalism*, p. 41.

67 FO 371 A 87/86/26.

68 An interesting discussion of presidential power in foreign policymaking during this and other periods appears in A. Schlesinger, *The Imperial Presidency* (Boston, 1973).

69 British Minister Ovey complained that 'Mr Sheffield belongs utterly to the school of thought which preaches force, force and nothing but force' (FO 371 A 948/40/26, 4 February 1927). Ovey's more conciliatory line was supported in London despite opposition from the USA and also from El Aguila and he received an official congratulation after the Calles–Morrow agreement was signed. It is a pity that the same wisdom did not govern British policy towards Mexico during the 1930s.

70 FO 371 A 5272/40/26, 19 August 1927.

71 *Ibid.* A 948/40/26, 4 February 1927.

72 Kane, *Diplomatic History*, from which the quotations in this paragraph are taken.

73 Meyer, *México y los Estados Unidos*, pp. 233–89, provides a full account of this period.

74 Apart from John de Novo, 'The Movement for an Aggressive Oil Policy', see also M. J. Hogan, 'Informal Entente: Public Policy and Private Management in Anglo-American Petroleum Affairs', *Business History Review* (1974), J. S. Tulchin, *The Aftermath of War: World War I and US Policy Toward Latin America* (New York, 1971), and B. McBeth, 'Juan Vicente Gómez'.

75 Pearson Collection, box C 25, file 1, Ribon to Murray, 25 January 1914. See also Iturralde's speech quoted in chapter 9, below. For more scholarly studies of this period, see Smith, *The United States and Revolutionary Nationalism*, and Calvert, *The Mexican Revolution*.

76 F. P. Baran, *The Political Economy of Growth* (Stanford, 1957), contains the most famous statement of the case that 'The principal impact of foreign enterprise on the development of the underdeveloped countries lies in hardening and strengthening the sway of mercheant capitalism, in slowing down and indeed preventing its transformation into industrial capitalism' (p. 194). Thorp and Bertram also explore this theme in *Peru 1890–1977*.

Regarding the oil industry, however, the mercheant (comprador) class lost its political grip as the state apparatus throughout Latin America became increasingly sophisticated, generally between 1930 and 1945. Local capitalists involved with oil after 1945 were a much more genuine bourgeoisie in the sense that, although they traded in part upon their political connections, they were interested in developing their own production capacity rather than simply mediating between foreign capital and the state.

2 Retrenchment and concentration 1928–41

1 Williamson *et al.*, *The American Petroleum Industry*.
2 FO 371, A 3410/3410/35, *Annual Report for Peru 1930*.
3 *Ibid*. A 59830/5930/11, 23 July 1934.
4 In Venezuela, Gulf, Jersey Standard and Shell entered into a production agreement in November 1933 which was strengthened in September 1936. See McBeth, 'Oil in Venezuela', p. 19.
5 P. H. Giddens, *Standard Oil Company (Indiana): Oil Pioneer of the Middle West* (New York, 1955), p. 489.
6 Royal Dutch/Shell, *Annual Reports*.
7 *Ibid*.
8 FO 371 A 9676/5930/11, 15 November 1934.
9 It is in fact the case that Mexican Eagle was legally a separate company from Canadian Eagle and that the list of shareholders in each was not identical; but it is also true that the Canadian Eagle was deliberately created for tax purposes. The objective was not to use transfer prices to take profits out of Mexico, but to prevent transfer prices from increasing the profits allocated to Mexico.
10 The US tariff also had the effect of weakening the position of host governments *vis-à-vis* international companies. On this, see McBeth, 'Oil in Venezuela', pp. 39–42.
11 On this period, see McBeth, 'Juan Vicente Gómez', and Knudson, 'Petroleum: Venezuela and the United States'.
12 FO 371 A 2389/1732/47, 28 March 1938.
13 Thorp and Bertram, *Peru 1890–1977*, pp. 165–6.
14 J. Fred Rippy, *British Investments in Latin America 1822–1949: a Case Study in the Operation of Private Enterprise in Retarded Regions* (Minneapolis, 1959), p. 132.
15 Thorp and Bertram, *Peru 1890–1977*, p. 139.
16 The file FO 371 A 410/410/54 *et seq.* covers this story quite neatly.
17 FO 371 A 1397/344/9, 17 March 1932.
18 *Ibid*. A 977/344/9, 17 February 1932.
19 *Ibid*. A 443/11/9, 8 February 1939.
20 *Ibid*. A 2624/1166/26, 4 April 1934.
21 Larson, Knowlton and Pople, *New Horizons*, p. 350. To add to the above examples, Jersey Standard lost $250,000 in Uruguay in 1935 and made little money in that country during the decade. See US State Department Memo, 'Relations of the Uruguayan Government Petroleum Corporation with the Foreign Companies', 31 January 1948; Declassified Document C 322, released 1979.
22 *Proyecto de refinería de petróleo del estado* (Santiago, 1939).

23 FO 371 A 8565/667/26, 8 October 1935. Daniels's memoirs, *Shirt-sleeved Diplomat,* reinforce the accuracy of this judgement.
24 FO 371 A 7891/132/26, 13 October 1937.
25 *Ibid.*
26 *Ibid.* A 6299/132/26, 30 August 1937.
27 *Ibid.* A 6299/10/26, 4 March 1938.
28 *Ibid.* A 2004/10/26, 15 March 1938.
29 F. Gellman, *Good Neighbour Diplomacy: United States Policies in Latin America 1933–45* (Baltimore, 1979). Another good treatment of this topic is provided by Cole Blasier, *The Hovering Giant: US Responses to Revolutionary Change in Latin America* (Pittsburgh, 1976), p. 122.
30 The tone of the British protests revealed clear interference in Mexican affairs as well as a very low opinion of the Mexican government. It is interesting that the most 'hawkish' view of the issue came from London although Ambassador O'Malley was still able, after the expropriation, to describe Cárdenas (and the Mexican people in general) as 'a mixture of Indian inferiority and Spanish arrogance'. It is also interesting that pressures from El Aguila shareholders carried very little weight in London, where national security – in terms of access to crude oil supplies – was seen as the main issue. London, unlike Washington, feared a 'domino effect'.
31 Bryce Wood, *The Making of the Good Neighbour Policy* (New York, 1961).
32 *Ibid.* p. 194.
33 *Ibid.* p. 196.
34 Meyer, *México y los Estados Unidos,* pp. 413–14.
35 *Ibid.* pp. 456–7.

3 The making of the post-war oil world 1942–55

1 Ministry of Fuel and Power, Power 33, vol. 224, Van Hassalt to Godber, 24 June 1941.
2 *Ibid.* vol. 224, Godber to Hopwood, 27 August 1942.
3 *Ibid.* vol. 224, Godber to Starling, 1 October 1942. Linam was head of Jersey Standard in Venezuela, Crebbs and Greer were representatives of Gulf Oil. Linam, then aged 41, was described by the British Ambassador (Gainer) as follows: 'he has no social or educational background and outside of business, where he is admittedly a brilliant figure, he has nothing but a number of deep seated prejudices' (FO 371 A 7435/4224/47, Gainer to Eden, 18 September 1941).
4 FO 371 A 8412/503/47, 31 August 1942.
5 Wood, *The Making of the Good Neighbour Policy,* p. 267. At this point it was Welles and Thornburg who took the initiative within the State Department. In October 1942 Manrique Pacanins, speaking for the Venezuelan government, informed Welles that Venezuela had retained a firm of US oil consultants (Hoover and Curtice) to make recommendations for new legislation; if the companies did not cooperate, this new law would be passed and any companies refusing to comply would be harassed by legal challenges to their earlier concessions. Some of Lago's concessions (now owned by Jersey Standard) were to be examined first.
6 *Ibid.* p. 270. In London, the Petroleum Department was relatively hard line (as it was regarding Mexico) whereas the Foreign Office was much more conciliatory.

On 27 May 1942 Anthony Eden minuted that 'the oil companies will be wise if they accept these additional burdens with good grace' (FO 371 A 4797/503).

7 Ministry of Fuel and Power, Power 33, vol. 224, Van Hassalt to Godber, 6 September 1942. This point was certainly arguable but by no means self-evident. In fact, there had long been misgivings within the Venezuelan elite regarding the position of the oil companies. See Lieuwen, *Petroleum in Venezuela*. Moreover, AD was flexing its political muscles by calling for higher taxes from oil and better treatment for the workers. See R. Betancourt, *Política y petróleo*, p. 174.

8 Ministry of Fuel and Power, Power 33, vol. 224. This insistence was undoubtedly based on a genuine dislike of Linam on the part of Medina and Manrique Pacanins, who was in charge of the actual negotiations. Nevertheless, it is likely that Welles and Thornburg independently welcomed an initiative to transfer responsibility for negotiations to themselves. In late September 1942, just before the State Department intervened directly, Welles told Hopwood (the British oil representative in Washington) that 'it had been made clear to him that it was felt that Henry Linam and also to some extent Greer were unsuitable to do the negotiations on behalf of the American companies'. (FO 371 A 8946/503/47, Hopwood to Godber, 29 September 1942). Welles's original idea was to persuade the New York office of Jersey Standard to negotiate a settlement which would then have to be accepted by the other companies. After opposition from Gulf Oil, the task fell directly on Thornburg himself to draft out the basis of a settlement with Venezuela, the companies filling in the details.

9 Larson, Knowlton and Pople, *New Horizons;* but see also n. 3, above.

10 See Wilkins, *The Maturing of Multinational Enterprise,* p. 276.

11 Once Jersey Standard had decided, under pressure from Welles, to shift responsibility from its Caracas office to its New York one, it became the most conciliatory of the companies. Shell saw no alternative but to go along with Jersey Standard but Gulf was for a time obdurate. This may have been because Gulf had paid $10m. to the Venezuelan government in 1940 in order to have its concession titles recognised; Gulf's position changed, however, when the Venezuelan government discovered a different kind of possible legal claim against the company.

12 *Ibid.* p. 276. According to Ambassador Gainer, after Welles's intervention in late September 1942, 'the companies are alarmed and are prepared now to go very much further to meet views of the Venezuelan government than at any time previously' (FO 371 A 9273/503/47 Gainer to Eden, 6 Oct. 1942). The complete terms of the new law are set out in the *Petroleum Press Service* of 1943 (pp. 102–4). Essentially they involved an increase in the royalty payment to 16.67% and a multiplicity of other taxes which the government expected would yield about 50% of total company profits in any one year. This projection was contested by the Venezuelan opposition and in fact proved over-optimistic in view of rising oil prices. In return for these tax changes, the companies were confirmed in their existing holdings for a further 40 years.

13 Betancourt also argued that 'a regime which planned to maintain its autocratic character was historically incapable of confronting this problem. It lacked the courage and moral authority which only comes from the support of the majority of the people' (*Política y petróleo,* p. 176). This argument and its variations have been heard often in Latin America.

14 *Petroleum Press Service,* July 1948.

15 *Fortune,* February 1949, p. 96. Much of the information in the next two paragraphs is taken from this article.

16 *Ibid.* p. 178.

17 *Ibid.* It is also worth consulting *Foreign Relations of the United States, 1946,* and *1947.* The documents bear out the essential accuracy of the *Fortune* article.

18 FO 371 AS 1840/273/43, 17 March 1948.

19 *Fortune,* February 1949, p. 178. Some readers may find it difficult to see how an oil company can be both non-political and pro-government. Some of the ambiguities of the Venezuelan case will be explored in chapter 15.

20 *Petroleum Press Service,* July 1949.

21 *Ibid.*

22 Thorp and Bertram, *Peru 1890–1977,* p. 168.

23 The British Embassy reported that opposition to the contracts came from 'the extreme Right and the Communists [who] are united in their desire to embarrass APRA . . . APRA justly claimed authorship of the project' (FO 371 AS 3805/1267/35, 3 July 1946).

24 The British Ambassador reported in 1947 that 'the acting manager of this company [IPC] told the commercial secretary that there is likely to be a considerable drop in production in the Talara oilfields within the next few years' and that Peru might even become a net importer of oil (FO 371 AS 5217/533/35, 8 September 1947).

25 *Ibid.* AS 3549/553/35, 16 June 1947.

26 Thorp and Bertram discuss this point in *Peru 1890–1977,* pp. 221–9.

27 Larson, Knowlton and Pople, *New Horizons,* p. 731.

28 *Foreign Relations of the United States, 1946,* pp. 679–80.

29 *Foreign Relations of the United States, 1948,* p. 451. The Communist Oil-Workers' Movement, CTAL, held a meeting in Mexico in October 1948 in which it was resolved, among other things (numerical order as in original):

3. To struggle for the development of national industry . . . as a basis for opposing the anti-national policies of the oil trusts.

4. To interest in this patriotic struggle not only the working class of each country, but all progressive sectors which for historical reasons should necessarily be concerned about the present absolute dominion of the oil companies.

To these provisions were added others which called for better pay and treatment for oil-workers, while certain spokesmen also made it clear that they would try to cut off oil supplies to the USA in the event of a war with the USSR.

The British Foreign Office noted that 'Venezuelan representatives were a minority group but militant Mexican and Colombian representatives must be taken seriously' (FO 371, AN 3719/0088/26, 14 October 1948).

30 *Foreign Relations of the United States, 1951,* p. 1303.

31 Ministry of Fuel and Power, Power 33, vol. 343, Godber to Starling, 9 October 1941.

32 *Ibid.* vol. 343, Shell memo, 4 April 1946.

33 See, for example, E. Penrose, *The Large International Firm in Developing Countries: the International Petroleum Industry* (London, 1968), and J. M. Blair, *The Control of Oil* (New York, 1977).

34 A British Foreign Office official remarked that 'the US have succeeded in getting into Bolivian oil exploration quite ingeniously and . . . the same tactics may be tried in Mexico and Chile' (FO 371 AS 7072/341/5, 15 November 1946). Damn clever these Yankees!

35 L. Fanning, *American Oil Operations Abroad* (New York, 1947), p. 19.

36 A. Silenzo de Stagni, *El petróleo argentino* (Buenos Aires, 1955). The British government, however, believed that Argentina was 'unreceptive to these approaches' even before the 1943 coup (Power 33, vol. 224, telegram 28998 from Washington, 4 October 1942).

37 See R. B. Woods, 'Hull and Argentina: Wilsonian Diplomacy in the Age of Roosevelt', *Journal of Inter-American Studies and World Affairs,* vol. 16, no. 3 (August 1974), and Gellman, *Good Neighbour Diplomacy,* ch. 14.

38 *Foreign Relations of the United States, 1946,* p. 627.

39 The British government actively discouraged UK companies from entering Chile except under concession contracts.

40 A. Sampson, *The Seven Sisters* (London, 1975), H. Feis, *Three International Episodes as seen from E.A.* (New York, 1946), and M. B. Stoff, *Oil, War and American Security: the Search for a National Policy on Foreign Oil 1941–7.* (New Haven, 1980).

41 H. Feis, *Petroleum and American Foreign Policy* (Stanford, 1944), p. 54.

42 L. Meyer, 'La resistencia al capital privado extranjero: el caso del petróleo 1938–50', in B. Sepúlveda *et al., Las empresas transnacionales en México* (Mexico City, 1974), and M. Alemán *La verdad sobre petróleo mexicano* (Mexico City, 1977).

43 *Foreign Relations of the United States, 1945,* p. 1160.

44 *Foreign Relations of the United States, 1950,* pp. 949–53.

45 *Ibid.* p. 937.

46 *Ibid.* p. 956.

47 *Ibid.* p. 938.

48 It was Mexico that suggested that a non-oil loan could in practice be treated as an oil loan; Bermúdez later wrote that 'It was well understood that the Mexican government would, in turn, make available to Petróleos Mexicanos a sum in pesos equivalent to the $150m.' (*The Mexican National Petroleum Industry: a Case Study in Nationalisation* (Stanford, 1963), p. 181).

49 IBRD, *Annual Report.* There can be no doubt that the World Bank consistently sought to persuade Third World governments to be liberal towards foreign investors. Thus, according to R. Vedavalli, the Bank in three separate missions to India discouraged the setting up of state-owned oil refineries. R. Vedavalli, *Private Foreign Investment and Economic Development: a Case Study of Petroleum in India* (Cambridge, 1976).

50 Cole Blasier, 'The United States and the Revolution', in J. M. Mallory and R. S. Thorn (eds.), *Beyond the Revolution: Bolivia since 1952* (Pittsburgh, 1971), pp. 53–110.

51 L. A. Whitehead, *The United States and Bolivia: a Case of Neo-colonialism* (London, 1969), p. 10.

52 S. G. Hanson, 'The End of the Good Partner Policy', *Inter-American Economic Affairs,* vol. 14, no. 1 (Summer 1960). See also chapter 4, below.

53 J. E. Hartshorn, *Oil Companies and Governments: an Account of the International Oil Industry in its Political Environment* (London, 1967), ch. 8.

54 M. A. Adelman, *The World Petroleum Market* (Baltimore, 1973), p. 98.

55 Adelman reports that, as of 1968, 'contractors do about 60 percent in the United States but 90/95 per cent in the Middle East and about 86 percent in Africa' (*ibid.* p. 201).

56 'Oil Exploration in Latin America', by J. Herbert Sawyer, p. 1167, in Wesley Owen, *Trek of the Oil Finders.*

57 Quoted in *NACLA Newsletter,* February 1969.

58 It would be nice to think that Gulf Oil lavished its gifts on President Barrientos in the same state of mind. Gulf Oil appears to have followed the advice of a nineteenth-century US businessman: 'If you have to pay money to have the right thing done, it is only just and fair to do it', quoted in R. Hofstadter, *The American Political Tradition and the Men Who Made It* (New York, 1967), p. 163. R. A. Packenham, *Liberal America and the Third World* (Princeton, 1973), is excellent on the ideas behind US foreign policy.

4 The major companies in retreat 1955–70

1 On these, see Penrose, *The Large International Firm,* ch. 5, and compare also Adelman's conclusion that 'the price increases of 1957 marked the zenith of post-war control of the market' (*The World Petroleum Market,* p. 159).

2 N. Jacoby, *Multinational Oil* (New York, 1974), p. 82, provides the following data on the allocation of US oil investment abroad.

($000)

	1946	1961	1972
Sector			
Production	2,410	15,810	32,220
Pipelines	225	3,095	8,590
Marine	1,325	10,170	26,950
Refineries and petrochemicals	1,220	11,390	42,030
Others	145	1,210	3,045

3 *Ibid.* p. 248.

4 Blair, *The Control of Oil.* It should be noted, however, that book-value based estimates such as these may be misleading for two reasons, both of which would suggest that downstream profits were higher and upstream ones lower than these figures might suggest. The first involves transfer prices. There is evidence that the major companies preferred to allocate their profitability disproportionately to the upstream sector in order to take advantage of tax credit arrangements and the depletion allowance and also because the political sensitivity of the Middle East was greater than that of Europe. There is also the point that the depreciation provisions for capital assets in the oil industry practically guarantee that the older the asset, the greater the divergence that is likely between book and market value. There will therefore be a bias towards overstating the real profitability of assets in areas where there has been little reinvestment (notably, in this case, the producing

areas) and understating it in areas (notably downstream and in transportation sectors) where it has been heavy and depreciation costs consequently large. Thus, according to G. Gals, the lower aggregate returns for downstream investment during the period 'may be interpreted as reflecting the rapid growth and investment expansion in which major companies were engaged during that period', in R. F. Mikesell (ed.), *US Private and Government Investment Abroad* (Portland, 1962), p. 424. Gals notes, however, that the major companies with key Middle Eastern concessions were generally more profitable than smaller independent companies.

5 But see note 4, above.

6 This worked in three different ways:

a. Under the 'law of capture', the legal system provided that any individual had the right to develop any oil found beneath his property. Consequently, in the event of any oilfield being discovered, the neighbours of the oil finder were forced to drill quickly to prevent the oil beneath their property being depleted by his exploitation of the entire field through a single well. Overdrilling, however, is likely to reduce the amount of recoverable oil *in situ*.

b. The depletion allowance and some specific tax concessions encouraged drilling, as did the fact that certain development costs may be treated for tax purposes as expenses (immediately deductible) rather than investments (deductible only over a period).

c. Until 1973 production (allowables) in many US states (including Texas, which was the largest) was regulated in order to maintain the price. (Allowables were exemptions from quota limits to oil production.) Although output in most wells was held back, very small 'stripper' wells and newly drilled wells were immune from regulation.

After noting these, and particularly the last, M. Adelman noted that 'waiving any claim to precision, it is difficult to escape the conclusion that the bulk of the development work in these eight years [1955–63] was waste and done largely to get additional allowables' ('The World Oil Outlook', p. 57, in M. Clawson (ed.), *Natural Resources and International Development* (Baltimore, 1964), pp. 27–126).

7 The story of this transformation regarding the Middle East has been well told elsewhere and need not be repeated here. See, for example, Sampson, *The Seven Sisters,* and the US Senate Committee on Foreign Relations, *Multinational Corporations and US Foreign Policy,* vol. 5, January/February 1975.

8 F. Tugwell, *The Politics of Oil in Venezuela* (Stanford, 1975).

9 E. H. Shaffer, *The Oil Import Program of the United States: an Evaluation* (New York, 1968), pp. 107–10.

10 According to Shaffer, the tax increases imposed by Venezuela in 1958 were a major factor in this decision. He argues that 'Since the US government had no desire to encourage other governments to follow Venezuela's lead, it did not wish to grant Venezuela exempt status in the mandatory program which went into effect shortly after the enactment of Venezuela's new tax law. To have done so might have provided other countries with an incentive to follow suit. By differentiating between Venezuela and Canada, the US government let the other oil countries know that it did not favour such action' (*ibid.* p. 124). This may well be true, although Shaffer provides no evidence. On the other hand, exports from Venezuela

to the USA were rising rapidly at the time, from 384,000 b/d to 611,000 b/d, particularly from 'newcomer' companies. These were discriminated against by the provisions which treated residual fuel oil exports from Venezuela far more generously than exports of crude oil.

Moreover, it is significant that the US State Department knew of proposed restrictions in the form of a 20% cutback on Venezuelan oil prior to the 1958 elections (and the 1958 tax increase) and urged the Commerce Department not to make its proposals public before these elections lest this benefit the Communists. (See US Declassified Document C 453, released 1979, Herter to Strauss, 21 November 1958). The fact that this proposal was different from that actually applied in 1959 helps Shaffer's argument.

11 Tugwell, *The Politics of Oil*, p. 54.
12 K. Faud, 'Venezuela's Role in OPEC: Past, Present and Future', p. 16, in R. D. Bond (ed.), *Contemporary Venezuela and its Role in International Affairs* (New York, 1977), pp. 120–55.
13 Venezuela had significantly shifted the composition of its exports by encouraging foreign companies to build refineries within the country under the terms of the 1943 oil law. The refineries that were built were large and simple and were set up with the aim of supplying fuel oil to the USA to complement the 'lighter' products processed by refineries within the USA.
14 Shaffer, *The Oil Import Program*, p. 95.
15 *Peru 1890–1977*, p. 229.
16 *Ibid.* pp. 221–9.
17 Quoted in P. Odell, 'Oil in Latin America', pp. 176–7, in Penrose, *The Large International Firm*.
18 For example, Belco Petroleum bought up several offshore Peruvian concessions in 1959–60 and began an energetic programme of exploration despite the fact that, in the early 1960s, Peru had so much difficulty in finding markets that it was exporting on a very small scale to Chile, Indonesia, New Zealand and Australia. As *World Oil* (15 August 1963) pointed out, 'these shipments indicated the difficulty of finding markets'. The following year, *World Oil* (15 August 1964) reported that Belco 'was still hampered by its difficulty of marketing the crude. Nearly half of its potential production was shut in and 14 wells were temporarily closed. At year end 47 wells were producing.' Nevertheless, Belco continued to invest aggressively and, from the end of 1967, was able to sell its production to the state company EPF for refining in its La Pampilla refinery. At the end of 1967 Belco's investment in Peru was calculated at $32m. (*World Oil*, 1 August 1968), and it was a major supplier of the domestic market. Moreover, Gulf Oil had some difficulty in finding markets for all of its Bolivian production. In 1967 it made an exceptionally favourable offer of low-cost oil supply to EPF for the La Pampilla refinery which was to include technical help for the state company, even though Gulf was to be allowed to market a certain amount of gasoline in Peru in exchange.

The point, however, is not that these companies faced some marketing difficulties, but rather that they were nonetheless willing to invest.
19 R. Vernon, *Sovereignty at Bay: the Multinational Spread of US Enterprises* (London, 1973), pp. 116–17.
20 A detailed account of company motivations in one major exploration campaign, Peru in 1971–3, is provided in G. Philip, 'Policymaking in the Peruvian Oil

Industry, with special reference to the period October 1968 to September 1973'
(DPhil thesis, Oxford, 1975).

21 Hartshorn, *Oil Companies and Governments.*

22 Interview with Arturo Sabato, Buenos Aires, September 1979. It is interesting
that the president of Amoco Petroleum defended his company's decision to enter
Argentina under contract on the ground that 'a ready market exists for the crude
that will be developed and produced'. Quoted in Gals, in Mikesell (ed.), *US Private
and Government Investment Abroad,* p. 422.

23 Quoted in Sampson, *The Seven Sisters,* p. 190. The same author, however, also
quotes an exchange in which Exxon manager Howard Page 'was once told by one
of the Exxon geologists who had just come back from Oman: "I am sure there's a
billion [barrel] oilfield there." Page replied, "Well then, I'm absolutely sure that
we don't want to go into it, and that settles it. I might put some money in it if I
was sure that we weren't going to get some oil, but not if we are going to get oil
because we are liable to those the Aramco concessions" ' (p. 181). It would seem
that individual or group judgement was particularly important here.

24 P. Odell, 'Oil and the State in Latin America', *International Affairs,* vol. 40 (October 1964), p. 662.

25 On the Indian case, see M. Tanzer, *The Political Economy of International Oil in the
Underdeveloped Countries* (Boston, 1969). An interesting discussion of the majors'
refining policies and government response in Africa is provided by T. Turner,
'Two Refineries: a Comparative Study of Technology Transfer to the Nigerian
Refining Industry', in *World Development,* vol. 5, no. 3 (March 1977), pp. 235–
56.

26 *World Oil,* 15 August 1956.

27 Betancourt, *Política y petróleo,* p. 323.

28 Banco Central de Venezuela, *La economia venezolana 1940–73* (Caracas, 1973), p.
122. This series is slightly different from that provided by the *Petroleum Press Service*
and shown in table 3.4, above.

29 The *Petroleum Press Service* in October 1951 reported that the 'distributing companies are losing heavily' and Petrovén made a similar complaint about the domestic
market in 1976 and 1977.

30 Peru, Ministerio de Minas y Energía, *Estadística petrolera* (1968).

31 Odell, 'Oil and the State, p. 663.

32 Brazil, Petrobrás, *Annual Report for 1956* declared that the company was opposed
to any suggestion that it should move into marketing.

33 For example, M. Adelman and M. Zimmermann, *La industria petroquímica en un
pais subdesarrollado* (Bogotá, 1973).

34 *Latin America,* 21 June 1968.

35 E. Acosta Hermoso, *Petroquímica: ¿desastre o realidad?* (Caracas, 1977), p. 110.

36 R. J. Alexander, *The Venezuelan Democratic Revolution* (New York, 1964), p. 212.

37 *Petroquímica,* p. 55.

38 IDB, *Annual Report for 1963.*

39 *Annual Report for 1965.*

40 *Annual Report for 1967.*

41 *Petroleum Press Service,* 1967.

42 *Business Latin America,* 7 May 1975.

43 'Multinationals, State-Owned Corporations and the Transformation of Imperial-

ism: a Brazilian Case-Study', in *Economic Development and Cultural Change* (October 1977), p. 47.

44 Quoted in *ibid.* p. 57.

45 R. Engler, *The Brotherhood of Oil: Energy Policy and the Public Interest* (Chicago, 1977), pp. 119–20.

46 Quoted in *ibid.* p. 121.

47 Hanson, 'The End of the Good Partner Policy', pp. 74–5.

48 *HAR* (January 1958).

49 F. Parkinson, *Latin America: the Cold War and the World Powers 1945–73* (London, 1974).

50 *HAR,* November 1957.

51 Parkinson, *Latin America,* p. 56.

52 E. Mariaca Bilbao, *Mito y realidad del petróleo boliviano* (La Paz, 1966).

53 *HAR,* September 1959.

54 *New York Times,* 16 April 1960. This point was not made only by the MNR left; more conservative figures within the MNR had similar perceptions even if their objectives were different. Thus, on 19 August 1960, the *New York Times* quoted Guevara Arce, a right-wing *movimientista,* as being 'critical of the United States refusal, on general policy grounds, to lend money to the state oil company . . . A breakdown of the state company could produce a political reaction jeopardizing foreign oil investments'.

55 Parkinson, *Latin America,* p. 114.

56 *HAR,* May 1961. It is worth noting that even in late 1960 Washington appears to have been hoping that it could find a way of avoiding an open change of policy. Thus, on November 24, the *New York Times* reported that 'Officials here said that the United States at first sought to persuade West Germany to counter the Soviet offer. However, as the political situation in Bolivia grew worse, the Administration evidently decided that it could not risk waiting until Bonn agreed to underwrite the full amount of aid needed'. Subsequently, the West German government did provide some finance for the state-run Bolivian mining industry.

57 For example, according to J. O'Connor, 'The companies fully expected to be taken over sooner or later and decided to force a showdown over the issue of Soviet crude' (*The Origins of Socialism in Cuba* (New York, 1964), p. 163).

58 P. Bonsal, *Cuba, Castro and the United States* (Pittsburgh, 1971), p. 149.

59 This appears to have been generally, although not universally, true of oil company behaviour after 1945.

60 Bonsal, *Cuba,* p. 117, points out that the companies had offered some minor favours to the Cuban government during 1959 in the hope that these would buy Cuban goodwill.

61 The IBRD commissioned W. J. Levy to write a report on this question. When it appeared, the report, 'The Search for Oil in Developing Countries: A Problem of Scarce Resources and its Implications for State and Private Enterprise', was broadly opposed to any policy of World Bank lending to state companies.

   The Bank was, however, generally less reluctant to lend to projects which had private sector participation. Thus, in 1959 it made a $50m. loan to CFP (the Compagnie Française de Pétrole) and the French government for an oil pipeline in the colony of Algeria. In 1963 it followed this up with a $20.5m. loan to a gas liquefaction project in independent Algeria; this was a joint venture in which the state held only 20% of the capital. In 1968 it lent $23.75m. to Bolivia for a joint venture between Gulf Oil and YPFB to build a gas pipeline to Argentina. The consequences of this will be discussed in chapter 13.

62 US Declassified Document 45 F, released 1975, McLintock to Washington, 2 December 1963.
63 *Ibid.*
64 4 December 1963. US Declassified Document 46 B, released 1975.
65 20 June 1964, US Declassified Document 172 E, released 1975.
66 *Ibid.*
67 *Ibid.*
68 *Ibid.*
69 10 March 1965, US Declassified Document 173 B, released 1975.
70 On this point, see for example, R. J. Smith, 'The United States Government Perspective on Expropriation and Investment in Developing Countries', *Vanderbilt Journal of Transnational Law,* vol. 9, no. 3 (Summer 1975).
71 J. Levingstone and J. De Onis, *The Alliance that Lost its Way* (Chicago, 1970).
72 Quoted in R. Goodwin, 'Letter from Peru', in *New Yorker,* 17 May 1969.
73 G. Treverton, 'US Foreign Policymaking in the IPC Case' (mimeo, Washington, 1974).
74 There was a tendency within the USA, well exemplified by Goodwin's *New Yorker* article, to exaggerate the extent to which Peru was dependent on US aid. This perception appears to have been shared by the US Embassy, which appeared to believe prior to 1968 that cutting aid was an effective substitute for intelligent diplomacy.
75 Quoted in the *Financial Times,* 25 February 1969. Against this, however, the regime worked hard behind the scenes to reassure other US businessmen that they would not be affected, whatever happened. The Velasco regime always used the technique of being radical in Spanish and moderate in English.
76 *El comercio* (Lima), 20 and 22 March 1969. As is now clear from US State Department documents, however, Occidental was prepared to act as an indirect medium for compensating IPC. See Paul Sigmund, *Multinationals in Latin America: the Politics of Nationalisation* (Madison, Wisconsin, 1980), p. 92.
77 This period is discussed in more detail in G. Philip, 'The Political Economy of Expropriation: Three Peruvian Cases', in *Millennium,* vol. 6, no. 3, 1977–8 (Spring 1978), pp. 221–35.
78 J. Einhorn, *Expropriation Politics* (Lexington, Mass., 1974), pp. 58–9. Einhorn provides a very interesting picture of US policymaking during this period.
79 See G. Ingram, *Expropriation of US Property in South America: Nationalization of Oil and Copper Companies in Peru, Bolivia and Chile* (New York, 1974), pp. 175–80. However, according to V. Andrade, Bolivia did in fact approach the USSR but 'the Kremlin showed no interest whatever in marketing natural gas, in exploration for new deposits, or in financing the completion of the pipeline to the Argentine border' (*My Missions for Revolutionary Bolivia 1944–52* (Pittsburgh, 1976), p. 186). There had been some press reports that Moscow might be interested in buying Bolivian crude in order to supply Cuba.
80 *Peruvian Times,* 3 April 1970.
81 The fullest account of this period was provided by *Informe politico–económico* on 12 May 1975 when *Informe* took advantage of the revelations surrounding the conduct

of Gulf Oil in Bolivia to provide a full account of the post-expropriation period in
Bolivia. Although the editor would not comment, several interview sources in La
Paz confirmed that the report was essentially accurate.

82 Ingram, *Expropriation,* p. 182.

83 *Presencia,* 10 March 1971.

84 Einhorn, *Expropriation Politics,* p. 79. (Original italic.)

5 The oil market revolution and its consequences for Latin America 1971–9

1 It will not be possible here to discuss these events in any detail, except in as far as
they affected Latin America. For fuller treatment the reader is referred to L.
Turner, *Oil Companies in the International System* (London, 1978), Sampson, *The
Seven Sisters,* and R. Weisburg, *The Politics of Crude Oil Pricing in the Middle East*
(Berkeley, 1977).

2 'Why the Multinational Tide is Ebbing', *Fortune,* August 1977, p. 118.

3 From the point of view of Shell, of particular importance was the unique suitability
of a particular Venezuelan crude oil for manufacture into a very popular and highly
profitable lubricant. For this and other reasons, one executive told me that around
10% of Shell's pre-tax profits continued to be attributable to the company's operations in Venezuela.

4 *Fortune,* August 1977, p. 118.

5 Interview data.

6 Interview data.

7 Petroleum Economist: *Latin American and Caribbean Oil Report* (London, 1979), p.
153.

8 F. R. Wyant finds that there is a 'strong relationship between an OPEC member's
level of shut-in capacity and need for current revenues' (*The United States, OPEC
and Multinational Oil* (Lexington, 1977), p. 105).

9 Admiral Jarrín Ampudia's speech to the Universidad Central de Guayaquil, 6 June
1976.

10 *New York Times,* 12 October 1974.

11 *Ibid.* 20 October 1974.

12 *Financial Times,* 20 March 1975.

13 'El debate nacional sobre el petróleo', in *Vuelta* (January 1979).

14 Quoted in *Documentos fundamentales sobre petróleo,* Universidad Central de Guayaquil
(Guayaquil 1976), p. 116.

15 F. Tugwell, 'Venezuela's Oil Nationalization: the Politics of Aftermath' in R. D.
Bond (ed.), *Contemporary Venezuela,* p. 113.

16 Interview data.

17 This objection was powerfully stated in an article in *Uno más uno,* 30 December
1978. This article was written under a pseudonym by an influential Mexican and
argued, among other things, that 'the possibility of a rapid inflation following the
export of oil is, whatever happens, something to consider carefully and objectively.
We already know about the political and economic effects of a major inflow of oil
money; the risks that these will sustain or increase the speculationist tendencies in
the economy are very serious or at least considerable.'

18 *Petroleum Economist,* 1979, p. 145.

19 This touches on an old problem considered, for example, in Vernon's *Sovereignty at*

Bay. Any company deciding to invest in oil exploration considers its venture on the basis that there is a chance of finding oil but a probability that it will not. Very successful ventures both compensate for, and help finance, the failures, and expected rates of return need to be high. Adelman in *The World Petroleum Market,* ch. 2, estimates that companies would require a rate of return of 20% on a successful venture if they were to invest in Latin America; this figure is much the same as that provided by my own interview sources. However, once oil is found the risk is substantially lessened. Under these circumstances, a host government will be able to reduce company profitability to a level which takes into account only the maintenance of existing operations and (possibly) reinvestment in areas of lower risk (development drilling, etc.). Unless a company believes that a government can be prevented from so acting, at least for a limited period while high profits can be made, it will consider a new investment not on the basis of the actual terms offered but on what these terms might be following renegotiation.

Clearly, international conditions in the 1970s lent weight to company suspicions that speedy renegotiation was likely. In Peru in 1974 the government responded to the oil price increases by making clear its intention to renegotiate its contracts for exploration of the Selva (signed in 1971–3) even before oil production had begun on a significant scale, and in 1975 the Mines and Energy Minister declared that Peru would join OPEC once reserves of a sufficient size had been discovered. Moreover, as we shall see in chapter 14, renegotiation in Ecuador in 1972–3 was also very harsh and Gulf Oil later said that it was making only 5–10% on its capital in Ecuador before it sold out at the end of 1976.

For these reasons, a number of Latin American governments in the 1970s tried to attract foreign investment on terms that provided for automatic renegotiation after a certain period of time.

20 Questions such as this are discussed further in Philip, 'Policymaking in the Peruvian Oil Industry', ch. 9.
21 See *ibid.* chs. 7–9.
22 Armand Hammer of Occidental talked to President Velasco of Peru about the opportunities of the Amazon as early as 1969 – two years before the exploration contract was signed – and spent around 40 minutes in Velasco's ante-room telling another oil company executive about the riches of the Amazon. (Interview data.)
23 According to Bernardo Grossling, 'When reviewing the petroleum opportunities through Latin America it becomes apparent that outstanding possibilities are met in the Argentine continental shelf' (*Latin America's Petroleum Prospects in the Energy Crisis* (Washington, 1975), p. 30).
24 *Latin America Economic Report,* 30 September 1977.
25 *Petroleum Economist,* May 1979.
26 See various reports in the *Petroleum Economist* and, from the beginning of 1980, in *Brazil Energy.*
27 *Latin America Economic Report,* 7 July 1978.
28 Grossling, *Latin American Petroleum Prospects,* p. 33.
29 *Ibid.* p. 8.
30 The IDB also increased its lending to energy projects and reduced its restrictions on lending for oil projects. In 1980 it lent $23.5m. to Jamaica to finance offshore wildcat drilling and in 1981 it lent to both Peru and Brazil for seismic work.
31 *Latin America Economic Report,* 13 September 1974. The report stated that ENAP

was looking for some $150m. to build an LNG plant at Cabo Negro, Magallanes. ENAP was hoping for support from the IDB. The project was intended eventually to substitute gas for fuel oil imports in the copper mines but before this could be arranged exports would be necessary. ENAP's original idea was to use the gas for various petrochemical ventures and to finance the LNG exports on the basis of loans or trade credits but not partnerships. As we have seen, these plans were later somewhat changed.

32 P. Evans, 'Multinationals', p. 53.

33 The Pact originally included Colombia, Ecuador, Peru, Bolivia and Chile. Venezuela joined at the end of 1974 and Chile left in 1975.

34 See the article in the *Economist,* 1 April 1979.

35 See note 1, above.

36 Turner, *Oil Companies in the International System,* ch. 9.

37 Tugwell, *The Politics of Oil in Venezuela,* pp. 134–5.

38 The classic case was Nixon's statement in September 1973 that 'The radical elements that [*sic*] presently seem to be on [*sic*] ascendancy in various countries in the Mid-East, like Libya. Those elements, of course, we are not in a position to control, although we may be in a position to influence them, influence them for this reason; oil without a market, as Mr Mossadegh learned many, many years ago, does not do a country much good.' And a market without oil?

39 *Financial Times,* 22 December 1977.

40 *New York Times,* 19 July 1974.

41 *New York Times,* 21 July 1974. It would be interesting to know how he would have regarded the Ayatollah Khomeni.

42 *El comercio* (Quito), 13 July 1974.

43 *New York Times,* 27 September 1974.

44 *Washington Post,* 8 January 1975.

45 Turner, *Oil Companies in the International System,* pp. 179–86.

46 See J. Petras, M. Morley and S. Smith, *The Nationalisation of Venezuelan Oil* (New York, 1977). This book is not always reliable in its discussion of Venezuela, but quite useful on the US response.

47 When I spoke to Jarrín in Quito he emphasised that OPEC, having achieved surprising success, was not certain how best to continue. Consequently, countries with new ideas, such as Ecuador and Algeria, had an influence far greater than their economic importance. Moreover, since Saudi Arabia and Iran were far from friendly at this time, it was important to conciliate and try to hold OPEC together. It is certain that Jarrín was strongly supported by the government of Venezuela.

48 *New York Times,* 30 June 1975.

49 Olga Pellicier de Brody provides an excellent account of Mexican–US diplomacy in 'El petróleo en la política de Estados Unidos hacia México 1976–80' (unpublished paper, Cuadernos sobre perspectiva energética, no. 2, Colegio de México, 1980). She is surely right to link changes in US foreign policy to changes in the internal political situation of the USA and particularly to the passage of the US energy bill through Congress.

6 Latin America in the twentieth-century oil system

1 J. Cotler and R. Fagan (eds.), *Latin America and the United States: the Changing Political Realities* (Stanford, 1974), provides a fascinating example of the debate

between those who believe that the essentially variable internal political processes of the USA are crucial in policymaking toward Latin America and those who believe the policies are determined more 'structurally' by economic or ideological factors. In the Cotler and Fagan book almost every North American wrote from the first standpoint and almost every Latin American from the latter.

2 P. H. Frankel, *Essentials of Petroleum* (London, 1946), put forward the classic argument that 'there has been, always and everywhere, an overwhelming tendency towards concentration, integration and cartelization in the petroleum industry' (p. 127). Some of his arguments do appear to rely upon specific institutional factors such as the US 'law of capture' rather than any universal inevitability, but there can be no doubt that he has proved a far better guide to subsequent events than those writers who assumed that oil would be guided by the logic of a free market and that prices would fall towards the cost of production in the cheapest and most prolific oilfields in the world. Institutional factors play a part in any market and are clearly of unusual importance in the case of oil. Nevertheless Peter Odell appears to be going too far when he argues that 'the present high degree of concentration of both reserves and production is nothing more than a series of historical accidents arising out of recent imperial and colonial history' ('A Personal View of "Missing Oil" ', *Petroleum Economist* (January 1980)). However only time will tell.

3 *Ibid.*

7 Politics and the concession contract

1 Two of the most explicit and useful writings from this approach are R. F. Mikesell (ed.), *Foreign Investment in the Petroleum and Mineral Industries: Case Studies of Investor – Host Country Relations* (Baltimore, 1971), and T. H. Moran, *Multinational Corporations and the Politics of Dependence: Copper in Chile* (Princeton, 1974).

2 M. Bronfenbrenner in his interesting article, 'The Appeal of Confiscation in Economic Development,' in *Economic Development and Cultural Change,* vol. 4 (April 1955), argued that confiscation of foreign companies might in fact make a country better off. Such a position lies well within the bargaining approach as defined here since it is based on the assumption of coherent rationality on the part of the host government. Bronfenbrenner, however, was considering the socialisation of an entire economy where the assumption of economic maximisation is highly implausible; this kind of rational and coherent maximisation is more likely when we are talking of a single industry within a given overall framework. Under the latter conditions confiscation will very rarely pay since the company involved will probably be able to exercise sufficient leverage in Washington or elsewhere to ensure that it does not. It is a valid point, however, that there is an 'appeal of confiscation' and that multinational oil companies, among others, have prepared strategies to protect themselves, as far as possible, against this threat.

3 See, for example, Bertram, 'Development Problems', ch. 4, which argued this explicitly with reference to the Leguia government in Peru (1919–30).

4 This logic can also be inverted with the argument that economic nationalism strengthens middle-class control over the economy to the detriment of broader national interests which lie in the faster rate of economic growth that private ownership can bring about. See H. G. Johnson, 'A Theoretical Model of Economic Nationalism in New and Developing States', in Johnson (ed.), *Economic Nationalism in Old and New States* (Chicago 1967).

8 Argentina: YPF, Yrigoyen and the 1935 oil law

1 Grossling, *Latin America's Petroleum Prospects,* p. 29.

2 Sceptics include F. A. Hollander, 'Oligarchy and the Politics of Petroleum in Argentina: the Case of the Salta Oligarchy and Standard Oil 1918–33' (PhD thesis, University of California at Los Angeles, 1975), and Solberg, *Oil and Nationalism in Argentina.* Solberg, who looked through the Argentine literature of the period, points out that the government was indeed interested in looking for oil, but there is still no serious evidence that it intended to find any in Comodoro Rivadavia. Captain Luce, of H.M.S. *Glasgow,* reported to the British government in 1914 that, in the course of a visit to the oilfield, 'I enquired of the French inspector whether the country gave the appearance typical of an oil-bearing country and he informed me that, although the experts since the discovery of oil said that it did so, in his opinion there was nothing to indicate oil in any way previous to its accidental discovery when boring for water six years ago' (FO 368 A 102/20829/12, 13 April 1914).

3 Pearson Collection, box C 29, file 1, Purdy to Body, 19 September 1913.

4 *Ibid.* 20 November 1913.

5 *Ibid.* 19 September 1913. He might have had in mind Huergo's assertion that 'Throughout the world Standard Oil acts like a band of cruel, usurious pirates, headed by an ex-clerk, who began by carrying thousands among his own countrymen to ruin. Like an octopus, it has extended its tentacles everywhere, accumulating colossal fortunes of millions of pesos on the basis of human blood and tears.'

6 *Ibid.* 28 November 1916. Selected papers from *La Razón* appear in the Pearson Collection.

7 *Ibid.* box C 29, file 2, memo to Body, 20 February 1917.

8 YPF, *Desarrollo de la industria petrolifera fiscal 1907–32* (Buenos Aires, 1932).

9 Pearson Collection, box C 29, file 2, Anderson to Pearson, 15 October 1917.

10 Gibb and Knowlton, *The Resurgent Years,* p. 381.

11 Pearson Collection, box C 29, file 1, Purdy to Body, 19 September 1913.

12 FO 371 A 4934/1455/2, June 1920. There is also considerable discussion of this episode in the Pearson Collection. There were, in fact, some areas open to private capital just outside the reserve area, but most exploration here was unsuccessful. On June 22 Pearson were told by their representative that 'The only concerns that are getting satisfactory results are the Argentine government fields, the Cía Ferrocarrilera de Petróleo and the Cía Astra Argentina' (Pearson Collection box C 29, file 4).

13 *Revista de economia argentina,* June 1930.

14 *Oil and Nationalism,* p. 70. The reader is referred to this source for a detailed account of the state oil commission during this period.

15 In 1930 T. Serghiesco, head of YPF's geological division, complained that YPF had 'lived more for the present than the future' and that Mosconi frequently overruled his geologists. Within Rivadavia output per well in 1928 was less than half its 1924 level (Solberg, *Oil and Nationalism,* ch. 4).

16 Malumphy, quoted in Herbert Sawyer, 'Oil Exploration in Latin America', p. 1175, in Wesley Owen (ed.), *Trek of the Oil Finders.*

17 FO 371, *Annual Report for 1923.*

18 This situation was foreseen by Pearson's representative in Argentina in 1917 who

advised the company not to enter Argentina unless under contract with the state company: 'A further reason to doubt the desirability of undertaking operations in Argentina is that the prospect of entering into competition with the government is not alluring. One of the considerations leading the government to undertake and continue the exploitation at Comodoro Rivadavia is that it will afford it a means to control the price of oil' (Pearson Collection, box C 29, file 2, Anderson to Pearson, 15 October 1917).

19 Gibb and Knowlton, *The Resurgent Years,* p. 563.
20 Pearson Collection, box C 29, file 2, Anderson to Body, 25 April 1920.
21 Solberg, *Oil and Nationalism,* and Mayo *et al., Diplomacia,* are both good on the politics of this campaign; the next section is largely derived from their accounts.
22 Mayo, *Diplomacia,* p. 60.
23 *Ibid.* especially ch. 4. See also chapter 1, above.
24 FO 371 A 5922/2062/2, 1927. It is only fair to point out, however, that the British Embassy in Buenos Aires was never very perceptive on the oil question.
25 *Argentina and the Failure of Democracy: Conflict among Political Elites 1904–55* (Madison, 1974). Smith, together with Mayo and Solberg, offers something of a revisionist view against earlier writers, notably A. Frondizi, *Petróleo y política* (Buenos Aires, 1956), who saw Yrigoyen as a genuinely committed neutralist and nationalist in a way that his opponents were not.
26 D. Rock, *Politics in Argentina 1890–1930; the Rise and Fall of Radicalism* (Cambridge, 1975), p. 239.
27 Solberg, *Oil and Nationalism,* p. 118. There was also considerable academic support for policies of oil nationalism; see *El petróleo argentino,* Comité Universitario Radical, Junta Central (Buenos Aires, 1930).
28 Solberg, *Oil and Nationalism,* p. 117.
29 Rock, *Politics in Argentina,* p. 236. Solberg shares the conclusion that the oil issue essentially mobilised the Buenos Aires middle class.
30 E. Mosconi, *El petróleo argentino* (Buenos Aires, 1936), p. 181.
31 Quoted in Mayo *et al., Diplomacia,* p. 99.
32 Buchanan, 'Politics and Petroleum Development', ch. 6.
33 Hollander, 'Oligarchy', pp. 312–13.
34 In November 1926 Jersey Standard wrote to the State Department that 'we feel that this district may well develop into the most important producing area in the Argentine, and that our concessions cover by all means the greatest part of the prospective productive area'. Quoted in Solberg, *Oil and Nationalism,* p. 106.
35 FO 371 A 468/468/2, 1932.
36 Solberg, *Oil and Nationalism,* pp. 59–63, provides evidence of a mysterious Bolivia–Argentina company (possibly a Standard Oil subsidiary) which planned to force its way into Argentina by flooding the market with cheap Bolivian oil. This plan, which proved abortive, anticipated support from certain northern governors.
37 Other explanations have certainly been put forward for this fact. Some writers have seen a secret British influence in this campaign, and it is certainly true that the British railway companies, which produced significant amounts of oil, were never part of a united company front. Nevertheless the railway companies were less influential in Argentina than is often imagined. Colin Lewis, for example, concludes that 'seemingly so powerful, the railway lobby had to be seen to be controlled by the government if politicians were to maintain their credibility. In Argentina,

despite the apparent strength and power of the British railway community, the state was paramount, its task made easier by an absence of concerted action among railway managers . . . despite all the literature that now exists on the theme of direct and co-ordinated pressure, little scope for such pressure and coercion in fact existed (C. M. Lewis, 'British Railway Companies and the Argentine government', p. 427, in D. C. M. Platt (ed.), *Business Imperialism: an Analysis based on the British Experience in Latin America before 1930* (Oxford, 1977). A more plausible, but partial, explanation for the same feature lies in the simple fact that a US company was inevitably an easier target than a British one in Argentina at that time.

38 Quoted in Mayo *et al., Diplomacia,* p. 149. This is not just a statement taken out of context. Mayo shows that many punches were surprisingly pulled during the oil campaign in 1929 and 1930.

39 Smith, *Argentina and the Failure of Democracy,* p. 95.

40 Mayo *et al., Diplomacia,* p. 149.

41 R. Potash, *The Army and Politics in Argentina 1928–45* (Stanford, 1969), p. 23. Potash provides a very full account of the politics of the military during this period but has very little to say about oil. This suggests that the issue was not particularly intrusive at that time.

42 For a discussion of this episode see Hollander, 'Oligarchy'.

43 27 June 1934. See also R. Silveyra, the head of YPF, arguing the government's case, in *YPF rectifica: aclarando y puntualizando manifestaciones vertidas en la H. Cámera de Diputados* (Buenos Aires, 1934).

44 FO 371 A 7013/7013/2, Shell memo to Foreign Office, 12 November 1934.

45 Pearson Collection, box C 29, file 2, Adams to Body, 14 April 1920.

9 Some nationalisations of the 1930s: Chile, Uruguay, Bolivia

1 Senator Vicuna's speech to Congress, 22 June 1927, reported in FO 371 A 4592/4592/9.

2 *Ibid.* A 870/344/9, 10 February 1932.

3 *Foreign Relations of the United States, 1932,* pp. 507–8.

4 FO 371 A 870/344/9, 10 February 1932.

5 *Ibid.* A 1488/344/9, 10 March 1932.

6 *Ibid.* A 1639/344/9, 18 March 1932.

7 *Ibid.* A 2244/344/9, 12 April 1932.

8 *Ibid.* A 3503/344/9, 10 June 1932.

9 *Ibid.*

10 *Ibid.* A 5874/344/9, 8 September 1932.

11 *Ibid.*

12 *Ibid.* A 7105/344/9, 21 September 1932.

13 *Ibid.* A 6647/344/9, 6 September 1932.

14 *Ibid.* A 6157/2578/9, 9 July 1935.

15 *Ibid.*

16 *Ibid.* A 562/353/9, 14 January 1939.

17 See M. Puga Vega, *El petróleo chileno* (Santiago, 1964), and O. Wenzel, 'El petróleo en Chile', *Boletin del Instituto Sudamericano del Petróleo,* vol. 1, no. 5 (February 1945). In 1930 German and Belgian companies were contracted to carry out geo-

physical and seismic work in the south of Chile, but work ended in October 1932 when the Central Bank refused to finance further spending.

18 FO 371 A 562/353/9, 14 January 1939.

19 *Ibid.* A 1364/353/9, 17 February 1939.

20 *Ibid.* A 3804/353/9, Starling to Balfour (of the Petroleum Department), 16 May 1939.

21 *Proyecto de refinería de petróleo del estado* (Santiago, 1939).

22 FO 371 AS 3582/200/9, 2 June 1947.

23 M. Weinstein, *Uruguay: the Politics of Failure* (New York, 1975), p. 69.

24 FO 371 A 6140/950/46, 12 October 1931.

25 E. Pérez Prins, 'La refinería del petróleo de la ANCAP', *Boletin del Instituto Sudamericano del Petróleo* vol. 1, no. 1 (April 1943).

26 The US State Department described oil company reaction as follows: 'Both at the time of ANCAP's creation and subsequently the companies maintained a negative attitude toward the government company and apparently contented themselves with placing obstacles in its way and yielding ground when forced to do so' (State Department memo, 'Relations of the Uruguayan Government Petroleum Corporation with the Foreign Companies', 31 January 1948. Declassified Document C 322, released 1979).

27 FO 371 A 484/3/46, 26 January 1934.

28 *Ibid.* A 3048/26/46, 26 November 1932, Shell memo to the British Embassy.

29 S. G. Hanson, *Utopia in Uruguay* (Oxford, 1938), pp. 61–4.

30 FO 371, *Annual Report for 1932*.

31 *Ibid.* A 1317/2/46, 26 January 1934. The political opposition, naturally enough, alleged that Terra, a military dictator who took power in 1933, was connected with the oil companies and this charge has sometimes been repeated later; see E. H. Galeano, *Open Veins of Latin America: Five Centuries of the Pillage of a Continent* (New York, 1973), and V. Trías, *Imperialismo, geopolitica y petróleo* (Montevideo, 1971).

32 Prins, 'La refinería del petróleo'.

33 *Ibid.*

34 *Ibid.* See also State Department memo, 'Relations of the Uruguayan Government', Declassified Document C 322.

35 Klein, *Parties and Political Change,* pp. 47–8.

36 *Ibid.* pp. 80–1.

37 A. Iturralde, *Petición de informe del H. Senador por La Paz . . . sobre la concesión de un millión de hectares petroliferas* (La Paz, 1922), p. 53.

38 Klein, *Parties and Political Change,* p. 82.

39 L. B. Rout, Jr, *The Politics of the Chaco Peace Conference 1935–9* (Austin, Texas, 1970), pp. 46–7.

40 *Financial Times,* 4 August 1932.

41 Rout, *The Politics of the Chaco,* p. 47. Indeed, as late as 1930 the Bolivian government included in its budget estimates an income of 446,000 pesos from oil. See FO 371, *Annual Report for 1931*.

42 Klein, *Parties and Political Change,* p. 147.

43 Rout, *The Politics of the Chaco,* p. 47.

44 *Ibid.* p. 47.

45 *Ibid.* p. 25.
46 FO 371 A 388/388/5, 13 December 1933.
47 *Ibid.* A 2907/388/5, 15 March 1934.
48 Klein, *Parties and Political Change,* p. 36.
49 Ministry of Fuel and Power, Power 33, file 346, Report of Press Attaché, British Embassy, 14 September 1942.
50 It should be clear from what has already been said that this accusation – still sometimes made by left-wing journalists – has no foundation. It was, however, widely publicised both in Argentina (which had its own reasons for doing so) and, via Senator Huey Long, in the USA. A recent account of the period is provided by James Dunkerley, 'The Politics of the Bolivian Army: Institutional Development to 1935' (DPhil thesis, Oxford, 1980). Dunkerley points out that 'what has become increasingly clear is that neither Bolivia nor Paraguay, which faced problems of equal magnitude and was virtually totally dependent on Argentine aid, received major financial backing from the two oil companies [Standard Oil and Shell]' (p. 231).
51 Quoted in Rout, *The Politics of the Chaco,* p. 148.
52 *Ibid.*
53 *Foreign Relations of the United States, 1937,* p. 276.
54 Rout, *The Politics of the Chaco,* p. 148.
55 Ministry of Fuel and Power, Power 33, file 346, Rees to Eden, 4 October 1944.

10 Cárdenas and the Mexican oil nationalisation

1 FO 371 A 524/10/26, 21 January 1938.
2 Meyer, *México y los Estados Unidos,* p. 8.
3 Smith, *The United States and Revolutionary Nationalism,* p. 78.
4 A. S. Knight, 'Nationalism, Xenophobia and Revolution: the place of Foreigners and Foreign Interests in Mexico 1910–15' (DPhil thesis, Oxford, 1974), pp. 203–4.
5 *Ibid.*
6 *México y los Estados Unidos,* p. 145.
7 Quoted in W. C. Gordon, *Expropriation of Foreign Owned Property in Mexico* (Washington, 1941), p. 51.
8 Quoted in A. Cordova, *La ideología de la revolución mexicana: la formación del nuevo régimen* (Mexico, 1973), p. 255.
9 *Ibid.* p. 255.
10 *Ibid.* p. 256.
11 *Foreign Relations of the United States, 1927,* p. 187. On 22 January 1927, British Minister Ovey noted that Calles 'has therefore up to the present been expending every effort to keep the peace between these two important supporters' Pani and Morones (FO 371 A 945/40/26).
12 Cowdray archive, box C 44, file 1. The quotations later in this paragraph are all from the same source.
13 FO 371 A 8565/667/26, 8 October 1935.
14 *Ibid.*
15 Pearson Collection, box C 44, file 1, memo to Godber, 6 January 1936.
16 *Ibid.* Cowdray to Body, 9 January 1925.

17 FO 371 A 732/86/26, 20 January 1926.
18 Larson *et al., New Horizons,* p. 128.
19 FO 371 A 481/10/26, 19 January 1938.
20 See *ibid.* A 581/10/26, 24 January 1938, and A 383/195/26, 11 January 1936.
21 I was able to look briefly at the Huasteca papers kept within the Pemex archive.
22 See Gordon, *Expropriation of Foreign Owned Property,* p. 49.
23 FO 371 A 1410/667/26, 31 January 1935.
24 *Ibid.* A 6295/667/26, 2 August 1935.
25 *Ibid.* A 1947/1166/26, 8 March 1934.
26 J. López Portillo y Weber, *El petróleo de México* (Mexico City, 1975), p. 161.
27 M. Hoodless, 'Mexico's Oil' (London, 1977), pp. 12–13.
28 J. Silva Herzog, *Petróleo mexicano* (Mexico City, 1942), p. 104.
29 FO 371 A 8565/667/26, 8 October 1935.
30 Lief Adelson, 'Legistas en Overoles: la lucha de los obreros industriales tampi-
    queños para definir y defender el derecho del trabajo en la ausencia de un régimen
    jurídico 1910–24' (mimeo, Mexico City, 1979).
31 On this period see Rebeca de Gortari Rabiela, 'Petróleo y clase obrera en la zona
    del Golfo de México 1920–38 (*Licenciatura,* Universidad Nacional Autónoma de
    México, 1978). This very good study can be supplemented by discussion of various
    specific incidents provided in *La huelga de los obreros de la compañia mexicana de
    petróleo 'El Aguila' S.A. en Minatitlán: su origen y caracteres* (Mexico City, 1925), and
    Barry Carr, *El movimiento obrero y la politica en México 1910–29,* 3 vols. (Mexico
    City, 1976), vol. 2. Calles's archives (available also at Pemex) also contain a good
    deal of material on particular strikes.
32 FO 371 A 2461/1166/26, 26 March 1934.
33 *Ibid.* A 4906/1166/26, 19 June 1934.
34 *Ibid.* A 667/667/26, 23 January 1935.
35 *Ibid.* A 5339/667/26, 17 June 1935.
36 *Ibid.* A 9043/95/26, 15 November 1936.
37 M. Wionczek, 'Electric Power, the Uneasy Partnership', p. 44 in R. Vernon (ed.),
    Public Policy and Private Enterprise in Mexico (Cambridge, Mass., 1963), pp. 19–
    110.
38 On this see E. Suárez, *Comentarios y recuerdos 1926–46* (Mexico City, 1977), pp.
    181–6. Suárez was Cárdenas's Finance Minister.
39 FO 371 A 6516/667/26, 14 August 1935.
40 *Ibid.* A 9047/363/26, translation as provided in the archive.
41 *Ibid.*
42 *Ibid.* A 5464/667/26, 30 June 1935.
43 *Ibid.* A 1692/196/26, 28 February 1936.
44 *Ibid.* A 6648/132/26, 2 September 1937.
45 *Ibid.* A 1451/132/26, 24 February 1937.
46 *Ibid.* A 2003/132/26, 9 March 1937. This draft law envisaged a 10% royalty
    demanded by the state on the ground that it was the owner of the subsoil under
    Article 27. See Meyer, *México y los Estados Unidos,* p. 156.
47 FO 371 A 6049/132/26, 20 August 1937.
48 *Ibid.* A 1822/132/26, 8 March 1937.
49 *Ibid.* A 2003/132/26, 9 March 1937.
50 *Ibid.* A 5859/132/26, 16 August 1937.

51 Silva Herzog, *Petróleo,* p. 110.

52 *Ibid.* p. 112.

53 FO 371 A 6648/132/26, 2 September 1937.

54 M. Hoodless, 'Mexico's Oil', argues that the companies' accounting practices were reasonable and that their finances would not easily bear more than around 19m. pesos ($5.3m.), which was in fact the companies' final offer.

55 FO 371 A 5926/132/26, 17 August 1937.

56 Hoodless points out ('Mexico's Oil', p. 20) that 'in June 1937 on the occasion of the railway nationalisation, Cárdenas wrote in his diary that the entire oil industry ought to come into the hands of the state so that the Nation could benefit from this essential resource and that for this they were following another procedure'. The British Embassy also believed that the railways were no more than a trial run for the likely oil nationalisation, but see note 69, below.

57 FO 371 A 7391/132/26, 13 October 1937.

58 *Ibid.* A 6682/132/26, 14 September 1937.

59 See Meyer, *México y los Estados Unidos,* pp. 305–6.

60 'Mexico's Oil', p. 13.

61 *Comentarios,* p. 185. Suárez is excellent on the financial negotiations surrounding Petromex during this period. He was not, however, at the centre of the labour question.

62 *Ibid.* pp. 182–3.

63 Meyer, *México y los Estados Unidos,* p. 161, provides some evidence that the Mexican government was trying to divide the companies. It is, on the other hand, quite clear that the Mexican government was willing to reciprocate in the event that the companies accepted the 26m. peso award.

64 FO 371 A 7992/132/26, 1 November 1937.

65 *Foreign Relations of the United States, 1937,* p. 649.

66 *Petróleo,* p. 124.

67 Meyer, *México y los Estados Unidos,* p. 323. Meyer writes that 'the companies were certain that, in the last analysis and as had happened in the past, the government would have to back down, and they informed Ambassador Daniels to this effect; in their opinion, Cárdenas could not take over their properties finally because he lacked the specialised personnel and, if he were to expropriate, he could not export oil due to a shortage of transport; the companies would also, although they did not say so, close those international markets under their influences'. While this is on the whole true, Meyer did not use the British records and so missed the serious differences of opinion within El Aguila between the local managers who (like the British Embassy in Mexico) were gloomy and the London directors of Shell who were more optimistic. As early as August 1937, the British Minister reported that 'I find Davidson and Van Hassalt in an extremely pessimistic frame of mind. The former went so far as to tell me that if he judged by the outward appearance of things he would expect the company to be out of the country within two years. It is only because in Mexico it is the unexpected that always happens that he is still hoping that 'something will turn up', but if the position shows no improvement by the end of the year he will begin to lose even that hope' (FO 371 A 5764/132/26, 13 August 1937). This led to considerable ill-feeling between the Mexican managers and Godber in London; the British Minister on one occasion went so far as to

describe Godber as 'obtuse', which led to a mild rebuke from London. Godber himself continued to believe that the Mexican government was bluffing until the very end. Indeed, in March 1938 the British Embassy in Mexico appeared more optimistic than previously and on 1 March wrote that the 'possibility cannot be excluded that [the] Mexican government have caused an adverse verdict to be delivered as an essential preliminary to further negotiation on their part' (FO 371 A 1682/10/26). It believed, therefore, that although the properties might be intervened, they would not be expropriated. An attempt at intervention which resulted in economic difficulties and technical failures would, of course, have rebounded to the advantage of the companies.

68 Quoted in Silva Herzog, *Petróleo,* pp. 119–20.

69 See Meyer, *México y los Estados Unidos.* It is possible that Cárdenas's diary, from which Meyer's evidence is taken, was influenced by hindsight; the diary was only released in 1970 and certain phrases in it may well have been added subsequently. Nevertheless, its general position seems to have reflected Cárdenas's real feeling at the time. Even so, the diary should be treated with care.

70 FO 371 A 2319/10/26, 21 March 1938.

71 Meyer, *México y los Estados Unidos,* p. 347.

72 Hoodless, 'Mexico's Oil', p. 18.

73 FO 371 A 948/40/26, Peter Snow's comments.

74 Silva Herzog, *Petróleo,* p. 106.

75 I discussed this point with Lorenzo Meyer who replied that 'The nationalisation was popular because Cárdenas was popular'.

76 This fact has led A. Cordova, in *La politica de masas del cardenismo* (Mexico City, 1974), to argue that Cárdenas essentially manipulated his mass support in the interests of long-run political stability and economic development. While this argument has its attractions, it should be clear from this chapter that Cárdenas's freedom of manoeuvre was limited; the CTM clearly enjoyed at least a certain independence and, after 1937, the fear of a reaction on the right forced Cárdenas to temper his policies. Hindsight may suggest a clearer pattern than actually existed at the time.

11 The formation of Petrobrás

1 Wilkins, 'Multinational Oil Companies in South America', *Business History Review* (Autumn 1974), p. 418.

2 P. S. Smith, *Oil and Politics in Modern Brazil* (Toronto, 1976), ch. 1, deals with the pre-1930 period in some detail. Apart from Smith, full-length studies of the formation of Petrobrás are provided by J. D. Wirth, *The Politics of Brazilian Development 1930–54* (Stanford, 1970), G. Cohn, *Petróleo e nacionalismo* (São Paulo, 1968), and L. Martins, *Pouvoir et développement économique: formation et évolution des structures politiques au Brésil* (Paris, 1976). It will be apparent, therefore, that this period has been extremely well covered in the literature and this chapter will be restricted to a short summary of the main points.

3 Martins, *Pouvoir et développement,* p. 271.

4 These categories appear in *ibid.* and are extremely useful in the case of both Brazil and other parts of Latin America.

5 See Smith, *Oil and Politics,* ch. 2.

6 Eli Diniz, *Empresário, estado e capitalismo no Brasil: 1930–45* (Rio de Janeiro, 1978), is interesting on the relationship between the two groups during the 1930s.

7 J. Soares Pereira, *Petróleo, energia eléctrica, siderúrgia: a luta pela emancipaçõ* (Rio de Janeiro, 1978), p. 66.

8 *Ibid.* pp. 58–9.

9 Cohn, *Petróleo,* p. 46.

10 *Ibid.* p. 46. Horta actually complained that 'Since exploration has been timid, nothing positive has been done in our country in order to obtain this precious fuel. The Department specialising in this matter and certain engineers hasten to proclaim that oil does not exist in our territory. The government, in turn, and despite the declarations of its technicians, has allowed private companies to search for oil.'

11 Wirth, *The Politics of Brazilian Development,* p. 144.

12 *Ibid.* pp. 148–9. Even the federal bureaucracy was apparently taken by surprise. The local Shell manager wrote to his superior that 'we have interviewed the Minister of Agriculture, who advised us that the Decree which had just been issued was as unexpected to him, and more so to his Ministry, as perhaps it was to the companies. In his Ministry and in direct collaboration with the War Council he was actually preparing a Project of Law whereby the refining industry would be subject only to proper control on the part of the government' (FO 371 A 4659/3392/6, 1938, Wright to Brousson).

13 Quoted in Cohn, *Petróleo,* p. 48.

14 *Ibid.* pp. 48–9.

15 In 1939 the Justice Minister Fransisco Campos said of the CNP that 'the immense importance of energy matters, closely linked as they are to the economy and to the defence of the state, cannot be subjected to bureaucratic procedures' (*ibid.* p. 57).

16 Pedro de Moura and Felisberto Carneiro, *Em busca do petróleo brasileiro* (Rio de Janeiro, 1978), p. 232.

17 Martins, *Politique et développement,* pp. 308–9.

18 *Foreign Relations of the United States, 1945,* p. 678.

19 *Ibid.* pp. 686–7.

20 *Petroleum Press Service,* 1947, p. 185.

21 In June 1947 the British Minister reported that US Ambassador Pauley 'gave me a long and frank account of a conversation he had recently with the President and the Ministers of Foreign Affairs, Finance and Agriculture on the subject of the new petroleum bill. On this occasion he seems to have laid it down in no uncertain terms that USA oil interests would not participate in any oil developments in this country which they could not control' (FO 371 AS 4113/124/6 30 June 1947).

22 Quoted in Cohn, *Petróleo,* p. 94.

23 Wirth, *The Politics of Brazilian Development,* p. 176.

24 *Ibid.* p. 178.

25 FO 371 AS 5664/5503/6, 5 October 1948.

26 N. W. Sodré, *História militar do Brasil* (Rio de Janeiro, 1965), p. 293.

27 *Ibid.* p. 300.

28 Martins, *Politique et développement,* p. 346.

29 Wirth, *The Politics of Brazilian Development,* p. 173.

30 *Ibid.* pp. 171–2.

31 *Foreign Relations of the United States, 1948,* p. 363.

32 Soares Pereira, *Petróleo*, p. 81.
33 Wirth, *The Politics of Brazilian Development*, p. 174.
34 Martins, *Pouvoir et développement*, p. 347.
35 FO 371 AS 5664/5503/6, 5 October 1948.
36 Wirth, *The Politics of Brazilian Development*, p. 179.
37 Martins, *Pouvoir et développement*, p. 346.
38 Rómulo de Almeida interview with *O estado de São Paulo*, 1 October 1978.
39 Soares Pereira, *Petróleo*, p. 91. Soares Pereira worked as assistant to Almeida over this project.
40 Wirth, *The Politics of Brazilian Development*, part 2.
41 See Almeida's introduction to Soares Pereira, *Petróleo*, p. 21.
42 Martins, *Pouvoir et développement*, p. 338. As Almeida points out, the nationalists were already suspicious of the technocracy.
43 Smith, *Oil and Politics*, p. 98.

12 The nationalisation of the IPC in Peru

1 FO 371 A 5165/2445/55, 19 July 1938.
2 C. Goodsell, *American Corporations and Peruvian Politics* (Harvard, 1974), pp. 141–4.
3 *Ibid.* pp. 142–3.
4 Thorp and Bertram, *Peru 1890–1977*.
5 R. Miller, 'Foreign Firms and the Peruvian Government', in D. C. M. Platt (ed.), *Business Imperialism: an Analysis based on the British Experience in Latin America before 1930* (Oxford, 1978).
6 See, for example, the data provided in Goodsell, *American Corporations and Peruvian Politics*, pp. 114–15.
7 See V. Villanueva, *Un año bajo el sable* (Lima, 1963), pp. 112–15.
8 Memo for US State Department, 20 December 1963. Declassified Document 339 B, declassified 1977.
9 P. P. Kuczynski, *Peruvian Democracy under Economic Stress: an Account of the Belaúnde Administration 1963–8* (Princeton, 1977), p. 119. Kuczynski provides a valuable insider's account of this period.
10 On this point see the report from the US Embassy in Lima, 6 May 1964. Declassified Document 340 C, released 1977.
11 A. J. Pinelo, *The Multinational Corporation as a Force in Latin American Politics: a Case Study of the International Petroleum Corporation* (New York, 1973). Pinelo provides some very useful material but his discussion of the period is very pro-company.
12 These points are discussed at greater length in ch. 2 of G. Philip, *The Rise and Fall of the Peruvian Military Radicals 1968–76* (London, 1978).
13 Pinelo, *The Multinational Corporation*, p. 173.
14 Although one cannot be certain, the story that APRA approached IPC in this way is compatible with Pinelo's discussion and is also hinted at by Levingstone and Onis, *The Alliance that Lost its Way*. This states that APRA 'concluded that if power was at hand, the time had come to resolve the IPC dispute . . . New management in IPC was able to convince the parent company that the political situation was favourable to a settlement' (p. 154).

15 Kuczynski, *Peruvian Democracy,* p. 261.
16 Full accounts are provided in Kuczynski, *Peruvian Democracy,* which is written from a pro-government position, in A. Zimmermann Zavala, *El plan inca: objectivo, revolución peruana* (Lima, 1974), which is an insider's account of the coup, in R. Goodwin, 'Letter from Peru', *New Yorker,* 17 May 1969, which is based largely on Loret de Mola's account, and in S. Lewis, 'The IPC v. Peru: a Case Study of Nationalism, Management and International Relations' (mimeo, University of California at Los Angeles, 1972), which is well balanced but was written before the most important inside information became available. See also G. Philip, *The Rise and Fall,* ch. 2.
17 Goodwin, 'Letter from Peru'.
18 *Caretas,* 12 December 1968.
19 Pinelo, however, does offer such a conclusion: *The Multinational Corporation,* p. 150.

13 The nationalisation of Gulf Oil in Bolivia 1969

1 See, for example, the *Petroleum Press Service* article 'Bolivian Bombshell', November 1969.
2 R. Alexander, *The Bolivian National Revolution* (Stanford, 1969).
3 The code provided for an 11% royalty, a 30% profits tax and various surface taxes. The effect of the income tax was greatly reduced by a depletion allowance to the value of 27% of gross production (with an upper limit of half of the profit level). A further tax was to be imposed if necessary, which would guarantee that the state's share of all taxes should not be less than 50% (Article 128). The main advantage of the code to potential investors was the generous depletion allowance which would, at the extreme, reduce the state's overall tax take to 25%.
   Despite the apparent generosity of these terms, it was still necessary for Jersey Standard to disclaim any further interest in Bolivia before other US companies would enter. See Andrade, *My Missions for Revolutionary Bolivia,* p. 185.
4 C. Zondag, *The Bolivian Economy 1952–65: the Revolution and its Aftermath* (New York, 1966), ch. 10.
5 Mariaca Bilbao, *Mito y realidad,* p. 229.
6 *Ibid.* p. 368.
7 Interview with René Zavaleta, Mines Minister in 1964, Quito 1977.
8 Whitehead, *The United States and Bolivia.* See also Blasier, *The Hovering Giant.*
9 Interview data.
10 M. Quiroga Santa Cruz, *Gas y petróleo en Bolivia: ¿liberación o dependencia?* (Cochabamba, 1967), p. 239.
11 I was allowed to look through a number of files in the Ministry of Mines and Energy in mid-1977. Although these could not really be described as an archive, they did include a number of documents which would not normally be made public.
12 Mariaca, *Mito y realidad,* p. 437.
13 *Ibid.* p. 438.
14 M. Tejada, *Aprovechamiento del gas natural en Bolivia* (La Paz, 1965), p. 33.
15 Ingram, *Expropriation.*
16 Ministry of Mines and Energy files.

17 Interview data.

18 See Arguedas's interview with the *Guardian,* 15 March 1969.

19 *Latin America,* 10 May 1968.

20 See Whitehead, *The United States and Bolivia,* especially the appendix.

21 *Latin America,* 10 May 1968.

22 Quoted in C. Corbett, 'Military Institutional Development and Socio-Political Change: the Bolivian Case', *Journal of Inter-American Studies,* vol. 14, no. 4 (November 1972), pp. 389–437.

23 Interview data.

24 Interview data.

25 One observer described Siles Salinas as 'a weak figure, associated with the economically privileged, lacking working class appeal and directly a target of peasant attacks for his associations with former landlords' (L. A. Whitehead, 'Bolivia's Conflict with the United States', *World Today* (April 1970), p. 174).

26 L. A. Whitehead, 'National Power and Local Power: the Case of Santa Cruz de la Sierra, Bolivia', *Latin American Urban Research,* vol. 3 (1974), p. 25.

27 *Ibid.* pp. 38–9. I also discussed this point with the author.

28 *Presencia,* 16 June 1968.

29 *Expropriation,* p. 175.

30 *New York Times,* 17 May 1975.

31 *Ibid.*

32 *Presencia,* 20 August 1969.

33 *Presencia,* 2 September 1969.

34 *New York Times,* 21 October 1969.

35 *Financial Times,* 1 January 1970.

36 *Ibid.*

37 Interview data.

38 Interview data.

39 *New York Times,* 9 September 1970.

40 It has been argued that Bolivia would have done better to wait for the completion of the gas pipeline before nationalising Gulf since this would have improved its bargaining position. This is very plausible, particularly now that we know Allende was in power in Chile in 1971 and that world oil prices were then rising. This only emphasised, however, that the motivations for the nationalisation were overwhelmingly political and had little to do with any expectation of national advantage.

41 On this point, see L. A. Whitehead, 'The State and Sectional Interests: the Bolivian Case', *European Journal of Political Research,* vol. 3 (Spring 1975), pp. 115–46.

14 Oil policies in Ecuador 1972–6

1 Quoted in IBRD, *Current Economic Position and Prospects of Ecuador* (Washington, 1973).

2 *New York Times,* 16 May 1972.

3 Ministerio de Planificación, *Junta plan,* book 3, part 2: *Programa de desarrollo del petróleo* (Quito, 1966).

4 J. S. Fitch, *The Military Coup d'Etat as a Political Process: Ecuador 1940–66* (Baltimore, 1977), p. 150.

5 The most notable of the foreigners were Salas, a Chilean who had worked with ENAP for 24 years, and Mariaca Bilbao, who had been both Bolivian Minister of Hydrocarbons and head of the state oil company YPFB.

6 IBRD, *Current Economic Position* (Washington, 1974), pp. 8–9.

7 Interview data.

8 A fuller account of Ecuadorian oil policy during this period is provided in G. Philip, *The Politics of Oil in Ecuador* (working paper, Institute of Latin American Studies, London, 1978). See also O. Hurtado *et al.*, *Ecuador, hoy* (Bogotá, 1978) for some more general treatments of this period.

9 *Financial Times*, 23 February 1973.

10 The best financial study of the Ecuadorian tax structure as it affects the oil industry is R. Sagasti, 'Análisis económico de la actividad petrolera en el Ecuador' (PhD thesis, Quito, 1974).

11 IBRD, *Current Position* (1973), p. 15.

12 The information provided here on Jarrín's own attitudes came from a personal interview with him in 1977.

13 *El telégrafo*, 22 December 1973.

14 *Weekly Analysis*, 21 April 1976.

15 *El tiempo*, 6 October 1974.

16 According to Ecuadorian law, all revenue earned by Texas–Gulf had to be paid into the Central Bank in Quito which would then return what it owed to the companies. The companies complained that the money was often returned late and that some of it was not returned at all.

17 One well placed diplomatic observer later reported that 'neither my diplomatic colleagues nor I were ever able to get clear briefings – or any briefings at all – on Ecuadorian policy from official sources, in contrast to René Bucaram's readiness to talk at all times and to answer questions with detailed facts and figures'. Bucaram and Jarrín were the two Ecuadorians who best understood the oil industry and both proved to be controversial; in 1977 Bucaram was moved to the USA by Texaco.

18 *Nueva*, April 1976.

19 *El universo*, 16 March 1976.

20 27 July 1976.

21 On 16 March 1976 Vargas met various university and other group leaders and together they discussed the formation of 'a broad front, only loosely connected with ideological positions, in order to support an eventual decision by the government to take full control of Oriente oil' (*El comercio*, 17 March 1976).

22 Fitch, *The Military Coup d'Etat*, p. 169.

15 The nationalisation of oil in Venezuela

1 J. Pérez Alfonzo, *Petróleo y dependencia* (Caracas, 1971), p. 54.

2 Tugwell, *The Politics of Oil*.

3 *HAR,* December 1958.

4 Tugwell, *The Politics of Oil*.

5 See, for example, *El nacional,* 29 September 1961.

6 Acosta Hermoso, *Petroquimica*.

7 Betancourt, in *Politica y petróleo* (Caracas, 1967), points out that no significant

domestic group supported nationalisation in the 1940s except as a long-term objective. This remained the position subsequently. In 1952, for example, *El universal* and 'all opposition parties' were in favour of the gradual nationalisation of oil. (See US National Security Council Report, December 1952, US Declassified Document 60 A, released 1978.)

8 Alexander, *The Venezuelan Democratic Revolution*, p. 79. The incident is also described in J. D. Martz, *Acción Democrática: Evolution of a Modern Political Party in Venezuela* (Princeton, 1966), pp. 180–3.

9 Quoted in J. D. Martz, 'The Venezuelan Elections of 1963', p. 66, in R. Fagan and W. Cornelius (eds.), *Political Power in Latin America: Seven Confrontations* (Newark, NJ, 1970).

10 Sampson, *The Seven Sisters*, p. 172.

11 Quoted in R. Betancourt, *Venezuela's Oil* (London, 1978), p. 100.

12 The capital investment figure is taken from p. 38 of United Nations, ECLA, *La industria del petróleo en América Latina* (Santiago, 1973).

13 *The Politics of Oil*, p. 89.

14 There is a series of recently released US State Department documents covering this period (US Declassified Documents, Microfiches 426–7, released 1980) from 30 June to 6 July. On this issue, see Bernbaum to State Department, 30 June 1966.

15 US Declassified Document 427 B, Bernbaum to State Department, 6 July 1966. This conversation took place on 4 July.

16 Creole (Standard Oil of New Jersey) calculated that the initial proposal would have changed the tax take from 65–35 to the government to 72–28; the distribution after the agreement was around 68–32. This, of course, does not include the back-taxes agreement.

17 *Business Venezuela*, July 1968.

18 Tugwell, *Politics of Oil*, p. 102.

19 *Resumen*, 13 June 1976.

20 Fuad, 'Venezuela's Role in OPEC', in Bond (ed.), *Contemporary Venezuela*.

21 Tugwell, *Politics of Oil*, p. 107.

22 US Senate Committee on Foreign Relations, *Multinational Corporations and US Foreign Policy*, vol. 5, Pierce Testimony, p. 71.

23 Tugwell, *The Politics of Oil*.

24 See *Business Venezuela*, no. 19 (1972).

25 *Ibid.*

26 This did lead to some post-nationalisation difficulties, however. As was provided in the 1971 law mentioned above, the companies were required to post a bond with the Venezuelan government which would be returned to them after the nationalisation or the reversion of the concessions to the state in 1983. The Venezuelan government was prevented from returning this bond after 1975 as a result of legal action aimed at proving that the companies owed taxes for underproduction in 1971. The matter is still unresolved.

27 Tugwell, *Politics of Oil*, p. 143.

28 N. Gall, 'The Challenge of Venezuelan Oil', *Foreign Policy*, no. 18 (Spring 1975).

29 *Business Venezuela*, no. 22 (1972).

30 *Petroleum Press Service*, December 1972.

31 *Financial Times*, 27 December 1973.

32 12 December 1973.

33 *New York Times,* 2 December 1974.
34 Venezuela, Secretaría de la Presidencia, *Nacionalización del petróleo en Venezuela: tesis y documentos fundamentales* (Caracas, 1975), p. 92.
35 23 June 1975.
36 *Resumen,* 21 December 1975.
37 J. Martz, 'Policy-making and the Quest for Consensus: Nationalizing Venezuelan Petroleum', *Journal of Inter-American Studies and World Affairs,* vol. 19, no. 4 (November 1977), p. 499. Martz provides a very useful account of the political infighting of the period.

16 Oil companies and governments in twentieth-century Latin America

1 The most relevant game structure for understanding this kind of situation is not the two-person non-zero-sum game appropriate to 'bargaining in one country' (which is brilliantly analysed by T. Schelling in *Strategy of Conflict* (Oxford, 1971)), but rather the 'prisoner's dilemma'. On this see T. Axelrod, *Conflict of Interest: a Theory of Divergent Goals with Application to Politics* (Chicago, 1971).
2 Frankel, *Essentials of Petroleum,* pp. 79–89, is good on the logic of 'free riding'.
3 F. H. Cardoso and E. Faletto, *Dependency and Development in Latin America* (Berkeley, 1979), use a similar but slightly different classification, based not on exports of oil but of minerals as opposed to agriculture.
4 Some of the main tactical considerations involved in Peruvian negotiations with IPC are discussed in G. Philip, 'The Limitations of Bargaining Theory: the IPC in Peru', *World Development,* vol. 4, no. 3 (May 1976), pp. 231–9.
5 T. H. Moran, *Copper in Chile,* ch. 7, provides an excellent account of the way in which Chilean conservatives broke off their unofficial alliance with the US copper companies in the early 1960s in revenge for Washington's espousal of the Alliance for Progress and support for the Christian Democrats. When the Christian Democrats grew tired of defending the companies, the nationalisation was passed unanimously by Congress in 1971.
    Outside Latin America, British oil companies have been expropriated on more than one occasion as a protest against British government policy.

17 Pemex in Mexican politics 1938–79

1 An excellent account of the technical side of the Mexican oil industry is provided by J. R. Powell, *The Mexican Petroleum Industry 1938–50* (Los Angeles, 1956).
2 Apart from Powell, see L. Meyer, 'La resistencia al capital privado extranjero', in Sepúlveda *et al., Las empresas transnacionales en México,* and Cárdenas's letter to Avila Camacho, pp. 437–9 in E. Vásquez Gómez (ed.), *Epistolario de Lázaro Cárdenas* (Mexico City, 1974). There is also, at much greater length, M. Alemán, *La verdad del petróleo en México.*
3 *Foreign Relations of the United States,* 1947, p. 787.
4 The best account of these conflicts is provided in Powell, *The Mexican Petroleum Industry.*
5 Vásquez Gómez (ed.), *Epistolario de Lázaro Cárdenas,* p. 45.
6 FO 371 AN 1859/88/26, 8 May 1948.
7 Quoted in Wionczek, 'Electric Power: the Uneasy Partnership', p. 103, in Vernon (ed.), *Public Policy and Private Enterprise in Mexico.*

8 Powell, *The Mexican Petroleum Industry,* pp. 106–7.
9 Bermúdez, *The Mexican National Petroleum Industry,* pp. 30–3.
10 Powell, *The Mexican Petroleum Industry,* p. 77.
11 *Ibid.* p. 73.
12 Meyer, 'Resistencia', in Sepúlveda, *Las empresas transnacionales,* p. 118.
13 IBRD, *Economic Report on Mexico* (1953).
14 Bermúdez, *The Mexican National Petroleum Industry,* table 6, appendix.
15 Meyer, 'Resistencia', pp. 140–1.
16 *Director's Report, 1951.* Some of these are translated from the Spanish, while others have been released in English as well.
17 *Foreign Relations of the United States, 1950,* pp. 947–50. Mexico was less well placed than those countries where oil production was in the hands of vertically integrated US companies which could count on a ready market and some political influence.
18 *Director's Report,* 1953.
19 *HAR,* July 1955.
20 *Ibid.* November 1955.
21 Secretaría de la Presidencia, *Inversión pública federal 1925–63* (Mexico City, 1964).
22 United Nations, Department of Economic and Social Affairs, *Petroleum Exploration: Capital Requirements and Methods of Financing* (1962).
23 A. J. Bermúdez, *La política petrolera mexicana* (Mexico City, 1976), pp. 54–5.
24 *Ibid.* p. 56.
25 Bermúdez, *The Mexican National Petroleum Industry,* ch. 4.
26 *HAR,* February 1959.
27 *Ibid.*
28 *HAR,* February 1960.
29 Bermúdez, *La política petrolera mexicana,* p. 58.
30 *World Oil,* 15 August 1959.
31 *Director's Report,* 1953.
32 *HAR,* June 1959.
33 *Ibid.* December 1959.
34 UN, Department of Economic and Social Affairs, *Petroleum Exploration,* p. 17.
35 R. Vernon, *The Dilemma of Mexico's Development: the Roles of the Private and Public Sectors* (Cambridge Mass., 1963), p. 119.
36 Bermúdez, *La política petrolera mexicana,* p. 69.
37 *HAR,* February 1959.
38 *Director's Report,* 1962.
39 Vernon, *The Dilemma,* p. 127.
40 F. J. Bullard, *Mexico's Natural Gas* (Austin, Texas, 1968).
41 UN, ECLA, *Annual Survey of Latin America for 1963,* p. 86.
42 Bermúdez, *La política petrolera,* p. 71.
43 *Director's Report,* 18 March 1965, p. 18.
44 *Director's Report,* 18 March 1968, p. 16.
45 *Director's Report,* 1971 (Dovali Jaime), p. 13.
46 Interview data.
47 *Director's Report,* 1966, pp. 18–19.
48 *Director's Report,* 1968.
49 *Director's Report,* 1970, p. 20.
50 *Director's Report,* 1976, pp. 29–30.
51 IBRD (Levy), 'The Search for Oil in Developing Countries', p. 94.

52 Bermúdez, *La política petrolera mexicana*, pp. 69–70.
53 *Ibid.* pp. 62.
54 *Director's Report*, 1965, pp. 13–15.
55 *Director's Report*, 1968, pp. 6–7.
56 *Director's Report*, 1970.
57 *Ibid.* p. 27.
58 Several of my interview sources stressed this point.
59 *Director's Report*, 1966, p. 7.
60 These figures are taken from Ramón Castro Melganejo, 'Participación de la industria petrolera en la balanza de pagos' (*Licenciatura* thesis, Universidad Nacional Autónoma de México, 1980).
61 Adelman, 'The World Oil Outlook'.
62 Even so, there is evidence that average costs rose during the 1960s as continued exploration of familiar territory led to smaller and smaller discoveries. On this see A. Megadelli, *Investment Policies of National Oil Companies: a Comparative Study of Sonatrech, Nioc and Pemex* (New York, 1980).
63 Interview data. The plan was finally produced in 1970: it was entitled 'Plan for the Development of the Oil and Basic Petrochemicals Industries 1970–80'. Additionally Pemex began to explore more costly and less familiar areas after 1969. See Megadelli, *Investment Policies of National Oil Companies*.
64 *Director's Report*, 1966.
65 *Director's Report*, 1970.
66 *Director's Report*, 1972, pp. 10–11.
67 *Director's Report*, 1973, pp. 6–7.
68 D. Fox, 'Mexico: the Development of the Oil Industry', *BOLSA Review* (October 1977), p. 525.
69 *Director's Report*, 1974, p. 6.
70 *Revisión presupuesta 1978. Obras capitaliares de la gerencia de petroquímica'.
71 December 26, 1972.
72 *Director's Report*, 1973, pp. 8–9.
73 October 12, 1974.
74 Interview data.
75 Megadelli, *Investment Policies of National Oil Companies*, p. 131.
76 A well-placed source told me that Echeverría told one of his Ministers some time in 1972 or 1973 that very large oil discoveries had been made in the south and that nothing was to be said about this. The strategy of secrecy was then partially undermined by us press coverage of October 1974.
77 Mexico, Pemex, Díaz Serrano, *Línea troncal nacional de distribución de gas natural* (speech to the Chamber of Deputies, 26 October 1977). An interview source close to this 'group of engineers' gave me a very similar account of the same incident, but added that it was clear from the meeting with López Portillo at that time that he was out of sympathy with their position.
78 *Financial Times*, 25 December 1976.
79 *Línea troncal*, pp. 10–12.
80 According to one informant, Pemex sent details of its geology to an operational research team in order to have computed the total potential reserves. This team submitted a figure of 170 billion barrels to the President and its members were told to keep silent on the matter since the figure would shortly be made official. It

was with some surprise, therefore, that they heard the presidential speech in which the figure of 200 billion barrels was given. It was later explained that the President was in receipt of new information. Whatever the nature of the new information, it remains true that on oil matters Díaz Serrano was no more royalist than the king.

81 The proportion of Pemex's income allocated to wages and salaries fell, as a result of the expansion, from 22% in 1976 to an estimated 14% in 1979 even though the absolute amount spent on wages and salaries continued to rise. See the *Director's Report,* 1979.

82 *Director's Report,* 1977, p. 15.

83 H. Sandeman, 'Pemex' (mimeo, London, 1977). An abbreviated and edited version of this article appeared in *Fortune,* April 1978.

84 See Jaime Corredor, 'El petróleo en México', *Uno más uno,* 18 March 1981.

85 Jose Z. Lasa, 'Chicontepec, un proyecto para abrir 16 mil pozos en 14 años', *Uno más uno,* 18 March 1981.

86 Pemex, *Memoria de labores,* 1980.

87 These mainly came in interviews, but see also Díaz Serrano's remarks about the petrochemical industry in the *Director's Report,* 1978.

88 For a more general discussion of these questions see G. Philip, 'Mexican Oil and Gas: the Politics of a New Resource' *International Affairs,* Summer 1980, pp. 474–83.

89 Sandeman, 'Pemex' (mimeo), p. 6.

90 Wionczek, 'Electric Power', in Vernon, *Public Policy,* p. 101.

91 M. Lourdes Orozco, 'Integración, estructura y funcionamiento de la empresa "Petróleos Mexicanos" ' (mimeo, Universidad Nacional Autónoma de México, 1980).

92 Bermúdez, *La política petrolera mexicana,* p. 103.

18 The development of Petrobrás: oil company to conglomerate?

1 'Petrobrás – 25 anos', in *O estado de São Paulo,* 1 October 1978.

2 'The Search for Oil in Developing Countries'.

3 'Petrobrás – 25 anos', *O estado de São Paulo,* 1 October 1978.

4 G. Carvalho, *Petrobrás: do monopólio aos contratos de risco* (Rio de Janeiro, 1976), p. 94.

5 'Petrobrás – 25 anos', *O estado de São Paulo,* 1 October 1978.

6 *Ibid.*

7 J. Soares Pereira, *Petróleo, energia eléctrica, siderúrgia: a luta pela emancipação* (Rio de Janeiro, 1978), p. 111.

8 Quoted in Smith, *Oil and Politics,* p. 103.

9 Moura and Carneiro, *Em busca do petróleo brasileiro.*

10 Petrobrás, *Annual Report for 1956.* It is interesting to compare Judith Tendler's account of the attitude of state sector engineers in the Brazilian power industry who 'wanted to build things, not to be bothered with the money making aspects of their ventures. Distribution meant going into and running a business, which was considered unexciting and almost undignified because of its details and routine' (*Electric Power in Brazil: Entrepreneurship in the Public Sector* (Cambridge, Mass., 1968), (p. 183). According to Getúlio Carvalho, who questioned Colonel Nunes

(head of Petrobrás 1956–8) on this point, the attitude of Petrobrás technicians was rather similar, at least with regard to priorities; some of them believed that control over distribution should be a long-term aim, but that the enterprise first 'had a pioneering role in other, higher priority sectors' (Petrobrás, *Annual Report for 1956*, p. 177).

11 'Petrobrás – 25 anos', *O estado de São Paulo*, 1 October 1978.

12 Soares Pereira, *Petróleo*, p. 112.

13 This point comes out remarkably often in conversations with Brazilians. Smith makes it the central theme of his *Oil and Politics*.

14 Lima Rocha article in 'Petrobrás – 25 anos', *O estado de São Paulo*', 1 October 1978.

15 J. W. F. Dulles, *Castello Branco: The Making of a Brazilian President* (Texas, 1979), p. 226.

16 Carvalho, *Petrobrás*, p. 111.

17 Labour conflict during this period is well described in K. P. Erickson, *Corporatism and Working Class Politics in Brazil* (Los Angeles, 1977).

18 Smith, *Oil and Politics*, p. 128.

19 *Ibid.* pp. 133 *et seq.*

20 *Ibid.* p. 134.

21 *HAR*, December 1960.

22 Smith, *Oil and Politics*, p. 154.

23 'Petrobrás – 25 anos', *O estado de São Paulo*, 1 October 1978.

24 *Ibid.*

25 *Oil and Politics.*

26 A. Stepan, *The Military in Politics: Changing Patterns in Brazil* (Princeton, 1971), p. 231. I discussed this point later with the author, who said that the proposal was mooted by Castelo Branco and objected to strongly by Ernesto Geisel, at that time head of the President's military household. There was so little public discussion that at least one Cabinet Minister was not even aware that the proposal had been made.

27 *O estado de São Paulo*, 27 May 1964.

28 See Evans, 'Multinationals'.

29 Carvalho, *Petrobrás.*

30 Evans, 'Multinationals.'

31 A. Stumpf and M. Pereira Filho, *A segunda guerra: sucessão de Geisel* (São Paulo, 1979), p. 20.

32 See *Jornal de tarde*, 3 October 1978.

33 Carvalho, *Petrobrás.*

34 A. Tamer, *Petróleo: o preço da dependência: o Brasil na crise mundial* (Rio de Janeiro, 1980), pp. 72–4, reproduces the letter sent by David Martin of Occidental to Professor Dias Leite. Tamer devotes a chapter to the incident described here.

35 *O estado de São Paulo*, 12 March 1968.

36 Quoted in M. Gomes, 'Petrobrás: uma "octava irmã" do Petróleo', p. 87, in B. Kucinski (ed.), *Petróleo: contratos de risco de dependência: ensaio e reportagem* (São Paulo, 1977).

37 *Ibid.* p. 88.

38 *O estado de São Paulo*, 7 August 1977.

39 *Ibid.*

40 Quoted in B. Kucinski, 'A campanha contra o monopólio', p. 35, in Kucinski, *Petróleo.*

41 Lima Rocha's interview in 'Petrobrás – 25 anos', *O estado de São Paulo,* 1 October 1978.
42 This point is highlighted in, for example, W. Baer, *The Brazilian Economy: its Growth and Development* (Columbus, Ohio, 1979), ch. 7.
43 Interview with Carlos Isnard, Finance Director of Petrobrás 1973–8, in Rio de Janeiro, August 1979.
44 1 June 1977.
45 3 June 1977.
46 *Latin America Regional Report: Brazil,* 17 April 1981.
47 Tamer, *Petróleo,* p. 169. The information provided in this paragraph is taken from this source.
48 *Ibid.* p. 170.
49 *Ibid.* p. 265.
50 25 May 1977.
51 *Petrobrás News,* October 1979.
52 Hilnor Cangaçu interview in 'Petrobrás – 25 anos', *O estado de São Paulo,* 1 October 1978.
53 This secrecy has also been attributed in part to a desire to strengthen, as far as possible, the negotiating position of Petrobrás when seeking supplies from abroad.
54 *O estado de São Paulo,* 20 January 1978.
55 See Tamer, *Petróleo,* Kucinski, *Petróleo,* Stumpf and Filho, *A segunda guerra,* and also P. Cotta, *O petróleo é nosso?* (São Paulo, 1975).
56 This is clear from conversations I had in both Rio and Brasilia.
57 Simonsen, at that time Planning Minister, had expressed considerable doubt on this score in an internal policy document which was later leaked to the press and appeared in the *Latin American Daily Post* on 22 July 1979. Maluf also publicly questioned the need for Braspetro in August 1979.
 However, despite selling its holdings in Iraq, Braspetro continued to be active downstream and has signed a number of exploration contracts since.
58 These ideas stimulated considerable press comment at the time of Ueki's appointment. See *O estado de São Paulo,* 30 January 1979, *Jornal do Brasil,* 18 March 1979.
59 In 'Multinationals', p. 63.
60 This is very much the theme of Kucinski, *Petróleo.*
61 22 May 1977.
62 In 1973, for example, Petrobrás prepared to take over two refineries in Italy for the purpose of supplying oil from the Middle East to Continental Europe at a profit. The venture was aborted when the Italian government changed its tax regulations.
63 *Annual Report for 1978.*
64 Interview with Carlos Isnard, July 1979. It is of course true that private sector companies do not maximise profits in straightforward, simple-minded sense.
65 *The Brazilian Economy.*
66 Evans, 'Multinationals'.
67 The main proponent of this approach is Carvalho, in *Petrobrás.*
68 Survey work carried out by Luciano Martins suggests this conclusion.
69 Tendler, *Electric Power in Brazil.*
70 Quoted in Moura and Carneiro, *Em busca do petróleo,* p. 242.
71 Interview data.
72 Petrobras, *Annual Report for 1978.* The position did not change very much in 1979 and 1980, as is shown in the following table.

Profits by sector
(percentages)

	1979	1980
Production, transport and refining	81.4	82.8
Petrochemicals	10.8	6.4
Distribution	11.6	12.7
Trading	0.8	0.7
Fertilizers	(4.6)	(2.6)
TOTAL	100.0	100.0

Note: Figures in parentheses denote losses.
Sources; Petrobrás, *Annual Reports.*

19 YPF 1972–79: public enterprise or bureaucracy?

1 This point was made by a number of Argentines; see also R. D. Mallon, *Economic Policymaking in a Conflict Society: the Argentine Case* (Cambridge, Mass., 1975).

2 A. Ferrer, *Crisis y alternativas de la política económica argentina* (Buenos Aires, 1977), pp. 9–10.

3 Solberg, *Oil and Nationalism,* ch. 6.

4 Mario Villa and Enrique Canepa, 'El petróleo argentino en el último decenio', in *La ingenieria,* May 1956.

5 On this point, as on a number of others, the author is indebted to Jorge Katz and his research team at Cepal, Buenos Aires, for some of the findings from their work on the economics of oil refining in Argentina. Moreover, according to a reputable contemporary observer, 'it may be affirmed that few if any national industries use modern technology and expertise to a greater extent than does YPF in all its tasks of organisation and development' (*Revista de economia argentina* (1937), p. 348). Moreover, in 1938 YPF had 5,413 b/d of 'cracking' capacity in its refineries – more than Germany or France. See 'El Petróleo argentino en la economía, en la doctrina y en la legislación, *Boletin de Informes* (Buenos Aires, 1938).

6 J. V. Canessa, *La verdad sobre el petróleo argentino* (Buenos Aires, 1957).

7 M. Kaplan, *Economia y politica del petróleo argentino 1939–56* (Buenos Aires, 1957), p. 56.

8 Villa and Canepa, 'El petróleo argentino', present statistics which show a decline in geophysical activity during the 1945–9 period and conclude that 'Argentine geologists specialising in oil were no longer being trained and a number of those who had already been trained left the country.' The exodus of trained Argentine technicians and engineers during this period is a well-attested fact.

9 *Ibid.* It is not clear that Perón can be personally blamed for more than appointing

inept people to senior positions of YPF. Arturo Sabato, who left YPF in 1948, described one key figure as 'a madman who simply fired everybody who disagreed with him'.

The Peronist government itself put much of the blame for its problems on the US government's unwillingness to export oilfield equipment to YPF during this period, although this point is contested by Villa and Canepa who assert that 'the government in Washington never denied or delayed permission for export to YPF'. In fact there is some evidence in the US archives that YPF encountered some purchasing difficulties but this is likely to have been, at best, only a minor factor in YPF's difficulties.

10 On these 1946–7 negotiations see R. A. Potash, *The Army and Politics in Argentina 1945–62: Perón to Frondizi* (Stanford and London, 1980), pp. 67–75.

11 *Ibid.* p. 70.

12 *Ibid.* pp. 72–4.

13 Quoted in Laura Randall, *An Economic History of Argentina in the Twentieth Century* (New York, 1978), p. 234. Gómez Morales repeated this account to Potash, *Army and Politics 1945–62*, p. 162.

14 Villa and Canepa, in 'El petróleo argentino', assert that the government came close to signing agreements with Glenn McCarthy, Dresser Industries and the Atlas Corporation. The evidence presented is very far from being conclusive on this, but it is highly probable that some serious negotiations did take place.

15 See FO 371 AS file 1532/2, 1949.

16 British Foreign Office papers make it clear that Shell and Jersey Standard, supported by their home governments, were ready to use their control over crude oil supplies to apply pressure where necessary. Thus during trade negotiations with Argentina in 1949 a British official wrote that 'it might be admirable to arrange for an oil famine towards the end of March' (FO 371 AS 339/1532/2, 15 January 1949).

17 *HAR*, December 1957.

18 A detailed and influential but very hostile treatment of this concession appears in A. Silenzo de Stagni, *El petróleo argentino.*

19 *HAR, April 1955.*

20 Report prepared for IBRD: Levy, *The Search for Oil in Developing Countries,* p. 122.

21 United Nations, Department of Economic and Social Affairs, *Petroleum Exploration.*

22 ECLA, *Bulletin for Latin America, 1957,* p. 114.

23 *HAR*, May and August 1956.

24 Canessa, *La verdad.* Many of these engineers went to work for private sector companies.

25 D. James, 'Unions and Politics: the Development of Peronist Trade Unions 1955–66' (PhD thesis, London, 1979), p. 132.

26 This accusation is made by Juan Sabato, *Ficción y realidad de la política y del plan energético del gobierno revolucionario* (Buenos Aires, 1969), p. 11.

27 *Ibid.* pp. 12–14.

28 This accusation was made, for example, in E. Mosconi, *Los delitos petroleros,* published by the General Mosconi institute in 1962.

29 Argentina, Secretaría de la Presidencia, A. Frondizi, *La batalla del petróleo,* 24 July 1958. Frondizi also proposed more decentralisation and a pricing system more favourable to YPF.

30 G. Edwards, 'The Frondizi Contracts and Petroleum Self-sufficiency in Argentina', in R. F. Mikesell (ed.), *Foreign Investment*.

31 A. Sabato, *Historia de los contratos petrolíferos* (Buenos Aires, 1963), p. 25.

32 Interview with Arturo Sabato, Buenos Aires, September 1979.

33 James, 'Argentine Trade Unions', p. 150.

34 *Ibid.* p. 150.

35 *Ibid.* p. 151.

36 *Ibid.* p. 152.

37 *Political Parties in Latin America* (Penguin Handbook), pp. 75–6.

38 The dispatches from US Ambassador McLintock during this period give some idea of the Illia government's internal political arguments.

39 Sabato, *Ficción y realidad,* pp. 14–17.

40 Edwards, 'The Frondizi Contracts', in Mikesell (ed.), *Foreign Investment,* p. 174.

41 *Ibid.* p. 164.

42 Juan Sabato, *Ficción y realidad,* pp. 51–5.

43 *Ibid.* p. 65.

44 23 June 1967.

45 Sr Thibaud, at that time Secretary of Energy, remarked that there was surprisingly little military interest in the question of oil and very little controversy over the oil law within the government. This would tie in with comments made by Arturo Sabato, Juan Sabato and Aldo Ferrer, all of whom stated that during their own periods in government there was little interference from the military in oil policies, which were throughout this period defined by civilians. Potash, *Army and Politics 1945–62* (p. 75), comments of the 1946–7 oil debate that 'the most striking aspect of the Army's role in the oil policy controversy was its relative passivity'.

46 Thibaud recalled that Amoco and the Illia government were close to a cash settlement at the time of the coup but that the incoming government insisted on a full renegotiation of any compensation terms with all the ensuing delays unless Amoco agreed to continue to operate within the country.

47 Daniel Brunella, *La administración de las empresas públicas: la experiencia de YPF* (Santiago, 1969).

48 *Ibid.* p. 15.

49 Ministerio de Economía, *Serie histórica,* 1978.

50 *Petroleum Press Service,* 1972, p. 98.

51 *La provincia,* March 1975.

52 Interview data.

53 C. J. Rosker, 'Argentina's Energy Program 1977–85' (British Engineering Association, August 1979), p. 25.

54 Interview with Ing. Piegari, Secretaría de Energía, September 1979.

55 Raúl Ondarts's seminar to the Instituto Torcuato di Tella, September 1979.

56 Sabato, *Petróleo,* p. 56.

57 Quoted in Brunella, *La administración.*

20 Petroperú 1968–80: achievements and hard lessons

1 *El comercio,* 2 September 1969.

2 F. Baca, 'La empresa pública'.

3 The classic case of this form of manipulation took place when US President Theo-

dore Roosevelt reacted to congressional refusal to vote funds to send the navy on a world trip by sending it to the Philippines and telling Congress that it would remain there until the money was found to bring it back.

4 Interview data.

5 Interview data.

6 Interview data.

7 *Oil and Gas Journal,* 23 April 1973.

8 A. Stepan, *The State and Society: Peru in Comparative Perspective* (Princeton, 1978), p. 264.

9 See Philip, 'Policymaking in the Peruvian Oil Industry', especially chs. 7, 8 and 9.

10 'Estamos explorando en la Selva' (Petroperú handout, 1971).

11 Personal communication.

12 Interview data.

13 *Andean Report,* June 1978.

14 See the interview with G. Bischoff in *Caretas,* 9 March 1972. My own interview sources tended to confirm this point.

15 According to my interview sources, Petrobrás initially showed interest in Selva exploration but was refused a contract by the Peruvian government for political reasons.

16 *State and Society,* p. 264.

17 *Peruvian Times,* 20 September 1974. Interview sources (in this case company officials) were extremely critical of the performance of the Peruvian air force.

18 This was a military tradition and was due partly to the need to maintain morale within the army by keeping access to top jobs open and partly to the fact that rotation makes military conspiracy far more difficult. It should be noted, however, that this strategy of rotation applied more to the directorate than to the actual management where turnover was far slower.

19 Peru, Comisión de Trabajo sobre las Empresas Públicas, report dated December 1976, section on Petroperú.

20 For broader discussion of the politics of the Velasco regime see G. Philip, *The Rise and Fall,* and Stepan, *State and Society.*

21 Government agencies did, however, eventually come to have a clear idea of the true state of Petroperú's finances. According to the Ministerio de Economía y Finanzas in February 1978 (*El problema de caja de Petroperú en 1978*), Petroperú's short-term debt rose from $195m. in 1974 to $228m. in 1975, $357m. in 1976 and $421m. by the end of 1977.

22 Patricio Ricketts in *Correo,* 26 March 1973.

23 According to one journalistic source, Velasco rejected Petroperú's proposal for a price increase on the ground that the Lima poor would have difficulty getting to the beach if gasoline prices were higher.

24 Peru, Comisión de Trabajo report.

25 *Andean Report,* June 1977.

26 Peru, Comisión de Trabajo report.

27 *Andean Report,* March 1979.

28 *Ibid.*

29 The *Andean Report* in July 1980 estimated Petroperú's reserves at 184.1 million barrels, and the company made a significant new oil find in January 1981.

30 See Rosemary Thorp, 'The Peruvian Experiment in Historical Perspective', Working Paper no. 31, Woodrow Wilson Center, 1979. She notes (p. 12) that in and after 1974 there was a 'rise in short-term borrowing . . . This was in large part a product of the inadequate financial arrangements made for the wide range of new state enterprises. Without proper provision for their working capital needs, and limited by law as to local borrowing, these enterprises were also in many cases unable to generate their own resources through pricing policy, either because they lacked market or political power or because, as we have mentioned, the distributional policies of the Velasco regime made low prices of basic products of overwhelming importance.'

31 The consequences of this were neatly described in the *Andean Report*, May 1978. 'President Morales Bermúdez continued to try to keep a balance between different views within the army. This strategy ended up this month in his governing through a hasty shell game procedure in which moves seemed to be made only to counter-balance the political effect of previous decisions, not because any measures taken were either right or timely in themselves. The result has been a succession of wildly swinging decisions and counter-decisions, statements and counter-statements that . . . have been unpredictable from one day to the next.'

32 Thorp and Bertram, *Peru 1890–1977*.

33 February 1977.

34 P. J. Cleaves and M. J. Scurrah, *Agriculture, Bureaucracy and Military Government in Peru* (Ithaca, NY, 1980), p. 412.

35 *Ibid.* p. 213.

36 See also Philip, 'Policymaking in the Peruvian Oil Industry', ch. 7.

37 CADE, *Annual Proceedings for 1976*.

38 *Andean Report*, July 1980. There is an interesting analysis in *Actualidad económica*, no. 20 (October 1979), by Carlos Romero. This appears to underestimate Occidental's production costs and final prices by roughly the same amount so that his estimate of Occidental's gross profit (before amortisation and depreciation) of between $340m. and $410m. may not be far wide of the mark.

39 Philip, 'Policymaking in the Peruvian Oil Industry', ch. 7.

40 For a detailed discussion of these changes, see *Andean Report*, July 1980.

41 IBRD, *Peru: Major Development Policy Issues and Recommendations* (Washington, 1981).

42 *Andean Report*, April 1981.

43 A number of senior geologists working for private companies were very surprised by the difficulty of finding significant oil reserves in the Amazon. Moreover, a study carried out by a private US firm, commissioned by the Peruvian government, found that Petroperú alone could expect to produce 200,000 b/d from the Amazon basin. On the other hand, the sharp increase in world oil prices during the 1970s eventually worked to Peru's advantage and this was not easily foreseeable either.

21 YPFB and the development of oil in Bolivia

1 Mariaca Bilbao, *Mito y realidad*.

2 FO 371 AS 6770/1817/5, 24 November 1947.

3 *HAR*, September 1950.

4 G. J. Eder, *Inflation and Development in Latin America: a Case Study of Inflation and Stabilisation in Bolivia* (Ann Arbor, Michigan, 1968), p. 58.

5 *Ibid.* p. 80.

6 *Ibid.* p. 506.

7 FO 371 AS 6512/341/5, 23 October 1946.

8 Quoted in FO 371 AS 4369/1817/5, 4 July 1947.

9 15 August 1952.

10 According to the *South American Journal* (30 June 1951), YPFB was in the process of negotiating a $3m. loan from the Export–Import Bank in order to contract a US drilling firm to develop YPFB's own areas, while attracting direct foreign investment into other areas of Bolivia. It is not known how close these negotiations were to completion at the time of the Bolivian Revolution, but the USA appears to have been closely involved from the beginning. Thus, according to the *Journal*, 'The US Ambassador is known to have taken part in conversations in La Paz leading to the change' in Bolivian policy. See also *Foreign Relations of the United States, 1951*, pp. 1143–4.

11 Zondag, *The Bolivian Economy*, ch. 10.

12 Eder, *Inflation and Development*, p. 60.

13 See Mariaca, *Mito y realidad*, ch. 3, and also Bolivia, YPFB, José Paz, *Radiografía del petróleo boliviano* (La Paz, 1956).

14 Zondag, *The Bolivian Economy*, ch. 10.

15 YPFB, *Informe técnico–estadístico 1956–60* (La Paz, 1960).

16 S. Almaraz, *Petróleo en Bolivia* (La Paz, 1958).

17 *Washington Post*, 7 November 1960.

18 Eder, *Inflation and Development*, p. 194.

19 *Ibid.* p. 195.

20 *Ibid.* p. 408. Eder complained that the YPFB 'management's understanding of corporation accounting and finance was practically nil'. This, however, appears to have been something of a naive view. It is highly probable that YPFB, which 'of all government enterprises . . . appeared to be the only one that was competently administered and which gave some promise of fulfilling the high hopes of its managers' (*ibid.* p. 193), was also the most resentful of heavy and imposed cuts in its permitted level of spending. Indeed, the same author remarked that 'Even . . . when it was illegal for any government department or entity to contract new obligations without the prior approval of the Council, YPFB and other agencies violated the law without a qualm, leaving the Council to deal with the creditors as best it could' (p. 124).

 Eder's book contains much valuable material and was certainly honestly written, but many of the judgements in it are extremely questionable.

21 *Ibid.* p. 291.

22 *Ibid.* p. 407.

23 *Mito y realidad*, p. 223.

24 According to José Paz, the plan for the pipeline was drawn up by the YPFB directorate from the very beginning of 1955 and a treaty was agreed with Chile to permit construction of the line at the end of January 1955. See YPFB, Paz, *Radiografía*.

 It is interesting that ECLA reported severe doubts about this export pipeline. It argued that 'it appears logical that YPFB should concentrate its investments principally on the tasks of exploration and subsequently of assuring a level of production sufficient to justify the construction of the pipeline . . . If, for political reasons or because the interest of the country requires it, Bolivia ought to take charge of the construction of the pipeline it would be best to find a form of financing which does not worsen the difficult financial situation of YPFB' (UN, ECLA, *Análysis y proyecciones del desarrollo económico: 4. El desarrollo económico de Bolivia* (1958) p. 199).

25 Quoted in Eder, *Inflation and Development*, p. 553. I have not been able to obtain a copy of this report.

26 See *Oil and Gas Journal*, 20 September 1964, which discussed a conflict between Gulf Oil and YPFB on the terms under which the Arica pipeline was to be used.

27 These figures were provided in *Petróleo interamericano*, March 1969.

28 A. del Castillo Crespo, 'Las industrias extractivas en Bolivia', in *Estudios andinos*, vol. 1 (1970), p. 112.

29 Quoted in *Diario*, 5 January 1971.

30 *Presencia*, 20 April 1971.

31 Decree Law 09723.

32 *Financial Times*, 8 February 1977.

33 Interview data. By mid-1977 this loss had reached serious proportions.

34 The political significance of Santa Cruz and its importance on the oil issue were discussed in chapter 13.

35 8 February 1977.

36 Bolivia, Ministerio de Minas e Hidrocarburos, *Diagnostico del sector de hidrocarburos* (La Paz, 1977).

37 These figures, however, were later challenged by Luis Salinas after the fall of the Banzer government in 1978. Salinas stated that, in the exploration division, 'in 1975, US$29.22m. was set aside for investment in the industry but only US$11.13m. was paid out. In 1977 the figures were US$49.27m. and US$13m. respectively' (*Latin America*, 20 October 1978).

38 See, for example, *Informe politico-económico* (La Paz, 18 July 1977), which headlined an article 'YPFB está en crisis'.

39 Interview data.

40 *Petroleum Economist*, January 1978.

41 *Latin America*, 10 November 1978. The Bolivian left has consistently stressed the importance of oil conservation and at various times accused Gulf Oil and the Banzer government of irresponsibly ignoring the future. See, for example, M. Quiroga Santa Cruz, *El saqueo de Bolivia* (Buenos Aires, 1973). It has rarely considered the question, however, of how a reasonable rate of oil exploration and development could be maintained unless the necessary income could be generated by producing oil and gas.

42 Interview data.

43 Interview data.

44 *Latin America*, 20 October 1978.

45 *Latin America*, 5 January 1979. It is, in fact, quite untrue that production from the Tita field 'has never been expected to be more than 5,000 b/d'. I was informed both by the British Embassy and by YPFB officials in August 1977 that production would reach at least 10,000 b/d and might go higher. It is, however, true that Bolivian geology is highly complicated and mistakes of this kind are easy to make. Thus, when YPFB drilled a particularly prolific well in its Montecristo field in 1977, it decided to call it the 'Banzer well' after the President; no sooner had the well been renamed than it dried up entirely.

46 Quoted in the *Financial Times*, 15 October 1974.

22 Petrovén: the birth of a giant

1 See, for example, Carlos Blanco *et al.*, *C.A.P.: 5 años* (Caracas, 1978), p. 178.
2 See the article by Kim Fuad in *Resumen*, 11 September 1977.
3 General Ravard, interviewed in *Resumen* 11 September 1977.
4 Petrovén, *Annual Report for 1979*.
5 *Ibid. 1978*.
6 *Business Venezuela*, July–August 1976.
7 30 January 1980.
8 *Resumen*, 13 June 1976.
9 *Ibid.* 16 January 1977.
10 *Business Venezuela*, May–June 1979.
11 *Ibid.*
12 Quoted in *Resumen*, 16 January 1977.
13 *Business Venezuela*, November–December 1974.

23 State oil companies in Latin America

1 Work being undertaken by Jorge Katz and Julio Fidel at Cepal in Buenos Aires inclines towards this conclusion.
2 See, for example, IBRD (Levy) 'The Search for Oil in Developing Countries'. The thinking behind the Levy report has greatly influenced World Bank policy and has become something of an orthodoxy among the private oil companies.
3 Much depends here upon the relative amount at stake. At one extreme one might put together a notional 'rate of return' based upon the best available assumptions about the cost of exploration and the probability of success and compare this with the social rate of return on the best alternative project available. At the other extreme one might regard oil exploration as purely speculative and simply allocate a fixed amount to it. An intermediate approach might be to discount any expected rate of return according to an uncertainty factor, or alternatively to vary the oil exploration budget according to whether or not previous exploration ventures were successful.
4 See B. Dasgupta, *The Oil Industry in India: Some Economic Aspects* (London, 1971), and Turner, 'Two Refineries: a Comparative Study of Technology Transfer to the Nigerian Refining Industry'.
5 The Mexican government deliberately used Pemex in the late 1970s as a strategically located borrower so as to channel credit into less appealing sectors via taxation or low oil-product prices.
6 James Corredor, 'El petróleo en México', *Uno más uno*, 18 March 1981.
7 For the 1960s see A. Gantt and G. Dutto, 'The Financial Performance of Government-owned Corporations in less Developed Countries', *IMF Staff Papers*, vol. 15 (March 1968), pp. 102–41. The authors find that Latin American oil companies during 1958–64 were more profitable than other state companies as a group both by sector and by continent. It is my impression that profitability has, if anything, increased since then.
8 At least one economist has attributed the failure of the Velasco government in Peru to its unwillingness or inability to raise the prices of outputs from state companies to levels sufficient to enable the public sector to generate a surplus. See E. V. K.

Fitzgerald, *The Political Economy of Peru 1956–78: Economic Development and the Restructuring of Capital* (Cambridge, 1979).

9 One official in the Peruvian Mines and Energy Ministry, to which Petroperú is nominally responsible, was at one point under the impression that oil flowed in underground rivers between countries and that Peru's share had not been collected in time and had therefore moved downriver to Venezuela.

10 Interview data.

11 Pertamina provides an obvious example. On this company see R. Fabrikant, 'Pertamina: a Legal and Financial Analysis of a National Oil Company in a Developing Country'. *Texas International Law Journal,* vol. 10 (1975), pp. 495–536.

12 R. Thorp, 'The Stabilisation Crisis in Peru 1975–78', in R. Thorp and L. Whitehead (eds.), *Inflation and Stabilisation in Latin America* (London, 1979), p. 139.

Bibliography

Official documents

Argentina. Ministerio de Economía. *Serie histórica de estado de fuentes y usos de fondos y balances generales.* Vol. 2 (Buenos Aires August 1978)
  Síntesis estadística anual de las empresas del estado (Buenos Aires November 1978)
  Secretaría de la Presidencia. President A. Frondizi. *La batalla del petróleo* (Buenos Aires July 1958)
  President J. C. Onganía *Petróleo y gas* (Buenos Aires 1969)
  YPF *Annual Report* (*Memoria anual*) (Buenos Aires)
  Boletín de informes (Buenos Aires, annually)
  Desarrollo de la industria petrolífera fiscal 1907–32 (Buenos Aires 1932)
  Política nacional de la energía (Buenos Aires 1949)
  La verdad sobre el petróleo argentino (Buenos Aires 1949)
Bolivia. Ministerio de Minas e Hidrocarburos. *Diagnóstico del sector de hidrocarburos* (La Paz 1977)
  Ministerio de Planificación. *Cuentas nacionales 1950–69* (La Paz 1970)
  Estrategia socio-económica (La Paz 1970)
  Plan nacional 1976–80 (La Paz 1977)
  YPFB *Annual Report* (*Memoria anual*) (La Paz)
  (José Paz) *Radiografía del petróleo boliviano* (La Paz 1956)
  Informe técnico-estadístico 1956–60 (La Paz 1960)
Brazil. Petrobrás. *Annual Report* (*Relatório das atividades*) (Rio de Janeiro)
  Petrobrás News (Rio de Janeiro, monthly)
Chile. ENAP. *Annual Report* (*Memoria anual*) (Santiago)
  Ministerio de Minas. *Proyecto de refinería de petróleo del estado* (Santiago 1939)
Ecuador. Banco Central. *Información estadística* (Quito, fortnightly)
  CEPE. *Informe* (Quito, annually)
  Ministerio de Planificación. *Junta plan* (Quito 1966)
  Plan nacional 1973–7 (Quito 1973)
IBRD. *Annual Reports* (Washington)
  Current Economic Position and Prospects of Ecuador (Washington 1972, 1973, 1974)
  Economic Report on Mexico (Washington 1953)
  Peru: Major Development Policy Issues and Recommendations (Washington 1981)
  (W. J. Levy) 'The Search for Oil in Developing Countries: a Problem of Scarce Resources and its Implications for the State and Private Enterprise' (Washington 1960)

IDB. *Annual Reports* (Washington)

IMF. Peru: Staff Report for the 1980 Article IV Constitution' (Washington 1981)

Mexico. Banco Nacional de Comercio Exterior. *Comercio exterior* (Mexico City monthly)

Government of Mexico. *Anuario de estadística* (Mexico City 1919–38)

Pemex. *Annual Report* (in two parts: *Informe del director* (*Director's Report*) and *Memoria de labores* (*Report of Work Done*) (Mexico City))

(Díaz Serrano) *Línea troncal nacional de distribución de gas natural* (Mexico City 1977)

Plan sexenal (Mexico City 1977)

Revisión presupuesta 1978. Obras capitiliares de la gerencia de petroquímica (Mexico City 1978)

Secretaría de la Presidencia. *Anuario estadístico*

Inversión pública federal 1925–63 (Mexico City 1964)

Inversión pública federal 1964–70 (Mexico City 1971)

Peru. CADE. *Annual Proceedings (Informe anual)*

(Fernández Baca) 'La empresa pública' (speech to CADE, 1969)

(Carlos Bobbio) 'Los contratos petrolíferos' (speech to CADE, 1970)

Comisión de Trabajo sobre las Empresas Públicas. Report (no title) dated December 1976. Chairman F. Bruce.

Comisión Multisectoral. *Primer informe* (Lima 1977)

EPF/Petroperú. *Annual Report (Memoria)* (Lima)

Instituto Nacional de Planificación. *Estudio sobre los contratos de operación petrolífera* (Lima 1973)

Plan nacional 1971–5 (Lima 1971)

Plan nacional 1975–8 (Lima 1975)

Ministerio de Economía y Finanzas. *El problema de caja de Petroperú en 1978* (Lima 1979)

Ministerio de Minas y Energía (until 1969 Ministerio de Fomento). *Estadística petrolera* (Lima, annually)

Sector hidrocarburos: política petrolera (Lima 1974)

Petroperú. *Carta de noticias* (Lima, various copies)

(Fernández Baca) *Operations Contract: Peruvian Model* (Lima 1973)

(Gerhardt Bischoff) 'Estamos explorando en la Selva' (Lima 1972)

United Nations (including Economic Commission for Latin America (Cepal)).

ECLA. *Análisis y proyecciones del desarrollo económico:4. El desarrollo económico de Bolivia (Mexico 1958)*

Análisis y proyecciones del desarrollo económica:5. El desarrollo económico de la Argentina (Mexico 1958)

Economic Survey of Latin America (New York), esp. 'The Economic Policy of Bolivia', in *Economic Survey* (1967)

'Energy in Latin America', in *Economic Bulletin for Latin America* (New York 1980)

(J. W. Mullin) *Energy in Latin America: the Historical Record* (Santiago 1978)

La industria del petróleo en América Latina: notas sobre su evolución reciente y perspectiva (New York 1973)

Survey of Latin America (annual)

(J. W. Mullin) *World Oil Prices: Prospects and Implications for Energy Policy-makers in Latin American Oil Deficit Countries* (Santiago 1978)

UN Department of Economic and Social Affairs, *Petroleum Exploration: Capital Requirements and Methods of Financing* (New York 1962)

United States of America. Department of Commerce. *Investments in Latin America and the British West Indies* (Washington 1918)
  Survey of Current Business
Department of Energy. *Petroleum Yearbook* (Washington)
Energy Statistics (Washington, annually)
Department of State. *Foreign Relations of the United States* (Washington, annually) (All references are to the volume *The American Republics,* which has a different volume number each year.)
Senate Committee on Foreign Relations. *Multinational Corporations and US Foreign Policy.* Vol. 5 (Washington 1975)
Uruguay. ANCAP. *Annual Report (Memoria)* (Montevideo)
Venezuela. Banco Central de Venezuela. *La economia venezolana 1940–73* (Caracas 1975)
Petrovén. *Annual Report (Informe anual)* (Caracas)
Secretaría de la Presidencia. *Anuario estadístico de Venezuela* (Caracas 1920–35)
  Nacionalización del petróleo en Venezuela: tesis y documentos fundamentales (Caracas 1975)
  Reversión petrolera en Venezuela (Caracas 1975)

Archives

British Government. General Foreign Office Correspondence (FO 368 and 371) Ministry of Fuel and Power (Petroleum Department) (Power 33)
Pearson Collection. Archives Collection. Science Museum Library, London
Peruvian Corporation Archive, University College, London
United States of America. Declassified Documents series published by Carrollton Press, Washington

Note. the US Declassified Documents service is provided by a Washington publisher. It contains documents which are not eligible for inclusion in the *Foreign Relations of the United States* service because they cover the last thirty years. These documents were, however, released under the 1975 United States Freedom of Information Act. References to this material give both the date of the original and the year and reference number under which they have subsequently been published.

Interview Sources

Companies involved with oil, private and public sector
Around one hundred present or former company executives were interviewed. Since a number of these requested secrecy, I have simply indicated the name of the company, the place and year of interview or interviews.
Amoco (Lima 1974, London 1974)
Arco (Lima 1973)
Arthur Anderson (Lima 1973)
Bank of Boston (São Paulo 1979)
Banco Continental, Lima (Lima 1973, 1974, 1977)
Belco Petroleum (Lima 1974, 1977)

British Petroleum (Lima 1973, 1974, London 1974)
Cayman Oil (Quito 1974)
Cities Service (Lima 1977)
Clyde Petroleum (Quito 1977)
Continental Oil (Lima 1974)
Davy International (São Paulo 1979)
Deminex (Lima 1974)
Dettco (Buenos Aires 1979)
Elf/Erap (Lima 1974, Rio de Janeiro 1979)
El Oriente (Lima 1974)
ENAP (London 1976)
Gulf Oil (Lima 1973, Quito 1974, 1977)
Iparanga (Rio de Janeiro 1979)
Lobitos Oilfields Ltd (Lima 1973)
Occidental Petroleum (Lima 1973, 1977)
Petrobrás (Rio de Janeiro 1979)
Pemex (Mexico 1978, 1979)
Petroperú (Lima 1973, 1974, 1977)
Petrovén (Caracas 1977)
Phillips Petroleum (Lima 1974)
Price Waterhouse (Lima 1974)
Royal Dutch/Shell (Buenos Aires 1979, Caracas 1977, Lima 1974, London several
    times, Mexico City 1979, 1981, Rio de Janeiro 1979)
Signal Oil (Lima 1974)
Society of British Engineers (Buenos Aires 1979)
Standard Oil of California (London 1974)
Sun Oil (Lima 1974)
Tenneco Petroleum (Lima 1973)
Texas Oil Company (Lima 1974)
Total (Lima 1973)
Union Oil (Lima 1974)
YPF (Buenos Aires 1979)
YPFB (La Paz 1977)

Political figures directly involved in oil policymaking

Lucho Arrauz, *asesor* to Jarrín Ampudia (Quito 1977)
Edgardo Camacho, Bolivian Foreign Minister 1969–70 (Lima 1977)
Ignacio Chavez de Mendonça, Chairman of Brazilian Energy Commission 1979–
    (Brasilia 1979)
Aldo Ferrer, Argentine Economics Minister 1970–1 (Buenos Aires 1979)
Gustavo Jarrín Ampudia, Ecuadorian Minister of Energy and Natural Resources 1972–
    4, President of OPEC 1974 (Quito 1977)
Jesús Puente Leyva, Chairman (in 1979) of Mexico's Energy Committee in the Cham-
    ber of Deputies (Mexico City 1979)
Ezequiel Ramírez Novoa, lawyer, anti-IPC nationalist (Lima 1974)
Juan Sabato, Argentine Deputy Minister with responsibility for oil 1963–6 (Buenos
    Aires 1979)
Luis Siles Salinas, President of Bolivia 1969 (La Paz 1977)

Rolando Thibaud, Argentine Deputy Minister with responsibility for oil 1967–70 (Buenos Aires 1979)
René Zavaleta, Bolivian Minister of Mines and Energy 1964 (Quito 1977)

Journalists covering oil politics or policy

Andean Report (Lima 1973, 1974, 1977) Nick Asheshov, Michelle Proud, Doreen Gillespie
Brazil Energy (Rio de Janeiro 1979) George Hawrylyshyn
Business Venezuela (Caracas 1977) Kim Fuad
Correo (Lima 1977) Patricio Ricketts
Daily Journal (Caracas 1977) Keith Grant
Financial Times (Quito 1977) Sarita Kendall
Financial Times (Mexico City 1978, 1981) William Chislett
Financial Times (Rio de Janeiro 1979) Diana Smith
Freelance (Buenos Aires 1979) Armando Ribas
O estado de São Paulo (São Paulo 1979) Alberto Tamer
Review of the River Plate (Buenos Aires 1979) Archie Norman

Others

There are a number of others who, for various reasons, cannot be named. Within the ministries of Latin American governments are included Central Bank officials in Peru, Mexico and Ecuador, officials from the Planning Institutes in Lima and La Paz, from the Mines and Oil Ministries in Lima and La Paz, from the Secretaría de Energía in Buenos Aires and the Technological Research Institute in São Paulo. There were also officials of the British Embassy in Brasilia (1979), Caracas (1977), La Paz (1977), Lima (1974, 1977), Mexico City (1978, 1981), Quito (1977), Rio de Janeiro (1979) and São Paulo (1979).

Periodicals

Actualidad económica (Lima)
Andean Report (Lima)
Brazil Energy (Rio de Janeiro)
Briefing Service, Shell Transport and Trading (London)
Business Latin America (New York)
Business Venezuela (Caracas)
Caretas (Lima)
El comercio (Lima)
El comercio (Quito)
Daily Journal (Caracas)
Diario (La Paz)
O estado de São Paulo (São Paulo)
Excelsior (Mexico City)
Ficha de información socio-política (Quito)
Financial Times (London)
Fortune (New York)
Guardian (London)
Hispanic American Report (1948–64) (Stanford, California).

Industria y quimica (Buenos Aires)
Informe politico–económico (La Paz)
International Herald Tribune (New York and Paris)
Jornal de tarde (São Paulo)
Jornal do Brasil (Rio de Janeiro)
Latin America (London)
Latin America Economic Report (London)
Latin America Regional Report (London)
Latin America Weekly Report (London)
El nacional (Caracas)
NACLA Newsletter (Washington)
New York Times (New York)
Nueva (Quito)
Oil and Gas Journal (Tulsa, Oklahoma)
Peruvian Times (Lima)
Petróleo interamericano (Tulsa, Oklahoma)
Petroleum Press Service (later *Petroleum Economist*) (London)
Platt's Oilgram (Houston, Texas)
La prensa (Lima)
Presencia (La Paz)
Proceso (Mexico)
Resumen (Caracas)
Review of the River Plate (Buenos Aires)
Revista de economia argentina (pre-1939) (Buenos Aires)
South American Journal (pre-1951) (London)
El telégrafo (Quito)
El tiempo (Quito)
El universal (Caracas)
El universo (Guayaquil)
Uno más uno (Mexico)
Vuelta (Mexico)
Washington Post (Washington)
World Oil (Washington)

Published works

Acosta Hermoso, E. *Petroquimica: ¿ desastre o realidad?* (Caracas 1977)
Adelman, M. 'The World Oil Outlook' in M. Clawson (ed.), *Natural Resources and International Development* (Baltimore 1964), pp. 27–126
  The World Petroleum Market (Baltimore 1973)
  with M. B. Zimmermann. *La industria petroquimica en un país subdesarrollado* (Bogotá 1973)
Alascio Cortázar, M. *Murguesia argentina y petróleo nacional* (Buenos Aires 1969)
Alemán, M. *La verdad del petróleo en México* (Mexico City 1977)
Alexander, R. *The Venezuelan Democratic Revolution* (New York 1964)
  The Bolivian National Revolution (Stanford 1969)
  The Communist Party of Venezuela (Stanford 1969)
Almaraz, S. *Petróleo en Bolivia* (La Paz 1958)

Anderson, I. H., Jr *The Standard–Vacuum Oil Company and United States East Asian Policy 1933–41* (Princeton 1975)

Andrade, V. *My Missions for Revolutionary Bolivia 1944–52* (Pittsburgh 1976)

Axelrod, T. *Conflict of Interest: a Theory of Divergent Goals with Application to Politics* (Chicago 1971)

Baer, W. *The Development of the Brazilian Steel Industry* (Vanderbilt University, Nashville, Tenn., 1969)
The Brazilian Economy: Its Growth and Development (Columbus, Ohio, 1979)
with I. Kerstensky and R. Villela. 'The Changing Role of the State in the Brazilian Economy', *World Development,* vol. 1, no. 11 (November 1973), pp. 23–35

Balestrini Contreras, G. *La industria petrolera en América Latina* (Caracas 1971)

Baloyra, R. 'Oil Policies and Budgets in Venezuela' *Latin American Research Review,* vol. 9, no. 4 (1974), pp. 28–72

Baran, P. *The Political Economy of Growth* (Stanford 1957)

Barrett Brown, R. *The Economics of Imperialism* (Harmondsworth, Middx, 1972)

Basurto, J. *El conflicto internacional en torno al petróleo de México* (Mexico 1978)

Benavides, M. V. de M. *O governo Kubitchek: desenvolvimento econômico e estabilidade política 1956–61* (Rio de Janeiro 1976).

Bermúdez, A. J. *The Mexican National Petroleum Industry: a Case Study in Nationalisation* (Stanford 1963)
La politica petrolera mexicana (Mexico City, 1976)

Bernard, J.-P. et al. *Guide to the Political Parties of South America* (Harmondsworth, Middx, 1973)

Betancourt, R. *Politica y petróleo.* 2nd edn (Caracas 1967)
Venezuela's Oil (London 1978)

Blair, J. M. *The Control of Oil* (New York 1977)

Blanco, C. et al. *C.A.P.: 5 años* (Caracas 1978)

Blasier, C. 'The United States and the Revolution', in J. M. Mallory and R. S. Thorn (eds.), *Beyond the Revolution: Bolivia since 1952* (Pittsburgh 1971), pp. 53–110.
The Hovering Giant: US responses to revolutionary change in Latin America (Pittsburgh 1976)

Bond, R. D. (ed.). *Contemporary Venezuela and its Role in International Affairs* (New York 1977)

Bonsal, P. *Cuba, Castro and the United States* (Pittsburgh 1971)

Braden, S. *Diplomats and Demagogues* (La Rochelle 1971)

Brandenburg, F. *The Making of Modern Mexico* (Newark, NJ, 1964)

British Petroleum. *Statistical Reviews of the World Oil Industry*

Bronfenbrenner, M. 'The Appeal of Confiscation in Economic Development', *Economic Development and Cultural Change,* vol. 4 (April 1955)

Brunella, D. *La administración de las empresas públicas: la experiencia de YPF* (Santiago 1969)

Bullard, F. J. *Mexico's Natural Gas* (Austin, Texas, 1968)

Bunge, A. *La guerra del petróleo en la Argentina* (Buenos Aires 1933)

Burgraaff, W. J. *The Venezuelan Armed Forces in Politics 1935–59* (St Louis 1972)

Calvert, P. *The Mexican Revolution 1910–14: the Diplomacy of Anglo-American Conflict* (Cambridge 1968)

Canessa, J. V. *La verdad sobre el petróleo argentino* (Buenos Aires 1957)

Cardoso, F. and E. Faletto. *Dependency and Development in Latin America* (Berkeley 1979)
'On the Characterization of Authoritarian Regimes in Latin America' in D. Collier
(ed.). *The New Authoritarianism in Latin America* (Princeton 1979)

Carr, B. *El movimiento obrero y la política en México 1910–29* (Mexico City 1976)

Carvalho, G. *Petrobrás: do monopólio aos contratos de risco* (Rio de Janeiro 1976)

Castillo Crespo, A. del. 'Las industrias extractivas en Bolivia', *Estudios andinos,* vol 1
(1970)

Chase Manhattan Bank. *Report on the World Oil Industry* (New York, annual)

Cleaves, P. J. and M. J. Scurrah. *Agriculture, Bureaucracy and Military Government in
Peru* (Ithaca, NY 1980)

Cohn, G. *Petróleo e nacionalismo* (São Paulo 1968)

Corbett, C. 'Military Institutional Development and Socio-Political Change: the
Bolivian Case', *Journal of Inter-American Studies,* vol. 14, no. 4 (November 1972)

Cordova, A. *La ideologia de la revolución mexicana: la formación del nuevo régimen* (Mexico
City 1973)
La política de masas del cardenismo (Mexico City 1974)

Corredor, J. 'El petróleo en México', *Uno más uno* (18 March 1981)

Cotler, J. and R. Fagan (eds.), *Latin America and the United States: the Changing Political
Realities* (Stanford, 1974)

Cotta, P. *O petróleo é nosso?* (São Paulo 1975)

Cronon, E. D. *Josephus Daniels in Mexico* (Madison, 1960)

Daniels, Josephus. *Shirt-sleeved Diplomat* (Chapel Hill, N. Carolina 1947)

Darmstadter, J. and H. H. Landsberg, 'The European Background', in 'The Oil Crisis
in Perspective', *Daedalus,* vol. 104 (Fall 1975)

Dasgupta, B. *The Oil Industry in India: Some Economic Aspects* (London 1971)

Delitos petroleros, Los. General Mosconi Centre (Buenos Aires 1962)

De Novo, J. 'The Movement for an Aggressive Oil Policy abroad, 1918–20', *American
Historical Review,* vol. 62 (1956), pp. 854–76

Díaz Alejandro, C. 'The Argentine State and Economic Growth: a Historical Overview'
in G. Ranis (ed.), *Government and Economic Development* (New Haven 1971)

Díaz Goitía, E. *La riqueza argentina en peligro* (Buenos Aires 1936)

Diniz, Eli. *Empresário, estado e capitalismo no Brasil 1930–45* (Rio de Janeiro 1978)

Dobkin, W. W. *Petroleum Industry and Trade of Peru and Equador (sic)* (US Dept. of
Commerce 1924)

Documentos fundamentales sobre petróleo, Universidad Central de Guayaquil (1976)

Dulles, J. W. F. *Castello Branco: the Making of a Brazilian President* (College Station,
Texas, 1979)

Eder, G. J. *Inflation and Development in Latin America: a Case Study of Inflation and
Stabilisation in Bolivia* (Ann Arbor, Michigan, 1968)

Egana, Manuel, *et al. Nacionalización petrolera en Venezuela* (Caracas 1971)

Einhorn, J. *Expropriation Politics* (Lexington, Mass., 1974)

Ellsworth, P. T. *Chile: an Economy in Transition* (London 1945)

Engler, R. *The Politics of Oil: a Study of Private Power and Democratic Directions* (New
York 1961)
The Brotherhood of Oil: Energy Policy and the Public Interest (Chicago 1977)

Erickson, K. P. *Corporatism and Working Class Politics in Brazil* (Los Angeles, 1977)

Evans, Peter. 'Multinationals, State-owned Corporations and the Transformation of

Imperialism: a Brazilian Case Study', *Economic Development and Cultural Change* (October 1977), pp. 43–64

Dependent Development: the Alliance of Multinational, State and Local Capital in Brazil (Princeton 1979)

Fabrikant, R. 'PERTAMINA: a Legal and Financial Analysis of a National Oil Company in a Developing Country', *Texas International Law Journal*, vol. 10 (1975), pp. 495–536

Fagan, R. and W. Cornelius (eds.). *Political Power in Latin America: Seven Confrontations* (Newark, NJ, 1970)

Fanning, L. W. *American Oil Operations Abroad*. (New York 1947)

Foreign Oil and the Free World (New York 1954)

Feis, H. *Petroleum and American Foreign Policy* (Stanford 1944)

Three International Episodes as seen from E. A. (New York, 1946)

Ferrer, A. *Crisis y alternativas de la política económica argentina* (Buenos Aires 1977)

Fitch, J. S. *The Military Coup d'Etat as a Political Process: Ecuador 1940–66* (Baltimore 1977)

Fitzgerald, E. *The Political Economy of Peru 1956–78: Economic Development and the Restructuring of Capital* (Cambridge 1979)

Fox, D. 'Mexico: the Development of an Oil Industry', *BOLSA Review*, vol. 11 (October 1977), pp. 520–33

Frank, A. G. *Capitalism and Underdevelopment in Latin America* (New York 1967)

Frankel, P. H. *Essentials of Petroleum* (London 1946)

Frigerio, R. *Petróleo* (speech to Chamber of Deputies, Buenos Aires, 1964)

Frondizi, A. *Petróleo y política* (Buenos Aires, 1956)

Petróleo y nación (Buenos Aires, 1963)

Fundación Eugenio Blanco. *El Ministro Eugenio A. Blanco y la anulación de los contratos de petróleo* (Buenos Aires 1975)

Furnish, D. 'Peruvian Domestic Law Aspects of the La Brea y Pariñas Controversy', *Kentucky Law Journal* vol. 59 (1970), pp. 351–85

Galeano, E. H. *Open Veins of Latin America: Five Centuries of the Pillage of a Continent* (New York 1973)

Gall, N. 'The Challenge of Venezuelan Oil', *Foreign Policy*, no. 18 (Spring 1975)

Gallardo Lozada, J. *De Torres a Banzer: diez meses de emergencia en Bolivia* (Buenos Aires 1972)

Gantt, A. and G. Dutto. 'The Financial Performance of Government-owned Corporations in less Developed Countries', *IMF Staff Papers*, vol. 15 (March 1968), pp. 102–41

Geithman, D. T. (ed.). *Fiscal Policy for Industrialisation and Development in Latin America* (Gainesville, Florida, 1974)

Gellman, F. *Good Neighbour Diplomacy: United States Policies in Latin America 1933–45* (Baltimore 1979)

Gerretson, C. *Geschiedenis der 'Koninlijke'*, vol. 5 (Shell, The Hague, n.d.)

Ghadar, F. *The Evolution of OPEC Strategy* (Lexington, Mass., 1977)

Gibb, G. and H. Knowlton. *The Resurgent Years 1911–27: History of Standard Oil Company, New Jersey* (New York 1956)

Giddens, P. H. *Standard Oil Company (Indiana): Oil Pioneer of the Middle West* (New York, 1955)

562   *Bibliography*

Girvan, N. 'Multinational Corporations and Dependent Underdevelopment in Mineral Export Economies', *Social and Economic Studies* (1971), pp. 490–526

Goff, I. and G. Locker. 'The Violence of Domination: US Power and the Dominican Republic' in I. L. Horowitz *et al. Latin American Radicalism: a Documentary Report on Left and Nationalist Movements* (London 1969)

Goldwert, M. *Democracy, Militarism and Nationalism in Argentina, 1930–66* (Austin, Texas, 1972)

Gómez, O. *Infamia y verdad* (Quito 1973)

Goodsell, C. *American Corporations and Peruvian Politics* (Cambridge, Mass., 1974)

Goodwin, R. 'Letter from Peru', *New Yorker* (17 May 1969), pp. 41–108

Gordon, W. *Expropriation of Foreign Owned Property in Mexico* (Washington 1941)

Grayson, G. 'Mexico's Opportunity: the Oil Boom', *Foreign Policy*, vol. 29 (Winter 1977–8), pp. 65–89

Griffin, K. (ed.) *Financing Development in Latin America* (London 1971)

Grossling, Bernardo F. *Latin America's Petroleum Prospects in the Energy Crisis* (Washington 1975)

Guzmán Velasco, E. *Aprovechamiento del gas natural en Bolivia* (La Paz 1966)

Hanson, A. H. *Public Enterprise and Economic Development* (London 1959)

Hanson, S. G. *Utopia in Uruguay* (Oxford 1938)

'The End of the Good Partner Policy', in *Inter-American Economic Affairs*, vol. 14, no. 1 (Summer 1960)

Hartshorn, J. E. *Oil Companies and Governments: an Account of the International Oil Industry in its Political Environment* (London 1967)

Hermida Ruiz, A. J. *Bermúdez y la batalla por el petróleo* (Mexico City 1974)

Hidy, R. and M. Hidy. *Pioneering in Big Business 1882–1911: History of Standard Oil New Jersey* (New York 1956)

Hirschman, A. *How to Divest in Latin America and Why* (Essays in International Finance, no. 76, Princeton 1969)

Hirst, D. *Oil and Public Opinion in the Middle East* (London 1966)

Hofstadter, R. *The American Political Tradition and the Men who made it* (New York 1967)

Hogan, M. J. 'Informal Entente: Public Policy and Private Management in Anglo-American Petroleum Affairs', *Business History Review*, vol. 48 (1974), pp. 187–205

Huelga de los obreros de la compañia mexicana de petróleo 'El Aguila', S.A. en Minatitlán: su origen y caracteres, La (Mexico City 1925)

Hugo Salamanca, F. *El fraude de la nacionalización de 'Bolivian Gulf Oil Co.'* (Oruro, Bolivia, 1978)

Hurtado, O. *et al. Ecuador, hoy* (Bogotá 1978)

Ingram, G. *Expropriation of U.S. Property in South America: Nationalization of Oil and Copper Companies in Peru, Bolivia and Chile* (New York 1974)

Iturralde, A. *Petición de informe del H. Senador por La Paz . . . sobre la concesión de un millón de hectares petroliferas* (La Paz 1922)

Jacoby, N. *Multinational Oil* (New York 1974)

Jarrín Ampudia, G. 'Situación de la política petrolera ecuatoriana', in *Por la nacionalización del petróleo* (Guayaquil 1976)

Johnson, H. G. (ed.). *Economic Nationalism in Old and New States* (Chicago 1967)

Justiniano Canedo, O. *Tesis de nacionalización de los bienes de la empresa boliviana Gulf Oil Co.* (La Paz 1969)

Kane, N. Stephen. 'Corporate Power and Foreign Policy: Efforts of American Oil Companies to Influence United States Relations with Mexico', *Diplomatic History*, vol. 1 (1977), pp. 170–98

Kaplan, M. *Economía y política del petróleo argentino 1939–56* (Buenos Aires 1957)
Petróleo, estado y empresas en Argentina (Caracas 1972)

Klein, H. 'American Oil Companies in Latin America: the Bolivian Experience', *Inter-American Economic Affairs*, vol. 18, no. 2 (Autumn 1964), pp. 47–72
Parties and Political Change in Bolivia 1880–1952 (Cambridge 1969)

Kucinski, B. (ed.). *Petróleo: contratos de risco e dependência: ensaio e reportagem* (São Paulo 1977)

Kuczynski, P. P. *Peruvian Democracy under Economic Stress: an Account of the Belaúnde Administration 1963–68* (Princeton 1977)

Larson, H., K. Knowlton and C. Pople. *New Horizons 1927–50: History of the Standard Oil Company, New Jersey* (New York 1971)

Lasa, J. 'Chicontepec, un proyecto para abrir 16 mil pozos en 14 años', *Uno más uno* (18 March 1981)

Latin American and Caribbean Oil Report (Petroleum Economist, London 1979)

Leff, N. *Economic Policy-making and Development in Brazil 1947–64* (New York 1968)

Levingstone, J. and J. De Onis. *The Alliance that Lost its Way* (Chicago 1970)

Lewis, Cleona, *America's Stake in International Investments* (Washington 1938)

Lewis, C. M. 'British Railway Companies and the Argentine Government' in D. C. M. Platt (ed.), *Business Imperialism: an Analysis based on the British Experience in Latin America before 1930* (Oxford 1978)

Lieuwen, E. *Petroleum in Venezuela: a History* (Stanford 1954)

López Portillo y Weber, J. *El petróleo de México* (Mexico City 1975)

Luna, Félix (ed.). *El petróleo nacional* (Buenos Aires 1976)

Malave Mata, H. *Petróleo y desarrollo económico de Venezuela* (Caracas 1962)

Mallon, R. D. *Economic Policymaking in a Conflict Society: the Argentine Case* (Cambridge, Mass., 1975)

Malpica, C. *Los dueños del Perú*. 3rd edn. (Ensayos Sociales, Lima 1968)

Mamelakis, M. 'The Theory of Sectoral Clashes', *Latin American Research Review* (1969), pp. 9–43

Mancke, L. *Mexican Oil and Natural Gas, Political, Strategic and Economic Implications* (New York 1979)

Mariaca Bilbao, E. *Mito y realidad del petróleo boliviano* (La Paz 1966)

Martínez, A. R. *Chronology of Venezuelan Oil* (London 1969)

Martins, C. E. (ed.). *Estado e capitalismo no Brasil* (São Paulo 1977)

Martins, Luciano. *Pouvoir et développement économique: formation et évolution des structures politiques au Brésil* (Paris 1976)

Martz, J. D. *Acción Democrática: Evolution of a Modern Political Party in Venezuela* (Princeton 1966)
'Policy-making and the Quest for Consensus: Nationalizing Venezuelan Petroleum', *Journal of Inter-American Studies and World Affairs*, vol. 19, no. 4 (November 1977), pp. 483–508

Mayo, C. et al. *Diplomacia, política y petróleo en la Argentina 1927–30* (Buenos Aires 1976)

Medeiros Lima, C. *Petróleo: desenvolvimento o vassalagem (a defecção de Frondizi)* (Rio de Janeiro 1960)

Megadelli, A. *Investment Policies of National Oil Companies: a Comparative Study of Sonatrech, Nioc and Pemex* (New York 1980)

Meyer, L. *México y los Estados Unidos en el conflicto petrolero 1917–42*. 2nd edn (Mexico City 1972)

'La resistencia al capital privado extranjero: el caso del petróleo 1938–50' in B. Sepúlveda *et al.*, *Las empresas transnacionales en México* (Mexico City 1974)

Mikdashi, Z. *The Community of Oil Exporting Countries: a Study of Governmental Co-operation* (London 1971)

Mikesell, R. F. (ed.). *U.S. Private and Government Investment Abroad* (Portland 1962)
Foreign Investment in the Petroleum and Mineral Industries: Case Studies of Investor–Host Country Relations (Baltimore 1971)

Miller, R. 'Foreign Firms and the Peruvian Government' in D. C. M. Platt (ed.), *Business Imperialism: an Analysis based on the British Experience in Latin America before 1930* (Oxford 1978)

Moran, T. H. *Multinational Corporations and the Politics of Dependence: Copper in Chile* (Princeton 1974)

Mosconi, E. *El petróleo argentino* (Buenos Aires 1936)
La batalla del petróleo (Buenos Aires 1938)

Moura, Pedro de, and Felisberto Carneiro. *Em busca do petróleo brasileiro* (Rio de Janeiro 1978)

Nove, Alec. *Efficiency Criteria for Nationalised Industries* (London 1973)

O'Connor, H. *World Crisis in Oil* (London 1962)

O'Connor, J. *The Origins of Socialism in Cuba* (New York 1964)

Odell, P. 'Oil and the State in Latin America', *International Affairs*, vol. 40 (October 1964), pp. 659–73

'A Personal View of "Missing Oil" ', *Petroleum Economist* (January 1980)

O'Shaughnessy, H. *Oil in Latin America* (*Financial Times*, London, 1976)

Packenham, R. *Liberal America and the Third World* (Princeton 1973)

Parkinson, F. *Latin America, the Cold War and the World Powers 1945–73* (London 1974)

Payne, D. *Initiative in Energy: Dresser Industries Inc. 1880–1979* (New York 1979)

Penrose, E. 'Profit-sharing between Producing Countries and Oil Companies in the Middle East' in *Economic Journal*, vol. 70 (1959), pp. 238–62
The Large International Firm in Developing Countries: the International Petroleum Industry (London 1968)

Pérez Alfonzo, J. P. *La dinámica del petróleo en el progresso de Venezuela* (Caracas 1965)
El pentágono petrolero (Caracas 1967)
Petróleo y dependencia (Caracas 1971)

Pérez Prins, E. 'La refinería del petróleo de la ANCAP', *Boletín del Instituto Sudamericano del Petróleo*, vol. 1, no. 1 (April 1943), pp. 15–36

Peterson, H., and T. Ungar. *Petróleo: hora cero* (Lima 1964)

Petras, J. F., M. Morley and S. Smith. *The Nationalisation of Venezuelan Oil* (New York 1977)

Petróleo argentino, El. Comité Universitario Radical, Junta Central (Buenos Aires 1930)

'Petróleo argentino en la economía, en la doctrina y en la legislación', *Boletín de informaciones petroleras* (Buenos Aires 1938)

Philip, G. 'The Limitations of Bargaining Theory', *World Development*, vol. 4, no. 3 (May 1976), pp. 231–9

'The Political Economy of Expropriation: Three Peruvian Cases', *Millennium,* vol. 6, no. 3 (Spring 1978), pp. 221–35
The Politics of Oil in Ecuador (Working Paper, Institute of Latin American Studies, London 1978)
The Rise and Fall of the Peruvian Military Radicals 1968–76 (London 1978)
'Mexican Oil and Gas: the Politics of a New Resource', *International Affairs,* vol. 56, no. 3 (Summer 1980), pp. 474–83
Pike, F. *Chile and the United States 1880–1962* (Notre Dame, Indiana, 1963)
Pinelo, A. *The Multinational Corporation as a Force in Latin American Politics: a Case Study of the International Petroleum Company* (New York 1973)
Plaza, S. de la. 'Foreign Exploitation of Oil and National Development' in I. L. Horowitz *et al.* (eds.), *Latin American Radicalism* (New York 1969)
Potash, R. A. *The Army and Politics in Argentina 1928–45* (Stanford 1969)
The Army and Politics in Argentina 1945–62: Perón to Frondizi (Stanford and London 1980)
Powell, J. R. *The Mexican Petroleum Industry 1938–50* (Los Angeles 1956)
Primer seminario de investigación sobre la industria del petróleo en Colombia (Bogotá 1960)
Puga Vega, M. *El petróleo chileno* (Santiago 1964)
Quiroga Santa Cruz, M. *La desnacionalización del petróleo: desarrollo con soberanía* (Cochabamba 1967)
El saqueo de Bolivia (Buenos Aires 1973)
(with others). *Gas y petróleo: ¿liberación o dependencia?* (Cochabamba 1967)
(with others). *La dramática lucha por los hidrocarburos en Bolivia* (Cochabamba 1970)
Ramírez Novoa, E. *Recuperación de La Brea y Pariñas* (Lima 1964)
Petróleo y revolución nacional (Lima 1970)
Randall, Laura, *An Economic History of Argentina in the Twentieth Century* (New York 1978)
Randall, S. J. 'The International Corporation and American Foreign Policy: the United States and Colombian Petroleum 1920–40', *Canadian Journal of History,* vol. 9, no. 2 (1974), pp. 174–96
'The "Barco Concession" in Colombian–American Relations 1926–32' *The Americas,* vol. 9, no. 1 (July 1976), pp. 96–108
The Diplomacy of Modernization: Colombian–American Relations 1920–40 (Toronto 1977)
Ranis, G. (ed.). *Government and Economic Development* (New Haven 1971)
Ricketts, P. 'El rol empresarial del estado', *La prensa* (12 December 1976)
Rippy, J. Fred *British Investments in Latin America 1822–1949: a Case Study in the Operations of Private Enterprise in Retarded Regions* (Minneapolis 1959)
Rock, D. (ed.). *Argentina in the Twentieth Century* (London 1974)
Politics in Argentina 1890–1930: the Rise and Fall of Radicalism (Cambridge 1975)
Romero, C. 'Petróleo peruano: el Japón y la OXY', *Actualidad económica,* vol. 2, no. 20 (October 1979), pp. 5–7
Rout, L. B., Jr. *The Politics of the Chaco Peace Conference 1935–39* (Austin, Texas, 1970)
Royal Dutch/Shell *Annual Reports*
Sabato, A. *Historia de los contratos petrolíferos* (Buenos Aires 1963)
Petróleo: ¿dependencia o liberación? (Buenos Aires 1974)
Sabato, J. *Ficción y realidad de la política y del plan energético del gobierno revolucionario* (Buenos Aires 1969)

El ministro Eugenio A. Blanco y la anulación de los contratos de petróleo (Buenos Aires 1969)

Sader Pérez, J. *The Venezuelan State Oil Reports to the People* (Caracas 1967)

Sampson, A. *The Seven Sisters* (London 1975)

Sandeman, H. 'Pemex comes out of its Shell', *Fortune* (10 April 1978)

Sandino, D. (pseud.) *El mar, el político nacional y los políticos criollos* (La Paz 1964)

Scalabrini Ortiz, J. *La industria del petróleo en Argentina y la política petrolera* (Buenos Aires 1977)

Schelling, T. *Strategy of Conflict* (Oxford 1971)

Schlesinger, A. *The Imperial Presidency* (Boston 1973)

Schneider, R. M. *Brasil: Foreign Policy of a Future World Power* (Boulder, Colorado, 1974)

Sepúlveda, B. *et al. Las empresas transnacionales en Mexico* (Mexico City 1974)

Serrato, M. 'La expansión de Pemex', *Uno más uno* (18 March 1981)

— Shaffer, E. *The Oil Import Program of the United States: an Evaluation* (New York 1968)

Sigmund, P. *Multinationals in Latin America: the Politics of Nationalisation* (Madison 1980)

Silenzo de Stagni, A. *El petróleo argentino* (Buenos Aires 1955)

Silva Herzog, J. *Petróleo mexicano* (Mexico City 1942)

México y su petróleo: una lección para América (Buenos Aires 1959)

Silveyra, R. *YPF rectifica: aclarando y puntualizando manifestaciones vertidas en la H. Cámera de Diputados* (Buenos Aires 1934)

Smith, P. *Argentina and the Failure of Democracy: Conflict among Political Elites 1904–55* (Madison 1974)

Smith, P. S. 'Brazilian Oil: from Myth to Reality', *Inter-American Economic Affairs*, vol. 30, no. 4 (Spring 1977), pp. 45–61.

Oil and Politics in Modern Brazil (Toronto 1976).

Smith, R. F. *The United States and Revolutionary Nationalism in Mexico 1916–32* (Chicago 1972)

— Smith, R. J. 'The United States Government Perspective on Expropriation and Investment in Developing Countries', *Vanderbilt Journal of Transnational Law*, vol. 9, no. 3 (Summer 1975), pp 526–43

Soares Pereira, J. (with help from C. Medeiros Lima). *Petróleo, energia eléctrica, siderúrgia; a luta pela emancipação* (Rio de Janeiro 1978)

Sodré, N. W. *História militar do Brasil* (Rio de Janeiro 1965)

Solberg, Carl. *Oil and Nationalism in Argentina: a History* (Stanford 1979)

Stepan, A. *The Military in Politics: Changing Patterns in Brazil* (Princeton 1971)

(ed.). *Authoritarian Brazil: Origins, Policies and Future* (New Haven 1973)

The State and Society: Peru in Comparative Perspective (Princeton 1978)

Stoff, M. B. *Oil, War and American Security: the Search for a National Policy on Foreign Oil 1941–7* (New Haven 1980)

Stumpf, A. and M. Pereira Filho. *A segunda guerra: sucessão de Geisel* (São Paulo 1979)

Suárez, E. *Comentarios y recuerdos 1926–46* (Mexico City 1977)

Tama Paz, C. *Petróleo: drama ecuatoriana* (Guayaquil 1970)

Tamer, A. *Petróleo: o preço da dependência: o Brasil na crise mundial* (Rio de Janeiro 1980)

Tanzer, M. *The Political Economy of International Oil in the Underdeveloped Countries* (Boston 1969)

Tejada, M. *Aprovechamiento del gas natural en Bolivia* (La Paz 1965)

Tendler, J. *Electric Power in Brazil: Entrepreneurship in the Public Sector* (Cambridge, Mass., 1968)

Thorp, R. and G. Bertram. *Peru 1890–1977: Growth and Policy in an Export Economy* (London 1978)

and L. Whitehead (eds.). *Inflation and Stabilisation in Latin America* (London 1979)

Trias, V. *Imperialismo, geopolitica y petróleo* (Montevideo 1971)

Tugwell, F. *The Politics of Oil in Venezuela* (Stanford 1975)

Tulchin, J. S. *The Aftermath of War: World War I and US Policy Toward Latin America* (New York 1971)

Turner, L. *Oil Companies in the International System* (London 1978)

Turner, T. 'Two Refineries: a Comparative Study of Technology Transfer to the Nigerian Refining Industry', *World Development,* vol. 5, no. 3. (March 1977), pp. 235–56

Vallenilla, L. *Auge, declinación y porvenir del petróleo venezolano* (Caracas 1973)

Oil: the Making of a New Economic Order: Venezuelan Oil and OPEC (New York 1975)

Vargas McDonald, A. *Hacia una nueva política petrolera* (Mexico City 1959)

Vásquez Gómez, E. (ed.). *Epistolario de Lázaro Cárdenas* (Mexico City 1974)

Vedavalli, R. *Private Foreign Investment and Economic Development: a Case Study of Petroleum in India* (Cambridge 1976)

Vernon, R. *The Dilemma of Mexico's Development: the Roles of the Private and Public Sectors* (Cambridge, Mass., 1963).

(ed.) *Public Policy and Private Enterprise in Mexico* (Cambridge, Mass., 1963)

(ed.) *The Oil Crisis* (New York 1970)

Sovereignty at Bay: the Multinational Spread of US Enterprises (London 1973)

Villa, M., and E. Canepa. 'El petróleo argentino en el último decenio', *La ingeniería* (May 1956)

Villanueva, V. *Un año bajo el sable* (Lima 1963)

Villegas, J. *Petróleo oligarquía e imperio* (Bogotá 1975)

Votaw, Dow. *The Six-legged Dog: Mattei and ENI – a Study in Power* (Berkeley 1964)

Weinstein, M. *Uruguay, the Politics of Failure* (New York 1975).

Weisburg, R. *The Politics of Crude Oil Pricing in the Middle East* (Berkeley 1977)

Wenzel, O. 'El petróleo en Chile', *Boletin del Instituto Sudamericano del Petróleo,* vol. 1, no. 5 (February 1945)

with R. Muller. 'El petróleo en Chile', *Boletin de Información Petrólero* (Buenos Aires) (September 1945)

Wesley Owen, E. *Trek of the Oil Finders: a History of Exploration for Petroleum* (Tulsa 1975)

Whitehead, L. A. *The United States and Bolivia: a Case of Neo-colonialism* (London 1969)

'Bolivia's Conflict with the United States', *World Today* (April 1970), pp. 167–78

'The State and Sectional Interests; the Bolivian Case', *European Journal of Political Research,* vol. 3 (Spring 1975), pp. 115–46

'National Power and Local Power: the Case of Santa Cruz de la Sierra', *Latin American Urban Research,* vol. 3 (1974), pp. 1–23

Wilkins, M. *The Emergence of Multinational Enterprise: American Business abroad from the Colonial Era to 1914* (Cambridge, Mass., 1970)

The Maturing of Multinational Enterprise: American Business Abroad from 1914 to 1970 (Cambridge, Mass., 1974)

'Multinational Oil Companies in South America in the 1920s; Argentina, Bolivia,

Brazil, Chile, Colombia, Ecuador and Peru', *Business History Review,* vol. 48 (Autumn 1974), pp. 415–38

Williamson, H. F., *et al. The American Petroleum Industry: the Age of Energy 1899–1959* (Seattle 1963)

Wionczek, M. 'Electric Power: the Uneasy Partnership' in R. Vernon (ed.), *Public Policy and Private Enterprise in Mexico* (Cambridge, Mass., 1963), pp. 19–110

Wirth, J. D. *The Politics of Brazilian Development 1930–54* (Stanford 1970)

Wood, Bryce, *The Making of the Good Neighbour Policy* (New York 1961).

Woods, R. B. 'Hull and Argentina; Wilsonian Diplomacy in the Age of Roosevelt', *Journal of Inter-American Studies and World Affairs,* vol. 16, no. 3 (August 1974), pp. 350–71

Wright, W. *British-owned Railways in Argentina: their Effect on the Growth of Economic Nationalism 1854–1948* (Austin, Texas, 1974)

Wyant, F. R. *The United States, OPEC and Multinational Oil* (Lexington, Mass., 1977)

Yornet, Mario *Los precios del petróleo en la República Argentina* (Buenos Aires 1977)

Zaharia, H. S. 'State Petroleum Companies', in *Journal of World Trade Law,* vol. 12, no. 6 (November–December 1978), pp. 481–500

Zimmermann Zavala, A. *La historia secreta del petróleo* (Lima 1968)

El plan inca: objectivo, revolución peruana (Lima 1974)

Zondag, C. *The Bolivian Economy 1952–65: the Revolution and its Aftermath* (New York 1966)

Unpublished works

Adelson, Lief. 'Legistas en Overoles: la lucha de los obreros industriales tampiqueños para definir y defender el derecho del trabajo en la ausencia de un régimen jurídico 1910–24' (mimeo, Mexico City 1979)

Bates, L. W. 'The Petroleum Industry in Brazil' (PhD, University of Texas, 1975)

Bertram, I. G. 'Development Problems in an Export Economy: a Study of Domestic Capitalists, Foreign Firms and Government in Peru 1919–30 (DPhil, Oxford 1974)

Buchanan, J. E. 'Politics and Petroleum Development in Argentina 1916–30' (PhD, University of Massachusetts 1973)

Castro Melganejo, Ramón. 'Participación de la industria petrolera en la balanza de pagos' (*licenciatura* thesis, Universidad Nacional Autónoma de México 1980)

Corkill, Dave. 'The Political Impact of Oil in Ecuador: the Rodríguez Lara Regime' (mimeo, Manchester 1976)

Dunkerley, James. 'The Politics of the Bolivian Army: Institutional Development to 1935' (DPhil, Oxford 1980)

Durán de Seade, E. 'Mexico's Relations with the Great Powers during the Great War' (DPhil, Oxford 1980)

Gortari Rabiela, R. N. de 'Petróleo y clase obrera en la zona del Golfo de México 1920–38' (*licenciatura* thesis, Universidad Nacional Autónoma de México, 1978)

Gutiérrez, T. 'La intervención del estado mexicano en la economía a través de los organismos descentralizados: el caso de Petróleos Mexicanos' (*licenciatura* thesis, Instituto Politécnico Nacional, 1978)

Hollander, F. A. 'Oligarchy and the Politics of Petroleum in Argentina: the Case of the Salta Oligarchy and Standard Oil' (PhD, University of California at Los Angeles 1975)

Hoodless, M. 'Mexico's Oil' (mimeo, London 1977)

James, D. 'Unions and Politics: the Development of Peronist Trade Unions 1955–66' (PhD, London 1979)

Knight, A. S. 'Nationalism, Xenophobia and Revolution: the Place of Foreigners and Foreign Interests in Mexico 1910–15' (DPhil Oxford 1974)

Knudson, David 'Petroleum: Venezuela and the United States 1920–41' (PhD, University of Michigan 1975)

Lewis, S. 'The IPC v. Peru; a Case Study of Nationalism, Management and International Relations' (mimeo, University of California at Los Angeles 1972)

Lourdes Orozco, M. 'Integración, estructura y funcionamiento de la empresa "Petróleos Mexicanos" ' (mimeo, Universidad Nacional Autónama de México 1980)

McBeth, Brian. 'Venezuelan Oil' (mimeo, London 1979)

'Juan Vicente Gómez and the Venezuelan Oil Industry' (BPhil, Oxford 1975)

'The Venezuelan Oil Industry under Juan Vicente Gómez' (DPhil, Oxford 1980)

Miller, Rory. 'The Forgotten Firm: Lobitos Oilfields Limited and the Early Development of the Peruvian Petroleum Industry' (mimeo, Liverpool 1979)

'British Business in Peru 1883–1930' (PhD, Cambridge 1979)

Pellicier de Brody, Olga. 'El petróleo en la política de Estados Unidos hacia México 1976–80' (unpublished paper, Cuadernos sobre Perspectiva Energética, no. 2, Colegio de México 1980)

Philip, G. 'Policymaking in the Peruvian Oil Industry, with special reference to the period October 1968 to September 1973' (DPhil, Oxford 1975)

Price Waterhouse, 'Petroleum Industry: Basic Legal Treatment' (Lima 1973)

Rosker, C. J. 'Argentina's Energy Program 1977–85' (British Engineering Association, August 1979)

Sagasti, R. 'Análisis económico de la actividad petrolera en el Ecuador' (PhD, Quito 1974)

Sandeman, H. 'Pemex' (mimeo, London 1979)

Thorp, Rosemary. 'The Peruvian Experiment in Historical Perspective' (Working Paper no. 31, Woodrow Wilson Center, Washington 1979)

Treverton, G. 'Politics and Petroleum: the IPC in Peru' (BA thesis, Princeton 1969)

'US Foreign Policymaking in the IPC Case' (mimeo, Washington 1974)

Index

CAMBRIDGE LATIN AMERICAN STUDIES